D1463542

Samba
Black Book

Dominic Baines

President, CEO
Keith Weiskamp

Publisher
Steve Sayre

Acquisitions Editor
Stephanie Wall

Marketing Specialist
Tracy Schofield

Project Editor
Tom Lamoureux

Technical Reviewer
Ivan McDonagh
George Ashlansvili

Production Coordinator
Wendy Littley

Cover Designer
Jody Winkler

Layout Designer
April Nielsen

CD-ROM Developer
Robert Clarfield

Samba Black Book

© 2000 Dominic Baines. All Rights Reserved.

This book may not be duplicated in any way without the express written consent of the publisher, except in the form of brief excerpts or quotations for the purposes of review. The information contained herein is for the personal use of the reader and may not be incorporated in any commercial programs, other books, databases, or any kind of software without written consent of the publisher. Making copies of this book or any portion for any purpose other than your own is a violation of United States copyright laws.

Limits Of Liability And Disclaimer Of Warranty

The author and publisher of this book have used their best efforts in preparing the book and the programs contained in it. These efforts include the development, research, and testing of the theories and programs to determine their effectiveness. The author and publisher make no warranty of any kind, expressed or implied, with regard to these programs or the documentation contained in this book.

The author and publisher shall not be liable in the event of incidental or consequential damages in connection with, or arising out of, the furnishing, performance, or use of the programs, associated instructions, and/or claims of productivity gains.

Trademarks

Trademarked names appear throughout this book. Rather than list the names and entities that own the trademarks or insert a trademark symbol with each mention of the trademarked name, the publisher states that it is using the names for editorial purposes only and to the benefit of the trademark owner, with no intention of infringing upon that trademark.

The Coriolis Group, LLC
14455 N. Hayden Road, Suite 220
Scottsdale, Arizona 85260

480/483-0192
FAX 480/483-0193
http://www.coriolis.com

Library of Congress Cataloging-in-Publication Data
Baines, Dominic.
Samba black book / by Dominic Baines.
p. cm.
Includes index.
ISBN 1-57610-455-9
1. Samba (Computer file) 2. UNIX (Computer file) 3. Microsoft Windows (Computer file) I. Title.
QA76.76.O63 B3446 2000
005.4'476--dc21 99-043503
CIP

Printed in the United States of America
10 9 8 7 6 5 4 3 2 1

14455 North Hayden Road • Suite 220 • Scottsdale, Arizona 85260

Dear Reader:

Coriolis Technology Press was founded to create a very elite group of books: the ones you keep closest to your machine. Sure, everyone would like to have the Library of Congress at arm's reach, but in the real world, you have to choose the books you rely on every day *very* carefully.

To win a place for our books on that coveted shelf beside your PC, we guarantee several important qualities in every book we publish. These qualities are:

- *Technical accuracy*—It's no good if it doesn't work. Every Coriolis Technology Press book is reviewed by technical experts in the topic field, and is sent through several editing and proofreading passes in order to create the piece of work you now hold in your hands.
- *Innovative editorial design*—We've put years of research and refinement into the ways we present information in our books. Our books' editorial approach is uniquely designed to reflect the way people learn new technologies and search for solutions to technology problems.
- *Practical focus*—We put only pertinent information into our books and avoid any fluff. Every fact included between these two covers must serve the mission of the book as a whole.
- *Accessibility*—The information in a book is worthless unless you can find it quickly when you need it. We put a lot of effort into our indexes, and heavily cross-reference our chapters, to make it easy for you to move right to the information you need.

Here at The Coriolis Group we have been publishing and packaging books, technical journals, and training materials since 1989. We're programmers and authors ourselves, and we take an ongoing active role in defining what we publish and how we publish it. We have put a lot of thought into our books; please write to us at **ctp@coriolis.com** and let us know what you think. We hope that you're happy with the book in your hands, and that in the future, when you reach for software development and networking information, you'll turn to one of our books first.

Keith Weiskamp
President and CEO

Jeff Duntemann
VP and Editorial Director

Look For These Other Books From CoriolisOpen™ Press:

Apache Server Commentary
Greg Holden, Nicholas Wells, and Matthew Keller

GIMP: The Official Handbook
Olof and Karin Kylander

Linux Core Kernel Commentary
Scott Maxwell

Linux Install and Configuration Little Black Book
Dee-Ann LeBlanc and Isaac-Hajime Yates

Linux Programming White Papers
Rusling, Pomerantz, Goldt, Van Der Meer, Burkett, Welsh, & Bowman

Linux System Administration White Papers
Olaf Kirch and Lars Wirzenius

Open Source Development with CVS
Karl Franz Fogel

Setting Up A Linux Intranet Server Visual Black Book
Hidenori Tsuji and Takashi Watanabe

To Ben, my brother, for his memorable comment "Why not! You can write can't you?" when I asked him about writing this.

❧

About The Author

Dominic Baines is the Prinicipal Database Consultant for Recognition Systems Group, plc, global leaders in the development of intelligent computer software products used in marketing. His work takes him all over the world, where he sees Samba being used in many locations. He is a director of a family-owned, IT management consulting firm, providing services to businesses in the pharmaceutical, finance, media, marketing, and retail industries.

Acknowledgments

I would like to acknowledge the following:

Andrew Trigdell, the original author of Samba, without whose work Samba would not exist.

All the members of the Samba Team who have created a suite of software that has been accepted into and used by many of the largest companies and universities in the world. These team members are constantly updating and improving the software.

Numerous others from the Samba mailing lists (**www.samba.org/listproc**) who have helped and guided so many.

Linus Torvalds, the original creator of the Unix clone—Linux—that has proven invaluable to millions

Richard Stallman and the others from the Free Software Foundation who have been instrumental in the establishment of GPL licensing and GNU software.

The staff, members, and fellows of Cambridge University, especially Pembroke College, the University Computing Service, and the Chemistry Department. I studied in Cambridge first as a Ph.D. student, later becoming a Computer Officer (Network Administration and Desktop Support Role) for one of the University Departments, the University Centre (Grad Pad to those who know Cambridge).

My parents for buying me my first computer in 1986, a Z80A-based Sinclair Computers ZX81, capable of being programmed in Basic and Assembler; they started me off into IT and provided continued support through all these years.

Marsden, McClure, Baines & Quinn Limited and Generic Software Consultants, for graciously allowing me to pursue my use of Linux and Samba whilst working for clients.

Mark Terry, for being a friend for so many years and for convincing me to continue in IT at a time when I could have easily moved off into other sciences.

Christine, who has suffered the most from the long periods where weekends and evenings were taken up writing and re-writing sections of various chapters instead of going out.

Coriolis, for providing me with the opportunity to write this book. Special thanks to Stephanie Wall who has managed to keep this project alive for so long, prompting me when I was late all too often. Thanks also to all the staff who have worked on the book, including Ann Waggoner-Aken, Tom Lamoureux, Paula Kmetz, Wendy Littley, Jesse Dunn, and April Nielsen.

Contents At A Glance

Table Of Contents

Immediate Solutions 374

Introduction

This book is all about using Samba to provide Microsoft Windows or SMB (server message block) networking services from a Unix (or other non-Microsoft Windows) machine. Samba, like the underlying operating system that it is often found on and associated with Linux is free, and is available under the GNU Public License.

My own experience with Linux and Samba goes back to 1994, when I was a new Ph.D. student at Cambridge University. I needed a way to get data produced on Linux servers for my Physical Chemistry Ph.D. (which involved experimentation data collection and theoretical calculations). I then needed to make the data available to Microsoft Windows clients so I could write my first year thesis.

I will discuss some of my early experiences with Samba and Linux that at the time caused me long periods of frustration before they were resolved.

Audience

Samba Black Book describes in detail the requirements commonly experienced in organizations both large and small, and how an administrator can use Samba to solve common requests.

This book is aimed at network administrators who have an increasingly complex combination of operating systems that need to share resources. I make no secret that this book has been written primarily from an approach that favors the NT administrator who is trying to come to grips with Unix integration. Due in no large part to my own background, I think I have included sufficient "guts" so that these chapters will prove useful to IT students and Unix gurus alike—all who desire to learn to install and administer a network where SMB rules as King. *Samba Black Book* is not a book on Unix administration, and it is definitely NOT a book solely on Linux. You are advised to obtain a copy of *Linux System Administration Black Book* from Coriolis if you have not encountered Linux before.

***WARNING!* Whatever your background, before you attempt any operations described in this book, you should consult the appropriate operating system documentation before making your system's vulnerable underbelly available over a network.**

In addition to that word of caution, please consult with your network administration before attempting some of the configurations detailed in the chapters due to conflicts that could occur.

How This Book Works

This book is task orientated and is designed to take you right to the heart of the steps involved in building a successful Samba server and configuring and using resources throughout a mixed operating system network. You will find chapters that take you directly to the solutions without having to read the whole book consecutively. Having said that, let me say that reading the chapters in the order in which they appear will lead you through simple tasks and their solutions and gradually bring you to the more complex and "real world" examples that are included in the later chapters. These examples may be expected to appear in any network.

Examples of almost every challenge that you are likely to face are included in this book. *Samba Black Book* does not run high on theory or vague references to how tasks might be accomplished. Instead, it gets right down to specifics—all the specifics—that give you the understanding you need to implement and use Samba.

Samba is closely related to Linux and the Open Source community, where it has become popular lately to "bash" Microsoft Corporation and their products for their adherence to closed source software and operating systems. This book does not take any part in this argument and does not intend to show allegiance to any specific operating system or Unix distribution.

Although I endorse the Open Source philosophy, a great deal of work still needs to be done on its software. I also recognize that unfortunately we don't all work in an Open Source software world. Frankly, if each of us had the will to make our environment an entirely Open Source one, then it is ultimately possible to achieve a type of software utopia. But we still have a long way to go. So, recognizing the status quo, this book is designed to provide you with the solutions you need today to make Samba work in whatever environment you happen to be in.

What's In This Book

Well, the list is extensive, but this book does discuss the following:

- A brief tour of networking
- Obtaining Samba, building (compiling) and installing it with configuration details listed for various versions of Unix
- Setting up a Samba server as a file server for the network
- Use of Linux/Unix file servers by Microsoft clients
- Setting up a Samba server as a print server for the network
- Use of Linux/Unix printer servers by Microsoft clients

- Microsoft Windows 95 and 98 setup, both as client and server
- Microsoft Windows NT setup, both as client and server
- Windows 95, 98, NT 4, and various service-pack password encryption and access control configuration issues
- Microsoft Windows NT domains, their control, and Microsoft networking
- Oracle databases on Samba servers
- Operation though an IP filtering firewall
- RAS and WAN services

The CD-ROM at the back of this book includes:

- A copy of a Linux distribution (a reduced, cut-down version to get you started if you do not have access to a full distribution)
- A complete copy of the Samba FTP distribution site
- Copies of all the configuration scripts mentioned in the text (including brief firewall information)

What You'll Need

To use this book profitably, you should have some experience with either Linux (Unix) or Windows (95, 98, or NT) and have at least two computers with either operating system on them and a network connection between them. The contents of Chapter 1 should be enough to get you through networking. If you have trouble with either Unix or Microsoft Windows operating systems, you might want to look at an introductory book on those operating systems before proceeding.

As far as software goes, just about everything you will need to accomplish the tasks is included on the CD-ROM, apart from the Microsoft operating systems.

This book is as self-contained as possible. Nonetheless, there are a number of other locations where you can get support, and there are considerable Internet resources accessible today to the users of Microsoft, Unix, Linux, and Samba. In addition to the online help systems available as Microsoft Help files and Unix Man pages, there are hundreds of Usenet discussion groups and emailing lists dedicated to the specific operating system that you use. Some of the more helpful ones include:

- comp.os.linux
- comp.os.linux.setup
- comp.os.linux.networking
- alt.os.linux
- alt.os.linux.slackware

- alt.os.linux.caldera
- alt.os.linux.turbolinux
- aus.computers.linux
- linux.debian
- linux.redhat
- linux.samba
- linux.samba.announce
- uk.comp.os.linux

Microsoft has several dozen newsgroups. The most helpful include:

- comp.os.ms-windows.win-nt
- comp.os.ms-windows.networking.misc
- comp.os.ms-windows.networking.ras
- comp.os.ms-windows.networking.tcp-ip
- comp.os.ms-windows.networking.win95
- comp.os.ms-windows.networking.windows
- comp.os.ms-windows.
- microsoft.public.

Linux has a central site at **www.linux.org** that contains a number of jumping-off points to the support, distribution, and other project pages; it is worth bookmarking. (Look for local mirrors of this site.)

Last but not least, Samba has it's own dedicated website at **www.samba.org**. It is well worth the visit, even if only to locate the latest releases.

Errata—Oops!

I and the Coriolis publishing staff have done our best to remove any bugs in the scripts or errors in the text. But even the best laid plans sometimes go astray, and errors may have crept in. If mistakes are found, you will find an errata list and perhaps updates on any sections at **http://mmbq.demon.co.uk/samba** and **http://www.coriolis.com**. If you find a problem, or have a suggestion or criticism, please direct it to me at **sambablackbook@mmbq.demon.co.uk**.

Errata and possible problems with the Samba software should be directed to the Samba authors; you will find details of how and where to contact them in Appendix A. You can also follow any of the links to the support email lists on **http://www.samba.org**.

Chapter 1
Getting Started

This book covers the practical how-to of using and integrating the resources of two families of very different operating systems currently in use today. These are Unix (Linux is a well-known version) and Microsoft Windows (Windows for Workgroups, Windows 95/98, Windows NT, and Windows 2000).

However, Samba is not limited to use with Linux and Windows; many different platforms run Samba successfully. Linux and SunOS are the platforms that have been the most widely used and thus are the best tested.

At the time of this writing, the Samba Makefile claimed support for the following:

- Altos Series 386/1000
- Amiga
- Apollo Domain/OS sr10.3
- A/UX 3.0
- B.O.S. (Bull Operating System)
- BSDI
- Convex
- Cray, Unicos 8.0
- DGUX
- DNIX
- FreeBSD
- HP-UX
- Intergraph
- Linux (with and without shadow passwords and quota)
- LYNX 2.3.0
- MachTen (a Unix-like system for Macintosh)

- Motorola 88xxx/9xx range of machines
- NetBSD
- NEXTSTEP release 2.x, 3.0, and greater (including OPENSTEP for Mach)
- OS/2 using EMX 0.9b
- OSF1
- QNX 4.22
- RiscIX
- RISCOs 5.0B
- SCO (including 3.2v2, European distribution, OpenServer 5)
- SEQUENT
- SGI
- SMP_DC.OSx 1.1-94c079 on Pyramid S series
- SONY NEWS, NEWS-OS (4.2.x and 6.1.x)
- SUNOS 4
- SUNOS 5.2, 5.3, and 5.4 (Solaris 2.2 and later)
- Sunsoft ISC SVR3V4
- SVR4
- System V with some berkely extensions (Motorola 88k R32V3.2)
- ULTRIX
- UNIXWARE
- UXP/DS

So What Exactly Is Samba?

Samba, as written by Andrew Tridgell and The Samba Team, is a suite of different programs that are capable of running on Unix and Unix-like operating systems. These systems allow these machines to provide services and share resources over a network using the Microsoft networking protocols. In essence, this makes it possible to set up a Unix file server for clients that might be using Microsoft Windows or another operating system that either already has support for the Microsoft networking protocol or already has the Samba client program suite installed.

This has considerable impact for those who have a mixed client environment to administer. No longer is it necessary to FTP or copy files from one operating system to another. It is now possible to make those same files available on their current hosts to any number of different clients running a number of different operating systems. If you use only the Unix or the Microsoft operating system, this might not mean much, but it has a huge impact for support in a mixed environment.

Making files available to other clients is not new. FTP and its derivatives have been around for some time. However, FTP involves the physical copying of files from a server to the client where the work is needed and then involves the return of those files, possibly after they have been worked on at the client. If in the meantime the original has been copied to another location and worked on separately, the added problem of multiple copies and versions of files now exists throughout the network. The disadvantage of using FTP is tracking large amounts of data, managing hard drive space, and more network traffic. Samba makes the files from an original host drive available to Windows or Unix clients, where they can be created, edited, or deleted as if they were on the client's own drive without moving from the host.

This is possible by implementing the Server Message Block (SMB) networking protocol between the hosts involved. SMB runs on a number of different networking protocols, but essentially uses NetBIOS to provide the facilities for naming services, establishing sessions, and sending datagrams between hosts. NetBIOS is capable of running over a number of different networking protocols, namely, NetBEUI, IPX, DECNet, and TCP/IP. Utilizing SMB in this way makes it possible to use SMB between any number of different types of hosts and networks. The examples in this book concentrate on the use of SMB services running on top of NetBIOS over TCP/IP. The examples are based on the Unix host operating system, Linux, running TCP/IP as its standard network protocol stack, and the Windows NT default installing TCP/IP as the networking protocol.

It is possible to run SMB services over networking protocols other than TCP/IP, so a brief description of the major networking protocols is included in Chapter 2. If any major difference in configuration is required in the operation of Samba because of the alternate networking protocols, the details are included in the relevant chapters.

The Difference Between NFS And Samba

The Unix method of sharing files, directories, and even whole file systems between Unix hosts is Network File System (NFS) (a non-Unix PC-based version is PC-NFS). Samba and NFS differ mainly in that NFS uses host-based authentication, in which no client authentication is possible other than that available on the client host. Samba can also be made to authenticate the user. The usual way to provide an NFS file system share is a directory and host listing in the /etc/exports file on the server. An example is shown in Listing 1.1.

Listing 1.1 An example of how to provide an NFS file system share according to the /etc/exports configuration file.

```
(for a description, see the manpages exports[5]).
# This file contains a list of all directories exported to other
# computers.
# It is used by rpc.nfsd and rpc.mountd.
/projects 192.168.10. (rw,no_root_squash)
/cdrom (ro,no_root_squash)
```

In this case, the /projects directory is being shared to all hosts in the 192.168.10.0 network with read/write access; /cdrom is being shared to all hosts that can reach this server; and, as it is a CD-ROM, the file system is made available read-only.

On a Unix client, these directories would be made available to local users using the /etc/fstab configuration file on the client. An example is shown in Listing 1.2.

Listing 1.2 An example of an /etc/fstab client configuration file showing how to use an NFS file system share.

```
/dev/hda2              swap                 swap     defaults   0  0
/dev/hda3              /                    ext2     defaults   1  1
/dev/hdb1              /home                ext2     defaults   1  1
/dev/hda1              /dosc                vfat     defaults   1  0
/dev/hdd               /cdrom               iso9660  ro,noauto  0  0
192.168.10.1:projects/ /nfsmounts/projects  nfs      defaults   1  1
192.168.10.1:cdrom/    /nfsmounts/cdrom     nfs      defaults   1  1
none                   /proc                proc     defaults   0  0
```

This works well if you happen to be at the correct host. If you are not at the correct host, you cannot share the files on the server. In the increasingly diverse office environment, it is sometimes a requirement that a user be able to sit at any one of a dozen or more hosts, even every host on a whole network, and be able to log in and see his or her work or project. NFS simply cannot offer the user authentication security that SMB (protocol) or Samba provide. This might not be a drawback in a closed office environment in which everyone shares the same project directory or set of files, but such a situation is not the norm.

Samba is also able to offer printer services between Unix and Windows hosts in a much more user-friendly way than other current Line Printer Daemon (LPD) printer services. Samba can successfully make use of the browsing service while operating in a Microsoft network by adding the Samba server to Network Neighborhood. This is part of the series of Microsoft graphic user interfaces (GUIs) that is used to find shared resources between network clients. Samba can even control certain aspects of Microsoft Windows networking and user account authentication. In fact, Samba can implement several of the different user account authentication schemes currently used by both Windows and Unix clients, so that sharing account databases is possible. While using Samba to share the files between a Unix host and a Windows host or vice versa, it is possible to use one central server to back up a mixed network.

If you have a network that spans several subnets, it is possible to configure Samba to utilize the Microsoft Windows Internet Name Service (WINS) to share resources across your network. Samba can even be configured to become a WINS server, thus releasing a Microsoft host from the overhead and the costs associated with operating system client access licenses. In a mixed operating system network, Samba could provide a simple solution to your resource and authentication requirements at a fraction of the cost of the licenses and software add-ons required for other operating systems.

You can use Samba to provide simple file and printer sharing to a network of Microsoft Windows and Unix clients, and you could stop there; however, as you progress through this book, you will see complex solutions to the real networking challenges that network administrators of mixed operating systems face. Some are handled by Samba, others by Linux. These examples include the following:

- User login authentication
- Microsoft WINS management
- Microsoft Windows roaming profile support
- Microsoft Windows domain control
- Password encryption and access control configuration issues
- Web servers and email
- Backup and recovery of a mixed operating system network
- Databases on Samba servers
- Samba servers as application servers
- Operation though an IP-filtering firewall and other security issues
- Remote Access Service (RAS) and wide area network (WAN) services

Introduction To Microsoft Windows And Unix (Linux)

Detailing the general use of each individual variant of Microsoft Windows or Unix operating systems would require a whole series of books. Many such books are available, and some are listed in Appendix B. This section details both operating systems and the platforms on which they are capable of running. It also covers where to get information on these systems and the resources that they control.

Linux

In the late 1980s, a number of different projects sought to develop a Unix clone that was capable of running on the new x86 series of microprocessor. Dr. Andrew Tanenbaum developed MINIX as a teaching aid, basing his work on the Intel 8086 microprocessor, which at the time was widely available and relatively inexpensive.

The major drawback to using the 8086 was that it had neither virtual- nor protected-memory capabilities, and it could address only 1MB of memory at a time. Compare this to today's systems, in which multiple tasks and large amounts of memory are required. Thus, although the MINIX operating system represented a groundbreaking step, it was limited, almost from its origin, to remain only a teaching tool. (MINIX is a great place to start if you want to learn more about operating system design and kernel internals.) Eventually, MINIX moved on to the 80386 and other microprocessors.

NOTE: *MINIX has evolved over the years, and several versions exist. Two of these are still current, and the rest are obsolete. The current versions are the following:*

- *MINIX 2.0 (Intel CPUs from 8088 to Pentium)*
- *MINIX 1.5 (Intel, Macintosh, Amiga, Atari, and SPARC)*

Legal Status Of MINIX

Although MINIX is supplied with the complete source code, it is copyrighted software and is not public domain. It is also not like GNU software. However, the copyright owner, Prentice-Hall, has granted permission for anyone to download MINIX and use it for educational or research purposes. Companies that want to embed MINIX in commercial systems or sell MINIX-based products need permission from Prentice-Hall **www.minix.org/minix.html**.

Linus Torvalds was a student at the University of Helsinki in the late 1980s. He realized that the Intel 80386 microprocessor was the ideal candidate for running a fully functional Unix clone. Although it was rather expensive, it was the only microprocessor that was available. This choice of microprocessor was perhaps the single most important "happy accident" in the history of Linux, because a growing number of hackers were willing to code and support the x86 microprocessor architecture.

Linus went further and built a kernel that featured virtual memory, preemptive multitasking, and multiuser capability. It is staggering to think that one information technology (IT) student built and designed a Unix clone almost single-handedly. In the spring of 1991, Linus started his project. At this point, MINIX had begun to incorporate some of the advanced features of the Intel x86 processors. In September 1991, version 0.01 of Linux appeared, and new versions (such as 0.02 and 0.03) appeared at monthly intervals. During the development period, many others became involved in the development of Linux, and the whole project started to gather momentum. Enhancements and bug fixes were done daily by way of the Usenet (comp.os.minix) and email. The kernel quickly became a Unix clone.

The Internet was still in its infancy, relative to today's standards, but the key to the growth of Linux was the inspirational way in which Torvalds obtained the help of many others in what was and still is a massive project.

As Linux continued to grow and develop and the kernel started to take shape, news of it spread, especially within academic communities worldwide, and other GNU functions started to be ported to it. In version 0.12, the compiler and bash shell were included, and the compilations were done by way of MINIX. Version 0.12 came online in January 1992.

Richard Stallman created the Free Software Foundation (GNU Project) in 1993, and GNU tools and software have been widely available since then. In most cases, the GNU counterpart to a commercial software variant is more stable and has a better quality in use, mainly because of the open and rapid development of its code and the manner in which any bugs are isolated and fixed. Where a bug fix or an enhancement is required, the user typically makes the needed change himself (assuming that he has the knowledge to do so) and makes it public. In this case, the personal pride and responsibility of the user completely surpasses anything that a major commercial software organization could bestow on one of its own developers. The support and use of the GNU community in this way was essential for the success of Linux.

Linux continued to develop rapidly and approached the point at which it was ready to be released generally. At that time, the complex issue of maintaining the development while releasing updates was addressed. The now-successful practice was established of using even numbers to indicate a stable release (or one that would not alter greatly over time) and odd numbers to indicate those releases that would undergo rapid change and development and require enhancements and fixes.

In early 1994, Torvalds finalized his prerelease version 0.99pl15 to be made available on the Internet from a server in Helsinki. In manner that is now legendary, the news of this release spread out through the Internet, becoming available to the average PC user. In 1994, I was in the second year of a doctoral program at Cambridge University when I stumbled across Linux. I was looking for an alternative PC-based operating system that would be capable of running some gas-phase kinetics calculations (C programs). DOS versions of C compilers simply could not cope with the code I had written to run on the much larger Unix systems that belonged to the Cambridge University Computing Service (**www.cam.ac.uk/CS/**). I had some code rewrites to do, and CPU time was limited, so an alternative had to be found. A rumor was circulating in one of the newsgroups that such an alternative existed that could run on an i386DX40, which I was fortunate enough to own. I still have that original PC running Linux today, albeit a much more recent version. Many others discovered Linux from 1994 to 1995 and adopted it readily; even at those early stages, Linux was becoming a success.

Another major stage in the development of Linux was the concept of distribution. The initial methods involved the establishment of FTP sites, through which one could download all the distributions from one location. This led to the decision to make the distribution available on floppies. Slackware was and still is arranged in this manner. The ultimate step was to make the whole distribution and all the documentation associated with this new operating system available on CD-ROM. Yggdrasil released the first CD-ROM distribution in late 1992. This step, occurring so early in the development of Linux, was a key step in its success.

Since those early days, the development of Linux has continued at an incredible pace. In a recent series of interviews and articles, Linus Torvalds has estimated that he has written only 10 percent of the current Linux code—the rest was written by many unpaid developers worldwide. Torvalds, who eventually graduated from the University of Helsinki, now works in California.

Linux is still under constant development and is now in kernel release 2.2. The following is an excerpt from a *PC Week* interview with Torvalds (it can be found at **www.zdnet.co.uk/news/1999/4/ns-6808.html**):

> *PC Week*: What's next in Linux development?
>
> Torvalds: Right now we have a lot of developers with four-processor machines, some eight. With those, Linux already works fine, but if you want to scale to a larger number, to tens or even hundreds of processors, which has been discussed, there will be a need to change things there. There's a lot of stuff that people always want. Linux 2.0 to Linux 2.2 should not be a big deal. The 2.2 kernel is faster, especially on machines with more memory. It's more aggressive with caching, but frankly I don't think you should have to upgrade every year. If people are happy with 2.2, there's not that much reason to look too far forward.

Intel, the manufacturer of one of the microprocessors on which Linux is now capable of running, has invested in Red Hat, one of the leading distributors of Linux, so it is expected that this development will continue into the foreseeable future. You will find a list of currently available software that has been ported to Linux in Appendix C. Visit the main Linux Web site **www.linux.org** to check out the latest distributions. The *Linux System Administration Black Book* (The Coriolis Group, ISBN 1-57610-419-2) discusses Linux in great depth and is a suitable supplement to this book if you have not yet experienced Linux.

DOS

DOS 1.0, introduced in 1981, is a text-based, 16-bit, single-user, single-tasking operating system. Because IBM chose DOS as the operating system for its PCs, it soon became the most important operating system for PCs. The success of Microsoft is based mainly on the success of DOS.

Later versions of DOS brought some changes in memory handling and peripheral support, but, because of its architecture, DOS is unable to use the capabilities of modern computers. Although technically obsolete, DOS is preferred by many programmers (mainly developers of games) because the application has full control over all resources in the PC.

Microsoft's Web site, **www.microsoft.com**, contains little information on DOS; however, bookstores carry suitable titles for you to review. The DOS operating system is inexpensive and should be available on older desktop PCs.

Microsoft Windows

Microsoft Windows is an operating system that was developed by Microsoft Corporation. For the past several years, it has been the most popular operating environment for IBM-compatible computers. Its great contribution to the PC community has been the graphical interface. The desktop metaphor, as well as the idea that programs would share a similar interface, has been one of the enduring legacies of the Windows revolution. Microsoft did not invent these metaphors and interface methods; the credit for these ideas belongs to Xerox PARC (**www.parc.xerox.com**.) The mass-market acceptance of Windows 3.x has been instrumental in promoting the idea of interacting with the computer by pointing and clicking as well as typing.

In addition to changing our ideas about how to interact with computers, the first versions of Microsoft Windows opened up new possibilities about what could be done with the hardware on our desks.

Microsoft Windows was designed as an extension of DOS. It was announced in November 1983 and became available in November 1985. Windows was a graphical user environment and featured window management capability that enabled the user to run different applications at the same time. It also offered the capability to transfer data from one application to another. Version 2.0 was introduced in 1987 and offered significant enhancements in performance as well as memory handling (i.e., expanded memory support).

Microsoft Windows 3, introduced in 1990, offered a dramatic increase in performance as well as a reworked appearance and was probably the greatest breakthrough for Microsoft Windows. For the first time, Windows was more a multitasking system than a task switcher. The improvements in graphic support and memory handling enabled more complex applications to run under Windows. This was even more the case for Microsoft Windows 3.1. With Windows 3.x, users could run multiple programs at the same time, but this resulted in instability (e.g., frozen screens and general protection fault errors). After losing enough work to this sort of problem, most users played it safe, using only one program at a time.

Microsoft Windows for Workgroups 3.1 and 3.11 (launched in 1992 and 1994, respectively) added real network support and more performance.

Microsoft has addressed the shortcomings of Windows 3.x with two different products: Windows NT and Windows 95. Aided by a huge marketing campaign, Windows 95, code-named "Chicago," was a big success. Seven million copies were sold only two months after it became available. Windows 95 offered a new graphical environment and real 32-bit support. Microsoft also developed Windows NT. The first version, which was presented in 1993, was developed as a platform for client/server solutions. As a step toward a broader market, Windows NT was available not only for Intel-based computers but also for computers with a RISC CPU (e.g., the DEC ALPHA).

Microsoft Windows NT 4, which followed on the success of versions 3.1 and 3.51, adopted the newer Windows 95 GUI and can be said to be the most successful operating system today. It exists in several variants, the two classes of which are servers and workstations. Both share common kernels and are capable of running on identical hardware.

The latest additions to the Microsoft Windows operating systems are Windows 98 and the much-anticipated Windows NT 5, now called Windows 2000. If you are interested in following the cutting-edge Windows technology, read *NT5: The Next Revolution*, by Ari Kaplan and Morten Strunge Nielsen (The Coriolis Group, ISBN 1-57610-288-2). Microsoft's Web site has plenty of information on the Windows operating systems. Appendix B lists some titles that can help get you started.

Samba, The Internet, And GNU/Free Software Foundation

Thus far, I have mentioned only the different families of operating systems that are the focus of this book. However, you also need to be aware of other factors that played a role in the development of Samba.

Samba

Samba was created by Andrew Tridgell, who, like Linus Torvalds, was someone who saw a need and filled it. As he has stated himself, the idea of Samba was a project for his own use that grew to become greater than expected.

Samba began life in December 1991 while Tridgell was a doctoral student in the Computer Sciences Laboratory at the Australian National University in Canberra, Australia. The following is reprinted by permission of Andrew Tridgell:

> We had just got a beta copy of eXcursion from Digital, and I was testing it on my PC. At this stage I was an MS-DOS user, dabbling in Microsoft Windows. eXcursion ran (at the time) only with Dec's 'Pathworks' network for DOS. I had up till then been using PC-NFS to connect to our local sun workstations, and was reasonably happy with it. In order to run pathworks I had to stop using PC-NFS and try using pathworks to mount disk space. Unfortunately pathworks was only available for digital workstations running VMS or Ultrix so I couldn't mount from the suns anymore.
>
> I had access to a decstation 3100 running Ultrix that I used to administer, and I got the crazy notion that the protocol that pathworks used to talk to ultrix couldn't be that hard, and maybe I could work it out. I had never written a network program before, and certainly didn't know what a socket was.
>
> In a few days, after looking at some example code for sockets, I discovered it was pretty easy to write a program to "spy" on the file sharing protocol. I wrote and installed this program (the sockspy.c program supplied with this package) and captured everything that the pathworks client said to the pathworks server.
>
> I then tried writing short C programs (using Turbo C under DOS) to do simple file operations on the network drive (open, read, cd, etc.) and looked at the packets that the server and client exchanged. From this I worked out what some of the bytes in the packets meant, and started to write my own program to do the same thing on a sun.

After a day or so more I had my first successes and actually managed to get a connection and to read a file. From there it was 'all downhill', and a week later I was happily (if a little unreliably) mounting disk space from a sun to my PC running pathworks. The server code had a lot of 'magic' values in it, which seemed to be always present with the ultrix server. It was not till 2 years later that I found out what all these values meant.

Anyway, I thought other people might be interested in what I had done, so I asked a few people at uni, and noone seemed much interested. I also spoke to a person at Digital in Canberra (the person who had organised a beta test of eXcursion) and asked if I could distribute what I'd done, or was it illegal. It was then that I first heard the word "netbios" when he told me that he thought it was all covered by a spec of some sort (the netbios spec) and thus what I'd done was not only legal, but silly.

I found the netbios spec after asking around a bit (the RFC1001 and RFC1002 specs) and found they looked nothing like what I'd written, so I thought maybe the Digital person was mistaken. I didn't realise RFCs referred to the name negotiation and packet encapsulation over TCP/IP, and what I'd written was really a SMB implementation.

Anyway, he encouraged me to release it so I put out "Server 0.1" in January 1992. I got quite a good response from people wanting to use pathworks with non-digital Unix workstations, and I soon fixed a few bugs, and released "Server 0.5" closely followed by "Server 1.0". All three releases came out within about a month of each other.

At this point I got an X Terminal on my desk, and I no longer needed eXcursion and I promptly forgot about the whole project, apart from a few people who e-mailed me occasionally about it.

Nearly two years then passed with just occasional emails asking about new versions and bugs. I even added a note to the ftp site asking for a volunteer to take over the code as I no longer used it. No one volunteered.

During this time I did hear from a couple of people who said it should be possible to use my code with Lanmanager, but I never got any definite confirmation.

One email I got about the code did, however, make an impression. It was from Dan Shearer at the University of South Australia, and he said this:

> I heard a hint about a free Pathworks server for Unix in the Net channel of the Linux list. After quite a bit of chasing (and lots of interested followups from other Linux people) I got hold of a release news article from you, posted in Jan 92, from someone in the UK. Can you tell me what the latest status is? I think you might suddenly find a whole lot of interested hackers in the Linux world at least, which is a place where things tend to happen fast (and even some reliable code gets written, BION!)

I asked him what Linux was, and he told me it was a free Unix for PCs.

This was in November 1992 and a few months later I was a Linux convert! I still didn't need a pathworks server though, so I didn't do the port, but I think Dan did.

At about this time I received an e-mail from Digital, from a person working on the Alpha software distribution. He asked if I would mind if they included my server with the "contributed" cd-rom. This was a bit of a shock to me, as I never expected Dec to ask me if they could use my code! I wrote back saying it was OK, but never heard from him again. I don't know if it went on the cd-rom.

Anyway, the next big event was in December 1993, when Dan again sent me an e-mail saying my server had "raised its ugly head" on comp.protocols.tcpip.ibmpc. I had a quick look on the group, and was surprised to see that there were people interested in this thing.

At this time a person from our computer center offered me a couple of cheap ethernet cards (3c505s for $15 each) and coincidentially someone announced on one of the Linux channels that he had written a 3c505 driver for Linux. I bought the cards, hacked the driver a little and setup a home network between my wife's PC and my Linux box. I then needed some way to connect the two, and I didn't own PC-NFS at home, so I thought maybe my server could be useful. On the newsgroup among the discussions of my server someone had mentioned that there was a free client that might work with my server that Microsoft had put up for ftp. I downloaded it and found to my surprise that it worked first time with my 'pathworks' server!

Well, I then did a bit of hacking, asked around a bit and found (I think from Dan) that the spec I needed was for the "SMB" protocol, and that it was available via ftp. I grabbed it and started removing all those ugly constants from the code, now that all was explained.

> On December 1st 1993 I announced the start of the "Netbios for Unix" project, seeding the mailing list with all the people who had e-mailed me over the years asking about the server.
>
> About 35 versions (and two months) later I wrote a short history of the project, which you have just read.
>
> Andrew Tridgell
> 6 February 1994

Why the name "Samba"? Originally, Tridgell wrote the code, which he called simply "server." It was then renamed "smb-server," a name that was already trademarked by Syntax, maker of the "TotalNet advanced server," a commercial SMB server. Tridgell was informed that he would have to change the name. He ran an egrep search for words containing the letters "S," "M," and "B" on /usr/dict/words and "Samba" looked like the best choice. He now admits that if he reruns the same process, Samba is no longer in his /usr/dict/words!

NOTE: *egrep is a Unix utility that looks for occurrences of a search string from a file, a running process, a directory structure and any input that may be piped to it.*

The Internet

Linux and Samba were originally designed and coded without the Internet in mind, but their use and development have grown largely because of the Internet.

NOTE: *For those who do not know the Internet's history, I will briefly detail it here; those who know all about the information superhighway might want to skip this section.*

As it currently exists, the Internet is an evolving organism. It grows and expands, and bits of it die off. It consumes information, and it passes information through itself. It is probably safe to say that it has no real "life" or intelligence beyond an ability to pass information about the world through any number of routes.

In the beginning, as far back as the 1960s, the U.S. Department of Defense realized that in the event of war, its command-and-control structures would be extremely vulnerable because of the highly centralized nature of most of its facilities. To reduce this risk, a project was begun by the Defense Advanced Research Projects Agency (DARPA) to decentralize its communications.

DARPA was provided with the resources to establish nationwide communications networks and to obtain the very best hardware and personnel available at the time. One project the agency created, ARPANET, experimented with the models and protocols that have led to the systems in use today. In 1969 the Interface Message Processor (IMP; basically a router) was installed at the University of California, Los Angeles (UCLA). This was mirrored at several other sites, both university and defense research sites, around the United States. These were interconnected to create ARPANET, which then was connected to sites outside the United States, including the United Kingdom in 1973. Research was conducted over the next 10 years that eventually led to the communications protocols in use today.

The main protocols that emerged were TCP, UDP, and ICMP/IP. (Today, when these three are used in combination they are shortened to TCP/IP.) The National Science Foundation (NSF) adopted this protocol to connect supercomputers. The physical wiring used between the sites was the Public Switched Telephone network (PSTN) in the form of fast leased lines. The NSF set up NSFNET, and using these connections, government departments and institutions could communicate and share resources all over the United States. Within a few years, the major commercial organizations saw that they could use this facility as well. The Internet as we know it today began from this point in the early 1980s. However, only the really large institutions and organizations were connected to it. The phenomenon continued to grow, expanding beyond the continental United States and connecting most of the major academic and government institutions in Europe.

Growth continued, although the facilities were available only to large organizations until the late 1980s and early 1990s, when Internet Service Providers (ISPs) started to offer services to individuals by dial-up telephone line. The first of these was CompuServe, which offered email and its own customer services. At first the service was expensive (up to $20,000 per year). Eventually, the Serial Line Internet Protocol (SLIP) and the Point-To-Point Protocol (PPP) were offered at "reasonable" prices. This meant that you could connect your home PC or small office network to the Internet at minimal cost. As prices continued to fall and the numbers of connected PCs and networks increased, the Internet grew into the form that we know it as today.

An important point about the Internet should be made here: Whether your PC is connected to a network or individually through an ISP PPP connection, it is equal to all the others on the Internet once it is connected. It might be able to offer the same services and make use of all the other available services, although perhaps at a slower speed. It will have an IP address allocated to it, perhaps only for the duration of that connection, which means that it can be seen by others on the Internet (ignoring firewalls) and can also see other hosts on the Internet.

Because TCP/IP networks are interconnected widely across networks, both large and small and some that span the whole world, every machine on the Internet must have a unique address to make sure that transmitted data reaches the correct destination. IP addresses assignment duties are given to ARIN (The American Registry for Internet Numbers) **www.arin.net**, APNIC (Asia-Pacific Network Information Center) **www.apnic.net**, and RIPE NCC (Reseaux IP Europeens) **www.ripe.net**. Individual users and small organizations can obtain their addresses either from one of these organizations or from an ISP.

The whole network now has so many hosts on it that the current network numbering scheme is filling up fast and a new scheme is being formed. Currently, IP addresses use a 32-bit address structure that usually is written in dot notation (also called dotted-decimal notation), in which each group of 8 bits is written in decimal form, separated by decimal points. For example, the binary address 00001010 00000001 00000001 00000001 is normally written as 10.1.1.1, which is easier to remember and easier to enter into a computer's network configuration application.

GNU

The link between Linux and the GNU Project is a critical but often overlooked part of the existence of, and success of what most users refer to as Linux. In this context, Linux is the Linux kernel and a series of other software written by others under a GNU/GPL or other free software license. From my own perspective, that of an end user, this fact does not have much impact. I use the software that others develop. I might have hacked or tweaked something in the past or aided in debugging a hardware driver or two, but I cannot remember when or what. Before I started to write this book, the relationship of Linux and GNU was vague even for me. Every system I had used that involved Linux had presented the notices for a GPL or GNU license, but I never completely understood the link.

This link is probably best explained by Richard Stallman, who founded the Free Software Foundation and is the founder of the GNU Project (copyright 1997, 1998 by Richard Stallman; from **www.gnu.org/gnu/linux-and-gnu.html**):

> Linux And The GNU Project, by Richard Stallman
>
> Many computer users run a modified version of the GNU system every day, without realizing it. Through a peculiar turn of events, the version of GNU which is widely used today is more often known as "Linux," and many users are not aware of the extent of its connection with the GNU Project.
>
> There really is a Linux; it is a kernel, and these people are using it. But you can't use a kernel by itself; a kernel is useful only as part of a whole operating system. The system in which Linux is typically used

is a modified variant of the GNU system—in other words, a Linux-based GNU system.

Many users are not fully aware of the distinction between the kernel, which is Linux, and the whole system, which they also call "Linux". The ambiguous use of the name doesn't promote understanding.

Programmers generally know that Linux is a kernel. But since they have generally heard the whole system called "Linux" as well, they often envisage a history which fits that name. For example, many believe that once Linus Torvalds finished writing the kernel, his friends looked around for other free software, and for no particular reason most everything necessary to make a Unix-like system was already available.

What they found was no accident—it was the GNU system. The available free software added up to a complete system because the GNU Project had been working since 1984 to make one. The GNU Manifesto had set forth the goal of developing a free Unix-like system, called GNU. By the time Linux was written, the system was almost finished.

Most free software projects have the goal of developing a particular program for a particular job. For example, Linus Torvalds set out to write a Unix-like kernel (Linux); Donald Knuth set out to write a text formatter (TeX); Bob Scheifler set out to develop a window system (X Windows). It's natural to measure the contribution of this kind of project by specific programs that came from the project.

If we tried to measure the GNU Project's contribution in this way, what would we conclude? One CD-ROM vendor found that in their "Linux distribution", GNU software was the largest single contingent, around 28% of the total source code, and this included some of the essential major components without which there could be no system. Linux itself was about 3%. So if you were going to pick a name for the system based on who wrote the programs in the system, the most appropriate single choice would be "GNU."

But we don't think that is the right way to consider the question. The GNU Project was not, is not, a project to develop specific software packages. It was not a project to develop a C compiler, although we did. It was not a project to develop a text editor, although we developed one. The GNU Project's aim was to develop a complete free Unix-like system.

Many people have made major contributions to the free software in the system, and they all deserve credit. But the reason it is a system—and not just a collection of useful programs—is because the GNU Project set out to make it one. We made a list of the programs needed to make a complete free system, and we systematically found, wrote, or found people to write everything on the list. We wrote essential but unexciting major components, such as the assembler and linker, because you can't have a system without them. A complete system needs more than just programming tools; the Bourne Again SHell, the PostScript interpreter Ghostscript, and the GNU C library are just as important.

By the early 90s we had put together the whole system aside from the kernel (and we were also working on a kernel, the GNU Hurd, which runs on top of Mach). Developing this kernel has been a lot harder than we expected, and we are still working on finishing it.

Fortunately, you don't have to wait for it, because Linux is working now. When Linus Torvalds wrote Linux, he filled the last major gap. People could then put Linux together with the GNU system to make a complete free system: a Linux-based GNU system (or GNU/Linux system, for short).

Putting them together sounds simple, but it was not a trivial job. The GNU C library (called glibc for short) needed substantial changes. Integrating a complete system as a distribution that would work "out of the box" was a big job, too. It required addressing the issue of how to install and boot the system—a problem we had not tackled, because we hadn't yet reached that point. The people who developed the various system distributions made a substantial contribution.

Aside from GNU, one other project has independently produced a free Unix-like operating system. This system is known as BSD, and it was developed at UC Berkeley. The BSD developers were inspired by the example of the GNU Project, and occasionally encouraged by GNU activists, but their actual work had little overlap with GNU. BSD systems today use some GNU software, just as the GNU system and its variants use some BSD software; but taken as wholes, they are two different systems which evolved separately. A free operating system that exists today is almost certainly either a variant of the GNU system, or a kind of BSD system.

The GNU Project supports GNU/Linux systems as well as the GNU system—even with funds. We funded the rewriting of the Linux-related extensions to the GNU C library, so that now they are well

> integrated, and the newest GNU/Linux systems use the current library release with no changes. We also funded an early stage of the development of Debian GNU/Linux.
>
> We use Linux-based GNU systems today for most of our work, and we hope you use them too. But please don't confuse the public by using the name "Linux" ambiguously. Linux is the kernel, one of the essential major components of the system. The system as a whole is more or less the GNU system.

To find out more about the GNU Project, visit the Free Software Foundation at **www.fsf.org**. If you use free software in a commercial setting, you might consider making a donation to the Free Software Foundation.

Real-World Examples

Having described the origins of the major operating systems and having introduced Samba, the Internet, and GNU software, it is time to give some examples of where and how these systems are used.

Over the years, I have experienced some fairly complex networking challenges as well as the simpler flat networks of offices or groups of laboratories. In some cases, these have been networks that used only one type of operating system; others were not as clearly defined. However, this book, to be a useful reference for you, details networking models, encompassing a number of different operating systems and their different resource requirements that might commonly be expected to occur in the networks of a hypothetical group of companies. Although hypothetical, these examples are drawn from real networks and include many common challenges so that you can see where your own requirements might fit in. Throughout the chapters in this book, you will locate the fine details of the different challenges you might face and the solutions that can be employed.

I expect that most readers are network administrators or students of such who want to learn how to implement a mixed operating system network and how to make the best use of the available resources. The details of the functions carried out by some of these organizations might be somewhat simplistic in their presentation, and I apologize for this. However, these organizations have the same common requirement in that all require users to be able to securely log on to their own networks and to share resources between them.

Background On These Firms

The Blue Jumper Company is a small-family IT and software consulting firm. It has offices in three locations in the United Kingdom. One of the directors has offices as well in Canada and the Far East, to which he travels often. These locations are the bases of production and manufacture for The Red Shoe Company. The Green

Soup Company has grown over the years and is now the major client of the Blue Jumper Company. Its offices and manufacturing and sales operations span continental Europe.

Recent additions to the client list are the following:

- *The Big Pill Company*—Runs databases and email operations out of three bases in the United Kingdom, the United States, and Australia. The company is eager to link up its research and marketing departments to the Internet.
- *Wholesome Legal Advisors*—Is a law firm with three small regional offices and partners in each location, all of whom tend to work out of one of the offices about 30 percent of the time when in court.
- A university department has administration, stores, catering, finance, and laboratory sections. The department has about 500 student who regularly use the facilities for teaching purposes and about 200 postgraduates who are involved in research.
- A number of members of an association and the members of a club have been advised over time on setting up their networks.

For those who have never experienced networking at this level, detailed networking diagrams and a NetBIOS and DNS naming and IP numbering strategy are suggested in Chapter 2. Appendix B provides a selection of reference materials for networking. The more advanced reader is well advised to note the information concerning IPv6 in Chapter 13.

Chapter 2

Networking

In Depth

If Unix and Windows machines are to start sharing resources with each other, you will need to be able to communicate between them. This chapter covers obtaining and installing the hardware and configuring the software for networking to take place.

Although it is expected that you will be learning to use Samba in a networked environment, a fair amount can be accomplished on a single PC with Linux installed on it.

Throughout this book, it is assumed that the Unix operating system being used is Linux. The installation, configuration, and use on two of the main distributions (Red Hat and Slackware) are demonstrated throughout. Major differences for other Unix operating systems are noted, although very few such requirements exist.

It is also assumed that the major Microsoft operating system being used is Windows NT 4.0. The installation, configuration, and use are demonstrated throughout, and major differences for other Microsoft operating systems are noted.

The OSI Model

Any network communication process may be described in terms of the layers that make up that data exchange. In a model of the network communication process, each layer can be said to represent a specific network process; this means that changes or enhancements to a network make it possible to isolate the processes involved in terms of the layers that are affected.

This layered model of networking is known as the OSI (Open Systems Interconnect) reference model. It was defined by the International Standards Organization (ISO). The OSI model breaks the various elements of a computer network into seven distinct layers. You can think of these levels like the layers of an onion, with each layer enveloping the layer below, hiding its details from the levels above. In itself, the OSI model is not a networking standard in the same way that Ethernet or token ring is, and no networking system in general use has elements that relate to every layer in the model. The OSI model specifies which aspects of a network's operation can be addressed by various network standards. In one sense, the OSI model is a whole series of standards used by other standards.

The seven layers in the OSI model are shown in Figure 2.1.

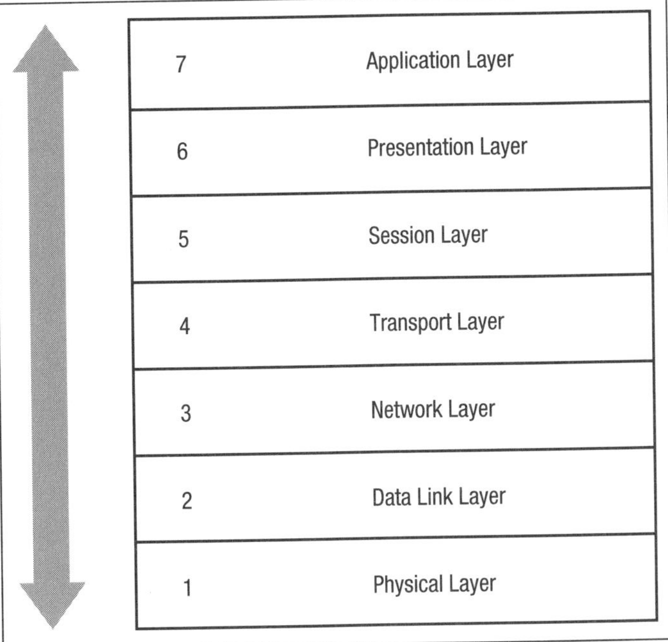

Figure 2.1 Diagram of the OSI model.

Layer 1: The Physical Layer

The foundation for the OSI model is the Physical layer. It details the physical characteristics of the network: the types of media used to connect devices, the types of connectors used, the length of media, the connector pin configurations, and how the connectors should be utilized.

For example, the Ethernet standard for 10baseT media specifies the electrical characteristics of the twisted-pair cables, the size and shape of the connectors, and the maximum length of the cables.

The Physical layer also defines the electrical characteristics of the signals that are used to transmit data over the cables from one end system of a network (node) to another. No interpretation of those signals occurs at the Physical layer, only a low or a high voltage transmission (less than 5 volts), corresponding to a 0 or 1 (binary) value. The higher levels of the OSI model interpret the meaning of the bits that are transmitted at the Physical layer.

Layer 2: The Data Link Layer

The Data Link layer is the layer concerned with translating the bits that are transmitted over the network. A standard for the Data Link layer might address the size of the data packets sent and a means of addressing each packet so that it is delivered to the intended recipient. It might also include details of a way to ensure that two or more nodes do not try to transmit data on the network at the same time.

The Data Link layer also must provide for basic flow control and error correction to ensure that the data received is the same as the data that has been sent. If an uncorrectable error occurs, the Data Link layer standard must specify how the node is to be informed so that the data packet can be retransmitted. (It should be noted that the Data Link layer contains MAC (physical or hardware addresses, it also contains two smaller sublayers: LLC and MAC)

Layer 3: The Network Layer

The Network layer defines logical addressing and data routing from a sending host to a receiving host. These may be on separate networks or even different types of networks, such as Ethernet and token ring. This is the beauty of the OSI model: Even though the underlying Physical and Data Link layers use different standards, it doesn't matter because the Network layer can handle the routing requirements.

Layer 4: The Transport Layer

The Transport layer is responsible for managing the communications between two computers on a network. It accepts data from the session layer above and, if necessary, divides them into smaller pieces to be sent over the network; it then manages the passage of the message through the Network layer to the correct host. It also accepts messages from the Network layer and manages their passage onto the correct process. The Network layer can be seen as a simple receipt-and-delivery layer, whereas the Transport layer allows the Network layer to send and receive messages from multiple processes on each host and to ensure that each message is delivered to the correct process.

Layer 5: The Session Layer

The Session layer establishes sessions between communicating network nodes. A session must be established before data can be transmitted over the network. The Session layer ensures that all sessions are properly established and maintained.

The Server Message Block (SMB) protocol establishes its sessions at this layer to allow login to remote terminals and to provide or use shares with other nodes. Network File System (NFS) is also implemented at this layer.

Level 6: The Presentation Layer

The Presentation layer is responsible for translating the data sent over the network from one type of presentation to another. It compresses or encrypts data transmitted over the network to render the packets smaller or unintelligible without using the necessary compression and decryption utilities.

Layer 7: The Application Layer

The Application layer is the top layer in the OSI model and deals with the techniques for how the applications on a host communicate with the network. The smbd and nmbd and many other daemon processes operate here. The name of this layer can be confusing. The application's programs are not part of the Application layer; rather, the networking components and systems that operate at the Application layer are. The daemon processes are capable of communicating with the networking modules at this level.

The Application layer provides the following:

- Resource sharing and device redirection
- Remote file access
- Remote printer access
- Interprocess communication support
- Remote procedure call support
- Network management
- Directory services
- Electronic messaging and Internet email.
- Virtual terminal simulation

Immediate Solutions

TCP/IP Networking

The easiest way to get a Samba network running is to set up TCP/IP networking. TCP/IP networks can be both large and small. They can also be so widely interconnected that they span the whole world. This means that every machine on the Internet must have a unique address to make sure that transmitted data reaches the correct destination. You could think of this as basically similar to a telephone number with a country and area code, but in reality it's a little different. The blocks of IP addresses are assigned to organizations by ARIN (The American Registry for Internet Numbers) **www.arin.net**, APNIC (Asia-Pacific Network Information Center) **www.apnic.net**, and RIPE NCC (Reseaux IP Europeens) **www.ripe.net**. Individual users and small organizations may obtain their addresses either from the IANA or from an Internet Service Provider (ISP). Note that no correlation exists between IP addresses and geographic location.

Currently, IP addresses have a 32-bit address structure. The IP address is usually written in dot notation (also called dotted-decimal notation), in which each group of 8 bits is written in decimal form, separated by a decimal point. For example, the binary address 00001010 00000001 00000001 00000001 is normally written as 10.1.1.1.

Unless you converse in binary, you will probably find the condensed form easier to remember; for our purposes, it is the format most often entered into a computer's network configuration application.

In addition, the 32 bits of the address are divided into two parts. The first part of the address identifies the network, and the second part identifies the host node or station on the network. The dividing point can vary, depending on the address range and application.

There are five classes of IP addresses. These address classes determine the network and host sections of the address in different ways, allowing for different numbers of hosts on a network. Each address type begins with a unique bit pattern that is used by the TCP/IP software to identify the address class. After the address class has been determined, the software can correctly identify the host section of the address. The three commercial address classes are illustrated in Figure 2.2, which shows the network and host sections of the address for each address type in both dotted-decimal and binary formats.

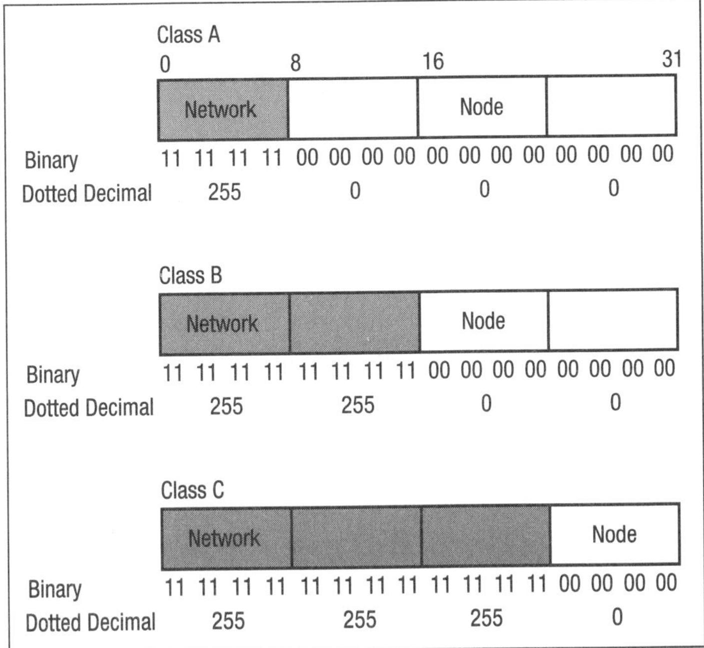

Figure 2.2 The three commercial address classes.

Class A addresses can have up to 16,777,214 hosts on a single network. They use an 8-bit network number and a 24-bit host number and are in the range 1.xxx.xxx.xxx to 126.xxx.xxx.xxx.

Class B addresses can have up to 65,534 hosts on a network. Class B addresses use a 16-bit network number and a 16-bit node number and are in the range 128.0.xxx.xxx to 191.255.xxx.xxx.

Class C addresses can have 254 hosts on a network. They use 24 bits for the network address and 8 bits for the node and are in the range 192.0.0.xxx to 223.255.255.xxx.

Class D addresses are used for multicasts (messages sent to many hosts) and are in the range 224.0.0.0 to 239.255.255.255.

Class E addresses are for experimental use. This addressing structure allows IP to uniquely identify each physical node on each physical network.

For each unique value of the network portion of the address, the base address of the range (host addresses of all zeroes) is known as the network address and is not usually assigned to a host. Also, the top of the range (host address of all ones) is not assigned but is used as the broadcast address for sending a packet simultaneously to all hosts with the same network address.

Netmask (Or Subnet Mask)

In each of the previous address classes, the address class implies the size of the two parts—the network address and host address. This partitioning scheme can also be expressed by a netmask associated with the IP address. A netmask is a 32-bit quantity that, when logically ANDed with an IP address, yields the network address. For example, the default netmasks for Class A, B, and C addresses are 255.0.0.0, 255.255.0.0, and 255.255.255.0, respectively.

For example, the address 192.168.1.1 is a Class C IP address whose network portion is the upper 24 bits. When ANDed with the Class C netmask, as shown in the following example, only the network portion of the address remains:

```
11000000 10101000 00000001 00000001 (192.168.1.1)
```

ANDed with:

```
11111111 11111111 11111111 00000000 (255.255.255.0)
```

equals:

```
11000000 10101000 00000001 00000000 (192.168.1.0)
```

NOTE: *An explanation of the math involved with the logical AND process:*

1 and 1 give 0 and 0 with 0 or 1 will give 1.

As a shorter alternative to dotted-decimal notation, the netmask can also be expressed in terms of the number of ones from the left. This number is appended to the IP address, following a backslash (/), as "/n." In this example, the address could be written as 192.168.1.0/24, indicating that the netmask is 24 ones followed by 8 zeroes.

Subnet Addressing

By looking at the addressing structures, you can see that, even with a Class C address, a large number of hosts per network are present. Such an address structure is inefficient, because each end of a routed link requires a different network number. It is unlikely that the smaller home or office local area networks (LANs) would have that many devices. You can resolve this problem by using a technique known as subnet addressing.

Subnet addressing allows you to split one IP network address into smaller, multiple physical networks known as *subnetworks*. Some of the node numbers are used as a subnet number instead. A Class B address gives you 16 bits of node numbers, translating to more than 65,000 nodes. Most organizations do not use 65,000 nodes, so free bits are available that can be reassigned. Subnet addressing makes use of free bits, as shown in Figure 2.3.

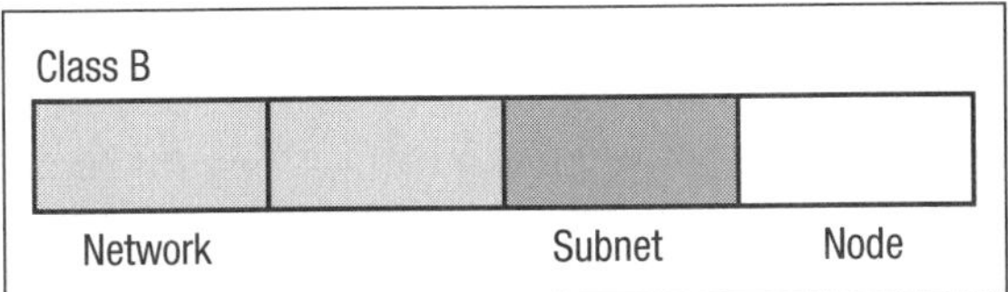

Figure 2.3 Subnetting a Class B address.

A Class B address can be translated into multiple Class C addresses. For example, the IP address of 172.16.0.0 is assigned, but node addresses are limited to a maximum of 254, allowing 8 extra bits to use as a subnet address. The IP address of 172.16.90.125 would be interpreted as IP network address 172.16, subnet 90, and node number 125. In addition to extending the number of addresses available, subnet addressing allows a network manager to construct an address scheme for the network by using different subnets for other geographic locations in the network or for other departments in the organization.

Although the preceding example uses the entire third octet for a subnet address, note that you are not restricted to octet boundaries in subnetting. To create more network numbers, you need only shift some bits from the host address to the network address. For example, to partition a Class C network address number (192.168.100.0) in two, shift 1 bit from the host address to the network address. The new netmask (or subnet mask) is now 255.255.255.128. The first subnet has network number 192.168.100.0 with hosts 192.168.100.1 to 192.168.100.126, and the second subnet has network number 192.168.100.128 with hosts 192.168.100.129 to 192.168.100.254.

NOTE: *The number 192.168.100.127 is not assigned because it is the broadcast address of the first subnet. Likewise, 192.168.100.128 is not assigned because it is the network address of the second subnet.*

Please note that in the above Class C example only up to 6 bits could be borrowed, with Class B, up to 14 bits, and with Class A, up to 22 bits.

Table 2.1 lists the additional subnet mask bits in dotted-decimal notation. To use the table, write down the original class netmask and replace the zero-value octets with the dotted-decimal value of the additional subnet bits. For example, to partition your Class C network 192.168.100.0 with subnet mask 255.255.255.0 into 16 subnets (4 bits), the new subnet mask becomes 255.255.255.240.

Table 2.2 displays several common netmask values for both dotted-decimal and mask-length formats.

I strongly recommend that all hosts on a LAN segment use the same netmask for the following reasons:

- Hosts must recognize local IP broadcast packets.

- When a device broadcasts to its segment neighbors, it uses a destination address of the local network address with all the ones for the host address. For this scheme to work, all devices on the segment must agree on which bits constitute the host address.
- A local router will know which addresses are local and which are remote.

Private IP Addresses

If your networks are isolated from the Internet (e.g., they exist only in a home or an office), you could assign any IP addresses to the hosts without any problem. However, the IANA has reserved the following three blocks of IP addresses specifically for private networks: 10.0.0.0 to 10.255.255.255, 172.16.0.0 to 172.31.255.255, and 192.168.0.0 to 192.168.255.255.

Table 2.1 Netmask notation translation table for one octet.

Number Of Bits	Dotted-Decimal Value
1	128
2	192
3	224
4	240
5	248
6	252
7	254
8	255

Table 2.2 Netmask formats.

Dotted-Decimal Value	Mask-Length Value
255.0.0.0	/8
255.255.0.0	/16
255.255.255.0	/24
255.255.255.128	/25
255.255.255.192	/26
255.255.255.224	/27
255.255.255.240	/28
255.255.255.248	/29
255.255.255.252	/30
255.255.255.254	/31
255.255.255.255	/32

If your network is not on the Internet or you do not have an IANA- or ISP-assigned IP address range for your network, I suggest that you choose a private network address range from this list. Whatever your circumstances, do not assign an IP address arbitrarily, as this might affect your local network. For more information on address assignment, refer to RFC 1597, Address Allocation for Private Internets, and RFC 1466, Guidelines for Management of IP Address Space. You'll find a copy of both on this book's CD-ROM in /docs/RFC.

IP Numbering Strategy

You can often simplify administration at work by adopting IP numbering strategies. You may not have a whole Class B or C subnet of real IPs to use, but if you are using one of the private IP addresses, IP numbering strategies can make network administration much easier. An example of this can be seen in Table 2.3, which shows a suggested IP numbering strategy covering one Class C subnet.

For reasons that might be obvious to you, such strategies might not work in all situations; however, if you are new to networking, adopting a policy of grouping IP addresses by function can help in administration. The administration and use of the Dynamic Host Configuration Protocol (DHCP) for any host in your network would be much easier if continuous blocks of IP addresses were made available in this manner.

At this time, IPv4 is the current IP numbering strategy; here, the number of possible IPs is based on the 32-bit, or 255.255.255.255, format. This is a considerable number, although the range of these strategies is running out rapidly. An update to IPv4 known as IPv6, where the number of possible hosts is greatly increased to reflect the larger 128-bit IP addresses, is under development and is being used in some areas already. A further enhancement to this, IPv9, was suggested on April 1, 1994, and the humor in

Table 2.3 A suggested IP numbering strategy.

Host Type	IP Range
Miscellaneous	a.b.c.1 to 9
Normal desktop hosts	a.b.c.10 to 180
Routers and gateways	a.b.c.190 to 200
DNS	a.b.c.201 to 205
WINS	a.b.c.201 to 205
Email, news	a.b.c.206 to 210
SMB servers	a.b.c.210 to 240
Administration	a.b.c.240 to 245
Firewall	a.b.c.246 to 250
Miscellaneous	a.b.c.250 to 254

RFC1606 is worth reading. A copy of RFC1883, which details IPv6, is available on this book's CD-ROM under /docs/RFC. The detailed diagrams for TCP/IP networks for the companies listed in Chapter 1 are given at the end of this chapter.

IP Routing

When you have more than one TCP/IP network or subnet operating within any organization, you must have routers between the networks so that the IP packets or traffic from one TCP/IP network can be passed to another TCP/IP network.

The individual hosts on a TCP/IP network also maintain a list of entries or tables of IP for every other host you might want to communicate with outside your local network. This is called the hosts file, and it can be seen in Unix systems in /etc/hosts, as shown in Listing 2.1, or in Windows NT in \winnt\system32\drivers\etc\hosts, as shown in Listing 2.2; both listings are from a 192.168.1.x network host.

Listing 2.1 The /etc/hosts file in Unix.

```
# Linux cluster hostnames and IP's
192.168.3.1  kirk.domscluster  kirk
192.168.3.2  mccoy.domscluster  mccoy
192.168.3.3  spock.domscluster  spock
192.168.3.4  scotty.domscluster  scotty
192.168.3.5  sulu.domscluster  sulu
192.168.3.6  uhura.domscluster  uhura
192.168.3.7  chekov.domscluster  chekov
192.168.3.8  enterprise.domscluster  enterprise
```

Listing 2.2 The \winnt\system32\drivers\etc\hosts file in Windows NT.

```
# Copyright (c) 1993-1995 Microsoft Corp.
#
# This is a sample HOSTS file used by Microsoft TCP/IP for Windows NT.
#
# This file contains the mappings of IP addresses to host names. Each
# entry should be kept on an individual line. The IP address should
# be placed in the first column followed by the corresponding host name.
# The IP address and the host name should be separated by at least one
# space.
#
# Additionally, comments (such as these) may be inserted on individual
# lines or following the machine name denoted by a '#' symbol.
#
```

```
# For example:
#
#      102.54.94.97     rhino.acme.com          # source server
#       38.25.63.10     x.acme.com              # x client host

127.0.0.1   localhost

# Office PC's
192.168.10.2            linuxfirewall2.domain  linuxfirewall2
192.168.10.1            linuxrouter1.domain           linuxrouter1
192.168.3.100           linuxresearch.domain   linuxresearch
# Lab PC's
131.111.117.54     dominics.ch.cam.ac.uk
# MMB&Q
194.222.159.25     mmbq.demon.co.uk
# Linux cluster hostnames and IP's
192.168.3.1        kirk.domscluster       kirk
192.168.3.2        mccoy.domscluster      mccoy
192.168.3.3        spock.domscluster      spock
192.168.3.4        scotty.domscluster     scotty
192.168.3.5        sulu.domscluster       sulu
192.168.3.6        uhura.domscluster      uhura
192.168.3.7        chekov.domscluster     chekov
192.168.3.8        enterprise.domscluster enterprise
```

You can see that the structures of the listings are identical. However, maintaining such files can be impractical and cumbersome. An alternative, called the *default gateway*, is available. This is the IP address for a host on your network that is connected to the local network and to other networks. This host has a series of routing tables that list the details of the possible networks that can be connected to. When an IP packet from an originating host is prepared for sending, the local, or *source*, IP address and the IP address of the destination host are inserted into the packet header. The sending host then examines the destination address and, after comparing it with the host's routing table, sends the packet either to a host on the local network or to a gateway host on the local network that connects to the remote network. If a gateway does not exist and the destination host is not on the local network, the IP packet is discarded.

Routing IP can be refined into three types of routing:

- *Minimal routing*—This is where all the hosts that are to be connected are on the same TCP/IP network (e.g., 192.168.1.0) with a netmask of 255.255.255.0. All hosts would expect to see all other hosts on the local network, and no external connections would be required. This can be limiting, but it still allows for about 250 hosts and might be sufficient in many cases.

- *Static routing*—This is where networks are separated by a limited but well-defined number of gateways to other networks. Static routing tables to these other networks can be established. These are usually configured by hand on individual hosts. When remote networks and hosts can be reached through one or more router, static routes might be the easiest option to use.
- *Dynamic routing*—When you have a network that might have any number of routes to the same destination that might or might not have different network usage and performance during a working period, you should use dynamic routing. This involves using routing protocols to build dynamic routing tables that are written from the information exchanged by the routing protocols. This is often used where networks connected in large organizations need to be flexible for purposes of redundancy and network load. During the operation of a network, sometimes a specific route through the larger network that was appropriate in one period may not be appropriate in a later period. This may be due to the number of hops involved or the amount of network traffic on an intermediate network. Likewise, when a router is unavailable because of hardware failure, a scheduled maintenance, or some other reason, one network can send its packets by means of another route. Routing protocols are designed to be "intelligent" so that the chosen route is the best available one.

Although the principles of routing are the same for Unix and Microsoft TCP/IP networks, the commands that create or interrogate the routing that is used can appear to be different.

The Various Routing Options In Action

An example of minimal routing is shown in Figure 2.4.

The routing tables for the hosts within the diagram are shown in Listing 2.3, 2.4, and 2.5.

Listing 2.3 A route table for a Windows 95 system.

```
Active Routes:
Network Address  Netmask          Gateway Address  Interface    Metric
127.0.0.0        255.0.0.0        127.0.0.1        127.0.0.1      1
192.168.1.0      255.255.255.0    192.168.1.3      192.168.1.3  1
192.168.1.3      255.255.255.255  127.0.0.1        127.0.0.1      1
192.168.1.255    255.255.255.255  192.168.1.3      192.168.1.3  1
224.0.0.0        224.0.0.0        192.168.1.3      192.168.1.3  1
255.255.255.255  255.255.255.255  192.168.1.3      192.168.1.3  1
```

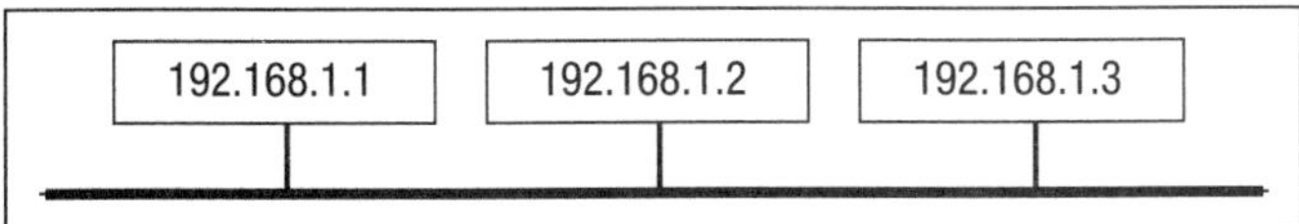

Figure 2.4 Minimal routing diagram.

Listing 2.4 A route table for a Windows NT system.

```
===========================================================================
Interface List0x1 ......................... MS TCP Loopback interface
0x2 ...00 48 45 00 15 21 ...... Novell 2000 Adapter.
===========================================================================
===========================================================================
Active Routes:
Network Destination        Netmask          Gateway       Interface  Metric
          127.0.0.0        255.0.0.0        127.0.0.1       127.0.0.1     1
        192.168.1.0    255.255.255.0      192.168.1.8     192.168.1.8     1
        192.168.1.8  255.255.255.255        127.0.0.1       127.0.0.1     1
      192.168.1.255  255.255.255.255      192.168.1.8     192.168.1.8     1
          224.0.0.0        224.0.0.0      192.168.1.8     192.168.1.8     1
    255.255.255.255  255.255.255.255      192.168.1.8     192.168.1.8     1
===========================================================================
```

Listing 2.5 A route table for a Linux system.

```
linuxrouter1:~# netstat -rn
Kernel IP routing table
Destination     Gateway         Genmask         Flags   MSS Window  irtt Iface
192.168.1.0     0.0.0.0         255.255.255.0   U      1500 0          0 eth0
127.0.0.0       0.0.0.0         255.0.0.0       U      3584 0          0 lo
linuxrouter1:~#
```

In all the previous cases, an entry for the local host is created when TCP/IP networking is installed. The Linux system refers to this as the interface. The other entries are the route to network 192.168.1.0 through the interface eth0. The 192.168.1.1 entry under **Gateway** is the IP address assigned to the eth0 interface; it is not a remote gateway.

If you try to ping a host on the 192.168.1.0 network from this location, you will obtain a response similar to the ones shown in Listings 2.6 and 2.7.

Listing 2.6 Pinging a host on the local subnet (Microsoft version).

```
C:\> ping 192.168.1.2
Pinging 192.168.1.2 with 32 bytes of data:
Reply from 192.168.1.2: bytes=32 time=1ms TTL=128
Reply from 192.168.1.2: bytes=32 time=1ms TTL=128
Reply from 192.168.1.2: bytes=32 time<10ms TTL=128
Reply from 192.168.1.2: bytes=32 time<10ms TTL=128
```

Listing 2.7 Pinging a host on a local subnet (Linux version).

```
linuxserver1:~$ ping 192.168.1.2
PING 192.168.1.2 (192.168.1.2): 56 data bytes
64 bytes from 192.168.1.2: icmp_seq=0 ttl=128 time=1.8 ms
64 bytes from 192.168.1.2: icmp_seq=1 ttl=128 time=1.5 ms
64 bytes from 192.168.1.2: icmp_seq=2 ttl=128 time=1.5 ms
-- 192.168.1.2 ping statistics --
3 packets transmitted, 3 packets received, 0% packet loss
round-trip min/avg/max = 1.5/1.6/1.8 ms
linuxserver1:~$
```

In both cases, because the "hosts" file was on the local network and the host had an entry to its Ethernet card in its routing table, a response to the ping occurred. If this is attempted to a host that is not on the local network, the response will be as shown in Listings 2.8 and 2.9.

Listing 2.8 Pinging a host on a different subnet, without routing (Microsoft version).

```
C:\> ping 192.168.10.1
Pinging 192.168.10.1 with 32 bytes of data:
Destination host unreachable.
Destination host unreachable.
Destination host unreachable.
Destination host unreachable.
```

Listing 2.9 Pinging a host on a different subnet, without routing (Linux version).

```
linuxrouter1:~# ping 192.168.10.1
PING 131.111.117.54 (192.168.10.1): 56 data bytes
ping: sendto: Network is unreachable
ping: wrote 192.168.10.1 64 chars, ret=-1
-- 192.168.10.1 ping statistics --
1 packets transmitted, 0 packets received, 100% packet loss
linuxrouter1:~#
```

In both cases, the response states that the network is unreachable, which is true because no route exists off this network to the 192.168.10.0 network and the 192.168.10.1 host. This is exactly what will happen if you install TCP/IP networking without adding any gateway entries. An example of static routing is shown in Figure 2.5.

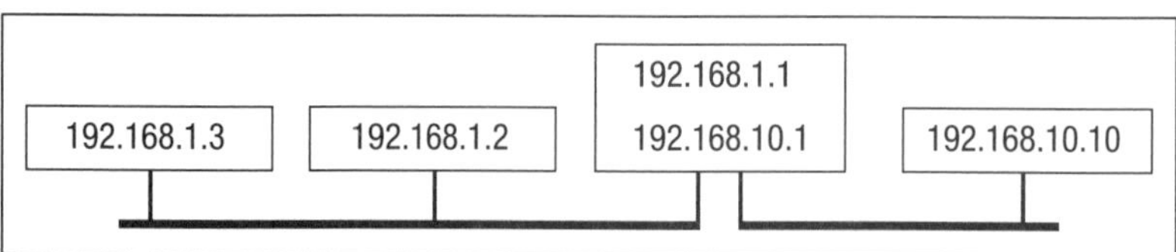

Figure 2.5 Static routing diagram.

The static routing tables for Linux and Windows NT are shown in Listings 2.10 and 2.11.

Listing 2.10 The Linux kernel IP routing table.

```
Linux version:
ntrouter1:~# netstat -rn
Kernel IP routing table
Destination     Gateway         Genmask         Flags   MSS Window  irtt Iface
192.168.1.0     0.0.0.0         255.255.255.0   U      1500 0          0 eth0
127.0.0.0       0.0.0.0         255.0.0.0       U      3584 0          0 lo
0.0.0.0         192.168.1.1     0.0.0.0         UG     1500 0          0 eth0
ntrouter1:~#
```


The response in Listing 2.11 is for Windows NT.

Listing 2.11 The Windows NT IP routing table.

```
===========================================================================
Interface List
0x1 ........................... MS TCP Loopback interface
0x2 ...00 48 45 00 15 21 ...... Novell 2000 Adapter.
===========================================================================
Active Routes:
Network Destination        Netmask          Gateway       Interface  Metric
          0.0.0.0          0.0.0.0      192.168.1.1     192.168.1.8     1
        127.0.0.0        255.0.0.0        127.0.0.1       127.0.0.1     1
      192.168.1.0    255.255.255.0      192.168.1.8     192.168.1.8     1
      192.168.1.8  255.255.255.255        127.0.0.1       127.0.0.1     1
    192.168.1.255  255.255.255.255      192.168.1.8     192.168.1.8     1
        224.0.0.0        224.0.0.0      192.168.1.8     192.168.1.8     1
  255.255.255.255  255.255.255.255      192.168.1.8     192.168.1.8     1
===========================================================================
```

In this case, the 192.168.1.0 network has a gateway set to host 192.168.1.1, which is a dual-homed Linux server that is connected to 192.168.10.0 by another Ethernet interface, 192.168.10.1. Now, a ping to a host in 192.168.10.0 will result in success (see Listings 2.12 and 2.13).

Listing 2.12 Microsoft version of pinging a host.

```
C:\> ping 192.168.10.10
Pinging 192.168.10.10 with 32 bytes of data:
Reply from 192.168.10.10: bytes=32 time=<10ms TTL=128
Reply from 192.168.10.10: bytes=32 time=<10ms TTL=128
Reply from 192.168.10.10: bytes=32 time<10ms TTL=128
Reply from 192.168.10.10: bytes=32 time<10ms TTL=128
```

Listing 2.13 Linux version of pinging a host.

```
linuxserver1:~$ ping 192.168.10.10
PING 192.168.10.10 (192.168.10.10): 56 data bytes
64 bytes from 192.168.10.10: icmp_seq=0 ttl=128 time=9.8 ms
64 bytes from 192.168.10.10: icmp_seq=1 ttl=128 time=9.5 ms
64 bytes from 192.168.10.10: icmp_seq=2 ttl=128 time=10.5 ms
-- 192.168.10.10 ping statistics --
3 packets transmitted, 3 packets received, 0% packet loss
round-trip min/avg/max = 9.5/9.9/10.5 ms
linuxserver1:~$
```

Likewise, this Linux server will also act as a gateway for all traffic outside the 192.168.1.0 network. If the connection to that other host is not in the 192.168.10.0 network, the traffic will still go through the 192.168.1.1 gateway. Let's look at, say, 131.111.117.54, which is a host within the network at Cambridge University (see Listing 2.14).

Listing 2.14 Pinging the 131.111.117.54 host.

```
Pinging 131.111.117.54 with 32 bytes of data:
Reply from 131.111.117.54: bytes=32 time=159ms TTL=59
Reply from 131.111.117.54: bytes=32 time=141ms TTL=59
Reply from 131.111.117.54: bytes=32 time=158ms TTL=59
Reply from 131.111.117.54: bytes=32 time=145ms TTL=59
```

If no route exists to this from the 192.168.10.0 network—say, because a router was not working—the ping will fail with a response that tells you that the destination network is unreachable (see Listing 2.15).

Listing 2.15 An Unreachable Network.

```
Pinging 131.111.117.54 with 32 bytes of data:
Reply from 192.168.1.1: Destination net unreachable.
Reply from 192.168.1.1: Destination net unreachable.
Reply from 192.168.1.1: Destination net unreachable.
Reply from 192.168.1.1: Destination net unreachable.
```

Setting Up These Routes

The commands to edit or add to the routing tables are similar for both Unix and Microsoft operating systems and involve the use of the **route** command.

The Linux Version

route - show / manipulates the kernel's IP routing table. Its primary use is to set up static routes to specific hosts or networks by means of an interface after it has been configured with the ifconfig (8) program.

```
route [-CFvnee]
route [-v] [-A  family] add [-net-host] target [netmask Nm] [gw Gw] [metric
M] [mss M] [window W] [irtt I] [reject] [mod] [dyn] [reinstate] [[dev] If]
```

```
route [-v] [-A family] del [-net|-host] target [gw Gw] [netmask Nm] [metric
N] [[dev] If]
route [-V] [--version] [-h] [--help]
```

The options are as follows:

- **-v**—Selects verbose operation.
- **-A *family***—Uses the specified address family (e.g., inet, inet6).
- **-n**—Shows numerical addresses instead of trying to determine symbolic hostnames. This is useful if you are trying to determine why the route to your name server has vanished.
- **-e**—Uses netstat (8) format for displaying the routing table. **-ee** will generate a very long line with all parameters from the routing table.
- **-net**—The target is a network.
- **-host**—The target is a host.
- **-F**—Displays the kernel FIB routing table. The layout can be changed with **-e** and **-ee**.
- **-C**—Displays the kernel's route cache.
- **del**—Deletes a route.
- **add**—Adds a route.
- **target**—The destination network or host. You can provide IP addresses in dotted-decimal or host/network names.
- **netmask *Nm modifier***—Specifies the netmask of the route to be added.
- **gw *Gw***—Any IP packets for the target network/host will be routed through the specified gateway. Note that the specified gateway must be reachable first. This usually means that you must set up a static route to the gateway beforehand. If you specify the address of one of your local interfaces, the address will be used to determine which interface the packets should be routed to. This is a BSDism compatibility hack.
- **metric *M***—Sets the metric field in the routing table (used by routing daemons) to ***M***.
- **mss *M***—Sets the TCP maximum segment size (MSS) for connections over this route to ***M*** bytes. Normally, this is used only for fine optimization of routing setups. The default is 536.
- **window *W***—Sets the TCP window size for connections over this route to ***W*** bytes. This is typically only used on X.25 networks and with drivers that cannot handle back-to-back frames.

- **irtt *I***—Sets the initial round-trip time (IRTT) for TCP connections over this route to ***I*** milliseconds (1 to 12,000). Typically, this is used only on AX.25 or X.25 networks. If this is omitted, the RFC 1122 default of 300 milliseconds is used.
- **reject**—Installs a blocking route, which will force a route lookup to fail. This is used to mask out networks before using the default route and is not used for firewalling.
- **mod, dyn, reinstate**—Installs a dynamic or modified route. Generally, both flags are set only by a routing daemon. This is used only for diagnostic purposes.
- **dev If**—Forces the route to be associated with the specified device, as the kernel will otherwise try to determine the device on its own (by checking existing routes and device specifications and by checking where the route is added to). In most normal networks, you will not need this. When dev If is the last option on the command line, the word "dev" may be omitted, as it is the default. Otherwise, the order of the route modifiers (metric, netmask, gw, dev) does not matter.

The Microsoft Version

```
Route [-f] [-p] [command] [destination] [mask netmask] [gateway]
```

The options are as follows:

- **-f**—This flushes or resets all the routes currently in the routing tables. If you use it before any other option, it clears the routing table before the command is executed.
- **-p**—You can create this as a permanent route entry in the routing tables so that it is remembered for the next reboot.
- ***command***—Four general commands are available:
  - **Add**—Adds a route
  - **Delete**—Deletes a route
  - **Change**—Modifies an existing routing table entry
  - **Print**—Displays the routing table
- ***destination***—This is the network or host that is reached using this route.
- **Mask *netmask***—The netmask is an additional component that is applied to the address from the destination field to determine the final destination of the route. For example, if the netmask is 255.255.0.0 and the destination is 192.168.3.1, the route will be defined to the 192.168.0.0 network. A bit in the netmask corresponds to a significant bit in the destination address. If no netmask is defined, it is assumed that the netmask is 255.255.255.255, so the entire destination address is used to find the route.

- ***gateway***—This is the IP address of the gateway host for this route.
- ***metric***—Specifies the metric or cost for the destination.

Examples

The following examples assume that the local IP address in all cases is 192.168.1.3, that the netmask is 255.255.255.0, and that the default gateway address is 192.168.1.1.

Not all entries are possible with both Windows and Linux; the GUI Network interface in Windows is used for most Windows entries. However, the addition of IP routes by the command line method is useful to know. Red Hat has available a network configurator that provides a graphic user interface (GUI) for this procedure.

1. Adds the normal loopback entry, using netmask 255.0.0.0 (Class A net, determined from the destination address) and associated with the lo device (assuming that this device was previously set up correctly).

   Linux:

   ```
   /sbin/route add -net 127.0.0.0
   ```

   Windows:

   ```
   route add 127.0.0.0
   ```

2. Adds a route for the host for all hosts in 192.168.4.x by means of eth0. The Class C netmask modifier is not really necessary here because 192.* is a Class C IP address. The word "dev" can be omitted for the Linux entry.

   Linux:

   ```
   /sbin/route add -net 192.168.4.0 netmask 255.255.255.0 dev eth0
   ```

   Windows:

   ```
   route add 192.168.4.0 mask 255.255.255.0 192.168.1.1
   ```

3. Adds a default route (which will be used if no other route matches). All packets using this route will be gatewayed through router1. The device that will be used for that route depends on how you can reach router1; the static route to router1 must be set up beforehand.

   Linux:

   ```
   /sbin/route add default gw router1
   ```

4. Adds the route to the sliprouter host by means of the SLIP interface.

   Linux:

   ```
   /sbin/route add sliprouter sl0
   ```

5. Adds the net 192.168.3.x to be gatewayed through the former route to the SLIP interface.

   Linux:

   ```
   /sbin/route add -net 192.168.3.0 netmask 255.255.255.0 gw sliprouter
   ```


6. An obscure entry whose details have been obtained from the "man route" manual pages on a Red Hat 5.2 system. I have included them here so that you can see how to do it. This sets all the Class D (multicast) IP routes to go by means of eth0. This is the correct normal configuration line with a multicasting kernel.

   Linux:

   ```
   /sbin/route add 224.0.0.0 netmask 240.0.0.0 dev eth0
   ```

7. Rejects all traffic for the private network 10.x.x.x. This command should not be used as a firewall.

   Linux:

   ```
   /sbin/route add 10.0.0.0 netmask 255.0.0.0 reject
   ```

In all cases, it is possible to read the output of the IP routing tables, and it is shown in the following columns:

- *Destination or network address*—The destination network or destination host.
- *Gateway*—The gateway address, or "*" if none is set.
- *Genmask or netmask*—The netmask for the destination net; 255.255.255.255 is for a host destination, and 0.0.0.0 is for the default route.

With Linux, additional entry flags are also seen. These flags are detailed in Table 2.4.

An example of dynamic routing is shown in Figure 2.6.

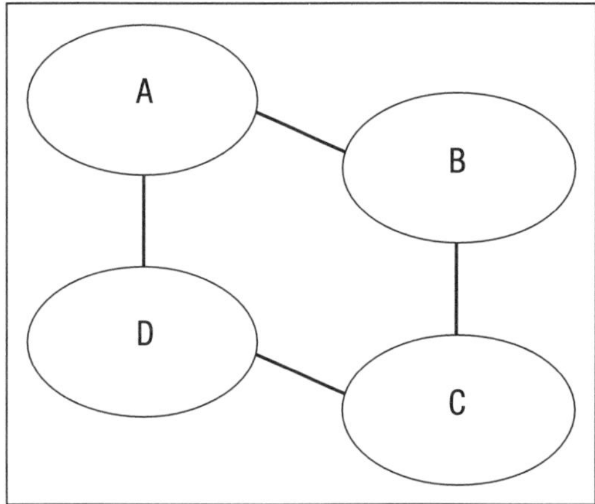

Figure 2.6 Dynamic routing diagram.

Table 2.4 The kernel IP routing table flags.

Flag	Description
U	Route is up.
H	Target is a host.
G	Use gateway.
R	Reinstates route for dynamic routing.
D	Dynamically installed by daemon or redirect.
M	Modified from routing daemon or redirect.
!	Reject route.
Metric	The *distance* to the target (usually counted in hops); not used by recent kernels but might be needed by routing daemons.
Ref	Number of references to this route (not used in the Linux kernel).
Use	Count of lookups for the route. Depending on whether **-F** or **-C** is used, this will be either route cache misses (**-F**) or route cache hits (**-C**).
Iface	Interface to which packets for this route will be sent.
MSS	Default maximum segment size for TCP connections over this route.
Window	Default window size for TCP connections over this route.
Irtt	Initial round trip time. The kernel uses this to estimate the best TCP protocol parameters without waiting on (possibly slow) answers.
HH	Cached only. The number of ARP entries and cached routes that refer to the hardware header cache for the cached route. This will be -1 if a hardware address is not needed for the interface of the cached route (e.g., lo).
Arp	Cached only. Indicates whether the hardware address for the cached route is up-to-date.

Dynamic routing uses a routing protocol. This involves the use of a routing process on your routers that advertise themselves to the other networks using routing protocols. They then learn the routing tables of the routers on the network so that when a client sends a packet to a remote host through the router, the router will choose the best route for that packet to use.

The two generic classes of routing protocols are referred to as interior and exterior routing protocols. The best-known interior routing protocol, Routing Information Protocol (RIP), is available for both Unix and Windows NT. If a routing protocol already exists on your network, it likely is RIP.

RIP operates by selecting the route with the shortest (maximum of 15) number of hops taken to reach a host. It assumes that the fewest number of hops is the better option; this may or may not be the case and depends on the network in-between. The Unix implementation of RIP is handled by **routed**. Although RIP is included in **gated** as well, Microsoft has its own implementation of RIP that is included with Windows NT; it is augmented by the Microsoft Routing and Remote Access Service (RRAS) add-on or supplement.

Exterior routing protocols are used to exchange routing information between whole networks or network systems. The information that is shared between routers indicates which networks or systems can be reached using the specific system router. The commonly used implementation of exterior routing protocol is in the Exterior Gateway Protocol (EGP), which is included in Unix **gated**.

RIP

To use RIP on a Unix system: log in as "root" and simply type "routed" at the command prompt or add it to your system startup configuration /etc/rc.local. A suitable entry is shown in Listing 2.16.

Listing 2.16 Starting routed.

```
# Start routed (RIP daemon):
if [ -f /etc/routed ]; then
  routed; echo -n ' routed' > /dev/console
fi
```

The routing daemon that is routed will then advertise and listen to all routes advertised by other systems. The addition of **-q** to the **routed** command will instruct the daemon to listen to all the announced routes but not to broadcast its own. This option is appropriate if the host in question is not a gateway between network segments.

An additional option is to set up routes with **routed**; on a Unix system, the /etc/gateways file contains this information. This involves entries of the type shown in Listing 2.17.

Listing 2.17 An example /etc/gateways file.

```
net 0.0.0.0 gateway a.b.c.d metric 1 active
```

Each entry starts net; 0.0.0.0 refers to this as the default route. The a.b.c.d IP address is that of the gateway host. The metric 1 indicates that only one hop to the network is needed, and active indicates that the gateway host will make RIP updates. If the host is not capable of providing RIP updates, this should read "passive," so that the routing entry is maintained and not removed. It then becomes a static route for the system.

Microsoft's implementation of RIP involves the addition of the RIP service through the Network configuration in the Control Panel or using the Microsoft RRAS add-on for Windows NT.

EGP

To use EGP on a Unix system as the implementation gated at startup, you simply enter "gated" or add it to your system startup configuration /etc/rc.local, as shown in Listing 2.18.

Listing 2.18 Starting gated.

```
# Start gated (EGP daemon):
if [ -f /etc/gated -a -f /etc/gated.conf ]; then
  gated; echo -n ' gated' > /dev/console
fi
```

However, **gated** does require a configuration file—gated.conf in this example—it is placed in /etc, and the gated.conf file structure depends on your local configuration. Also, this example has two subnets and a router connecting them. RIP is used on both interfaces and EGP to advertise the network to the external connection, as shown in Listing 2.19.

Listing 2.19 An example gated.conf configuration file.

```
# gated (RIP/EGP daemon) configuration
options gendefault ;
#
# This is an example AS number and is fake do
# not use it in your own configuration
# obtain a REAL AS number when you register
# your network or use a private network only
autonomoussytem 200 ;
#
rip yes;
#
# announce to the neighbor hello packets 120 seconds apart
# set the announce interval to 600 seconds
# remote routers are at 192.168.10.1 and 192.168.100.1
egp yes
{group minhello 120 minpoll 600
       {   neighbor 192.168.10.1;
           neighbor 192.168.100.1;
    } ;
};
# send the EGP information to the remote routers
propogate proto egp as 8
           {
           proto direct {
                  announce 192.168.1.0 metric 0;
                         } ;
           };
```

```
# announce the default route via RIP with a cost of 3
propgate proto rip interface 192.168.1.1
            {
            proto default {
                    announce 0.0.0.0 metric 3;
                            };
            };
```


Understanding Internet Domains

As already noted, most systems use both names and numbers to identify hosts, and the same is true of the networks on which those hosts reside. At the level of the underlying networking protocol, the systems require only the IP addresses to operate; however, this is not user friendly. This is where domain names become useful.

It is common practice to group the systems of networks together so that in naming the networks they are on groups of similar systems by either physical location or organization. These groupings are known as *domains*. Each domain is a logical grouping that includes the whole domain, including all the subdomains of that domain and all the hosts within the domain and subdomains.

In real terms, this means that for all networks and systems in the United Kingdom, the domain is known as “uk”. “.uk” is just an end portion of the registered domain name that points out that this entity has been registered in the United Kingdom. The same is true for other countries’ domain names, such as “.fr” for France and so forth. It uses ISO symbols for indicating country. For all networks and systems in academic institutions in the United Kingdom, the subdomain is “ac.uk”. For Cambridge University, the subdomain goes one stage further, to “cam.ac.uk” The Chemistry Department in that domain is “ch.cam.ac.uk” and the PC that sat on the desk in my lab for so long is “dominics.ch.cam.ac.uk”. Figure 2.7 shows this graphically.

Each of the separate subdomains (ch.cam.ac.uk, cam.ac.uk, ac.uk, and so on) must maintain an accurate record of all systems and networks and the names and IP addresses. This local record set is referred to in DNS-speak as a *zone*. It is a requirement to have a server (and sometimes two, the other server often being held on another network) in each of these zones to hold the records of names and IP addresses for every host within the zone. This is not strictly true and sometimes a DNS server can hold the records for several zones. This server may be queried by a host on another network so that it is possible to determine the IP address, or name of a host within that remote zone. This is referred to as domain name server (DNS) resolution.

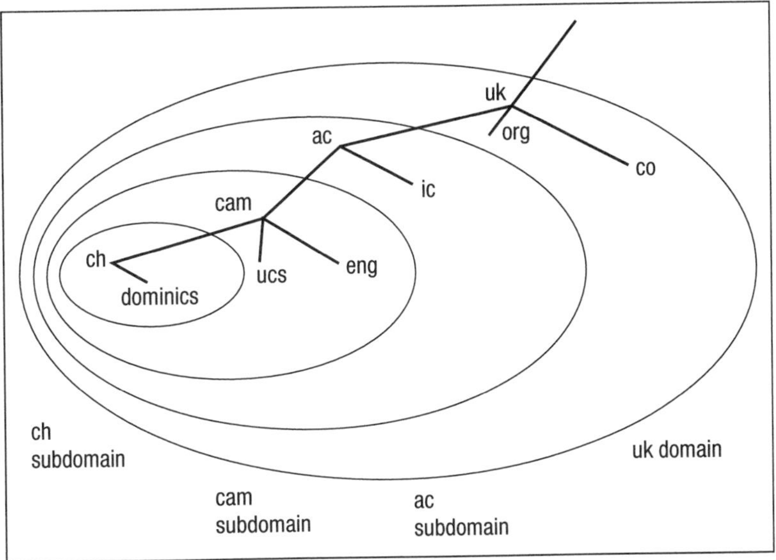

Figure 2.7 The domain structure for the host dominics.ch.cam.ac.uk.

The main domain names from the original Internet network are com, org, mil, edu, net, and gov. As the Internet has grown, the number of domain names has increased, and it is now common to see country abbreviations and suffixes added with other groups such as ac, co, ltd, and many others. A whole series of subdomain names, such as co.uk, are used by corporate bodies in the United Kingdom. For further details, see /docs/DNS on this book's CD-ROM.

Setting Up DNS

The DNS server software that responds to these requests for IP address and DNS name resolution is available for both Unix and Microsoft operating systems.

You can find information on how to set up and establish DNS in the DNS HOWTO written by Nicolai Langfeldt that can be found with most Linux distributions. A current copy can be found in /doc/HOWTO/DNS-HOWTO on this book's CD-ROM. In addition, several excellent books are available on DNS services and how to create and run them (see Appendix B). The DNS service can be run by many operating systems, but here I discuss two: Linux and Windows NT. Both systems give the same results, but they are set up differently.

For computers to communicate with each other over a network, only the IP addresses are necessary. However, we humans prefer to use names for things, including PCs. DNS acts as a translator that converts the machine names to the IP numbers that the PC addresses. DNS holds records of the *name to address* and *from address to name* for the specific parts of the network in which a DNS server is located.

The three types of DNS servers are discussed in the following sections.

Primary DNS

The primary name server for a domain and subdomains contains the master copy of name and the IP information related to that domain and subdomain. It contains the record information for all the hosts in a zone; that is, the domain or subdomain that the server holds. It can be considered the authoritative database for all information regarding hosts in the zone.

Secondary DNS

The secondary DNS contains copies of the information held in the primary name server. When the information related to a host is added, deleted, or altered, this change occurs at the primary name server. The secondary name servers then replicate this information.

Caching DNS

The caching name server holds a cache of host information that is built up over time from the information obtained following name queries from some remote name server. The server resolves the name query and caches the information locally, then uses it to respond to further queries for the same information.

In a large network, it is standard practice to have a primary name server and at least one secondary name server, possibly with some caching name servers being present in some parts of the network. This arrangement ensures that network load on the primary name servers and the traffic from all the hosts in the network attempting to resolve the name/IP information does not automatically use the primary name server.

A DNS entry is an association between two things: a machine name, such as mmbq.demon.co.uk, and the machine's IP number, such as 194.222.159.25. It is really that simple; however, the maintenance of this information and how it is gathered and provided to hosts when resolution queries are made can require intensive administration, and the consequences of getting this wrong can be serious.

A Real-World Example

In 1998 an operator for one of the main Internet host-naming companies made an error in updating some of the primary name server records on its DNS server. The DNS server had the main DNS database for a whole chunk of the Internet, and although the error was corrected rapidly, the impact was felt worldwide for at least 48 hours. This resulted in the apparent disappearance of whole companies from the Internet and caused worldwide havoc with email.

This was and is due to the fact that primary name servers from different zones depend on correct information being present in the primary name server databases of other zones. When a name resolution query from one zone is made to another, the responding zone's DNS server provides IP/name information that then becomes cached in the requesting zone's DNS server. This information is then used by the clients in that zone that are resolving the name queries to the zone's primary DNS, which is unaware of the mistake. Thus, errors in one primary DNS might affect more than one zone.

The main DNS services that exist are implementations by Microsoft of its own DNS software and by Unix of its BIND software. The RFC 1033 document (the Domain Administrators Operations Guide) defines the records used to construct zone files (a copy of this document can be found in /docs/RFC on this book's CD-ROM). The number and type of these records differ, depending on which server is being used (primary, secondary, or caching).

Deciding Which DNS Service To Use

Which DNS service to use depends on your local requirements. However, the primary DNS server would be used in a large organization that has a central computing facility containing a number of other servers, the best networking facilities, and key administration staff. The primary DNS server would also be located closely to your WINS (Windows Internet Naming Service) server and, if you are using real IPs, a reliable Internet connection so that Internet hosts can obtain access to your server and query responses about your zone. If the latter is the case, you will also require a secondary DNS server that should have an independent Internet connection, usually in a building separate from the first. It is not uncommon for institutions to swap or share secondary DNS servers off site in case the primary one fails. Depending on the size of your network, you might find that you either have or need to use other secondary DNS servers in your network to reduce the network load on the primary DNS server because of local network conditions.

The manner in which the DNS zone is named and partitioned between parts of your organization will depend on local requirements, but usually this follows administrative, geographic, or functional boundaries.

Types Of DNS Servers

We'll be talking about five different types of DNS servers in this section.

Microsoft DNS Server

This follows the Internet standards and communicates with other DNS servers (an important factor) and will respond to client name resolution requests for any number of different clients. The database files and resource files required by a Windows NT DNS server are identical to those used with a Unix DNS server.

NOTE: *Microsoft's implementation of DNS is capable of integrating with WINS servers as well, so if you use DHCP and WINS on your network, name resolution is possible using both WINS or DNS. Non-WINS clients might also be able to use DNS to resolve a WINS host even if the IP address is dynamically assigned with DHCP. This topic is worth exploring in some detail if you are in an NT-dominated environment. Some books that discuss the mix of DHCP/WINS and DNS are referenced in Appendix B.*

The traditional way to maintain zone files is by using simple ASCII text editors. The Microsoft DNS implementation also provides a standard GUI to these records that should help manage DNS zones.

To install the Microsoft DNS server, you need to open the Network Services tab of the Network Configuration utility from the Control Panel. Click on Add to display the Select Network Service dialog box, then choose the Microsoft DNS server and install it. The DNS service will start automatically when you restart Windows NT, although at this stage it is not configured and you should follow the configuration options that are listed.

When you first open the DNS Manager application for the Administration Tools (Common) program group, you will obtain the window shown in Figure 2.8.

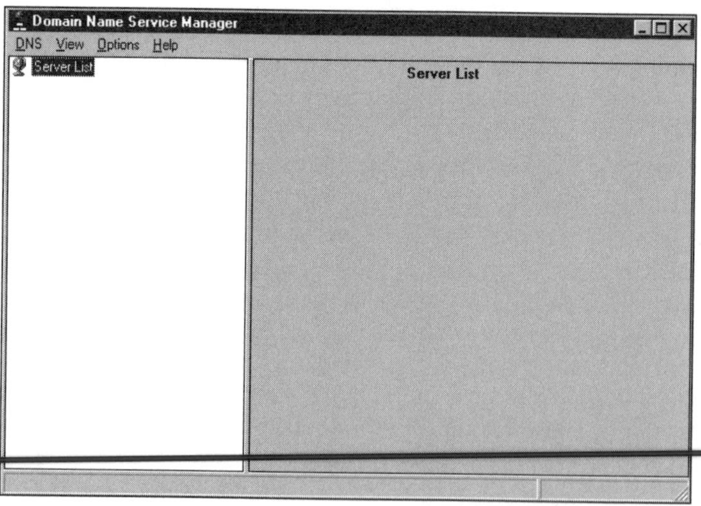

Figure 2.8 The DNS Manager following a new installation.

You will also see this window if no other Microsoft DNS server is present in your network. The first task is to add your server to the server list. This is accomplished by highlighting the server list and adding a new server from the DNS menu dialog box, as shown in Figure 2.9.

Simply enter the IP address of the server and click on OK.

The server will now appear in the server list, as shown in Figure 2.10. At this point the Microsoft DNS server is configured as a caching-only DNS server.

Unix (BIND) DNS Server

Before you start on this you should configure your machine so that you can telnet in and out of it, be able to successfully make all kinds of connections to the net, and you should especially be able to do telnet 127.0.0.1 and get your own machine. In addition, you also need a /etc/resolv.conf and /etc/hosts file.

A program called *named* performs name serving on Unix. This is a part of the BIND package, which is coordinated by Paul Vixie for The Internet Software Consortium. *Named* is included in most Linux distributions and is usually installed as

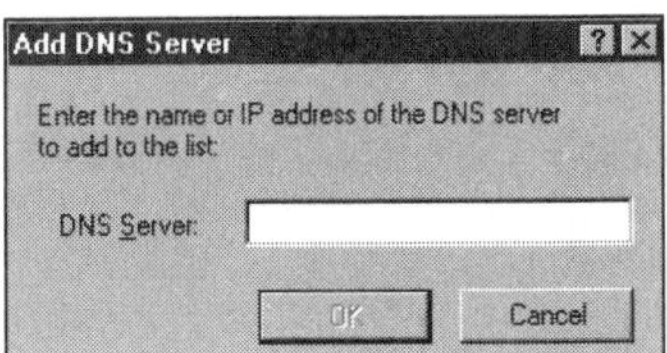

Figure 2.9 Adding a DNS server.

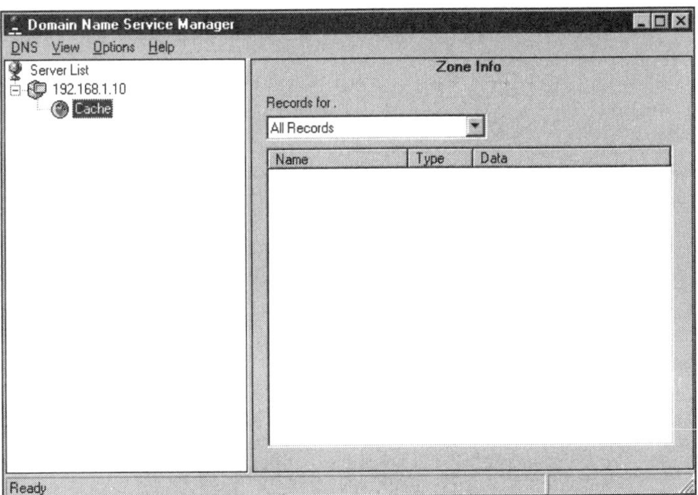

Figure 2.10 The DNS Manager showing the caching-only server.

/usr/sbin/named. You might be able to get a binary off a Linux FTP site or get the latest and greatest source from **ftp.isc.org/isc/bind/src/cur/bind-8**.

A couple of major versions are available with the different Linux distributions. You should always try to use the most recent of these. Remember that because DNS is an information database that is used to identify hosts, it is important to maintain its content correctly.

Caching-Only Name Server

The first option is to run a caching-only name server. The Microsoft version of the DNS service installs the caching-only DNS server as detailed previously with no further effort.

Although not all files are used, the file names used with a Unix-named configuration are as follows:

- *named.boot*—This is the general parameters file; it indicates the source of the domain information for the DNS server.
- *named.ca*—This points to the root domain servers (you need to edit this file if you are not connected to the Internet).
- *named.local*—This resolves the loopback device address.
- *named.domainhosts*—This is the zone file that maps the hostnames for the domain to IP addresses.
- *named.reversedomain*—This is the zone file that maps the reverse domain IP addresses to hostnames.

A caching-only DNS server is a simple DNS configuration and often is useful for dial-up users or small remote networks, and it might be all that you require. A caching-only name server will find the answer to name queries and remember the answer the next time you need it. This will significantly shorten the time you spend waiting, especially if you are on a slow connection.

To start the process of installing a caching-only DNS server, the cache.dns (Windows NT) or named.ca (Unix) file should be updated by downloading the domain/named.root file from rs.internic.net on a regular basis. This file can be obtained by anonymous FTP from **rs.internic.net**. The procedure is similar to the one shown in Listing 2.20.

Listing 2.20 Obtaining an example named.root file.

```
C:\DNSSTUFF>ftp rs.internic.net
Connected to rs.internic.net
(a pile of messages)
user (rs.internic.net: (none)): anonymous
331 Guest login ok, send your complete e-mail address as password.
Password: dombaines@host.somewhere
```

```
230 Guest login ok, access restrictions apply.
ftp>BIN
200 Type set to I.
ftp> get domain/named.root
200 PORT command successful.
150 Opening data connection for domain/named.root (2769 bytes).
226 transfer complete
2769 bytes received in 1.3 secs (2 Kbytes/sec)
ftp>quit
221 Goodbye.
C:\DNSSTUFF>copy named.root cache.dns
C:\DNSSTUFF>copy named.root named.ca
```


This code is in the correct format for Windows NT or Linux use. The code shown in Listing 2.21 shows a copy of the named.ca file for use with Unix DNS or cache.dns for use with Windows NT DNS service.

Listing 2.21 An example named.ca file.

```
;       This file holds the information on root name servers needed to
;       initialize cache of Internet domain name servers
;       (e.g. reference this file in the "cache  .  <file>"
;       configuration file of BIND domain name servers).
;
;       This file is made available by InterNIC registration services
;       under anonymous FTP as
;           file                /domain/named.root
;           on server           FTP.RS.INTERNIC.NET
;       -OR- under Gopher at    RS.INTERNIC.NET
;           under menu          InterNIC Registration Services (NSI)
;              submenu          InterNIC Registration Archives
;           file                named.root
;
;       last update:    Aug 22, 1997
;       related version of root zone:   1997082200
;
;
; formerly NS.INTERNIC.NET
;
.                        3600000  IN  NS    A.ROOT-SERVERS.NET.
A.ROOT-SERVERS.NET.      3600000      A     198.41.0.4
;
; formerly NS1.ISI.EDU
;
.                        3600000      NS    B.ROOT-SERVERS.NET.
B.ROOT-SERVERS.NET.      3600000      A     128.9.0.107
;
```

```
; formerly C.PSI.NET
;
.                           3600000      NS     C.ROOT-SERVERS.NET.
C.ROOT-SERVERS.NET.         3600000      A      192.33.4.12
;
; formerly TERP.UMD.EDU
;
.                           3600000      NS     D.ROOT-SERVERS.NET.
D.ROOT-SERVERS.NET.         3600000      A      128.8.10.90
;
; formerly NS.NASA.GOV
;
.                           3600000      NS     E.ROOT-SERVERS.NET.
E.ROOT-SERVERS.NET.         3600000      A      192.203.230.10
;
; formerly NS.ISC.ORG
;
.                           3600000      NS     F.ROOT-SERVERS.NET.
F.ROOT-SERVERS.NET.         3600000      A      192.5.5.241
;
; formerly NS.NIC.DDN.MIL
;
.                           3600000      NS     G.ROOT-SERVERS.NET.
G.ROOT-SERVERS.NET.         3600000      A      192.112.36.4
;
; formerly AOS.ARL.ARMY.MIL
;
.                           3600000      NS     H.ROOT-SERVERS.NET.
H.ROOT-SERVERS.NET.         3600000      A      128.63.2.53
;
; formerly NIC.NORDU.NET
;
.                           3600000      NS     I.ROOT-SERVERS.NET.
I.ROOT-SERVERS.NET.         3600000      A      192.36.148.17
;
; temporarily housed at NSI (InterNIC)
;
.                           3600000      NS     J.ROOT-SERVERS.NET.
J.ROOT-SERVERS.NET.         3600000      A      198.41.0.10
;
; housed in LINX, operated by RIPE NCC
;
.                           3600000      NS     K.ROOT-SERVERS.NET.
K.ROOT-SERVERS.NET.         3600000      A      193.0.14.129
;
; temporarily housed at ISI (IANA)
```

```
;
.                           3600000      NS     L.ROOT-SERVERS.NET.
L.ROOT-SERVERS.NET.         3600000      A      198.32.64.12
;
; housed in Japan, operated by WIDE
;
.                           3600000      NS     M.ROOT-SERVERS.NET.
M.ROOT-SERVERS.NET.         3600000      A      202.12.27.33
; End of File
```

If your network is connected to the Internet, you can use this file as it is. If your network is not connected to the Internet, remove all the records and then replace them with the NS and A records for the DNS server that is authoritative for the root domain at your site.

In a Windows NT DNS server, this file is located in the \%System32%\dns\ directory.

The one extra file that exists in Unix systems is the named.local file, which is used to convert the address 127.0.0.1 into the name localhost. This is the zone file for the reverse domain 0.0.127.IN-ADDR.ARPA. Most, if not all, systems use a localhost 127.0.0.1 loopback address, so this file is similar on every server. A sample named.local file is shown in Listing 2.22.

Listing 2.22 An example named.local file.

```
@    IN SOA  linuxdns1.domain.      root.linuxdns1.domain. (
             1                 ;serial
             360000            ;refresh every 100 hours
             3600              ;retry after 1 hour
             3600000 ;expire after 1000 hours
             360000  ;default ttl is 100 hours
             )
     IN NS   linuxdns1.domain.
1    IN PTR  localhost.
```

The SOA and NS record is for a system called linuxdns1.domain, with an IP address 192.168.1.1, and will vary from system to system. The root.linuxdns1.domain is the email address of the administrator of that system. The "@" that normally is included within an email address is not present; the "." is used instead.

The Unix DNS server is then created simply by using a named.boot file that contains the code shown in Listing 2.23.

Listing 2.23 An example caching server named.boot file.

```
; a caching-only DNS server
primary    0.0.127-IN-ADDR.ARPA    /etc/named.local
cache                              /etc/named.ca
```

That is all that is required to run the caching-only DNS server.

Primary DNS Server

For a Microsoft DNS server, the setup of a primary DNS server is fairly straightforward. Select the server from the server list and select New Zone from the DNS menu. The display to create a new zone appears, as shown in Figure 2.11.

In this case, I am dealing with a primary DNS server, so I have selected that option and will enter the name of the zone. The DNS Manager automatically creates the zone file as it appears in Figure 2.12.

The DNS Manager then has the zone for the domain added to its list, as shown in Figure 2.13.

It is advisable to add the reserve DNS lookup as well; this is shown in Figures 2.14 and 2.15.

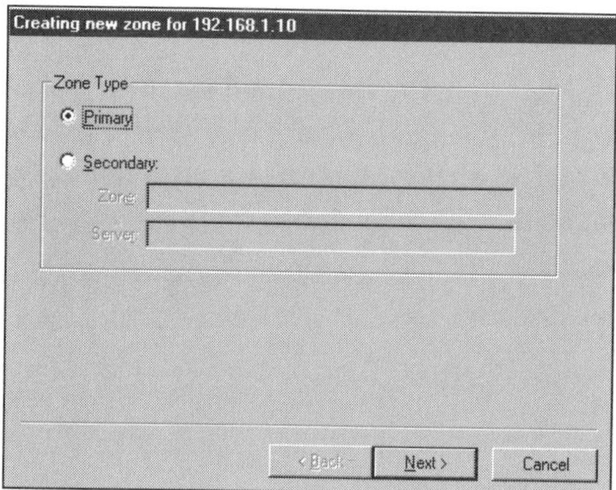

Figure 2.11 Creating a new DNS zone.

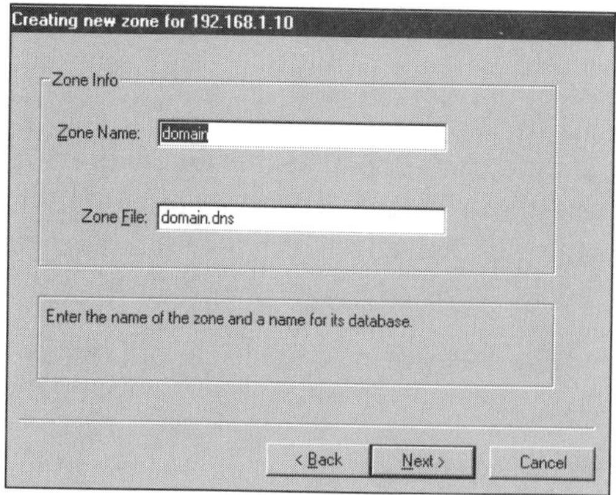

Figure 2.12 The new zone is created.

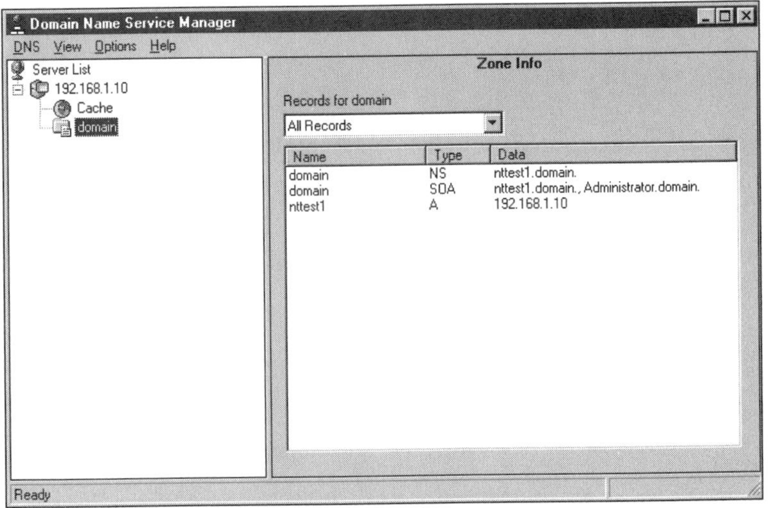

Figure 2.13 The new zone added to the list.

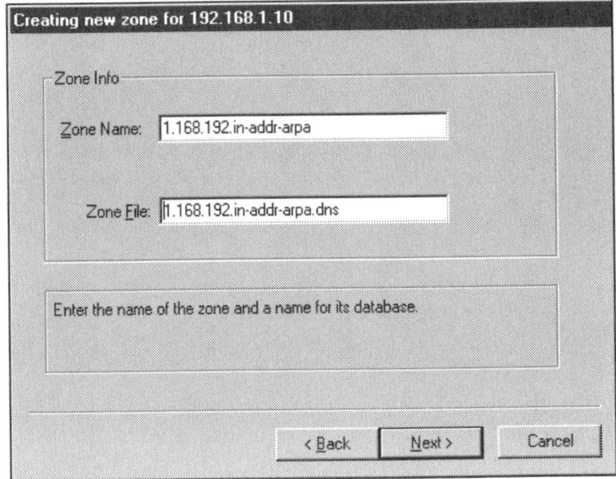

Figure 2.14 Adding the reverse zone.

Now the DNS records for the zone must be created. Select the zone from the server list, then select New Host from the DNS menu. A dialog box for the host record appears, as shown in Figure 2.16.

Continue to add hosts until the hosts are added to the database. You can see that these have been added in Figure 2.15.

The DNS manager automatically creates the Address (A) record and, if requested, the Pointer (PTR) record for each host. The other records, such as MX, are added manually using the New Record option from the DNS menu.

For a Unix DNS server called linuxdns1.domain with an IP address of 192.168.1.1, the named.boot file would be altered to the code shown in Listing 2.24.

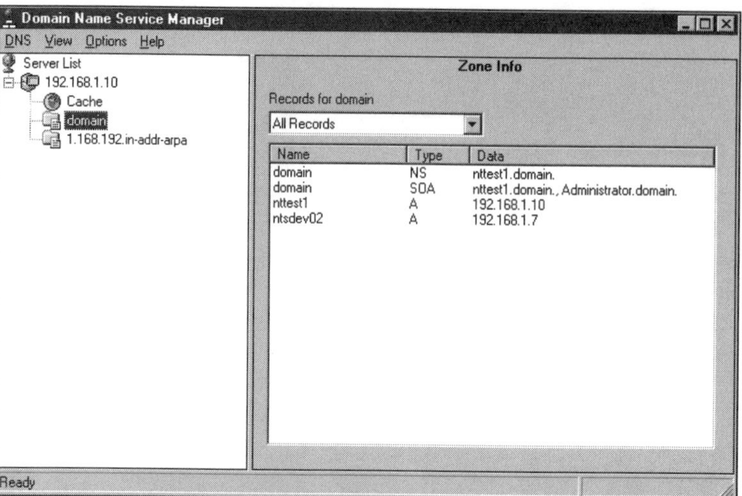

Figure 2.15 The reverse zone in the list.

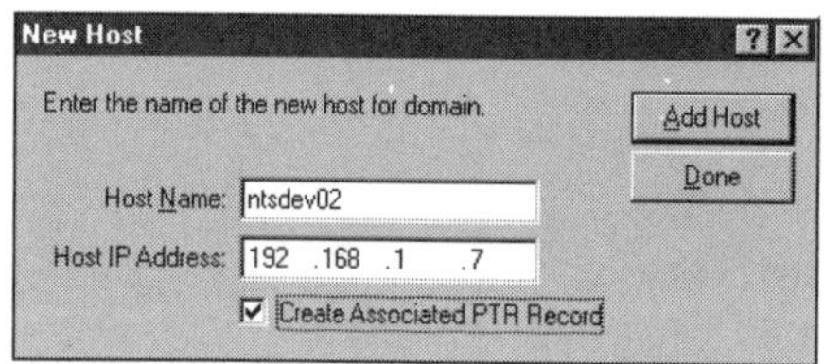

Figure 2.16 The New Host entry.

Listing 2.24 An example named.boot file.

```
; a primary DNS server
directory                                          /etc
primary     domain                                 named.domainhosts
primary     1.168.192-IN-ADDR.ARPA                 named.reversedomain
primary     0.0.127-IN-ADDR.ARPA                   named.local
cache                                              named.ca
```

The key line in this file is the first primary statement, which indicates that this is the primary server for the "domain" domain. The information for this domain is present in the named.domainhosts zone file. The line with named.reversedomain makes the local server the primary DNS server for the reverse domain 1.168.192-IN-ADDR.ARPA, and the resolution information for the domain is loaded from the named.reversedomain file.

The named.reversedomain file structure is almost identical to the named.local file. An example is shown in Listing 2.25.

Listing 2.25 An example named.reversedomain file.

```
; IP address to hostname mappings
@   IN SOA linuxdns1.domain.      root.linuxdns1.domain. (
           10000          ;serial
           36000          ;refresh every 10 hours
           3600           ;retry after 1 hour
           3600000 ;expire after 1000 hours
           2592000) ; Minimum
    IN NS  linuxdns1.domain.
1   IN PTR localhost.
```


The named.domainhosts file is the zone file that contains most of the domain information.

A sample named.domainhosts file for this system is shown in Listing 2.26.

Listing 2.26 An example named.domainhosts file.

```
; IP addresses and other hostname information for the 'domain' zone
@           IN SOA  linuxdns1.domain.      root.linuxdns1.domain. (
            10000          ;serial
            36000          ;refresh every 10 hours
            3600           ;retry after 1 hour
            3600000 ;expire after 1000 hours
            2592000) ; Minimum
; this zone has a couple of nameservers and a mail server
            IN NS   linuxdns1.domain.
            IN NS   linuxdns2.domain.
            IN MX   10      linuxmail1.domain.
            IN MX   20      linuxmail2.domain.
; it is necessary to define the localhost
localhost   IN      A       127.0.0.1
; list the hosts in this zone
linuxdns1   IN      A       192.168.1.1
linuxdns2   IN      A       192.168.1.2
linuxmail1  IN      A       192.168.1.3
            IN      MX      5       linuxmail1.domain.
            IN      CNAME   linuxmail1.domain.
linuxmail2  IN      A       192.168.1.4
            IN      MX      5       linuxmail2.domain.
            IN      CNAME   linuxmail2.domain.
linuxsmb1   IN      A       192.168.1.10
```

Secondary DNS Server

For a Microsoft DNS server, following the installation of the DNS service, the secondary DNS server can be installed by following the same method for creating an initial zone in the primary DNS server. The difference is that the secondary

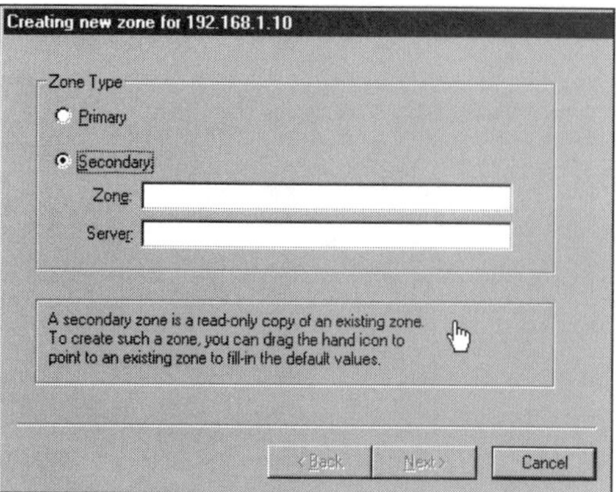

Figure 2.17 Secondary DNS zone created.

zone option is selected and the zone name and IP address of the primary DNS are entered as shown in Figure 2.17. The Microsoft DNS Manager will then create a secondary DNS server.

For a Unix DNS server called linuxdns2.domain with an IP address 192.168.1.2, the named.boot file would be altered to the code shown in Listing 2.27:

Listing 2.27 The named.boot file for a secondary DNS server.

```
; a secondary DNS server
directory                                                      /etc
secondary    domain                   192.168.1.1    named.domainhosts
secondary    1.168.192-IN-ADDR.ARPA   192.168.1.1    named.reversedomain
primary      0.0.127-IN-ADDR.ARPA                    named.local
cache                                                named.ca
```

The key line in this file is the first secondary statement, which indicates that this is a secondary server for the "domain" domain. The information for this domain is present in the primary server at 192.168.1.1, and the information for this zone should be stored in the named.domainhosts file. Likewise, the reverse domain information should be stored in the named.reversedomain file obtained from the primary server at 192.168.1.1. In all cases, entering "named" at the command prompt or entering it as command in a system startup starts the DNS service. The hosts on your network then make use of the DNS service by referring to the DNS server, be it in the primary, secondary, or cache in the network configuration.

The Windows 95/98 and NT versions are almost identical; under the DNS tab through Network icon, the entries will read as in Figure 2.18.

In Unix systems, this is in the /etc/resolv.conf file, and a suitable entry for the network is shown in Listing 2.28.

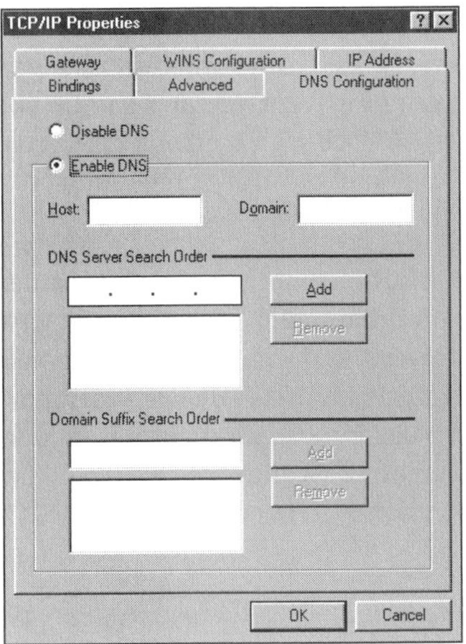

Figure 2.18 Windows client DNS entry.

Listing 2.28 The /etc/resolv.conf file.

```
# /etc/resolv.conf
domain      domain
nameserver 192.168.1.1
nameserver 192.168.1.2
```

Using DHCP

Dynamic Host Configuration Protocol (DHCP) is used to dynamically assign IP addresses to network clients. This protocol has been available for some time; it was not a Microsoft design, although the use of DHCP has expanded considerably in Microsoft Windows desktop networking. DHCP is defined in RFC 1533, RFC 1534, RFC 1541, and RFC 1542. Copies of all these can be found on this book's CD-ROM in /doc/RFC.

DHCP is a client/server service. At a minimum, you will need to have one server running a DHCP service and one or more clients using TCP/IP networking with a running DHCP client. DHCP is part of the TCP/IP stack. Originally the different server platforms were restricted to Microsoft and Novell; however, various DHCP servers now exist for Windows NT, Novell, and Unix.

The normal DHCP setup would be to use the DHCP service that is present in the Windows NT server and can be installed from the Network configuration|Services tab in Control Panel. In addition, Linux has a DHCP service and can be configured to operate as either a DHCP server or a DHCP client. The Linux mini-HOWTO on DHCP and related documents on setup and configuration can be found on this book's CD-ROM in /doc/HOWTO/Linux-mini-HOWTOs/.

Why DHCP? DHCP allows for considerable flexibility and lower maintenance in a large network. The configuration of a very large number of hosts on a network with the correct IP addresses, netmask, gateways, and so on can place a considerable burden on the support staff, and the presence of a DHCP server on a network can lessen this administrative burden considerably. The centralized location of the TCP/IP and network information can greatly ease the challenges faced when networks are structurally changed or when an incorrect configuration of TCP/IP network settings has occurred.

One common use of DHCP is to reduce the number of IP addresses that are physically used. Let's say that a pool of 256 IP addresses was available for the laptop PCs of a company's sales force. In this case, it would be possible to allocate these when they were needed rather than assigning them to machines that connect infrequently and thus use up the IP addresses. Likewise, ISPs commonly use DHCP to dynamically allocate a different IP address every time you dial in.

The use of DHCP can occur safely alongside machines with fixed IP addresses. To aid in NetBIOS name to IP address resolution WINS could be utilized. The WINS service was designed for use with DHCP where the temporary nature of a machine having a specific IP address exists.

How is DHCP configured? As already stated, the DHCP service should exist on a server. Although it might seem obvious, it is worth noting that you should not configure the DHCP server to obtain its IP using DHCP and then assign it a fixed IP address. The assignment of an IP address using DHCP is the default when installing or configuring TCP/IP networking for Windows NT Workstation clients.

When the software is installed on the server you intend to use, your first task is to configure the DHCP server with some essential information:

- A defined range of IP addresses that may be given out to clients
- The subnet mask, default gateway, primary and secondary DNS IP address (if any), and WINS server IP address.
- The duration of the DHCP lease for an IP address (how long it will be allocated to a specific machine).

The Windows NT configuration for all this information is done through the DHCP Manager. Note that DHCP deals only with the TCP/IP fully qualified domain names (FQDNs) and does not recognize NetBIOS names.

It is possible to configure both client and server to reserve IP addresses for hosts; this might be important if you are using network applications that depend on the same IP address being used every time. Further details of the DHCP service can be found in many of the books listed in Appendix B.

Configuring Ports And Services

An application that needs to operate between two machines needs to know what to do with the network packets that it sends over TCP and UDP between the machines. The process involves the use of sockets, which are a combination of the machine's IP number and TCP port number. Table 2.5 shows these ports and service. An application that communicates between one machine and an application on another machines does so by using a port number to identify the TCP layer.

An example of the way in which these are used follows. A PC requests a Telnet connection (port 23 is used in Telnet) from another PC. The TCP protocol assembles the socket for this connection and assigns it to the packet to be transmitted. In this example, the sending machine is at IP 192.168.1.1 and the receiving machine at 192.168.1.2. The socket number for this connection would be 192.168.1.1 and 23. If the connection request is successful, the receiving PC transmits a packet with its socket number attached at 192.168.1.2 and 23 once the necessary exchanges have taken place. Then a Telnet connection and session will exist between the two PCs. An SMB session request would occur in a similar way, the various port numbers being added to the IP addresses as the SMB session is established.

When a PC wants to create more than one service session, it adds another number, a source port number—which is usually a value of 1,024 (or greater) higher than the original port number—along with the destination port number to the socket identifier. Thus, a Samba server would have the destination ports 137, 138, and 139 and might have several connections and sessions in progress, all with different source numbers being used with the IP addresses of the remote PCs.

The use of ports and IP addresses has clear implications when routers and firewalls, which act as IP filters, are in place between the two connected PCs. These would need to be configured to allow for these services.

Table 2.5 NetBIOS and SMB services and ports.

Port Number	Process Name	Description
137	NETBIOS-NS	NetBIOS Name Service
138	NETBIOS-DG	NetBIOS Datagram Service
139	NETBIOS-SS	NetBIOS Session Service

Using RAS

Sometimes it is necessary to connect clients or remote offices to networks. This is easily accomplished using RAS, which is available for most operating systems. Linux and Microsoft Windows include the client software with the standard installations. The setup of RAS servers to allow dial-in to a network is somewhat more difficult to achieve, as it involves installing or configuring RAS software to allow dial-in. Chapter 8 details the steps required to connect a remote PC to an office to make use of Samba and to establish a RAS dial-in server for use with Linux and Microsoft Windows clients.

Configuring Microsoft Windows Networking

Microsoft Windows networking is configured and managed on Windows 9.x and NT clients and servers through the Network icon in the Control Panel. In addition, Windows networking is visible through the Explorer or Network Neighborhood applications. However, the underlying protocol for Windows networking is NetBIOS over IP, also known as NBT or NetBT (SPX is not discussed here) and the SMB protocol that makes use of NetBIOS over IP.

Using NetBIOS

In a manner similar to that used with hostname and IP addresses, NetBIOS allows you to provide names for your hosts so that you can use those names more easily. In a TCP/IP network, instead of 192.168.2.15, you could use, say, "goofy" to identify the host on the local subnet. The NetBIOS name is usually, but not always, the same as the Internet hostname. For matters of security, you might find that hiding the NetBIOS name and using a generic hostname is advisable. Chapter 11 details where this difference can be applied and the problems that this practice can introduce.

The naming practices allowed are defined in RFC 1001 and 1002, copies of which are located on this book's CD-ROM in /doc/RFC. The NetBIOS name, unlike the DNS name, is a flat namespace, means that unlike DNS, no hierarchy of names exists; the namespace is limited to 16 alphanumeric characters that include a to z, A to Z, 0 to 9, and the special characters: !, @, #, $, %, ^, &, (), -, ', {}, /, and ~. Of these 16 characters, 15 are available for the name; the 16th character is reserved to describe the resource type of the name.

The NT Server Resource Kit Networking Guide, one of the NetBIOS references listed in Appendix B, is an extensive source of information on NetBIOS names and includes a more thorough treatment of the topic than space allows here. The types of NetBIOS name are included in Tables 2.6 and 2.7.

The NetBIOS name and resource character used on, say, a Windows NT workstation can be identified by using the **nbtstat** command. An example is shown in Listing 2.29.

Table 2.6 NetBIOS unique names.

Resource Character	Description Of Resource
<00>	The NetBIOS name for the workstation service name
<03>	The messenger service name used for sending and receiving messages
<1B>	The domain master browser name, used by a machine to contact a domain's primary domain controller
<06>	RAS server service
<1F>	NetDDE service
<20>	Server service name that provides an access point for file sharing
<21>	RAS client
<BE>	Network monitor agent
<BF>	Network monitor utility

Table 2.7 NetBIOS group names.

Resource Character	Description Of Resource
<1C>	The domain group name, registered by the domain controller, that contains a list of the computers that have registered the domain name
<1D>	The master browser name used by clients to access the domain's master browser
<1E>	The normal group name that is involved with the election of master browsers; browsers broadcast to this name and listen on it to elect a master browser
<20>	The Internet group that is registered with WINS servers and identifies groups of machines for administration purposes
MSBROWSE	A string that is appended to the domain name and broadcast on the local subnet to announce the domain to other master browsers

Listing 2.29 The nbtstat command.

```
C:\nbtstat -a ntwdev01

       NetBIOS Remote Machine Name Table

   Name               Type         Status
---------------------------------------------
NTWDEV01       <00>  UNIQUE      Registered
DOMAIN         <00>  GROUP       Registered
NTWDEV01       <03>  UNIQUE      Registered
NTWDEV01       <20>  UNIQUE      Registered
DOMAIN         <1E>  GROUP       Registered
CHRISTINE      <03>  UNIQUE      Registered

MAC Address = 00-20-18-2D-25-88
```

NetBIOS Names

Discussions of possible standards for NetBIOS names have occurred in places where I have worked. These standards fall into three main categories. I have included an example of the outcome of these discussions to provide some guidance on naming conventions that you might want to use.

First, you could simply choose a real name, a person's name, an object, or a reference name, for example, ORANGE, PARIS, or TOPCAT. Second, you could simply name according to function or location, for example, FRONTDESK1, RECEPTION1, or FINANCE1. Finally, you could incorporate the details of the domain, the operating system, the location, or the asset number, for example, UKNTS40PRD01 or USNTW40DEV02.

You also could include combinations or variations on any of these. The 15 characters provide a fair amount of flexibility, but you should definitely attempt to rationalize any naming strategy you use. For example, LINUXSERVER1 may not be very helpful, as it doesn't aid in identifying a function or location; perhaps UKLNX52DEV01 might be a better choice even though it is somewhat difficult to say.

The names of the machines I use most are based on cartoon characters. Workstations are named after sidekicks (e.g., Benny, from Top Cat), the servers are named after main cartoon characters (e.g., Roadrunner), and the domains are the major cartoon studios (HB and MGM), so you can see that you can be flexible with your naming.

It is also possible to subdivide the NetBIOS namespace using the **scope** parameter. The use of this parameter is discussed in Chapter 8.

LMHOSTS

Whereas TCP/IP uses the hosts configuration file to retain a local copy of hosts that are regularly used (thus avoiding DNS resolution), a similar file in ASCII, known as LMHOSTS, is used for name resolution from NetBIOS to IP. The layout can be seen in the sample LMHOSTS file shown in Listing 2.30.

Listing 2.30 A sample LMHOSTS file.

```
# NTSDEV01 LMHOSTS file
#
192.168.1.7     ntsdev01        #PRE #DOM:domain  #PDC
192.168.1.8     ntsdev02        #PRE       #source server
192.168.1.100   ntscfg01        #PRE       #needed for the include
#
#BEGIN_ALTERNATE
#INCLUDE \\ntscfg01\public\lmhosts
#INCLUDE \\ntsdev01\public\lmhosts
#END_ALTERNATE
#
```

This file's format is such that the IP address should be placed in the first column followed by the corresponding NetBIOS name. One or more spaces or tabs separate the columns. Any "#" character at the beginning or end of a line is used to indicate a comment. Exceptions to this are shown in Listing 2.31.

Listing 2.31 lmhosts file exceptions.

```
#PRE
#DOM:<domain>
#INCLUDE <filename>
#BEGIN_ALTERNATE
#END_ALTERNATE
\0xnn (non-printing character support)
```

An entry on the line with the characters **#PRE** will cause that entry to be preloaded into the NetBIOS name cache. By default, entries are not preloaded but are parsed only after dynamic name resolution fails.

An entry with the **#DOM:*domain*** tag will associate the entry with the domain specified by ***domain***. This affects how the browser and logon services behave in TCP/IP environments. To preload the hostname associated with the **#DOM** entry, you must add a **#PRE** to the line. The ***domain*** is always preloaded, although it will not be shown when the name cache is viewed.

An **#INCLUDE *filename*** is a very useful method of centrally controlling the NetBIOS entries because it forces the RFC NetBIOS (NBT) software to seek the specified ***filename*** and parse it as if it were on the local host. ***filename*** is generally an UNC-based name, allowing a centralized lmhosts file to be maintained on a server.

Note that you must always provide a mapping for the IP address of the server prior to the **#INCLUDE**. This mapping must use the **#PRE** directive. In addition, the share "public" in the example below must be in the LanManServer list of NullSessionShares in order for client machines to be able to read the lmhosts file successfully. This key is under HKEY_LOCAL_MACHINE\System\system\currentcontrolset\services\lanmanserver\parameters\nullsessionshares in the Registry. Simply add "public" to the list found there.

The **#BEGIN_** and **#END_ALTERNATE** keywords allow multiple **#INCLUDE** statements to be grouped together. Any single successful include will cause the group to succeed.

Finally, nonprinting characters can be embedded in mappings by first surrounding the NetBIOS name in quotations and then using the \0xnn notation to specify a hex value for a nonprinting character.

Configuration

No additional configuration is required to enable use of this file. The Windows operating systems include support for this file in the standard network software where TCP/IP and NetBIOS over IP are used. However, the location might be different for the different versions. The option by which a central lmhosts file can be read by individual hosts—by including it in use—can be useful and is probably the only configuration detail that requires attention to detail.

Why use lmhosts? The lmhosts file works on a similar basis to the hosts file that exists on Unix (/etc/hosts) and Windows (/%system32%/drivers/etc or /win95/system) that is used to resolve the DNS hostname and/or IP address for a remote host. There is a sample or lmhosts.sam file installed in these locations following network installation. The function is to act as a shortcut to, or local copy of, the most commonly-referenced NetBIOS hostnames and to maintain a copy of the information required for name or IP resolution locally. It might be common practice to populate this file with the NetBIOS name and IP information for the primary domain controller (PDC) and backup domain controller (BDC) of a network along with the file, in which case printer servers should have fixed IP addresses. This is useful for a number of hosts, especially when fixed IP addresses are used; however, this file can become laborious to maintain if the number of hosts in it exceeds 100, which is a lot of hosts. When large numbers of hostname to IP address resolutions are required, especially when DHCP is utilized, the only realistic option is to use WINS.

NetBIOS Elections

Microsoft clients can access other hosts on a network through browsing. This is most evident in the Network Neighborhood dialog box, which allows the client to browse the hosts on the network and, with the appropriate permissions, to make use of the identified resources.

Browsing involves sending broadcasts over a local subnet using NetBIOS over IP. All hosts on that network would then respond to the broadcast in time, informing the network what services were available from each host. Rather than having excessive network traffic with all hosts on a network notifying their presence and every host requesting what services were available, an enhancement to this method enables a host to adopt the role of master browser. This host sends broadcasts to other hosts on a network to learn the nature of the available services and responds to clients who want to learn which resources and hosts exist on the local network. The master browser on a Microsoft network is also the machine with the latest version of the operating system. This host announces itself as the master browser, and other hosts on the network interrogate it to determine the resources on the network. When a new NetBIOS host first starts up on a network, it sends a broadcast to the network announcing its presence. This broadcast includes details of the host's operating system level. The master browser responds to this host, and if the master browser's operating system level is lower, a process known as a NetBIOS election starts; the new host then becomes the master browser. If the new host has an identical operating system level, the original master browser remains in place. The standard operating-system-level values for the various operating systems are listed in Table 2.8.

Normally, Samba announces itself with an operating system level of 0; however, a number of relevant parameters in the smb.conf file are involved in setting the NetBIOS election criteria. Details on the use and setting of these values are discussed in Chapter 8.

Table 2.8 Operating-system-level values.

Operating System	Operating System Level
DOS	1
Windows for Workgroups	1
Windows 95	1
Windows NT 3.51 Workstation	16
Windows NT 3.51 Server	32
Windows NT 4.0 Workstation	16
Windows NT 4.0 Server	32

Working With WINS

The use of the lmhosts file provides the necessary local NetBIOS name to IP address resolution that most hosts require. However, when many hosts and/or DHCP are used on a network, this might not be a viable option; this is where WINS comes into play. In summary, WINS is to *NetBIOS name to IP resolution* what DNS is to *hostname to IP resolution*. The major difference is that WINS is a dynamic service and uses the periodic NetBIOS broadcasts and elections to build its database.

In practice, a WINS server collects the broadcasts from various hosts on a network and so learns the IP addresses associated with those hosts on the network. This reduces network traffic in two ways. One (or more if you are using a Microsoft NT server) WINS server and database act as the central location for both the registration and the resolution of NetBIOS name to IP addresses. Before attempting to locate the host, a client configured to use the WINS server first interrogates the local lmhosts file, then the WINS server, and then the DNS server (should networking have been configured that way). If a WINS server does not exist, the NetBIOS client hosts on the network regularly generate traffic to both announce and determine the NetBIOS names and IP addresses of those hosts for which a service is required. This will still occur from time to time, but then you will no longer have the large numbers of broadcasts associated with every client attempting to determine which service is to be connected to. This can greatly reduce the network load for a NetBIOS- or Windows-dominated network.

The broadcasts are also restricted to the local subnet only. Although this might not affect small networks, larger networks that span several subnets are not able to communicate with each other in this manner. Even though lmhosts can be used in this situation, WINS might be more flexible in the long run.

WINS solves both sets of problems by design and can be used by configuring clients to make use of the WINS server for NetBIOS name to IP address registration and resolution, including hosts on different subnets on your network.

The standard Microsoft NT WINS server includes a WINS server as part of the possible network management administration tools and is installed through the Network icon in the Control Panel. Figure 2.19 shows the NT version of the WINS server.

The creation of a WINS server on a Samba server is as simple as adding **wins support = yes** to the smb.conf file. Note that if you already have a Microsoft NT server performing this duty on your network, you need not add a Samba WINS server to your network. This is because of the property that a Windows NT server

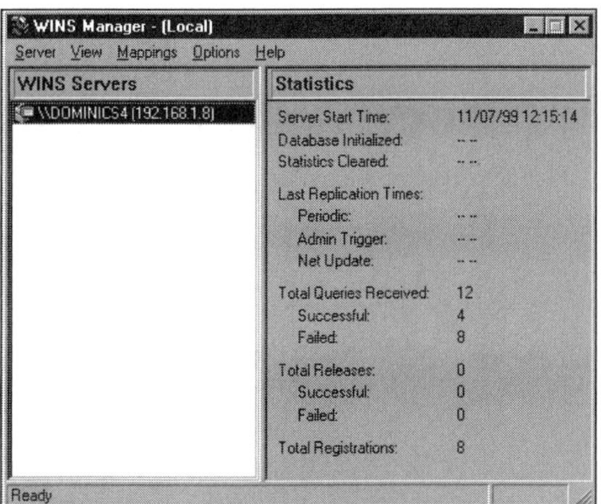

Figure 2.19 The NT WINS Manager.

would expect to adopt this function. Also, the Microsoft WINS server is able to replicate its database with another NT WINS server, say, at a company's other location; Samba does not yet support this ability and can be used only in a single configuration. The WINS database for a Samba server is contained in the WINS.DAT file, which is an ACSII text file in the <samba_home>/var/locks/ directory. Listing 2.32 shows this file.

Listing 2.32 Entries in the WINS.DAT file.

```
VERSION 1 160619
"DOMAIN#00" 930008238 255.255.255.255 c4R
"DOMAIN#1e" 930008238 255.255.255.255 c4R
"LINUXROUTER1#00" 930008238 192.168.1.1 46R
"LINUXROUTER1#03" 930008238 192.168.1.1 46R
"LINUXROUTER1#20" 930008238 192.168.1.1 46R
```

In case of failure, say, for a WINS server that held the database for a couple of hundred hosts, it would make sense to be able to create a copy of this database for purposes of recovery. However, you cannot copy this file on a running Samba server. You need to shut down the nmbd service first. However, if the WINS server fails—either because of Samba or otherwise—and needs to be restarted, the NetBIOS hosts on the network will quickly re-announce themselves on the server starting, and the database is quickly re-created (see Listing 2.33).

Listing 2.33 A copy of the entries in BROWSE.DAT.

```
"DOMAIN"                    c0001000 "DOMINICS4"                    "DOMAIN"
"LINUXROUTER1"              40019a03 "Linux Router Samba Server"    "DOMAIN"
"DOMINICS4"                 4006120b "Tower Server - BDC"           "DOMAIN"
```

Understanding SMB

Currently, five SMB protocol extensions are available. These are listed in Table 2.9.

The different protocol extensions were developed as Microsoft released new versions of its operating systems. The later versions are enhancements on the earlier versions.

What happens in a normal SMB exchange? First, let's take a simple example. I'm using an application sitting on my desktop PC running Windows NT; say, Microsoft Word. I need to look at Chapter 2 of the book on Samba that I'm writing, and it is actually stored on the hard drive of one of my Linux servers. Let's say that the Word document is called Chapter2.doc and is stored in a directory on the Linux server that is mapped to the workstation as drive S: . When I choose to open the Word document using File|Open and then selecting S:\Chapter2.doc., Windows NT fires off an SMB request to the Linux server, and a series of transactions takes place between the Windows NT workstations and the Linux server to open and send the Word document Chapter2.doc to the desktop PC. The process is shown in Figure 2.20.

Table 2.9 SMB protocol extensions.

Version	Explanation
CORE	The first version of SMB; has no concept of usernames
COREPLUS	An enhancement of the original
LANMAN1	Included support for long file names
LANMAN2	Enhanced version of LANMAN1
NT1 (and NT2)	The current version, which is included with Samba and Windows NT 4.0 Service Pack 3 (Service Pack 4 and later implement SMB with a newer version but are backward compatible); also known as NT LM 0.12

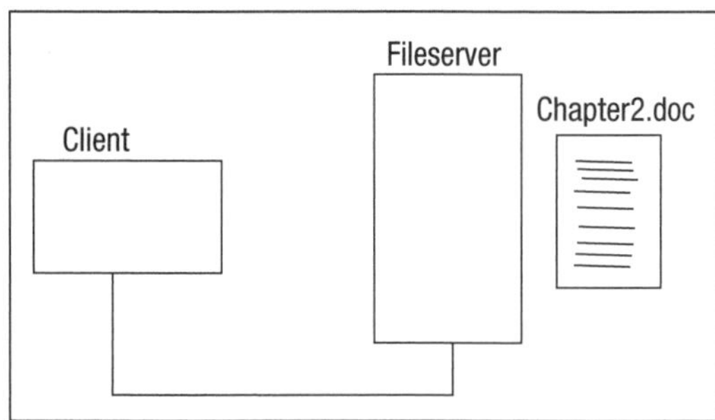

Figure 2.20 An SMB session to open a document on a server by a client.

The actual capture of an SMB session that involved this request is analyzed here. It begins with a **negotiate** command from the SMB client being sent to the server:

```
C negotiate, Dialect = NT LM 0.12
```

This indicates that the client, an NT server in this case, will understand the NT LM 0.12 or NT1 protocol extension. The server responds with a response that indicates the level of the protocol extension that it will use:

```
R negotiate, Dialect #=7
```

The next series of exchanges depends on the security level being used by the SMB server. In this example, share-level security is being used. The client connects to the server requesting the directory contents first:

```
SMB: C session setup & X, Username = ADMINISTRATOR, and C tree connect & X,
Share = \\LAPTOP\D
```

The tree connect is similar to the mount command used with NFS. The server responds with the directory details:

```
R session setup & X, and R tree connect & X, Type = A:
```

In addition, if there are no errors in the connection, it will respond with an identifier that the client will use for all future SMB connections for this session:

```
Tree ID      (TID) = 2 (0x2)
```

The client then confirms the attributes for the file:

```
C get attributes, File = \SambaBook\Chapter 2.doc
```

This includes the TID value. The server then determines the permissions on the file:

```
R get attributes
```

The client requests that it be opened:

```
C open & X, File = \SambaBook\Chapter 2.doc (R -Share Deny None)
```

The server sends the file to the client one piece at a time:

```
R open & X, FID = 0x1, File Size = 0x1c600
```

The client then acknowledges receipt of the file until the whole file has been transferred to the client:

```
C read & X, FID = 0x1, Read 0x800 at 0x00000000
```

How Did I Capture This Information?

Many "network sniffer" packages are available that will "snoop" on all or a selected part of the traffic on your network. These can aid in the analysis of a network by capturing all the traffic that passes on a network. In this case, I used Microsoft NT's Network Monitor from the SMS version of the software and captured all traffic between the client and server, filtered it to look only at SMB traffic, and extracted the previous sections from it.

Several other programs are regularly used; one of the most common being tcpdump. The Samba Team (Andrew Tridgell) has written a series of patches for this program that enable SMB sessions to be captured more easily than in the original.

Chapter 12 will give you details on how to use both tools to aid diagnosis. You will find netmon and tcpdump captures included and analyzed for several different SMB processes.

The use of these tools has also been fundamental in the design and coding of Samba when reengineering other operating systems. I was fortunate enough to carry out a series of SMB captures from a session between an NT PDC and a new BDC. This was useful when attempting to re-create the Microsoft NT functionality when setting up a PDC with a BDC to view the RPC calls made during the setup of a new BDC on an NT network. This was passed on to members of the Samba Team.

The SMB protocol is used by Microsoft Windows 3.11, NT, and 95 to share disks and printers. Using the Samba suite of tools by Andrew Tridgell, Unix (including Linux) machines can share disk and printers with Windows hosts.

Sample Networking Setups

Samba uses the TCP/IP protocol. If you are investigating the use of Samba within a non-Microsoft Windows network, you need to be sure that you have TCP/IP networking configured for your operating system.

Microsoft Windows Networking Setup

I am assuming that most readers will already have a PC running Windows 95/98 or NT and are exploring the possibility of using Samba either at home or at work. If you already have either operating system set up, this discussion assumes that the network instructions are for configuring the network following a fresh installation. If you do not have a network card installed or have not yet configured your network settings, these instructions can be followed completely. If you do not have either operating system installed, it is a relatively painless process. Simply follow the instructions that came with your Microsoft operating system. Many books are available to help you (see Appendix B).

Whenever you are configuring networking for Microsoft operating systems, you will need to have access to the original CD-ROM. Insert the it into your CD-ROM drive.

The essential difference between the Microsoft operating systems is that for NT you must be logged on to the PC as an administrator to carry out this process.

If you do not have the network adapter installed in the PC, you must first install your network adapter into the PC. Shut it down in the normal manner and install the network adapter as directed by the instructions that came with it. Switch the PC back on. The Microsoft operating system, depending on the hardware, might or might not detect the network adapter. If it detects it as a plug-and-play device, enter the software driver for the network adapter and operating system CD-ROM when requested. This will set up and configure the operating system to use the new network adapter. This might have entered the adapter information into the networking configuration as set out in the following steps:

1. Open the Control Panel. You can do this in two ways.

    - The first option is to select and open (by double-clicking) the My Computer icon on your desktop. Once the Control Panel icon appears, you need to select and open it (see Figures 2.21 and 2.22).

    - The second option is to click on the Start menu and then select Settings|Control Panel (see Figure 2.23).

    You will be presented with the Control Panel window.

Figure 2.21 My Computer.

Figure 2.22 The Control Panel.

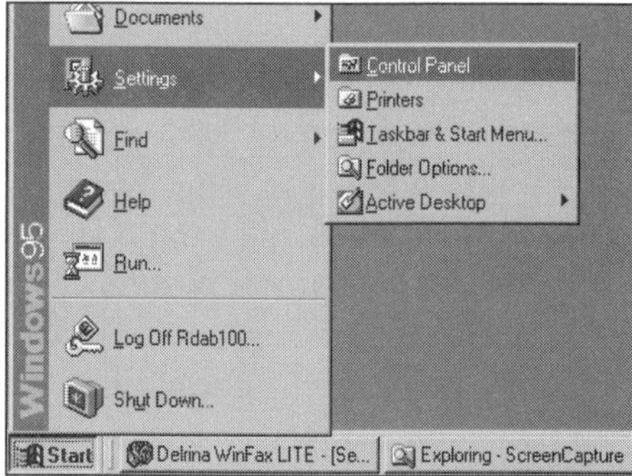

Figure 2.23 Opening the Control Panel from the Start menu.

2. In the Control Panel window, select and open the Network icon that was highlighted in Figure 2.22. This will open the Network configuration dialog boxes for either Windows 95/98 or Windows NT. Figure 2.24 shows the Windows 95 Network dialog box.

   To set up a network for use with Samba, you will need to have the following network components installed:

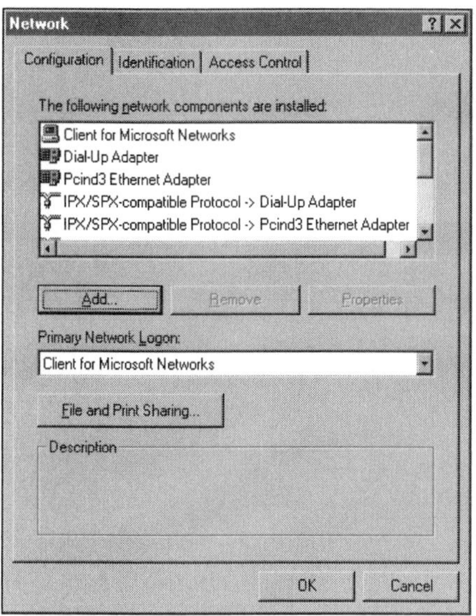

Figure 2.24 Windows 95 network setup.

- *Client for Microsoft Networks*
- *Network adapter*—Ethernet card of some description
- *Protocol*—TCP/IP (IPX and NetBEUI are optional because they do not interfere with a TCP/IP network)

It is also optional at this point to install file and printer sharing, which will allow others to use or access the files on your PC or use your printers. Details for doing this are covered in Chapter 7.

3. If your adapter is not detected automatically, you will need to manually add the Client for Microsoft Networking. To do this, click on Add. This will open the Select Network Component Type dialog box, as shown in Figure 2.25. Highlight the Client option, then click on Add; this is activated only after you have selected an option.

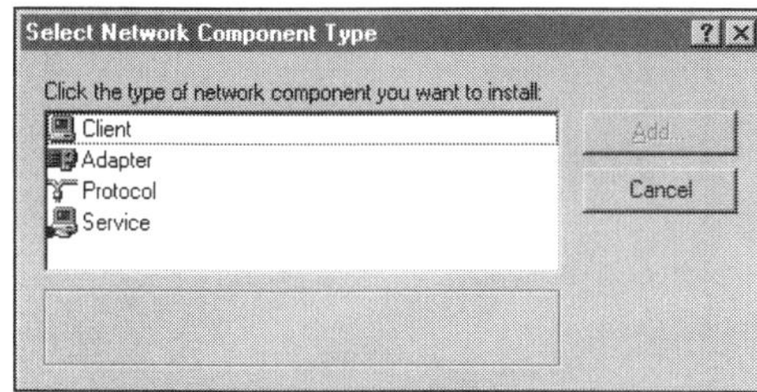

Figure 2.25 Windows 95 Select Network Component Type dialog box.

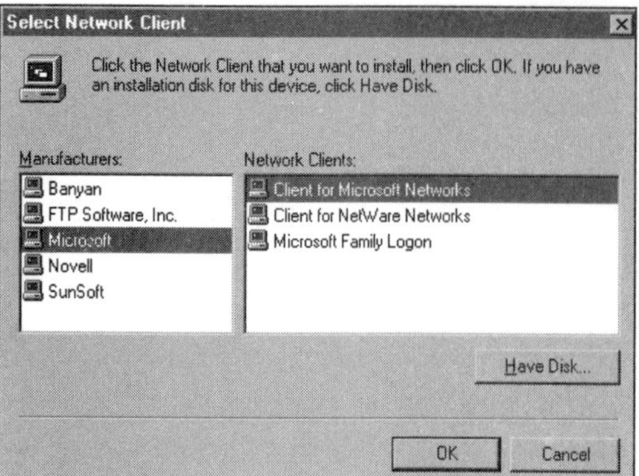

Figure 2.26 Windows 95 Select Network Client dialog box.

The Select Network Client dialog box, shown in Figure 2.26, contains several choices, depending on what software is installed on your PC. Select the Microsoft option from the manufacturer's list and the Client for Microsoft Networks. Click on OK.

4. You should then be prompted with the Select Network Adapters dialog box, as shown in Figure 2.27. You will need to select the manufacturer and model of your network adapter. Not all the currently available network adapters are included in this list. If no options appear, insert the floppy or the CD containing software drivers that came with your network adapter into the PC and select Have Disk. Find and select the appropriate choices for your system and click on OK.
5. You should be returned to the Network dialog box. Four components should be listed.

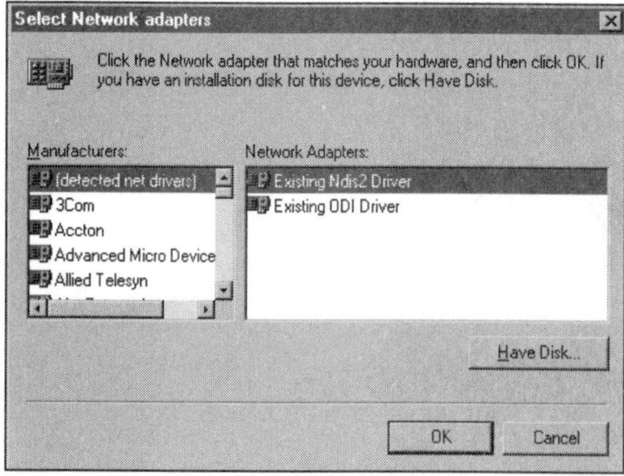

Figure 2.27 Windows 95 Select Network Adapters dialog box.

You need to add the TCP/IP protocol, so, as in Step 3, click on Add to bring up the Select Network Component Type dialog box. Select the protocol component and click on Add. The dialog box presented will list a number of manufacturers. Select Microsoft from the Manufacturers list and TCP/IP from the Network Protocols list, as shown in Figure 2.28, then click on OK.

You will now be returned to the Network dialog box again. As mentioned previously, the IPX and NetBEUI protocols are not required for Samba networking and may be removed.

NOTE: *Serious networking implications on you particular setup can occur if you do this, so be sure to check with your network administrator or networking documentation if any of these protocols are already present on your system.*

6. You will need to configure the Client for Microsoft Networks properties. Select Client for Microsoft Networks and then click on Properties. A dialog box similar to that shown in Figure 2.29 will appear. Ensure that the Log On To Windows NT Domain checkbox is selected and that the Windows NT domain is identified correctly.

   This assumes that you already have either a Microsoft NT domain or a Samba server operational. This allows you to log on to the network. If you do not have either, it might be prudent to ignore this step for the moment and move on to Step 7. You can always return to this step later.

   The default domain name for a Samba server is WORKGROUP; for an NT controlled domain it is DOMAIN. These might be appropriate entries if no other networks exist that use these names. Chapter 9 includes more information on Microsoft domain control and domain names. A normal operation is to select the Logon And Restore Network Connections checkbox. Click on OK, and you will return to the Network dialog box.

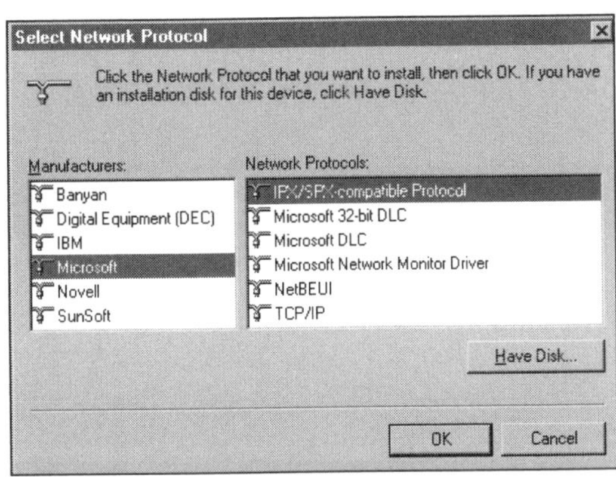

Figure 2.28 Windows 95 Select Network Protocol.

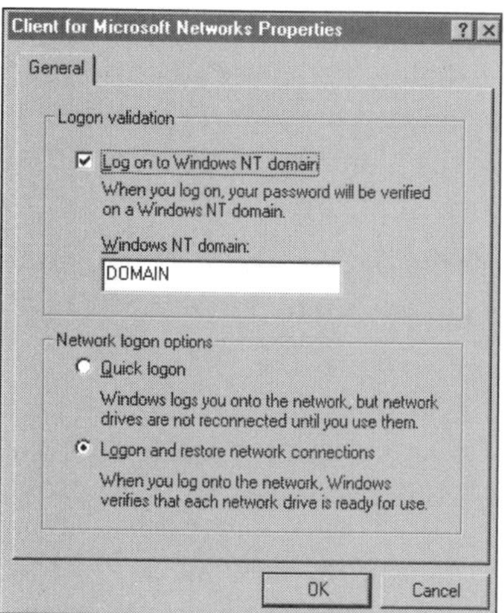

Figure 2.29 Client for Microsoft Networks Properties dialog box.

7. You now need to configure the TCP/IP properties of your network connection. Select the TCP/IP protocol and then click on Properties. The TCP/IP Properties dialog box appears. This dialog box has six sections, but in this case we will install only simple TCP/IP networking and provide your network adapter with an IP address.

   Select the Specify An IP Address radio button on the IP Address tab and enter the IP address and subnet mask for your network. The IP address should be unique in your network; otherwise, conflicts will occur. The other entries in this dialog box are not relevant at this time.

   As shown in Figure 2.30, the entries for a sample PC have been made for network 192.168.1.0 with a subnet mask of 255.255.255.0. The exact settings you will use depend on your own circumstances.

8. You need to name your PC for the network. In the Network dialog box, select the Identification tab and enter the computer name and computer description. The default under Windows 95 for Workgroups is WORKGROUP. See Figure 2.31 for a selection of these entries.

9. In the Network dialog box, select the Access Control tab. The default is set to share-level access control. Select the User-Level Access Control radio button and complete the Obtain List Of Users And Groups From box, setting the entry to YOUR WORKGROUP NAME, as in Figure 2.32. Click on OK.

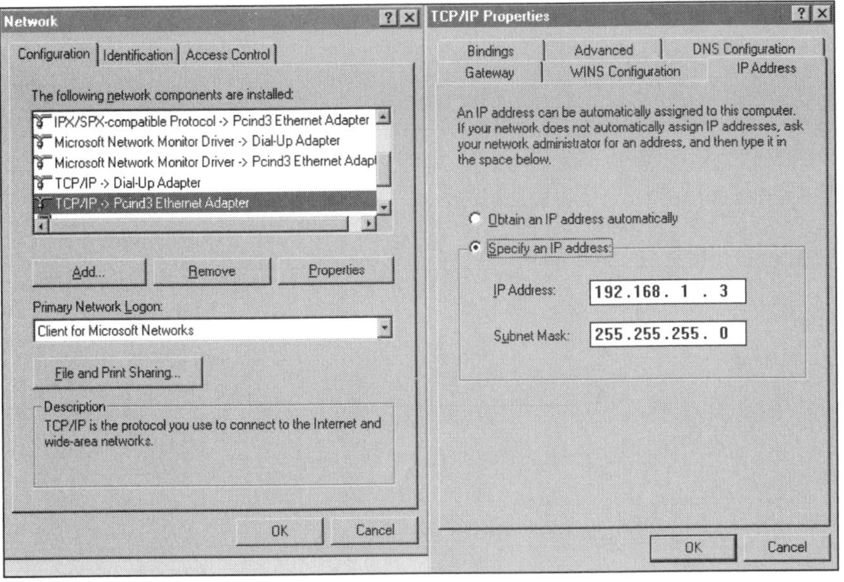

Figure 2.30 Windows 95 TCP/IP Properties.

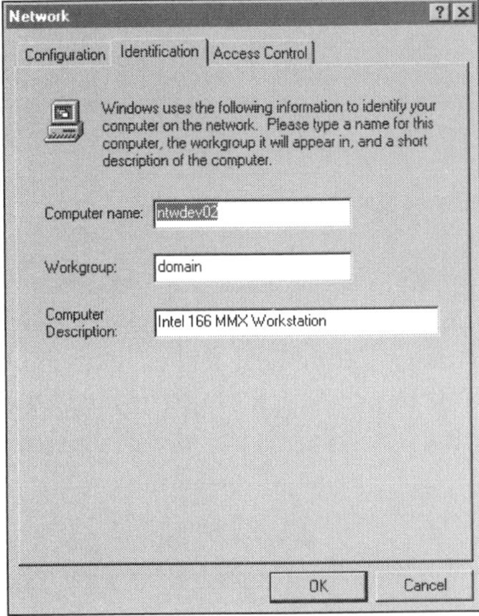

Figure 2.31 Windows 95 Network Identification Tab.

2. Networking

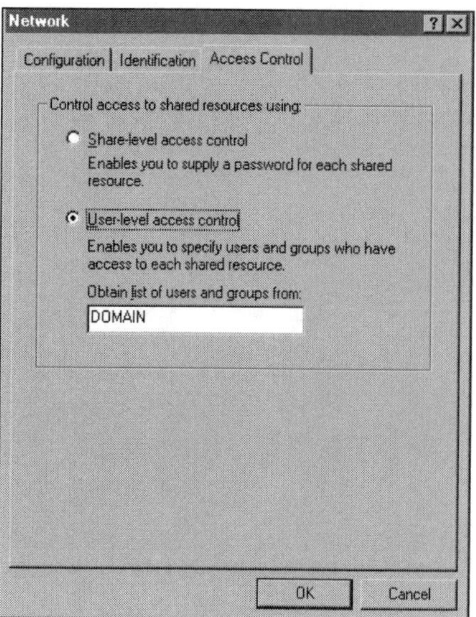

Figure 2.32 Windows 95 Access Control tab.

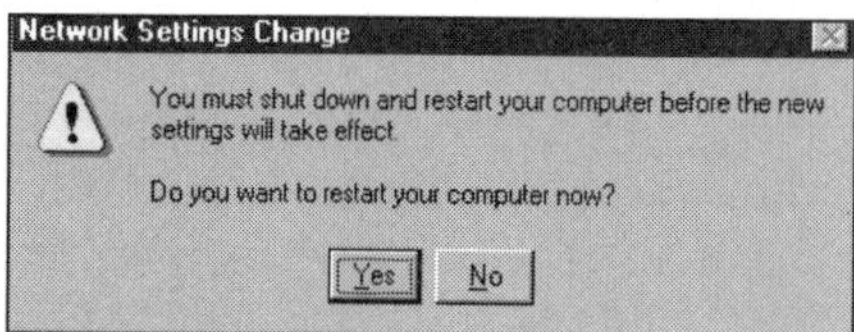

Figure 2.33 Request to restart following a network configuration change.

> After installing all the software, you might be asked to enter floppies or CD-ROMs for adding driver or operating system software. You will be presented with the System Settings Change dialog box, as in Figure 2.33. You will need to reboot the PC to enable to configuration to be altered as entered and to be made active. Selecting Yes will restart your computer and allow this process to occur.

Your new networking setting will now be in place, and you should have a PC installed with Microsoft 95/98 or NT and installed and configured with TCP/IP networking. Many books are available to help you with the details of installing network adapters into Microsoft Windows PCs (see Appendix B).

Red Hat Linux Networking Setup

If you already have either operating system set up, this discussion assumes that the network instructions are for configuring the network following a fresh installation. If you do not have a network card installed or have not yet configured your network settings, these instructions can be followed completely. If you do not have either operating system installed, it is a relatively simple process. Many books are available to help you with the details of installing network adapters into Linux PCs (see Appendix B).

You will need to configure TCP/IP. If you are not able to use a genuine IP address, you will need to use one of the IP addresses from the private ranges listed in the following:

- 10.0.0.0 to 10.255.255.255 (subnet mask 255.0.0.0)
- 172.16.0.0 to 172.31.255.255 (subnet Mask 255.255.0.0)
- 192.168.0.0 to 192.168.255.255 (subnet Mask 255.255.255.0)

The IP addresses used for your setup should be such that the PCs that are to be connected need to share the same network address. I will use 192.168.1.0 as the network address with a netmask value of 255.255.255.0. For now, I will not list any gateway IP address or DNS nameserver, although I will indicate the locations of these values.

When a new system is being installed and configured, and if the networking options are installed, Linux will automatically try to install networking regardless of whether a network adapter is present. In the case of either Linux distribution, simply select Yes for the networking option. Red Hat goes further, asking what type of network adapter is to be used and asks for any needed module options. In this example, I have selected ne2k-pci as the adapter module. I am using an RTL8029AS-based PCI network adapter and have chosen autoprobe to set the module options.

The next option is to configure the TCP/IP settings of the adapter. Enter the IP address, netmask, gateway, and DNS name server values as appropriate for your network.

Red Hat then requires you to enter a domain and hostname for your network. If this is not in a current network environment or is not likely to be connected to the Internet directly, you may be creative in your choice, because your network is private. If this is not the case, request the necessary details from your network administrator. In this example, I have chosen lnxsmbsvr1, as it is a private network and the hostnames here indicate the machine type and location; the network domain name is simply "domain" (lnxsmbsvr1.domain).

Your new networking setting will now be in place, and you should have a Linux-installed PC with TCP/IP networking installed and configured.

Chapter 3

Obtaining And Installing

In Depth

If Unix and Windows machines are to start sharing resources with each other, you will need to add software to your Unix machines and arrange to have them configured correctly. This chapter covers obtaining and installing this software for the nearly 100 different Unix variants now supported by Samba.

You will have the option either of installing a binary or executable that will have been created for your specific operating system or of compiling your own. The current distributions of Linux have already included one version of Samba or another. This chapter details where to locate this version in the installation or how to upgrade it to a more recent version.

Throughout this book, it is assumed that the Unix operating system being used is Linux. The installation, configuration, and use of two of the main distributions (Red Hat and Slackware, chosen because of their different installation methods) are demonstrated throughout. Major differences for other Unix operating systems are noted, although very few such requirements exist.

Immediate Solutions

Getting Samba

Although a current copy of Samba is included with this book's CD-ROM, this is not the only source you should refer to. Samba has been available on the Internet almost since its inception, and since the end of 1998 a new Web domain has been available to Samba developers; thus, any information, including the latest version, can always be obtained from **www.samba.org**. You should consider obtaining Samba from one of the many worldwide mirror sites to reduce the bandwidth demands on the main site, which is located in Australia (or was at the time of writing). (A complete list of mirror sites known to date is given in Appendix A.) The main site also contains a link to these mirrors, one of which is the popular Sunsite in the United States, mirrored worldwide. My local Sunsite mirror is at **http://sunsite.org.uk** and it carries copies of all the major Linux distributions and links to many FTP sites for other software (both full copies and patches). I recommend that you visit Sunsite regardless of your needs.

An alternative is to purchase one of the many CD-ROM snapshots of the Sunsite, Linux, and Samba sites that are becoming more commonly available by mail order. Walnut Creek and InfoMagic incorporate these and other reference site images into several of their bundled Linux packages.

Currently, somewhat earlier versions of Samba than are available from the Samba mirrors are included in the Linux distributions by Red Hat and Slackware. At the time of this writing, the latest Slackware 3.6 and Red Hat 5.2 distributions included Samba version 1.9.18.p10. You are well advised to upgrade this to a more recent version. These distributions make the process easier by including in the CD-ROM a precompiled binary package of a later release. This chapter gives you details on how to upgrade your Samba installation.

To make use of the NT primary domain controller (PDC) and other capabilities described here, you should either use the versions 2.05a or 2.06 distributions of Samba included on this book's CD-ROM or obtain the latest version you can. In January and February 1999, version 2.0.x went through at least two subreleases, so you can see that it is developing rapidly. Table 3.1 gives several sources for Samba.

Table 3.1 Where to obtain Samba.

Operating System	Samba Version	Precompiled Required	Will Compile Your Own
Red Hat	1.9.18p10	Red Hat 5.2 CD-ROM	CD-ROM or a Samba mirror
Red Hat	2.0.5a	CD-ROM	CD-ROM or a Samba mirror
Red Hat	2.0.x or later	Samba Mirror	Samba mirror
Slackware	1.9.18p10	Slackware 3.6 distribution	CD-ROM or a Samba mirror
Slackware	2.0.5a	CD-ROM	CD-ROM or a Samba mirror
Slackware	2.0.x or later	Samba Mirror	Samba mirror
Debian	1.9.18p10	CD-ROM	CD-ROM or a Samba mirror
Debian	2.0.3	CD-ROM	CD-ROM or a Samba mirror
Debian	2.0.x or later	Samba mirror	Samba mirror
AIX	1.9.18p10	CD-ROM	CD-ROM or a Samba mirror
Solaris	2.0.3	CD-ROM	CD-ROM or a Samba mirror
Other Operating System	2.0.x or later	Samba Mirror	Samba mirror

At last check, the Samba mirrors carried various binary packages for different releases ranging from version 1.8 through 2.0.3 and later depending on which operating system is included. A copy of these binaries is included on this book's CD-ROM and are listed here:

- AIX
- BSDI
- Bull
- Caldera
- Debian
- DigitalUnix
- Hewlett-Packard
- IRIX
- MVS
- Novell
- OSF
- Red Hat Linux
- SCO
- Sinix

- Slackware
- Solaris
- SuSE
- TurboLinux
- VMS

You have two choices for obtaining and installing Samba. You can use a precompiled version of the Samba executables, or you can create your own.

Samba is available from the previously mentioned locations as precompiled binaries; the main Samba distribution site might also include precompiled binaries for use with your particular operating system. In addition, these sites should provide a copy of the Samba source that will allow you to compile your own binary if one is not available.

The choice between using a precompiled binary and creating your own is a question that only you can answer. Considerable advantages exist in taking and using a precompiled binary for use on a system that is the result of a standard installation or that has been optimized for your platform. This is especially the case with Red Hat and the RPM package system, the latter of which is capable of using a precompiled binary and updating your system by adding a new version using the RPM Package Manager, a short summary of which appears in this chapter. A fuller investigation should be obtained from one of the Red Hat–specific books listed in Appendix B. The Red Hat binaries (and several others as well) are available from the main Samba archive. Likewise, Debian has a binary for many Debian systems that is available from the Debian archives. Slackware binaries are available as a standard tar-gzipped ("tarball") package for download from the Samba site.

However, I prefer to obtain the source, which might include the latest enhancements, and create my own binary to reflect my own system. In later chapters I indicate when it is necessary to obtain the source and create your own binary. This is especially true for areas that are still under development in Samba and in cases in which Samba is considered an alpha or a beta release. In such cases, you play at your own risk, and not everything is expected to work.

Using CVS

If you want to use the very latest source from development, you might consider using Concurrent Version System (CVS) to download the latest source from the main Samba site.

Accessing Source Code Via CVSWEB

You can access the source code via your favorite Web browser. This allows you to access the contents of individual files in the repository and to look at the revision history and commit logs of individual files. Using CVS, it is possible to request a copy of the source that is different from the local version. This is known as a diff listing. See **http://samba.org/cgi-bin/cvsweb**.

Accessing Source Code Via CVS

You can also access the source code through a normal CVS client. This gives you much more control than using the repository, and it allows you to check out whole source trees and keep them up-to-date through normal CVS commands. This is the preferred method of access if you are a developer and not just a casual browser.

To download the latest CVS source code, point your browser at **www.cyclic.com** and click on the How To Get CVS link. CVS is free software under the GNU GPL (as is Samba). Chapter 1 included a section on this.

To gain access through anonymous CVS, use the following steps. For this example, it is assumed that you want a copy of the Samba source code. For other source code repositories on this system, simply substitute the correct package name:

1. Install a recent copy of CVS. All you need is a copy of the CVS client binary.
2. Run the command **cvs -d :pserver:cvs@samba.org:/cvsroot login**. When it asks you for a password, enter "cvs".
3. Run the command **cvs -d :pserver:cvs@samba.org:/cvsroot co samba**. This will create a directory called Samba containing the latest Samba source code. This corresponds to the current development tree.
4. Whenever you want to merge in the latest code changes, use the following command from within the Samba directory: **cvs update -d -P**. If you instead want the latest source code for the 2.0.2 stable tree, use the command **cvs -d :pserver:cvs@samba.org:/cvsroot co -r BRANCH_2_0_2 samba**.

Accessing The NT Domain Controller Code

The Samba PDC code is being separately developed on a branch named BRANCH_NTDOM. To gain access to the latest source code (this changes daily), follow these steps:

1. Log on to CVS at **cvs -d :pserver:cvs@samba.org:/cvsroot login**. When it asks you for a password, enter "cvs".

2. Check out the BRANCH_NTDOM by entering “cvs -d :pserver:cvs@ samba.org:/cvsroot co -r BRANCH_NTDOM samba”. This will create a directory called Samba containing the latest snapshot of the domain controller code.
3. To keep this code up-to-date after it has been changed in the CVS repository, change to the Samba directory you created previously and enter “cvs update -d -P”.

You should be able to produce a usable system by sticking with the latest binaries or compiling your own binary from the most recent stable source code tree.

Understanding Samba Executables

What exactly are the programs involved in the Samba distributions? Note first where they are usually located. The default location for the Samba executables is /usr/local/samba/bin.

On my current Linux system, the Samba executables are in the default /usr/local/ samba/bin; these are detailed in Listing 3.1. The backup subdirectory contains a whole series of sub-versions and earlier versions of the Samba executables that I keep, but you need not keep these. All these are installed and owned by root, with permissions set readable and executable by all.

Listing 3.1 The Samba executables.

```
Linuxserver1:/usr/local/samba/bin# ls -l
total 4148
-rwxr-xr-x   1 root     root         1708 Mar  1 20:37 addtosmbpass*
drwxr-xr-x   2 root     root         1024 Mar  1 20:40 backup/
-rwxr-xr-x   1 root     root          446 Mar  1 20:37 convert_smbpasswd*
-rwxr-xr-x   1 root     root       194341 Mar  1 20:37 make_printerdef*
-rwxr-xr-x   1 root     root       193534 Mar  1 20:37 make_smbcodepage*
-rwxr-xr-x   1 root     root       391924 Mar  1 20:37 nmbd*
-rwxr-xr-x   1 root     root       269183 Mar  1 20:37 nmblookup*
-rwxr-xr-x   1 root     root       481730 Mar  1 20:37 rpcclient*
-rwxr-xr-x   1 root     root       319297 Mar  1 20:37 smbclient*
-rwxr-xr-x   1 root     root       774901 Mar  1 20:37 smbd*
-rwxr-xr-x   1 root     root       445224 Mar  1 20:37 smbpasswd*
-rwxr-xr-x   1 root     root        26447 Mar  1 20:37 smbrun*
-rwxr-xr-x   1 root     root       216854 Mar  1 20:37 smbstatus*
-rwxr-xr-x   1 root     root         4795 Mar  1 20:37 smbtar*
-rwxr-xr-x   1 root     root       499244 Mar  1 20:37 *
-rwxr-xr-x   1 root     root       191933 Mar  1 20:37 testparm*
-rwxr-xr-x   1 root     root       202970 Mar  1 20:37 testprns*
Linuxserver1:/usr/local/samba/bin#
```

Three other directories are included: lib, var, and private. These are usually located in the /usr/local/samba directory:

- *bin*—Contains all the Samba programs.
- *lib*—Contains the configuration files for Samba.
- *var*—Contains all the log files and share mode files.
- *private*—Should be readable only by root, and it is used to store the Samba encrypted password file used in encrypted password support.

All the man pages for these programs are included as well.

The different programs can be divided into two categories: server programs and utility programs. The following are the programs and utilities that will provide SMB services to your client hosts:

- **smbd**
- **nmbd**
- **nmblookup**
- **smbprint**
- **smbrun**
- **smbstatus**
- **addtosmbpass**
- **convert_smbpasswd**
- **smbpasswd**
- **swat**

Server Programs: smbd

The program **smbd** is the server program that will provide SMB/CIFS services to clients. The syntax for launching the program from the command line is:

```
smbd [-D] [-a] [-o] [-d debuglevel] [-l log file] [-p port number]
  [-O socket options] [-s configuration file] [-i scope] [-P] [-h]
```

An extensive description of the services that the server can provide is given in the man page for the server and it details the parameters available in the configuration file that controls the attributes of those services. Note that significant security implications to running this server exist, and the smb.conf (5) man page should be regarded as mandatory reading before proceeding with installation.

NOTE: *A copy of the smb.conf(5) man page as an HTML document (some 130 pages if you were to print it out) is included in the Samba source distribution. The most recent version at the time of this writing can be found in the /docs/HTML directory on this book's CD-ROM, as can other HTML documentation.*

A session is created whenever a client requests one. Each client gets a copy of the server for each session. This copy then services all connections made by the client during that session. When all connections from its client are closed, the copy of the server for that client terminates.

The configuration file and any files that it references are automatically reloaded every minute, should they change. You can force a reload by sending a SIGHUP to the server. Reloading the configuration file will not affect connections to any service that is already established. Either the user will have to disconnect from the service or **smbd** is killed and restarted. The following options may follow the **smbd** command:

- **-D**—If specified, this parameter causes the server to operate as a daemon. That is, it detaches itself and runs in the background, fielding requests on the appropriate port. Operating the server as a daemon is the recommended way of running **smbd** for servers that provide more than casual user file and print services. By default, the server will not operate as a daemon.
- **-a**—If this parameter is specified, each new connection will append log messages to the log file. This is the default.
- **-o**—If this parameter is specified, the log files will be overwritten when opened. By default, the log files that exist already on the server will be appended to.
- **-d *debuglevel***—This parameter is an integer from 0 to 10. If this parameter is not specified, the default value is zero. The higher this value, the more detail will be logged to the log files about the activities of the server. At level 0, only critical errors and serious warnings will be logged. Level 1 is a reasonable level for day-to-day running, as it generates a small amount of information about the operations that are carried out. Levels above 1 will generate considerable amounts of log data and should be used only when investigating a problem. Levels above 3 are designed for use only by developers; these generate huge amounts of log data, most of this is extremely cryptic. Note that specifying this parameter here will override the log-level parameter in the smb.conf file.
- **-l *log file***—If specified, ***log file*** specifies a log file name into which informational and debug messages from the running server are logged. The server never removes the log file that is generated, although its size may be controlled by the **Max Log Size** parameter in the smb.conf file. The default log file name is specified at compile time.

- **-p *port number***—This parameter is a positive integer value. If this parameter is not specified, the default value is 139. This number is the port number that will be used when making connections to the server from client software. The standard (well-known) port number for the SMB over TCP is 139, thus the default. If you want to run the server as an ordinary user rather than as root, most systems require you to use a port number greater than 1024; ask your system administrator for help if you are in this situation. For the server to be useful by most clients, if you configure the server on a port other than 139, you will require port redirection services on port 139, details of which are outlined in rfc1002.txt section 4.3.5. This parameter is not normally specified, except in the previously described situation.
- **-O *socket options***—For details, see the **socket options** parameter in the smb.conf file.

NOTE: *Copies of the Requests For Comment (RFCs) related to networking, Samba, and other such topics are included in the /doc/RFC directory on this book's CD-ROM.*

- **-s *configuration file***—The specified file contains the configuration details required by the server. The information in this file includes server-specific information, such as which printcap file to use, as well as descriptions of all the services that the server is to provide. For more information, see smb.conf. The default configuration file name is determined at compile time.
- **-i *scope***—This specifies a NetBIOS scope that the server will use to communicate with when generating NetBIOS names. For details on the use of NetBIOS scopes, see rfc1001.txt and rfc1002.txt. NetBIOS scopes are very rarely used, so set this parameter only if you are the system administrator in charge of all the NetBIOS systems you communicate with.
- **-P**—This is the Passive option. It causes **smbd** not to send any network traffic out and is used for debugging only by developers.
- **-h**—Prints the help information (usage) for **smbd**.

Limitations: On some systems, **smbd** cannot change uid back to root after a **setuid()** call. Such systems are called "trapdoor" uid systems. If you have such a system, you will be unable to connect from a client (such as a PC) as two different users at once. Attempts to connect the second user will result in Access Denied or similar messages.

Environment Variables: Printer

If no printer name is specified to printable services, most systems will use the value of this variable (or "lp" if this variable is not defined) as the name of the printer to use. However, such an action is not printer-specific.

Environment Variables: Signals

Sending the **smbd** a SIGHUP will cause it to reload its smb.conf configuration file within a short period of time.

To shut down a user's **smbd** process, it is recommended that SIGKILL (-9) not be used except as a last resort, as this can leave the shared memory area in an inconsistent state. A safe way to terminate an **smbd** is to send it a SIGTERM (-15) signal and wait for it to die on its own.

The debug log level of **smbd** can be raised by sending it a SIGUSR1 (**kill -USR1 <smbd-pid>**) and lowered by sending it a SIGUSR2 (**kill -USR2 <smbd-pid>**). This allows transient problems to be diagnosed while running at a normally low log level.

Note that as the signal handlers send a debug write, they are not reentrant in **smbd**. Thus, you should wait until **smbd** is in a state of waiting for an incoming SMB before issuing them. It is possible to make the signal handlers safe by unblocking the signals before the select call and then reblocking them afterward, but this would affect performance.

Server Programs: nmbd

The program **nmbd** is the NetBIOS name server that will provide NetBIOS over IP naming services to clients. The syntax for launching the program from the command line is:

```
nmbd [-D] [-o] [-a] [-H lmhosts file] [-d debuglevel] [-l log file basename]
[-n primary NetBIOS name] [-p port number] [-s configuration file]
[-i NetBIOS scope] [-h]
```

The **nmbd** program is a server that understands and can reply to NetBIOS over IP name service requests, such as those produced by SMB/CIFS clients (e.g., Windows 95/98, Windows NT, and LanManager clients). It also participates in the browsing protocols that make up the Windows Network Neighborhood view. SMB/CIFS clients, when they start up, might want to locate an SMB/CIFS server. That is, they might want to know which IP number a specified host is using.

Among other services, **nmbd** will listen for such requests and respond with the IP number of the host on which it is running if its own NetBIOS name is specified. By default, its own NetBIOS name is the primary domain name server (DNS) name of the host on which it is running, but this can be overridden with the **-n** option (see following discussion of this option). Thus, **nmbd** will reply to broadcast queries for its own name(s). Additional names on which **nmbd** can respond can be set through parameters in the smb.conf configuration file.

In addition, **nmbd** can be used as a Windows Internet Name Server (WINS). That is, it will act as a WINS database server, creating a database from name registration requests that it receives and replying to queries from clients for these names.

Also, **nmbd** can act as a WINS proxy, relaying broadcast queries from clients that do not understand how to communicate with a WINS server. The following options may follow the **nmbd** program from the command line:

- **-D**—If specified, this parameter causes **nmbd** to operate as a daemon. That is, it detaches itself and runs in the background, fielding requests on the appropriate port. By default, **nmbd** will not operate as a daemon. Also, **nmbd** can be operated from the inetd meta-daemon, although this is not recommended.
- **-o**—If this parameter is specified, the log files will be overwritten when opened. By default, the log files that exist already on the server will be appended to.
- **-a**—If this parameter is specified, each new connection will append log messages to the log file. This is the default.
- **-H *lmhosts filename***—The lmhosts file is a list of NetBIOS names to IP addresses that is loaded by the **nmbd** server. It is used through the name resolution mechanism's name resolve order described in smb.conf to resolve any NetBIOS name queries needed by the server. Note that the contents of this file are not used by **nmbd** to answer any name queries. Adding a line to this file affects name NetBIOS resolution from this host only. The default path to this file is compiled into Samba as part of the build process. Common defaults are /usr/local/samba/lib/lmhosts, /usr/samba/lib/lmhosts, and /etc/lmhosts. For details on the contents of this file, see the lmhosts (5) man page.

NOTE: *A copy of the lmhosts (5) man page as an HTML document is included in the Samba source distribution. The most recent version at the time of this writing can be found in the /docs/HTML directory on this book's CD-ROM, as can other HTML documentation.*

- **-d *debuglevel***—This parameter is an integer from 0 to 10. If this parameter is not specified, the default value is zero. The higher this value, the more detail will be logged to the log files about the activities of the server. At level 0, only critical errors and serious warnings will be logged. Level 1 is a reasonable level for day-to-day running, as it generates a small amount of information about the operations that are carried out. Levels above 1 will generate considerable amounts of log data and should be used only when investigating a problem. Levels above 3 are designed for use only by developers; these generate huge amounts of log data, and most of this is extremely cryptic.

Note that specifying this parameter here will override the **log level** parameter in the smb.conf file.

- **-l *log file***—The **-l** parameter specifies a pathname and base file name into which operational data from the running **nmbd** server will be logged. The actual log file name is generated by appending the .nmb extension to the specified base name. For example, if the name specified were "log", the file log.nmb would contain the debugging data. The default log file path is compiled into Samba as part of the build process. Common defaults are /usr/local/samba/var/log.nmb, /usr/samba/var/log.nmb, and /var/log/log.nmb.
- **-n *primary NetBIOS name***—This option allows you to override the NetBIOS name that Samba uses for itself. This is identical to setting the NetBIOS name parameter in the smb.conf file but will override the setting in the smb.conf file.
- **-p *UDP port number***—The ***UDP port number*** is a positive integer value. This option changes the default UDP port number (normally 137) on which **nmbd** responds to name queries. Do not use this option unless you are an expert, in which case you will not need help!
- **-s *configuration file***—The default configuration file name is set at build time, typically as /usr/local/samba/lib/smb.conf, but this might be changed when Samba is autoconfigured. The specified file contains the configuration details required by the server. For more information, see smb.conf.
- **-i *NetBIOS scope***—This specifies a NetBIOS scope that **nmbd** will use to communicate with when generating NetBIOS names. For details on the use of NetBIOS scopes, see rfc1001.txt and rfc1002.txt. NetBIOS scopes are very rarely used, so set this parameter only if you are the system administrator in charge of all the NetBIOS systems you communicate with.
- **-h**—This prints the help information (usage) for **nmbd**.

When run as a WINS server (see the WINS support parameter in the smb.conf [5] man page), **nmbd** will store the WINS database in the wins.dat file in the var/locks directory configured under wherever Samba was configured to install itself.

If **nmbd** is acting as a browse master (this is a parameter set in the smb.conf file; details of this and other parameters can be obtained from the smb.conf [5] man page. smb.conf (5) is the entry to view these), **nmbd** will store the browsing database in the browse.dat file in the var/locks directory configured under wherever Samba was configured to install itself.

Signals

To shut down an **nmbd** process, it is recommended that SIGKILL (-9) not be used, except as a last resort, as this can leave the name database in an inconsistent state. The correct way to terminate **nmbd** is to send it a SIGTERM (-15) signal and wait for it to die on its own.

The **nmbd** will accept SIGHUP, which will cause it to dump out its name lists into the namelist.debug file in the /usr/local/samba/var/locks directory (or the var/locks directory configured under wherever Samba was configured to install itself). This will also cause **nmbd** to dump out its server database in the log.nmb file. In addition, the debug log level of **nmbd** can be raised by sending it a SIGUSR1 (**kill -USR1 <nmbd-pid>**) and lowered by sending it a SIGUSR2 (**kill -USR2 <nmbd-pid>**). This allows transient problems to be diagnosed while still running at a normally low log level.

Utility Programs: nmblookup

nmblookup is a NetBIOS over TCP/IP client used to look up NetBIOS names:

```
nmblookup [-M] [-R] [-S] [-r] [-A] [-h] [-B broadcast address]
[-U unicast address][-d debuglevel] [-s smb config file]
[-i NetBIOS scope] [-T] name
```

The **nmblookup** program is used to query NetBIOS names and map them to IP addresses in a network using NetBIOS over TCP/IP queries. The options allow the name queries to be directed at a particular IP broadcast area or to a particular machine. All queries are done over User Datagram Protocol (UDP).

The following options may follow the **nmblookup** command from the command line:

- **-M**—Searches for a master browser by looking up the NetBIOS name with a type of 0x1d. If name is "-", it does a lookup on the special name __MSBROWSE__.
- **-R**—Sets the recursion desired bit in the packet to do a recursive lookup. This is used when sending a name query to a machine running a WINS server and the user wants to query the names in the WINS server. If this bit is unset, the normal (broadcast responding) NetBIOS processing code on a machine is used instead. For details, see rfc1001.txt and rfc1002.txt on this book's CD-ROM.
- **-S**—Once the name query has returned an IP address, do a node status query as well. A node status query returns the NetBIOS names registered by a host.
- **-r**—This attempts to bind to UDP port 137 to send and receive UDP datagrams. This option has been made available because of a bug in Windows 95 that ignores the source port of the requesting packet and replies only to UDP port 137. Unfortunately, on most Unix systems, root privilege is needed to bind to this port; the **nmbd** daemon, if running on this machine, also binds to this port.

- **-A**—This interprets **<name>** as an IP address and does a node status query on this address.
- **-h**—This prints a help (usage) message.
- **-B *broadcast address***—This sends the query to the given broadcast address. Without this option, the default behavior of **nmblookup** is to send the query to the broadcast address of the primary network interface as either autodetected or defined in the interfaces parameter of the smb.conf file.
- **-U *unicast address***—This does a unicast query to the specified address or host ***unicast address***. This option (along with the **-R** option) is needed to query a WINS server.
- **-d *debuglevel***—This parameter is an integer from 0 to 10. If this parameter is not specified, the default value is zero. The higher this value, the more detail will be logged about the activities of **nmblookup**. At level 0, only critical errors and serious warnings will be logged. Levels above 1 will generate considerable amounts of log data and should be used only when investigating a problem. Levels above 3 are designed for use only by developers; these generate huge amounts of data, most of which is extremely cryptic. Note that specifying this parameter here will override the log level parameter in the smb.conf file.
- **-s *smb.conf***—This parameter specifies the pathname to the Samba smb.conf configuration file. This file controls all aspects of the Samba setup on the machine.
- **-i *NetBIOS scope***—This specifies a NetBIOS scope that **nmblookup** will use to communicate with when generating NetBIOS names. For details on the use of NetBIOS scopes, see rfc1001.txt and rfc1002.txt. NetBIOS scopes are very rarely used, so set this parameter only if you are the system administrator in charge of all the NetBIOS systems you communicate with.
- **-T**—This causes any IP addresses found in the lookup to be looked up through a reverse DNS lookup into a DNS name and printed out before each "IP address NetBIOS name" pair that is the normal output.
- ***name***—This is the NetBIOS name being queried. Depending on the previous options, this might be a NetBIOS name or an IP address. If it is a NetBIOS name, the different name types can be specified by appending "**#<type>**" to the name. This name may also be "*", which will return all registered names within a broadcast area.

nmblookup Examples

nmblookup can be used to query a WINS server (in the same way that **nslookup** is used to query DNS servers). To query a WINS server, **nmblookup** must be called as follows:

```
nmblookup -U server -R 'name'
```

For example, running

```
nmblookup -U samba.org -R IRIX#1B'
```

would query the WINS server **samba.org** for the domain master browser (**1B** name type) for the **IRIX** workgroup.

smbprint

This is not so much a program as it is a shell script that makes it possible to use a printer on an alternate SMB server. Unix printing utilizes the printcap entries to control how the **lpr** command sends commands to a printer. Much like the way another printcap filter acts, **smbprint** acts as an input filter to the printer's printcap entry, piping the data submitted to the print job into **smbclient**, which then sends this to the remote SMB server. Chapters 5 and 8 discuss in more detail how to configure and use printers in a mixed Unix and Windows environment.

smbrun

This is an interface program between **smbd** and external programs.

The **smbrun** program is a very small "glue" program that runs shell commands for the **smbd** daemon. It first changes to the highest effective user and group ID that it can, then it runs the command line that is provided by using the **system()** call. This program is necessary to allow some operating systems to run external programs as nonroot.

The following option may follow the **smbrun** command from the command prompt:

- **shell-command**—This is the shell command to execute. The command should have a fully qualified path.

Environment Variables

The PATH variable set for the environment in which **smbrun** is executed will affect which executables are located and executed if a fully qualified path is not given in the command.

smbrun Diagnostics

If **smbrun** cannot be located or cannot be executed by **smbd**, appropriate messages will be found in the **smbd** logs. Other diagnostics depend on the shell command being run. It is advisable for your shell commands to issue suitable diagnostics to aid troubleshooting.

smbstatus reports on current Samba connections

```
smbstatus [-b] [-d] [-L] [-p] [-S] [-s configuration file] [-u username]
```

smbstatus is a very simple program by which to list the current Samba connections.

The following options may follow the **smbstatus** command:

- **-b**—This gives brief output.
- **-d**—This gives verbose output.
- **-L**—This causes **smbstatus** to only list locks.
- **-p**—This prints a list of **smbd** processes and exits. It is useful for scripting.
- **-S**—This causes **smbstatus** to only list shares.
- **-s *configuration file***—The default configuration file name is determined at compile time. The file specified contains the configuration details required by the server. For more information, see smb.conf.
- **-u *username***—Selects information relevant to username only.

addtosmbpass

addtosmbpass is an awk script program used to add new entries in **smbpasswd** files. The script arguments are account names to add. Passing it an existing Samba password file on stdin will cause it to be written on stdout.

convert_smbpasswd

This program converts a Samba 1.9.18 smbpasswd file format into a Samba 2.0 smbpasswd file format.

smbpasswd changes a user's SMB password:

```
smbpasswd [-a] [-d] [-e] [-D debuglevel] [-n] [-r remote_machine] [-R name
resolve order] [-m] [-j DOMAIN] [-U username] [-h] [-s] username
```

The **smbpasswd** program has several different functions, depending on whether it is run by the root user. When run as a normal user, it allows the user to change the password used for his or her SMB sessions on any machines that store SMB passwords. By default (when run with no arguments), it will attempt to change the current user's SMB password on the local machine. This is similar to the way in which the **passwd** program works. However, **smbpasswd** differs from how the **passwd** program works in that it is not setuid root but works in a client/server mode and communicates with a locally running **smbd**. Thus, for this to succeed, the **smbd** daemon must be running on the local machine. On a Unix machine, the encrypted SMB passwords are usually stored in the smbpasswd file.

When run by ordinary users with no options, **smbpasswd** will prompt them for their old SMB password and then ask them for their new password twice to ensure that the new password was entered correctly. No passwords will be echoed on the screen while being typed. If you have a blank smb password (specified by the string "NO PASSWORD" in the smbpasswd file), simply press Enter when asked for your old password.

smbpasswd may be used by a normal user to change his or her SMB password on remote machines. These could be Windows NT PDCs. See the **-r** and **-U** options in the following discussion.

When run by root, **smbpasswd** allows new users to be added and deleted in the smbpasswd file and allows changes to the attributes of the user in this file to be made. When run by root, **smbpasswd** accesses the local smbpasswd file directly, enabling changes to be made even if **smbd** is not running.

The following options may follow the **smbpasswd** command:

- **-a**—This option specifies that the username following should be added to the local smbpasswd file, with the new password entered (press Enter for the old password). This option is ignored if the user name following already exists in the smbpasswd file and is treated like a regular change password command. Note that the user to be added must already exist in the system password file (usually /etc/passwd); otherwise, the request to add the user will fail. This option is available only when running **smbpasswd** as root.
- **-d**—This option specifies that the user name following should be disabled in the local smbpasswd file. Writing a "D" flag into the account control space in the smbpasswd file accomplished this. Once this is done, all attempts to authenticate by way of SMB using this user name will fail. If the smbpasswd file is in a pre-Samba 2.0 format, no space is given in the user's password entry to write this information, so the user is disabled by writing "X" characters into the password space in the smbpasswd file. For details on the old and new password file formats, see **smbpasswd** (5). This option is available only when running **smbpasswd** as root.
- **-e**—This option specifies that the user name following should be enabled in the local smbpasswd file if the account was previously disabled. If the account was not disabled, this option has no effect. Once the account is enabled, the user will be able to authenticate by way of SMB again. If the smbpasswd file is in the old format, **smbpasswd** will prompt for a new password for this user; otherwise, the account will be enabled by removing the "D" flag from account control space in the smbpasswd file. For details on the old and new password file formats, see **smbpasswd** (5). This option is available only when running **smbpasswd** as root.

- **-D *debuglevel***—This parameter is an integer from 0 to 10. If this parameter is not specified, the default value is zero. The higher this value, the more detail will be logged to the log files about the activities of **smbpasswd**. At level 0, only critical errors and serious warnings will be logged. Levels above 1 will generate considerable amounts of log data and should be used only when investigating a problem. Levels above 3 are designed for use only by developers and generate huge amounts of log data, most of which is extremely cryptic.
- **-n**—This option specifies that the user name following should have its password set to null (i.e., a blank password) in the local smbpasswd file. This is done by writing the string "NO PASSWORD" as the first part of the first password stored in the smbpasswd file. Note that to allow users to log on to a Samba server once the password has been set to "NO PASSWORD" in the smbpasswd file, the administrator must set the null passwords parameter in the [global] section of the smb.conf file:
- **null passwords = true**—This option is available only when running **smbpasswd** as root.
- **-r *remote machine name***—This option allows users to specify which machine they want to change their password on. Without this parameter, **smbpasswd** defaults to the local host. The remote machine name is the NetBIOS name of the SMB/CIFS server to contact to attempt the password change. This name is resolved into an IP address using the standard name resolution mechanism in all programs of the Samba suite. For details on changing this resolution mechanism, see the **-R *name resolve order*** parameter. The user name whose password is changed is that of the current logged-on Unix user. For details on changing the password for a different username, see the **-U *username*** parameter. Note that if changing a Windows NT Domain password, the remote machine specified must be the PDC for the backup domain controllers (BDCs); it will have only a read-only copy of the user account database and will not allow the password change. Note also that Windows 95/98 do not have a real password database, so it is not possible to change passwords specifying a Windows 95/98 machine as a remote machine target.
- **-R *name resolve order***—This option allows the user of **smbclient** to determine which name resolution services to use when looking up the NetBIOS name of the host being connected to. The options are **lmhosts**, **host**, **wins**, and **bcast**. These cause names to be resolved as detailed in the following sidebar.

Name Resolve Order

- **lmhosts**—This looks up an IP address in the Samba lmhosts file.
- **host**—This does a standard hostname-to-IP address resolution, using the system /etc/hosts, NIS, or DNS lookups. This method of name resolution is operating system-dependent. For example, on IRIX or Solaris, this may be controlled by the /etc/nsswitch.conf file.
- **wins**—This queries a name with the IP address listed in the WINS server parameter in the smb.conf file. If no WINS server has been specified, this method is ignored.
- **bcast**—This does a broadcast on each of the known local interfaces listed in the interfaces parameter in the smb.conf file. This is the least reliable of the name resolution methods, as it depends on the target host being on a locally connected subnet. If this parameter is not set, the name resolve order defined in the smb.conf file parameter name resolve order will be used.

The default order is **lmhosts**, **host**, **wins**, and **bcast**; without this parameter or any entry in the smb.conf file, the name resolution methods will be attempted in this order.

- **-m**—This option tells **smbpasswd** that the account being changed is a MACHINE account. Currently, this is used when Samba is being used as an NT PDC; PDC support is not a supported feature in Samba 2.0. However, this will become supported in a later release. (If you want to know more about using Samba as an NT PDC, you can subscribe to a mailing list at **samba-ntdom@samba.org**.) This option is available only when running **smbpasswd** as root.
- **-j *DOMAIN***—This option is used to add a Samba server into a Windows NT domain as a domain member capable of authenticating user accounts to any domain controller in the same way that a Windows NT server does. See the security=domain option in the smb.conf (5) man page. To be used in this way, the administrator for the Windows NT domain must have used the Server Manager for Domains program to add the primary NetBIOS name of the Samba server as a member of the domain. After this has been done, you can join the domain by invoking **smbpasswd** with this parameter; **smbpasswd** will then look up the PDC for the domain (found in the smb.conf file in the parameter password server) and change the machine account password used to create the secure domain communication. This password is then stored by **smbpasswd** in a file, read only by root, called ***Domain.Machine.mac***, where ***Domain*** is the name of the domain being joined and ***Machine*** is the primary NetBIOS name of the machine being run. Once this operation has been performed, the smb.conf file may be updated to set the security=domain option, and all future logins to the Samba server will be authenticated to the Windows NT PDC. Note that even though the authentication is being done to the PDC, all users accessing the Samba server must still have a valid Unix account on that machine. This option is available only when running **smbpasswd** as root.

- **-U *username***—This option may be used only in conjunction with the **-r** option. When changing a password on a remote machine, it allows the user to specify the user name on that machine whose password will be changed. This option exists so users who have different user names on different systems can change these passwords.
- **-h**—This option prints the help string for **smbpasswd**, selecting the correct one for running as root or as an ordinary user.
- **-s**—This option causes **smbpasswd** to be silent (i.e., not issue prompts) and to read its old and new passwords from standard input rather than from /dev/tty (like the **passwd** [1] program does). This option helps people writing scripts to drive **smbpasswd** username. This specifies the user name for all the root-only options to operate on. Only root can specify this parameter, as only root has the permission needed to modify attributes directly in the local smbpasswd file.

NOTE: *Because **smbpasswd** works in client-server mode communicating with a local **smbd** for a non-root user, the **smbd** daemon must be running for this to work. A common problem is to add a restriction to the hosts that may access the **smbd** running on the local machine by specifying an allow hosts or deny hosts entry in the smb.conf file and neglecting to allow localhost access to the **smbd**.*

*In addition, the **smbpasswd** command is useful only if Samba has been set up to use encrypted passwords. For details on how to do this, see the ENCRYPTION.txt file in the docs directory of this book's CD-ROM.*

SWAT is the Samba Web Administration Tool:

```
swat [-s smb config file] [-a]
```

The Samba Web Administration Tool (SWAT) program allows a Samba administrator to configure the complex smb.conf file via a Web browser. In addition, a SWAT configuration page has help links to all the configurable options in the smb.conf file, allowing an administrator to easily look up the effects of any change. SWAT is run from inetd, usually as service 901/tcp.

The following options may follow the swat command:

- **-s *smb configuration file***—The default configuration file path is determined at compile time. The specified file contains the configuration details required by the **smbd** server. This is the file that SWAT will modify. The information in this file includes server-specific information, such as which printcap file to use, and descriptions of all the services that the server is to provide. For more information, see man smb.conf (5).
- **-a**—This option disables authentication and puts SWAT in demo mode, in which anyone will be able to modify the smb.conf file. Do not enable this option on a production server.

make_smbcodepage constructs a code-page file for Samba:

```
make_smbcodepage [c|d] codepage inputfile outputfile
```

The program **make_smbcodepage** compiles or decompiles code-page files for use with the internationalization features of Samba 2.0.

The following options may follow the **make_smbcodepage** command:

- **c|d**—This tells **make_smbcodepage** whether it is compiling (**c**) a text format code-page file to binary, or decompiling (**d**) a binary code-page file to text.
- ***codepage***—This is the code page being processed (a number, e.g., 850).
- ***inputfile***—This is the input file to process. In the "c" case, this will be a text code-page definition file, such as the ones found in the Samba source/code pages directory. In the "d" case, this will be the binary format code-page definition file normally found in the lib/codepages directory in the Samba install directory path.
- ***outputfile***—This is the output file to produce.

Samba Code-Page Files

A text Samba code-page definition file is a description that tells Samba how to map from upper- to lowercase for characters greater than ASCII 127 in the specified DOS code page. Note that for certain DOS code pages (e.g., 437), mapping from lower- to uppercase can be nonsymmetrical. For example, in code page 437, lowercase "a" acute maps to plain uppercase "a" when going from lower- to uppercase. But that plain uppercase "a" maps to plain lowercase "a" when lowercasing a character.

A binary Samba code-page definition file is a binary representation of the same information, including a value that specifies which code page this file is describing.

Because Samba does not yet use UNICODE (current for Samba version 2.0), you must specify the client code page that your DOS and Windows clients are using if you want to have case insensitivity done correctly for your particular language. The default code page that Samba uses is 850 (Western European). Text code-page definition sample files are provided in the Samba distribution for code pages 437 (United States), 737 (Greek), 850 (Western European), 852 (DOS Latin 2), 861 (Icelandic), 866 (Cyrillic), 932 (Kanji SJIS), 936 (Simplified Chinese), 949 (Hangul), and 950 (Traditional Chinese). Users are encouraged to write text code-page definition files for their own code pages and donate them to **samba-bugs@samba.org**. All code-page files in the Samba source/codepages directory are compiled and installed when a "make install" command is issued there.

The client code page used by the **smbd** server is configured using the client code-page parameter in the smb.conf file.

The Files Used By **make_smbcodepage**

make_smbcodepage uses the following files:

- ***codepage_def.<codepage>***—These are the input (text) code-page files provided in the Samba source/codepages directory. A text code-page definition file consists of multiple lines containing four fields. These fields are "lower," which is the (hex) lowercase character mapped on this line; "upper," which is the (hex) uppercase character that the lowercase character will map to; "map upper to lower," which is a boolean value (either True or False) that tells Samba whether it is to map the given uppercase character to the given lowercase character when lowercasing a file name; and "map lower to upper," which is a boolean value (either True or False) that tells Samba whether it is to map the given lowercase character to the given uppercase character when uppercasing a file name.
- ***codepage.<codepage>***—These are the output (binary) code-page files produced and placed in the Samba destination lib/codepage directory.

Installation

The location of the server and its support files is a matter for individual system administrators. Thus, the following are only suggestions.

It is recommended that the **make_smbcodepage** program be installed under the /usr/local/samba hierarchy in a directory readable by all and writeable only by root. The program itself should be executable by all. The program should not be setuid or setgid.

A useful addition to SWAT is the **debug2html** program added by Chris Hertel.

NOTE: *Until the release of Samba 2.0.3, you had to hand compile this from the source in /source/utils/debug2html.c; however, the Makefile.in configuration file that creates the Makefile now contains a reference to it so that it is included in the compile.*

---

debug2html is the Samba DEBUG-to-HTML translation filter:

```
debug2html [input-file [output-file]]
```

The **debug2html** program generates HTML files from Samba log files. A Web browser may then be used to view the log files output by either the **nmbd** or **smbd** programs. The output conforms to the HTML 3.2 specification.

The file names specified on the command line are optional. If the output file is omitted, output will go to stdout. If the input file is omitted, **debug2html** will read from stdin. The filename "-" can be used to indicate that input should be read from stdin. For example:

```
cat /usr/local/samba/var/log.nmb | debug2html - nmblog.html
```

The Client Programs

The following are the client programs that allow you to use your Unix or other system as if it were an SMB client:

- **smbtar**
- **smbclient**
- **rpcclient**

smbtar is the shell script for backing up SMB/CIFS shares directly to Unix tape drives:

```
smbtar -s server [-p password] [-x service] [-X] [-d directory]
[-u user] [-t tape] [-b blocksize] [-N filename] [-i] [-r]
[-l log level] [-v] filenames
```

The **smbtar** program is a very small shell script on top of **smbclient** that dumps SMB shares directly to tape.

The following options may follow the **smbtar** command:

- **-s *server***—This is the SMB/CIFS server that the share resides on.
- **-p *password***—This is the password to use to access a share. The default is None.
- **-x *service***—This is the share name on the server to connect to. The default is backup.
- **-X**—This is exclude mode. The filenames following this option will be excluded from a tar create or restore
- **-d *directory***—this changes to initial directory before restoring or backing up files.
- **-u *user***—This is the user ID to connect as. The default is the Unix login name.
- **-t *tape***—This may be a regular file or a tape device. The default is a TAPE environmental variable; if it is not set, a file called tar.out is written.
- **-b *blocksize***—This is a blocking factor. The default is 20. For a fuller explanation, see tar (1).

- **-N *filename***—This backs up only files that are newer than the file name. Could be used, for example, on a log file to implement incremental backups.
- **-i**—Incremental mode; tar files are backed up only if they have the archive bit set. The archive bit is reset after each file is read.
- **-r**—Restore; files are restored to the share from the tar file.
- **-l *log level***—This is the log (debug) level. It corresponds to the **-d** flag of **smbclient** (1).
- **-v**—This is verbose mode.

Environment Variables

The **TAPE** variable specifies the default tape device to write to. It may be overridden with the **-t** option.

Bugs

The **smbtar** script has different options, ranging from ordinary tar and tar called from **smbclient**.

Caveats

Sites that are more careful about security might not like the way in which the script handles PC passwords. Backing up and restoring work on entire shares should work on file lists; **smbtar** works best with GNU tar and might not work well with other versions.

smbclient is the FTP-like client to access SMB/CIFS resources on servers:

```
smbclient servicename [password] [-s smb.conf] [-B IP addr]
[-O socket options][-R name resolve order] [-M NetBIOS name] [-i scope]
[-N] [-n NetBIOS name] [-d debuglevel] [-P] [-p port] [-l log basename]
[-h] [-I dest IP] [-E] [-U username] [-L NetBIOS name] [-t terminal code]
[-m max protocol] [-W workgroup] [-T<c|x>IXFqgbNan] [-D directory]
[-c command string]
```

The **smbclient** program is a client that can "talk" to an SMB/CIFS server. It offers an interface similar to that of the FTP program (see **ftp** [1]). Operations include getting files from the server to the local machine, putting files from the local machine to the server, and retrieving directory information from the server.

The following options may follow the **smbclient** command:

- ***servicename***—This is the name of the service you want to use on the server. A service name takes the form //server/service, where *server* is the NetBIOS name of the SMB/CIFS server offering the desired service and *service* is the name of the service offered. Thus, to connect to the service printer on the SMB/CIFS server **smbserver**, you would use the service name //smbserver/

printer. Note that the server name required is not necessarily the IP (DNS) hostname of the server. The name required is a NetBIOS server name, which might or might not be the same as the IP hostname of the machine running the server. The server name is looked up either according to the **-R** parameter to **smbclient** or using the name resolve order parameter in the smb.conf file, allowing an administrator to change the order and methods by which server names are looked up.

- ***password***—This is the password required to access the specified service on the specified server. If this parameter is supplied, the **-N** option (suppress password prompt) is assumed. There is no default password. If no password is supplied on the command line (either by using this parameter or adding a password to the **-U** option; see the following discussion) and the **-N** option is not specified, the client will prompt for a password, even if the desired service does not require one. (If no password is required, simply press Enter to provide a null password.) Note: Some servers (including OS/2 and Windows for Workgroups) insist on an uppercase password. Lowercase or mixed-case passwords might be rejected by these servers. Be cautious about including passwords in scripts.
- **-s *smb.conf***—This parameter specifies the pathname to the Samba configuration file, smb.conf. This file controls all aspects of the Samba setup on the machine; **smbclient** also needs to read this file.
- -**B *IP addr***—This is the IP address to use when sending a broadcast packet.
- -**O *socket options***—These are the TCP socket options to set on the client socket. For the list of valid options, see the socket options parameter in the smb.conf (5) man page.
- -**R *name resolve order***—This option allows the user of **smbclient** to determine which name resolution services to use when looking up the NetBIOS name of the host being connected to. The options are **lmhosts**, **host**, **wins**, and **bcast**. They cause names to be resolved as explained in the following sidebar.

Name Resolve Order

- ***lmhosts***—This looks up an IP address in the Samba lmhosts file. The lmhosts file is stored in the same directory as the smb.conf file.
- ***host***—This does a standard hostname-to-IP address resolution, using the system /etc/hosts, NIS, or DNS lookups. This method of name resolution is operating system-dependent; for example, on IRIX and Solaris this might be controlled by the /etc/nsswitch.conf file.
- ***wins***—This queries a name with the IP address listed in the WINS server parameter in the smb.conf file. If no WINS server has been specified, this method will be ignored.

- ***bcast***—This does a broadcast on each of the known local interfaces listed in the interfaces parameter in the smb.conf file. This is the least reliable of the name resolution methods, as it depends on the target host being on a locally connected subnet. To specify a particular broadcast address, the **-B** option may be used. If this parameter is not set, the name resolve order defined in the smb.conf file parameter (name resolve order) will be used. The default order is **lmhosts**, **host**, **wins**, and **bcast**, and without this parameter or any entry in the "name resolve order" parameter of the smb.conf file, the name resolution methods will be attempted in this order.

- **-M *NetBIOS name***—This option allows you to send messages, using the WinPopup protocol, to another computer. Once a connection is established, you enter your message, pressing Ctrl+D to end. If the receiving computer is running WinPopup, the users will receive the message and probably a beep. If they are not running WinPopup, the message will be lost and no error message will occur. The message is also automatically truncated if the message is over 1,600 bytes, as this is the limit of the protocol. One useful trick is to cat the message through **smbclient**. For example:

  ```
  cat mymessage.txt | smbclient -M FRED
  ```

  will send the message in the mymessage.txt file to the machine **FRED**. You might also find the **-U** and **-I** options useful, as they allow you to control the FROM and TO parts of the message. For a description of how to handle incoming WinPopup messages in Samba, see the message command parameter in the smb.conf (5). Note: Copy WinPopup into the startup group on your WfWg PCs if you want them always to be able to receive messages.

- **-i *scope***—This specifies a NetBIOS scope that **smbclient** will use to communicate with when generating NetBIOS names. For details on the use of NetBIOS scopes, see rfc1001.txt and rfc1002.txt. NetBIOS scopes are very rarely used; set this parameter only if you are the system administrator in charge of all the NetBIOS systems you communicate with.
- **-N**—If specified, this parameter suppresses the normal password prompt from the client to the user. This is useful when accessing a service that does not require a password. Unless a password is specified on the command line or this parameter is specified, the client will request a password.
- **-n *NetBIOS name***—By default, the client will use the local machine's hostname (in uppercase) as its NetBIOS name. This parameter allows you to override the hostname and use whatever NetBIOS name you want.
- **-d *debuglevel***—This parameter is an integer from 0 to 10 or the letter "A." If this parameter is not specified, the default value is zero. The higher this value, the more detail will be logged to the log files about the activities of the client.

At level 0, only critical errors and serious warnings will be logged. Level 1 is a reasonable level for day-to-day running, as it generates a small amount of information about operations carried out. Levels greater than 1 will generate considerable amounts of log data and should be used only when investigating a problem. Levels greater than 3 are designed for use only by developers and generate huge amounts of log data, most of which is extremely cryptic. If debuglevel is set to the letter "A," all debug messages will be printed. This setting is for developers only (and people who really want to know how the code works internally). Note that specifying this parameter here will override the log level parameter in the smb.conf (5) file.

- **-P**—This option is no longer used. The code in Samba 2.0 now lets the server decide the device type, so no printer-specific flag is needed.
- **-p *port***—This number is the TCP port number that will be used when making connections to the server. The standard (well-known) TCP port number for an SMB/CIFS server is 139, which is the default.
- **-l *logfilename***—If specified, ***logfilename*** specifies a base file name into which operational data from the running client will be logged. The default base name is specified at compile time. The base name is used to generate actual log file names. For example, if the name specified were "log," the debug file would be log.client. The log file that is generated is never removed by the client.
- **-h**—This prints the usage message for the client.
- **-I *IP address***—This is the address of the server to connect to. It should be specified in standard "a.b.c.d" notation. Normally, the client would attempt to locate a named SMB/CIFS server by looking it up by way of the NetBIOS name resolution mechanism described previously in the name resolve order parameter. Using this parameter will force the client to assume that the server is on the machine with the specified IP address, and the NetBIOS name component of the resource being connected to will be ignored. This parameter has no default. If not supplied, it will be determined automatically by the client as described previously.
- **-E**—This parameter causes the client to write messages to the standard error stream (stderr) rather than to the standard output stream. By default, the client writes messages to standard output, typically the user's terminal (TTY).
- **-U *username***—This specifies the user name that will be used by the client to make a connection, assuming that your server is not a down-level server that is running a protocol level that uses passwords on shares, not on user names. Some servers are fussy about this name's use of upper- or lowercasing, and some insist that the name must be a valid NetBIOS name. If no user name is supplied, it will default to an uppercase version of the environment variable

USER or **LOGNAME**, in that order. If no user name is supplied and neither environment variable exists, the user name "GUEST" will be used. If the **USER** environment variable contains a "%" character, everything after that will be treated as a password. This allows you to set the environment variable to be **USER=username%password** so that a password is not passed on the command line (where it might be seen by the **ps** command). If the service you are connecting to requires a password, it can be supplied using the **–U** option by appending a percent symbol (%) and then the password to user name. For example, to attach to a service as user "fred" with password "secret," you would specify "-U fred%secret" on the command line. Note that no spaces are present around the percent symbol. If you specify the password as part of the user name, the **-N** option (suppress password prompt) is assumed. If you specify the password both as a parameter and as part of user name, the password as part of username will take precedence. Putting nothing before or nothing after the percent symbol will cause an empty user name or an empty password to be used, respectively. The password can also be specified by setting up an environment variable called **PASSWORD** that contains the user's password. Note that this can be very insecure on some systems, but on others it allows users to script **smbclient** commands without having a password appear in the command line of a process listing. Note: Some servers (including OS/2 and Windows for Workgroups) insist on an uppercase password. These servers can reject lowercase or mixed-case passwords. Be cautious about including passwords in scripts or in the **PASSWORD** environment variable. Also, on many systems, the command line of a running process can be seen by way of the **ps** command; to be safe, always allow **smbclient** to prompt for a password and enter it directly.

- **-L**—This option allows you to look at what services are available on a server. You use it as "smbclient -L host," and a list should appear. The **-I** option can be useful if your NetBIOS names do not match your TCP/IP DNS hostnames or if you are trying to reach a host on another network.
- **-t *terminal code***—This option tells **smbclient** how to interpret file names coming from the remote server. Usually, Asian-language multibyte Unix implementations use different character sets than SMB/CIFS servers (e.g., EUC instead of SJIS). Setting this parameter will let **smbclient** convert between the Unix file names and the SMB file names correctly. This option has not been seriously tested and might have some problems. The terminal codes include **sjis**, **euc**, **jis7**, **jis8**, **junet**, **hex**, and **cap**. This is not a complete list, so check the Samba source code for the complete list.
- **-m *maximum protocol level***—With the new code in Samba 2.0, **smbclient** always attempts to connect at the maximum protocol level that the server supports. This parameter is preserved for backward-compatibility, but any string following the **-m** will be ignored.

- **-W *WORKGROUP***—This overrides the default workgroup specified in the workgroup parameter of the smb.conf file for this connection. This might be required to connect to some servers.
- **-T *tar options*—smbclient** may be used to create tar (1)-compatible backups of all the files on an SMB/CIFS share.

The secondary tar flags that can be given to the tar option are as follows:

- **c**—This creates a tar file on Unix and must be followed by the name of a tar file, tape device, or "-" for standard output. If using standard output, you must turn the log level to its lowest value, **-d0**, to avoid corrupting your tar file. This flag is mutually exclusive with the **x** flag.
- **x**—This extract (restores) a local tar file back to a share. Unless the **-D** option is given, the tar files will be restored from the top level of the share. This must be followed by the name of the tar file, device, or "-" for standard input. This flag is mutually exclusive with the **c** flag. Restored files have their creation times (**mtime**) set to the date saved in the tar file. Directories currently do not get their creation dates restored properly.
- **I *include files and directories***—This is the default behavior when file names are those specified previously. It causes tar files to be included in an extract or create (and thus everything else to be excluded). File name globbing works in one of two ways (see **r**).
- **X *exclude files and directories***—This causes tar files to be excluded from an extract or create (see example). File name globbing works in one of two ways now (see r).
- **b *blocksize***—This must be followed by a valid (greater than zero) block size. It causes the tar file to be written out in blocksize*TBLOCK (usually 512-byte) blocks.
- **g *incremental***—This backs up only files that have the archive bit set and is useful only with the **c** flag.
- **q *quiet***—This keeps tar from printing diagnostics as it works and is the same as tarmode quiet.
- **r *regular expression include or exclude***—This uses regular expression matching for including or excluding files if compiled with HAVE_REGEX_H. However, this mode can be very slow. If this is not compiled with HAVE_REGEX_H, it does a limited wildcard match on * and ?.
- **N *newer than***—This must be followed by the name of a file whose date is compared against files found on the share during a create. Only files newer than the file specified are backed up to the tar file. This is useful only with the **c** flag.

- **a** ***set archive bit***—This causes the archive bit to be reset when a file is backed up. It is useful with the **g** and **c** flags.

Tar Long File Names

smbclient's tar option now supports long file names both on backup and on restore. However, the full pathname of the file must be less than 1,024 bytes. Also, when a tar archive is created, **smbclient**'s tar option places all files in the archive with relative, not absolute, names.

Tar File Names

All file names can be given as DOS pathnames (with \ as the component separator) or as Unix pathnames (with / as the component separator).

Examples of **smbclient** used in tar mode appear in the following list:

- Restore from tar file backup.tar into myshare on mypc (no password on share):

```
smbclient //mypc/myshare "" -N -Tx backup.tar
```

- Restore everything except users/docs:

```
smbclient //mypc/myshare "" -N -TXx backup.tar users/docs
```

- Create a tar file of the files beneath users/docs:

```
smbclient //mypc/myshare "" -N -Tc backup.tar users/docs
```

- Create the same tar file as in the previous entry but now use a DOS pathname:

```
smbclient //mypc/myshare "" -N -tc backup.tar users\edocs
```

- Create a tar file of all the files and directories in the share:

```
smbclient //mypc/myshare "" -N -Tc backup.tar *
```

The final options for use with **smbclient** are:

- **-D** ***initial directory***—This changes to initial directory before starting and is probably of any use only with the tar **-T** option.
- **-c** ***command string***—This is a semicolon-separated list of commands to be executed instead of prompting from stdin. **-N** is implied by **-c**. This is especially useful in scripts and for printing stdin to the server (e.g., **-c 'print -'**).

Operations

Once the client is running, the user is presented with a prompt: smb:\>. The backslash (\) indicates the current working directory on the server and will change if the current working directory is changed. The prompt indicates that the client is ready and waiting to carry out a user command. Each command is a single word, optionally followed by parameters specific to that command. Command and parameters are space delimited unless these notes specifically state otherwise. All commands are case insensitive. Parameters to commands might or might not be case sensitive, depending on the command. You can specify file names that have spaces in them by quoting the name with double quotes, for example, "a long file name." Parameters shown in square brackets (e.g., [parameter]) are optional. If not given, the command will use suitable defaults. Parameters shown in angle brackets (e.g., <parameter>) are required.

Note that all commands operating on the server are actually performed by issuing a request to the server. Thus, the behavior might vary from server to server, depending on how the server was implemented.

The available commands are given here in alphabetical order:

- **?** [***command***]—If ***command*** is specified, the **?** command will display a brief informative message about the specified command. If no command is specified, a list of available commands will be displayed.
- **!** [***shell command***]—If ***shell command*** is specified, the **!** command will execute a shell locally and run the specified shell command. If no command is specified, a local shell will be run.
- **cd** [***directory name***]—If ***directory name*** is specified, the current working directory on the server will be changed to the directory specified. This operation will fail if, for any reason, the specified directory is inaccessible. If no directory name is specified, the current working directory on the server will be reported.
- **del** ***mask***—The client will request that the server attempt to delete all files matching ***mask*** from the current working directory on the server.
- **dir** ***mask***—A list of the files matching ***mask*** in the current working directory on the server will be retrieved from the server and displayed.
- **exit**—This terminates the connection with the server and exits from the program.
- **get** ***remote file name*** [***local file name***]—This copies the file called ***remote file name*** from the server to the machine running the client. If specified, name the local copy ***local file name***. Note that all transfers in **smbclient** are binary. See also the **lowercase** command.

- **help** [***command***]—See the **?** command.
- **lcd** [***directory name***]—If ***directory name*** is specified, the current working directory on the local machine will be changed to the directory specified. This operation will fail if for any reason the specified directory is inaccessible. If no directory name is specified, the name of the current working directory on the local machine will be reported.
- **lowercase**—This is toggle lowercasing of file names for the **get** and **mget** commands. When lowercasing is toggled **On**, local file names are converted to lowercase when using the **get** and **mget** commands. This is often useful when copying, for example, DOS files from a server because lowercase file names are the norm on Unix systems.
- **ls** ***mask***—See the **dir** command.
- **mask** ***mask***—This command allows the user to set up a mask that will be used during recursive operation of the **mget** and **mput** commands. The masks specified to the **mget** and **mput** commands act as filters for directories rather than files when recursion is toggled **On**. The mask specified with the **.B mask** command is necessary to filter files within those directories. For example, if the mask specified in an **mget** command is "source*", and the mask specified with the **mask** command is "*.c", and recursion is toggled **On**, the **mget** command will retrieve all files matching "*.c" from all directories below, including all directories matching "source*" in the current working directory. Note that the value for mask defaults to blank (equivalent to "*") and remains so until the **mask** command is used to change it. It retains the most recently specified value indefinitely. To avoid unexpected results, it would be wise to change the value of **.I** mask back to "*" after using the **mget** or **mput** commands.
- **md** ***directory name***—See the **mkdir** command.
- **mget** ***mask***—This copies all files matching ***mask*** from the server to the machine running the client. Note that mask is interpreted differently during recursive operation and nonrecursive operation; for more information, refer to the **recurse** and **mask** commands. Note that all transfers in **.B smbclient** are binary. See also the **lowercase** command.
- **mkdir** ***directory name***—This creates a new directory on the server (user access privileges permitting) with the specified name.
- **mput** ***mask***—This copies all files matching **mask** in the current working directory on the local machine to the current working directory on the server. Note that mask is interpreted differently during recursive operation and nonrecursive operation; for more information, refer to the **recurse** and **mask** commands. Note that all transfers in **smbclient** are binary.

- **print** ***file name***—This prints the specified file from the local machine through a printable service on the server. See also the **printmode** command.
- **printmode** ***graphics*** or ***text***—This sets the print mode to suit either binary data (such as graphical information) or text. Subsequent print commands will use the currently set print mode.
- **prompt**—This is a toggle prompting for file names during operation of the **mget** and **mput** commands. When toggled **On**, the user will be prompted to confirm the transfer of each file during these commands. When toggled **Off**, all specified files will be transferred without prompting.
- **put** ***local file name [remote file name]***—This copies the ***local file name*** file from the machine running the client to the server. If specified, name the remote copy ***remote file name***. Note that all transfers in **smbclient** are binary. See also the **lowercase** command.
- **queue**—This displays the print queue, showing the job ID, name, size, and current status.
- **quit**—See the **exit** command.
- **rd** ***directory name***—See the **rmdir** command.
- **recurse**—This is toggle directory recursion for the **mget** and **mput** commands. When toggled **On**, these commands will process all directories in the source directory (i.e., the directory they are copying **.IR** from) and will recurse into any that match the mask specified to the command. Only files that match the mask specified by using the **mask** command will be retrieved. See also the **mask** command. When recursion is toggled **Off**, only files from the current working directory on the source machine that match the mask specified to the **mget** or **mput** commands will be copied, and any mask specified using the **mask** command will be ignored.
- **rm** ***mask***—This removes all files matching ***mask*** from the current working directory on the server.
- **rmdir** ***directory name***—This removes the specified directory (user access privileges permitting) from the server.
- **tar c|x[IXbgNa]**—This performs a tar operation. See the **-T** command line option. Behavior may be affected by the **tarmode** command. Using **g** (incremental) and **N** (newer) will affect **tarmode** settings. Note that using the "-" option with tar x might not work, so use the command line option instead.
- **blocksize** ***blocksize***—This must be followed by a valid (greater than zero) block size. It causes tar file to be written out in blocksize*TBLOCK (usually 512-byte) blocks.
- **tarmode full|inc|reset|noreset**—This changes tar's behavior with regard to archive bits. In full mode, tar will back up everything regardless of the

archive bit setting (this is the default mode). In incremental mode, tar will back up only files with the archive bit set. In reset mode, tar will reset the archive bit on all files it backs up (implies read/write share).

- **setmode** ***filename*** **<perm=[+|\-]rsha>**—This is a version of the DOS **attrib** command to set file permissions. For example, **setmode myfile +r** would make myfile read-only.

NOTE: *Some servers are fussy about the case of supplied user names, passwords, share names (or service names), and machine names. If you fail to connect, try giving all parameters in uppercase.*

It is often necessary to use the ***-n*** *option when connecting to some types of servers. For example, OS/2 LanManager insists that a valid NetBIOS name be used, so you need to supply a valid name that would be known to the server.*

smbclient *supports long file names where the server supports the LANMAN2 protocol or above.*

Environment Variables

The **USER** variable may contain the user name of the person using the client. This information is used only if the protocol level is high enough to support session-level passwords.

The **PASSWORD** variable may contain the password of the person using the client. This information is used only if the protocol level is high enough to support session-level passwords.

Installation

The location of the client program is a matter for individual system administrators. Thus, the following are suggestions only.

It is recommended that the **smbclient** software be installed in the /usr/local/samba/bin or /usr/samba/bin directory, which is readable by all and writeable only by root. The client program itself should be executable by all. The client should not be setuid or setgid. The client log files should be put in a directory that is readable and writeable only by the user.

To test the client, you will need to know the name of a running SMB/CIFS server. It is possible to run **smbd** (8) as an ordinary user; running that server as a daemon on a user-accessible port (typically any port number over 1024) would provide a suitable test server.

Diagnostics

Most diagnostics issued by the client are logged in a specified log file. The log file name is specified at compile time but can be overridden on the command line.

The number and nature of diagnostics available depends on the debug level used by the client. If you have problems, set the debug level to 3 and peruse the log files.

rpcclient

The last program that is available is **rpcclient,** which was specifically designed for use in interrogating SMB/CIFS servers for network information:

```
rpcclient service <password> [-d debuglevel] [-l log]
```

The options for **rpcclient** are as follows:

- **-d *debuglevel***—This sets the debuglevel.
- **-l *log base name***—This is the base name for log/debug files.
- **-n *NetBIOS name***—This is used as a NetBIOS name.
- **-N**—This means "do not ask for a password."
- **-m *maximum protocol***—This sets the maximum protocol level.
- **-I *destination IP***—This is the IP to connect to.
- **-E**—This writes messages to stderr instead of stdout.
- **-U *user name***—This sets the network user name.
- **-W *workgroup***—This sets the workgroup name.
- **-c *command string***—This executes semicolon-separated commands.
- **-t *terminal code***—This is the terminal I/O code {**sjis**|**euc**|**jis7**|**jis8**|**junet**|**hex**}.

Using A Precompiled Version Of The Samba Executables

Two different options will be looked at here: Red Hat RPM package management and Slackware "tarball" package installation. The latter choice has many similarities across the different Unix environments that Samba has been ported to. Traditionally, software was transferred to Unix systems using tape archive (tar) files. These tar files can store many separate files in a single file that can be saved to a removable storage device; depending on the size of the resultant tar file, this can be as small as a floppy disk or can run to some very large tapes. In addition, the **tar** command can pipe the resultant file through compression utility. In any case, the actual sequence of creation or utilization of the tar file has offered a reliable method of distributing software widely throughout the Unix and Linux operating systems.

The usual sequence of events involved in the use of a tarball is as follows:

1. Untar the tar file contents, which involves extracting the individual files from the tarball into one or more directories on the computer.
2. Move or copy the new binaries to their appropriate location on the system.

Precompiled Samba packages can often be found in the following files:

- /usr/local/bin
- /usr/local/sbin
- /usr/bin
- /usr/sbin
- /opt/samba
- /usr/lib
- /usr/local/man

Alternatively, with the Linux distribution Slackware, this is handled by using the pkgtool utility, which takes a binary package or tarball and installs it into the appropriate directories. This utility helps in the installation and removal of packages under Slackware Linux. It is available in both a menu and a command line version, depending on how it is called. Issuing the **pkgtool** command as the root without options usually launches the menu-based version; with options runs **pkgtool** at the command line. Listing 3.2 details the man page for **pkgtool**.

Listing 3.2 The man page for pkgtool.

```
PKGTOOL(8)                                              PKGTOOL(8)

NAME
       pkgtool - software package maintenance tool.

SYNOPSIS
       pkgtool

       pkgtool  [  -sets #a#b#c# ] [ -source_mounted ] [ -ignore_tagfiles ]
[ -tagfile tagfile ] [ -source_dir directory ]
[       -target_dir directory ] [ -source_device directory ]

DESCRIPTION
       pkgtool is the standard package maintenance tool provided with the
Slackware Linux distribution. It is called by the setup utility to perform
system installation. It can also be called without any arguments, and will
then allow the user to install, remove, (or view, in the case of the color
version) software packages through an interactive menu system. There are
```

```
two versions of the pkgtool utility - /sbin/pkgtool.tty and
/usr/lib/setup/cpkgtool. These function in a similar fashion, but the first
one uses standard tty text output, while the second uses full screen (and
possibly color) ncurses output. The color version depends on the presence of
the /usr/lib/terminfo terminal library.

OPTIONS
        Most users will not want to use any options when running pkgtool.
These are generally used only when pkgtool is run by setup. Feel free to
Try them, but be careful.

        -sets #A#B#C#
                Install the disk sets A, B, C. Seperate the disk set names
                by '#' symbols.

        -source_mounted
                When this flag is present, pkgtool will not attempt to
                unmount and remount the source device with each disk.

        -ignore_tagfiles
                When this flag is present, pkgtool will install every *.tgz
                package encountered no matter what the tagfiles say.

        -tagfile tagfile
                This flag is used to specify from the command line which
                tagfile should be used for the installation.

        -source_dir directory
                Used when installing multiple packages from disk sets. This
                Is the directory in which the subdirectories for
                each disk are found. This isn't used when installing from
                floppy.

        -target_dir directory
                The directory where the target root directory is located.
                This is '/' when installing on the hard drive, or
                typically '/mnt' when installing from an install disk.

        -source_device device
                The source device to install from. This is not used if you've
                provided the -source_mounted flag. It's usually used when
                installing from floppy, as in:
                 -source_device /dev/fd0H1440 or
                 -source_device /dev/fd1h1200.
```

3. Obtaining And Installing

```
AUTHOR
       Patrick J. Volkerding <volkerdi@mhd1.moorhead.msus.edu>

SEE ALSO
       makepkg(8), explodepkg(8), installpkg(8), removepkg(8), setup(8)
Slackware Version 3.1.0    24 Nov 1995
```

The menu-based version of **pkgtool** is shown in Figures 3.1 to 3.7.

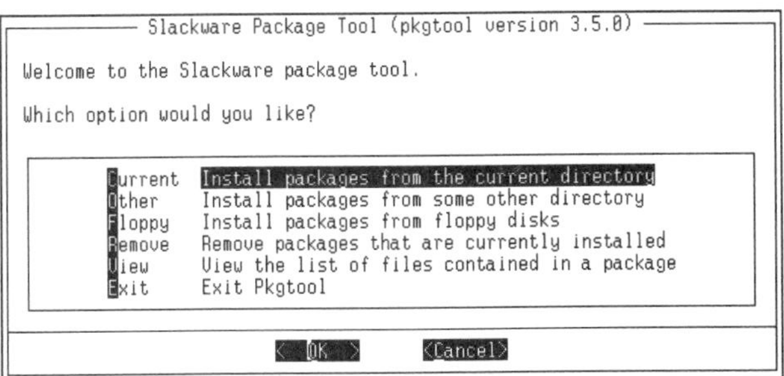

Figure 3.1 Slackware's **pkgtool** main screen.

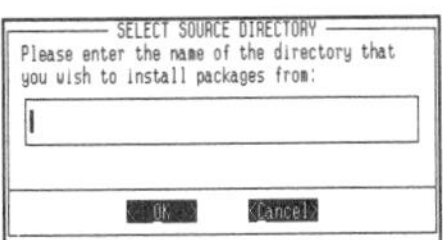

Figure 3.2 Slackware's **pkgtool** installation from other directory dialog.

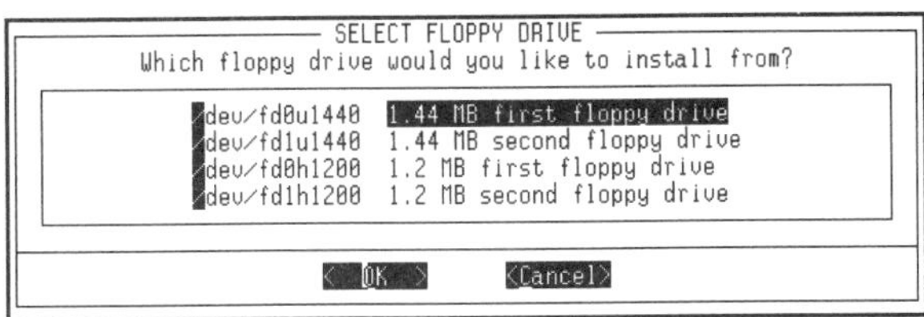

Figure 3.3 Slackware's **pkgtool** installation from floppy.

```
SCANNING
Please wait while Pkgtool scans your
system to determine which packages
you have installed and prepares a
list for you. This will take
3.51E+13 BogoMipSeconds.
```

Figure 3.4 Slackware's **pkgtool** package removal scanning notice.

```
                    SELECT PACKAGES TO REMOVE
Please select the packages you wish to Remove. Use the spacebar to
select packages to delete, and the UP/DOWN arrow keys to scroll up and
down through the entire list.
        ^(-)
    [ ] quota                 Linux disk quota utilities (1.51)
    [ ] rcs                   GNU revision control system.  (v. 5
    [ ] rdist                 rdist-6.1.3.
    [X] samba-2.0.2.tar.gz
    [ ] sastroid              Sasteroids 1.3
    [ ] sc                    The 'sc' spreadsheet. (v. 6.21)
    [ ] scsi                  Linux kernel version 2.0.34, with S
    [ ] scsimods              Linux SCSI kernel modules for 2.0.3
    [ ] seejpeg               seejpeg-1.6.1
    [ ] sendmail              BSD sendmail 8.9.0.
    [ ] seyon                 Seyon 2.14c.
    [ ] sh_utils              GNU sh-utils-1.16
    [ ] shadow                Shadow password suite (shadow-98052
        v(+)

                  <  OK  >      <Cancel>
```

Figure 3.5 Slackware's **pkgtool** package removal menu.

```
            CONTENTS OF PACKAGE: samba-2.0.2.tar.gz
PACKAGE NAME:      samba-2.0.2.tar.gz
COMPRESSED PACKAGE SIZE:      2004 K
UNCOMPRESSED PACKAGE SIZE:      9860 K
PACKAGE LOCATION: samba-2.0.2.tar.gz
FILE LIST:
samba-2.0.2/
samba-2.0.2/COPYING
samba-2.0.2/docs/
samba-2.0.2/docs/faq/
samba-2.0.2/docs/faq/Samba-Server-FAQ-2.html
samba-2.0.2/docs/faq/Samba-Server-FAQ-1.html
samba-2.0.2/docs/faq/Samba-meta-FAQ.txt
samba-2.0.2/docs/faq/sambafaq-2.html
samba-2.0.2/docs/faq/sambafaq-3.html
samba-2.0.2/docs/faq/sambafaq-1.html
samba-2.0.2/docs/faq/sambafaq-4.html
samba-2.0.2/docs/faq/sambafaq-5.html
samba-2.0.2/docs/faq/sambafaq.sgml
                                                      ( 2%)
                         < EXIT >
```

Figure 3.6 Slackware's **pkgtool** has the ability to view the contents of a package.

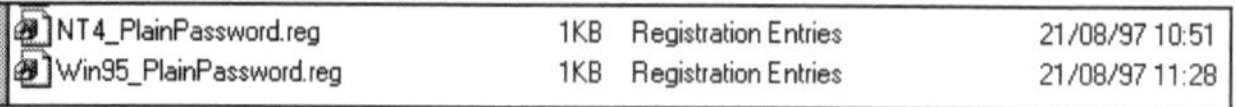

NT4_PlainPassword.reg	1KB	Registration Entries	21/08/97 10:51
Win95_PlainPassword.reg	1KB	Registration Entries	21/08/97 11:28

Figure 3.7 Some of the Samba package content.

The Linux Red Hat distribution developers have spent considerable time and effort on a new method of distribution of software called Red Hat Package Manager (RPM). This is a sophisticated addition to the Linux operating system; it is part of the administrator's toolkit, and it offers considerable advantages over the tarball approach when you need to manage software packages and systems. Adding, deleting, modifying (upgrading), and software list management on any server are constant drains on resources. In the past, a detailed knowledge of the interdependency of one package on another had to be maintained, so that when one package needed upgrading or had to be modified, you knew which other packages were affected. This is even more important in cases in which some libraries affect and are used by many of the installed packages available today. **pkgtool** does not offer this level of support.

RPM for the user exists in a format that is just like another Unix command with the necessary syntax and command line options. It operates by maintaining its own database of the packages you have on your system, their location, and the interdependencies and relationships between them.

Thus, an RPM package is more than simply a collection of binaries; it contains considerably more information than you might expect, including the detailed information on its contents, name, and version. RPM packages have been created, in a way similar to the older tarball, to provide either a single function or a collection of functions for a Linux system. In this case, we are interested in the Samba RPM package that contains the Samba executables, configuration files, manual pages, and other documentation.

Fortunately, the RPM system has also been made available for use with other Unix systems. The main requirement to run RPM is CPIO 2.4.2 or greater. Although the RPM system is included with Red Hat Linux, it has been ported to Slackware so that you can use the RPM packages. It has been ported to a large number of other Unix systems. I believe that it has been compiled on Sun OS, Solaris, AIX, IRIX, AmigaOS, and others. The very best source of information on RPM is **www.redhat.com**, the Red Hat Web site.

NOTE: *The binary packages generated on a different type of Unix system will not be compatible. Do not attempt to install a Red Hat Samba RPM package on your AIX or other system, as the result might not be productive.*

On my current system, entering "rpm" at the command prompt returns the code in Listing 3.3.

Listing 3.3 Output after entering "rpm" at the command prompt.

```
RPM version 2.3.11
  Copyright (C) 1997 - Red Hat Software
  This may be freely redistributed under the terms of the GNU Public
  License
  usage: rpm {--help}
         rpm {--version}
         rpm {--initdb}   [--dbpath <dir>]
         rpm {--install -i} [-v] [--hash -h] [--percent] [--force] [--test]
                          [--replacepkgs] [--replacefiles] [--root <dir>]
                          [--excludedocs] [--includedocs] [--noscripts]
                          [--rcfile <file>] [--ignorearch] [--dbpath <dir>]
                          [--prefix <dir>] [--ignoreos] [--nodeps]
                          [--ftpproxy <host>] [--ftpport <port>]
                          file1.rpm ... fileN.rpm
         rpm {--upgrade -U} [-v] [--hash -h] [--percent] [--force] [--test]
                          [--oldpackage] [--root <dir>] [--noscripts]
```

```
                          [--excludedocs] [--includedocs] [--rcfile <file>]
                          [--ignorearch]  [--dbpath <dir>] [--prefix <dir>]
                          [--ftpproxy <host>] [--ftpport <port>]
                          [--ignoreos] [--nodeps] file1.rpm ... fileN.rpm
        rpm {--query -q} [-afpg] [-i] [-l] [-s] [-d] [-c] [-v] [-R]
                          [--scripts] [--root <dir>] [--rcfile <file>]
                          [--whatprovides] [--whatrequires] [--requires]
                          [--ftpuseport] [--ftpproxy <host>]
                          [--ftpport <port>]
                          [--provides] [--dump] [--dbpath <dir>] [targets]
        rpm {--verify -V -y} [-afpg] [--root <dir>] [--rcfile <file>]
                          [--dbpath <dir>] [--nodeps] [--nofiles]
                          [--noscripts]
                          [--nomd5] [targets]
        rpm {--setperms} [-afpg] [target]
        rpm {--setugids} [-afpg] [target]
        rpm {--erase -e} [--root <dir>] [--noscripts] [--rcfile <file>]
                          [--dbpath <dir>] [--nodeps] [--allmatches]
                          package1 ... packageN
        rpm {-b|t}[plciba] [-v] [--short-circuit] [--clean]
                          [--rcfile  <file>]
                          [--sign] [--test] [--timecheck <s>] specfile
        rpm {--rebuild} [--rcfile <file>] [-v] source1.rpm ... sourceN.rpm
        rpm {--recompile} [--rcfile <file>] [-v]
                           source1.rpm ... sourceN.rpm
        rpm {--resign} [--rcfile <file>] package1 package2 ... packageN
        rpm {--addsign} [--rcfile <file>] package1 package2 ... packageN
        rpm {--checksig -K} [--nopgp] [--nomd5] [--rcfile <file>]
                             package1 ... packageN
        rpm {--rebuilddb} [--rcfile <file>] [--dbpath <dir>]
        rpm {--querytags}
```

Thus, it is clear that several functions and options are available under RPM. These are summarized in Table 3.2.

An interesting option is that RPM is also capable of installing and querying a package over an FTP link. It could be used to install the Samba package directly from a mirror site, although I do not recommend doing so. However, this means that it would be possible to install or upgrade any number of Samba servers in your organization from a central FTP site copy. The syntax would be as follows:

```
rpm -i ftp://localhost/pub/linux/redhat/RPMS/foobar-1.0-1.i386.rpm
```

Table 3.2 RPM functions.

Command Line	Use
rpm -i install-options package_file	Installs the package with the given options.
rpm -U upgrade-options package_file	Upgrades the package with the given options.
rpm -e erase-options package_file	Erases or uninstalls the package with the given options (removing all possible dependencies).
rpm -q query-options package_file	Determines whether a specific package has been installed and where it is located.
rpm -Vl-yl--verify verify-options	Compares an installed package with the original, "virgin" package. This comparison could include size, a checksum, permissions, type, owner, and group of each file that makes up the package.
rpm -b0 build-options <package_spec>+ B	Creates an RPM package (possibly of limited use if you plan to use Samba only as a file print server; however, should you eventually create software or a specific Samba configuration for your organization, this might be a useful option).
rpm -rebuilddb	Rebuilds the database with the configuration information for all currently installed packages on your system.
rpm --setperms package_file	Resets the original file permissions to the files belonging to a package.
rpm --checksig package_file	Verifies that a package's integrity and origin are correct. This function checks the digital signature of a package to make sure that it has not been tampered with.
rpm --setugids package_file	Resets the original owner and group to the files belonging to a package.
rpm --showrc package_file	Displays the values of the rpmrc file, which is used to set various parameters used by RPM.
rpm -[main option] --test	Tests the package; may be used during installation, erasure, and rebuilding.

Here, **localhost** is your FTP server, **/pub/linux/redhat/RPMS** is the package directory, and **foobar-1.0.1.i386.rpm** is the corresponding package.

Red Hat 5.2 no longer includes a single tar.gz package archive in its distribution, and the source even exists as RPM packages as well.

Installing Samba: First Steps

Let us assume that you have a system without Samba installed on it. Your available options can be summarized as shown in Table 3.3.

If you have a version of Samba installed already, as might be the case with many Linux distributions, you can confirm whether you do by running **smbstatus**, which would return an output similar to the one in Listing 3.4.

Listing 3.4 Output from running smbstatus.

```
linuxserver1:~$ smbstatus

Samba version 2.0.2
Service      uid      gid      pid     machine
----------------------------------------------


No locked files


Share mode memory usage (bytes):
   102216(99%) free + 128(0%) used + 56(0%) overhead = 102400(100%) total
```

Should the Samba programs be present but no smb.conf exists or the services are not started, you will obtain an error message, depending on whether the smb.conf file is not present or the services have not started or have not been installed as in Listing 3.5 or Listing 3.6.

Listing 3.5 Output from running smbstatus when smb.conf is not present.

```
dh012:/etc# smbstatus
params.c:OpenConfFile() - Unable to open configuration file
"/usr/local/samba/lib/smb.conf":
        No such file or directory
Can't load /usr/local/samba/lib/smb.conf - run testparm to debug it
dh012:/etc#
```

Listing 3.6 Output from running smbstatus.

```
dh012:~# smbstatus
Samba version 2.0.2
Service      uid      gid      pid     machine
----------------------------------------------


ERROR smb_shm_open : open failed with code No such file or directory
ERROR: Failed to initialise share modes!
Can't initialise shared memory - exiting
```

Now, your options are either to remove the currently installed version of Samba or to install a new version. You can then use one of the package tools (RPM, **pkgtool**, or **removepkg**) or manually remove the executables.

Table 3.3 Installation options.

Method	When To Use
Rpm	Red Hat- or RPM-capable system
pkgtool or installpkg	Slackware system
Configure, make, and make install	Non-RPM system or any other situation

Creating Your Own Version Of The Samba Executables

In this option, you will need to obtain a copy of the Samba source (a copy is located on this book's CD-ROM) and extract it onto your system into a suitable location; /usr/src/samba would be advisable.

Are Encrypted Passwords Used On Your Network?

If you are using Samba on a network with either Microsoft NT 4.0 with Service Pack 3 or later, you are probably using encrypted passwords on your network. This is because Microsoft NT uses encrypted passwords for authentication as of Service Pack 3; the default is to deny access to clients using plain-text password authentication. Furthermore, if you want to authenticate users against the Security Account Manager (SAM) database in a Windows NT Server on your network, the DES (Data Encryption Standard) must be compiled into your Samba binaries. Chapter 9 investigates the use of an NT server to authenticate users on Unix systems. Some users of Unix systems also allow encrypted password authentication. It is possible to switch this requirement off by using plain-text passwords by setting the NT Registry entry (Run regedt32.exe) for

HKEY_LOCAL_MACHINE\system\CurrentControlSet\Services\Rdr\Parameters\

by adding the following value: EnablePlainTextPassword:REG_DWORD=1. Alternatively, in the Samba distribution you will find the NT4_PlainPassword.reg file as shown in Figure 3.8; copy it to the NT workstation or server and double-click on it while in an open folder. It will add the appropriate entry in the Registry.

Likewise, for Windows 95 it is possible to switch this requirement off by using plain-text passwords by setting the NT Registry entry (Run regedit.exe) for

HKEY_LOCAL_MACHINE\System\CurrentControlSet\Services\VxD\VNETSUP

by adding the following value: EnablePlainTextPassword:Value data=1. Alternatively, in the Samba distribution you will find the Win95_PlainPassword.reg file as in Figure 3.8; copy it to the Windows 95 workstation and double-click on it while in an open folder. It will add the appropriate entry in the Registry.

Note that to turn Plain Text Password authentication off, you need to either remove this Registry key or set the value to 0.

Versions of Samba earlier than 1.9.18 required a separate compile in support of encrypted passwords using a DES library called libdes. This added an extra step to the compile and install process because U.S. distributors of Samba were unable to export strong encryption technology (DES being one of these) because of an export ban. This is controlled under the International Traffic in Arms Regulation (ITAR) laws, which stop anyone from exporting technology with potential military applications from the United States. You might have come across this ban already with Netscape (www.netscape.com), which has different versions that support 40- or 128-bit encryption. The latter is available in the continental United States to U.S. citizens. The same laws are applied to Samba. The developers of Samba 1.9.18 included a modified, cut-down version of the DES algorithm that can be used for authentication of SMB passwords.

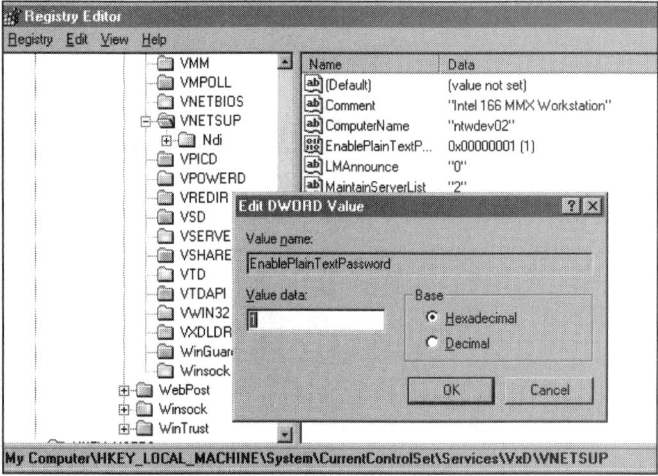

Figure 3.8 Plain-text password Registry files included in distribution for Windows 95 and NT4.

Building Samba

If you have decided to build your own copy of the Samba executables, you need to know a few requirements. First, you must have a system that has a GNU C compiler and the **make** utility installed on it. In both the Slackware and the Red Hat Linux distributions, this involves making sure that the GNU development tools suite has been installed. On a Slackware system, the software is available from the disk "D" set. On a Red Hat system, the software required is listed under development. In any other system, you will need a C compiler (either GNU gcc or egcs) and **make** to build the Samba executables.

Unpacking The Distribution

The Samba source distribution, available from one of the Samba mirror sites, is usually found as a tar.gz or gzipped tar archive. The naming of this file should immediately indicate the version of the source contained within it. The structure of this file is samba-n.x.mm.tar.gz, where n.x.mm is the full version number of the distribution source within.

On a Linux system, the command to extract the individual files from this archive while viewing the extraction is **gzip -dc samba-n.x.mm.tar.gz | tar xvf-** or **tar zxvf samba-n.x.mm.tar.gz**.

What Do The Version Numbers Mean?

In samba-n.x.mmpXX.tar.gz, n is currently at 2 (Samba is at major release version 2), x is a subversion, and mm indicates a major transition within subversions.

When a new or the latest piece of code that needs testing is included, the subversion number is increased by one, and the word *alpha* is included in the name; as the development of this code continues, a number might be appended to *alpha* to show further revisions.

Once alphas have become stable enough, then, depending on the size of the changes involved, Andrew Tridgell will either rename by removing the word *alpha,* indicating a stable release, or increase the major or subversion numbers (usually at the alpha stage this would have been set, as in the transition from 1.9.18 to 2.0.0).

Should a bug fix be required in a stable release, a minor patch release would occur so that the appended pXX series would apply. If no patch level exists, the pXX does not appear in the name.

I do not recommend that you run a version of Samba with the word *alpha* in its name unless you know what you are doing and are willing to do some debugging. The introduction of some code in one part of the source might have resulted in another part's breaking. This can lead to unreliable results on a production platform.

Should you log in to any of the FTP mirror sites, they should indicate the latest stable release of Samba (usually in the root of the Samba tree). The latest stable release version should allow you to produce a production Samba server. If you are so inclined, use an alpha release and help with the testing and development—but do not install it on your departmental server. Do not forget to join the Samba mailing lists if you do. For details, see Appendix A.

The latest Samba production release is typically very stable and safe, mainly due to the many public releases that follow extensive testing.

This works in the following example:

1.9.18p10 (production)

2.0.0alpha1 (test sites only)

:

2.0.0alpha17 (test sites only)

2.0.0 (production)

This system means that whenever someone looks at the Samba FTP site, he or she will be able to grab the highest numbered release without an alpha in the name and be sure he or she is getting the current recommended version. This is listed as samba-latest.tar.gz, which links to the correct version.

The version 2.0.0 also introduced a series of beta releases (e.g., Samba-2.0.0beta4.tar.gz).

The Samba site contains a document called "Roadmap," which will tell you at a glance which changes are envisioned for coming releases. The copy included with 2.0.2 reads as follows:

Copyright (C) 1997-1998 - Samba-Team

The Samba-Team is committed to an aggressive program to deliver quality controlled software to a well defined roadmap.

The current Samba release 2.0.0 is called the "Domain Client Release."

It correctly implements the Windows NT specific SMB calls, and will operate correctly as a client in a Windows NT Domain environment.

In addition, the first implementation of the Web-based GUI management tool ships with 2.0.0, thus fulfilling some of the commitments made in the 1.9.18 release Roadmap document.

Some work has been done on ensuring compatibility with Windows NT 5.0 (now Windows 2000 :-) although this is a somewhat (slowly) moving target.

The following development objectives for future releases are in place:

2.0.x - "NT Security update" - Allowing Windows NT Clients to manipulate file security and ownership using native tools.

2.0.xx - "Thin Server" mode, allowing a Samba server to be inserted into a network with no UNIX setup required.

Some management capabilities for Samba using native NT tools.

Provision of command-line equivalents to native NT tools.

2.X - "Domain Controller" - able to serve as a Windows NT PDC.

X.XX - "Full Domain Integration" - allowing both PDC and BDC modes.

Note that it is a given that the Samba Team will continue to track Windows (NT/2000) update releases, ensuring that Samba will work well with whatever "Beta" releases Redmond throws our way :-).

You may also note that the release numbers get fuzzier the further into the future the objectives get. This is intentional as we cannot yet commit to exact timeframes.

Understanding What Is In The Source Distribution

The contents from an example Samba distribution from a distribution file samba-2.0.2.tar.gz are included in Listing 3.6.

Listing 3.6 The distribution contents.

```
Linuxserver1:/downloads/samba/samba-2.0.2# ls -l
total 45
-rw-r--r--   1 1002     1002         17982 May  4  1996 COPYING
-rw-r--r--   1 1002     1002          3311 Nov 23 22:50 Manifest
-rw-r--r--   1 1002     1002          6750 Nov 23 22:50 README
-rw-r--r--   1 1002     1002             0 Aug 21  1997 Read-Manifest-Now
-rw-r--r--   1 1002     1002          1789 Nov 12 20:41 Roadmap
-rw-r--r--   1 1002     1002          7692 Feb  6 22:56 WHATSNEW.txt
drwxr-xr-x   7 1002     1002          1024 Nov 23 22:50 docs/
drwxr-xr-x  12 1002     1002          1024 Feb  6 22:43 examples/
drwxr-xr-x  12 1002     1002          1024 Jan 14 20:07 packaging/
drwxr-xr-x  25 1002     1002          1024 Mar  1 19:41 source/
drwxr-xr-x   5 1002     1002          1024 Dec  7 21:50 swat/
```


The Non-Operating-System-Specific Compile-Time Configuration Options

The latest versions of Samba have an increased portability because Samba is now self-configuring using GNU autoconfiguration; this ends the need for people installing Samba to configure the Makefile.

When in the source directory, you now configure and build Samba by running **./configure** and then **make**. For further details, see this book's CD-ROM or the latest Samba distribution docs/textdocs/UNIX_INSTALL.txt file. The source directory listing before and after**./configure** has been run is shown in Listings 3.7 and 3.8, respectively.

Listing 3.7 The source directory listing before running ./configure.

```
Linuxserver1:/downloads/samba/samba-2.0.2/source# ls -l M
-rw-r--r--   1 1002     1002         19676 Feb  6 22:51 Makefile.in
```

Listing 3.8 The source directory listing after running ./configure.

```
Linuxserver1:/downloads/samba/samba-2.0.2/source# ls -l M*
-rw-r--r--   1 root     root         19517 Mar  1 20:13 Makefile
-rw-r--r--   1 1002     1002         19676 Feb  6 22:51 Makefile.in
```

The header contents of the Makefile are shown in Listing 3.9.

Listing 3.9 Makefile.

```
# Generated automatically from Makefile.in by configure.
###########################################################################
# Makefile.in for Samba - rewritten for autoconf support
# Copyright Andrew Tridgell 1992-1998
###########################################################################

prefix=/usr/local/samba
exec_prefix=${prefix}
mandir=${prefix}/man

LIBS=
CC=gcc
CFLAGS=-O
CPPFLAGS=
LDFLAGS=
AWK=gawk

INSTALLCMD=/usr/bin/ginstall -c

srcdir=.
builddir=/downloads/samba/samba-2.0.2/source
SHELL=/bin/sh

BASEDIR= /usr/local/samba
BINDIR = ${exec_prefix}/bin
# we don't use sbindir because we want full compatibility with
# the previous releases of Samba
SBINDIR = ${exec_prefix}/bin
LIBDIR = ${exec_prefix}/lib
VARDIR = ${prefix}/var
MANDIR = ${prefix}/man

# The permissions to give the executables
INSTALLPERMS = 0755

# set these to where to find various files
# These can be overridden by command line switches (see smbd(8))
# or in smb.conf (see smb.conf(5))
SMBLOGFILE = $(VARDIR)/log.smb
NMBLOGFILE = $(VARDIR)/log.nmb
CONFIGFILE = $(LIBDIR)/smb.conf
LMHOSTSFILE = $(LIBDIR)/lmhosts
DRIVERFILE = $(LIBDIR)/printers.def
```

```
PASSWD_PROGRAM = /bin/passwd
# This is where smbpasswd et al go
PRIVATEDIR = ${prefix}/private

SMB_PASSWD_FILE = $(PRIVATEDIR)/smbpasswd

# This is where SWAT images and help files go
SWATDIR = ${prefix}/swat

# the directory where lock files go
LOCKDIR = $(VARDIR)/locks

# The directory where code page definition files go
CODEPAGEDIR = $(LIBDIR)/codepages

# The current codepage definition list.
CODEPAGELIST= 437 737 850 852 861 932 866 949 950 936

# where you are going to have the smbrun binary. This defaults to the
# install directory. This binary is needed for correct printing
# and magic script execution. This should be an absolute path!
# Also not that this should include the name "smbrun" on the end (the
# name of the executable)
SMBRUN = $(BINDIR)/smbrun


PASSWD_FLAGS = -DPASSWD_PROGRAM=\"$(PASSWD_PROGRAM)\" -
DSMB_PASSWD_FILE=\"$(SMB_PASSWD_FILE)\"
FLAGS1 = $(CFLAGS) -Iinclude -I$(srcdir)/include -I$(srcdir)/ubiqx -
I$(srcdir)/smbwrapper $(CPPFLAGS) -DSMBLOGFILE=\"$(SMBLOGFILE)\" -
DNMBLOGFILE=\"$(NMBLOGFILE)\"
FLAGS2 = -DCONFIGFILE=\"$(CONFIGFILE)\" -DLMHOSTSFILE=\"$(LMHOSTSFILE)\"
FLAGS3 = -DSWATDIR=\"$(SWATDIR)\" -DSBINDIR=\"$(SBINDIR)\" -
DLOCKDIR=\"$(LOCKDIR)\" -DSMBRUN=\"$(SMBRUN)\" -
DCODEPAGEDIR=\"$(CODEPAGEDIR)\"
FLAGS4 = -DDRIVERFILE=\"$(DRIVERFILE)\" -DBINDIR=\"$(BINDIR)\"
FLAGS5 = $(FLAGS1) $(FLAGS2) $(FLAGS3) $(FLAGS4) -DHAVE_INCLUDES_H
FLAGS  = $(ISA) $(FLAGS5) $(PASSWD_FLAGS)
FLAGS32  = $(ISA32) $(FLAGS5) $(PASSWD_FLAGS)

SPROGS = bin/smbd bin/nmbd bin/swat
PROGS1 = bin/smbclient bin/testparm bin/testprns bin/smbrun bin/smbstatus
PROGS2 = bin/rpcclient bin/smbpasswd bin/make_smbcodepage
MPROGS =
PROGS = $(PROGS1) $(PROGS2) $(MPROGS) bin/nmblookup bin/make_printerdef
```

```
SCRIPTS = $(srcdir)/script/smbtar $(srcdir)/script/addtosmbpass $(srcdir)/
script/convert_smbpasswd

QUOTAOBJS=noquotas.o
. . .
```

Knowing Your Installation Options

You may still hand edit the Makefile for your specific system. Editing this file after running **./configure** and before **make** can allow you to install Samba according to your preferences for base directory or elsewhere.

The default directory for an installation in this case is BASEDIR=/usr/local/samba; prefix=/usr/local/samba is the variable that sets the other directories in the Makefile.

Samba and its associated programs are commonly installed in an alternative location; these are /usr/local/bin, /usr/local/sbin, /usr/bin, /usr/sbin, /opt/samba, /usr/lib, and /usr/local/man.

Default Configuration Options

Default configuration options set the locations for various files that the Samba executables use. These can be overridden by command line switches or in smb.conf as follows:

```
SMBLOGFILE = $(VARDIR)/log.smb
NMBLOGFILE = $(VARDIR)/log.nmb
CONFIGFILE = $(LIBDIR)/smb.conf
LMHOSTSFILE = $(LIBDIR)/lmhosts
DRIVERFILE = $(LIBDIR)/printers.def
PASSWD_PROGRAM = /bin/passwd
# This is where smbpasswd et al go
PRIVATEDIR = ${prefix}/private
SMB_PASSWD_FILE = $(PRIVATEDIR)/smbpasswd
```

SWAT, the new Web-based configuration utility, also has a series of programs and files. The locations of any lock files and code pages and other programs are also listed in the Makefile:

```
# This is where SWAT images and help files go
SWATDIR = ${prefix}/swat

# the directory where lock files go
LOCKDIR = $(VARDIR)/locks
```

```
# The directory where code page definition files go
CODEPAGEDIR = $(LIBDIR)/codepages

# The current codepage definition list.
CODEPAGELIST= 437 737 850 852 861 932 866 949 950 936

# where you are going to have the smbrun binary. This defaults to the
# install directory. This binary is needed for correct printing
# and magic script execution. This should be an absolute path!
# Also note that this should include the name "smbrun" on the end (the
# name of the executable)
SMBRUN = $(BINDIR)/smbrun
```


In addition, the compilation of the executables will use several header files. In the /include directory, the header files also contain other options used when producing executables. If you are interested, you should take time to read these. The header files include comments that explain their use and purpose. One of these header files, local.h, includes several of these options, the first of which sets the default workgroup that your Samba server will participate in:

```
/* The default workgroup - usually overridden in smb.conf */
#define WORKGROUP "WORKGROUP"
```

In addition, the default guest account user is stated in this file:

```
/* the default guest account - normally set in the Makefile or smb.conf */
#define GUEST_ACCOUNT "nobody"
```

A number of other options are listed in the local.h file; all these files are commented. If you want to get involved in tuning your version of Samba, you can locate the default options here. Some of the more important ones are the following:

```
#define GLOBAL_NAME "global"
#define GLOBAL_NAME2 "globals"
This defines the section name in the configuration file that will contain
global parameters - that is, parameters relating to the whole server, not
just services. This name is then reserved, and may not be used as a service
name. It will default to "global" if not defined here.

#define HOMES_NAME "homes"
This defines the section name in the configuration file that will refer to
the special "homes" service
```

```
#define PRINTERS_NAME "printers"
This defines the section name in the configuration file that will refer to
the special "printers" service

#define MAXPRINTERLEN 15
Yves Gaige <yvesg@hptnodur.grenoble.hp.com> requested this set this to a
maximum of 8 if old smb clients break because of long printer names.


#define MAX_OPEN_DIRECTORIES 256
/* max number of directories open at once */
/* note that with the new directory code this no longer requires a
   file handle per directory, but large numbers do use more memory */


#define MAX_DIRECTORY_HANDLES 2048
/* max number of directory handles */
/* As this now uses the bitmap code this can be
   quite large. */

#define SYSLOG_FACILITY LOG_DAEMON
/* define what facility to use for syslog */

#define SHMEM_SIZE (1024*1024)
/* Default size of shared memory used for share mode locking */

#define MAX_OPEN_FILES 10000
/*Default number of maximum open files per smbd. This is
 * also limited by the maximum available file descriptors
 * per process and can also be set in smb.conf as "max open files"
 * in the [global] section.
 */

#define MAXSTATUS 100000
/* the max number of simultanous connections to the server by all clients */

#define MAX_PASS_LEN 200
/* the maximum password length before we declare a likely attack */

#define MANGLE_LONG_FILENAMES
/*shall filenames with illegal chars in them get mangled in long filename
listings?*/

#define PAGER "more"
/*the default pager to use for the client "more" command. Users can
   override this with the PAGER environment variable*/
```

3. Obtaining And Installing

The /include directory contains several other header files; the smb.h file contains the port details for the different services. These are at ports 137, 138, and 139:

```
#define NMB_PORT 137
#define DGRAM_PORT 138
#define SMB_PORT 139
```

It is possible to set these to alternative ports if you want. However, this would become a nonstandard installation.

This same header file, smb.h, also lists the standard code pages and defaults to 850:

```
/* Defines needed for multi-codepage support. */
#define MSDOS_LATIN_1_CODEPAGE 850
#define KANJI_CODEPAGE 932
#define HANGUL_CODEPAGE 949
#define BIG5_CODEPAGE 950
#define SIMPLIFIED_CHINESE_CODEPAGE 936

#ifdef KANJI
/*
 * Default client code page - Japanese
 */
#define DEFAULT_CLIENT_CODE_PAGE KANJI_CODEPAGE
#else /* KANJI */
/*
 * Default client code page - 850 - Western European
 */
#define DEFAULT_CLIENT_CODE_PAGE MSDOS_LATIN_1_CODEPAGE
#endif /* KANJI */
```

The header file version.h contains the text variable to identify the version number for the Samba executables:

```
#define VERSION "2.0.1"
```

Authentication Options

Authentication Options are set using the autoconfiguration facility, which will detect and create the necessary entries for authentication options in the Makefile. The general form of the configure.in file entry that the autoconfiguration facility would use in this case is as follows:

```
# check for the AFS filesystem
AC_MSG_CHECKING(whether to use AFS)
```

```
AC_ARG_WITH(afs,
[  --with-afs     Include AFS support
  --without-afs  Don't include AFS support (default)],
[ case "$withval" in
  yes)
    AC_MSG_RESULT(yes)
    AC_DEFINE(WITH_AFS)
    ;;
  *)
    AC_MSG_RESULT(no)
    ;;
  esac ],
  AC_MSG_RESULT(no)
)
```


The options are passed into the facility that would create the Makefile with the appropriate option. The default is that these options are not included. These authentication options include the following:

- Andrews File System (AFS)
- Distributed Computing Environment (DCE)
- Distributed File System (DFS)
- Kerberos IV auth system
- Kerberos 5 auth system
- LDAP password database
- NISPLUS password database
- NISPLUS_HOME support
- Secure Socket Layer

Operating-System-Specific Compile-Time Configuration Options

These are now included in the configure.in file that is used by autoconfiguration to produce the Makefile.

In previous releases (i.e., 1.9.18 and earlier) of Samba, before the use of the autoconfiguration facility, these options were uncommented in the appropriate line in the Makefile. An example Makefile from the 1.9.18 Samba release is included on this book's CD-ROM so that you can see these options.

The following options are set:

- FLAGSM
- LIBSM

These include compiler settings for specific operating systems and versions. Other options that are set are the following:

- CC
- AWK

These detail the compiler to use and the **awk** facility to use if broken. In the Solaris operating system, this is the case, and **nawk** is specificed.

Compiling Samba

Enter "make" after the Makefile has been configured either using the **./configure** option or following manual editing. The Samba binaries will then be compiled.

Completing The Installation

At this point, it makes no difference whether you have decided to use a binary that came with your operating system, you have installed a pre-built binary, or you have compiled your own. (Take a look at Chapter 11 and the available troubleshooting options.) The created binaries now need to be installed.

If you have compiled your own binaries from source, these are installed by entering "make install". The binaries and the man pages or documentation and support files will then be installed into the appropriate locations as per the Makefile. You can also refine this to install either only the binaries or the man pages using make installbin or make installman.

NOTE: *If you are not happy with your new Samba executables, you have the option of returning to your previous installation by entering "make revert". While installing or upgrading to a new version, the old binaries will have been renamed with the .old extension. You are well advised to back up these before proceeding. Care is required during this installation process if you are compiling your own binaries, as rebuilding and reinstalling the binaries a second time will completely overwrite those original copies.*

If you are using binaries that already have been created for your system, be it Red Hat, Slackware, Debian, or even Sun OS and AIX, you should follow the instructions that accompany these binaries. Refer to the section on the **rpm** and pkgtool earlier in this chapter.

It is recommended that the server software be installed under the /usr/local/samba hierarchy in a directory readable by all and writeable only by root. The server program itself should be executable by all, because users might want to run the server themselves (in which case it will run with their privileges). The server should not be setuid. On some systems, it might be worthwhile to make **smbd** setgid to an empty group. This is because some systems might have a security hole; daemon processes that become a user can be attached to that hole with a debugger. Making the **smbd** file setgid to an empty group can prevent this hole from being exploited. This security hole and the suggested fix have been confirmed only on old versions (pre-kernel 2.0) of Linux at the time of this writing. It is possible that this hole exists only in Linux, because testing on other systems has thus far shown them to be immune.

setuid: Set User Identity

setuid sets the effective user ID of the current process. If the effective userid of the caller is root, the real and saved user IDs are also set. Under Linux, setuid is implemented like the POSIX version with the _POSIX_SAVED_IDS feature. This allows a setuid (other than root) program to drop all its user privileges, do some unprivileged work, and then reengage the original effective user ID in a secure manner.

If the user is root or the program is setuid root, special care must be taken. The setuid function checks the effective uid of the caller, and if it is the superuser, all process-related user IDs are set to uid. After this has occurred, it is impossible for the program to regain root privileges.

So, if a program wishes to temporarily drop root privileges to assume the identity of a non-root user, regaining root privileges again after the activity, it may not use setuid. You can accomplish this with the (non-POSIX, BSD) call seteuid.

Linux has the concept of file system user ID, normally equal to the effective user ID. The setuid call also sets the file system user ID of the current process. See setfsuid (2).

If uid is different from the old effective uid, the process will be forbidden from leaving core dumps.

setgid: Set Group Identity

setgid sets the effective group ID of the current process. If the caller is the superuser, the real and saved group IDs are also set.

Under Linux, setgid is implemented like the POSIX version with the _POSIX _SAVED_IDS feature. This allows a setgid (other than root) program to drop all its group privileges, do some unprivileged work, and then reengage the original effective group ID in a secure manner.

If the user is **root** or the program is **setgid root**, special care must be taken. The setgid function checks the effective gid of the caller, and if it is the superuser, all process-related group IDs are set to gid. After this has occurred, it is impossible for the program to regain root privileges.

So, if a program wishes to temporarily drop root privileges to assume the identity of a non-root user, regaining root privileges again after the activity, it may not use setuid. You can accomplish this with the (non-POSIX, BSD) call setegid.

The server log files should be put in a directory readable and writeable only by root, as the log files might contain sensitive information.

The configuration file should be placed in a directory readable and writeable only by root, as the configuration file controls security for the services offered by the server. The configuration file can be made readable by all if desired, but this is not necessary for the correct operation of the server and is not recommended.

Running Samba

The **smbd** and **nmbd** daemons that make Samba work are the two processes that provide the sharing of file systems and printer services and that service incoming NetBIOS name server requests. It would be fair to say that without these running, you would not be able to provide Samba from your Unix machine.

These Samba services can be run two ways: First, you can start them using the main system startup scripts, where they can be run as standalone daemons that might or might not be invoked, on system startup. Second, you can use inetd, which is a general daemon that listens to all the preset ports on your server for incoming requests; when such a request arrives at your server, the corresponding process is started.

Listing 3.10 The man page for inetd.

```
INETD(8)                  UNIX System Manager's Manual
INETD(8)


NAME
     inetd - internet "super-server"


SYNOPSIS
     inetd [-d] [-q queuelength] [configuration file]


DESCRIPTION
     Inetd should be run at boot time by /etc/rc.local (see rc(8)). It then
     listens for connections on certain internet sockets. When a connection
     is found on one of its sockets, it decides what service the socket
     corresponds to, and invokes a program to service the request.
     After the program is finished, it continues to listen on the socket
     (except in some cases which will be described below). Essentially,
```

inetd allows running
one daemon to invoke several others, reducing load on the system.

The options available for inetd:

-d Turns on debugging.

-q queuelength
Sets the size of the socket listen queue to the specified value.
Default is 128.

Upon execution, inetd reads its configuration information from a configuration file which, by default, is /etc/inetd.conf. There must be an entry for each field of the configuration file, with entries for each field separated by a tab or a space. Comments are denoted by a "#" at the beginning of a line. There must be an entry for each field. The fields of the configuration file are as follows:

```
service name
socket type
protocol
wait/nowait[.max]
user[.group]
server program
server program arguments
```

To specify an Sun-RPC based service, the entry would contain these fields.

```
service name/version
socket type
rpc/protocol wait/nowait[.max]
user[.group]
server program
server program arguments
```

The service-name entry is the name of a valid service in the file /etc/services. For "internal" services (discussed below), the service name must be the official name of the service (that is, the first entry in /etc/services). When used to specify a Sun-RPC based service, this field is a valid RPC service name in the file /etc/rpc. The part on the right of the "/" is the RPC version number.

```
This can simply be a single
numeric argument or a range of versions.  A range is bounded by the low
version to the high version - "rusers/1-3".

The socket-type should be one of "stream", "dgram",
"raw", "rdm",
or "seqpacket", depending on whether the socket is a stream,
datagram, raw, reliably delivered message, or sequenced packet socket.

The protocol must be a valid protocol as given in /etc/protocols. Exam-
ples might be "tcp" or "udp". Rpc based services are specified with
the "rpc/tcp" or "rpc/udp" service type.

The wait/nowait entry is applicable to datagram sockets only (other
sockets should have a "nowait" entry in this space).  If a datagram
server connects to its peer, freeing the socket so inetd can receive
further messages on the socket, it is said to be a "multi-threaded"
server, and should use the "nowait" entry.  For datagram servers
which process all incoming datagrams on a socket and eventually time
out, the server is said to be "single-threaded" and should use a "wait"
entry.  Com-sat(8) (biff(1))  and talkd(8) are both examples of the
latter type of datagram server.  Tftpd(8) is an exception; it is a
datagram server that establishes pseudo-connections.  It must be listed
as "wait" in order to avoid a race; the server reads the first packet,
creates a new socket, and then forks and exits to allow inetd to check
for new service requests to spawn new servers.  The optional "max"
suffix (separated from "wait" or "nowait" by a dot) specifies the
maximum number of server instances that may be spawned from inetd
within an interval of 60 seconds. When omitted, "max" defaults to 40.

The user entry should contain the user name of the user as whom the
server should run.  This allows for servers to be given less permission
than root. An optional group name can be specified by appending a dot
to the user name followed by the group name. This allows for servers to
run with a different (primary) group id than specified in the password
file. If a group is specified and user is not root, the supplementary
groups associated with that user will still be set.

The server-program entry should contain the pathname of the program
which is to be executed by inetd when a request is found on its socket.
If inetd provides this service internally, this entry should be
"internal".

The server program arguments should be just as arguments normally are,
starting with argv[0], which is the name of the program.  If the
```

```
     service is provided internally, the word "internal" should take the
     place of this entry.

     Inetd provides several "trivial" services internally by use of
     routines within itself.  These services are "echo", "discard",
     "chargen" (character generator), "daytime" (human readable time),
     and "time" (machine readable time, in the form of the number of
     seconds since midnight, January 1, 1900).  All of these services are
     tcp based.  For details of these services, consult the appropriate RFC
     from the Network Information Center.

     Inetd rereads its configuration file when it receives a hangup signal,
     SIGHUP. Services may be added, deleted or modified when the
     configuration file is reread.  Inetd creates a file /etc/inetd.pid that
     contains its process identifier.

SEE ALSO
     comsat(8),  fingerd(8),  ftpd(8),  rexecd(8),  rlogind(8),  rshd(8),
     telnetd(8),  tftpd(8)

HISTORY
     The inetd command appeared in 4.3BSD. Support for Sun-RPC based
     services is modelled after that provided by SunOS 4.1.
```


Starting **smbd** And **nmbd** With inetd

The first step to enable Samba to start is to ensure that the SMB or NetBIOS services have the relevant entries in the systems /etc/services file. To provide SMB services, entries are required at both 139/tcp and 137/udp. Depending on whether either exists, you will need to add one or both of the following lines to your /etc/services file:

```
Netbios-ssn 139/tcp
Netbios-ns 137/udp
```

Then, you need to ensure that the appropriate program will service any requests for services on 137/udp or 139/tcp. This is accomplished by adding the following lines to your /etc/inetd.conf file:

```
Netbios-ssn stream tcp nowait root /usr/local/samba/bin/smbd smbd
Netbios-ns dgram udp wait root /usr/local/samba/bin/nmbd nmbd
```

The entry for the inetd configuration file might require an alternate syntax than the one listed, but the essential information is that the two services are set up so that a request for them starts the appropriate program.

If you are operating in an environment in which security is of paramount importance, it is becoming common for tcpwrappers to be placed around such daemon services so that they are restricted to specific IP addresses. This also requires that considerable logging and activity be available in the event that unauthorized access is attempted. This facility is already available as host-based access control with considerable independent logging in Samba.

Starting **smbd** And **nmbd** As Standalone Daemons

Running Samba from inetd might be adequate if you have a server that can handle the extra work involved in starting and stopping either the **smbd** or the **nmbd** process every time a request is made for that service. It also means that along with any other service, no system resources are used when it is not necessary. The major disadvantage is that an extra stage is involved in servicing every request received at your Samba server. Thus, the alternative option is to run the Samba **smbd** and **nmbd** processes as standalone daemons so that all requests are handled in the shortest time possible. This is accomplished by running the **smbd** and **nmbd** processes with the **-D** flag, which will cause them to run in the background as daemons. You then have the option of either starting them at system startup, thus including them in the startup scripts, or running them at a later stage.

In the current installations of Linux using Slackware or Red Hat distributions (and possibly others), the startup scripts have incorporated the necessary commands to start Samba as daemon processes for some time.

If the systems use BSD-style startup scripts, you may add the following lines to your rc.local file:

```
echo "Starting Samba..."
 /usr/local/samba/bin/smbd -D
 /usr/local/samba/bin/nmbd -D
echo "done"
```

You will need to edit these to account for where the **smbd** and **nmbd** programs were installed.

Slackware currently has an rc.samba script included in its distribution /etc/rc.d/rc.samba (see Listing 3.11) that is called from /etc/rc.d/rc.M (see Listing 3.12).

Both of these scripts run a check to see that the properties of either the called script or the Samba binaries are set as executable; if they are not, they exit without starting the Samba daemons. (This can be useful for security purposes on Samba servers on which security is important.)

Listing 3.11 The Samba daemon startup script /etc/rc.d/rc.samba.

```
# rc.samba: Start the samba server
#
if [ -x /usr/sbin/smbd -a -x /usr/sbin/nmbd ]; then
 echo "Starting Samba..."
 /usr/sbin/smbd -D
 /usr/sbin/nmbd -D
fi
```

Listing 3.12 The Samba part of /etc/rc.d/rc.M.

```
# Start Samba (a file/print server for Win95/NT machines):
if [ -x /etc/rc.d/rc.samba ]; then
  . /etc/rc.d/rc.samba
fi
```

Red Hat and other system V style startup scripts might use code similar to that shown in Listing 3.13.

Listing 3.13 System V–style startup script (/etc/rc.d/init.d/smb).

```
#!/bin/sh #
# description: Starts and stops the Samba smbd and nmbd daemons \
#          used to provide SMB network services.

# Source function library.
. /etc/rc.d/init.d/functions

# Source networking configuration.
. /etc/sysconfig/network

# Check that networking is up.
[ ${NETWORKING} = "no" ] && exit 0

# Check that smb.conf exists.
[ -f /etc/smb.conf ] || exit 0

# See how we were called.
case "$1" in
  start)
    echo -n "Starting SMB services: "
    daemon smbd -D
    daemon nmbd -D
    echo
    touch /var/lock/subsys/smb
    ;;
```

```
  stop)
    echo -n "Shutting down SMB services: "
    killproc smbd
    killproc nmbd
    rm -f /var/lock/subsys/smb
    echo ""
    ;;
  status)
    status smbd
    status nmbd
    ;;
  restart)
    echo -n "Restarting SMB services: "
    $0 stop
    $0 start
    echo "done."
    ;;
  *)
    echo "Usage: smb {start|stop|restart|status}"
    exit 1
```


The **smbd** daemon can be run by any user (execute permissions permitting). This is useful for testing purposes and might even be useful as a temporary substitute for something such as FTP. However, when run this way, the server will have the privileges only of the user who ran it.

So far, this chapter has been all about obtaining and installing the Samba programs. It is now necessary to configure these programs for use. To confirm the installation of the programs, Listing 3.14 shows a simple smb.conf configuration file that should allow you to confirm that the programs are operating. You should create the file with a text editor or use the copy on this book's CD-ROM and edit it where appropriate. By default, it should be installed to your /usr/local/samba/lib/ directory, unless you have requested an alternate location in your Makefile's LIBDIR = ${exec_prefix}/lib entry.

Listing 3.14 A simple smb.conf configuration file.

```
# A short test smb.conf file
#
# Set the workgroup to be that you are running in already
workgroup = YOURGROUP

[homes]
    guest ok = no
    read only = no
```

Testing The Installation

Chapter 12 includes much more information on testing and diagnosing a Samba server utilizing testparm and other Samba test programs. In this section, a simple check of whether you have a functional **smbd** and **nmbd** service is carried out. First, install a simple smb.conf file like the one shown in Listing 3.14.

Test NetBIOS Name Lookup

The **nmbd** service should respond to broadcast name queries using the **nmblookup** program. A command such as **nmblookup SERVERHOSTNAME** should respond with the IP address / hostname of the server as in:


```
Linuxserver1$ nmblookup Linuxserver1
192.168.1.1 Linuxserver1
```

Note that SERVERHOSTNAME is the Samba server's hostname alone and not the fully qualified domain name (FQDN).

If this response is not provided, there might be several causes: First, check that you have added an entry in the inetd.conf file or that you have started the **nmbd** service correctly. Second, check that your network interface is working correctly and that Samba automatically detects it. By default, Samba should bind the **nmbd** or **smbd** service to the first network interface, or eth0. You might need to specify the IP address of your Ethernet network interface in the simple smb.conf file. An additional line, such as interfaces=192.168.1.1/24, might be required. (This option can be used to provide interesting security options. See Chapter 11 for details.) Finally, the server hostname that you have provided might not be the hostname of your server. Check that **nmbd** is using the correct hostname either by using the **nmbd -n** option to set the hostname or by adding a NetBIOS name entry in your smb.conf file, such as netbios name=linuxserver1. This is a much more elegant method of setting your Samba server's NetBIOS name and ensures that regardless of the hostname the correct NetBIOS name is used. The command is as follows:

```
Linuxserver1$ nmbd -n SERVERHOSTNAME -D
```

Connecting With **smbclient**

With the Samba server running the expected **nmblookup** responses, you might try to connect to the home directory of the user that you are connected as. **Linuxserver1$ smbclient //SERVERHOSTNAME/username** should prompt you for the password and, if everything is functional, connect you to your home directory and provide you with the **smbclient** prompt:

```
Linuxserver1$ smbclient //linuxserver1/test
Password:
Domain = [TEST] OS = [Linux] Server = [Samba 2.0.2]
smb: \>
```

If this is not what you obtain or expect, do the following:

1. Make sure that **smbd** is started, then look at the inetd.conf entry or the syntax and path of the rc.local or other startup script.
2. Ensure that the content of the password entered is correct.

Should both of these simple tests prove successful, you might expect to have a set of workable Samba executables. Further diagnosis and troubleshooting details are covered at length in Chapter 12.

Using SWAT

The latest version of Samba includes a Web configuration tool known as SWAT, which allows a Samba administrator to configure the complex smb.conf file by way of a Web browser. In addition, a SWAT configuration page has help links to all the configurable options in the smb.conf file, allowing an administrator to easily look up the effects of any change. The SWAT daemon is run from inetd.

The SWAT options are as follows:

- **-s *SMB configuration file***—The default configuration file path is determined at compile time. The specified file contains the configuration details required by the **smbd** server. This is the file that SWAT will modify. The information in this file includes server-specific information, such as which printcap file to use, as well as descriptions of all the services that the server is to provide.
- **-a**—This option disables authentication and puts SWAT in demo mode. In this mode, anyone will be able to modify the smb.conf file. Do not enable this option on a production server.

Installing SWAT

After you compile SWAT, you need to run **make install** to install the SWAT binary and the various help files and images. If you are building Samba from the current version of the Samba source (2.0.5a), SWAT will have already been built. Running **make install** on a default install will install the following files:

- /usr/local/samba/bin/swat
- /usr/local/samba/swat/images/*
- /usr/local/samba/swat/help/*

inetd Installation

You need to edit your /etc/inetd.conf and /etc/services files to enable SWAT to be launched by way of inetd.

In /etc/services, you need to add a line such as the following:

```
swat 901/tcp
```

Note for NIS/YP users: You might need to rebuild the NIS service maps rather than alter your local /etc/services file. The choice of port number is important only in that it should be less than 1024 and not currently used (using a number above 1024 presents an obscure security hole, depending on the implementation details of your inetd daemon).

In /etc/inetd.conf, you should add a line such as the following:

```
swat stream tcp nowait.400 root /usr/local/samba/bin/swat swat
```

Once you have edited /etc/services and /etc/inetd.conf, you need to send a HUP signal to inetd. To do this, use "kill -1 PID," where PID is the process ID of the inetd daemon.

Launching SWAT

To launch SWAT, simply run your favorite Web browser and point it at **http://localhost:901/**. The result is a prompt for a user name and password of the administration account, as shown in Figure 3.9.

NOTE: *You can attach to SWAT from any IP-connected machine, but connecting from a remote machine leaves your connection open to password sniffing, as passwords will be sent over the wire.*

A successful connection will produce a screen that provides access to all the configuration and startup and shutdown capabilities of SWAT. The starting screen is shown in Figure 3.10. SWAT will be detailed for use in later chapters.

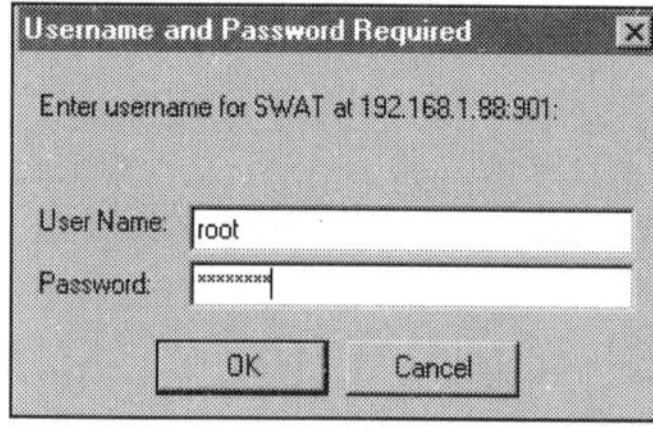

Figure 3.9 Authentication request for SWAT.

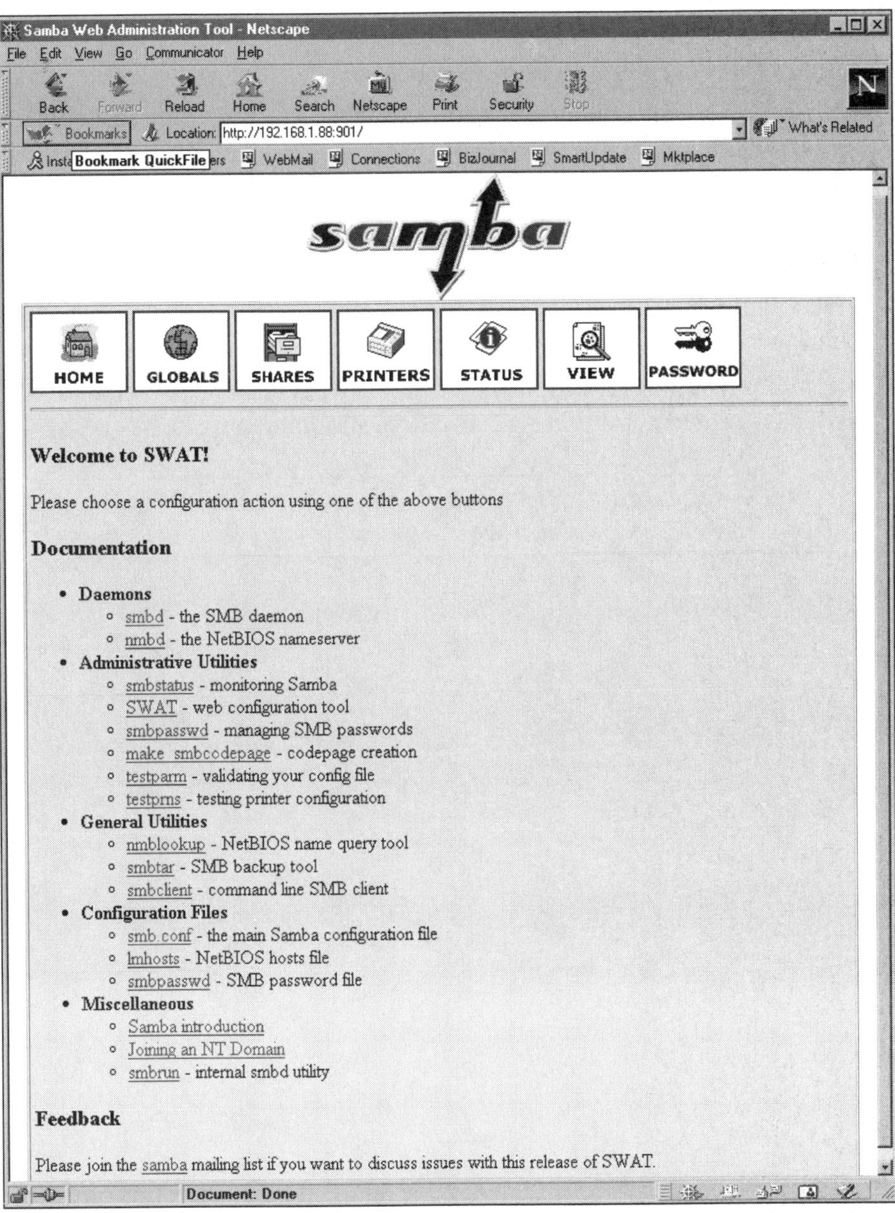

Figure 3.10 SWAT.

Files Used By SWAT

The following is a list of files used by SWAT:

- */etc/inetd.conf*—This file must contain suitable startup information for the meta-daemon.
- */etc/services*—This file must contain a mapping of service name (e.g., swat) to service port (e.g., 901) and protocol type (e.g., tcp).
- */usr/local/samba/lib/smb.conf*—This is the default location of the smb.conf server configuration file that SWAT edits. Other common places that systems install this file are /usr/samba/lib/smb.conf and /etc/smb.conf.
- */etc/smb.conf*—This file describes all the services that the server is to make available to clients. For more information, see smb.conf (5).

NOTE: *SWAT will rewrite your smb.conf file. It will rearrange the entries and delete all comments and the "include=" and "copy=" options. If you have a carefully crafted smb.conf, be sure to back it up or don't use SWAT.*

Chapter 4

Network File Server

In Depth

You have a Unix machine with Samba software installed on your network, and you want to make some of its resources available to another Samba server or a Windows PC. Although it is possible to use one of the graphic user interface (GUI) tools to configure Samba, I will begin by explaining the basic smb.conf file that you will need, what the contents of this file relate to, and the various options used with this file.

In many ways, the smb.conf file is similar to the windows.ini type of files that the older Microsoft operating systems used for applications. A similarity to the older Windows .ini files was included by design by the Samba Team so that familiarity with this method existed. The smb.conf file includes three main sections as well as sections that can be customized. An example is shown in Listing 4.1. These sections are known as global, homes, and printers, the contents of which are closely related to their names.

NOTE: *It is not necessary for the global section to be named within [] as [global], and it is normal that these parameters are set at the start of any smb.conf file.*

Listing 4.1 A sample smb.conf file.

```
# Global parameters
        workgroup = ENTERPRISE
        netbios name = KIRK
        server string = SMTP Server - See Unix Admin If Problem Exists
        security = USER
        printers = BSD
[homes]
        comment = Home Directories
        path = %H
        writeable = yes
        valid users = %S
[printers]
        comment = All Printers
        path = /var/spool/samba
        print ok = Yes
        browseable = No
```

The customized sections are as follows with the structure shown in Listing 4.2.

Listing 4.2 Sample customized sections of the smb.conf file.

```
['userdefined']                    #The share section and name
 comment = share comment
 path = /where this is on the server
 'option' =
```

A full list of these parameters and their descriptions is included in Appendix A. The complete list includes more than 100 options, and the Samba distribution HTML documentation for smb.conf and smb.conf.5.html runs to more than 100 pages.

Some of the more common and, in some cases, essential parameters are briefly described in Table 4.1. A full list of the currently available parameters is provided in Appendix A.

Table 4.1 Some smb.conf parameters.

Parameter	Description
Netbios name	The name that the smbd and nmbd service will announce the server as.
Netbios alias	The alias that the smbd and nmbd service will announce the server as.
Workgroup	The Microsoft-style workgroup or domain name that the Samba server is a member of.
Server string	A text string that accompanies the server name in NetBIOS announcements and can be seen in Network Neighborhood.
Security	The security mode of the server (**share**, **user**, **server**, or **domain**).
Comment	A comment for the service.
Path	The full path to the location of the file or files.
Log file	The location where the smbd and nmbd (usually) place the log files generated during operation. This is usually set at compile time to /usr/local/samba/log/ and may be overwritten by using this parameter. It is also possible to use macros; log file=/var/log/samba/log.%m will write a separate log file for each client connection.
Max log file	The maximum size of the log file in kilobytes. Defaults to 5MB.
Syslog	Should the option to include syslog entries have been chosen at compile time by ./configure --with-syslog, the integer value entered here will provide the debug level of the logs written to the syslog. These values are **0=LOG_ERR**, **1=LOG_WARNING**, **2=LOG_NOTICE**, **3=LOG_INFO**, and **>3=LOG_DEBUG**.
Syslog only	This requires that the syslog option be chosen at compile time and that an appropriate syslog entry exists in the smb.conf file. This option is a Boolean yes or no and indicates that only syslog entries are either made or not made.

(continued)

***Table 4.1 Some smb.conf parameters* (continued).**

Parameter	Description
Debug level	Also referred to as the log level, this specifies the level at which debug information is included when the smbd and nmbd information is written to the log files. The lower the value, the less information is written.
Lock directory	Samba is capable of allowing several users to access a service simultaneously. This is the directory location where Samba stores the information on its status, memory, WINS database (if active), and the lock files that are used in connection with the **max connections** parameter. This defaults to /usr/local/samba/var/locks and is set at compile time.
Name resolve order	In a similar manner to the host.conf file on Linux, this specifies the method in which name requests are attempted to be resolved. The parameter consists of ASCII space-delimited text; these values are **lmhosts** (uses the local lmhosts file), **hosts** (uses the local hosts file and works only if the NetBIOS name is the same as the first part of the Internet hostname), **wins** (uses the WINS servers), and **bcast** (uses a NetBIOS broadcast to determine the host location and works only for the local subnet). The default setting (acceptable for most conditions) is **lmhosts hosts wins bcast**. Setting this parameter without **bcast** ensures that the host never attempts to using a broadcast for hostname resolution.
Deadtime	Number of minutes of inactivity before an idle connection (with no open files) is dropped.
Smbrun	The location of the **smbrun** command. This defaults to /usr/local/samba/bin, but depending on your requirements, you might want to place it elsewhere.
Message command	Microsoft Windows applications commonly send pop-up messages that appear on the screen when some incident has occurred (such as UPS going offline or a virus appearing); this parameter sets what a Samba host should do with those messages. The default is to discard them, that is, no parameter set. You may write code to copy this to a log file or display it to a terminal session.
Protocol	There are five current SMB protocol extensions. This parameter specifies which of these you would attempt to use by default and indicates the highest level of protocol you want to use on the Samba server.
Time server	If you want to use the Samba server as a time server by your Windows clients (using net time \\server /y), set this parameter to **yes**. The default is **no**.

The smb.conf file allows extensive use of macros that are session-derived variables and that are replaced during operation, depending on the macro used. The macros that can be used in the Samba smb.conf file are shown in Table 4.2.

Table 4.2 Macros used in the Samba smb.conf file.

Macro	Explanation
%a	Architecture (operating system) of the connecting machines. The choices are Samba, Windows for Workgroups, Windows 95, and Windows NT. Windows 98 responds as Windows 95, and Windows NT 4 or Windows 2000 responds as Windows NT.
%d	Process ID (PID) of the current server process.
%g	Primary group of username from **%u**.
%G	Primary group of username from **%U**.
%h	Hostname part of the FQDN of the server.
%H	Home directory of the user from username **%u**.
%I	IP address of the client in dotted decimal format (e.g., a.b.c.d).
%L	NetBIOS name of the server.
%m	NetBIOS name of the client.
%M	Hostname part of the fully qualified domain name (FQDN) of the client.
%N	Name of the Network Information Service (NIS) home directory server as provided in auto.home map (for use with NIS). If NIS is not used, this returns the same value as **%L**.
%p	Path to the user's home directory if NIS is used. The value is obtained from your NIS auto.map entry, which is split up as **%N:%p**.
%P	Root directory of the current service.
%R	Protocol selected during the protocol negotiation stage of a session connection establishment. The possible values are **CORE**, **COREPLUS**, **LANMAN1**, **LANMAN2**, or **NT1**.
%S	Name of the current service.
%T	Current date and time of the server.
%u	Username for the current service.
%U	Username that the client requested in the session setup exchange.
%v	Samba version number (taken from version.h at compile time).

These macros can be incorporated for use in many useful ways, some of the more obvious of which are shown in Listing 4.3.

Listing 4.3 Examples of macros in use in a sample smb.conf file.

```
[global]
netbios name = server
comment = Samba Server %v       #appends the version number to the comment
log file = /var/log/log.%m      #generates a separate logfile for each
                                #client
logon script = %a.bat           #when a client logs on, run an OS dependant
                                #logon script
```

```
#logon script = scripts\%U.bat  #run a client specific script

[homes]
path = %H                       #The users home directory is substituted
valid users = %S                #Only the user that is the owner of the
    home
                                #directory may use the service
postexec = echo "%u disconnected from %S from %m (%I)" >> /tmp/log
                                #keep a useful log of who had used
                                #what from where
```

Although this is a short smb.conf file, it shows that many options are available.

Immediate Solutions

Recognizing Security Modes For A Samba Server

Before proceeding, we need to take a look at the Samba's authentication process. Currently, four main options are possible; these are listed under the global smb.conf parameter **security=** as **share**, **user**, **server**, and **domain**. Descriptions of the four modes are outlined in the following sections.

Share

In share-level security (the default with pre-Samba 2.x), the client authenticates itself separately for each share. The client sends a password along with each "tree connection" (share mount) and does not explicitly send a username with this operation. The client is expecting a password to be associated with each share independent of the user. In this mode of operation the client never explicitly sends the username of the session. Some commercial SMB servers, such as Windows NT, actually associate passwords directly with shares in share-level security, but Samba always uses the Unix authentication scheme, by which the username/password is authenticated, not a "share/password."

In practice, this means that a connection request to a share contains a password. Samba attempts to validate that password against all the usernames contained in its account database. Should none of the username/password pairs match the request, the tree connection is refused.

This form of validation closely resembles the default validation method used in a Windows 95 file or printer server.

User

In user-level security (the default with post-Samba 2.x), when a session request is made, Samba first requires the client to log on to the server. The username/password combination is then checked against the Samba account database and is authenticated; if the session request is successful, then the tree connect proceeds. If the session is maintained, subsequent client connection requests will not require that the authentication process be repeated.

Server

This is a modification of the user option that allows the Samba server to pass all authentication off to another server (Samba or otherwise) running in user mode. An additional parameter, **password server=**, identifies the authentication server and is included in the smb.conf configuration file. This parameter is commonly used with Samba servers that are in an NT-controlled domain, in which case the NT server controls the authentication. However, it would be just as simple to use another Samba server to achieve authentication. Beginning with NT 4 Service Pack 3, password encryption is used with the normal method of authentication.

If the remote server refuses to authenticate the client session's request, the authentication will revert to the local Samba server for authentication. Note that if the remote server refuses the request following an authentication that involves encrypted passwords, the local Samba server cannot return to using unencrypted passwords (as in the Unix password file). A valid local smb password file must be present for client sessions to be authenticated. If this file is missing, the request will be denied. The Samba distribution documentation includes an ENCRYPTION.txt file that provides details on setting up this file.

Domain

Domain security has been available since Samba 2.0.0 and, for client purposes, is essentially the same as server-mode security. The Samba server must become a member of the Windows NT domain and thereby is capable of participating in domain trust relationships. When a client session request occurs, the Samba server passes the authentication request for validation over to a Windows NT primary domain controller (PDC) or backup domain controller (BDC), validating the user against its account database. This is very similar to the process that occurs during server-mode operation.

NOTE: *The Samba documentation picks up on a bug in the older version of Windows, Windows for Workgroups that can cause some headaches with the security setting. Although a Samba server is in either user- or server-level security, an earlier Windows for Workgroups client will totally ignore the password that you enter in the Connect Drive dialog box. This makes it very difficult (if not impossible) to connect to a Samba service as anyone except the user that is logged in to Windows for Workgroups.*

For simplicity, the choice of security level to use can be summarized as follows:

- If usernames are the same on the PC and Unix computer, use **security=user**.
- If you mainly use usernames that do not exist on the Unix computer, use **security=share**.

You should also use **security=share** if you want to mainly set up shares without a password (guest shares). This parameter is commonly used for a shared printer server. It is more difficult to set up guest shares with **security=user**; for details, see the **map to guest** parameter.

It is possible to use smbd in a hybrid mode, where it offers both user- and share-level security under different NetBIOS aliases. For more information, see the NetBIOS aliases and the include parameters. The final choice of settings for security will have different implications. The process is fairly simple. The details in the smb.conf configuration file are altered to reflect the properties of the shares.

Utilizing Username Notes

Setting a security level is only the first part of controlling access to your server. Further security options would involve the details of the usernames and passwords.

By default, all Unix usernames consist of lowercase characters. Samba first attempts to authenticate users by means of all lowercase characters, then it attempts to authenticate users with the first character as uppercase.

The **username level** parameter allows you to set the number of username characters (provided in the sessions setup request) that are allowed to have their case changed so that the Samba server can authenticate the session. The Samba server will then attempt a brute-force lookup of every possible combination of that number of uppercase characters in each username against the account database. The larger this number, the more combinations exist and the longer the authentication process might take. If all the usernames are lowercase, password authentication will not require that this parameter be used.

TIP: *Always use lowercase usernames when possible.*

Another smb.conf parameter, **username map**, sets the pathname and file name for an ASCII text file that contains a mapping of Unix to other system usernames. This parameter allows the Administrator user of an NT system to map to, for example, the root or another user of your Samba server. Thus, you can use completely separate systems that might already have well-established usernames or different users that perform the same function. This parameter has no default setting.

The entries occupy a single line for each Unix username and follow this format:

```
Unix username = other system username, and another...
```

In all cases, the user must provide a password for the original Unix usernames account. This username map is operational for all but the **security=server** mode when the username included in the session is attempted with that usernames password.

Passwords

Normally, the passwords used with Unix systems are accepted in both upper- and lowercase characters. However, some Samba clients send uppercase passwords when using plain-text passwords. Once again, Samba will attempt to authenticate the user's password as provided, although all the characters of the password might be uppercase.

The **password level** parameter allows you to set the number of characters in the password (provided in the sessions setup request) that are allowed to have their case changed so that the Samba server can authenticate the session. The Samba server will attempt a brute-force lookup of every possible combination of that number of uppercase characters in the password against the account database. The larger this number, the more combinations exist and the longer the authentication process might take.

Some of the security features incorporated by design into Samba will not allow access to services using null password accounts, that is, accounts with no passwords. The **null passwords** parameter should be set to **yes** if you want to allow this option, which carries obvious security implications.

Password Encryption

Any discussion of passwords and Microsoft operating systems would not be complete without mentioning the use of password encryption. In Windows NT 4, from Windows NT 4 Service Pack 3 on, password encryption has been natively supported. This means that all authentication uses password encryption.

The major impact of using Windows NT service packs on the operation of Samba first appears as access control and configuration issues. (This is a major problem for most users and involves extra configuration after installing Samba.) Samba defaults to using plain-text passwords. The newer versions of Windows NT service packs default to sending and allowing only encrypted password authentication.

Two parameters are involved—**update encrypted** and **encrypt passwords**—both of which have a possible value of **yes** or **no**. The default is **no**. If you want to use encrypted passwords with the Samba server, these parameters need to be set to **yes**. Two other parameters that are used with encrypted passwords are **smb password file** and **null passwords**. If encrypted passwords are used, these parameters are usually set to **/etc/smbpasswd** and **yes**. Using password encryption on a Samba server requires password synchronization to occur between systems so that user accounts can be kept up to date.

An alternative is to make a change to allow or force Windows NT to use plain passwords by making a Registry entry alteration. Notes on the methods employed to set up and use plain-text passwords are included with the Samba distribution under Win95.txt and WinNT.txt. These documents include the required Registry entry changes to allow plain text passwords. The Samba distribution also includes the exported Registry entries that can be added to the Registry as well.

In a Windows NT system, the process requires setting the following Registry key to allow plain-text password authentication:

```
HKEY_LOCAL_MACHINE\system\CurrentControlSet\Services\Rdr\Parameters\
```

Add the following value:

```
EnablePlainTextPassword:REG_DWORD=1
```

Windows 95 and 98 allow similar plain password alterations that can be made at the Registry level:

```
/HKEY_LOCAL_MACHINE/System/CurrentControlSet/Services/VxD/VNETSUP
```

From the menu bar, select Edit/New/DWORD Value. Rename the New Value #1 entry to the following:

```
EnablePlainTextPassword
```

Alternatively, you can use the NT 4_PlainPassword.reg Registry export file included in the /docs directory of the Samba distribution. Windows 95 and 98 have similar files. To use this file, double-click on it to add its contents to the Registry directly or open the Registry editor by running regedt32.exe (Windows NT) or regedit (Windows 9x) and select Import Registry File from the Registry menu, then point at this *.reg file. Figure 4.1 shows these Registry export files in the Samba distribution.

Although making these alterations will allow you to use plain-text passwords in your systems, serious security risks are associated with this practice. A full treatment of password encryption and password synchronization issues is outlined in Chapter 11.

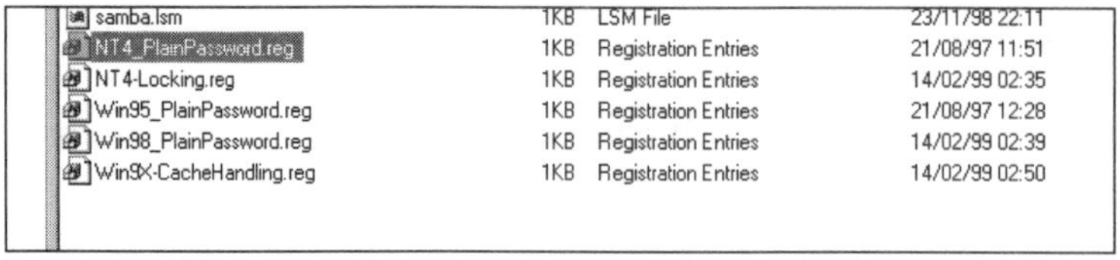

samba.lsm	1KB	LSM File	23/11/98 22:11
NT4_PlainPassword.reg	1KB	Registration Entries	21/08/97 11:51
NT4-Locking.reg	1KB	Registration Entries	14/02/99 02:35
Win95_PlainPassword.reg	1KB	Registration Entries	21/08/97 12:28
Win98_PlainPassword.reg	1KB	Registration Entries	14/02/99 02:39
Win9X-CacheHandling.reg	1KB	Registration Entries	14/02/99 02:50

Figure 4.1 The Registry export files for plain-text passwords.

Access Control

In addition to username and password authentication, some fairly simple additional parameters can be applied to help restrict access to your Samba server. These access control parameters provide the basic information to set up at least some security for your server, as shown in Table 4.3. Normally, they are present only in the [share] sections; however, if they are present in the [global] section, they will apply to all the possible services.

Table 4.3 Some access control parameters.

Parameter	Description
Hosts allow	Only the hosts that are listed may connect to a service. The syntax can take the form of specific IP addresses, a subnetwork IP address (such as 192.168.), or an FQDN (such as goodhost.net). It is also possible to use an additional parameter except within the list, so that ranges of IP addresses can be selected with members of that range being excluded. It is also possible to include the netmask to refine the hosts allowed if you have more than one subnet within your network. The default is that all hosts may access the server.
Hosts deny	This parameter lists those hosts or network of hosts that are denied access. The default is to deny no hosts.
Hosts equiv	This parameter has its roots in the Unix /etc/hosts.equiv file entries that allow other servers to access the server without having to use any authentication. The entry indicates that file. Major security problems can result if this file is not configured properly or, worse, if a nontrusted host exists in the remote server. The default is no entry.
User hosts	This parameter simply indicates whether the Unix user's ~/.rhosts file can be used to determine which host may access the server without authenticating using a valid username and password. Like the Hosts equiv parameter, this might be a security risk for your server. The default is **no**.
Map to guest	When a connection or user session fails because of a bad or an incorrect username or password or combinations thereof, it is possible to allow access to the guest-capable shares and services. The default is **no**.

(continued)

Table 4.3 Some access control parameters (continued).

Parameter	Description
Admin users	This is a list of users that have been granted administrative privileges on the share. When connected to the share, these users may perform operations on the share as *root*. This parameter may also be used with the "@" symbol and group name, as in "@users," which can refer to a whole group of users specified in the users group from /etc/group in Unix. With NIS support in Samba, this @groupname will refer to the NIS group first and then the Unix group. An alternate option of "+" denotes the Unix group, and "&" denotes the NIS group, should the two exist and contain exclusive lists of users.
Guest account	The default is set to **nobody** at compile time. Normally, this account does not have logon privileges, and the user home is set to /dev/null. If this parameter is used, the account must exist in the account database on the server. When the parameter is set at share level, the share value of guest account will override any global value.
Guest ok	When set to **yes**, no username or password is required to access the share. The default is no.
Guest only	When set to **yes**, only guest or nonauthenticated access is allowed to this share. The default is **no**.
Read list	This sets which users are to be given read access to the share even if the share is set to writable. The **@group** option may also be used to specify a group of users.
Read only	The default is **yes**, which sets the share to read only. Setting the share to **no** means that the share is writeable.
Writeable	The default is **no**, which sets the share to read only. Setting the share to **yes** means that the share is writable.
Write list	This sets which users are to be given read access to the share even if the share is set to writable. The **@group** option may also be used to specify a group of users.
Valid users	This sets which users may access the share. The options are the same as those for **Admin users**.
Invalid users	This sets which users may not access the share. The options are the same as those for **Admin users**.
Default service	If the requested service does not exist, this specifies which service should be returned as the default. A typical service might be a temporary share with **guest ok** set to **yes** and **read only** set to **yes**.
Max connections	The default is set to 0, which implies no limit to the number of connections. In practice, the larger the number of connections, the greater the chance that the share's contents will be contended for and the larger the resource requirement. The use of this parameter can provide a "backdoor" method of enforcing licensing for a number of users of some software contained within the share. Likewise, it can help reduce or administer the load placed on the Samba server. Note that this parameter sets the number of connected users, not active users, so it might not be advisable to set this on a public share that most users would map to.

Examining Unix File And Directory Permissions

A discussion on the use and administration of a Samba server would not be complete without a small diversion into how Unix file and directory permissions work. The setup of a Samba share might be easy to accomplish within the smb.conf file; however, if the Samba user does not have the permissions required to carry out actions within that share directory, the action will fail. The file and directory permissions can be broken down into three sections:

- The owner of the file or directory
- The group associated with the file or directory
- World permissions on the file or directory

In short, these permissions are R (Read), W (Write), and X (Execute).

Although the same permissions structure is used for both directories and files, subtle differences exist between file and directory permissions (see Table 4.4).

Read, Write, and Execute may exist in combination or not at all, depending on the situation, as shown in Table 4.5.

Table 4.4 File permissions compared with directory permissions.

Permission	File	Directory
r (Read)	Read the file contents	Search the directory
w (Write)	Write to the file	Write to the directory
x (Execute)	Run an executable file	Change to the current directory (cd into it)

Table 4.5 Complete file permissions compared with directory permissions.

Permission	File	Directory
---	Nothing possible	No access to directory
r--	Read the contents	Can list the directory contents
rw-	Read and write to the contents	Can list and add to the directory contents
rwx	Read and write to the contents and execute the file	Can list and add to the directory contents and make the directory the current directory (cd into it)
r-x	If executable, execute it	Able to read the contents Able to change to directory and to list or read the contents but not capable of directory alterations
--x	Execute the file if it is of the correct type	Execute a known binary

The combinations of the various r, w, and x permissions are available in some systems numerically as well. The numerical value 4 is assigned to r, 2 to w, and 1 to x. Through simple addition, combining these permissions would result in 7 for rwx, 5 for r-x, and so on.

By using the **chmod**, **chown**, and **chgrp** commands, an authorized user can alter the different permissions on files and directories. **chmod** changes the permissions on a file or directory at the user, group, or world level. The command to alter a file to rwx at the user level, r-x at the group level, and r-- at the world level follows:

```
chmod 754 <filename>
```

chown changes the current owner of the file or directory, and the syntax is of the following form:

```
chown <username> file or directory
```

Finally, **chgrp** changes the group that a file or directory can be accessed by:

```
chgrp <group> file or directory
```

An example of the permissions that exist on a directory that contains files and other directories is shown in Listing 4.4.

Listing 4.4 An example of a directory listing showing permissions.

```
linuxrouter1:/home# ls -l
total 4
drwxrwxr-x   8 root     wheel       1024 Aug  1  1994 ftp/
drwx--x--x   2 rdab100  users       1024 Aug 23 10:55 rdab100/
drwx--x--x   2 samba    samba       1024 Aug 23 09:10 samba/
lrwxrwxrwx   1 root     root          13 Aug 23 17:39 smb.conf ->
    /etc/smb.conf
-rwxr-xr--   1 rdab100  root          24 Aug 23 17:39 test*
linuxrouter1:/home#
```

An extra bit is present at the start of all the permission entries; this example has three variants: "l," "d," and "-". This is the object-type identifier, and in this case the choices are "l" for symbolic link, "d" for directory, and "-" for a simple file. The other options are "b" for block special file, "c" for character special file, "p" for named pipe, and "s" for socket.

The full file and directory permissions also include a leading bit that has a setting of setuid, setgid, "t," or "sticky." This means that this file's executable permissions are set to run either with an alternate user or group or with whatever the directory permissions are set to. These are seen in the permissions as an "s" where the "x" normally would appear.

Listing 4.5 shows three options. The first file has the suid set, the second has the sgid set, and the third has the "sticky" bit set.

Listing 4.5 The suid and sgid options in use.

```
linux1:/tmp# ls -l
total 3
-rwsrwxr-x   1 rdab100  users        1024 Aug  1  1994 runme
-rwx--sr--   1 rdab100  users        1024 Aug 23 10:55 runme2
-rwx--x--t   1 rdab100  users        1024 Aug 23 09:10 runme3
linux1:/tmp#
```


To set these, run the **chmod** command with the suffix 2, 4, or 1 for suid, sgid, or t. For example:

```
chmod 2### <filename>
chmod 4### <filename>
chmod 1### <filename>
```

Thus, to correctly create and use a share on your Samba server, a user should have user, group, or world permissions on that share, depending on the permission level that will allow that operation.

> ***NOTE:*** *Red Hat Linux adds users to its system, each user being given its own group ID (GID) as well.*

Samba also has a series of file- and directory-related permissions; these are listed in Table 4.6.

Table 4.6 Some file and directory parameters.

Parameter	Description
Create mask	This sets the permissions on a file when it is created. This defaults to 0744, or rwx permissions, for the owner and to r-- for everyone else. The format set here applies to all new files in the share, so the setting should be chosen with care.
Directory mask	This sets the permissions on a directory when it is created. This defaults to 0755, or rwx permissions, for the owner and to r-x for everyone else. This allows users other than the owner to change to the directory and list the contents. The format set here applies to all new directories and new subdirectories created in the share, so the setting should be chosen with care.

(continued)

***Table 4.6 Some file and directory parameters* (continued).**

Parameter	Description
Force create mode	This defaults to 0000, which means that no additional parameters are set on new files created in the share. A setting of 0644 will overwrite the previous setting in create mask and set the permissions to rw-r--r--.
Force directory mode	This defaults to 0000, which means that no additional parameters are set on new directories in the share. A setting of 0744 will overwrite the previous setting in create mask and set the permissions to rwxr--r--.
Force group	All Unix users will exist in a group. This parameter will force all new files in the share to be created with the group owner set to the value provided. This defaults to no entry, which normally means that any files created in the share are given the group of the parent directory.
Force user	This forces all new files in the share to be created with the owner set to the value provided. This defaults to no entry, which normally means that any files created in the share are given to the owner of the user accessing the share.

Setting Up A Share

Now that we have looked at the issues of security and permissions, it's time to see how a share is set up. The smb.conf file used in this example will be built up as further options are added; however, the starting smb.conf file shown in Listing 4.6 will be sufficient to start with.

Listing 4.6 The smb.conf file.

```
[global]
  netbios name = linuxserver1
  workgroup = local
  server string = example file server
  guest account = nobody
  security = user
  password level = 8
[example-share]
  comment = an example share
  path = /home/example
```

This simple smb.conf file provides a share called example-share on the file server with user permissions.

Using the Network Neighborhood dialog box on a Windows PC on the same network will show the share with the name; if Details is selected from the View menu, the value of the comment in the [example-share] section shown in Listing 4.6 will be seen as well. Figure 4.2 shows this share.

I had connected to the machine using the rdab100 user, which also had a home directory on the Samba server. The smb.conf file also had a [homes] section. so the share for the rdab100 user was like that shown in Figure 4.3. Listing 4.7 shows the smb.conf entry for the [homes] section.

Listing 4.7 The smb.conf entry for the [homes] section.

```
[homes]
   comment = Home Directories
   browseable = no
   writable = yes
```

If you open the example-share and create a new document with Notepad as shown in Figure 4.4, you'll see that you cannot save it to the share you created as shown in Figure 4.5.

You cannot save the share because the property that the share's default created is read-only, and the directory must have the appropriate Unix permissions. The current permissions and contents of the directory are shown in Listing 4.8.

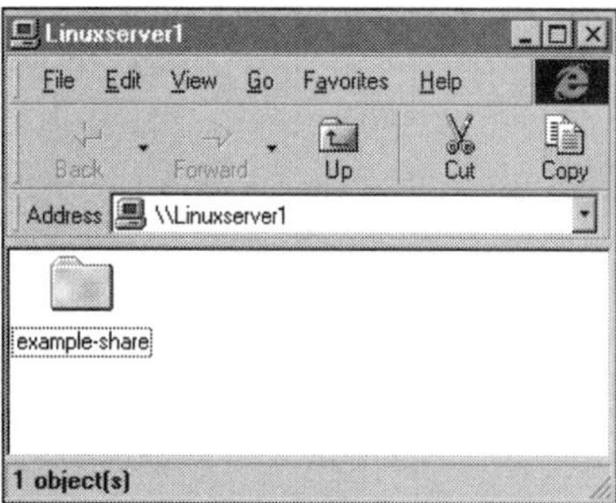

Figure 4.2 The simple example-share.

Figure 4.3 The simple example-share and the rdab100 home directory share.

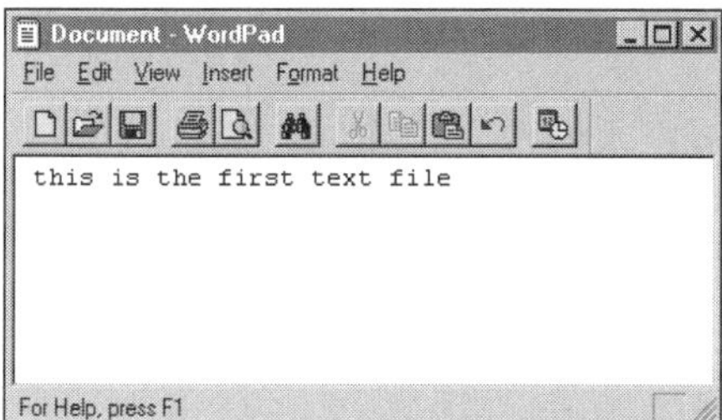

Figure 4.4 The example text document in Notepad.

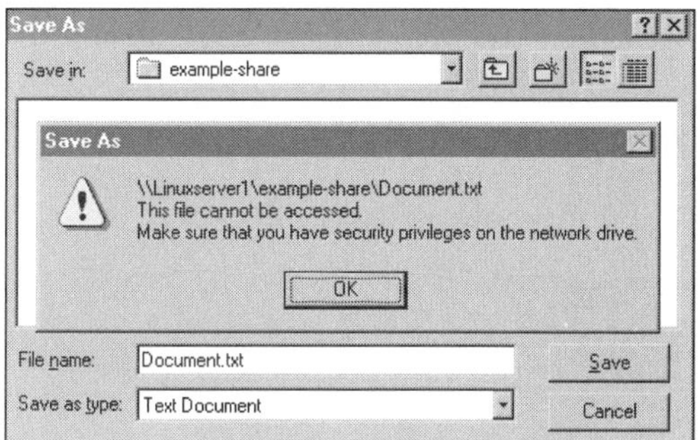

Figure 4.5 The error message that appears when you attempt to save this file to the new share.

Listing 4.8 Directory permissions on the new share.

```
linuxserver1:/home/example# ls -al
total 3
drwxr-xr-x   2 root     root         1024 Aug 25 10:48 ./
drwxr-xr-x  23 root     root         1024 Aug 25 08:47 ../
-rw-r--r--   1 root     root          214 Aug 25 11:01 smb.conf
linuxserver1:/home/example#
```

To be able to write the file to the share that you have created, you need to set the Unix directory permissions to allow the editing and addition of entries to it. Currently, the directory is world-readable only. You need to relax this condition to allow the current user (rdab100) to write to this directory. The command that will allow anyone to write to this directory follows:

```
chmod 0777 /home/example
```

The section "Examining Unix File And Directory Permissions" can guide you in setting up the correct permissions for use. Listing 4.9 shows the new permissions on the new share.

Listing 4.9 New permissions on the new share directory.

```
linuxserver1:/home/example# ls -al
total 3
drwxrwxrwx   2 root     root          1024 Aug 25 11:13 ./
drwxr-xr-x  23 root     root          1024 Aug 25 08:47 ../
-rw-r--r--   1 root     root           214 Aug 25 11:01 smb.conf
linuxserver1:/home/example#
```

If you again try to save the file to the share, another error message will appear. You have created the Unix permissions to allow the file to be saved, but you also need to alter the share parameters in the smb.conf file to make the share writable, as shown in Listing 4.10.

Listing 4.10 The smb.conf file altered to make the share writable.

```
[global]
netbios name = linuxserver1
workgroup = local
server string = example file server
guest account = nobody
security = user
password level = 8
[example-share]
comment = an example share
path = /home/example
writable = yes
```

Now the share will have the new document saved into it, as shown in Figure 4.6.

In addition, the directory listing clearly shows who created the file, as shown in Listing 4.11.

Listing 4.11 The new document saved to the share with the user permission details.

```
linuxserver1:/home/example# ls -al
total 4
drwxrwxrwx   2 root     root          1024 Aug 25 11:21 ./
drwxr-xr-x  23 root     root          1024 Aug 25 08:47 ../
-rwxr--r--   1 rdab100  users           29 Sep 24 10:09 document.txt*
-rw-r--r--   1 root     root           214 Aug 25 11:01 smb_conf.txt
linuxserver1:/home/example#
```

The share also contains a copy of the smb.conf file used; this file was copied there by the root user. (It has been saved with the .TXT suffix because that is the default that Notepad uses.) This file is owned by root, although it is possible to read the file because the permissions are world-readable. When you open the file

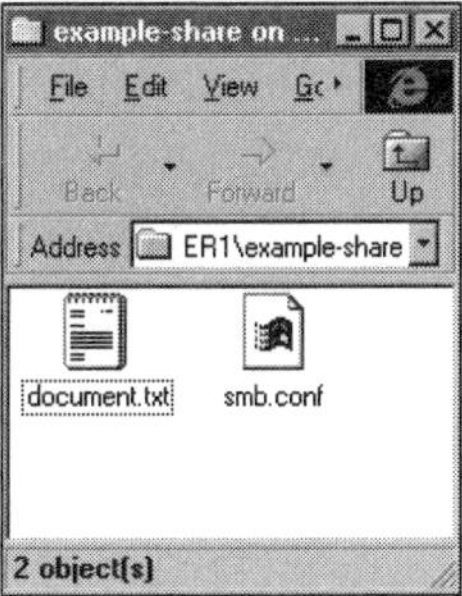

Figure 4.6 The new share with the document saved into it.

in Notepad, notice that the file does not appear to be formatted in the manner in which you entered it. This is because Unix and Windows store the end of a line in simple text files differently. If you immediately attempt to save the file again, Notepad will respond with an error message stating that the file already exists and that the file is read-only for your user. You may save it only as a different name.

So, what is happening now? The Samba permissions are set up so that you should be able to carry out the operation, but the underlying Unix operating system permissions are not allowing you to carry out the operation. When using Samba file servers, remember that the user attempting the operation must have permissions on the Unix file system to permit the operation.

Setting Up A Share Available To All Users For Read Access And To A Few For Write Access

The previous sample smb.conf file allows you to set up a simple share that is available to all users. Keeping the directory's settings the same, you can add parameters to the smb.conf file:

```
[example-share]
  comment = an example share
  path = /home/example
  writable = yes
  write list = user1 user2 user3 @admin
```

The share is now readable by all users, but only user1, user2, user3, and those in the admin group will have write access to the share.

The parameters that control which users have read and write access to the share are the following:

- **read list**
- **write list**
- **valid users**
- **invalid users**
- **guest account**
- **guest only**
- **admin users**

Setting Up A CD-ROM For Mounting By All Users

CD-ROMs must be mounted before they can be used on a Unix system. A useful application of the **preexec** and **postexec** parameters with a CD-ROM share is to use these parameters to send a **mount** and **unmount** command to the operating system as the clients are connected and then disconnected to the share.

For a CD-ROM share that is the fourth device on a SCSI controller (e.g., with a mount point of /cdromusers), a share syntax and layout might be the following:

```
[The-CDROM]
  comment = the CDROM on the server that may be used by users
  browsable = yes
  read only = yes
  path = /cdromusers
  root preexec = /sbin/mount /dev/sdd /cdromusers
  root postexec = /sbin/umount /dev/sdd /cdromusers
  #max connections = 1
  #set the maximum number of users that may use the share
```

Setting Up A Removable Device For Mounting And Unmounting By All Users

The same procedure used in the CD-ROM example can be used for any number of removable devices, including CD-ROMs, LS-120 floppies, Zip disks, Jaz disks, and tape devices. The smb.conf share format will then be as follows:

```
[sharename]
  comment = the <DEVICE> on the server that may be used by users
  browsable = yes
  read only = yes
  path = /<device mount point>
  root preexec = /sbin/mount /<device> /<device mount point>
  root postexec = /sbin/umount /<device> /<device mount point>
  #max connections = 1
  #set the maximum number of users that may use the share
```

This should allow Samba servers to offer a central location for often-expensive removable devices.

NOTE: *This type of share practice has been used successfully with operations that offer a central "data station" with large multimedia files or data extracts that are used offsite.*

Handling Symbolic Links

By default, symbolic links in Samba are set so that Samba will follow symbolic links that reside within the share directory tree but not those that reside outside it.

Two parameters can be set that involve symbolic links: **follow symlinks** (default value is **yes**) and **wide links** (default value is **no**). Because you are dealing with Unix, in which symbolic links are common, and Microsoft networking, in which they are not, taking a closer look at these can help you deal with any system. Symbolic links that refer to other directories outside the current share and that thus require the **wide links** parameter to be set to **yes** perhaps should be viewed as candidates for separate shares. Setting **follow symlinks** to **no** introduces a small performance drop, which is much more obvious when setting **wide links** to **yes**.

Mangled File Names On A Samba Share

Try running a dir in a DOS session on a Windows 9x or Windows NT session where long file names have been used! DOS file names are limited to the 8.3 length. Windows 95 and Windows NT support long file names. Running the **dir** command within a DOS session of the Linux-mini-HOWTO directory from the CD-ROM from this book, when inserted into a Windows System, produces the output shown in Listing 4.12, where you can clearly see both the long file names and the abbreviated DOS 8.3 file names.

Listing 4.12 Part of a directory output showing name mangling.

```
The volume in the E: drive has no label.
Volume Serial Number is CC63-43E1
Directory of E:\Linux\HOWTO\Linux-mini-HOWTOs

.              <DIR>         05-27-99 11:46a .
..             <DIR>         05-27-99 11:46a ..
3-BUTT~1            28,750   05-27-99 11:46a 3-Button-Mouse
ADSL                44,046   05-27-99 11:46a ADSL
ADSM-B~1             5,001   05-27-99 11:46a ADSM-Backup
ADVOCACY            20,822   05-27-99 11:46a Advocacy
AI-ALIFE           110,707   05-27-99 11:46a AI-Alife
APACHE~1            15,425   05-27-99 11:46a Apache+SSL+PHP+fp
AUTOMO~1             8,042   05-27-99 11:46a Automount
BACKUP~1            18,466   05-27-99 11:46a Backup-With-MSDOS
BATTER~1            32,300   05-27-99 11:46a Battery-Powered
BOCA                12,809   05-27-99 11:46a Boca
```

Fortunately, Unix allows very long file names, and almost any character can be used (except "/," which is reserved for directory identification and for escape). In addition, Unix is case sensitive, meaning that both upper- and lowercase names may be used. This provides for considerable flexibility when creating file names. The paths may also be very long, up to 1,024 characters, depending on the Unix variant.

As you have seen, DOS is restricted to the 8.3 format, and although Windows 95 and NT appear to be unlimited in pathname and file name length, they are limited to 127 characters for a file name. When the total pathname and file name exceeds 255 characters, problems can occur.

NOTE: *I first encountered this problem when attempting to create OFA-compliant Oracle database installations on an NT 3.51 server.*

Samba provides the ability to deal with these long file names through a number of parameters, shown in Table 4.7.

Table 4.7 Name-mangling parameters.

Parameter	Description
Mangled names	The default is **yes**. Samba will be default mangling file names into the 8.3 format so that DOS-based clients can read the files. If set to **no**, any files or directories with long names will not appear in listings for those clients.
Mangle case	The default is **no**. Samba will not mangle mixed-case file names if they are not in the default case, unless this parameter is set to **yes**.
Mangling char	The default character, "~," can be replaced by another character specified in this parameter.
Case sensitive	The default is **no**. If set to **yes**, Samba regards file names as case sensitive. If set to **no**, Samba must search directories and perform a case-insensitive file name match for all file names to check whether another file with the same name exists.
Default case	The default is **lowercase**.
Preserve case	The default is to preserve case when files are created.
Short preserve case	The default is **yes**. The short (mangled) names are set to uppercase.

Fortunately, such mangling follows a standard method. As many as the first five alphanumeric characters before the rightmost period in the file name are forced to uppercase and appear as the first five characters of the mangled name. By default, a notification character (~) is appended to the first part of the new file name, followed by two more uppercase characters that are generated from a hash of the original file name without the extension. The first three alphanumeric characters of the extension after the rightmost period are forced to uppercase and appear as the extension of the mangled name. If no period and no extension are used, the mangled name will not use them either. A file that starts with a period is treated as if it is a DOS hidden file; however, now three leading underscores are added to the mangled file name.

Restricting User Numbers And Inactive Users

The **max connections** parameter will allow you to set the number connections that may exist on a share. Setting **max connections=10** will restrict this share to 10 connections at any one time. However, it will not manage inactive connections. The parameter's dead time is useful in monitoring connections that are no longer active and would drops them after a specified number of minutes. This defaults to 0, a value that indicates never to drop the connection. If you needed to drop nonactive connections after 30 minutes (a generous amount of time), the share definitions should contain the following code:

```
[apps]
  ... the rest of the share definition
  max connections = 10
  dead time = 30
```

Setting Access Rights On Shares For Different User Groups

As an example, say that the members of the Accounting Department require read (R)/write (W) access to the share ACCOUNTS, RW to INVOICES, RW to PO, and R to PRODUCTS. Meanwhile, the Stores Department needs R to ACCOUNTS, R to INVOICES, RW to PO, and RW to PRODUCTS, and the Admin section needs R to INVOICES, PRODUCTS & PO.

A total of 50 users make up the three departments: 22 in Accounting, 15 in Stores, and 13 in Admin. The most manageable method is to create a number of groups called Accounts, Stores, and Admin in the Unix group (/etc/group) file or in NIS and to place the users into their respective groups. The shares should then be defined to make use of these groups, as shown in Listing 4.13 (share directory details are omitted for clarity).

Listing 4.13 The share details showing the write and read lists.

```
[accounts]
...
write list    @accounts
read list     @stores
[po]
...
write list    @accounts, @stores
read list     @admin
[products]
...
write list    @stores
read list     @accounts, @admin
[invoices]
...
write list    @accounts
read list     @stores, @admin
```

Setting Up A Share Where All The Files Belong To One User Group

In the share definition, set the **force group** parameter, then set the value to the user group:

```
force group = usergroup
```

Setting Permissions To Stop A Share From Being World-Readable

In the share definition, set the **create mask** and **directory mask** parameters with the world bit set to reflect the permissions required. The numeric values of the permissions are as follows:

- R 4
- W 2
- X 1

A suitable option for both is 0750, which would give user (RWX), group (RW-), and world (---) permissions. In addition, at the Unix operating system, you could (should) alter the directory permissions to reflect the correct requirements.

Currently, Samba does not fully support user mode access levels for Windows 95/98 and this will be implemented in futures releases of Samba. This is seen when a Windows 95 user attempts to access the permissions option (within Explorer for the files on a Samba server) with the intention of setting these permissions. The Remote Procedure Calls are not complete for this mode of operation and so the request fails. Chapter 13 includes a section on the future of Samba and includes details of some of the limitations and expected enhancements.

Chapter 5

Network Print Server

In Depth

Why would you want to use a printer connected to a Samba server if you had no problem printing to one connected to your own PC? If you had the money and the resources, you could connect a printer to every PC, but especially in an office environment, would it not be better to have one or two larger, higher-spec printers and arrange to have these shared around the network? Likewise, would it not be better to have a printer shared so users with different operating systems could use the same printer? Perhaps you have only one printer, and you and a friend need to share it.

First let's examine what happens when a Samba server offers printing services. This is accomplished with printer spooling. When a client has an open document that needs to be printed, the client would request that the document be printed using a print manager tool. The document is sent to the printer and the printer manager spools the documents to the printer. The printer spool operates in the following order:

1. The client print manager opens a print file.
2. The client print manager writes the required information to this file.
3. The client print manager closes the file once the write is complete.
4. The server sends the contents of this print file as a print job to the printer.

As you might have noticed in previous chapters, Samba sets up all its resources as shares, and any printer is set up the same way. Thus, for your Samba server to operate as a print server, you need to perform the following steps:

1. Create a share entry for a specific printer if you are not using it already in the /etc/printcap file.
2. Set up a directory to which to spool the print jobs. This must be world writeable with the other permissions set so that a user cannot remove the jobs of other users from the print queue. (The initial bit is set to "t" or 1### for the directory. For more information, see the discussion of Unix permissions in Chapter 4.)
3. Set the parameter for this share to act as a printer (set the **printable=yes** parameter in the smb.conf file).

A suitable printer share is included in the Samba distribution sample smb.conf.default file in the samples directory. Listing 5.1 shows the Global parameters from the example smb.conf file from the Samba distribution.

Listing 5.1 Global parameters that relate to printing.

```
# If you want to automatically load your printer list rather
# than setting them up individually then you'll need this
   load printers = yes

# you may wish to override the location of the printcap file
;   printcap name = /etc/printcap

# on SystemV system setting printcap name to lpstat should allow
# you to automatically obtain a printer list from the SystemV spool
# system
;   printcap name = lpstat

# It should not be necessary to specify the print system type unless
# it is non-standard. Currently supported print systems include:
# bsd, sysv, plp, lprng, aix, hpux, qnx
;   printing = bsd
```

Listing 5.2 shows the [printers] section definition.

Listing 5.2 The [printers] share definition in the smb.conf file.

```
# NOTE: If you have a BSD-style print system there is no need to
# specifically define each individual printer
[printers]
   comment = All Printers
   path = /usr/spool/samba
   browseable = no
# Set public = yes to allow user 'guest account' to print
   guest ok = no
   writeable = no
   printable = yes
```

Listing 5.3 shows an example of a private printer definition.

Listing 5.3 An example of a private printer definition.

```
# A private printer, usable only by fred. Spool data will be placed in
# fred's home directory.
# Note that fred must have write access to the spool directory,
# wherever it is.
[fredsprn]
```

```
comment = Fred's Printer
valid users = fred
path = /homes/fred
printer = freds_printer
public = no
writable = no
printable = yes
```

Listing 5.1 shows an option to read the printer definitions from the /etc/printcap or /lpstat file. This option allows you to use the printer definitions that have already been created in your system. Samba automatically includes these printers should the **load printers** parameter be set to **yes**. Likewise, the default printer style is set to BSD at compile time, that is, when you run ./configure. If you have a non-BSD type of printer system, you should investigate using the other printer styles.

The currently supported printer systems include the following:

- BSD
- SYSV
- PLP (portable line printer)
- LPRNG
- AIX (specific to the AIX flavor of Unix)
- HPUX (specific to the HPUX flavor of Unix)
- QNX (specific to a QNX system)

The printer style is set with the following parameter:

```
printing = bsd
```

If you can print to the printer using the Unix operating system, you should be able to use this printer with Samba. This printer should include most of the currently available parallel port and serial printers. However, because of the Printing Performance Architecture (PPA), several printers require special software drivers that are written only for Microsoft Windows systems. Unfortunately, these printers (which include some of the Hewlett-Packard DeskJet printers, such as the 720, 820, and 1000 series) cannot be used with most versions of Unix. However, at the speed at which device drivers are written for Linux, they might be able to soon. The best choice is a PostScript laser printer, if you can afford one.

TIP: *At the command prompt of the Samba server, enter "ls >/dev/lpx", where x is the parallel port number your printer is connected to. If you already have a printer set up, the current directory listing should be printed. Do not be too concerned with the output; if the printer is activated by this command and some sort of output is generated, at least you know that you have access to the printer and should be able to use it. (Note: This might not apply if the printer is a plotter, in which case I do not recommend trying this!) If you get nothing, see whether the printer device has been included with your kernel or has been loaded.*

Enter "cat /proc/devices". You should see listed a number of character devices, one of which should be lp. If nothing is listed, you might need to either compile support of it into your kernel or obtain a device driver for it.

Linux, especially the Red Hat distribution, includes a useful utility known as **printtool**. You can activate this utility from the command line of an X term or by using the Control Panel in X windows. This utility natively supports more than 30 families of printers, both local and remote Unix (lpd) queues. In addition, it supports the remote local area network (LAN) manager printer. Figures 5.1 through 5.11 show some of the dialog boxes from the **printtool** utility running on a Linux server.

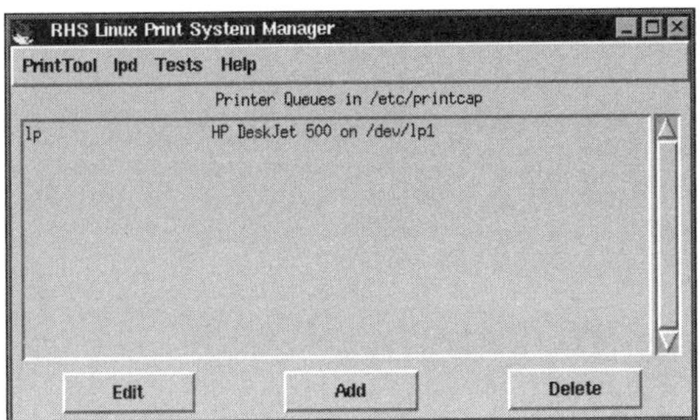

Figure 5.1 The Red Hat Linux **printtool** System Manager.

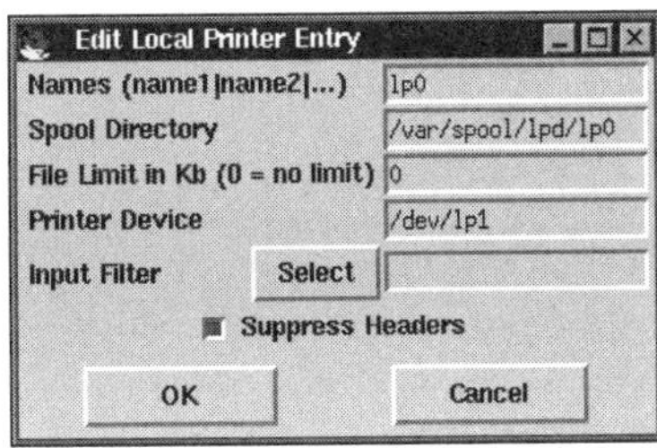

Figure 5.2 The Red Hat Linux **printtool** Edit Local Printer entry.

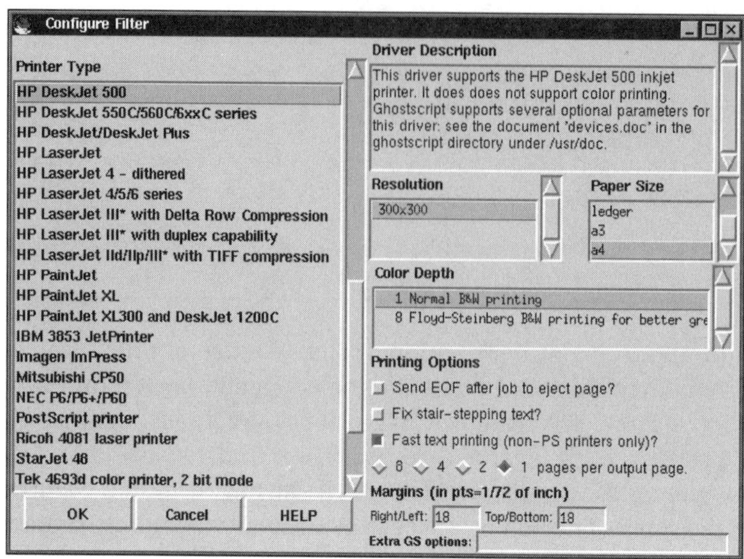

Figure 5.3 The Red Hat Linux **printtool** configuring a filter.

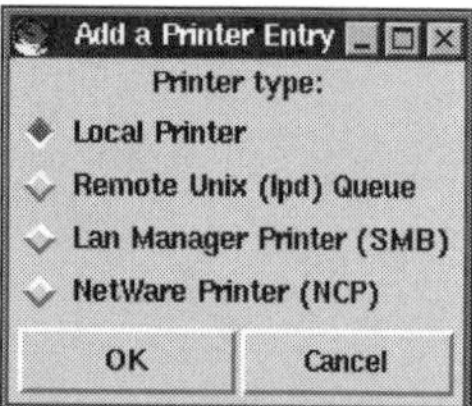

Figure 5.4 The Red Hat Linux **printtool** Add A Printer entry.

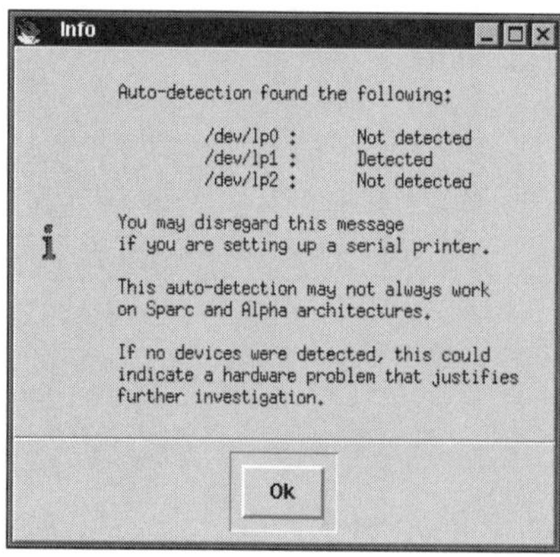

Figure 5.5 The Red Hat Linux **printtool** indicating which printer ports were detected.

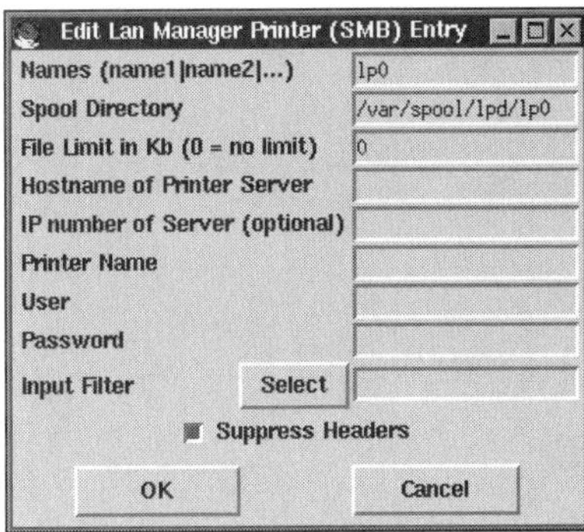

Figure 5.6 The Red Hat Linux **printtool** editing a local printer entry with the filter selected.

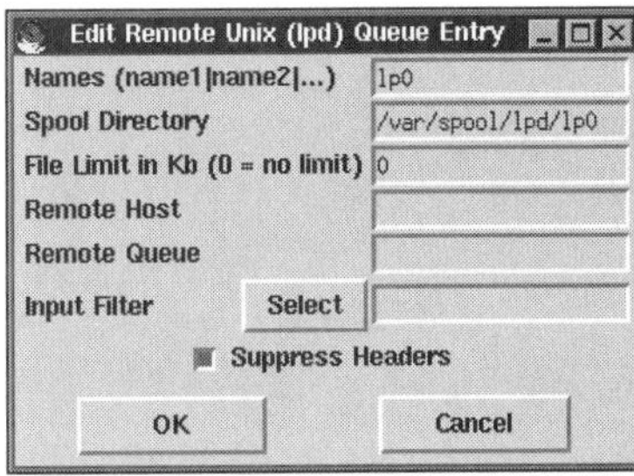

Figure 5.7 The Red Hat Linux **printtool** editing a remote Unix printer.

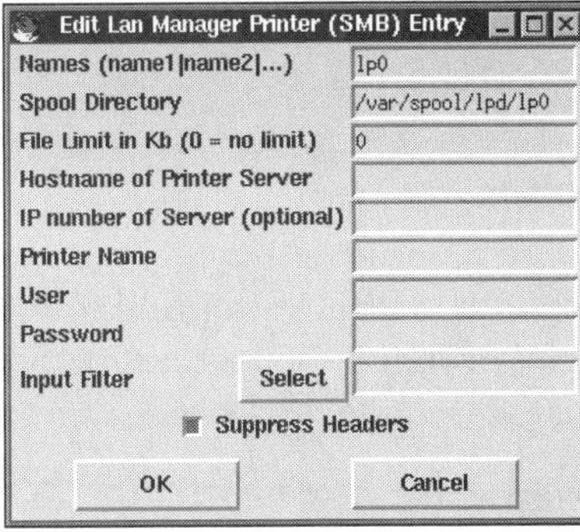

Figure 5.8 The Red Hat Linux **printtool** editing a remote LAN Manager (SMB) printer.

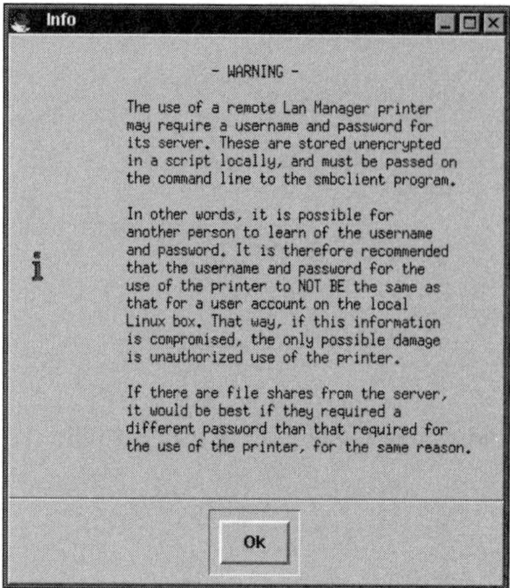

Figure 5.9 The Red Hat Linux **printtool** LAN Manager warning.

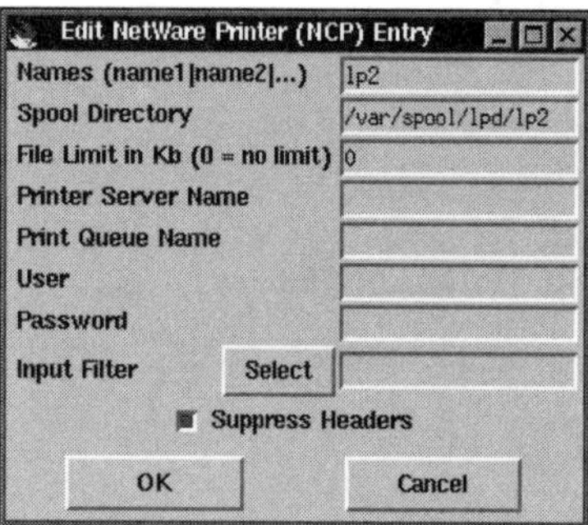

Figure 5.10 The Red Hat Linux **printtool** editing a NetWare printer.

In addition, Linux includes a Ghostscript interpreter that fully supports about 100 other printers and so allows your non-PostScript printer to behave as PostScript. The printers under Linux are held as devices, both parallel and serial.

The common LPT1 found on most PCs, usually at I/O port 0x378, is known as /dev/lp1. Other ports might be found at 0x3bc and 0x278 or /dev/lp0 and /dev/lp2. The serial printers are assigned to serial devices of the type /dev/ttySn, where n is a number from 0 to 3. However, if a serial printer is used, the port must be set to the highest possible speed, which requires the use of the **setserial** command.

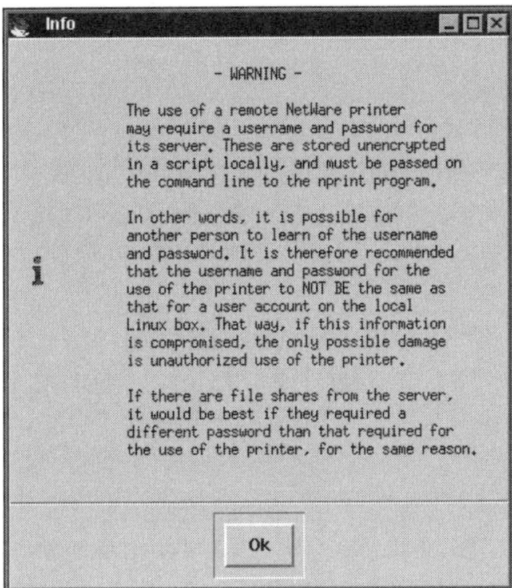

Figure 5.11 The Red Hat Linux **printtool** NetWare warning.

NOTE: *The security and authentication mode used to access a Samba server by any SMB client (covered in Chapter 4) forms the basis for the security required for printing. However, complications can arise when you attempt to set up a guest account that might print. Usually, such complications are related to permissions on the printer spool directory. You can find a solution to this problem in the Immediate Solutions section.*

Chapter 4 showed some smb.conf parameters and macros that are related to shares. A similar set of parameters and macros that are used mainly with printer shares are shown in Tables 5.1 and 5.2. A full list of smb.conf parameters and macros can be found in Appendix A.

Table 5.1 Printer-share-related smb.conf parameters.

Parameter	Description
load printers	If this is set to **yes** (the default), all the printers defined within the /etc/printcap file are loaded and made available for browsing. Set this parameter to **no** if you do not want the whole world to use your printers.
lppause command	This is one of the many parameters that you write into with the appropriate command line code to action something on the printer. It is used to stop the print job.
lpq command	This parameter reads the printer queue status for clients. With BSD, the default is **lpq**.
lpresume command	This parameter resumes the stopped print job using the lppause command.
lprm command	This parameter deletes the print job from the queue.

(continued)

Table 5.1 Printer-share-related smb.conf parameters (continued).

Parameter	Description
min print space	Specified in kilobytes, this parameter sets the minimum amount of space that must be available in the spool file location before a new print job can be accepted from a client. It is very useful when you have tree-size documents being produced on a busy printer. By default, this parameter is usually set to 0, meaning that all jobs are accepted.
postscript	Sometimes printers that are not PostScript seem to get confused because of the Ctrl+D characters appearing at the start of print jobs. The result is that the PostScript layout that is being printed is not PostScript. By default, this parameter is set to no, in which case it will add a "%!" to the beginning of each print job, forcing PostScript printing. It has been known to confuse real PostScript printers.
printable	This parameter defines what may or may not be a printer share and thus what may or may not be printed to. The default is **no**.
printcap name	Used in conjunction with the [printers] section, this parameter informs Samba of the printer definition file's location. This is an alternative to /etc/printcap.
printer	If the /etc/printcap file does not have an entry for the printer share you have defined, this parameter will tell Samba where to send the print job after spooling.
printing	This parameter sets the printer style to be used.

Table 5.2 Printer share macros used in smb.conf files.

Macro	Description
%p	Replace with the printer name
%j	Replace with the job number
%s	Replace with the full pathname and file name of the spool file
%S	Replace with the file name of the spool file

Immediate Solutions

Providing A List Of Printers In Network Neighborhood With No Printers Set Up

Without having to do anything but run the smbd service, Samba will respond to a request for a share in a defined sequence. First, the Samba server will search through the smb.conf file for a share of the appropriate name of the share request. If the share exists, it will return the share of that name. If no such share exists and a [homes] section does exist, it will look through the /etc/passwd file for a username with the same name as the requested share and return that user's home directory. If no share still exists, it will look for a [printers] section and look for a share with the same name as the requested share and return it as the share. If no share still exists, the Samba server will look for the default service and return that. If no default service exists, then it will respond with an error message.

If the smb.conf file has been set up to load the printers listed in the /etc/printcap file with the **load printers** parameter set to **yes** (the default), the printers listed in this file will be returned as individually-identified printer shares, all with the underlying properties of the [printers] section. Samba copies the properties from the [printers] section and passes these to the individual printers defined in the /etc/printcap file (or lpstat if SYSV). This can greatly improve the response time you would need to add a new printer to your machine and network. The Samba server simply relies on the /etc/printcap file for all its information, with the appropriate smb.conf entries. Adding or replacing a printer to a Samba server requires minimum effort when rewriting smb.conf files.

Creating A Printer Share

To create a printer share, you need a simple smb.conf file, such as that shown in Listing 5.4.

Listing 5.4 A simple smb.conf file.

```
netbios name  = linuxrouter1
server string = Samba example server
workgroup     = HOMENET
```

```
        printing      = bsd
        printcap name = /etc/printcap
        public        = no
   [printers]
        comment       = All the printers from /etc/printcap
        printable     = yes
        writeable     = no
```

Let's assume that the /etc/printcap file on your system appears similar to that shown in Listing 5.5.

Listing 5.5 A sample /etc/printcap file.

```
# Generic printer:
lp:lp=/dev/lp1
:sd=/var/spool/lpd
:sh
```

This is a simple entry for a generic dot-matrix printer. (I use such an entry with a Brother M-1109 9-pin dot-matrix printer for generating program listings and usage logs.) If you browse to the Samba server "linuxrouter1," the printer share lp will be listed as shown in Figure 5.12.

Another entry that includes two printers, such as that shown in Listing 5.6, will generate two entries in the Network Neighborhood. Figure 5.13 shows these two printers.

Listing 5.6 A sample /etc/printcap file for two printers.

```
# Generic printer:
lp:\
:lp=/dev/lp1
:sd=/var/spool/lpd
:sh
# HP Laser jet plus
hp:\
        :hp=/dev/lp0:\
        :sd=/usr/spool/lp0:\
        :mx#0:\
        :of=/usr/spool/lp0/hpjlp:
        :lf=/usr/spool/lp0/hp-log:
```

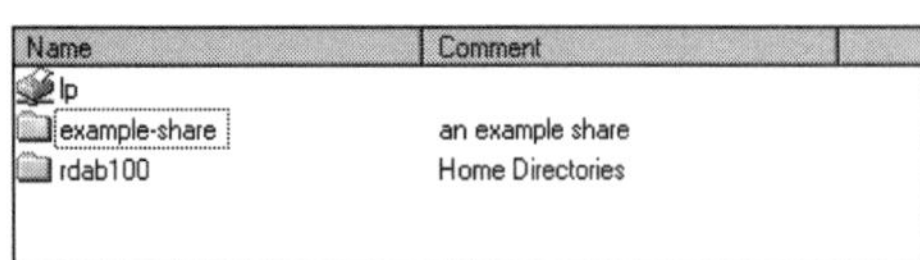

Figure 5.12 The lp printer share in a Network Neighborhood window.

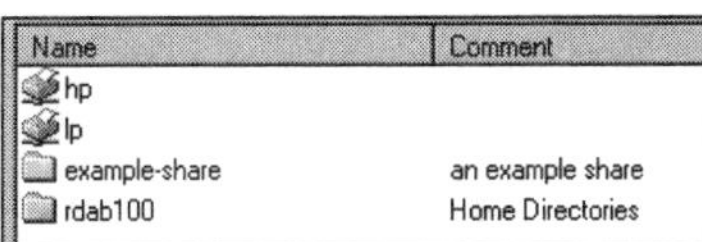
Name	Comment
hp	
lp	
example-share	an example share
rdab100	Home Directories

Figure 5.13 Two printers in a Network Neighborhood window.

Thus, to add a new printer into the smb.conf file that is a printer share and that might be used for a share named [trial-printer], you add the lines shown in Listing 5.7 to the smb.conf file.

Listing 5.7 The entry for a [trial-printer] for the smb.conf file.

```
[trial-printer]
 comment = trial printer
 path = /usr/spool/lpd
 printable = yes
```

Opening Network Neighborhood will now show three printers, as in Figure 5.14. However, at this stage you have not added a real printer to the system and will need to either add another printer to the system or edit the /etc/printcap file to reflect this new printer. This would effectively provide one of the printers listed earlier with another printer name. An amended /etc/printcap file, as in Listing 5.8, shows one option.

Listing 5.8 An /etc/printcap file with an alias for the trial-printer share.

```
# Generic printer:
lp:\
:lp=/dev/lp1
:sd=/var/spool/lpd
:sh
# HP Laser jet plus
trial-printer|hp:\
        :hp=/dev/lp0:\
        :sd=/usr/spool/lp0:\
        :mx#0:\
        :of=/usr/spool/lp0/hpjlp:
        :lf=/usr/spool/lp0/hp-log:
```

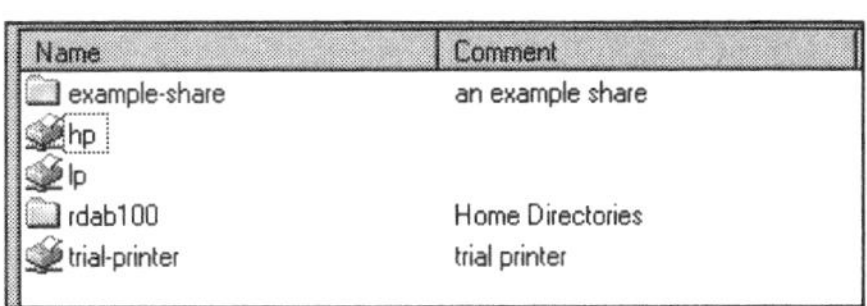
Name	Comment
example-share	an example share
hp	
lp	
rdab100	Home Directories
trial-printer	trial printer

Figure 5.14 A new printer "trial-printer" in a Network Neighborhood window.

Creating A Printer Share Only Certain Users Can Access

This is possible by creating a share and defining users for that share. The smb.conf.example from the distribution contains such a printer definition for a private share usable by user "fred" (see Listing 5.9).

Listing 5.9 A sample of a private printer definition.

```
# A private printer, usable only by fred. Spool data will be placed in
# fred's home directory.
# Note that fred must have write access to the spool directory,
# wherever it is.
[fredsprn]
   comment = Fred's Printer
   valid users = fred
   path = /homes/fred
   printer = freds_printer
   public = no
   writable = no
   printable = yes
```


You could just as easily add a number of users or even a group of users (@usergroup and add a user group with an appropriate entry in the /etc/group file) to the line "valid users."

Creating A Printer Share Only Guest Users Can Access

This is possible by creating a share and defining users for that share. Working from the base smb.conf.example from the distribution, you can create a printer share for a public share usable by guest users. Be sure to check that /dev/null is world writeable. Also, make sure that the **guest account** smb.conf parameter is set to a user with minimum access rights on the system and that the home is set to, for example, /dev/null and that the shell is set to /bin/false. The **nobody** user on most Unix systems is not capable of using the printers, mainly because of the user and group privileges on the printer spool directories, so you might need to create a new account to satisfy your requirements. In the past I have used a **printwho** user that has the minimum number of privileges required for access to the spool directory and that becomes the user listed in **guest account**. Listing 5.10 contains a sample public printer definition.

Listing 5.10 A sample of a public printer definition.

```
        guest account = printwho
# A public printer, usable by guests only.
 [public-printer]
        comment = A guest printer
```

```
path = /usr/spool/samba
guest ok = Yes
print ok = Yes
browseable = yes
guest only = yes
```

This definition has been set up so that the printer share is also browseable by guest users. You could also set this to no and require that the users know the share name to use, but that can complicate things, so it might be easier to leave this in place.

The SWAT Tool For Printer Administration

The GUI SWAT tool that comes with Samba has a separate section that will create and help administer printer shares. However, remember that printers that are auto-loaded through the /etc/printcap file cannot be deleted or modified if loaded with **load printers=yes**. The SWAT configuration tool entry dialog box (see Figure 5.15) under Printers allows you to configure current printers from a pick list or create a new printer share.

The parameters that can be configured using the SWAT printer configuration, which is available in the current version (2.0.4b) of Samba, are listed in Table 5.3.

Table 5.3 Parameters that can be configured using SWAT.

Parameter	Description
Base Options	
comment	This is a text field that accompanies the share to notify its use or function.
path	This is the server path for the spool directory for this server.
Security Options	
Guest account	The default is set to nobody at compile time. Normally, this account does not have any logon privileges, and the user home is set to /dev/null. If this option is used, the account must exist in the account database on the server. When set at share level, the share value of guest account will override any global value.
Guest ok	The default value is **no**. When set to **yes**, no username or password will be required to access the share.

(continued)

Table 5.3 Parameters that can be configured using SWAT (continued).

Parameter	Description
Security Options *(continued)*	
Hosts allow	Only those hosts listed may connect to a service. The syntax may take the form of specific IP addresses, a subnetwork IP address (e.g., 192.168.), or a fully qualified domain name (FQDN) (e.g., goodhost.net). It is also possible to use an additional parameter except within the list, so that ranges of IP can be selected with members of that range being excluded. Also, in case you have more than one subnet in your network, it is possible to include the netmask to refine the hosts allowed. The default is that all hosts may access the server.
Hosts deny	Whereas hosts allow indicates which hosts may access the services, hosts deny lists which hosts or network of hosts are denied access. The default is to deny no hosts.
Logging Options	
status	This parameter is a Boolean that sets the logging of connections to a status file that smbstatus can read. If set to no the smbstatus would not be capable of reporting on active connections. The default value is: **status = yes**. It is not advisable to alter this parameter.
Tuning Options	
min print space	Specified in kilobytes, this is the minimum space that must be available in the spool file location before a new print job can be accepted from a client. It is a very useful option if you have tree-size documents being produced on a busy printer. The default is usually **0**, meaning that all jobs are accepted.
Printing Options	
printable	This asks whether this share should appear as a printer. If it should, it will appear as one.
postscript	Sometimes printers that are not PostScript printers seem to get confused by the Ctrl+D characters appearing at the start of print jobs. The result is that the PostScript layout that is being printed is not PostScript. By default, this parameter is set to no, in which case it will add a "%!" to the beginning of each print job, forcing PostScript printing. It has been known to confuse real PostScript printers.
printing	As already noted, this is the printer style to be used.
print command	This is the command that Samba will use to run a print job. This should contain the **%s** macro and can contain **%p**. The default value depends on the printer style. Printing style bsd uses a default value of lpr **--r --P%p %s**.

(continued)

Table 5.3 Parameters that can be configured using SWAT **(continued).**

Parameter	Description
Printing Options *(continued)*	
lpq command	This parameter reads the printer queue status for clients. With BSD, the default is **lpq**.
lprm command	This parameter deletes the print job from the queue.
lppause command	This is one of the many parameters that you write into with the appropriate command line code needed to action something on the printer. It is used to stop the print job.
lpresume command	This parameter resumes the stopped print job using the **lppause** command.
queuepause command	If a pause is requested, Samba passes this command to pause the printer queue.
queueresume command	If a pause is requested, Samba passes this command to resume the printer queue.
printer name	This informs Samba of the location of the printcap entry; the default is /etc/printcap.
printer driver	This parameter has no default. If an entry exists, this informs Samba of the driver name to provide to client sessions.
printer driver location	This parameter has no default. If an entry exists, this informs Samba of the location of the printer driver definition file.
Browse Options	
browseable	If this printer is required to appear in Network Neighborhood browse lists, setting this value to **yes** will provide this functionality.
Miscellaneous Options	
postexec	After the print job is complete, this parameter holds the command to be run as the user connected.
root preexec	Before a print job is run, this parameter holds the command to be run as root.
root postexec	After the print job is complete, this parameter holds the command to be run as root.

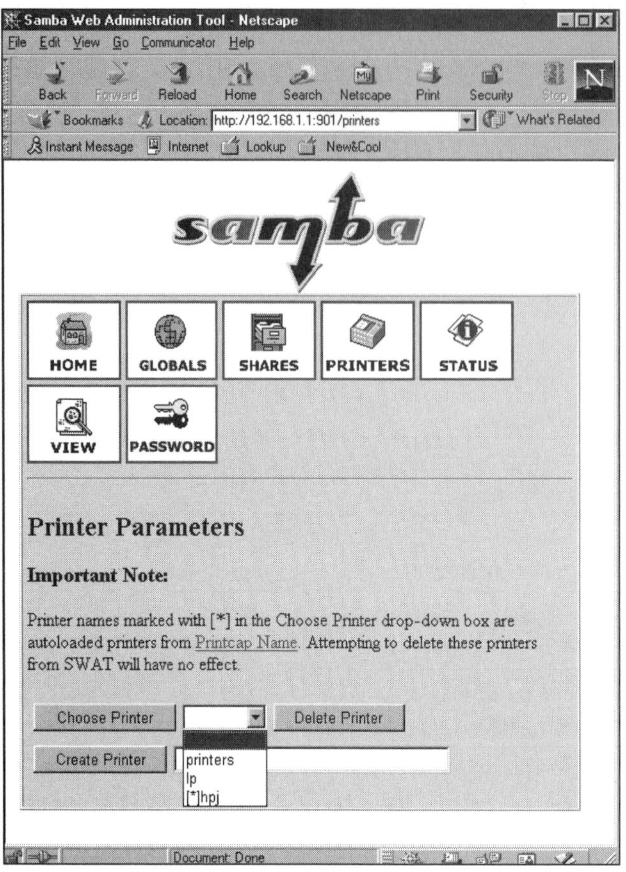

Figure 5.15 SWAT printer configuration.

Printing In Color

If the printer you are using is capable of printing in color from the system and operating system that it is connected to, it should be possible to print in color when using a client connected to it. The client might need to have the correct printer driver installed locally on it.

You should consult the printer manual for information on the drivers for different operating systems in this situation.

A Magic Printer Filter

The standard parallel port printer is not capable of processing PostScript images. A magic printer filter is a set of programs that work by defining and inserting the updated printer definitions into the /etc/printcap file. Within the amended printer entries are paths to scripts and programs that contain the necessary filter that will be run on the file before printing.

A number of these are available under the GNU/GPL distribution. The better-known ones in Linux are the following:

- APSfilter
- Bubbletools
- Magicfilter
- HPTools
- PPR for PostScript Printers

Managing Printer Queues

You can list all the pending jobs in a printer queue on a Samba (or SMB/CIFS) server by using the following command syntax (run as an appropriate user):

```
[somewhere]$ smbclient //servername/printer-share <PASSWORD> -c queue
```

This will respond (IPs are included in response) as follows:

```
Added interface ip=192.168.1.1 bcast=192.168.1.255 nmask=255.255.255.0
Client started (version 2.0.3).
Connecting to 192.168.1.8 at port 139
Domain=[DOMAIN] OS=[Linux] Server=[Samba 2.0.3]
119            20345               ntwdev01.b00012
120            20345               ntwdev01.b00098
```

You can see that two different jobs are pending on that printer queue.

Alternatively, from a Windows PC, you simply select and open the printer from the Printers dialog box and see the current printer queue, as shown in Figure 5.16.

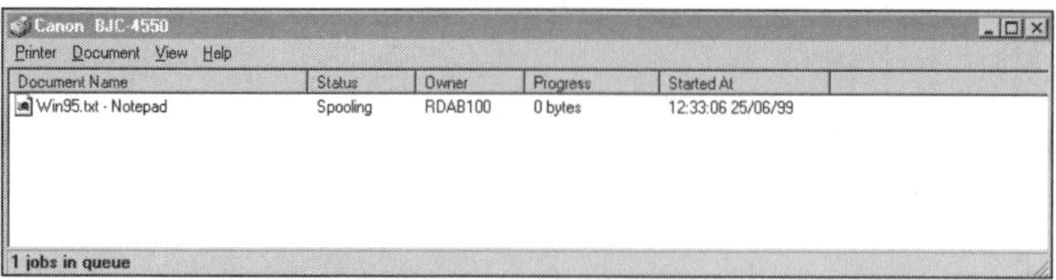

Figure 5.16 A printer queue from a Windows PC.

Running Printer Accounting

It is possible to run printer accounting so that you can manage and account for printer usage for users who like using trees. Linux has a package known as pac, which will help track costs and usage. Listing 5.11 provides the usage of pac from the Linux man page.

Listing 5.11 The pac man page.

```
PAC(8)                    UNIX System Manager's Manual

NAME
     pac - printer/plotter accounting information
SYNOPSIS
     pac [-Pprinter] [-c] [-m] [-pprice] [-s] [-r] [name ...]
DESCRIPTION
Pac reads the printer/plotter accounting files, accumulating the number of
pages (the usual case) or feet (for raster devices) of paper consumed by
each user, and printing out how much each user consumed in pages or feet and
dollars.
Options and operands available:
-Pprinter Accounting is done for the named printer. Normally, accounting is
done for the default printer (site dependent) or the value of the
environment variable PRINTER is used.
-c flag causes the output to be sorted by cost; usually the output is sorted
alphabetically by name.
-m flag causes the host name to be ignored in the accounting file. This
allows for a user on multiple machines to have all of his printing charges
grouped together.
-pprice The value price is used for the cost in dollars instead of the
default value of 0.02 or the price specified in /etc/printcap.
-r Reverse the sorting order.
-s Accounting information is summarized on the summary accounting file; this
summarization is necessary because on a busy system, the accounting file can
grow by several lines per day.
names Statistics are only printed for user(s) name; usually, statistics are
printed for every user who has used any paper.
```

```
FILES
     /var/log/?acct  raw accounting files
     /var/log/?_sum  summary accounting files
     /etc/printcap   printer capability data base
```

Native printer accounting software is not available for Windows NT. However, several shareware and freeware versions are becoming available, including pcounter, which has been used successfully; a trial version of this software can be obtained from **http://www.pcounter.com**.

Considering Infrared Printer Support

I recently discovered that I could use my laptop (a Toshiba Tecra 8000 that dual-boots to Linux and Windows 95) when running Windows 95 with either a Canon BJC80 or the Hewlett-Packard 340Cbi using an optional infrared port. This can be very useful when using laptops on the move because no printer cable is needed. Although I have not been able to use this option with Linux, you might be pleased to learn of some recent developments concerning Linux device drivers and infrared ports for both networking and printing. I have yet to find the time to get my own laptop infrared ports working while running Linux, but I understand that this is possible. The latest information on this can be found at **http://www.linuxdoc.org/HOWTO/IR-HOWTO.html**. This site is essential if you want to attempt infrared port usage

Finding Printer Support In The Linux Kernel

Printer support can be found under Character Devices in the kernel compile menu, which has options for both serial and parallel devices. Usually, the default Linux kernels include support for the standard parallel ports. For other operating systems, consult the operation manuals or documentation that accompany the system.

Chapter 6

Using SMB/CIFS Resources From Microsoft Clients

In Depth

As mentioned in Chapter 2, it is assumed that most readers will already have a PC running Windows 95/98 or NT and are exploring the possibility of using Samba either at home or at work. You need to confirm that Windows networking has been set up and configured to allow you to use the resources available on SMB/CIFS servers. A detailed description of setting up Microsoft Windows networking is included in the section "Immediate Solutions." Essentially, these are the same procedures as those required for setting up a 100 percent Microsoft Windows network, with a few additional Samba-related notes on password encryption.

Windows 95 and 98 share similar networking setups. The setup for Windows NT, although appearing identical to that of Windows 95/98, has some differences that are discussed later in this chapter. To use the SMB/CIFS services on a Samba server, you should at least have TCP/IP networking set up with an operational network. Also, to use the resources on the server, you should ensure that both the client and the server are in the same workgroup or domain.

For the purposes of the following solutions, it is assumed that the network has four PCs each installed with a different client or operating system (which could be the same PC running four different operating systems) and two SMB/CIFS servers. A diagram of the sample network is shown in Figure 6.1.

One server is known as LINUXSERVER, which is a Red Hat 5.2 Linux server with Samba 2.0.4b installed, and another server is known as NTSERVER, which is a Windows NT 4 server with no service pack applied, so that plain- or clear-text passwords are permitted.

The security employed is that of a workgroup, the name of which is SAMBABOOK. The NT server is installed as a standalone server with no NT domain existing, so security is username based, also known as 'User Level Security'. All machines on the network are members of the same workgroup. The servers have user accounts for a couple of named users and a guest user. The user details are shown in Table 6.1 and Listing 6.1.

Listing 6.1 The /etc/group file from LINUXSERVER.

```
root::0:root
bin::1:root,bin,daemon
daemon::2:root,bin,daemon
sys::3:root,bin,adm
```

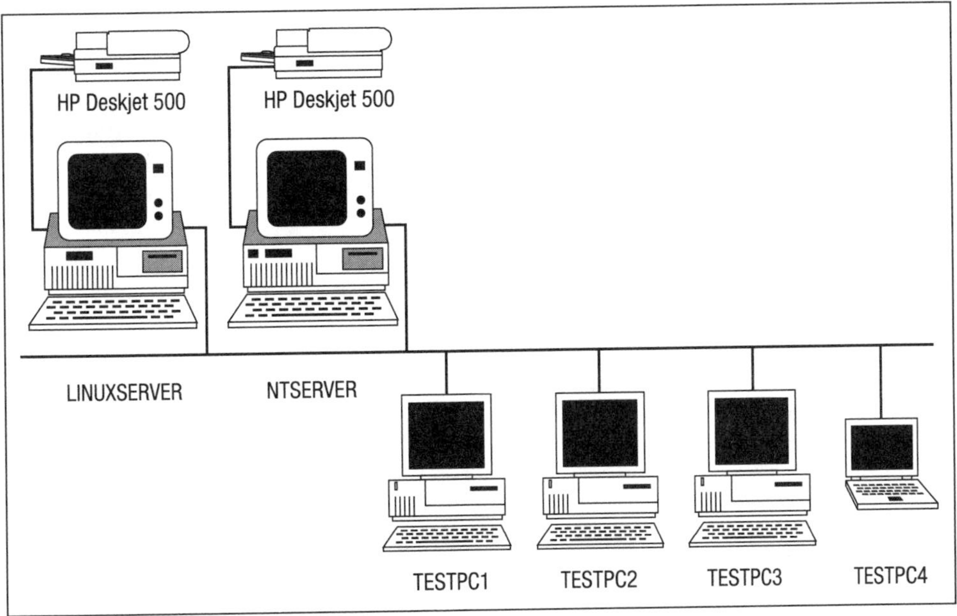

Figure 6.1 A sample network.

```
adm::4:root,adm,daemon
tty::5:
disk::6:root,adm
lp::7:lp
mem::8:
kmem::9:
wheel::10:root
floppy::11:root
mail::12:mail
news::13:news
uucp::14:uucp
man::15:man
users::100:games
nogroup::-2:
test::500:test1,test2
```


Table 6.1 Immediate Solutions user accounts.

Username	Password
test1	test1pass
test2	test1pass

No domain name server (DNS) or Windows Internet Name Service (WINS) server exists on this network, and all PCs have current hosts and lmhosts files that correctly identify all the hosts in the network. Each server has a printer connected to it (a Hewlett-Packard DeskJet 500 in both cases), and both have shares that are specific to named users as well as shares for groups of users and guest or anonymous users. The smb.conf file for LINUXSERVER is shown in Listing 6.2.

Listing 6.2 The smb.conf file from LINUXSERVER.

```
# Global parameters
        workgroup = SAMBABOOK
        netbios name = LINUXSERVER
        server string = Samba Server
        security = USER
        printers = BSD
[homes]
        comment = Home Directories
        path = %H
        writeable = yes
        valid users = %S
[printers]
        comment = All Printers
        path = /var/spool/samba
        print ok = Yes
        browseable = yes
[groupshare]
        comment = Group Share
        path = /home/group
        writeable = yes
        valid users = @test
```

The /home/group directory has permissions set as rwxrwx--for the test group so that the directory is not world readable and all members of the test group may read files, list directory contents, create files and directories, and change to other directories in this share. The /home/group directory contains the following file structure:

```
/home/group
            /test1work
            /test2work
            /jointwork
```

All the directories were created by the test1 user from a client machine.

The NTSERVER also has a share named groupshare and two users—test1 and test2—that have the same privileges on this share as on the Linux Samba version. The creation of the two users and the group test is accomplished in Windows NT using the User Manager dialog box, as shown in Figure 6.2.

The User Manager, through the main user dialog box, allows the ability to create groups for users. The creation of a user group is shown in Figure 6.3.

The share is created by selecting the drive or directory and using either the File And Sharing option from Explorer or a right-click pop-up menu, as shown in Figure 6.4, and creating a share in the dialog box, as shown in Figure 6.5, and allocating permissions to it, as shown in Figure 6.6.

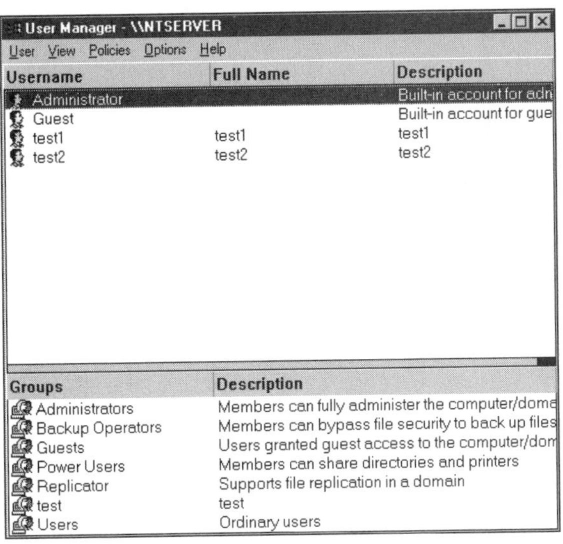

Figure 6.2 The User Manager dialog box.

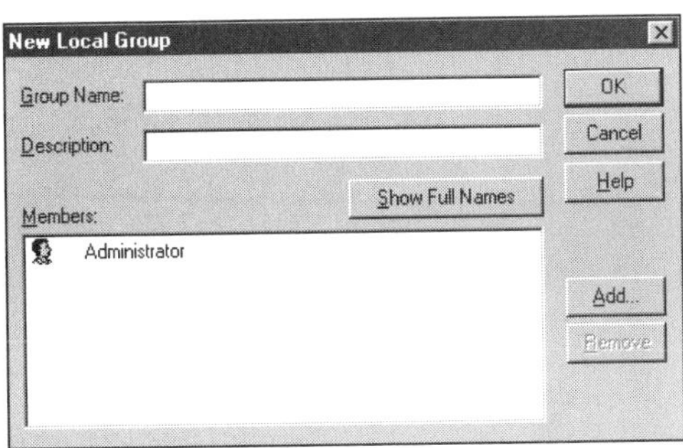

Figure 6.3 The New Local Group dialog box.

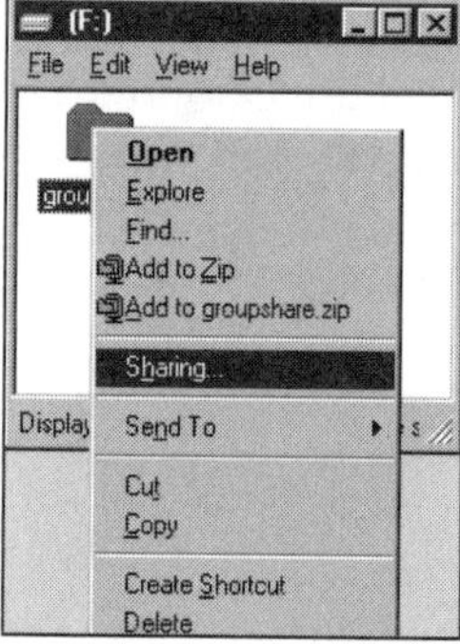

Figure 6.4 The Sharing option.

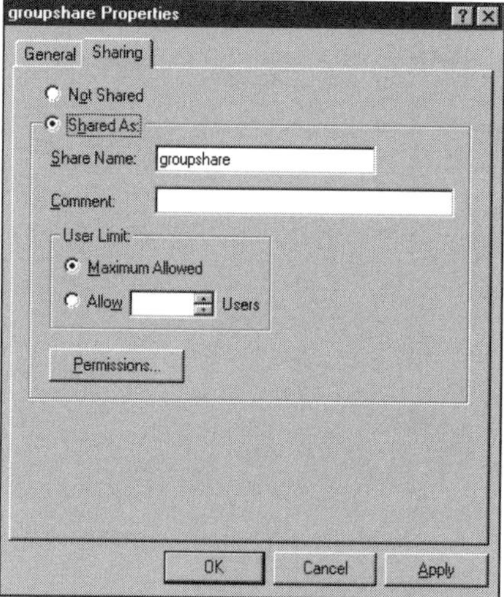

Figure 6.5 The Sharing dialog box.

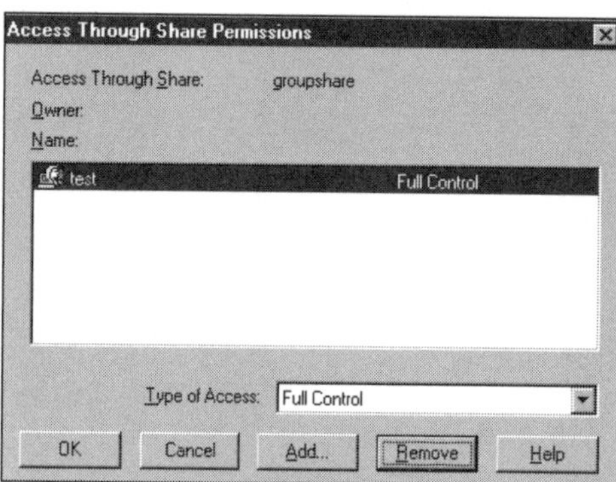

Figure 6.6 The Access Through Share Permissions dialog box.

By default, the share will be available to everyone with full control permissions; thus, the test1 and test2 users or the group of which those users are members need to be added to the permissions. It would be considered good practice to remove the 'Everyone' group unless explicitly needed. Again, the same directory structure is created in the share by user1 following a connection.

The printers are shared as **hp** on LINUXSERVER from the alias for the printer in the /etc/printcap entry on the Linux Samba server (also as **lp**) and as **hp** from the NT server. The /etc/printcap file for LINUXSERVER is shown in Listing 6.3.

Listing 6.3 The /etc/printcap file from LINUXSERVER.

```
# Global parameters
##PRINTTOOL3## LOCAL djet500 300x300 a4 {} DeskJet500Mono 1 {}
lp|hp:\
        :sd=/var/spool/lpd/lp:\
        :mx#0:\
        :sh:\
        :lp=/dev/lp1:\
        :if=/var/spool/lpd/lp/filter:
```

In Windows NT, you create a printer share by selecting the printer from the Printers dialog box. Then, using either the File And Sharing option from Explorer or a right-click pop-up menu, as shown in Figure 6.7, you create a share in the Sharing dialog box, as shown in Figure 6.8, and allocate permissions to it, as shown in Figure 6.9.

Figure 6.7 The Sharing option.

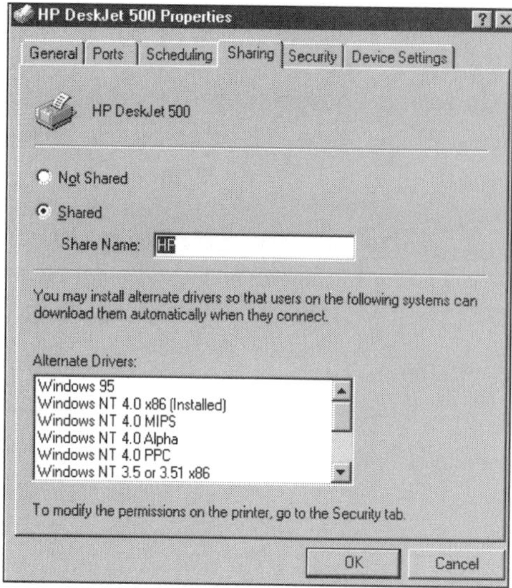

Figure 6.8 The Sharing dialog box.

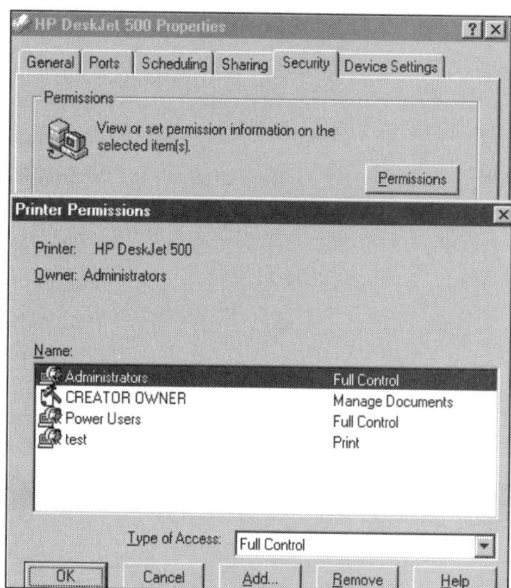

Figure 6.9 The Security dialog box.

Immediate Solutions

Setting Up Windows 95/98 To Use SMB/CIFS Resources

If you already have either operating system set up, these instructions assume that the network instructions are for configuring the network following a fresh installation. If you do not have a network card installed or have not yet configured your network settings, these instructions may be followed completely. If you don't have either operating system installed, it is a relatively simple process—just follow the instructions that came with your Microsoft operating system. Many good books are available to help you (see Appendix B).

Whenever you are configuring networking for Microsoft operating systems, you must have the original CD-ROM accessible during the process. Insert the disk into your CD-ROM drive.

If you do not have the network adapter installed on the PC, your first task is to install your network adapter into the PC. Shut the PC down in the normal manner, then install the network adapter according to the instructions. Switch the PC back on. Depending on the Microsoft Windows 9x operating system's hardware, your PC might or might not detect the network adapter. If it detects it as a plug-and-play device, enter the software driver for the network adapter and operating system CD-ROM when requested. This will set up and configure the operating system to use the new network adapter and might have entered the adapter information into the networking configuration as set out in the following steps:

1. Open the Control Panel. You can do this in either of two ways. The first option is to select and open (by double-clicking) the My Computer icon, as shown in Figure 6.10, on the desktop. Once the Control Panel icon appears, you need to select and open it, as shown in Figure 6.11.

   The second option is to use the Start button to select Settings and then Control Panel from the choices listed, as shown in Figure 6.12.

   You will be presented with the Control Panel window.

Figure 6.10 The My Computer icon.

Figure 6.11 The Control Panel.

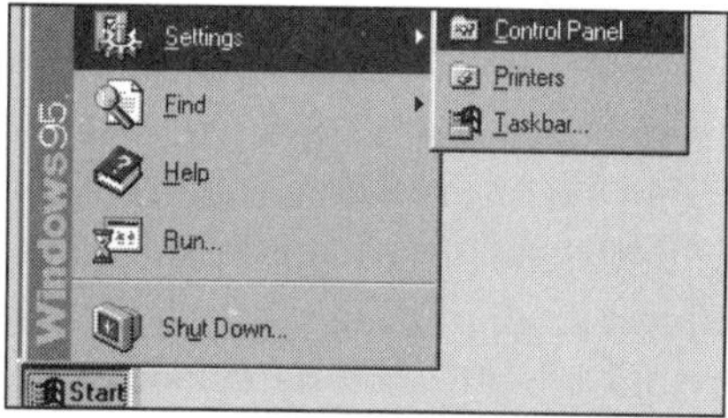

Figure 6.12 Opening the Control Panel from the Start menu.

2. In the Control Panel window, select and open the Network icon, as shown in Figure 6.13. This will open the Network dialog box for either Windows 95 or Windows 98.

   To set up a network for use with Samba, you need to have the following network components installed:

   - *Client for Microsoft Networks*
   - *Network adapter*—Some type of Ethernet card
   - *Protocol*—TCP/IP (IPX and NetBEUI are optional because they do not interfere with a TCP/IP network)

   It is also an option at this point to install the File And Printer Sharing service, which will allow others to use or access the files on your PC or to use your printers.

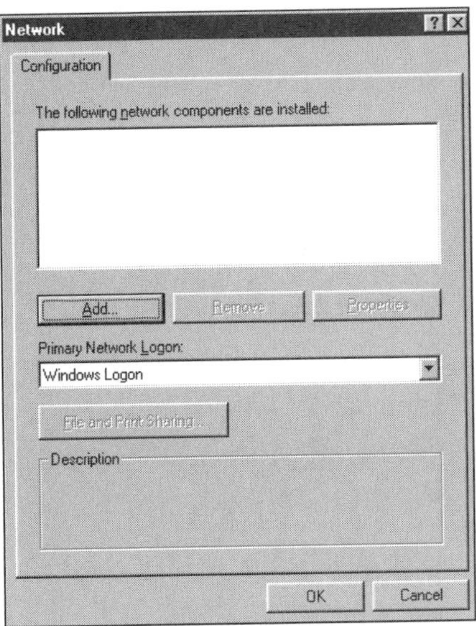

Figure 6.13 The Network dialog box.

3. If your adapter has not been detected automatically, you will need to manually add the Client for Microsoft Networking. To install Client for Microsoft Networking, click on Add. This will open the Select Network Component Type dialog box, as shown in Figure 6.14. Highlight the Client option, then click on Add; this is activated only after you have selected an option.

   The Select Network Client dialog box, shown in Figure 6.15, contains several choices, depending on which software is installed on your PC. Select the Microsoft option from the Manufacturers list and then on Client For Microsoft Networks from the Network Clients list, then click on OK.

4. You should be prompted with the Select Device dialog box, as shown in Figure 6.16. You will need to select the manufacturer and the model of your network adapter. Not all the currently available network adapters are included in this list. If yours does not appear, insert the floppy or CD-ROM containing the software drivers that came with your network adapter into the PC and click on Have Disk. Find and select the appropriate choices for your system, then click on OK.

5. You should be returned to the Network dialog box. As shown in Figure 6.17 (for a new installation), four components should be listed.

   You need to add the TCP/IP protocol, so, as in Step 3, click on Add to bring up the Select Network Component Type dialog box. Select the protocol component, then click on Add. The dialog box presented will list a number of manufacturers. Select Microsoft from the Manufacturers list and TCP/IP from the Network Protocols list, as shown in Figure 6.18, then click on OK.

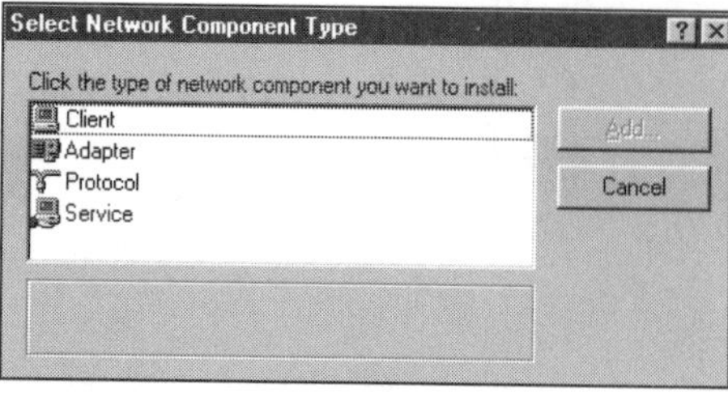

Figure 6.14 The Select Network Component Type dialog box.

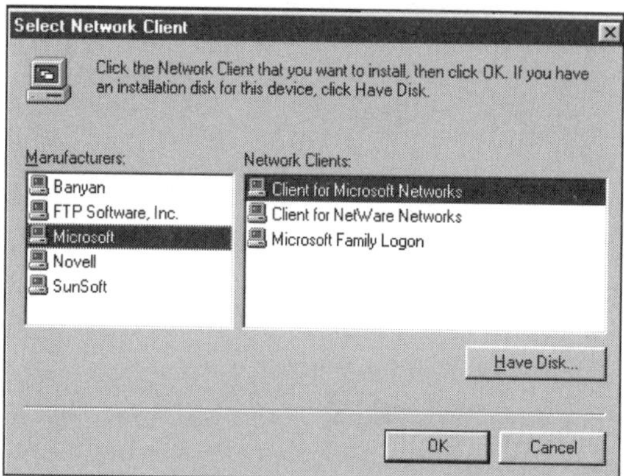

Figure 6.15 Windows 95 Network Setup.

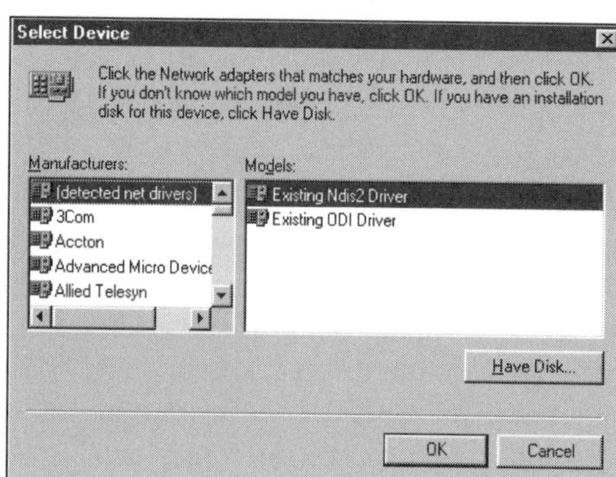

Figure 6.16 The Select Device dialog box.

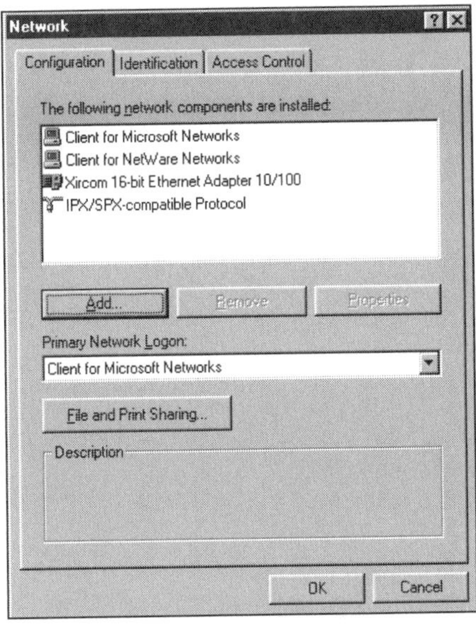

Figure 6.17 Four basic components installed.

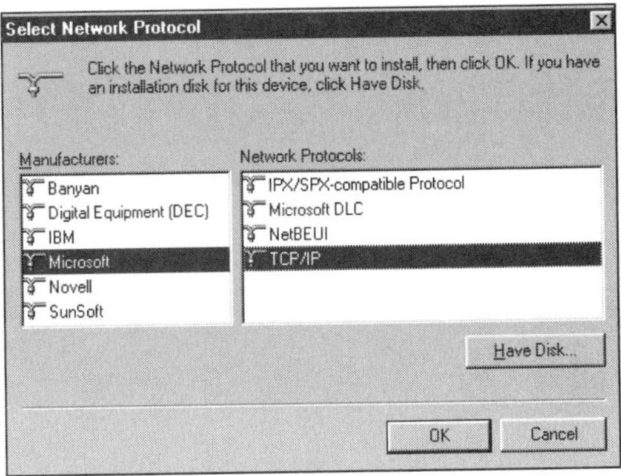

Figure 6.18 The Select Network Protocol dialog box.

You will again be returned to the Network dialog box. You should see the screen shown in Figure 6.19. As mentioned previously, the IPX and NetBEUI protocols are not required for Samba networking and may be removed.

NOTE: *Removing the IPX and NetBEUI protocols can have serious networking implications on your particular set up, so be sure to check with your network administrator or networking documentation if any of these protocols are already present on your system.*

6. You will need to configure the Client For Microsoft Networks Properties dialog box. Select Client For Microsoft Networks, then click on Properties. A dialog box similar to that shown in Figure 6.20 will appear.

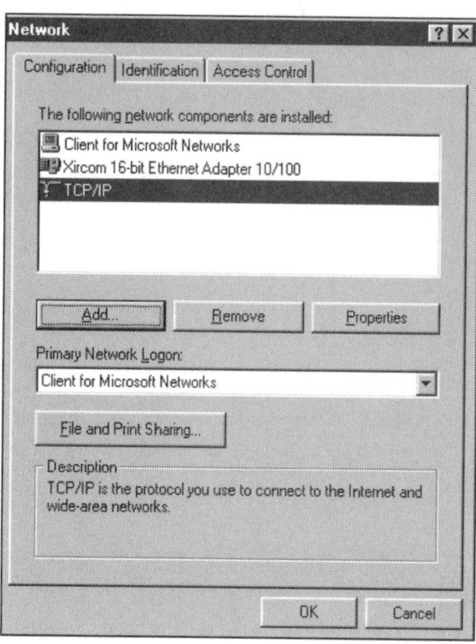

Figure 6.19 The initial setup of a client, adapter, and TCP/IP protocol.

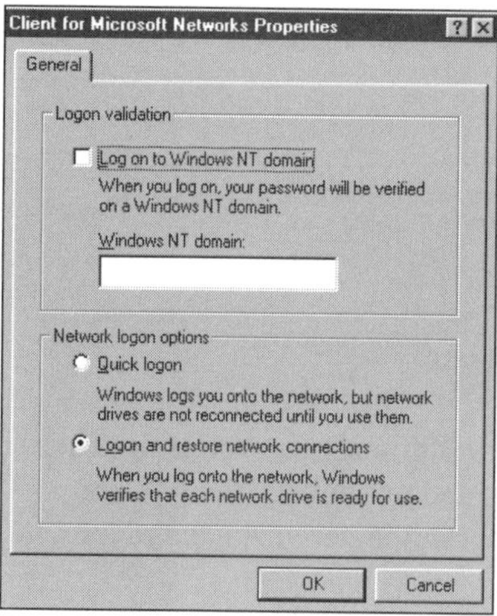

Figure 6.20 The Client For Microsoft Networks Properties dialog box.

NOTE: *In a Windows NT domain, this is where you ensure that the Log On To Windows NT Domain checkbox is selected and that the Windows NT domain is identified correctly. It assumes that you already have either a Microsoft NT domain or a Samba server that is operational as a domain controller. Selecting this checkbox allows you to log into the network. If you do not have either a Microsoft NT domain or a Samba server, it might be prudent to ignore this step for the moment and move on to Step 7. You can always return to this step later and allow the machine to log into a domain. The default domain name for a Samba server is WORKGROUP; for an NT-controlled domain it is DOMAIN. These are appropriate entries if no other networks exist that can use these names. Chapter 9 includes more information on Microsoft domain control and domain names.*

A normal operation is to select the Logon And Restore Network Connections checkbox. Click on OK, and you will return to the Network dialog box.

7. You need to configure the TCP/IP properties of your network connection. Select the TCP/IP protocol, then click on Properties. The TCP/IP Properties dialog box appears. This dialog box has six sections, but here we will install only simple TCP/IP networking and provide your network adapter with an IP address. Select the Specify An IP Address radio button on the IP Address tab and enter the IP address and subnet mask for your network. The IP address should be unique in your network, or else conflicts will occur. The other entries in this dialog box are not important at this time. In Figure 6.21, the entries for a sample PC have been made for network 192.168.1.0 with a subnet mask of 255.255.255.0. The exact settings you will use will depend on your own circumstances.

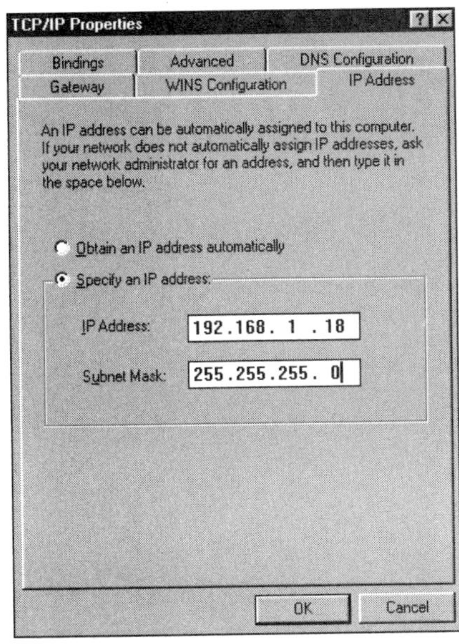

Figure 6.21 The TCP/IP Properties dialog box.

8. You need to name your PC for the network. In the Network dialog box, select the Identification tab and enter the computer name and the computer description. The default in Windows 95 for Workgroups is WORKGROUP. Figure 6.22 shows a selection of these entries.
9. In the Network dialog box, select the Access Control tab. The default is set to share-level access control. Select the User-Level Access Control radio button; the Obtain List Of Users And Groups From box is set to YOUR WORKGROUP, this PC is part of the SAMBABOOK workgroup, as shown in Figure 6.23. Click on OK.

   After installing all the software, you might be asked to insert floppies or CD-ROMs for adding driver or operating system software. You will be presented with a System Settings Change dialog box, as shown in Figure 6.24. You will need to reboot the PC to enable the configuration to be altered as entered and to be made active. Clicking on Yes will restart your computer and allow this process to occur.

   Your new networking setting will now be in place, and you should have Microsoft 95/98 or NT installed on your PC with TCP/IP networking installed and configured. Many good books are available to help you install network adapters into Microsoft Windows PCs (see Appendix B).

   The steps for Windows 98 are identical to those in the Windows 95 network setup. The Windows 98 setup differs from the network setup in Windows 98

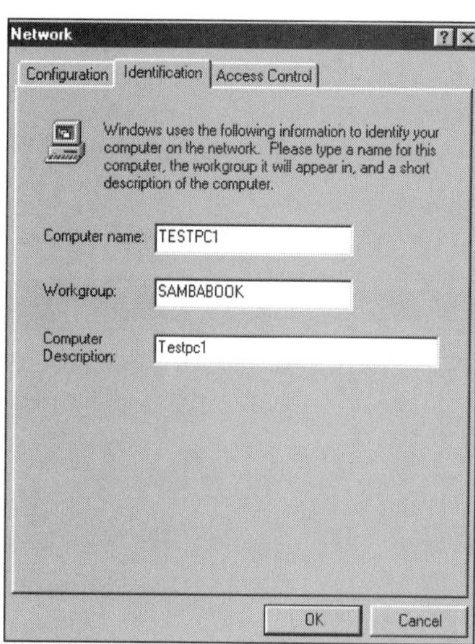

Figure 6.22 The Identification tab of the Network dialog box.

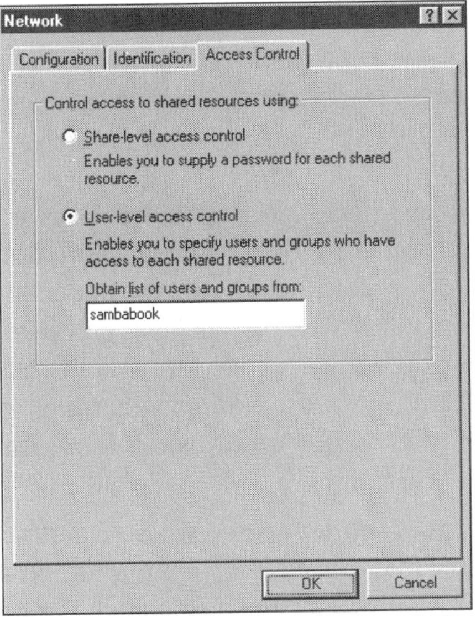

Figure 6.23 The Access Control tab of the Network dialog box.

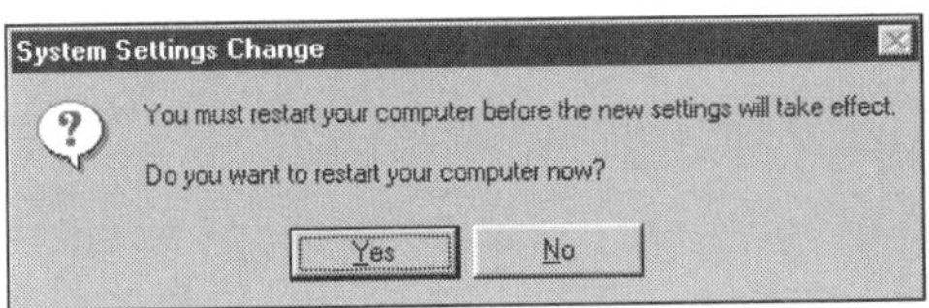

Figure 6.24 The System Settings Change dialog box.

in the default installed elements. By default, Windows 95 installs Client for Microsoft Networks, Client for Netware Networks, NetBEUI and IPX/SPX Compatible protocol, while Windows 98 defaults just to the Windows Family Logon and TCP/IP protocol.

Setting Up Windows NT To Use SMB/CIFS Resources

Setting up networking in Windows NT uses similar dialog boxes to those used in Windows 95/98, but some differences can be noted. Windows NT is not a plug-and-play operating system. This means that, unlike Windows 9x, you must manually add the networking adapter software to your system software once it is in place; unfortunately, Windows NT would not automatically detect the adapter and install the correct software for it. This can cause you some frustration, as you need to know the resources (IRQs and IO addresses) that your network card will use.

If you already have your Windows NT operating system set up with an adapter and TCP/IP networking, this discussion assumes that the network instructions are for configuring the network following a fresh installation. If you do not have a network card installed or have not yet configured your network settings, these instructions may be followed completely. Whenever you are configuring networking for Microsoft operating systems, you must have the original CD-ROM accessible during this process. Insert the disk into your CD-ROM drive. Note that for Windows NT, you must be logged on to the PC under the administrator account to be able to carry out this process. If you do not have the network adapter installed in the PC, your first task is to install your network adapter into the PC. Shut it down in the normal manner, then install the network adapter according to the instructions. Switch the PC back on. You will then need to install Windows NT networking according to the following instructions:

1. Open the Control Panel. You can do this in either of two ways. The first option is to select and open (by double-clicking) the My Computer icon, as shown in Figure 6.25, on the desktop. Once the Control Panel icon appears, you need to select and open it, as shown in Figure 6.26.

   The second option is to use the Start button to select Settings and then Control Panel from the choices listed, as shown in Figure 6.27.

   You will be presented with the Control Panel window.
2. In the Control Panel window, select and open the Network icon, as shown in Figure 6.28. This will open the Network dialog box, as shown in Figure 6.29.

Figure 6.25 The My Computer icon.

Figure 6.26 The Control Panel icon.

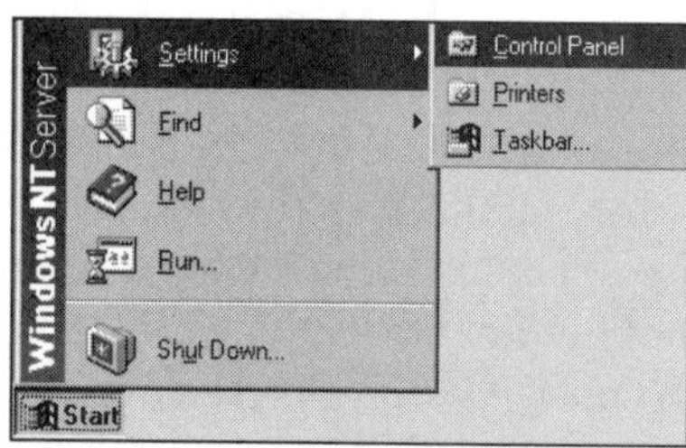

Figure 6.27 Opening the Control Panel from the Start menu.

Figure 6.28 The Control Panel with the Network icon selected.

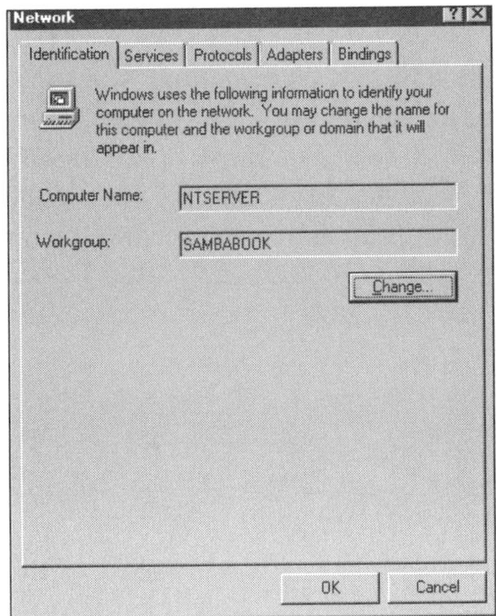

Figure 6.29 The Network dialog box.

To set up a network for use with Samba, you need to have the following network components installed:

- *Client for Microsoft Networks*
- *Network adapter*—Some type of Ethernet card
- *Protocol*—TCP/IP (NWLink IPX/SPX and NWLink NetBIOS are optional because they do not interfere with a TCP/IP network operating; however, you may remove these protocols if you plan to use only TCP/IP networking).

3. You need to manually add the adapter that you have added to the system. Select the Adapter tab, then click on Add. You should see the Select Network Adapter dialog box, as shown in Figure 6.30. You will need to select the manufacturer and model of your network adapter. Not all the currently available network adapters are included in this list. If yours does not appear, insert the floppy or CD-ROM containing the software drivers that came with your network adapter into the PC and click on Have Disk. Find and select the appropriate choices for your system, then click on OK.
4. You need to select the Protocols tab, which should appear as shown in Figure 6.31.

   Select the TCP/IP protocol, as shown in the figure. Insert the Windows NT CD-ROM or indicate the source of the Windows NT software when you are prompted to do so.
5. The TCP/IP protocol needs to be configured. Click on Properties on the Protocols tab. The dialog box should appear as shown in Figure 6.32.

   You need to enter the values for the IP address settings. Enter the appropriate values for your system. In this case, the Windows NT system is being set to 192.168.1.10 on network 192.168.1.0 with a netmask of 255.255.255.0 and a default gateway of 192.168.1.1. You need to set up the DNS settings for your system. Select the DNS tab of the dialog box to bring up the dialog box shown in Figure 6.33.

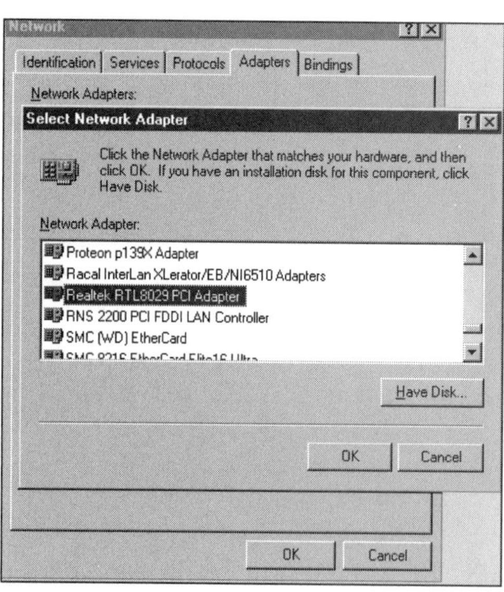

Figure 6.30 The Select Network Adapter dialog box.

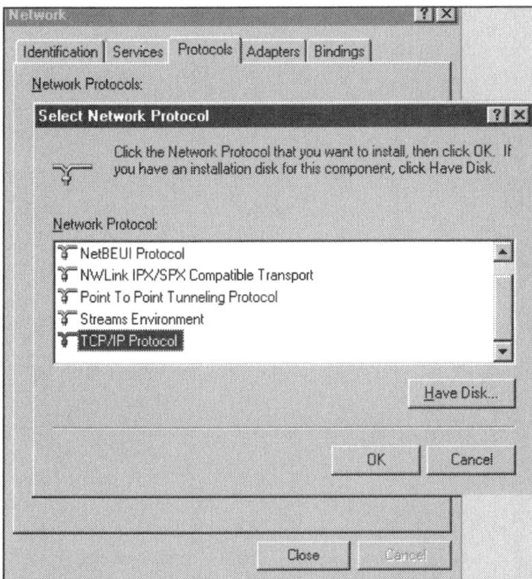

Figure 6.31 The Select Network Protocol dialog box.

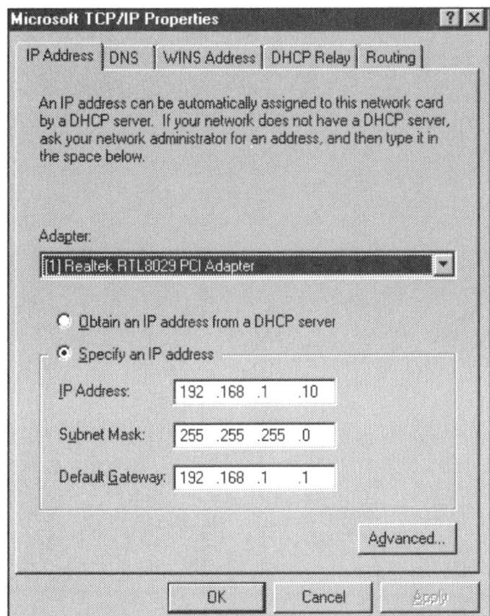

Figure 6.32 The Microsoft TCP/IP Properties dialog box.

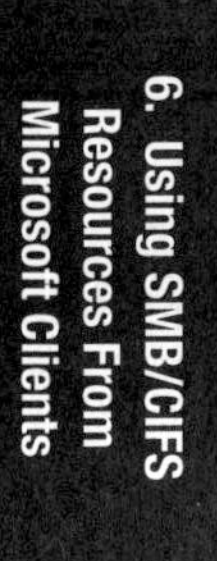

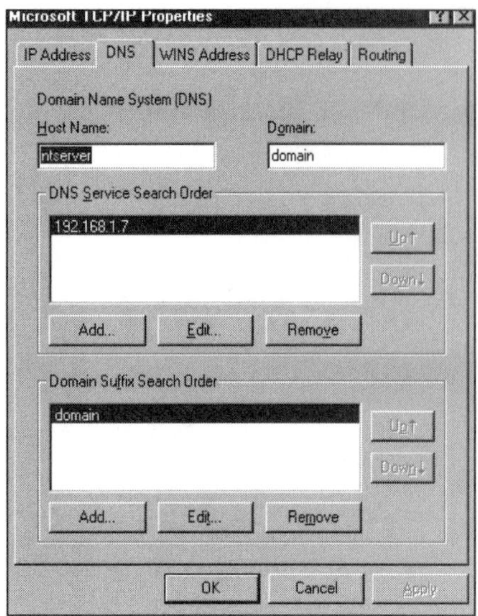

Figure 6.33   The DNS tab of the Microsoft TCP/IP Properties dialog box.

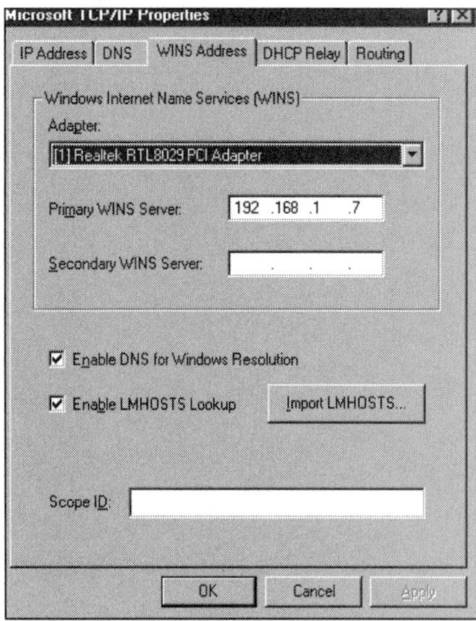

Figure 6.34   The WINS Address tab of the Microsoft TCP/IP Properties dialog box.

You now need to set up the WINS settings, as shown in Figure 6.34.

6. You need to name your PC for the network. In the Network dialog box, select the Identification tab and enter the computer name and the computer description. The default in Windows NT for Workgroups is DOMAIN. Figure 6.35 shows a selection of these entries.

7. The system will respond with a dialog box that welcomes you to the workgroup, as shown in Figure 6.36.
8. After installing all the software, you might be asked to insert floppies or CD-ROMs for adding driver or operating system software. You will be presented with a Network Settings Change dialog box, as shown in Figure 6.37. You will need to reboot the PC to enable the configuration to be altered as entered and to be made active. Clicking on Yes will restart your computer and allow this process to occur.

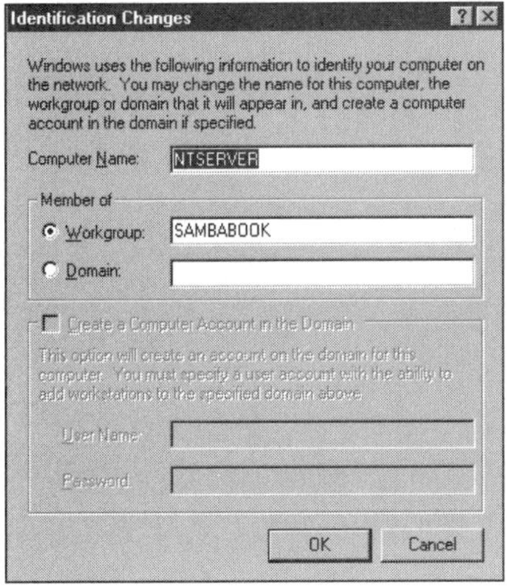

Figure 6.35 The Identification Changes dialog box.

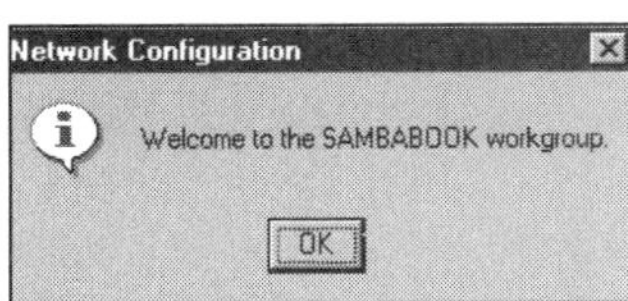

Figure 6.36 The Welcome dialog box.

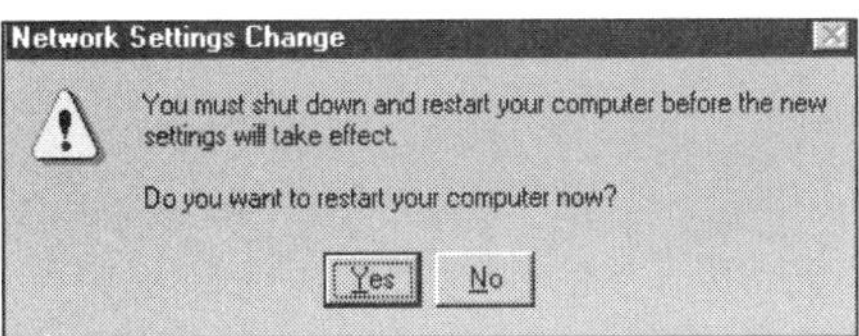

Figure 6.37 The Network Settings Change dialog box.

9. You need to ensure that the workstation service has been included and started on your machine. On the Services tab, be sure that the Workstation service exists, as shown in Figure 6.38, and on the Services tab in the Control Panel check that the Workstation service is set to start automatically, as shown in Figure 6.39.

   Your new networking setting will now be in place, and you should have Microsoft NT installed on your PC with TCP/IP networking installed and configured. Many good books are available to help you install network adapters into Microsoft Windows PCs (see Appendix B).

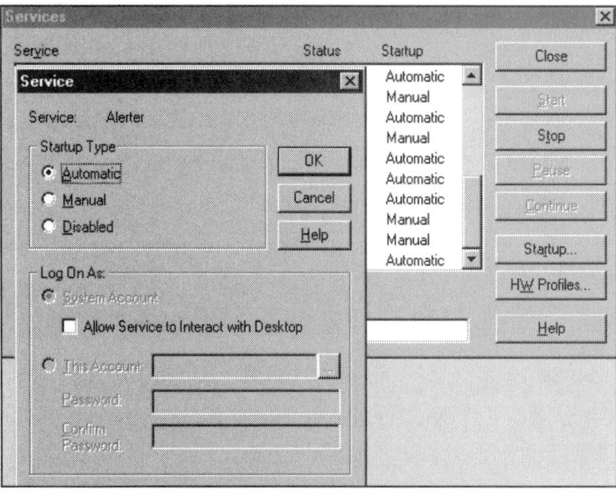

Figure 6.38 The Workstation service.

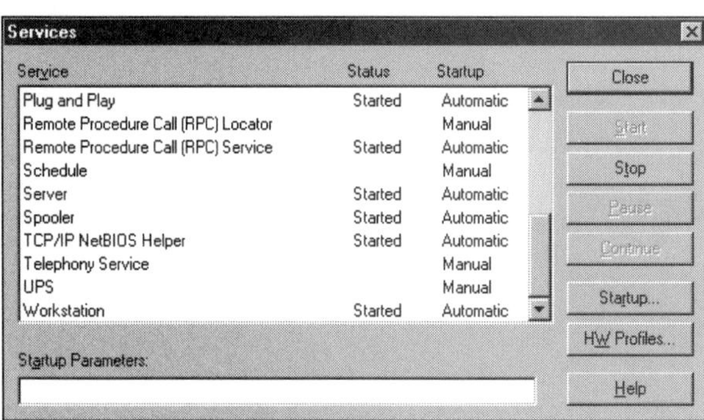

Figure 6.39 The Workstation service starts automatically.

Setting Up A DOS Client To Use SMB/CIFS Resources

Many people are surprised that Microsoft DOS is still in existence. The original version was being used on the Intel 8086 CPU over a decade and a half ago. This surprise is probably due to the limited ability of this operating system to use the types and kinds of software that we have become accustomed to. The graphical games and word processing packages commonly used today need large amounts of memory, and DOS is not able to offer these memory capabilities, being limited to 640KB.

However, DOS-based applications are seeing some considerable longevity in one area: in the setup of operating systems, software, and the current disk-copying software that will create disk images that can be placed onto a network volume. Setting up either Windows 95/98 or Windows NT on a machine without a CD-ROM is nearly impossible; however, it can be done with a network-mountable CD-ROM on either a Samba server or another SMB host.

To create the DOS client, you need to set up a DOS boot disk that contains Microsoft Network Client 3.0 for DOS software. This is available from Microsoft on the Internet at **ftp://ftp.microsoft.com/bussys/Clients/MSCLIENT/** and is included with the Windows NT Server operating system's CD-ROM. The software is available as two self-extracting executables contained in the \clients\msclient\disks directory. An already extracted source is present in the \clients\msclient\netsetup\ directory. You will find a readme.txt file that contains a set of release notes that you should read before proceeding.

If you use the two disk images DSK3-1.EXE and DSK3-2.EXE, you need to copy and then extract these to a staging location from which you will build the DOS client. To build the client, you need to run the setup program from the staging area. The initial screen of the program is shown in Figure 6.40.

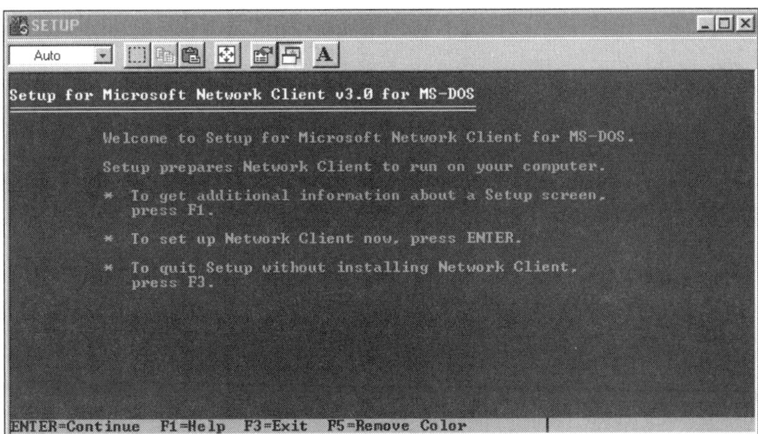

Figure 6.40 Initial Microsoft Client setup.

The system then requests that you specify the path for the setup files. It then prompts you for the default username, as shown in Figure 6.41.

The next option is to specify the default username, computer NetBIOS name, workgroup name, and domain name. The dialog box shown in Figure 6.42 provides a link to the dialog box for the names, setup options, and network configuration. The Names option is shown in Figure 6.43.

After the names have been entered, two more options are available. The first of these is to configure the setup options. These options are as follows:

- Change Redir options
- Change Startup options

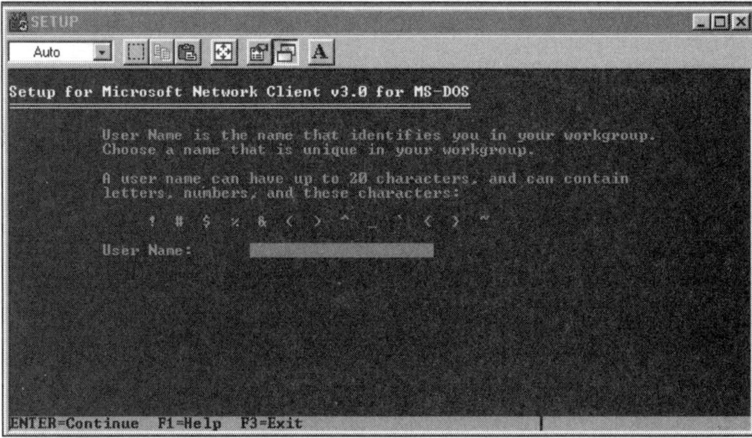

Figure 6.41 The default username.

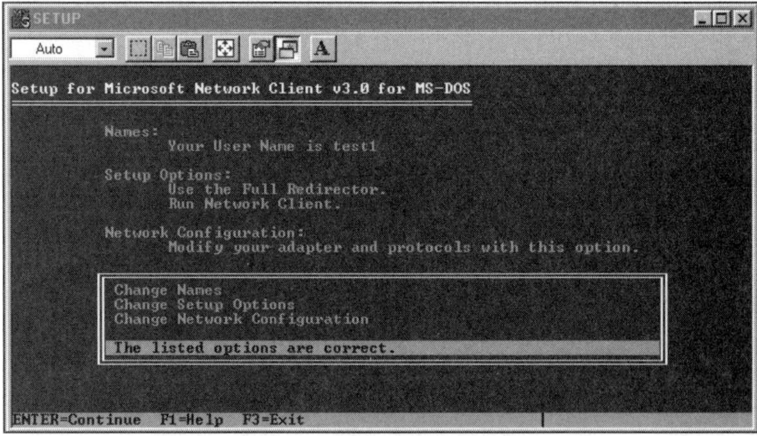

Figure 6.42 The options.

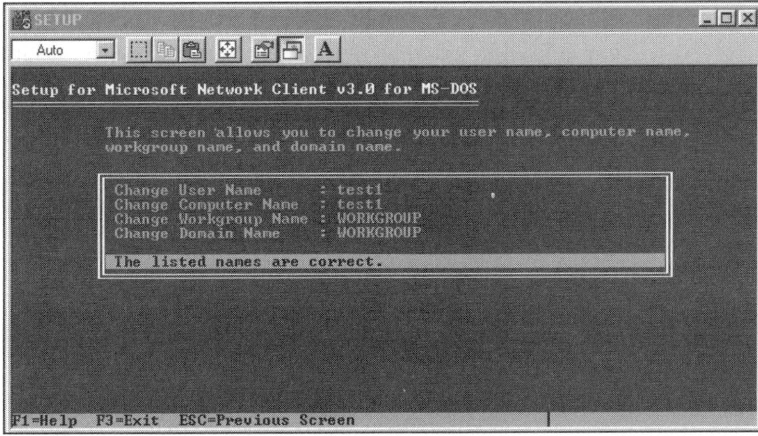

Figure 6.43 The Names option.

- Change Logon Validation
- Change Net Pop Hot Key

The first option specifies whether you will use the full or the basic redirector. If you choose to use the full one, you will be able to log on to a domain. The basic redirector will allow only mounting shares and printers. Startup Options gives you the choice of running the network client with and without a pop-up and no network client. Logon Validation specifies whether to log on to a domain. The Net Pop Hot Key is a hot key.

The next option is to change the network configuration. This will default to the IPX/SPX protocol. You need to delete the adapter and choose a network adapter to use from a list of network adapters, as shown in Figure 6.44.

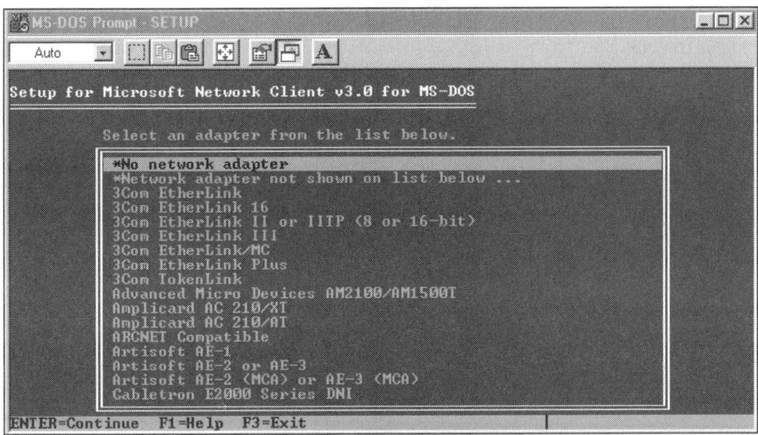

Figure 6.44 Network adapter choices.

This list is fairly limited but lengthy. You should ensure that the Ethernet card on the system has a disk driver available as an NDIS2 driver. Most Ethernet adapters include these as a matter of course.

The setup will then edit the autoexec.bat and config.sys files if they are present or will create them if they are not. The autoexec.bat and config.sys files on the system will appear, similar to those shown in Listings 6.4 and 6.5.

Listing 6.4 The autoexec.bat file.

```
PROMPT $p$g
PATH a:\NET;a:\dos
a:\NET\net initialize
a:\NET\netbind.com
a:\NET\umb.com
a:\NET\tcptsr.exe
a:\NET\tinyrfc.exe
a:\NET\nmtsr.exe
a:\NET\emsbfr.exe
a:\NET\net start
```

Listing 6.5 The config.sys file.

```
device=a:\dos\himem.sys
device=a:\dos\emm386.exe noems
buffers=40,0
files=100
dos=high, umb
device=a:\net\ifshlp.sys
lastdrive=z
```


The system then restarts, at which point you will be prompted for a username password, depending on the information provided during setup.

To create a bootable DOS client disk, you will need to create a boot floppy by issuing the format a: /s command to copy over the system to the floppy. Copy the autoexec.bat and config.sys files over and edit the paths for A:. Then create two directories on the floppy: a:\dos and a:\net. Into a:\dos, copy a few essential DOS utilities and programs. Into a:\net, copy over some of the files from the net directory. You are advised to copy the following files:

- net.exe
- netbind.com
- umb.com
- tcptsr.exe

- tinyrfc.exe
- nmtsr.exe
- emsbfr.exe
- netbind.com
- connect.dat
- protman.exe
- pcind.dos (the Ethernet NDIS2 driver)
- tcpdrv.dos
- nemm.dos
- system.ini
- protocol.ini
- tcputils.ini
- net.msg
- neth.msg
- shares.pwl
- ifshlp.sys
- ping.exe
- hosts
- lmhosts
- networks
- protocol
- services
- wfwsys.cfg

To use the boot floppy, restart the system with the floppy inserted. After the system reboots, you will be prompted for a username password, depending on the information provided during setup. Then, after creating a local entry for the password (if required), the **net use** and **net view** commands may be used as with the Windows 95 option. The disk could be used in the case in which a central file server contains copies of an operating system ready for installation or copies of other software, perhaps for disk copying.

Connecting To An SMB/CIFS Server

Connecting a Windows PC to an SMB/CIFS server, Samba or otherwise, using SMB (NetBIOS over TCP/IP) involves the same processes regardless of the server type.

Connecting to an SMB/CIFS server can be done by a few different methods. One method uses Windows Network Neighborhood. Another method uses a command line DOS-based interface. The Network Neighborhood is available from the desktop as the Network Neighborhood icon, as shown in Figure 6.45.

The Network Neighborhood also appears in the Explorer program, as shown in Figure 6.46.

A third method uses the Find: Computer option from the Start menu, as shown in Figure 6.47. This method also uses a version of the Network Neighborhood application.

Finally, the SMB/CIFS server can be accessed through a command line interface with the DOS **net** command. This command has a number of different options that can be displayed by entering "net" at a command prompt. Listing 6.6 shows the output produced.

Listing 6.6 The net command.

```
For more information about a specific Microsoft NET
command, type the command name followed by /?
(for example, NET VIEW /?).

NET CONFIG   Displays your current workgroup settings.
NET DIAG     Runs the Microsoft Network Diagnostics program to
             display diagnostic information about your network.
NET HELP     Provides information about commands and
             error messages.
NET INIT     Loads protocol and network-adapter drivers without
             binding them to Protocol Manager.
NET LOGOFF   Breaks the connection between your computer and
             the shared resources to which it is connected.
NET LOGON    Identifies you as a member of a workgroup.
NET PASSWORD Changes your logon password.
NET PRINT    Displays information about print queues
             and controls print jobs.
NET START    Starts services.
NET STOP     Stops services.
NET TIME     Displays the time on or synchronizes your computer's
             clock with the clock on a Microsoft Windows for
```

```
                Workgroups, Windows NT, Windows 95, or NetWare time
                server.
NET USE         Connects to or disconnects from a shared resource or displays
                information about connections.
NET VER         Displays the type and version number of the
                workgroup redirector you are using.
NET VIEW        Displays a list of computers that share
                resources or a list of shared resources
                on a specific computer.
The command was completed successfully.
```

Figure 6.45 The Network Neighborhood icon.

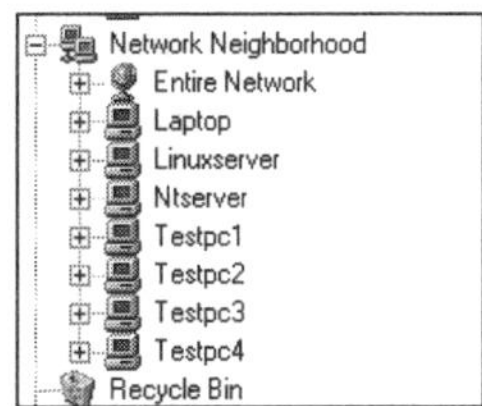

Figure 6.46 Network Neighborhood in Explorer.

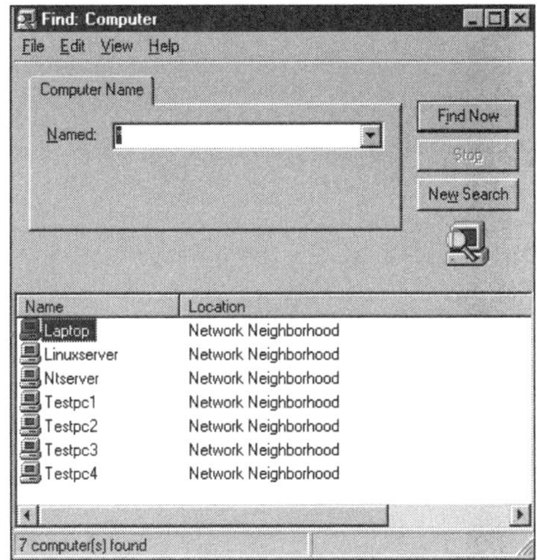

Figure 6.47 The Find: Computer dialog box.

The specific additional **net** parameters that we are concerned with are **use** and **view**, descriptions of which are shown in Listings 6.7 to 6.10.

Listing 6.7 The **net use** command in Windows 9x.

```
Connects or disconnects your computer from a shared
resource or displays information about your
connections.

NET USE [drive: | *] [\\computer\directory [password | ?]]
    [/SAVEPW:NO] [/YES] [/NO]
NET USE [port:] [\\computer\printer [password | ?]]
    [/SAVEPW:NO] [/YES] [/NO]

NET USE drive: | \\computer\directory /DELETE [/YES]
NET USE port: | \\computer\printer /DELETE [/YES]
NET USE * /DELETE [/YES]

NET USE drive: | * /HOME

  drive       Specifies the drive letter you assign to a
              shared directory.
  *           Specifies the next available drive letter.
              If used with /DELETE, specifies to
              disconnect all of your connections.
  port        Specifies the parallel (LPT) port name you
              assign to a shared printer.
  computer    Specifies the name of the computer sharing
              the resource.
  directory   Specifies the name of the shared directory.
  printer     Specifies the name of the shared printer.
  password    Specifies the password for the shared
              resource, if any.
  ?           Specifies that you want to be prompted for the
              password of the shared resource. You don't
              need to use this option unless the password is
              optional.
  /SAVEPW:NO  Specifies that the password you type
              should not be saved in your password-list
              file. You need to retype the password the
              next time you connect to this resource.
  /YES        Carries out the NET USE command without
              first prompting you to provide information or
              confirm actions.
  /DELETE     Breaks the specified connection to a shared
              resource.
```

```
  /NO         Carries out the NET USE command, responding
              with NO automatically when you are prompted
              to confirm actions.
  /HOME       Makes a connection to your HOME directory if
              one is specified in your LAN Manager or
              Windows NT user account.

To list all of your connections, type NET USE without
options.
```

Listing 6.8 The **net use** command in Windows NT.

```
NET USE [devicename | *] [\\computername\sharename [\volume]
  [password | *]]
    [/USER:[domainname]username]
    [[/DELETE] | [/PERSISTENT:{YES | NO}]]
NET USE [devicename | *] [password | *]] [/HOME]
NET USE [/PERSISTENT:{YES | NO}]

  devicename   Specifies the drive letter you assign to a
               shared directory.
  *            Specifies the next available drive letter.
               If used with /DELETE, specifies to
               disconnect all of your connections.
  computername Specifies the name of the computer sharing
               the resource.
  sharename    Specifies the name of the shared directory.
  password     Specifies the password for the shared
               resource, if any.
  /PERSISTENT  Specifies if the share should be maintained
               until the next time you reboot the PC.
  /DELETE      Breaks the specified connection to a shared
               resource.
  /HOME        Makes a connection to your HOME directory if
               one is specified in your LAN Manager or
               Windows NT user account.

To list all of your connections, type NET USE without
options.
```

Listing 6.9 The **net view** command in Windows 9x.

```
Displays a list of computers in a specified workgroup or
the shared resources available on a specified computer.

  NET VIEW [\\computer] [/YES]
  NET VIEW [/WORKGROUP:wgname] [/YES]
```

```
  computer     Specifies the name of the computer whose
               shared resources you want to see listed.
  /WORKGROUP   Specifies that you want to view the names
               of the computers in another workgroup that
               share resources.
  wgname       Specifies the name of the workgroup whose
               computer names you want to view.
  /YES         Carries out the NET VIEW command without
               first prompting you to provide information or
               confirm actions.

To display a list of computers in your workgroup that share
resources, type NET VIEW without options.
```

Listing 6.10 The net view command in Windows NT.

```
Displays a list of computers in a specified workgroup or
the shared resources available on a specified computer.

  NET VIEW [\\computername | /DOMAIN[:domainname]]

  computername Specifies the name of the computer whose
               shared resources you want to see listed.
  /DOMAIN      Specifies that you want to view the names
               of the computers in another domain that
               share resources.

To display a list of computers in your workgroup that share
resources, type NET VIEW without options.
```


Connecting To And Using A Share On An SMB/CIFS Server

Using the Network Neighborhood dialog box, select the server you want and open it by double-clicking on it or selecting File|Open or File|Explore from the menu. A window will appear, containing a list of the shares that you can browse in this session. Figure 6.48 shows the window that is displayed when connecting to the LINUXSERVER as the test1 user from a Windows 95 PC. You can immediately see that four shares are displayed: the file shares [groupshare] and [test1], and the printer shares [hp] and [printers].

Likewise, the same list can be obtained by entering "net view \\linuxserver" at the command prompt. This responds with a text version of the server share information. Listing 6.11 displays this information.

Listing 6.11 LINUXSERVER from the command line.

```
Shared resources at \\LINUXSERVER
Sharename     Type         Comment
---------------------------------
groupshare    Disk         Group Share
hp            Print        hp deskjet
printers      Print        All Printers
test1         Disk         Home Directories
The command was completed successfully.
```

By using either method to determine the share that you want to use, you are able to map this share to your local system so that it appears as if it is connected to the PC as either a permanent or a temporary connection. In the Windows version, you may browse to the share you want to use and make changes directly to a file or directory contained within, depending on permissions.

As an example, let's map the [test1] share to the local PC system as the H: drive. The process in the Network Neighborhood version involves highlighting or selecting the share and either right-clicking on it to bring up the options menu or using the File menu and selecting the Map Network Drive option. The right-click option list is shown in Figure 6.49.

Figure 6.48 LINUXSERVER in Network Neighborhood.

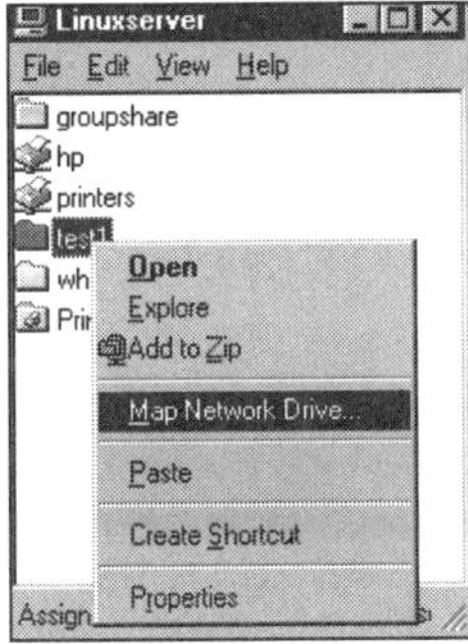

Figure 6.49 The Map Network Drive option.

With Windows 95/98 and NT, Network Neighborhood responds with a Map Network Drive dialog box, as shown in Figure 6.50 for Windows 9x and in Figure 6.51 for Windows NT, with choices for Drive: and Connect As: (Windows NT only) and a Reconnect At Logon checkbox. The choice of drive will default to the next available drive letter (only A: to Z: are available). In this case, we will make this a map to the H: drive, make it a temporary share, and connect as the test1 user.

The [test1] share will now be present on the local PC as the H: drive as in Figure 6.52.

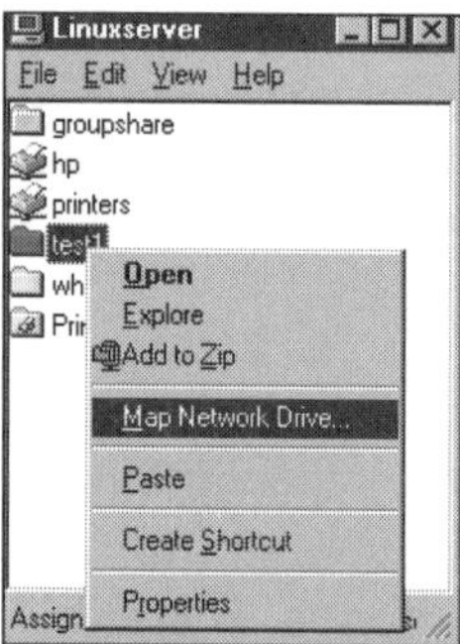

Figure 6.50 The Map Network Drive dialog box in Windows 95/98.

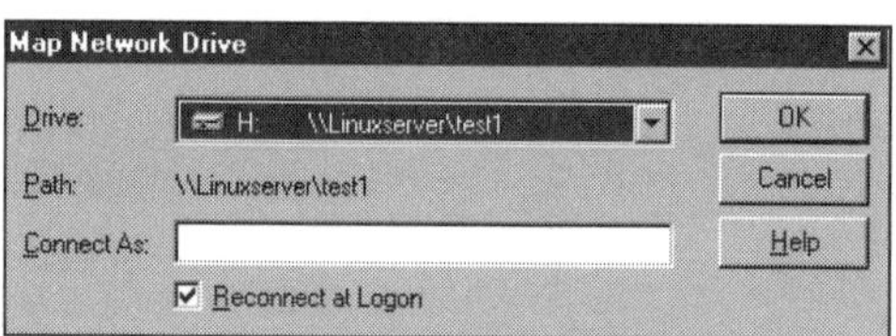

Figure 6.51 The Map Network Drive dialog box in Windows NT.

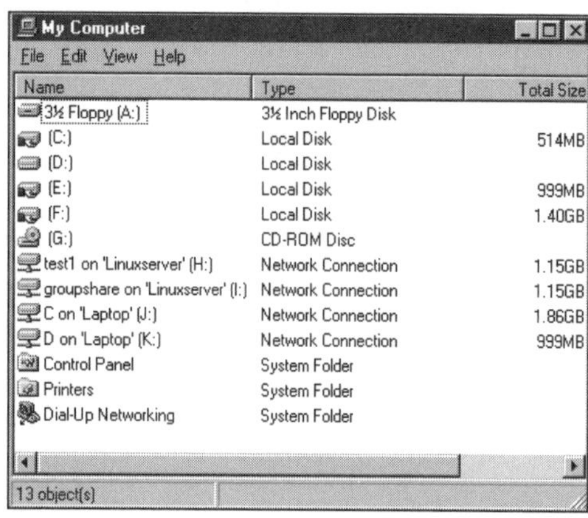

Figure 6.52 The mapped network drive.

The process in the command line version involves using the **net use** command with the full UNC path of the share required and specifying which drive you want to share the drive as on the local machine. The command line in this case is "net use H: \\LINUXSERVER\test1." This maps the share permanently in Windows 9x and temporarily in Windows NT (it is not possible to make this permanent by using the /persistent:yes switch); this mapping is then re-created at the next logon to the system. Likewise, it is possible to allow the mapping to use the first available drive letter by substituting the "*" character in place of the drive letter in the command line. As you can see from the options in Listings 6.7 and 6.8, it is also possible to alter the user and even the workgroup or domain to which the member belongs with the **net use** command.

The DOS client is able to map to the SMB/CIFS server using the **net view** and **net use** commands in an identical manner to that used in the Windows 95 option. When the DOS client system boots, you will be requested for a password to the server on the basis of the details that you entered when configuring the boot disk. The **net.exe** command can then be used to view and mount shares as before. The [test1] share will now be present on the local PC as the H: drive. The process is the same for mapping another drive on this or another SMB/CIFS server.

NOTE: *The DOS client and the Windows 95 client will exhibit the same property in that once a username and password pair to an SMB/CIFS server has been used in a session, the same username and password pair will be used for all subsequent connections from that client. Similarly, once an NT client has established one session to a server, all subsequent connections will attempt to use the same username and password even if you specify it correctly. Two possible workarounds involve "fooling" the smbd process into thinking that this is a new connection session. The options involve establishing an alternate NetBIOS name alias in the smb.conf file so that the server can announce it as a separate server. This way, several additional connections with different user credentials can exist on the server from the same client.*

Connecting To And Using A Printer On An SMB/CIFS Server

In an identical manner to that used when using the file shares on SMB/CIFS servers, use either the Network Neighborhood dialog box or the command line options to identify the printer share of interest. Figure 6.53 contains the window that is displayed when connecting to the LINUXSERVER as the test1 user from a Windows 95 PC. You can immediately see that four shares are displayed: the file shares [groupshare] and [test1], and the printer shares [hp] and [printers].

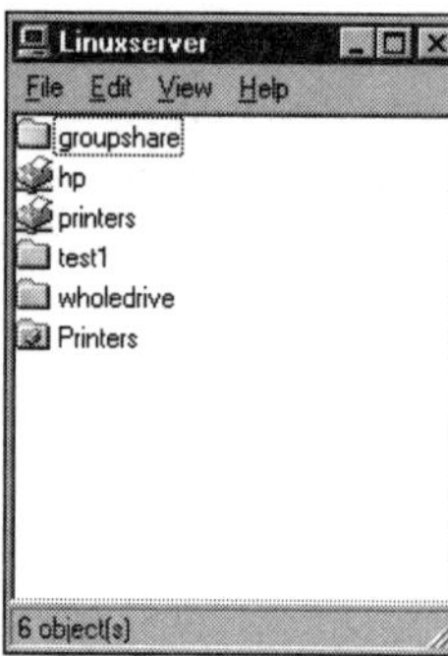

Figure 6.53 LINUXSERVER in Network Neighborhood.

Likewise, the same list can be obtained by entering "net view \\linuxserver" at the command prompt. This responds with a text version of the server share information. Listing 6.12 displays this information.

Listing 6.12 LINUXSERVER from the command line.

```
Shared resources at \\LINUXSERVER
Sharename    Type        Comment
--------------------------------
groupshare   Disk        Group Share
hp           Print       hp deskjet
printers     Print       All Printers
test1        Disk        Home Directories
The command was completed successfully.
```


By using either method to determine the share that you want to use, you are able to map this share to your local system so that it appears as if it is connected to the PC as either a permanent or a temporary connection. In the Windows version, you may browse to the share you want to use and make changes directly to a file or directory contained within, depending on permissions.

As an example, let's map the [hp] printer to the local PC system as LPT2. The process in the Network Neighborhood version involves highlighting or selecting the printer and either right-clicking on it to bring up the options menu or using the File menu and selecting the Capture Printer Port option. The right-click option list is shown in Figure 6.54.

With Windows 95/98, Network Neighborhood responds with a Capture Printer Port dialog box, shown in Figure 6.55 for Windows 9x, with a choice of Device: and a Reconnect At Logon checkbox. The choice of device will default to the next available port (options for LPT1 to LPT9 are available). In this case, we will make this a map to LPT2 and make it a temporary share.

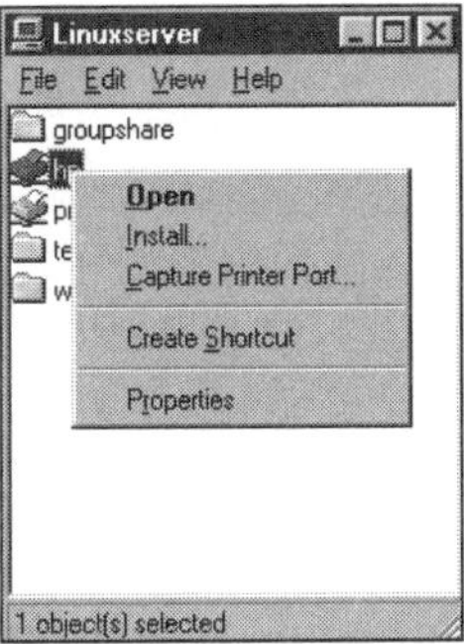

Figure 6.54 The Capture Printer Port option.

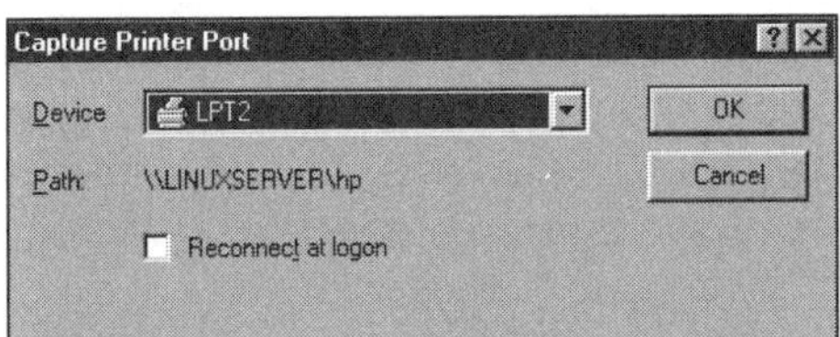

Figure 6.55 The Capture Printer Port dialog box.

The [hp] printer from LINUXSERVER will now be present on the local PC as LPT2.

The process in the command line version involves using the **net use** command with the full UNC path of the printer required, specifying which printer port you want to share the printer as on the local machine. The command line in this case is "net use LPT2 \\LINUXSERVER\hp." This maps the printer permanently in Windows 9x (in Windows NT, it is possible to make this permanent by using the /persistent:yes switch); this mapping is then re-created at the next logon to the system. Note that for printer shares it is not possible to use the wildcard option by substituting the "*" character in place of the printer port in the command line. This will result in a System Error 66, as the network resource type cannot be defined. As you can see from the options shown previously in Listings 6.7 and 6.8, it is also possible to alter the user and even the workgroup or domain to which the client belongs with the **net use** command.

The DOS client is able to map to the SMB/CIFS server using the **net view** and **net use** commands in an identical manner to that used in the Windows 95 option. When the DOS client system boots, you will be requested for a password to the server on the basis of the details that you entered when configuring the boot disk. The **net.exe** command can then be used to view and mount shares as before. The [hp] printer share will now be present on the local PC as LPT2 as in Figure 6.56.

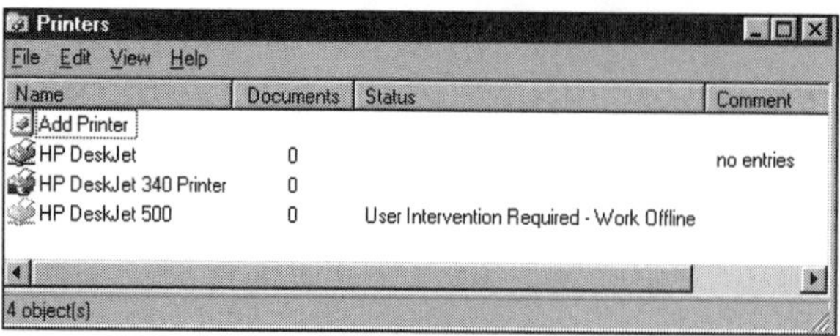

Figure 6.56 The mapped printer.

The same process is repeated to map another printer on this or another SMB/CIFS server.

NOTE: *The DOS client and the Windows 95 client will exhibit the same property in that once a username and password pair to an SMB/CIFS server has been used in a session, the same username and password pair will be used for all subsequent connections from that client. Similarly, once an NT client has established one session to a server, all subsequent connections will attempt to use the same username and password even if you specify it correctly. Two possible workarounds involve "fooling" the smbd process into thinking that this is a new connection session. The options involve establishing an alternate NetBIOS name alias in the smb.conf file so that the server can announce it as a separate server. This way, several additional connections with different user credentials can exist on the server from the same client.*

Disconnecting A File Or Printer Share From An SMB/CIFS Server

The PC "test1pc", which has shares to the [groupshare] on the LINUXSERVER as the H: drive and a share to the [groupshare] on the NTSERVER as the I: drive, and the two printers are shared as LPT2 and LPT3. The share that you want to disconnect is the I: drive.

Disconnecting a file or printer share can be done in two ways. The first involves selecting the share in My Computer or Explorer and selecting File|Disconnect, as shown in Figure 6.57.

Alternatively, you can use the command line options. This would require the user first confirming which services are currently being used with a **net use** command. The output of running the **net use** command is shown in Listing 6.13.

Listing 6.13 The net use command output.

```
C:\>net use
Status          Local name      Remote name
OK              H:              \\LINUXSERVER\groupshare
```

```
OK              I:              \\NTSERVER\groupshare
OK              LPT2            \\LINUXSERVER\hp
OK              LPT3            \\NTSERVER\hp
The command was completed successfully.
```

Once the resource that you want to remove has been identified, you should issue the following command:

```
net use H: /d
```

or

```
net use H: /DELETE
```

The share will no longer be available.

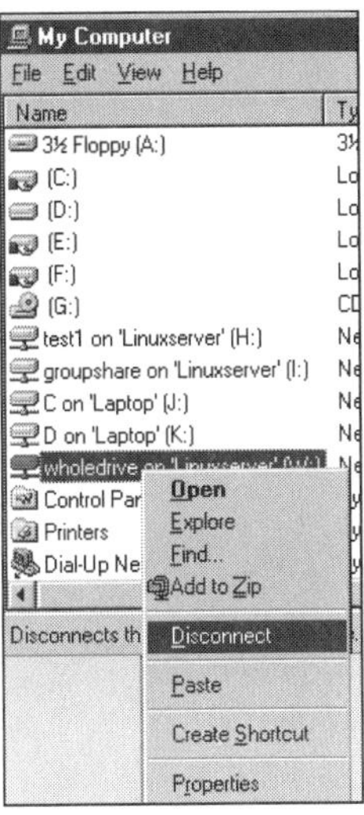

Figure 6.57 Disconnecting a file or printer share from an SMB/CIFS server.

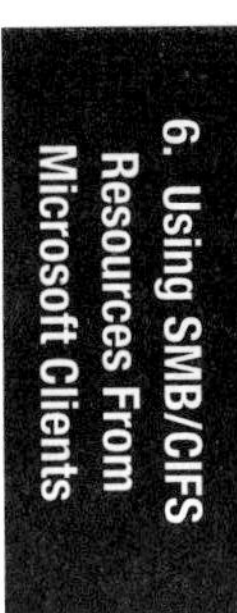

Chapter 7

Using SMB/CIFS Resources From Unix Machines

In Depth

Although it is usually expected that a Samba server and its resources will be used by Microsoft Windows clients, this is not always the case. Unix clients can also be configured to make use of SMB/CIFS resources. The core of these is available from the Samba distribution; however, smbfs SMB/CIFS file system support is available separately, and alternative versions of the smbmount and smbumount programs are available as well. These additional components require further steps to obtain or use them.

I first used the suite of software that is included in the Samba distribution to provide the ability to share data between several Unix systems rather than between Unix and Windows systems. The suite of software that can be used by Unix clients to access SMB/CIFS resources include the following:

- **smbclient**
- smbfs, **smbmount** (two versions), **smbumount** (two versions), and **smbmnt**
- **smbwrapper**
- smbprint
- smbtar

All of these are not part of the Samba distribution, but they will allow a Unix client to operate as an SMB/CIFS client and to access SMB/CIFS servers, including those of Microsoft and Samba.

smbclient

This program is run from a number of other programs, but it is also used from the command line, where it can operate in a similar manner to FTP. smbclient has more flexibility than the FTP program, and, in addition to the more usual file and directory operations that you would expect of FTP, it can be used to run commands on remote systems, use printers, and even run the archiving utility tar.

smbclient has many options, all of which follow the following syntax:

```
smbclient smbservicename password options
```

The ***smbservicename*** describes the SMB/CIFS service that is to be used. This can follow a number of different formats, which are shown here:

```
//smbserver/share (UNC style as //NetBIOS name/sharename )
```

or

```
//a.b.c.d/share (//IP address/sharename)
```

In Listing 7.1, the ***password*** is the password required by the user to log in to the SMB authentication server or the specific share password for the user associated with the session.

The ***options*** that follow are described in Table 7.1. You can see the options that are possible by using the **-h** option, as shown in Listing 7.1.

Listing 7.1 The smbclient options as seen from the command line.

```
[root@linuxserver root]# smbclient -h
Added interface ip=192.168.1.4 bcast=192.168.1.255 nmask=255.255.255.0
Usage: smbclient service <password> [options]
Version 2.0.4b
        -s smb.conf            pathname to smb.conf file
        -B IP addr             broadcast IP address to use
        -O socket_options      socket options to use
        -R name resolve order  use these name resolution services only
        -M host                send a winpopup message to the host
        -i scope               use this NetBIOS scope
        -N                     don't ask for a password
        -n netbios name.       use this name as my netbios name
        -d debuglevel          set the debuglevel
        -P                     connect to service as a printer
        -p port                connect to the specified port
        -l log basename.       basename for log/debug files
        -h                     print this help message
        -I dest IP             use this IP to connect to
        -E                     write messages to stderr instead of stdout
        -U username            set the network username
        -L host                get a list of shares available on a host
        -t terminal code       terminal i/o code
                               {sjis|euc|jis7|jis8|junet|hex}
        -m max protocol        set the max protocol level
        -W workgroup           set the workgroup name
        -T<c|x>IXFqgbNan       command line tar
        -D directory           start from directory
        -c command string      execute semicolon separated commands
[root@linuxserver root]#
```

Table 7.1 smbclient command line options.

Option	Description
-h	A common practice with most Unix commands is to offer a usage page, which is available with smbclient by using the **-h** option.
-s *smb.conf*	This option informs **smbclient** where to locate an alternative smb.conf file that can be used in operation.
-B *IP address*	Without this option, the **smbclient** program broadcasts NetBIOS name requests to determine the host. This option provides the client running the **smbclient** program with the necessary IP broadcast address that should be used to look up the declared host. This can be an advantage in a large network with many hosts.
-O *socket options*	With this option, it is possible to set the TCP options for this specific connection that override those in the smb.conf file.
-R *name resolve order*	Any Samba process uses a series of services to resolve the server name into an IP address. The order defaults to lmhosts, hosts, wins, and finally bcast. With this option, it is possible to set the order as appropriate. When a connection request is made, the resolution of the IP address is attempted with each service in order until no further service is available. If no IP address resolution is possible, the connection request will fail.
-M *NetBIOS name*	The **-M** option allows you to use **smbclient** to send a message to a specific host. This occurs in a similar method to the WinPopup protocol. The NetBIOS name is resolved into an IP address following the default name resolution order.
-N	This option allows for a connection to the service without using a password by suppressing the prompt for a password.
-n *NetBIOS name*	This allows the local client from which you are running the **smbclient** to adopt the NetBIOS name specified as the local system's NetBIOS name. This defaults to an uppercase name by default.
-d *debug level*	When using the **smbclient**, this option is useful when troubleshooting. The values are numerical, and the higher the number, the more information is written to the Samba logs. This defaults to 0, which reports only important warnings and critical errors.
-p *port*	The default SMB/CIFS TCP port number is 139. If you have an SMB/CIFS server that is operating on an alternate port, you should specify it with this option.
-I	Instead of using the normal resolution from NetBIOS name to IP name, the smbclient can be forced to use the IP address directly. This, used with the **-N** option, can be used with Microsoft servers.

(continued)

Table 7.1 ***smbclient command line options*** **(continued).**

Option	Description
-E	This writes any messages to STDERR rather than STDOUT. The default is to send messages to STDOUT.
-U *username*	This specifies the username used in the session request once connected to the server. A number of defaults occur with an **smbclient** session if this is not specified. The first of these is to use an uppercase version of the current session "user" or "logname" environment variable in order. If neither exist, the user "guest" will be specified. The environment variables may be viewed by entering "env" at the command prompt.
-L *NetBIOS name*	This instructs **smbclient** to obtain a list of the services available from the server specified.
-t *terminal code*	With various multibyte character sets in use and with Unix operating with different character sets than Windows, this option allows smbclient to translate from SMB file names to Windows file names. Setting this option indicates that **smbclient** should convert the file names using the appropriate character set. Possible character sets are **sjis** (Shift JIS, Japanese Industrial Standard), euc (Extended Unix Coding system), **jis7** (7-bit JIS), **jis8** (8-bit JIS), junet (Japanese Unix encoding), and **hex** (other multibyte character coding).
-m *max protocol*	This is no longer used in Samba 2.0.0 and later; it is now automatic. This was previously used to force smbclient to use the maximum protocol level the server supports.
-W *workgroup*	This option specifies the workgroup to use when looking up NetBIOS names of an SMB/CIFS server. This overrides the setting in the smb.conf file.
-P	In pre-Samba 2.0.0 versions this option specified the share as a printer. The current versions of Samba do not need to use this option.
-T *tar options*	You might use **smbclient** to create tar archives or files on SMB/CIFS servers. The use of tar in this manner includes a number of other options, which are detailed in Table 7.2.
-D *directory*	This sets the initial directory before starting an operation on the server. It is for use mainly with the tar option (**-T**).
-c *command string*	You can use **smbclient** to execute a command on the server as the connected user rather than the STDIN. The main usage of the **-c** option will be when scripts are to be run.

The **-T** (tar) option has a number of other possible secondary parameters. These are listed in Table 7.2.

To view the environment variables of the current session on the client machine, simply enter "env" at the command prompt. The system should respond with an output similar to that shown in Listing 7.2.

Listing 7.2 Viewing the environment variables.

```
[root@linuxserver root]# env
USERNAME=
HISTSIZE=1000
HOSTNAME=linuxserver.domain
LOGNAME=root
HISTFILESIZE=1000
MAIL=/var/spool/mail/root
TERM=vt100
HOSTTYPE=i386
PATH=/usr/local/bin:/bin:/usr/bin:/usr/X11R6/bin:/root/bin
HOME=/root
SHELL=/bin/bash
PS1=[\u@\h \W]\$
USER=root
BASH_ENV=/root/.bashrc
```

Table 7.2 smbclient -T tar options.

Option	Description
c *tarname file(s)*	Creates a tar of name *tarname*; if none is given, the default of the *file(s)* listed is assumed.
x *tarname file(s)*	Extracts the file(s) from the a tar of name *tarname* back to the remote system.
I *include expression*	Includes the list of files in the expression or directory; if the **r** option is specified, a recursive inclusion will occur.
X *exclude expression*	Excludes the list of files in the expression or directory; if the **r** option is specified, a recursive exclusion will occur.
b *blocksize*	Writes out the tar file in b * byte block sizes. Must be an integer greater than 0.
q	Creates the tar without notifications.
g	Adds the files that have the archive bit set to the tar file only. This option may be used only when the **c** option is included.
N *file*	Includes files into the tar archive that are newer than the specified file.
a	Resets the archive bit on a file once backed up. Used with the **g** and **c** options.
r	Uses the smbclient recursive option for including files or directories.

```
OSTYPE=Linux
SHLVL=2
_=/usr/bin/env
[root@linuxserver root]#
```

What happens when smbclient is invoked? Once a **smbclient** session has been created, the client is presented with a login prompt of the following form:

```
smb:\>
```

The prompt includes "\", which indicates the root level of the resource or share it's connected to. During any navigation through the remote file system, this prompt will show the current directory.

The **smbclient** session can also make use of a number of other options. These are shown in alphanumeric order in Table 7.3.

Table 7.3 smbclient session command options.

Option	Description
? *command* or **help *command***	Responds with a quick description of the command usage.
! *shell command*	Runs the ***shell command*** specified from the current location within the share.
archive *level*	Alters the behavior of the command mget with respect to the DOS/Windows archive bit being set or not on a file. Level 0: The default; instructs **mget** to ignore the archive bit and to retrieve all files and leave the archive bit alone. Level 1: Retrieves only files that have the archive bit set. Level 2: Functions the same as Level 1 but resets the archive bit once retrieved. Level 3: Ignores the archive bit and resets the archive bit on all files retrieved. To query the current archive level, simply use the command with no level set, and smbclient will return the current level.
blocksize *number*	Used by tar to determine how many blocks to read or write at once.
cancel *jobid*	Cancels the *jobid* in the print queue. The **smbclient** sessions need to be connected to the printer share to run this command.
cd *directory*	Changes to the directory specified. The prompt will reflect the new directory. If a long directory name that includes spaces is required, the directory name is enclosed in double quotation marks (for example, **cd "long directory name"**).

(continued)

Table 7.3 *smbclient session command options* (continued).

Option	Description
del *pattern*	Deletes the file or files that agree with the pattern. The standard wildcards of * and ? apply. **Del a*** deletes all files starting with a, **del *a*** deletes all files with an a in the name, and **del a????** deletes all files of five characters in length that start with an a.
dir or **ls**	Returns a directory list output for the current working directory.
du	Returns the space occupied by all files in the current working directory. If used with the recurse command, the directory contents, if they exist from the current working directory, will also be included. The values returned are the number of blocks, with a byte size for each block, and the number of free blocks available.
exit or **quit** or **q**	Terminates the current **smbclient** session.
Get *remote filename local filename*	Copies the remote file specified from the server to the client. If a local file name is given, it renames it; if no local file name is given, the remote file name is maintained.
lcd *directory*	Changes the local directory to the one specified during a smbclient session. Once changed, the new local directory is returned to the session. If no directory is provided, the current local directory is returned to the session prompt.
lowercase	A flag that is toggled on and off. When toggled on, the local file names are the lowercase versions of the remote file names when transferred. The default is **off**, maintaining the case.
mask *expression*	Used at the command prompt before an mput or mget command, this acts as a filter to specify which files to include in the operation. Files that match the given mask expression are included. The default is to include all files, unless specified. The * and ? wildcards can be used with this option.
md or **mkdir *directory***	Creates a directory with the given name in the remote share. The session user will be required to have the necessary permissions to carry out this operation.
mget *expression*	Retrieves all files that match the given expression from the remote server to the local client. Unlike the command line version of FTP from either Unix or Windows, the Samba version will create all subdirectories that are required when any recursive operation occurs. If a large structure of directories is involved, it can be extremely frustrating to create these individually. When used with recursion, the expression selects the directories and the mask will select the files.
more *file*	Retrieves the file specified and displays it within the session (similar to the standard Unix more facility).

(continued)

Table 7.3 ***smbclient session command options*** **(continued).**

Option	Description
mput ***expression***	Places multiple files on the remote SMB/CIFS server according to the expression given. When used with recursion, the expression selects the directories and the mask selects the files to be processed.
newer ***file***	A method of selecting files of a specific date. The date/time stamp of the file specified is used to define the oldest time when any file satisfying other expressions is to be selected for an operation.
print ***file***	Somewhat similar to the put command and functions in the same way. The specified file is printed to the local machine.
printmode ***mode***	The options for the ***mode*** are **graphics** or **text**. **printmode** sets the print mode for all the following print commands. However, this is no longer used with Samba version 2 and later.
prompt	When transferring files, it is possible to set for a confirmation before transfer takes place. The default is on, which then requests confirmation before carrying out any operation. Simply declaring prompt in a **smbclient** session turns this off until the prompt command is reissued. The command is reset between sessions.
put ***local file remote file***	Copies the file specified from the local machine to the remote server. The local file name must always be specified. If no remote file name is declared, the local file name is adopted. However, it is possible to rename the file during the copy operation.
pwd	Returns the current working directory on the remote SMB/CIFS server.
queue	This applies only when connected to printable shares on the remote SMB/CIFS server. The current print queue details are returned.
rd or **rmdir** ***directory***	Removes or deletes the remote directory specified from the SMB/CIFS server. However, the directory must be empty before this command will execute; if any content remains in the directory, the command returns an error. In addition, an error will occur if the connected user does not have the required permissions on the SMB/CIFS file system.
recurse	By default, this is set to off, meaning that all commands run against the current directory only. When set on the **all mput**, **mget**, or **du** command, this will execute against the directories and files that matched any mask or expression specified.
rm ***expression***	Deletes the files that match the given expression.
setmode ***file*** **<[+/-] [r s h a]>**	Sets (**+**) or removes (**-**) the DOS **r** (read only), **s** (system), **h** (hidden), and **a** (archive) attributes for a file or files on a server. Multiple operations are permitted at the same time on the same file or files. This works just like the **DOS attrib** command.

(continued)

***Table 7.3 smbclient session command options* (continued).**

Option	Description
tar **<c x *lxbgNarq parameters*>**	Executes the tar operation. The **c** means create the tar, and **x** means extract from the tar. The options specified are identical to those when using the **smbclient -T** option and are listed in Table 7.2.
tarmode <[no]<full, inc, reset, noreset, system, nosystem, hidden, nohidden, quiet, verbose>>	When running the **tar** command, if this option is set just prior to running it will allow the user to specify in more detail what the tar would include. The options are the following: **full**: The default, which will include all files in the tar **inc**: Includes only those files that have the archive bit set **reset**: Resets the archive bit on all backed-up files **noreset**: Does not change the archive bit on backed-up files **system**: Includes files with the system bit set **nosystem**: Does not include files with the system bit set **hidden**: Include files with the hidden bit set **nohidden**: Does not include files with the hidden bit set **verbose**: Reports on all files included and the status of the operation while running **quiet**: Does not report on the operation while running
translate	In simple text editors, Unix and DOS treat the ends of lines differently. DOS includes a CRLF (Carriage Return/Line Feed), whereas Unix uses only an LF (Line Feed).

smbfs

This is not a program but rather a supported file system. It is not part of the Samba distribution, although smbfs support has been available for some time on Linux systems. This provides support for and makes use of the SMB/CIFS protocol to share file systems between PCs. Its use is very similar to the more common NFS, and as such you could use it to gain access to the SMB/CIFS server's file system. Although support for smbfs might be included (usually in the kernel or a module), you cannot simply include smbfs support and use SMB/CIFS file systems. The NFS file system support makes use of the mount and unmount utilities, but these are not currently written to support smbfs, and alternatives must be used, two of which are the following:

- Use the **smbmount**, **smbumount**, and **smbmnt** programs that come with the current Samba distributions.

- Obtain the smbfs support utilities, including alternate versions of the smbmount and smbumount programs, and use these with the smbfs-capable system.

There is no difference between the functionality of the various **smbmount** and **smbumount** utilities. The major difference from the user's perspective is that the newer versions of the **smbmount**, **smbumount**, and **smbmnt** code included with current Samba releases require the Linux kernel source to be later than 2.1.70 or one of the latest 2.2 kernels.

An smbfs file system behaves similarly to any other NFS-style file system, with one notable exception: smbfs does not currently include support for the maintenance of owner or group privileges on the remote file system. In practice, what this means is that a Linux system utilizing smbfs would be able to mount a share within its local file system from an SMB/CIFS server; however, the real file and directory owner and group details would not necessarily coincide with the displayed values. Therefore, some activities might appear possible from the client's perspective, but the server would not necessarily allow the activity to occur.

To obtain the smbfs packages for Linux, you need to obtain smbfs-2.x from one of the Linux distribution sites. The current version is 2.0.2-1, which includes a security patch that overcomes a problem with root vulnerability in version 2.0.1. A copy of the tgz and RPM versions have been included on this book's CD-ROM under \smbfs.

The following is an excerpt from the readme file from the smbfs distribution from Volker Lendecke, with whose kind permission it is reproduced here:

> . . . smbfs is usable with Linux kernels 1.2 and above. For safe usage of smbfs, I strongly recommend to use Linux 2.0.28 and above.
>
> For the latest versions of smbfs & co., you might want to look at **http://www.kki.org/linux-lan/**.
>
> In release 2.0.0 of smbfs, I removed the kernel module for Linux 1.2.x. If you are still using 1.2.x, please get smbfs-0.10 from **ftp://ftp.gwdg.de/pub/linux/misc/smbfs**.
>
> INSTALLATION
>
> For using smbfs, I _strongly_ suggest to upgrade to Linux kernel 2.0.28. It fixes bugs in smbfs that severely affect the stability of your machine. To use smbfs, you have to enable it when you configure your kernel. If you have Windows 95 machines to connect to, please enable the switch in the configuration when you are asked for it. It slows down the listing of directories, to give Windows 95 a chance to answer the requests. If you will never connect to Windows 95, you can disable the option.

smbfs is an on-going effort. When I find bugs that affect the machine's stability, then I send the fixes to Linus. But there are others that fix problems with specific servers. I regard these as low priority fixes, which are not immediately sent to Linus. I will release them together with the smbfs packages. The patches are distributed as smbfs-2.0.xx-y.diff. Please do the following steps before configuring and building your kernel. Please always use a fresh, unpatched 2.0.28 source tree.

```
cd /usr/src/linux
patch -p1 </path/to/smbfs/smbfs-2.0.xx-y.diff
```

After this, you can build your kernel.

To compile and install the smbfs utilities smbmount and smbumount, please do a

```
make
make install
```

in the directory you find this README in. To do the make install, you have to be root. Please note that smbmount and smbumount are installed setuid root to allow normal users to mount their own shares.

LIMITATIONS

The limitations smbfs has are the natural limitations of the SMB protocol, which was designed with MS-DOS based PCs in mind. The first limitation is the lack of uid, gid and permission information per file. You have to assign those values once for a complete mounted directory.

The second limitation is just as annoying as the first: You cannot re-export a smb-mounted directory by nfs. It is not possible because the NFS protocol defines access to files through unique file handles, which can be mapped to the device and inode numbers in unix NFS servers. SMB does not have unique numbers per file, you only have the path name. I implemented a caching scheme for inode numbers, which gives unique inode numbers for every open file in the system. This is just sufficient for local use of the files, because you can tell when an inode number can be discarded. With NFS the situation is different. You can never know when the client will access the file-id you offered, so you would have to cache the inode numbers indefinitely long. I think this should not be done in kernel mode, as it would require an unlimited amount of RAM.

AUTOMOUNTING

I received the following amd map file entries from Andrew Tridgell:

laplandc type:=program;mount:="/sbin/smbmount smbmount //lapland/c ${fs} -P XXXX -u 148";unmount:="/sbin/umount umount ${fs}"

laplandd type:=program;mount:="/sbin/smbmount smbmount //lapland/d ${fs} -P XXXX -u 148";unmount:="/sbin/umount umount ${fs}"

Security Issue: Root Exploit Possible Using smbfs 2.0.1

Note that a security issue might exist using smbfs-2.0.1 because of a possible root exploit being available. However, a patch against the exploit does exist. The version of smbfs that is included on this book's CD-ROM in /smbfs is version 2.0.2-1, which includes the necessary patch. You are well advised to check the Web site listed in the extract for details of the current release.

smbmount, smbumount, And smbmnt

These programs or utilities are used with the smbfs file system support that is available with the Linux kernel-based operating systems. In a manner comparable to the more usual NFS counterparts, mount and unmount, these are used to mount the remote SMB/CIFS server share within the local file system.

The smbfs support has one supplier that might be included with the Linux kernel; some Linux distributions include this already, whereas others might need to obtain it separately. The utility programs **smbmount** and **smbumount** have two suppliers. The first is included with the smbfs distribution, and the second is from the Samba distribution. In both versions, the essential functionality of the **smbmount** and **smbumount** is the same. This functionality provides for the mounting or unmounting of the SMB/CIFS server shares.

The **smbmount** and **smbumount** utilities from the Samba distribution are cut-down versions of the **smbclient** program that functionally provide the mounting or unmounting of the SMB/CIFS server share. Because the common code parent of these programs is smbclient, the smbmount utility also has the flexibility to mount the remote share in the local file system with specific user and group definitions. The program smbmnt is the workhorse utility that makes the actual calls to the SMB/CIFS server.

The syntax of these utilities is shown here:

```
smbmount options
smbumount mount-point
smbmnt mount-point [-u uid] [-g gid] [-f file mode] [-d dir mode]
```

As previously stated, smbmount is a cut-down version of the smbclient program that is used to mount smbfs shares. In operation, **smbmount** applies only the **mount** command, which then calls the **smbmnt** program to do the actual mount. smbmount can accept most of the options that **smbclient** does. To use **smbmount** to mount an smb file system, the **-c** option, which in **smbclient** indicates passing a command to the program to execute, is invoked. In this case, the **smbmount** program passes the **mount** command to the **smbmnt** program. An example is shown here:

```
smbmount "\\\\linuxserver\\test" -c 'mount /mnt/smbfs/test -u 500 -g 500'
```

This mounts the test share of linuxserver on /mnt/smbfs/test, giving it a local uid of 500 and a local gid of 500. You could obtain these values from the /etc/passwd and /etc/group files. Note how the arguments supplied to the **mount** command are passed directly to the smbmnt utility for processing.

With the **smbumount** program, normal users can unmount SMB/CIFS file systems, provided that the program has been suid root. **smbumount** incorporates flexibility that would allow normal (nonroot) Linux users more control over their resources, thus allowing them to mount remote SMB/CIFS file systems within their home directories. Because of this usage, it is safe to install this program suid root because only the user who has mounted a file system is allowed to unmount it again.

The superusers on a system (root) can simply use the normal NFS umount program instead. For these users, it is not necessary to use smbumount. An example of smbumount is shown here:

```
smbumount /mnt/smbfs/test
```

In this case, /mnt/smbfs/test is the directory you want to unmount.

The **smbmnt** program is called and used by the **smbmount** and **smbumount** programs to do the actual mounting and unmounting of shares. When called, the calling program passes command line arguments directly to smbmnt. When **smbmnt** is installed, it is installed setuid root so that normal users can mount their smb shares. **smbmnt** checks to ensure that the user requesting the share has write permissions on the mount point and then mounts the directory.

The main options that are available with **smbmnt** are to specify which user and group the share should be mounted as within the local file system. Some SMB/CIFS servers, such as LAN Manager, will not pass on the details of the file owner. The Samba host operating system, Unix, requires that every file or directory in the file system has an owner and a group that the owner belongs to. The options that are available for **smbmnt** are **-u *uid*** and **-g *gid***, where the session user can inform smbmount of the Unix owner and groups that it needs to assign to the files in the mounted directory. The defaults for these values are the current uid and gid.

In addition, the permissions of a file must be specified, and LAN Manager does not apply file permissions. Unix requires this information. Two further options available with smbmnt are **-f *file mode*** and **-d *dir mode***, which apply file mode and directory mode permissions to the mounted files and directories.

The values within ***file mode*** and ***dir mode*** are given as octal numbers. Chapter 4 expanded on Unix file and directory permissions, so this information is not repeated here. If no values are specified for **-f** or **-d**, the default values employed are those from the current umask, where the ***file mode*** is the current umask, and the ***dir mode*** adds execute permissions, where the ***file mode*** gives read permissions.

The permissions you are allowed to set might differ from those of the server. It would be wise to avoid confusion by adopting file modes that are similar to those available on the server. It is not possible to use the **smbmnt** file and directory modes to override any permission that has been set at the server. Any implied restrictions will be enforced from the server.

An example of the syntax for the smbmnt command is shown here:

```
smbmnt /smbfs/mnt/test -u 500 -g 500 -f 744 -d 744
```

smbprint

This is not a program but rather a shell script that is written to the same location as the program executables on installation. It provides the necessary commands that will allow the Unix system, where it is called, to use the printers available on other SMB/CIFS servers.

Printing from a Unix system to a remote SMB/CIFS server requires that additional steps be taken when using a local printer; these steps involve setting the smbclient called parameters in configuration files and in printer filters. The printer filter is the smbprint script, and calling the **smbclient** program with the appropriate entries makes use of the remote resource as a printer.

The smbprint file contents on a newly installed Samba 2.0.4b system are included in Listing 7.3, which contains a lot of information on the usage of the smbprint script in setting up a Unix host to use the printer on a remote SMB/CIFS server.

Listing 7.3 The smbprint script.

```
#!/bin/sh

# This script is an input filter for printcap printing on a unix machine.
# It uses the smbclient program to print the file to the specified
# smb-based server and service.
# For example you could have a printcap entry like this
#
# smb:lp=/dev/null:sd=/usr/spool/smb:sh:if=/usr/local/samba/smbprint
#
# which would create a unix printer called "smb" that will print via this
# script. You will need to create the spool directory /usr/spool/smb with
# appropriate permissions and ownerships for your system.

# Set these to the server and service you wish to print to
# In this example I have a WfWg PC called "lapland" that has a printer
# exported called "printer" with no password.
#
# Script further altered by hamiltom@ecnz.co.nz (Michael Hamilton)
# so that the server, service, and password can be read from
# a /var/spool/lpd/PRINTNAME/.config file.
#
# In order for this to work the /etc/printcap entry must include an
# accounting file (af=...):
#
#   cdcolour:\
#      :cm=CD IBM Colorjet on 6th:\
#      :sd=/var/spool/lpd/cdcolour:\
#      :af=/var/spool/lpd/cdcolour/acct:\
#      :if=/usr/local/etc/smbprint:\
#      :mx=0:\
#      :lp=/dev/null:
#
# The /usr/var/spool/lpd/PRINTNAME/.config file should contain:
#   server=PC_SERVER
#   service=PR_SHARENAME
#   password="password"
#
# E.g.
#   server=PAULS_PC
#   service=CJET_371
#   password=""
#
# Debugging log file, change to /dev/null if you like.
#
# logfile=/tmp/smb-print.log
```

```
logfile=/dev/null
#
# The last parameter to the filter is the accounting file name.
#   Extract the directory name from the file name.
#   Concat this with /.config to get the config file.
#
eval acct_file=\${$#}
spool_dir='dirname $acct_file'
config_file=$spool_dir/.config
# Should read the following variables set in the config file:
#   server
#   service
#   password
eval 'cat $config_file'
#
# Some debugging help, change the >> to > if you want to same space.
#
echo "server $server, service $service" >> $logfile
(
# NOTE You may wish to add the line 'echo translate' if you want automatic
# CR/LF translation when printing.
#       echo translate
        echo "print -"
        cat
) | /usr/bin/smbclient "\\\\$server\\$service" $password -U $server -N -P >>
$logfile
```

To use a printer on a remote host using SMB/CIFS, the order of the configuration is as follows:

1. Define the printer entry in the /etc/printcap file.
2. Create a new spool directory for that printer, usually /usr/spool/lpd/*printer-name*.
3. In the newly created printer spool directory, create a file called .config (syntax includes a period before the file name) and create the entries in the file, as shown here:

    ```
    #   server=<remote SMB/CIFS server netBIOS name>
    #   service=<remote printer sharename>
    #   password="password"
    ```

4. Add a line for the smbprint filter to the printcap entry, as shown here:

    ```
    #    :if=/usr/local/samba/bin/smbprint:\
    ```

5. Restart the printer.

A Unix system that needs to print to another system running as an SMB/CIFS server with a printer connected is able to use this method easily for both Unix and Windows hosts.

smbtar

This is another shell script that sits on top of **smbclient**. The smbtar script is used when backing up SMB/CIFS shares to a local Unix tape drive. The script is included with the Samba distribution and is installed with the distribution executables in the /usr/bin directory. The copy that is included with the Samba 2.0.4b distribution is shown in Listing 7.4.

Listing 7.4 The smbtar script.

```
#!/bin/sh
#
# smbtar script - front end to smbclient
#
# Authors: Martin.Kraemer <Martin.Kraemer@mch.sni.de>
#          and Ricky Poulten (ricky@logcam.co.uk)
#
# (May need to change shell to ksh for HPUX or OSF for better getopts)
#
# sandy nov 3 '98 added -a flag
#
# Richard Sharpe, added -c 'tarmode full' so that we back up all files to
# fix a bug in clitar when a patch was added to stop system and hidden files
# being backed up.

case $0 in
    # when called by absolute path, assume smbclient is in the
    # same directory
    /*)
    SMBCLIENT="'dirname $0'/smbclient";;
    *)  # you may need to edit this to show where your smbclient is
    SMBCLIENT="smbclient";;
esac

# These are the default values. You could fill them in if you know what
# you're doing, but beware: better not store a plain text password!
server=""
service="backup"            # Default: a service called "backup"
password=""
username=$LOGNAME           # Default: same user name as in *nix
verbose="2>/dev/null"        # Default: no echo to stdout
log="-d 2"
newer=""
```

```
newerarg=""
blocksize=""
blocksizearg=""
clientargs="-c 'tarmode full'"
tarcmd="c"
tarargs=""
cdcmd="\\"
tapefile=${TAPE-tar.out}

Usage(){
    ex=$1
    shift
echo >&2 "Usage: `basename $0` [<options>] [<include/exclude files>]
Function: backup/restore Windows PC directories to a local tape file
Options:         (Description)                  (Default)
  -r             Restore from tape file to PC  Save from PC to tapefile
  -i             Incremental mode              Full backup mode
  -a             Reset archive bit mode        Don't reset archive bit
  -v             Verbose mode: echo command    Don't echo anything
  -s <server>    Specify PC Server             $server
  -p <password>  Specify PC Password           $password
  -x <share>     Specify PC Share              $service
  -X             Exclude mode                  Include
  -N <newer>     File for date comparison      'set - $newer; echo $2'
  -b <blocksize> Specify tape's blocksize      'set - $blocksize; echo $2'
  -d <dir>       Specify a directory in share  $cdcmd
  -l <log>       Specify a Samba Log Level     'set - $log; echo $2'
  -u <user>      Specify User Name             $username
  -t <tape>      Specify Tape device           $tapefile
"
  echo >&2 "$@"
  exit $ex
}

# echo Params count: $#

# DEC OSF AKA Digital UNIX does not seem to return a value in OPTIND if
# there are no command line params, so protect us against that ...
if [ $# = 0 ]; then

  Usage 2 "Please enter a command line parameter!"

fi

while getopts riavl:b:d:N:s:p:x:u:Xt: c; do
  case $c in
```

```
r) # [r]estore to Windows (instead of the default "Save from Windows")
   tarcmd="x"
   ;;
i) # [i]ncremental
   tarargs=${tarargs}g
   ;;
a) # [a]rchive
   tarargs=${tarargs}a
   ;;
l) # specify [l]og file
   log="-d $OPTARG"
   case "$OPTARG" in
     [0-9]*) ;;
     *)      echo >&2 "$0: Error, log level not numeric: -l $OPTARG"
     exit 1
   esac
   ;;
d) # specify [d]irectory to change to in server's share
   cdcmd="$OPTARG"
   ;;
N) # compare with a file, test if [n]ewer
   if [ -f $OPTARG ]; then
     newer=$OPTARG
     newerarg="N"
   else
     echo >&2 $0: Warning, $OPTARG not found
   fi
   ;;
X) # Add exclude flag
   tarargs=${tarargs}X
   ;;
s) # specify [s]erver's share to connect to - this MUST be given.
   server="$OPTARG"
   ;;
b) # specify [b]locksize
   blocksize="$OPTARG"
   case "$OPTARG" in
     [0-9]*) ;;
     *)      echo >&2 "$0: Error, block size not numeric: -b $OPTARG"
     exit 1
   esac
   blocksizearg="b"
   ;;
p) # specify [p]assword to use
   password="$OPTARG"
   ;;
```

```
    x) # specify windows [s]hare to use
       service="$OPTARG"
       ;;
    t) # specify [t]apefile on local host
       tapefile="$OPTARG"
       ;;
    u) # specify [u]sername for connection
       username="$OPTARG"
       ;;
    v) # be [v]erbose and display what's going on
       verbose=""
       ;;
    '?') # any other switch
        Usage 2 "Invalid switch specified - abort."
       ;;
  esac
done

shift 'expr $OPTIND - 1'

if [ "$server" = "" ] || [ "$service" = "" ]; then
  Usage 1 "No server or no service specified - abort."
fi

# if the -v switch is set, then echo the current parameters
if [ -z "$verbose" ]; then
      echo "server    is $server"
#     echo "share     is $service"
      echo "share     is $service\\$cdcmd"
      echo "tar args  is $tarargs"
#     echo "password  is $password" # passwords should never be sent to
            screen
      echo "tape      is $tapefile"
      echo "blocksize is $blocksize"
fi

tarargs=${tarargs}${blocksizearg}${newerarg}

eval $SMBCLIENT "'\\\\$server\\$service'" "'$password'" -U "'$username'" \
-E -N $log -D "'$cdcmd'" ${clientargs} \
-T${tarcmd}${tarargs} $blocksize $newer $tapefile $* $verbose
```

The script has several possible parameter options that are passed at the command line; these are shown in Table 7.4.

Table 7.4 The smbtar options.

Option	Description
-s *server*	The SMB/CIFS server that the share resides on.
-x *service*	The share name on the server to connect to. The default is **backup**.
-X	Exclude mode; excludes file names from tar create or restore.
-d *directory*	Changes to the initial directory before restoring or backing up files.
-v	Verbose mode.
-p *password*	The password to use to access a share. The default is none.
-u *user*	The user ID to connect as. The default is the Unix login name.
-t *tape*	Tape device; can be a regular file or a tape device. The default is the TAPE environmental variable; if this is not set, a file called tar.out is the default.
-b *blocksize*	Blocking factor. The default is **20**. The man pages for tar on the system have a full explanation of this parameter. This is the number of 512-byte blocks that the **tar** program will write at one time.
-N *filename*	Backs up only files that are newer than ***filename***. Could be used, for example, on a log file to implement incremental backups.
-i	Incremental mode; tar files are backed up only if they have the archive bit set. The archive bit is reset after each file is read.
-r	Restore; restores files to the share from the tar file.
-l *log level*	Log (debug) level; corresponds to the **-d** flag of **smbclient**.

The syntax of the **smbtar** command is shown here:

```
smbtar -s server [-p password] [-x service] [-X] [-d directory]
[-u user] [-t tape] [-b blocksize] [-N filename] [-i] [-r]
[-l log level] [-v] filenames
```


smbwrapper

This is a new addition to the Samba distribution and is still in development. The **smbwrapper** utility is not included by default, and to use it you need to recompile Samba with the **-with-smbwrapper** option; **smbwrapper** will then be installed with the Samba programs.

smbwrapper offers the **smbsh** command, which attempts to create a remote shell on the SMB/CIFS server, from which it is possible to run commands that are available as standard in a Unix operating system.

Much of the functionality is similar to **smbclient**, and the Samba distribution notes indicate that until **smbwrapper** development has progressed, **smbclient** and **smbwrapper** (smbsh) will be part of the distribution for some time to come.

Immediate Solutions

Listing The Shares On A Remote System

To list the shares on a remote SMB/CIFS server, you issue a command using **smbclient -L** followed by the server name and then, when prompted, enter the appropriate password. Alternatively, you can use **smbclient** with the **-N** option, which will suppress any password request, as shown in Listing 7.5.

Listing 7.5 Listing the shares on a remote SMB/CIFS server.

```
[test1@linuxclient test1]$ smbclient -L //linuxserver -N
Added interface ip=192.168.1.14 bcast=192.168.1.255 nmask=255.255.255.0
Domain=[SAMBABOOK] OS=[Unix] Server=[Samba 2.0.4b]

        Sharename      Type      Comment
        ---------      ----      -------
        homes          Disk      Home Directories
        printers       Printer   All Printers
        groupshare     Disk      Group Share
        IPC$           IPC       IPC Service (Linuxserver Samba Server)
        hp             Printer   hp deskjet

        Server               Comment
        ------               -------
        LINUXSERVER          Linuxserver Samba Server
        NTSERVER             NT Server

        Workgroup            Master
        --------             ------
        SAMBABOOK            NTSSERVER
[test1@linuxclient test1]$
```

This provides the share information and also details the workgroup, operating system, and SMB/CIFS server version. Also listed are the other servers and workgroups that this particular SMB/CIFS server knows about.

Connecting To An SMB/CIFS Server Using smbclient

Having determined which share on a remote SMB/CIFS server you want to connect to, you issue a command using **smbclient** followed by the server name and share name. When prompted, enter the appropriate password. Alternatively, you can use **smbclient** with the password included within the command (in the following listings, test1pass is the password for test1). The two different options and output are shown in Listings 7.6 and 7.7.

Listing 7.6 Connecting to the share not including the password initially.

```
[test1@linuxclient test1]$ smbclient //linuxserver/groupshare
Added interface ip=192.168.1.14 bcast=192.168.1.255 nmask=255.255.255.0
Password:
Domain=[SAMBABOOK] OS=[Unix] Server=[Samba 2.0.4b]
smb:\>
```

Listing 7.7 Connecting to the share including the password initially.

```
[test1@linuxclient test1]$ smbclient //linuxserver/groupshare test1pass
Added interface ip=192.168.1.14 bcast=192.168.1.255 nmask=255.255.255.0
Domain=[SAMBABOOK] OS=[Unix] Server=[Samba 2.0.4b]
smb:\>
```

Listing The Contents Of A Share Using smbclient

Having connected to the share on a remote SMB/CIFS server, you issue a command from the **smb** prompt, as shown in Listing 7.8, which is a continuation of the listings in the previous section.

Listing 7.8 Listing the share contents.

```
[test1@linuxclient test1]$ smbclient //linuxserver/groupshare test1pass
Added interface ip=192.168.1.14 bcast=192.168.1.255 nmask=255.255.255.0
Domain=[SAMBABOOK] OS=[Unix] Server=[Samba 2.0.4b]
smb: \>ls
  test1.txt                                          58 Sat Jun 20 11:22:45 1999
  test2.txt                                          59 Sat Jun 20 11:22:45 1999
  test3.txt                                          61 Sat Jun 20 11:22:45 1999
  test4.txt                                          35 Sat Jun 20 11:22:45 1999
  test1work                                    D      0 Sat Jun 20 11:22:45 1999
  test2work                                    D      0 Sat Jun 20 11:22:45 1999
  groupwork                                    D      0 Sat Jun 20 11:22:45 1999
           42567 blocks of size 16384. 11237 blocks available
smb: \>
```

Changing To Another Directory On A Remote Share

While in an smbclient session, to change to another directory within the remote share, simply issue the command **cd**. The session will change to the new directory and return the new directory in the smb prompt, as shown here:

```
smb: \> cd test1work
smb: \test1work\>
```

Adding Files To A Remote Share

While in an smbclient session, to add files to the remote share, simply issue the command **put *localfile remotefile***. However, it is not necessary to provide the remote file name, as the local file name will be used by default. If you want to change the file name, adding a remote file entry will create the file as necessary. The output from the two options are shown in Listings 7.9 and 7.10.

Listing 7.9 Adding a file to the remote share.

```
smb: \test1work\> put test5.txt
putting file test5.txt as \test5.txt (305.24 kb/s) (average 301.28 kb/s)
smb: \test1work\>
```

Listing 7.10 Adding a file to the remote share specifying a new file name.

```
smb: \test1work\> put test5.txt newtest5.txt
putting file test5.txt as \newtest5.txt (312.66 kb/s) (average 304.38 kb/s)
smb: \test1work\>
```

Adding Multiple Files To A Remote Share Using Wildcards

While in an **smbclient** session, to add files to the remote share with wildcards, simply issue the command **mput *expression***. In this case, also turn off the prompting for confirmation using the prompt command. The options available when using wildcards are *, which replaces all possible names with no length specified, or ?, which replaces single characters. The outputs from the two options are shown in Listings 7.11 and 7.12.

Listing 7.11 Adding multiple files to the remote share using *.

```
smb: \testlwork\>prompt
prompting is now off
smb: \testlwork\> mput *.txt
putting file test5.txt as \test5.txt (167.24 kb/s) (average 180.32 kb/s)
putting file test6.txt as \test6.txt (305.24 kb/s) (average 192.28 kb/s)
putting file test7.txt as \test7.txt (267.34 kb/s) (average 227.12 kb/s)
putting file test8.txt as \test8.txt (176.45 kb/s) (average 156.34 kb/s)
putting file alltest.txt as \alltest.txt (46.42 kb/s) (average 30.45 kb/s)
smb: \testlwork\>
```

Listing 7.12 Adding multiple files to the remote share using ?.

```
smb: \testlwork\>prompt
prompting is now off
smb: \testlwork\> mput test?.doc
putting file test5.doc as \test5.doc (209.64 kb/s) (average 184.32 kb/s)
putting file test6.doc as \test6.doc (213.24 kb/s) (average 197.28 kb/s)
putting file test7.doc as \test7.doc (224.74 kb/s) (average 223.12 kb/s)
putting file test8.doc as \test8.doc (198.55 kb/s) (average 163.34 kb/s)
smb: \testlwork\>
```

Adding Multiple Files To A Remote Share Using A Mask

While in an smbclient session, to add files to the remote share using a mask and with wildcards, simply issue the command **mask *expression*** and then **mput *expression***. In this case, also turn off the prompting for confirmation by using the **prompt** command. The options available when using wildcards are *, which replaces all possible names with no length specified, or ?, which replaces single characters. The output is shown in Listing 7.13.

Listing 7.13 Using a mask when adding multiple files to the remote share.

```
smb: \testlwork\>prompt
prompting is now off
smb: \testlwork\>mask test?.*
smb: \testlwork\>mput *.txt
putting file test5.txt as \test5.txt (167.24 kb/s) (average 180.32 kb/s)
putting file test6.txt as \test6.txt (305.24 kb/s) (average 192.28 kb/s)
putting file test7.txt as \test7.txt (267.34 kb/s) (average 227.12 kb/s)
putting file test8.txt as \test8.txt (176.45 kb/s) (average 156.34 kb/s)
smb: \testlwork\>
```

Adding Multiple Files From Directories Recursively To A Remote Share

While in an smbclient session, to add files contained within multiple directories to the remote share simply issue the command **recurse** and then **mput *expression***. In this case, also turn off the prompting for confirmation using the **prompt** command. It is possible to specify both file level (**mask**) and directory level (**mput**) options when issuing any command when recursively adding to or retrieving from shares and the subdirectories. The output of issuing the **recurse** command is shown here:

```
smb: \test1work\>prompt
prompting is now off
smb: \test1work\>recurse
directory recursion is now on
smb: \test1work\>
```

Retrieving Files From A Remote Share

While in an smbclient session, to retrieve files from the remote share simply issue the command **get *remotefile localfile***. However, it is not necessary to provide the local file name, as the remote file name will be used by default. If you want to change the file name, adding a local file name entry will create the file as necessary. The output from the two options are shown in Listings 7.14 and 7.15.

Listing 7.14 Retrieving a file from a remote share.

```
smb: \test1work\> get test.txt
getting file test.txt of size 65 as test.txt (305.24 kb/s) (average 301.28
kb/s)
smb: \test1work\>
```

Listing 7.15 Retrieving a file from a remote share specifying a new file name.

```
smb: \test1work\> get test.txt newtest.txt
getting file test.txt of size 65 as newtest.txt (312.66 kb/s) (average
304.38 kb/s)
smb: \test1work\>
```

Retrieving Files From A Remote Share Using Wildcards

In a similar manner to that available with **mput**, it is possible to use both the *, which replaces all possible names with no length specified, and **?** wildcards, which replaces single characters. In this case, also turn off the prompting for confirmation using the **prompt** command. Listing 7.16 shows both types of wildcards in operation.

Listing 7.16 Retrieving files using wildcards * or ?.

```
smb: \test1work\>prompt
prompting is now off
smb: \test1work\> mget *.txt
getting file test.txt of size 65 as test.txt  (167.24 kb/s)
 (average 180.32 kb/s)
getting file test1.txt of size 65 as test1.txt (267.34 kb/s)
 (average 227.12 kb/s)
getting file test2.txt of size 65 as test2.txt (176.45 kb/s)
 (average 156.34 kb/s)
getting file test3.txt of size 65 as test3.txt (305.24 kb/s)
 (average 301.28 kb/s)
smb: \test1work\>
smb: \test1work\> mget test?.doc
getting file test5.doc of size 69 as test5.doc (209.64 kb/s)
 (average 184.32 kb/s)
getting file test6.doc of size 69 as test6.doc (213.24 kb/s)
 (average 197.28 kb/s)
getting file test7.doc of size 69 as test7.doc (224.74 kb/s)
 (average 223.12 kb/s)
getting file test8.doc of size 69 as test8.doc (198.55 kb/s)
 (average 163.34 kb/s)
smb: \test1work\>
```


Retrieving Files From A Remote Share Using A Mask

While in an **smbclient** session, to retrieve files from the remote share using a mask and with wildcards, simply issue the command **mask *expression*** and then **mget *expression***. In this case, also turn off the prompting for confirmation using the **prompt** command. The options available when using wildcards are *, which replaces all possible names with no length specified, or **?**, which replaces single characters. The output is shown in Listing 7.17.

Listing 7.17 Using a mask when retrieving multiple files from a remote share.

```
smb: \test1work\>prompt
prompting is now off
smb: \test1work\>mask test?.*
smb: \test1work\>mget *.txt
getting file test.txt of size 65 as test.txt  (167.24 kb/s)
 (average 180.32 kb/s)
getting file test1.txt of size 65 as test1.txt (267.34 kb/s)
 (average 227.12 kb/s)
getting file test2.txt of size 65 as test2.txt (176.45 kb/s)
 (average 156.34 kb/s)
getting file test3.txt of size 65 as test3.txt (305.24 kb/s)
 (average 301.28 kb/s)
smb: \test1work\>
```

Retrieving Files From A Remote Share Selecting By Date

While in an **smbclient** session, to obtain files from the remote share, ensuring that only files newer than a specific date are retrieved, first determine the date of a file of interest on the local system (such as date.log) with the local **ls -l** command. Then simply issue the command **newer *filename***. This sets the date for files to be included on the basis of the local file date. The output from the session is shown here:

```
smb: \test1work\>newer date.log
Getting files newer that Sat Jun 22 13:45:26 1999
smb: \test1work\>
```

Retrieving Files From A Remote Share Recursively From Directories

While in an **smbclient** session, to retrieve files contained within multiple directories on the remote share, simply issue the command **recurse** and then **mget *expression***. It is possible to specify both file level (**mask**) and directory level (**mget**) options when issuing any command when recursively retrieving from shares and subdirectories. The output of issuing the **recurse** command is shown here:

```
smb: \test1work\>prompt
prompting is now off
smb: \test1work\>recurse
directory recursion is now on
smb: \test1work\>
```

Changing The Case Of The Files Obtained

While in an **smbclient** session, to change the case of files that are retrieved from remote SMB/CIFS servers, simply issue the command **lowercase**. The default is not to convert any file names. In use, issue the **get** or **mget *expression*** command to retrieve the file. The file obtained will be created with the file name in lowercase. The output of issuing the **lowercase** command is shown here:

```
smb: \test1work\>lowercase
filename lowercasing is now on
smb: \test1work\>
```

Deleting Files From A Remote Directory

To delete files from an SMB/CIFS server share directory, the smbclient sessions command **rm *expression*** can be used with wildcards. The following contains the output from a successful session when prompting has also been turned off:

```
smb :\> prompt
prompting is now off
smb :\> rm *.txt
smb :\>
```


Deleting A Directory From A Remote Share

To delete a directory from an SMB/CIFS server share, the smbclient sessions command **rmdir *expression*** (or the shorter form **rd *expression***) could be used with wildcards. The following contains the output from a successful session when prompting has also been turned off:

```
smb :\> prompt
prompting is now off
```

```
smb :\> rmdir test
smb :\>
```

If the directory is not empty or if insufficient permissions are available to perform the operation, an error will be displayed. The following error was obtained when some content remained in the test directory.

```
smb :\> rmdir test
ERRDOS - ERRnoaccess (Access denied.) removing remote directory file \test
smb :\>
```

Printing Using smbclient

To print a file using smbclient, you connect to a printer share and put the file onto the share. There are a couple of ways to achieve this with Samba utilities, all involving placing the file into the printer share.

The first option is to simply connect to the printer share and use the command **print** ***filename***; this file will be directly added to the printer queue of the SMB/CIFS server printer share":

```
smb :\> print test5.txt
putting file test5.txt as test5.txt (105.52 kb/s) (average 96.62 kb/s)
smb :\>
```

An alternative and perhaps more flexible approach is to use the | command in Unix. The following contains this option with the necessary command syntax and the successful response:

```
[test1@linuxclient test1]$ cat test5.txt | smbclient //linuxserver/hp
XXXXXXX \-N -c "put - hptest1"
Added interface ip=192.168.1.14 bcast=192.168.1.255 nmask=255.255.255.0
Domain=[SAMBABOOK] OS=[Unix] Server=[Samba 2.0.4b]
putting file - as \hptest1 (167.24 kb/s) (average 180.32 kb/s)
[test1@linuxclient test1]$
```

The ***XXXXXXX*** is the password of the user initiating the connection session to the SMB/CIFS server (in this case, test1 is the user).

This solution made use of **cat** and the | symbol. In Unix, | means to pipe the STDOUT output from the initial command as STDIN to the next command. In this case, the file was typed to STDOUT, output, and then piped as STDIN to **smbclient**, which finally writes this to a printer share. Alternatively, smbclient can be used to obtain a file and then, with the **smbclient** output acting as STDOUT, pipe this as STDIN to the local printer. The command to do this is shown in Listing 7.18.

Listing 7.18 Printing a file from an SMB/CIFS server to a local printer.

```
[test1@linuxclient test1]$ smbclient //linuxserver/hp XXXXXXX \-N -c
"get test5.txt -" | lpr -Plocalprinter
Added interface ip=192.168.1.14 bcast=192.168.1.255 nmask=255.255.255.0
Domain=[SAMBABOOK] OS=[Unix] Server=[Samba 2.0.4b]
getting file test5.txt of size 59 as testx.txt (167.24 kb/s)
(average 180.32 kb/s)
[test1@linuxclient test1]$
```

Viewing The Print Queue

It is possible to view all the printer jobs present on an SMB/CIFS server using the smbclient command with the **-c** queue option specified. The command and a successful response are shown in Listing 7.19, where ***XXXXXXX*** is the password for the user (in this case, test 1).

Listing 7.19 Listing the printer queue on an SMB/CIFS server.

```
[test1@linuxclient test1]$ smbclient //linuxserver/hp XXXXXXXX -c queue
Added interface ip=192.168.1.14 bcast=192.168.1.255 nmask=255.255.255.0
998         11876           test1.a00045
999         11876           test1.a00047
1000        11876           test1.a00052
[test1@linuxclient test1]$
```


Managing The Print Queue

The jobs that are held on a remote SMB/CIFS server printer queue can be deleted by using the smbclient session command **cancel *jobid***. The following shows an example of this based on the previous queue entries canceling job 1000:

```
smb :\> cancel 1000
Job 1000 cancelled
smb :\>
```

Creating A tar Of A Remote Directory

To create a tar archive of a remote share, issue the **smbclient** command with the **-T** option and any additional option from the **smbtar** or **-T** options listed in Tables 7.1 and 7.2, earlier in this chapter. Listing 7.20 shows the output created during a session involving the creation of a tar archive from smbclient.

Listing 7.20 Creating a tar of a remote SMB/CIFS directory.

```
[root@linuxserver rdab100]# smbclient //linuxserver/groupshare -U test1
 -Tcr test
Added interface ip=192.168.1.4 bcast=192.168.1.255 nmask=255.255.255.0
tar_re_search set
Password:
Domain=[SAMBABOOK] OS=[Unix] Server=[Samba 2.0.4b]
     27648 (  230.8 kb/s) \Document Scrap 'Listing 6_x net ...'.shs
       498 (   60.8 kb/s) \HOWTO-run_MPI_progs
       141 (   19.7 kb/s) \lamhosts
       189 (   20.5 kb/s) \lamhosts.domscluster.txt
       113 (   13.8 kb/s) \lamhosts.homecluster.txt
     11465 (  746.4 kb/s) \manroute.txt
    161679 ( 1409.7 kb/s) \parallelversionMPI
      8215 (  573.0 kb/s) \parallelversionMPI.c
    161679 ( 1475.6 kb/s) \parallelversionMPI2
      8211 (  572.8 kb/s) \parallelversionMPI2.c
       411 (   44.6 kb/s) \version2_0.dat
       501 (   61.2 kb/s) \version2_header.dat
tar: dumped 13 tar files
Total bytes written: 384512
[root@linuxserver rdab100]#
```

An alternative is to create an **smbclient** session and to issue the **tar** command, as shown in Listing 7.21.

Listing 7.21 Creating a tar of a remote SMB/CIFS directory from an smbclient session.

```
[root@linuxserver rdab100]# smbclient //linuxserver/groupshare test1pass
 -U test1
Added interface ip=192.168.1.4 bcast=192.168.1.255 nmask=255.255.255.0
Domain=[SAMBABOOK] OS=[Unix] Server=[Samba 2.0.4b]
smb :\>tar cr test
tar_re_search set
     27648 (  230.8 kb/s) \Document Scrap 'Listing 6_x net ...'.shs
       498 (   60.8 kb/s) \HOWTO-run_MPI_progs
       141 (   19.7 kb/s) \lamhosts
       189 (   20.5 kb/s) \lamhosts.domscluster.txt
       113 (   13.8 kb/s) \lamhosts.homecluster.txt
```

```
      11465 (  746.4 kb/s) \manroute.txt
     161679 ( 1409.7 kb/s) \parallelversionMPI
       8215 (  573.0 kb/s) \parallelversionMPI.c
     161679 ( 1475.6 kb/s) \parallelversionMPI2
       8211 (  572.8 kb/s) \parallelversionMPI2.c
        411 (   44.6 kb/s) \version2_0.dat
        501 (   61.2 kb/s) \version2_header.dat
tar: dumped 13 tar files
Total bytes written: 384512
[root@linuxserver rdab100]#
```

Setting The Mode Of A File On A Remote Share

From an **smbclient** session, issue the command **setmode *file expression*** with the expression appropriate for the setting. The details of the possible modes are detailed in Table 7.3, earlier in the chapter. The following shows the result of setting the mode on a file:

```
smb :\>setmode test.txt +r-a
per set 1 32
smb :\>
```

Changing The End-Of-Line Sequences Of The Files Retrieved

While in an **smbclient** session, to change the end-of-line sequences of files that are retrieved from remote SMB/CIFS servers, simply issue the command **translate** to toggle on the conversion of all end-of-line sequences. The default is not to convert any files.

In use, issue the **get** or **mget *expression*** to retrieve the file. The file obtained will be created with the end-of-line sequences in files converted to LF from CRLF. The output of issuing the **lowercase** command is shown here:

```
smb: \test1work\>translate
CRLF<->LF and print text translation is now on
smb: \test1work\>
```

Chapter 8

Complex Networking Challenges

In Depth

Previous chapters have discussed the principles of networking and the setup and use of SMB/CIFS resources involving relatively simple networks. This chapter will look at more complex real-world examples of Microsoft networking. The use of NetBIOS names brings many challenges that need to be dealt with when attempting to use Microsoft networking in real networks that are not simple, flat, single subnet networks. The real world involves networks that often span several subnets and often use Remote Access Services (RAS) to connect remote users to an office network.

Chapter 2 touched on NetBIOS names, DHCP, WINS, DNS, and the hosts and lmhosts configuration files on clients that are used in hostname resolution. The core of any solutions in this chapter will involve a fuller description of how to make the best use of the NetBIOS name resolution mechanisms alongside the necessary other networking solutions. First, however, we need to expand on what occurs when using NetBIOS and what challenges might be faced before moving on to the solutions.

Recall from Chapter 2 that NetBIOS names exist in flat name space and consist of 16 alphanumeric characters (a to z, A to Z, 0 to 9, and !, @, #, $, %, ^, &, (), -, ', {}, ., and ~). Only the first 15 characters may be used in naming the host. The 16th character (ACSII 0 to 255 or Hex 0x00 to 0xFF) is reserved and represents the resource type of the host. RFC 1001 and 1002, included on this book's CD-ROM in /doc/RFC, contain more information.

Earlier chapters provided examples of using Network Neighborhood but not much detail on the additional network traffic that can result when browsing a network. When a client needs to determine the IP address of a host on the basis of a NetBIOS name, a number of processes occur. The most costly process in terms of extra network traffic involves broadcasts to resolve NetBIOS names to IP addresses. This is because every time a client wants to determine the IP address of a NetBIOS host, the client, with no other option available, needs to broadcast to the subnet to locate the host. If the local subnet has many NetBIOS clients, a large number of broadcasts can occur. An additional issue is that NetBIOS broadcasts are limited to the local subnet, meaning that NetBIOS clients on different subnets cannot communicate with each other using broadcasts.

The first option involves the use of master browsers that assume the role of collecting NetBIOS name broadcasts on a subnet so that when other hosts request a host, the master browser responds on behalf of the intended host and thus reduces the network traffic. The method of determining which host is a network master browser involves NetBIOS elections (discussed in Chapter 2). This chapter expands on this to show what happens in a NetBIOS election, how to set the parameters that are available within the Samba smb.conf file to take part in these, and how to set up your Samba host to become a master browser.

The second option to reduce this extra network traffic involves the use of an lmhosts file that holds information on the resolution of NetBIOS name to IP address locally. Chapter 2 provided an introduction to the syntax and use of the lmhosts file.

The third option involves the establishment of a WINS service that acts as a centralized database for the resolution of NetBIOS name to IP address that is interrogated by clients to locate hosts both inside and outside the local subnet.

Browsing And NetBIOS Elections

Any of the computers on a network can be in one of a number of categories. These five categories are:

- *Nonbrowser*—This takes no part in maintaining a local network resource or browse list.
- *Potential browser*—This is the host that is maintained by the master browser in a ready state to become a backup browser if instructed to do so. It does not maintain a local network resource or browse list.
- *Backup browser*—The host receives a list of network resources from the master browser, and when a client host on the network requests a resource from the list, it distributes the information to the client on request. The backup browser synchronizes with the master browser every 15 minutes to obtain the latest information for the browse list, which will also include other domains and workgroups. The list is cached locally, and if any client host sends a **NetServerEnum** API call to the network, the backup browser will return the list. If the backup browser obtains no response after polling the master browser, it will force an election to the master browser.
- *Local master browser*—This is the central host that is responsible for collecting and maintaining the necessary information for browse lists. The information is collected when client hosts send a server announcement to the domain or workgroup master browser at startup. The master browser will then add that client host information to the list. In TCP/IP networks, the master

browser will operate within the local subnet only if a domain or workgroup spans multiple subnets. A master browser cannot operate across multiple subnets. If multiple workgroups or domains exist in a single subnet, each subnet will have its own master and backup browsers as required.

- *Domain master browser*—The primary domain controller (PDC) of an NT network usually performs this function. If the network spans several subnets, each subnet will have its own master and backup browsers. However, the domain master browser will collect the information from the local master browsers on the separate subnets. This is done when the master browsers send out a **MasterBrowserAnnouncement** datagram. The domain master browser will respond by sending a **NetServerEnum** API call to the local master browsers and retrieve the resource lists from the separate subnets. The domain master browser creates a master domain browse list that, in turn, is made available to the separate local master browsers through a remote **NetServerEnum** API call to the domain master browser and, in turn, to the client hosts on the remote subnet. The domain master browser repeats the **NetServerEnum** request every 15 minutes.

A NetBIOS election will occur when any of the following conditions exist:

- A client cannot locate a master browser on a network.
- A preferred master browser starts up on a network or the browser service (**nmbd** in Samba) is started on an existing machine and thus becomes active.
- A Windows NT domain controller system starts.

What Happens In A NetBIOS Election?

If any of the previously mentioned conditions occur, the host will send out a special broadcast datagram, called an *election datagram*. The election datagram contains election criteria that specify where within the election hierarchy the specific browser sits. Table 8.1 shows the hierarchy of election criteria for a browser election. It consists of 4 bytes as a 1-, 2-, and 1-byte group, the makeup of which can be controlled within the smb.conf parameters that are involved with NetBIOS browsing and elections. The first byte defines the operating system level, the next two bytes define the election version, and the final byte defines the browser level.

All browser hosts on a network are capable of receiving an election datagram. When a host receives such a datagram, it compares its own criteria and, according to a series of rules, either declares a NetBIOS election win over the sending host and attempts to make itself the master browser or does not. The rules are as follows:

Table 8.1 Election criteria hierarchy for a browser election.

Parameter	Byte Setting	Description
Operating system level	0xFF000000	Mask
	0x01000000	Windows for Workgroups, Windows 9x, or DOS
	0x10000000	Windows NT Workstation 4
	0x20000000	Windows NT Server 4
Election version	0x00FFFF00	Mask
Browser level	0x000000FF	Mask
	0x00000001	Current backup browser running
	0x00000002	Standby backup browser
	0x00000004	Current master browser running
	0x00000008	Preferred master browser
	0x00000020	WINS system
	0x00000080	PDC NT Server

- If the local host election version is greater than the sender's version, the local system wins. If it loses, it uses the next election criterion. The election version is connected to the browser election protocol and is not related to the operating system version.
- If the local host election criteria are greater than the sender's criteria, the local system wins. If it loses, it uses the next election criterion.
- If the local host has been running longer than the sender, and thus is more likely to have a complete browse list, the local system wins. If it loses, it uses the next election criterion.
- If the local host has a NetBIOS name that is "earlier" than the sender's NetBIOS name, the local system wins. The term "earlier" refers to a character-by-character comparison of the NetBIOS names, and lexically (alphabetically, by letter, number, and symbol), the lowest wins.
- If a local host wins an election, it will, depending on its current setting, send out an election request in a manner similar to the original request. To ensure that all the least likely browsers to win an election do not respond at the same time, a further set of criteria is followed that will stop them from responding. Master browsers and primary domain controllers delay 100 milliseconds (ms) before responding. Backup browsers and backup domain controllers delay from between 200 and 600 ms. Lower browsers delay between 800 and 3,000 ms. The host that is the most likely to win an election will probably have sent another election request before the less likely hosts on a network have even sent the first response. The "new" master browser

will make four election broadcasts before it will take over the role as master browser. If an election datagram is received during this confirmation process from a host higher on the election criteria, the local host will demote to a lesser browser as appropriate. The Windows NT system event logger will record that a browser election has been forced as well as the result that the local host has either won or lost.

NetBIOS Announcements

At startup, every host on an SMB/CIFS network will send out an announcement to the browser service that the host and its resources are available. This announcement is repeated every 1 to 12 minutes. The master browser on the local network sends out a list of the local subnet resources to the backup browsers every 15 minutes.

If the original master browser had been removed from the network and a new master browser had been elected, it is reasonable to expect that the browse list of the new server might be incomplete. When a new master browser wins an election, it sends out a **RequestAnnouncement** datagram. Any hosts on the local subnet will typically respond within 30 seconds. Any Windows host with its **MaintainServerList** parameter set to auto will have the master browser set to which browsers will become backup browsers.

The master browser browse list cannot be re-created without restarting the machine, thus forcing an election and a subsequent **RequestAnnouncement** or waiting for it to create the list from the directed datagrams sent periodically from every host to the master browser of the subnet.

The nonbrowsers periodically announce their presence every 12 minutes (on startup, 1, 2, 4, 8, and then 12 minutes pass between the initial announcements). Potential browsers follow the same period of announcements. Backup browsers announce themselves with the same periods as the previous examples, but they also participate in elections; thus, they also call the master browser every 15 minutes to obtain a new browse list.

TIP: *Two common questions seen in the Samba newsgroup lists involve NetBIOS announcements. Why can't I see my Samba server in client X Network Neighborhood once it is started? Why can I still see my Samba server in client X Network Neighborhood even long after it has been removed from the network?*

The answer in both cases is probably due to NetBIOS announcement periods between the server not being added to or removed from the local master browser browse list and thus either still appearing or not appearing for the client. It can take several minutes for a server to appear or disappear from a client's Network Neighborhood dialog box. In the case of a removed server, this could be 51 minutes, consisting of three 12-minute announcement periods during which the entry is not removed from a browser list and a 15-minute backup browser list update period.

This built-in delay in NetBIOS announcements can create some confusion and is not limited to Samba, but encompasses all NetBIOS networks.

When a client selects the host from Network Neighborhood (identical to using the **net view** command), the client sends a **NetShareEnum** request to the selected host and returns the shares available on that host. If this is the first time the client has used the Network Neighborhood and no other hosts are connected, the client will first send a **GetBackupList** datagram to the master browser. The master browser returns a list of active backup browsers in the local subnet to the client. The client caches the NetBIOS names of up to three backup browsers for later use.

If the client does not obtain any response from the workgroup or domain involved, the election of a new master browser is forced by sending an election datagram to the network.

Immediate Solutions

Browsing Using A Samba Host

To browse a network using a Samba host, use the **nmblookup** command to gather network information or the **smbclient** program to view the resources of a specific host.

The network involved is the simple network introduced earlier: The workgroup name is SAMBABOOK.

There are six hosts on this network—the two servers: ntserver (NT Server 4 Service Pack 1) and linuxserver (Red Hat 5.2), and the four client PCs: test1pc (Windows 95), test2pc (Windows 98), test3pc (Windows NT 4 Workstation), and test4pc (Red Hat 5.2). Figure 8.1 shows the sample network.

All the individual hosts are in the 192.168.1.0 network, and the hosts are numbered 192.168.1.x, where x = 1 to 6. The netmask is 255.255.255.0, and no gateway or DNS is defined. All hosts have no hosts or lmhosts file entries.

At this stage, no WINS server is running, and the smb.conf files for the linuxserver host are set as shown in Listing 8.1, which shows the use of the **netbios aliases** parameter. This parameter has the effect of adding three additional hosts to the network: fileserver, printerserver, and winsserver.

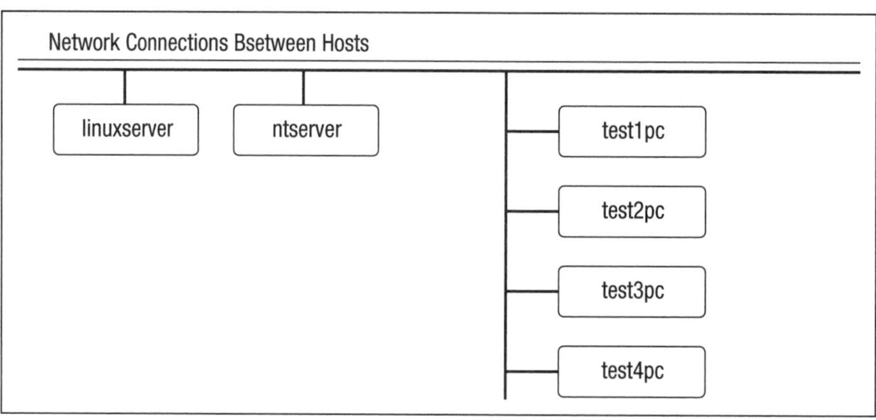

Figure 8.1 The SAMBABOOK workgroup.

Listing 8.1 The linuxserver smb.conf file.

```
[global]
workgroup = SAMBABOOK
server string = Version %v of Samba on host %h where %L is the NetBIOS name
# The string to identify the host name, NetBIOS name and Samba version
guest account = nobody
netbios name = linuxserver
netbios alias = fileserver printerserver winsserver # three
os level = 33 # Set at 33 because we want the server to win any NetBIOS
              # elections. See Table 8.5 for a list of the os level values
              # for different OSs
preferred master = yes # forces an election when the nmbd service starts
```

The host test4pc has no active **smbd** or **nmbd** service and no smb.conf file at this time. Thus, the view of the Network Neighborhood for the SAMBABOOK workgroup appears as shown in Figure 8.2.

Listings 8.2 and 8.3 show the output following running either the **smbclient** or the **nmblookup** program from the linuxserver host.

Listing 8.2 The smbclient command.

```
[root@linuxserver]$smbclient -L \\linuxserver -N
Added interface ip=192.168.1.88 bcast=192.168.1.255 nmask=255.255.255.0
Domain=[SAMBABOOK] OS=[Unix] Server=[Samba 2.0.4b]

   Sharename      Type      Comment
   --------       ----      ------
   homes          Disk      Home Directories
   tmp            Disk      Temporary file space
   public1        Disk      Public Stuff - read only except staff
   public2        Disk
   SambaBook      Disk      Samba Book stuff
   system         Disk      Root system - read only except staff
   groupshare     Disk
   C              Disk      DOS C:
   D              Disk      DOS D:
```

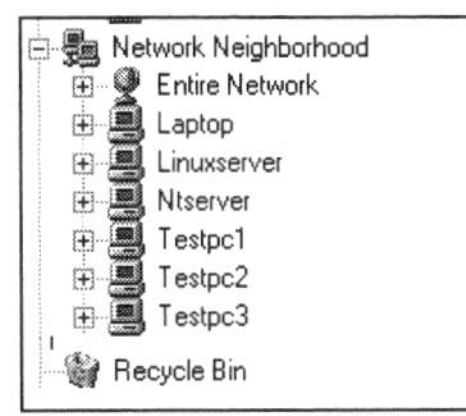

Figure 8.2 Network Neighborhood for the SAMBABOOK workgroup.

```
  wholedrive     Disk      Whole Samba server
  IPC$           IPC       IPC Service (Samba 2.0.4b on laptop laptop)
  deskjet        Printer   lp

  Server              Comment
  --------            ------
  LAPTOP              Samba 2.0.4b on laptop
  LINUXSERVER         Samba 2.0.4b on laptop
  NTSERVER
  TEST2PC
  TEST3PC
  TEST4PC
  TESTPC1             Testpc1

  Workgroup           Master
  --------            ------
  SAMBABOOK           LAPTOP
```

Listing 8.3 The nmblookup command.

```
[root@linuxserver]$ nmblookup -S linuxserver
Sending queries to 192.168.1.255
192.168.1.88 linuxserver<00>
Looking up status of 192.168.1.88
received 11 names
   LAPTOP           <00> -          B <ACTIVE>
   LAPTOP           <03> -          B <ACTIVE>
   LAPTOP           <20> -          B <ACTIVE>
   ..__MSBROWSE__.  <01> - <GROUP>  B <ACTIVE>
   LINUXSERVER      <00> -          B <ACTIVE>
   LINUXSERVER      <03> -          B <ACTIVE>
   LINUXSERVER      <20> -          B <ACTIVE>
   SAMBABOOK        <00> - <GROUP>  B <ACTIVE>
   SAMBABOOK        <1d> -          B <ACTIVE>
   SAMBABOOK        <1e> - <GROUP>  B <ACTIVE>
num_good_sends=0 num_good_receives=0
```

NOTE: *The SAMBABOOK <1d> entry in this output indicates that the Samba host linuxserver is the master browser for the workgroup SAMBABOOK.*

The syntax for using the **nmblookup** command is shown here:

```
nmblookup [-M] [-R] [-S] [-r] [-A] [-h] [-B broadcast address] [-U unicast
address] [-d debuglevel] [-s smb.conf] [-i NetBIOS scope] [-T] name
```

8. Complex Networking Challenges

The /doc/html folder on this book's CD-ROM and the Samba distribution both contain the HTML nmblookup.1.html page, which contains these options. The options are shown in Table 8.2.

The **nmblookup** command can be used to query a WINS server (in the same way that **nslookup** is used to query DNS servers). To query a WINS server, **nmblookup** must be called as follows:

```
nmblookup -U server -R 'name'
```

For example, running

```
nmblookup -U sambawins -R 'SAMBABOOK#1B'
```

would query the WINS server sambawins for the domain master browser (1B name type) for the SAMBABOOK workgroup.

Table 8.2 nmblookup options.

Option	Description
-M	Searches for a master browser by looking up the NetBIOS name with a type of 0x1d. If the name is "-", it does a lookup on the special name __MSBROWSE__.
-R	Does a recursive lookup by setting the recursion-desired bit in the packet. This is used when sending a name query to a machine running as a WINS server and the user wishes to query the names in the WINS server. If this bit is unset, the normal (broadcast responding) is employed.
-S	Once the name query has returned an IP address, it performs a node status query as well. A node status query returns the NetBIOS names registered by a host.
-r	Tries to bind to UDP port 137 to send and receive UDP datagrams. Windows 95 has a bug that ignores the source port of the requesting packet and replies only to UDP port 137. Unfortunately, on most Unix systems, root privilege is needed to bind to this port, and, in addition, if the nmbd daemon is running on this machine, it also binds to this port.
-A *name*	Interprets ***name*** as an IP address and performs a node status query on this address.
-h	Prints a help (usage) message.
-B *broadcast address*	Uses the provided broadcast address to send the query. By default, **nmblookup** sends the query to the broadcast address of the primary network interface as either auto-detected or defined in the interfaces parameter of the smb.conf file.
-U unicast address	Performs a unicast query to the specified address or host "unicast address." This option (along with the **-R** option) is needed to query a WINS server.

(continued)

Table 8.2 ***nmblookup options*** **(continued).**

Option	Description
-d *debuglevel*	An integer from 0 to 10. If this parameter is not specified, the default value is 0. The higher this value, the more detail is logged about the activities of **nmblookup**. At level 0, only critical errors and serious warnings are logged. Levels above 1 will generate considerable amounts of log data and should be used only when investigating a problem. Levels above 3 are generally of value only to developers, and requests for these can be seen in the Samba lists from time to time when resolving unexplained issues. Note that specifying this parameter here will override the log level parameter in the smb.conf file.
-s *smb.conf*	The pathname to the Samba configuration file, smb.conf, that contains all the settings and parameters that the Samba suite will use on the machine.
-i *NetBIOS scope*	Specifies a NetBIOS scope that **nmblookup** will use to communicate with when generating NetBIOS names. For extra details on the use of NetBIOS scopes, see rfc1001.txt and rfc1002.txt in /doc/rfc on this book's CD-ROM. NetBIOS scopes are very rarely used, and you should set this parameter only if you are the system administrator in charge of all the NetBIOS systems you communicate with.
-T	Requests that a reverse DNS lookup into a DNS name is performed for each IP address found in the lookup. The output should specify the DNS name before each "IP address-NetBIOS name" pair that is the normal output.
name	The NetBIOS name being queried. Depending on the previous options, this might be a NetBIOS name or an IP address. If it is a NetBIOS name, the different name types can be specified by appending ***#type*** to the name. This name might also be "*", which will return all registered names within a broadcast area.

Browsing Using A Windows Host

A Windows host allows two methods for browsing the network. The first uses the command line, and the second uses the GUI Network Neighborhood and related tools.

The available command line tools are the following:

- **net**
- **nbtstat**

The result of running the **net view linuxserver** command at the command prompt is shown on Listing 8.4 and is very similar to the output from the **smbclient -L \\linuxserver -N** command shown in Listing 8.2.

Listing 8.4 The net view linuxserver command.

```
C:\>net view linuxserver
Shared resources at linuxserver
Samba 2.0.4b on laptop linuxserver
Sharename      Type     Used as  Comment
---------------------------------------------------------
C              Disk              DOS C:
D              Disk              DOS D:
deskjet        Printer           lp
groupshare     Disk
homes          Disk              Home Directories
public1        Disk              Public Stuff - read only except staff
public2        Disk
SambaBook      Disk              Samba Book stuff
system         Disk              Root system - read only except staff
tmp            Disk              Temporary file space
wholedrive     Disk              Whole Samba server
The command completed successfully.
```

Note, however, that unlike the Samba **smbclient** command, this output does not contain the server list. The **net view /domain:sambabook** command will need to be run to return a list of each of the servers present on the network, as shown in Listing 8.5.

Listing 8.5 The net view /domain:sambabook command.

```
C:\>net view /domain:sambabook
Server Name              Remark
---------------------------------------
\\LAPTOP                 Samba 2.0.4b on laptop
\\LINUXSERVER            Samba 2.0.4b on laptop
\\NTSERVER
\\TEST2PC
\\TEST3PC
\\TEST4PC
\\TESTPC1                Testpc1
```

TIP: *The* ***net*** *command has many options that can be seen simply by entering "net" at the command prompt.*

The result of running the **nbtstat -c** command at the command prompt is shown in Listing 8.6. This outputs the cached list of NetBIOS name to IP address on the host.

Listing 8.6 The nbtstat -c command.

```
C:\>nbtstat -c

Node IpAddress: [192.168.2.99] Scope Id:[ ]
            NetBIOS Remote Cache name Table
```

```
    Name                Type          Host Address          Life [sec]
-----------------------------------------------------------------
LINUXSERVER   <20>   UNIQUE        192.168.2.88           60
```

The result of running the **nbtstat -n** command at the command prompt is shown in Listing 8.7. This outputs the NetBIOS local name table and is similar to the **nmblookup** command.

Listing 8.7 The nbtstat -n command run from test1pc.

```
C:\>nbtstat -n

Node IpAddress: [192.168.2.40] Scope Id:[ ]
            NetBIOS Local Name Table
Name                      Type          Status
-----------------------------------------------------------------
TESTPC1        <00>       UNIQUE        Registered
SAMBABOOK      <00>       GROUP         Registered
TESTPC1        <03>       UNIQUE        Registered
TESTPC1        <20>       UNIQUE        Registered
SAMBABOOK      <1E>       GROUP         Registered
TEST1          <03>       GROUP         Registered
SAMBABOOK      <00>       GROUP         Registered
.._MSBROWSE__.<01>        GROUP         Registered
```

When run at the command prompt, the **nbtstat** command will indicate its possible options. The syntax for the command is as follows:

```
NBTSTAT [-a RemoteName] [-A IP Address] [-c] [-n] [-r] [-R] [-s] [-S]
[interval]
```

Table 8.3 details the options for **nbtstat**.

NOTE: *For any of the resources detailed in Chapter 6, the **net use** command must be utilized to make use of the share.*

The GUI interfaces are the Network Neighborhood and the manifestations of it in the Explorer and the Find tools. The Network Neighborhood program will always populate first with the local network hosts, as can be seen in Figure 8.3, with the other possible networks being available from the Entire Network tree. The Entire Network tree includes all the other workgroups and domains that exist in that subnet or that can be reached from that client using remote browsing. The alternate is the Find tool, as shown in Figure 8.4.

Table 8.3 nbtstat options.

Option	Description
-a *RemoteName*	Lists the remote hosts name table given the NetBIOS name
-A *IP Address*	Lists the remote hosts name table given the IP address
-c	Lists the remote name cache including IP addresses
-n	Lists the local NetBIOS names
-r	Lists the names resolved by broadcast and via WINS
-R	Purges and reloads the remote cache name table
-S	Lists the sessions table with destination IP addresses
-s	Lists the sessions table on the remote host, converting destination IP addresses to hostnames through the hosts file
interval	Sets the period in seconds between displaying the statistics

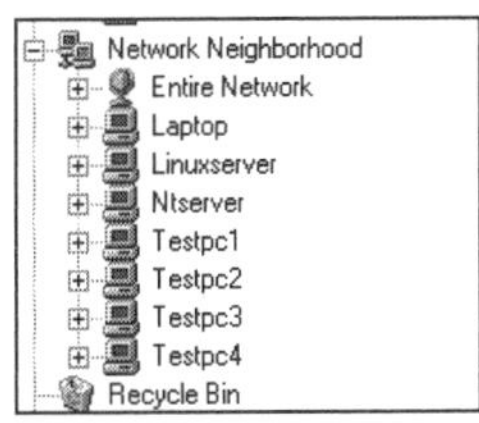

Figure 8.3 The Network Neighborhood.

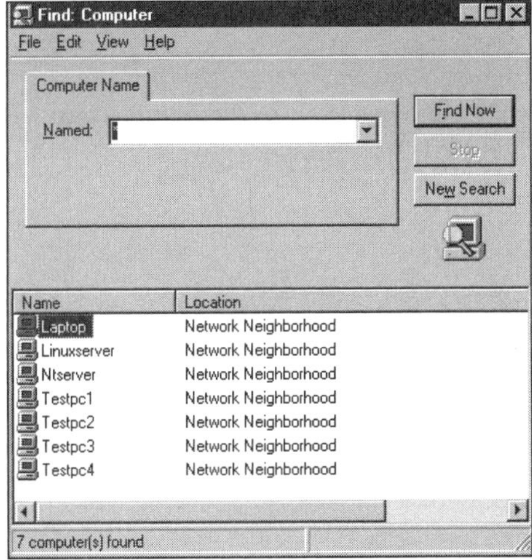

Figure 8.4 The Find: Computer tool.

After a host has been located, it is possible to view the resources on that host, as shown in Figure 8.5.

As discussed in Chapter 6, to administer the use of a share on a remote host, the option to map that resource, be it a folder or a printer, is available from either a menu or a pop-up option list. See Chapter 6 for more details.

In either a command line or a GUI interface, the Windows host sends a **QueryBrowserServers** request to the local network to request the list of local browser servers for the workgroup or domain involved. When the browser server or servers respond, the host chooses one randomly and sends a **NetServerEnum** call to the server, which responds with the contents of the browse list that the client caches locally.

Figure 8.5 The shares on a host.

Setting NetBIOS Election And Browsing Parameters In Samba

A number of parameters are relevant to NetBIOS elections and browsing that can be set in the smb.conf file. These are shown in Table 8.4.

The **os level** parameter has perhaps the largest impact on how a Samba host will participate in any NetBIOS election. The standard operating system level values for the various operating systems are listed in Table 8.5. The values were obtained from analysis of the election broadcasts captured between a host running Linux and **tcpdump** (with SMB extensions) and a Windows NT Server running **netmon** (both the SMS and the standard version). The output from the sessions involved in determining the operating system level were captured and can be seen in /sniffer/captures on this book's CD-ROM.

Table 8.4 The election and browsing parameters.

Parameter	Description
os level	This is a value that is set to determine the operating system level that Samba will advertise itself as during browsing elections. The **nmbd** program utilizes this parameter as part of the browsing process. The default is **0**, meaning that **nmbd** will lose elections to Windows machines.
lm announce	This has three possible values—**true**, **false**, or **auto**—and sets whether **nmbd** will produce Lanman announce broadcasts that are needed by OS/2 clients to allow them to see the Samba server in any network browse lists. By default, this is set to **auto**; **false** means that Samba will never produce these broadcasts, whereas **true** means that Lanman announcements are broadcast to the local network at the frequency set by the **lm interval** parameter. **auto** indicates that the server will listen for Lanman to announce broadcasts but will not send any. After the first Lanman broadcast is received, it will start to send broadcasts at a frequency set by the **lm interval** parameter.
lm interval	This sets the period, in seconds, between Lanman announcements.
preferred master	This defaults to **no**. If set to **yes**, the **nmbd** program will attempt to become the master browser for the local network.
local master	This defaults to **yes** and indicates that Samba will attempt to become the master browser for the local network. This translates to **nmbd** being instructed or not instructed to take part in browser elections.
domain master	This defaults to **no**. If this parameter is set, Samba will attempt to become the domain master browser.
browse list	This determines whether the Samba server will provide browse lists to clients. The default is **yes**.
protocol	This is the highest protocol level that will be supported by the server. The options include **CORE**, **COREPLUS**, **LANMAN1**, **LANMAN2**, and **NT1**. (**NT1** is used by Windows NT and is also known as **CIFS**.) Normally, this parameter need not be set because the automatic negotiation phase in a session setup usually sets the appropriate protocol. The default is **NT1**.
read raw	This sets the value of the number of bytes read in one packet to 65,535 bytes. The default is **yes**.
write raw	This specifies whether a server will support raw writes from a client. The default is **yes**.
nt smb support	This specifies whether **smbd** will negotiate NT SMB–specific support with Windows NT clients. The default is **yes**. Note that if the parameter is set to **no**, transfers involving NT clients can appear to be faster. Setting the parameter to **no** instructs **smbd** to use pre-Version 2 SMB calls, which were written to provide better NT support.

(continued)

***Table 8.4 The election and browsing parameters* (continued).**

Parameter	Description
nt pipe support	This allows a connection to NT SMB–specific IPC$ pipes. The default is **yes**.
nt acl support	This instructs **smbd** to map the Unix file permissions into NT Access Control Lists (ACLs).
announce version	Samba **nmbd** default announces itself at 4.2 (for Version 2.0.x currently) and specifies the major and minor version numbers used when announcing itself. This parameter normally is not altered.
announce as	Samba **nmbd** will announce itself as NT to a Network Neighborhood browse list. The possible choices are **NT** (a synonym for NT Server), **NT Server**, **NT Workstation**, **Win95**, or **WfW**, translating to Windows NT Server, Windows NT Workstation, Windows 95, and Windows for Workgroups, respectively. Altering this from the default NT can affect the way Samba acts as a browser server.
max mux	This sets the number of simultaneous SMB operations that are allowed by the server from any client. The default is **50**.
max xmit	This sets, in bytes, the maximum packet size that Samba will negotiate. The default is **65,535**, which is the maximum. Depending on the situation, setting this to a smaller value can improve performance. The workable minimum is 2,048 bytes.
name resolve order	This sets the order that is used to resolve name requests into IP addresses. The default is **lmhosts**, **hosts**, **wins**, **bcast**.
max packet	This is synonymous with **max xmit**.
max ttl	This sets the time to live, in seconds, of any NetBIOS name that **nmbd** attempts to resolve from WINS or broadcast. The default is **259,200**, or 3 days.
max wins ttl	If the Samba server is acting as a WINS server, this specifies the maximum time to live, in seconds, that **nmbd** will grant to NetBIOS names. The default is **518,400**, or 6 days.
min wins ttl	If the Samba server is acting as a WINS server, this specifies the minimum time to live, in seconds, that **nmbd** will grant to NetBIOS names. The default **21,600**, or 6 hours.
time server	This determines whether the Samba server will act as a time server to Windows clients. The default is **no**.
load printers	This global parameter instructs Samba to load the printers contained within the /etc/printcap file for browsing. Note that a [printers] section must be present with at least the parameter **browseable=yes** set to allow the printers to be included in any browse list. The default is **yes**.
netbios name	This global parameter sets the name given to the Samba host. This defaults to the first part of the Internet hostname if no value is given.

(continued)

***Table 8.4 The election and browsing parameters* (continued).**

Parameter	Description
server string	This global parameter appears next to the NetBIOS name in any browse list as a remark or comment that helps identify the Samba host. This parameter can make use of the macros **%v** (Samba version number), **%h** (real hostname), and **%L** (NetBIOS name) to make version and Samba host identification easier.
netbios aliases	The Samba host is capable of advertising itself as several different NetBIOS names, and this global parameter provides the names that will be used. No default aliases are set, and if the Samba host is performing the duty of browse server, the main NetBIOS name given with the netbios name parameter will be the only one associated with the browser service.
workgroup	This global parameter identifies which workgroup or domain the Samba host is to be a member of. The **nmbd** program will add the values of this parameter to the workgroup component of all host announcements.

Table 8.5 os level values.

Operating System	Value
DOS	1
Windows for Workgroups	1
Windows 95	1
Windows NT 3.51 Workstation	16
Windows NT 3.51 Server	32
Windows NT 4.0 Workstation	16
Windows NT 4.0 Server	32

Normally, Samba will announce itself with an **os level** of **0**; however, a number of relevant parameters in the smb.conf file are involved with the setting of NetBIOS election criteria: **os level**, **lm announce**, **lm interval**, **preferred master**, **local master**, and **domain master**. To set up a Samba host to at least stand a chance of winning an election, the host should have an **os level** value equal to or greater than that of any other operating system present. These parameters and their descriptions are listed in Table 8.4.

Setting NetBIOS Election And Browsing Parameters In Windows NT

On startup, a Windows NT system interrogates the Registry setting under HKEY_LOCAL_MACHINE\System\CurrentControlSet\Services\Browser\Parameters for the **MaintainServerList** parameter for the Browser service to determine whether the host should become a browser. The parameter has three possible values:

- **No**—Indicates that the host should never become a browser.
- **Yes**—Indicates that the host will become a browser. On startup of the browser service, the host will attempt to locate the local master browser to obtain a current browse list. If no master browser responds, the host will force a browser election. The host will then become either the master browser or a backup browser. Windows NT Server defaults to "yes" for this parameter.
- **Auto**—The host interrogates the master browser and, depending on the number of hosts on the network and other backup browsers, informs this host to act as a backup browser accordingly. For every 32 hosts on a network, a master browser attempts to add a backup browser. This setting is the default for Windows NT workstations. A BDC NT server automatically becomes a backup browser for the network.

On startup, a Windows NT system interrogates the Registry setting under HKEY_LOCAL_MACHINE\System\CurrentControlSet\Services\Browser\Parameters for the **IsDomainMasterBrowser** parameter for the Browser service to determine whether the host should become a master browser. The parameter has two possible values:

- **No**—Indicates that the host should never become a master browser.
- **Yes**—Indicates that the host will become a preferred master browser. On startup of the browser service, the host will immediately force an election to attempt to become the master browser for the local network. A preferred master browser will have priority over other, similar hosts in an election that do not have this setting. This setting can be used when you want one specific host to always be the master browser.

Setting The Time Between Browser Announcements

To alter the period between browser announcements for a host, be it Samba or Windows, certain settings control how often the LanManager announcements are made.

Settings For A Windows Host

Within the Windows NT Registry, HKEY_LOCAL_MACHINE\System\CurrentControlSet\Services\LanmanServer\Parameters add the **Announce** parameter if it does not already exist with a type REG_DWORD and set a value, in seconds, that the browser should wait between announcements. The default, if not set, is 720 seconds, or 12 minutes. Note that you should make corresponding changes to all hosts on the local subnet, or the browser announcement periods will become unsynchronized.

Settings For A Samba Host

Samba has two smb.conf parameters that can be used: **lm announce** (the values are **true**, **false**, and **auto**; see Table 8.4 for an explanation) and **lm interval** (the default is 60 seconds; if set to 0, no announcements are made regardless of what **lm announce** is set to). In combination, these parameters can be used to set the Samba host to make corresponding LanManager host announcements and the period between them.

Capturing NetBIOS Network Traffic

The facilities available to capture the network traffic during any sessions are either Windows or Unix based. The Windows option involves the **netmon** application that comes with Windows NT Server. A more expanded version comes with the SMS Server. Members of the Samba team have written some additions to the **netmon** tools that aid in the extraction of useful SMB/CIFS traffic from the network sniffer output. You will find details on this book's CD-ROM under /networksniffer. The Unix platform option involves using **tcpdump**. Again, the Samba team has written an extension to **tcpdump** known as **tcpdump-smb**, which captures and displays SMB packets in some detail. Using either tool will allow you to capture and report on the SMB traffic on your network.

A relatively simple example of the use of **tcpdump** is to capture the SMB traffic running between a client and an SMB/CIFS server that shows the various SMB exchanges between the two involving authentication and the use of a share, opening a file, and then closing it. This involved using Word 97 to open and close a file on the server. Listing 8.8 shows the reduced output obtained between a server named laptop and a client named test1pc. The output has been edited to indicate the SMB session commands that flow between the two hosts. Complete copies of sample outputs can be found in /network-sniffer/examples on the CD-ROM.

Listing 8.8 The SMB/CIFS traffic between a client and a server.

```
01:20:15.772642 test1pc.1028 > laptop.domain.netbios-ssn: P 73:231(158)
   ack 5 win 8756
>>> NBT Packet
NBT Session Packet
Flags=0x0
Length=154

SMB PACKET: SMBnegprot (REQUEST)

01:20:15.842642 laptop.domain.netbios-ssn > test1pc.1028: P 5:88(83)
   ack 231 win 32736
>>> NBT Packet
NBT Session Packet
Flags=0x0
Length=79

SMB PACKET: SMBnegprot (REPLY)

01:20:15.842642 test1pc.1028 > laptop.domain.netbios-ssn: P 231:395(164)
   ack 88 win 8673
>>> NBT Packet
NBT Session Packet
Flags=0x0
Length=160

SMB PACKET: SMBsesssetupX (REQUEST)
SMB PACKET: SMBtconX (REQUEST) (CHAINED)

01:20:16.022642 laptop.domain.netbios-ssn > test1pc.1028: P 88:178(90)
   ack 395 win 32736
>>> NBT Packet
NBT Session Packet
Flags=0x0
Length=86

SMB PACKET: SMBsesssetupX (REPLY)
SMB PACKET: SMBtconX (REPLY) (CHAINED)

01:20:16.022642 test1pc.1028 > laptop.domain.netbios-ssn: P 395:494(99)
```

```
   ack 178 win 8583
>>> NBT Packet
NBT Session Packet
Flags=0x0
Length=95

SMB PACKET: SMBtrans (REQUEST)

01:20:16.102642 laptop.domain.netbios-ssn > test1pc.1028: P 178:740(562)
   ack 494 win 32736
>>> NBT Packet
NBT Session Packet
Flags=0x0
Length=558

SMB PACKET: SMBtrans (REPLY)

01:20:17.692642 test1pc.1028 > laptop.domain.netbios-ssn: P 494:533(39)
   ack 740 win 8021
>>> NBT Packet
NBT Session Packet
Flags=0x0
Length=35

SMB PACKET: SMBtdis (REQUEST)

01:20:17.702642 laptop.domain.netbios-ssn > test1pc.1028: P 740:779(39)
   ack 533 win 32736
>>> NBT Packet
NBT Session Packet
Flags=0x0
Length=35

SMB PACKET: SMBtdis (REPLY)

01:20:17.722642 laptop.domain.netbios-ssn > test1pc.1028: F 779:779(0)
   ack 534 win 32736
01:20:21.702642 test1pc.1029 > laptop.domain.netbios-ssn: S 141195:141195(0)
   win 8192 <mss 1460> (DF)

>>> NBT Packet
NBT Session Request
Flags=0x81000044
Destination=LINUXSERVER     NameType=0x20 (Server)
Source=TESTPC1          NameType=0x00 (Workstation)
```

```
01:20:21.742642 laptop.domain.netbios-ssn > test1pc.1029: P 1:5(4)
   ack 73 win 32736
>>> NBT Packet
NBT Session Granted
Flags=0x82000000

 (DF)
01:20:21.742642 test1pc.1029 > laptop.domain.netbios-ssn: P 73:231(158)
   ack 5 win 8756
>>> NBT Packet
NBT Session Packet
Flags=0x0
Length=154

SMB PACKET: SMBnegprot (REQUEST)
SMB Command   =  0x72
Error class   =  0x0
Error code    =  0
Flags1        =  0x0
Flags2        =  0x0
Tree ID       =  0
Proc ID       =  5323
UID           =  0
MID           =  1154
Word Count    =  0
Dialect=PC NETWORK PROGRAM 1.0
Dialect=MICROSOFT NETWORKS 3.0
Dialect=DOS LM1.2X002
Dialect=DOS LANMAN2.1
Dialect=Windows for Workgroups 3.1a
Dialect=NT LM 0.12

 (DF)
01:20:21.752642 laptop.domain.netbios-ssn > test1pc.1029: P 5:88(83)
   ack 231 win 32736
>>> NBT Packet
NBT Session Packet
Flags=0x0
Length=79

SMB PACKET: SMBnegprot (REPLY)
SMB Command   =  0x72
Error class   =  0x0
Error code    =  0
Flags1        =  0x80
Flags2        =  0x1
```

```
Tree ID       =  0
Proc ID       =  5323
UID           =  0
MID           =  1154
Word Count    =  17
NT1 Protocol
DialectIndex=5
SecMode=0x1
MaxMux=50
NumVcs=1
MaxBuffer=65535
RawSize=65536
SessionKey=0xA0
Capabilities=0x331
ServerTime=Mon Aug  2 01:20:22 1999
TimeZone=0
CryptKey=Data: (1 bytes)
[000] 00                                                .
[000] 53 41 4D 42 41 42 4F 4F  4B 00                    SAMBABOO K.

 (DF)
01:20:21.752642 test1pc.1029 > laptop.domain.netbios-ssn: P 231:403(172)
   ack 88 win 8673
>>> NBT Packet
NBT Session Packet
Flags=0x0
Length=168

SMB PACKET: SMBsesssetupX (REQUEST)
SMB PACKET: SMBtconX (REQUEST) (CHAINED)
[000] 00 5C 5C 4C 49 4E 55 58  53 45 52 56 45 52 5C 47  .\\LINUX SERVER\G
[010] 52 4F 55 50 53 48 41 52  45 00 3F 3F 3F 3F 3F 00  ROUPSHAR E.?????.

01:20:21.992642 laptop.domain.netbios-ssn > test1pc.1029: P 88:178(90)
   ack 403 win 32736
>>> NBT Packet
NBT Session Packet
Flags=0x0
Length=86

SMB PACKET: SMBsesssetupX (REPLY)
SMB PACKET: SMBtconX (REPLY) (CHAINED)

01:20:22.152642 test1pc.1029 > laptop.domain.netbios-ssn: P 538:591(53)
   ack 335 win 8426
>>> NBT Packet
```

```
NBT Session Packet
Flags=0x0
Length=49

SMB PACKET: SMBtrans2 (REQUEST)
File=*

01:20:22.282642 laptop.domain.netbios-ssn > test1pc.1029: P 374:764(390)
   ack 676 win 32736
>>> NBT Packet
NBT Session Packet
Flags=0x0
Length=386

SMB PACKET: SMBtrans2 (REPLY)
data:
[000] 64 00 00 00 00 00 00 00  80 08 1C CF B8 D6 BE 01  d....... ........
[010] 80 58 4E F9 D9 DB BE 01  80 08 1C CF B8 D6 BE 01  .XN..... ........
[020] 80 08 1C CF B8 D6 BE 01  00 00 00 00 00 00 00 00  ........ ........
[030] 00 00 00 00 00 00 00 00  10 00 00 00 04 00 00 00  ........ ........
[040] 00 00 00 00 00 00 00 00  00 00 00 00 00 00 00 00  ........ ........
[050] 00 00 00 00 00 00 00 00  00 00 00 00 00 00 74 65  ........ ......te
[060] 73 74 00 00 6C 00 00 00  00 00 00 00 80 31 BA 51  st..l... .....1.Q
[070] AB DB BE 01 80 31 BA 51  AB DB BE 01 00 1B B8 E9  .....1.Q ........
[080] AB DB BE 01 00 1B B8 E9  AB DB BE 01 60 04 00 00  ........ ....'...
[090] 00 00 00 00 60 04 00 00  00 00 00 00 80 00 00 00  ....'... ........
[0A0] 0D 00 00 00 00 00 00 00  0C 00 4E 4D 42 4C 4F 7E  ........ ..NMBLO~
[0B0] 45 36 2E 54 58 54 00 00  00 00 00 00 00 00 00 00  E6.TXT.. ........
[0C0] 00 00 6E 6D 62 6C 6F 6F  6B 75 70 2E 74 78 74 00  ..nmbloo kup.txt.
[0D0] 6C 00 00 00 00 00 00 00  80 2A BD E6 AB DB BE 01  l....... .*......
[0E0] 00 0A D5 F6 AB DB BE 01  80 2A BD E6 AB DB BE 01  ........ .*......
[0F0] 80 2A BD E6 AB DB BE 01  B8 04 00 00 00 00 00 00  .*...... ........
[100] B8 04 00 00 00 00 00 00  80 00 00 00 0D 00 00 00  ........ ........
[110] 00 00 00 00 0C 00 53 4D  42 43 4C 7E 4F 55 2E 54  ......SM BCL~OU.T
[120] 58 54 00 00 00 00 00 00  00 00 00 00 00 00 73 6D  XT...... ......sm
[130] 62 63 6C 69 65 6E 74 2E  74 78 74 00              bclient. txt.

01:20:22.282642 test1pc.1029 > laptop.domain.netbios-ssn: P 676:772(96)
   ack 764 win 7997
>>> NBT Packet
NBT Session Packet
Flags=0x0
Length=92

SMB PACKET: SMBtrans2 (REQUEST)
Data: (26 bytes)
```

```
[000] 00 01 06 00 04 01 00 00  00 00 00 00 73 6D 62 63  ........ ....smbc
[010] 6C 69 65 6E 74 2E 74 78  74 00                    lient.tx t.

01:20:22.282642 laptop.domain.netbios-ssn > test1pc.1029: P 764:834(70)
   ack 772 win 32736
>>> NBT Packet
NBT Session Packet
Flags=0x0
Length=66

SMB PACKET: SMBtrans2 (REPLY)

01:20:22.282642 test1pc.1029 > laptop.domain.netbios-ssn: P 772:813(41)
   ack 834 win 7927
>>> NBT Packet
NBT Session Packet
Flags=0x0
Length=37

SMB PACKET: SMBfindclose (REQUEST)

01:20:22.292642 laptop.domain.netbios-ssn > test1pc.1029: P 834:873(39)
   ack 813 win 32736
>>> NBT Packet
NBT Session Packet
Flags=0x0
Length=35

SMB PACKET: SMBfindclose (REPLY)
```

The SMB commands and the host details involved in the session can clearly be seen in this listing.

Commands follow in specific patterns for the session setup, opening the share, opening the file (with data transfer), and finally closing the file. The groups of SMB commands for the session setup are the following:

- SMB PACKET: SMBnegprot (REQUEST)
- SMB PACKET: SMBnegprot (REPLY)
- SMB PACKET: SMBsesssetupX (REQUEST)
- SMB PACKET: SMBtconX (REQUEST) (CHAINED)
- SMB PACKET: SMBsesssetupX (REPLY)
- SMB PACKET: SMBtconX (REPLY) (CHAINED)

The groups of SMB commands for opening the share are the following:

- SMB PACKET: SMBtrans2 (REQUEST)
- SMB PACKET: SMBtrans2 (REPLY)

The groups of SMB commands for opening the file are the following:

- SMB PACKET: SMBtrans2 (REQUEST)
- SMB PACKET: SMBtrans2 (REPLY)

The groups of SMB commands for closing the file are the following:

- SMB PACKET: SMBfindclose (REQUEST)
- SMB PACKET: SMBfindclose (REPLY)

The more complex example in Listing 8.9 shows the SMB traffic that occurs between an SMB/CIFS server and another SMB host when it is added to the network and the resultant NetBIOS election occurs. Listing 8.9 shows the edited **tcpdump** capture.

Listing 8.9 The SMB/CIFS traffic between a client and a server.

```
01:20:10.342642 test1pc.1028 > laptop.domain.netbios-ssn: S 129832:129832(0)
   win 8192 <mss 1460> (DF)
01:20:10.342642 laptop.domain.netbios-ssn > test1pc.1028: S
   892731541:892731541(0) ack 129833 win 32736 <mss 1460>
01:20:10.342642 test1pc.1028 > laptop.domain.netbios-ssn: . ack 1
   win 8760 (DF)
01:20:10.342642 test1pc.1028 > laptop.domain.netbios-ssn: P 1:73(72)
   ack 1 win 8760
>>> NBT Packet
NBT Session Request
Flags=0x81000044
Destination=LINUXSERVER     NameType=0x20 (Server)
Source=TESTPC1          NameType=0x00 (Workstation)

01:20:10.842642 laptop.domain.netbios-ssn > test1pc.1028: P 1:5(4)
   ack 73 win 32736
>>> NBT Packet
NBT Session Granted
Flags=0x82000000
```

Running a network traffic monitor on your network to note the SMB traffic is both an interesting exercise and an important diagnostic tool; it is also an important addition to the administrator's toolbox. Whenever any problems are apparent, the output can be captured with either a pipe (|) or a send to (>) to provide you with the ability to capture as well as view the SMB sessions as they occur.

***WARNING!* The tcpdump application can produce enormous quantities of data, so you will need to exercise care when capturing the output for analysis.**

The Samba team has added an extra utility that simplifies the analysis of the data from sniffing network traffic. This allows the output from a **tcpdump** capture run on a Unix system to be converted to the CAP format used with the Windows **netmon** program. Two options are available. The first is for **tcpdump**-obtained output. The second is for use with Solaris 2.x operating systems that have their own network sniffer, known as snoop.

The source code for either is available from the Samba FTP site location for **tcpdump** at **ftp://ftp.samba.org/pub/tcpdump-smb/**. The files are called capconvert.c or snoop2cap.c. A copy of both can be found on this book's CD-ROM under /network-sniffer.

Browsing Without Broadcasts

All the previously mentioned methods indicate the browsing processes that occur. However, if the network has a large number of hosts, the broadcast method will produce a large amount of broadcast traffic between hosts. Alternate methods are available to help reduce this traffic. The first of these methods involves the use of the lmhosts file.

Using lmhosts

The hosts file used in the resolution of Internet hostname to IP address contains a list of the IP address and hostname pairs for hosts that are regularly used, thus avoiding the requests for DNS name resolution. The lmhosts file follows a similar function and is used for the resolution of NetBIOS name to IP. The layout and syntax of an lmhosts file for a network of a number of hosts can be seen in Listing 8.10. Chapter 2 provided details for the location of the lmhosts file and the lmhosts.sam sample file for different versions of Windows. These are installed at the same time as TCP/IP networking.

Listing 8.10 A sample lmhosts file (from a Windows client).

```
# LMHOSTS file
#
192.168.1.1     linuxserver     #PRE  #main Linux SMB/CIFS server
192.168.1.2     ntserver        #PRE  #workgroup NT SMB/CIFS server
192.168.1.3     test1pc               #test workstation
192.168.1.4     test2pc               #test workstation
192.168.1.5     test3pc               #test workstation
```

```
192.168.1.6     test4pc                 #test workstation
192.168.1.7     ntsdev01          #PRE  #DOM:sambabook  #PDC
192.168.1.8     ntsdev02          #PRE  #source server
192.168.1.9     ntsprint01        #PRE  #printer server
192.168.1.10    ntsfile01         #PRE  #file server
192.168.1.100   ntscfg01          #PRE  #needed for the include
#
#BEGIN_ALTERNATE
#INCLUDE \\ntscfg01\public\lmhosts
#INCLUDE \\ntsdev01\public\lmhosts
#END_ALTERNATE
#
```

This file's format is such that the IP address should be placed in the first column followed by the corresponding NetBIOS name. One or more spaces or tabs separate the columns. Any "#" character at the start or the end of a line is used to indicate a comment. The exceptions to this are shown here:

```
#PRE
#DOM:domain
#INCLUDE filename
#BEGIN_ALTERNATE
#END_ALTERNATE
\0xnn (non-printing character support)
```

An entry on a line of the characters **#PRE** will cause that entry to be preloaded into the NetBIOS name cache. By default, entries are not preloaded but are parsed only after dynamic name resolution fails.

An entry with the **#DOM:*domain*** tag will associate the entry with the domain specified by ***domain***. This affects how the browser and logon services behave in TCP/IP environments. To preload the hostname associated with the **#DOM** entry, it is necessary to also add **#PRE** to the line. The ***domain*** is always preloaded, although it will not be shown when the name cache is viewed.

An **#INCLUDE*filename*** is an extremely useful method of centrally controlling the NetBIOS entries, as it forces the RFC NetBIOS (NBT) software to seek the specified***filename*** and parse it as if it were on the local host.***filename*** is generally a UNC-based name, allowing a centralized lmhosts file to be maintained on a server.

Note that it is *always* necessary to provide a mapping for the IP address of the server prior to the **#INCLUDE**. This mapping must use the **#PRE** directive. In addition, if you intend to use the lmhosts **#INCLUDE** option, the share "public" must be present in the **LanManServer** list of **NullSessionShares** in order for client machines to be able to read the lmhosts file successfully. This key is under

HKEY_LOCAL_MACHINE\System\CurrentControlSet\Services\LanManServer\Parameters\NullSessionShares in the Registry. Simply add "public" to the list found there.

The **#BEGIN_ALTERNATE** and **#END_ALTERNATE** keywords allow multiple **#INCLUDE** statements to be grouped together. Any single successful include will cause the group to succeed.

Finally, nonprinting characters can be embedded in mappings by first surrounding the NetBIOS name in quotations and then using the \0xnn notation to specify a hex value for a nonprinting character.

Configuration Needed To Use lmhosts

For Windows operating systems, no added configuration is required to enable the use of this file. Windows networking will attempt a NetBIOS name lookup using this file automatically. Windows NT can be instructed to import an lmhosts file if instructed to do so within the Network dialog box under the WINS tab in the Control Panel.

TIP: *On your local network, make sure that all Windows clients have a properly configured lmhosts file that includes all the hosts that have fixed IP addresses. A better option is an lmhosts file that directs them to a central copy of the lmhosts entries for the local subnet that is maintained regularly. The operating system usually installs a sample copy, named lmhosts.sam, into /winnt/system32/drivers/etc on NT systems and /win9x on Windows 95 and Windows 98 systems. This simple configuration file will reduce the amount of NetBIOS name resolution broadcasts between clients on your local network. Likewise, it is recommended that you create a local hosts file on your clients at the same time.*

Additional Entries

Two additional types of entries have appeared recently in lmhosts files: **#SG** and **#MH**. The first, **#SG**, allows you to add user-defined special groups to the lmhosts file. This allows the grouping of resources, such as printers or computers. In use, the **#SG** keyword defines a special group in the lmhosts file. Special groups are limited to a total of 25 members. (If you are using WINS, they can also be defined by using the WINS Manager.)

Specify the name just as you would a domain name in lmhosts except that the keyword portion of the entry is **#SG**, as shown here:

```
192.168.2.100 printserver #SG:sambabook #SAMBABOOK group of computers
```

The special group "sambabook" will be created, and the computer "printserver" will become a part of that group. In some cases, you might want to simply specify the name of a special group without specifying an IP address. This can be done by giving the name of the group preceded by **#SG**, as shown here:

```
printserver #SG:sambabook #SAMBABOOK group of computers
```

Addresses entered by using the lmhosts file become permanent addresses in the special group and can be removed only by using the WINS Manager. The **#SG** keyword may only have 25 entries associated with it. The **#MH** keyword allows multiple homed computers to have more than one NetBIOS name occupy the same IP address. Specify the name just as you would for any other entry in the lmhosts file except that the **#MH** entry is added:

```
192.168.2.100 printserver #MH
192.168.2.101 printserver #MH
192.168.2.102 printserver #MH
```

The limit of IP entries possible for any NetBIOS name and **#MH** is 25.

For Samba clients, the support for this file is enabled by the parameter **name resolve order**, which takes four possible parameters—**hosts**, **lmhosts**, **wins**, and **bcast**—in the order in which these different options are to be used to resolve NetBIOS names. The list can be exclusive, meaning that it is possible to set the Samba client to never use **bcast** (NetBIOS broadcasts) to determine NetBIOS names and thus providing the option to reduce network traffic involving broadcasts. The standard Unix location for this file is /etc but can also be found in /usr/local/samba/lib, where the Samba distribution is expected to place a copy of the smb.conf file and searches this directory first. If an alternate location, such as /etc, is used, either create a link to it from /usr/local/samba/lib or start up **nmbd** specifying the /etc/lmhosts file with an **-h** flag. The following shows the two options for an inetd.conf start, or **nmbd**, and starting as a daemon process:

```
# inetd.conf
Netbios-ns dgram udp wait root /usr/local/samba/bin/nmbd -h /<location>
   nmbd -h /<location>
# Daemon process
/usr/local/samba/bin/nmbd -h /<location> -D
```

Unfortunately, the option in which a central lmhosts file can be read by individual hosts by including it in use is not available with the Samba version of the lmhosts file. In addition, it is not possible to use one Samba host to act as a central lmhosts lookup for many others (except perhaps using Network File System [NFS] to export the file location to other hosts). However, the same file can be used on both Samba and Windows, but the **#include** options will not be used.

How Does This Work?

The lmhosts file works on a similar basis to the hosts file that exists on either Unix (/etc/hosts) or Windows (/%system32%/drivers/etc or /win95/system) that is used to resolve the DNS hostname and/or IP address for a remote host. It functions as a shortcut or local copy of the most commonly referenced NetBIOS hostnames and maintains locally a copy of the information required for name or IP resolution. It's a common practice to populate this file with the NetBIOS name and IP information for the primary domain controller (PDC) and backup domain controller (BDC) of a network and the file and printer servers, should they have fixed IP addresses. This is useful for a number of hosts, especially when fixed IP addresses are used; however, this file can become very laborious to maintain if the number of hosts in it exceeds 100 (a large number of possible hosts). When a large number of resolutions of hostname to IP are required, especially when DHCP is utilized, the only realistic option is to use WINS.

Creating A WINS Service In Samba

The lmhosts file provides the necessary resolution of local NetBIOS name to IP that most hosts require. However, when many hosts are present and/or DHCP is used on a network, this might not be a viable option, and WINS can then be used. In summary, WINS is to NetBIOS-name-to-IP resolution what DNS is for hostname-to-IP resolution. The major difference is that WINS is a dynamic service and uses the periodic NetBIOS broadcasts and elections to build its database.

In practice, the WINS server collects the broadcasts from various hosts on a network and thus learns the IP addresses associated with those hosts. On startup, any NetBIOS host broadcasts to the network to announce that it is present. The WINS service has two important effects that reduce network traffic because it means that one (or more if you are using Microsoft NT Servers) WINS server and database act as the central location for both the registration and the resolution of NetBIOS name to IP addresses. Before attempting to locate the host, a client configured to use the WINS server first interrogates the local lmhosts file and then the WINS server and then the DNS server (if the networking has been configured that way). If a WINS server does not exist, the NetBIOS client hosts on the network will regularly generate traffic both to announce that a service is required and to determine the NetBIOS names and IP addresses of those hosts. This will still occur from time to time, but you will no longer have the large number of broadcasts associated with every client attempting to determine which service is to be connected to. This can greatly reduce the network load for a NetBIOS- or Windows-dominated network.

Importantly, the broadcasts are also restricted to the local subnet only. Although this might not affect small networks, larger networks that span several subnets are not able to communicate with one another in this manner. Although lmhosts can be used in this situation, WINS might be more flexible in the long run.

WINS solves both sets of problems by design and can be used by configuring clients to make use of the WINS server for the registration and resolution of NetBIOS to IP address, including hosts on different subnets on your network.

The creation of a WINS server on a Samba server is as simple as adding **wins support=yes** to the smb.conf file. Note that you need not add a Samba WINS server to your network if you already have a Microsoft NT Server performing this duty on your network. This is because a Windows NT Server would expect to adopt this function. In addition, the Microsoft WINS server is able to replicate its database with another NT WINS server, say, in a different building in a company. Samba does not support this ability and can be used only in a single configuration. The WINS database for a Samba server is contained in the WINS.DAT file, which is an ACSII text file in the <samba_home>/var/locks/ directory. An example is shown here:

```
VERSION 1 160619
"DOMAIN#00" 930008238 255.255.255.255 c4R
"DOMAIN#1e" 930008238 255.255.255.255 c4R
"LINUXROUTER1#00" 930008238 192.168.1.1 46R
"LINUXROUTER1#03" 930008238 192.168.1.1 46R
"LINUXROUTER1#20" 930008238 192.168.1.1 46R
```

In case of failure, say, for a WINS server that held the database for a couple of hundred hosts, it would make sense to be able to create a copy of this database for purposes of recovery. However, you cannot copy this file on a running Samba server. You need to shut down the **nmbd** service first. However, if the WINS server fails (Samba or otherwise) and needs to be restarted, the NetBIOS hosts on the network will quickly reannounce themselves when the server starts, and the database will be quickly re-created. Chapter 11 contains details of backup procedures that can be useful with complex networks in which Samba controls the WINS service. The browse service in Samba creates a database of machines that is held within the BROWSE.DAT file. An example of this is shown here:

```
"DOMAIN"                c0001000 "DOMINICS4"                     "DOMAIN"
"LINUXROUTER1"          40019a03 "Linux Router Samba Server"     "DOMAIN"
"DOMINICS4"             4006120b "Tower Server - BDC"            "DOMAIN"
```

Creating A WINS Service In Windows NT

The standard Microsoft NT WINS server includes a WINS server as one of the possible network management administration tools and is installed from the Network dialog box in the Control Panel. Figure 8.6 shows the NT version of the WINS server initial opening screen.

Once installed, there are a number of available options, as can be seen in Figures 8.7, 8.8, and 8.9. Figure 8.7 shows the WINS database. Several display options are possible, and the radio buttons will allow you to define the display.

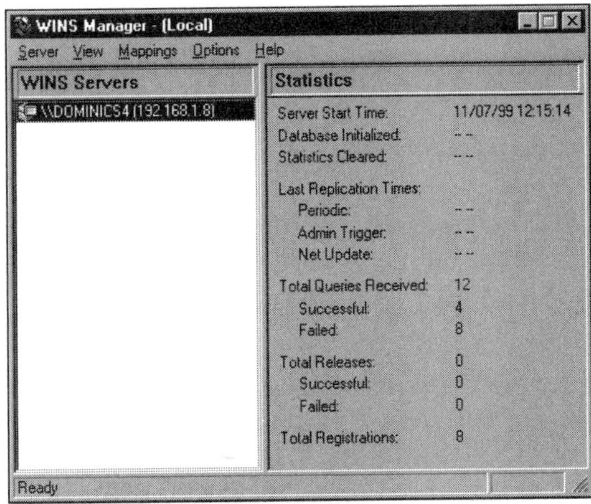

Figure 8.6 The NT WINS Manager.

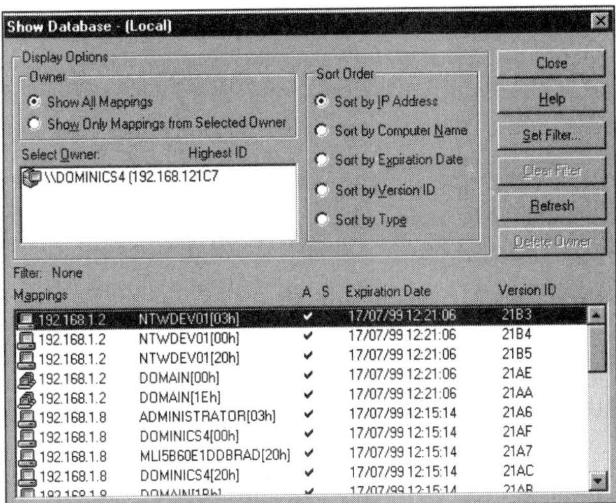

Figure 8.7 The WINS database.

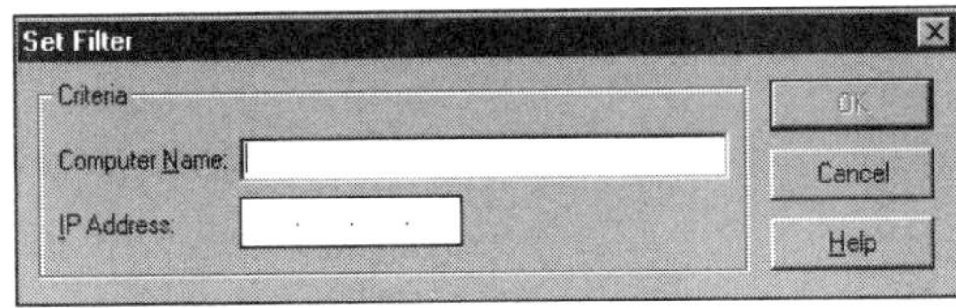

Figure 8.8 The NT WINS Manager filter.

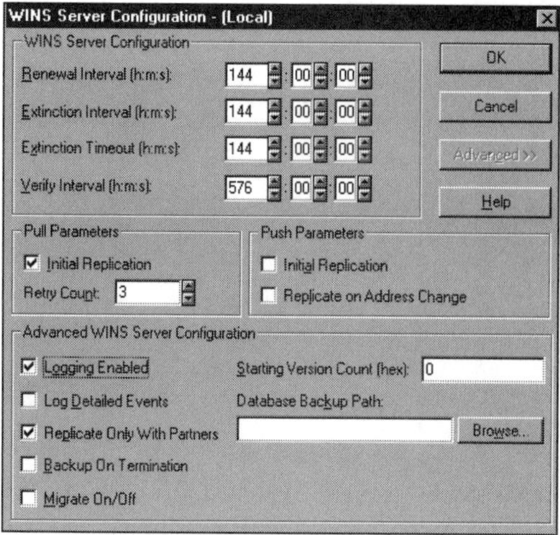

Figure 8.9 Configuring the NT WINS Manager.

Sometimes a WINS database contains many details on hosts, and a large number of entries are present. To view the data of one host, it is possible to use a filter by clicking on Set Filter, bringing up the dialog box shown in Figure 8.8. This will ask the WINS server to present the information for that host.

A key to the operation of the WINS NT server is a configuration screen, shown in Figure 8.9. The settings are defaults and can be modified to alter the periods for the WINS database update. You can also set the location of the WINS database backup.

Using WINS

To use WINS for Windows clients, the TCP/IP networking WINS tab should have the Enable WINS Resolution radio button selected and the IP address of the WINS server should be entered. The client will then attempt to resolve NetBIOS names to IP addresses using the designated server. Figure 8.10 shows the WINS tab with its appropriate entries. The WINS server can be a Samba server or an NT server performing the same function.

The Samba client specifies the WINS server IP address in the **wins server** parameter. Note that if the Samba server is itself acting as the WINS server, you need not add an entry to this parameter but need to set the **wins support** parameter to **yes**.

The Samba WINS support also provides two further options. The first option is similar to that offered with Windows clients where DNS can be used to resolve

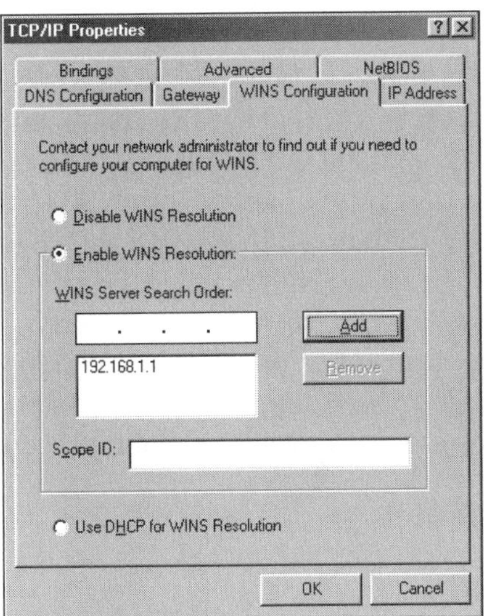

Figure 8.10 WINS configuration.

NetBIOS names if not found in the WINS database. Figure 8.10 shows this option as a checkbox. Samba WINS servers would set this option by making use of the **dns proxy** parameter and setting this to **yes**. In practice, if the WINS server database does not contain the required information, the WINS server, with **dns proxy** set to **yes**, will query the DNS server on behalf of the original client. The client need not send a request to the DNS server. Note that if the DNS servers are available only periodically—say, when you are using a dial-up connection from a remote location—it is advisable not to set this parameter, as the unconnected DNS will be queried, possibly delaying name resolution.

TIP: *Consider adding a secondary or cache DNS server to your remote office if the situation demands it.*

The second option is to configure a Samba WINS server on a remote subnet to make use of a central WINS server and to make the remote WINS server proxy the connection to the central WINS server. The Samba server will respond to name resolution requests on behalf of the remote server. The Samba server might or might not be acting as a WINS server. To make use of this facility, the smb.conf parameter **wins proxy** should be set to **yes**, along with (depending on the situation) the **wins support** or **wins server** parameter.

An additional smb.conf parameter, **name resolve order**, has four possible options: **hosts**, **lmhosts**, **wins**, and **bcast**. If these are set to **hosts**, **lmhosts**, and **wins**, the Samba host will attempt to determine the IP address of the required host using the options listed in order and will not attempt to broadcast name queries.

How Does This Work?

When a client is attached to the network, it broadcasts its presence to the network. If a WINS server exists on the network, it will register the client information in its database. The network's clients should be configured to make use of the WINS server, if it exists, so that when a NetBIOS name resolution is required, the client will send a name query to the WINS server to resolve the required NetBIOS name into an IP address. Because the WINS server will have a database of all NetBIOS names with IP addresses for hosts on the network, the server will respond to the client with the correct IP address that had been registered for that host. Thus, when any network spans multiple subnets, the use of WINS servers to provide NetBIOS name resolution for hosts outside the local subnet becomes necessary.

Browsing Through Single And Multiple Subnets

The examples outlined previously still assume that all the hosts exist on the same local subnet. In practice, it is not uncommon for hosts to be spread across several subnets separated by routers. Consider the possible network setup given in Figure 8.11, where the network spans several subnets: 192.168.2.0, 192.168.3.0, and 192.168.4.0.

The NetBIOS announcements will still occur on each of these subnets, and the practical existence of master and backup browsers in each of these subnets will remain. This will allow each of the hosts in the individual subnets to browse the local subnet with no further configuration. For a host to be able to browse the network outside its own subnet, the browse list contained on the master browser for that remote subnet must be made available to it. This is accomplished using a

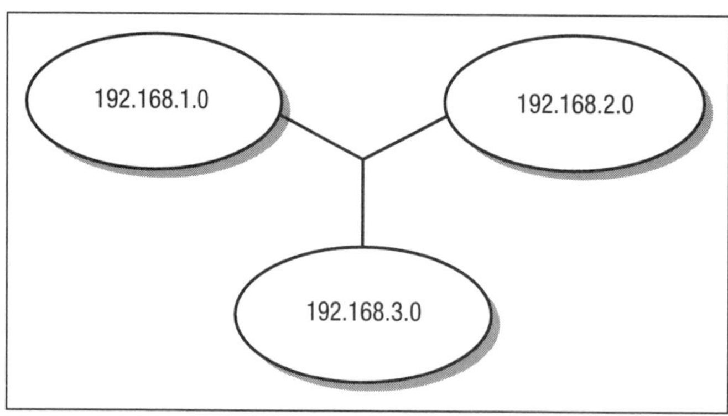

Figure 8.11 A network over several subnets.

domain master browser, which is a special designation of the master browser capable of communicating across subnets between master browsers sending **NetServerEnum** requests to the master browsers in each subnet and capturing and relaying the resultant merged domain master browser list across the domain. This process can take some time. The standard period between **NetServerEnum** requests from the domain master browser to the local master browser is 15 minutes. In turn, the local master browser will send a **NetServerEnum** request to the domain master browser to obtain an up-to-date list of all servers in the domain every 15 minutes.

In practice, two options are available to facilitate browsing across subnets. The first involves setting one Samba host in each subnet to be the local master browser and to make remote announcements to the other subnets. In addition, it is advisable to set these Samba hosts to synchronize the browse lists between them.

The second involves either setting a Samba host as a domain master browser or using an NT Server 4 machine as a PDC for the domain or workgroup. This will then synchronize the browse lists across the subnets.

In both cases, a WINS server (usually, but not necessarily, one of the master browsers) will be required to collect the NetBIOS names and IP addresses of all the hosts on the various subnets. The WINS server will then be able to reply to name queries for hosts across the subnets.

It is not considered good practice to attempt to create a domain master browser with a Samba host when an NT Server 4 PDC also exists on the network, as this would normally operate with this function. The reasoning is subtle, and one explanation is that Samba operates with the domain master browser and PDC functionality split, but NT Server does not. The result is that several Windows clients might attempt to use the Samba host as the logon server rather than the NT Server. This might disturb large sections of a network if not controlled carefully.

NOTE: *The smb.conf parameters that have relevance to browsing multiple subnets were shown earlier in the chapter in Table 8.4.*

Examples

For the hosts in the SAMBABOOK workgroup in the subnet 192.168.3.0 in Figure 8.11 to know of a Samba server in the 192.168.2.0 subnet, the smb.conf file for the server would have the parameter **remote announce=192.168.3.255/SAMBABOOK** set. The hosts in 192.168.3.0 would then be able to receive the broadcast announcements from that server.

If 192.168.1.0, 192.168.2.0, and 192.168.3.0 all had Samba hosts, it would be possible to make the Samba hosts synchronize the browse lists for the three subnets by doing the following:

1. Set one of the Samba servers (for example, in the 192.168.1.0 subnet) to a domain master browser with the smb.conf parameter **domain master=yes**.
2. Indicate which remote networks the domain master browser should synchronize with by using **remote browse sync=192.168.2.255 192.168.3.255**.
3. Set the parameters related to **os level**, **preferred master**, and **local master** on one of the Samba hosts in the other subnets such that they will become local master browsers; for example, **os level=33**, **local master=yes**, **preferred master=yes**.

RAS (Remote Access Service)

The detailed setup of a RAS server is beyond the scope of this book; however, most desktop operating systems that fall into the Windows or Unix family come with the necessary RAS software included as standard. Windows 9x and NT have a fairly simple GUI interface that aids in the establishment of a dial-up network (DUN) connection. The Unix variants, especially Linux, also have DUN capabilities with interfaces of various complexity, depending on whether the X-Windows interface is installed.

DUN from a Windows host will allow a network connection to many different kinds of networks and servers. This section discusses how to connect to and configure a Windows NT RAS server using TCP/IP so that SMB services on either a local or a remote network can be used. The section also includes details for other servers that are compatible with the Point-To-Point Protocol (PPP).

Connecting To A Windows NT RAS Server

Connecting to a Windows NT RAS server from another Windows host is relatively straightforward. All you need is the telephone number of the Windows NT server when creating a connection. DUN negotiates the proper protocols and server connection type. You need not specify a default server type.

The use of a Samba host to dial up a Windows NT Server depends on PPP and some Challenge Handshake Authentication Protocol (CHAP) or Password Authentication Protocol (PAP) authentication capabilities.

Windows NT RAS Servers

Windows NT Server 4 RAS supports PPP and RAS clients; PPP is the recommended protocol. Windows NT Server 4 also supports IPX/SPX, NetBEUI, and TCP/IP network protocols and can be configured to act as a NetBIOS gateway, IPX router, and IP router. Windows NT Server 4 and later can act as a virtual private network (VPN) server, so you can set up a VPN connection to Windows NT 4 RAS servers using the Point-to-Point Tunneling Protocol (PPTP). The latest RAS software for Windows NT Server 4, known as RRAS (or "steelhead"), incorporates many additional features that make wide area networking (WAN) considerably easier to configure.

Appendix B includes several references that provide much more detail on accessing Windows NT RAS servers.

Configuring A Windows NT Server For Dial-Up Clients

To configure a computer running Windows NT Server 4 so that dial-up clients can remotely access it, you need to install and configure RAS. This requires that you be logged into the server as a member of the Administrators group to install and configure RAS. It can be installed during custom setup of Windows NT or afterward. The RAS installation varies slightly, depending on which network protocols are installed. To use the TCP/IP protocol with RAS, you should install the protocol before you install RAS, although selecting the TCP/IP protocol when installing RAS (if it is not already present) will cause it to be installed at the conclusion of RAS setup. For detailed instructions on installing the TCP/IP protocol, see the section in Chapter 2 on installing the TCP/IP protocol for Windows hosts. Extra information can be obtained from the references in Appendix B.

NOTE: *The users that will need to dial into the server will have to have accounts on that server. If the server is patched to Service Pack 4 or later, the user authentication will utilize password encryption as standard.*

Another suggestion: Allow dial-in permission only to those accounts that require it. If you do allow dial-ins, be sure to maintain the security as necessary by ensuring that strong passwords are used and applying policies where applicable.

One advantage of using an NT Server in this role is that this server could act in a dual role and be used to authenticate the users in the local network as well as the remote users.

Connecting To PPP-Compatible Servers

The Windows NT Server 4 RAS is not the only possible dial-in server—you might want to consider several alternatives. Linux comes with a PPP daemon that is also capable of acting as a dial-in server when paired with mgetty or something similar. Many of the other Unix variants have their own PPP dial-in software.

To make use of Samba resources, the dial-in server should be PPP compatible. This section provides technical information about connecting to PPP-compatible servers. PPP is a standard method for transporting multiprotocol datagrams over point-to-point links. PPP does this by establishing and configuring different link and network-layer protocols to carry traffic from point to point.

Several elements make up the control and data flow in PPP. Figure 8.12 shows some of these, including PAP, CHAP, and Shiva Password Authentication Protocol (SPAP), which perform password authentication of PPP clients. Compression Control Protocol (CCP) is used to negotiate encryption with PPP clients. Internet Protocol Control Protocol (IPCP), Internet Packet Exchange Control Protocol (IPXCP), NetBIOS Frames Control Protocol (NBFCP), and Other are the IP, NetWare IPX, NetBIOS Extended User Interface (NetBEUI), and Other protocol modules, respectively, that control PPP client sessions. HDLC is the High-Level Data Link Control protocol. Figure 8.12 contains the modular breakdown of the different components of PPP.

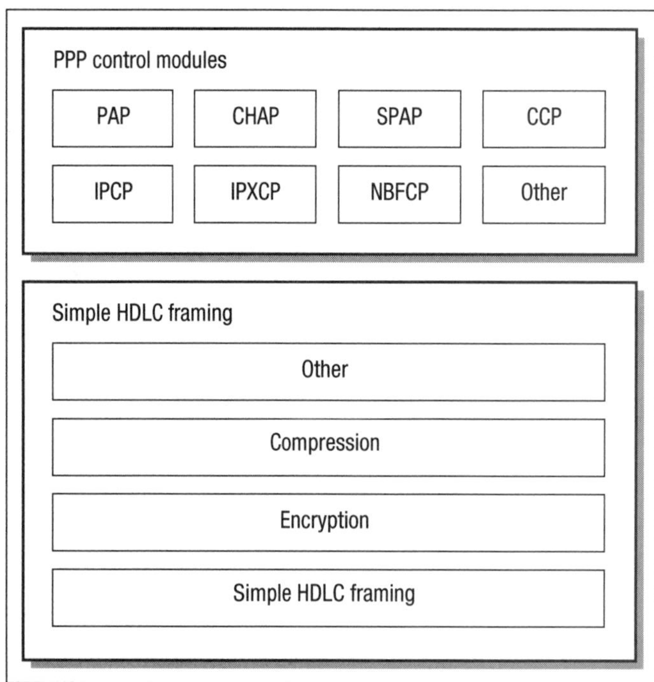

Figure 8.12 The elements of PPP.

What Happens During A PPP Dial-Up Session?

On dialing into a PPP-compatible server, there are several stages to establishing a connection. First, the HDLC defines how the data is encapsulated before transmission over the WAN link. The standard framing format of PPP ensures that the many different PPP solutions can communicate and distinguish data packets from one another. PPP is capable of using HDLC framing for serial, ISDN, and X.25 data transfer so that modem, cable, and packet-switched networks can all be used to establish PPP connections.

Next, the Link Control Protocol (LCP) establishes, configures, and tests the integrity of the data-link connection. The LCP will also negotiate which authentication protocol will be used and establish the method of authentication that the RAS server will perform and what the server requires.

The authentication methods that can be utilized are the following:

- *PAP*—Uses a two-way handshake once the link is established during which the user will establish identity. The passwords in PAP are sent in plain text.
- *SPAP*—Offers encryption of PAP passwords for user account information and is used mostly with Novell servers.
- *CHAP*—Verifies the user authentication once the connection is established and then periodically by using a three-way handshake. The server will send a challenge message to the user host. The user host returns the username and an MD5 hash of the challenge, session ID, and the user's password. The server then checks this response, and, if the values match, the authentication is acknowledged; otherwise, the connection is terminated. With CHAP, the password is sent encrypted over the connection.
- *MS-CHAP*—An encrypted authentication mechanism similar to but more secure than CHAP. As with CHAP, the server sends a challenge to the user host. The user host must return the username and an MD4 hash of the challenge string, the session ID, and the MD4-hashed password.

During the second stage of PPP link configuration, the server collects the authentication data and then validates the data against its own user database or against a central authentication database server. Following successful authentication, the client and the server begin negotiating to establish and configure the different network protocol parameters. The negotiation depends on which protocol (NetBEUI, TCP/IP, or IPX) is being used to establish the DUN connection.

Windows hosts support the following:

- *NBFCP*—Used to configure, enable, and disable the NetBEUI protocol modules on both ends of the link.

- *IPCP*—Used to configure, enable, and disable IP protocol modules at both ends of the link.
- *IPXCP*—Used to configure, enable, and disable IPX protocol modules on both ends of the link. IPXCP is widely implemented by PPP vendors.

RAS For Linux

All the current distributions of Linux include the capability to dial out to a PPP-compatible server. You probably already have all the hardware necessary: a modem, a modem cable if your modem is external, and a phone line. You will also need to be sure of your serial port or modem speed. However, if you can use your modem under Linux to dial out and connect by using the **minicom** program, it is very likely that you won't have any problems. The current Slackware and Red Hat Linux distributions include all the software required to establish a PPP connection.

The first stage in the setup of a PPP connection using Linux is to make sure that the Linux kernel supports PPP. If you have used the default kernel with your Linux installation, the kernel likely will have PPP support included. It is possible to have PPP support compiled into the kernel or loaded as a module when you start Linux. To check whether PPP support exists on your system, use the **dmesg** command to view the system messages. Running the **dmesg | more** command searches for a section that appears as in Listing 8.11.

Listing 8.11 Using dmesg | more to look for PPP support in the kernel.

```
# dmesg | more
(cut to reduce output)
PPP: version 2.2.0 (dynamic channel allocation)
TCP compression code copyright 1989 Regents of the University of California
PPP Dynamic channel allocation code copyright 1995 Caldera, Inc.
PPP line discipline registered.
(cut to reduce output)
```

These or similar lines should appear. If they are not present, you must recompile the kernel with built-in PPP support or build the PPP module and use the **insmod** command to load the driver. To use PPP, you will also need networking support enabled, especially TCP/IP.

The software program chat, usually installed in /usr/sbin, will also be required, although this is usually installed as part of the pppd package. The chat program is used during the dialing process to dial out and connect to your ISP's modem. Along with chat, you need the pppd daemon, also installed in the /usr/sbin directory. If pppd is installed, the directory /etc/ppp should exist, and the following files should reside in it: chap-secrets, options, ppp-on-dialer, connect-errors, pap-secrets, ppp-on, ip-up, and ppp-off. If they are missing, the ppp-on and ppp-on-dialer files are scripts, copies of which can be found in the /usr/doc/ppp-2.2.0f-3/scripts directory following the installation of the pppd package. It would also be wise to check whether the resolv.conf file exists in the /etc directory if you expect to use DNS; if the file does not exist, you can create it and enter the name(s) of your local networks and the IP address of the primary and secondary DNS name servers for your network. A suitable file is shown here:

```
search sambabook
nameserver 192.168.2.7
nameserver 192.168.3.9
```

The network tools **ifconfig**, **netstat**, **ping**, **route**, and **traceroute** will also help diagnose problems with PPP setup.

After you can confirm that the file is present on your system, you will need the following information to establish a PPP connection:

- A user account with a username and password.
- The dial-in PPP server modem number(s).
- Confirmation that the PPP server will assign either a static IP address or a dynamic IP address. (It is assumed that DHCP is used, but the changes for a static IP address will be listed.)
- The IP addresses and names of your networks' primary and secondary DNS servers if they exist. This information will go into the /etc/resolv.conf file.

Setting Up A PPP Connection

To set up a PPP connection, do the following:

1. Log in as the root operator.
2. Look in the /etc/ppp directory for a file called ppp-on. If the file is present, make a backup copy of this file. If the file is not present, copy it from the /usr/doc/ppp-2.20f-3/scripts directory. The salient details for a sample script included with the default installation are shown in Listing 8.12.

Listing 8.12 The ppp-on connection script.

```
...
TELEPHONE=123-4567 # The telephone number for the connection
ACCOUNT=username # The account name for logon
PASSWORD=password # The password for this account
LOCAL_IP=0.0.0.0 # Local IP address if known. Dynamic = 0.0.0.0
REMOTE_IP=0.0.0.0 # Remote IP address if desired. Normally 0.0.0.0
...
```

```
DIALER_SCRIPT=/etc/ppp/ppp-on-dialer
...
exec /usr/sbin/pppd lock modem crtscts /dev/modem 57600 \
asyncmap 20A0000 escape FF $LOCAL_IP:$REMOTE_IP \
noipdefault netmask $NETMASK defaultroute connect \
$DIALER_SCRIPT &
```

3. It will be necessary to alter several parts of this script, as follows:
   - **TELEPHONE**—Enter your modem connect number here.
   - **ACCOUNT**—Enter your username or login name.
   - **PASSWORD**—Enter your password here.
   - **DIALER_SCRIPT**—The complete pathname of the dialing script, which uses the pppd daemon's companion chat program. The chat program does the dialing, connecting, and login for you. If you can't find a copy of this script, which is called ppp-on-dialer, look under the /usr/doc/ppp-2.2.0f-3/scripts directory. Listing 8.13 shows the ppp-on-dialer script. If your computer does not present a login and password prompt, you'll have to change the **login:** and **password:** strings in this script to match the ones from your dial-in server.

Listing 8.13 The ppp-on-dialer dialing script.

```
...
exec chat -v \
TIMEOUT 3 \
ABORT '\nBUSY\r' \
ABORT '\nNO ANSWER\r' \
ABORT '\nRINGING\r\n\r\nRINGING\r' \
'' \rAT \
'OK-+++\c-OK' ATH0 \
TIMEOUT 30 \
OK ATDT$TELEPHONE \
CONNECT '' \
login: $ACCOUNT \
password: $PASSWORD
```

4. The pppd command line in the ppp-on script might need to be altered to change /dev/modem so that the device in your system is used. You can do this by creating a symbolic link to the modem and maintaining a /dev/modem device. If the PPP server assigns IP addresses using DHCP, the scripts are complete. If a static or fixed IP address is to be used, the scripts must be altered by removing the **noipdefault** option from the pppd command line and altering the **$REMOTE_IP** string to the IP address provided by the PPP server.

5. Make sure that the ppp-on and ppp-on-dialer scripts are executable by checking with **ls -l** or by modifying with the **chmod** program as shown here:

```
# chmod +x /etc/ppp/ppp-on*
```

6. Finally, check which mode of authentication the PPP server is using. If the server is using PAP or CHAP, the lines that relate to PAP or CHAP authentication should be uncommented in the options file. The file pap-secrets or chap-secrets will also need to be modified as appropriate.

It will now be possible to dial up to the PPP server to establish a PPP connection.

Using Your ppp-on Script To Connect

Using the ppp-on script to establish your PPP connection is easy:

1. Make sure that you are logged in as root, then execute the script. The following code will start the connection:

   ```
   # /etc/ppp/ppp-on
   ```

   Note that you will need to enter the entire pathname to the script, as no path is set for this directory.

2. If the PPP scripts are successful, create a symbolic link to the script and place it in /usr/local/bin, which should be in the path. A suitable command is shown in here:

   ```
   # ln -s /etc/ppp/ppp-on /usr/local/bin/start-ppp
   ```

When the script is run, the modem should connect to the telephone line, dial out, and then connect to the PPP server's modem. Following a wait of a few seconds, the exchange should complete, and the two should be connected!

Stopping The PPP Connection

To stop your PPP session, a ppp-off script, found in the /etc/ppp directory, can be used. To use it, enter "# /etc/ppp/ppp-off". This script works by finding your network interface, ppp0, which you can test by using some of the programs in the next section and then using the **kill** command to kill the process ID of ppp0.

Confirming The PPP Connection

The simplest way to confirm that you have a connection is to check which network connections you have at the Linux computer. The program **/sbin/ifconfig**, normally used to establish network interfaces and routes (as discussed in Chapter 2), will list all current network interfaces as shown in Listing 8.14 when used with no options.

Listing 8.14 /sbin/ifconfig output once a PPP connection established.

```
# ifconfig
lo Link encap:Local Loopback
inet addr:127.0.0.1 Bcast:127.255.255.255 Mask:255.0.0.0
UP BROADCAST LOOPBACK RUNNING MTU:3584 Metric:1
RX packets:1980 errors:0 dropped:0 overruns:0
TX packets:1980 errors:0 dropped:0 overruns:0

ppp0 Link encap:Point-Point Protocol
inet addr:192.168.2.50 P-t-P:192.168.2.100
Mask:255.255.255.0
UP POINTOPOINT RUNNING MTU:1500 Metric:1
RX packets:998 errors:0 dropped:0 overruns:0
TX packets:679 errors:0 dropped:0 overruns:0
```

The output shows the current, active network interfaces. The 127.0.0.1 interface is the loopback interface and will always appear. The section following the ppp0 listing shows the number of bytes received and transmitted (in the form of packets) over your PPP interface and the IP addresses of the local end (192.168.2.50) and remote end (192.168.2.100) of the PPP connections.

Using The **netstat** Command

The **netstat** command, is the definitive command for checking the network activity, connections, routing tables, and other network messages and statistics for a host. Once the PPP connection is established, the **netstat** command with no options will provide information that can be useful in diagnosis. Listing 8.15 shows such an output.

Listing 8.15 The netstat output following a PPP connection.

```
# netstat
Active Internet connections (w/o servers)
Proto Recv-Q Send-Q Local Address Foreign Address State
tcp 0 0 localhost:1988 localhost:80 ESTABLISHED
...
tcp 0 0 pppserver.sambabook.:1267 ntserver.sambabook.com:pop ESTABLISHED
Active UNIX domain sockets (w/o servers)
...
```

Using The **ping** Command

The **ping** command is useful for verifying that your PPP server's IP addresses are valid and for testing the response times of your remote network servers. The **ping** command sends small 56-byte test packets of data and records the time that it takes for the host to send back the information Listing 8.16 shows the pings for the sample PPP connection.

Listing 8.16 Pings for the PPP connection.

```
# ping ntserver.sambabook.com
PING ntserver.sambabook.com (192.168.2.200): 56 data bytes
64 bytes from 192.168.2.200: icmp_seq=0 ttl=254 time=184.7 ms
64 bytes from 192.168.2.200: icmp_seq=1 ttl=254 time=186.0 ms
64 bytes from 192.168.2.200: icmp_seq=2 ttl=254 time=190.0 ms
-- ntserver.sambabook.com ping statistics --
3 packets transmitted, 3 packets received, 0% packet loss
round-trip min/avg/max = 184.7/186.9/190.0 ms
```

In Linux, unlike in Windows, **ping** will continue to send and receive information until you tell it to quit with Ctrl+C. Windows usually sends only four pings and then halts. There are other options available. You can find more information by looking at the Unix man pages or Windows Help on the **ping** command.

Using The **route** Command

The **route** command is generally used to set up or delete networking routes for interfaces and can also be used to show the routing setup for the ppp0 interface. The output for this interface is shown in Listing 8.17.

Listing 8.17 The output for route for the PPP connection.

```
# /sbin/route
Kernel IP routing table
Destination Gateway Genmask Flags Metric Ref Use Iface
ppp2.sambabook.com * 255.255.255.255 UH 0 0 0 ppp0
127.0.0.0 * 255.0.0.0 U 0 0 2 lo
default ppp2.sambabook.com 0.0.0.0 UG 0 0 3 ppp0
```

Reading Your System Log

The PPP connection during establishment will also be recorded in the Linux system log, and this can be viewed in the /var/log/messages file. An example of the output produced during the creation of a PPP connection is shown in Listing 8.18.

Listing 8.18 The /var/log/messages file following a PPP connection.

```
...
Jun 22 17.32:49 localhost pppd[383]: pppd 2.2.0 started by root, uid 0
Jun 22 17:32:51 localhost chat[384]: timeout set to 3 seconds
Jun 22 17:32:51 localhost chat[384]: abort on (\nBUSY\r)
Jun 22 17:32:51 localhost chat[384]: abort on (\nNO ANSWER\r)
Jun 22 17:32:51 localhost chat[384]: abort on (\nRINGING\r\n\r\nRINGING\r)
Jun 22 17:32:51 localhost chat[384]: send (rAT^M)
Jun 22 17:32:51 localhost chat[384]: expect (OK)
Jun 22 17:32:51 localhost chat[384]: rAT^M^M
Jun 22 17:32:51 localhost chat[384]: OK -- got it
Jun 22 17:32:51 localhost chat[384]: send (ATH0^M)
Jun 22 17:32:51 localhost chat[384]: timeout set to 30 seconds
Jun 22 17:32:51 localhost chat[384]: expect (OK)
Jun 22 17:32:51 localhost chat[384]: ^M
Jun 22 17:32:51 localhost chat[384]: ATH0^M^M
Jun 22 17:32:51 localhost chat[384]: OK -- got it
Jun 22 17:32:51 localhost chat[384]: send (ATDT1234567^M)
Jun 22 17:32:51 localhost chat[384]: expect (CONNECT)
Jun 22 17:32:51 localhost chat[384]: ^M
Jun 22 17:33:10 localhost chat[384]: ATDT1234567^M^M
Jun 22 17:33:10 localhost chat[384]: CONNECT -- got it
Jun 22 17:33:10 localhost chat[384]: send (^M)
Jun 22 17:33:10 localhost chat[384]: expect (ogin:)
Jun 22 17:33:10 localhost chat[384]: 57600^M
Jun 22 17:33:12 localhost chat[384]: ^M
Jun 22 17:33:12 localhost chat[384]: ^M
Jun 22 17:33:12 localhost chat[384]: login: -- got it
Jun 22 17:33:12 localhost chat[384]: send (username^M)
Jun 22 17:33:12 localhost chat[384]: expect (assword:)
Jun 22 17:33:12 localhost chat[384]: username^M
Jun 22 17:33:12 localhost chat[384]: Password: -- got it
Jun 22 17:33:12 localhost chat[384]: send (password^M)
Jun 22 17:33:12 localhost pppd[383]: Serial connection established.
Jun 22 17:33:13 localhost pppd[383]: Using interface ppp0
Jun 22 17:33:13 localhost pppd[383]: Connect: ppp0 <--> /dev/modem
Jun 22 17:33:16 localhost pppd[383]: local IP address 192.168.2.50
Jun 22 17:33:16 localhost pppd[383]: remote IP address 192.168.2.200
...
```

The system log can be useful in determining the point at which a PPP connection is failing. Appendix B contains many references that will help establish a good PPP connection from Linux.

Browsing Across A RAS Or WAN Link

After the PPP or RAS connection has been established, browsing the remote network will be possible if the local host has been configured to use a WINS server on the remote network. Likewise, the local network will be available to the remote network as long as the routing over the PPP connection allows it and a master browser exists in the local network that performs a remote announce call to the remote network.

Chapter 9

Domain Control And Management

In Depth

Samba As A Domain Controller

The most exciting use of Samba is as a domain controller for either Windows NT or Windows 9x clients. It is also possible to allow Unix clients to take part in the domain and to use domain security when using shares and printers. This means that a Samba server can be used to provide the necessary user logon authentication for your network. This is possibly the most important feature currently available in Samba and will allow for a very tight integration between Windows and Unix clients and servers.

User account authentication is normally the responsibility of the host system. This added functionality also permits an enterprise-wide or a network-wide user authentication system to be established.

The Difference Between A Workgroup And A Domain

The SAMBABOOK workgroup example used elsewhere in this book enables SMB/CIFS resource sharing, with user authentication being undertaken at the individual SMB/CIFS server. The workgroup model is commonly referred to as a peer-to-peer network because it uses user authentication at the individual SMB/CIFS servers being accessed. Each SMB/CIFS server in a workgroup controls and manages the access to its own resources.

The domain model is different. Central to a domain is a domain controller, which maintains a user authentication database. When any user starts up a session on a PC in a domain, the user is authenticated with the domain authentication server. The individual SMB/CIFS servers are a part of the domain and adopt the security model of the domain. Now, when a user attempts to use a resource on an SMB/CIFS server, that server hands off the request for authentication to a domain controller.

In essence, the security definitions associated with a single user account (and the subsequent single username/password pair) in a domain model can be better defined for resources than that in a workgroup model, so that in a domain a greater level of security over those resources is possible.

For example, a PC running either Windows 95 or 98 that is a member of a workgroup can gain access to network resources even without using a correct login password. The user will appear to have logged in correctly, and no feedback will have occurred to inform the user otherwise. If any shares are created that offer guest or anonymous access, the user will have access to them.

The incorrect password becomes relevant only when the user attempts to connect to the first SMB/CIFS server that has been connected to with the user being authenticated using either the correct password or an alternate password. The local system will attempt to connect to the remote resource with the current username and password. If the correct password was entered at login, following failure the Windows 9x system will attempt to connect to the system using a password that would have been cached in the password cache file that exists in the c:\windows directory for that user. These files are encrypted and exist with the *.pwl extension. If the incorrect password was given at login, the user will not be able to use the password cache and will be prompted to enter the correct password. Considerable user confusion can arise from the ensuing multiple password requests. In a domain model, the user will be prompted immediately for a correct password on login with access to the other resources and then be granted access by virtue of the user account settings in the domain account database.

The possible lack of security in the encryption method that is used to maintain the password cache files can be an issue for those of us who are concerned with security (see Chapter 11 for details). The workgroup model will also demand that every SMB/CIFS server in the workgroup maintain a separate user account, so that several different passwords for that user might exist across the workgroup. Groups of users having common levels of security access, say, for administrative and functional purposes, will need to deal with a considerable amount of administrative overhead, especially if you have many SMB/CIFS servers in a workgroup with such unsynchronized account databases. In such a case, you might want to consider using a domain as an alternative configuration.

Immediate Solutions

Using Windows 9x Domain Control

A normal Windows 9x network is not able to centralize the user account database for all the individual workstations without using a domain controller. Normally, a Windows NT server performs this function satisfactorily, but an obvious cost is involved in the Windows NT client and server licenses. This is one area in which a Samba server can be employed as a direct replacement for an NT server even if not used for any other purpose.

Setting Up A Samba Windows 9x Domain Controller

For any Samba server to act as a Windows 9x domain controller, the first Samba parameter that must be set correctly is the **security** parameter. To be able to operate as a domain controller, the Samba server must be in one of the user-mode security levels: server or user. Set the **security** parameter to either value, as shown here:

```
security = user
#or
#security = server
#would be sufficient.
```

The preferred option is to set this to **user**, as **server** would require a separate server to be defined. To be able to act as a domain controller for a Windows 9x client, the NetBIOS settings need to be set so that the Samba server advertises itself as the master browser for the domain. This involves a NetBIOS resource announcement of <1b> being assigned to the server. Chapters 2 and 8 discuss the details behind the different configurations for the NetBIOS settings, so these are not repeated here. When the Samba server advertises itself as a resource type <1b>, the Windows 9x clients will recognize it as a host that should be capable of providing a netlogon service.

The minimum settings to achieve this are in the [global] section, as shown here:

```
os level = 33
domain master = yes
local master = yes
preferred master = yes
```

These settings only set the security authentication scheme and the NetBIOS network settings. To provide Windows 9x logon services, set the **domain logons** parameter, also in the [global] section, to make the Samba server act as a domain controller:

```
domain logons = yes
```

The Samba server is now ready to provide Windows 9x client logon services, and the netlogon share should now be added to the smb.conf file. The share parameters should contain the name as [netlogon] and a path that the users are capable of reading from only. This should not be set as writeable, as it is important that users are unable to modify or add files that another user's computer would then download when they log in. The Samba distribution DOMAIN.txt documentation file in /docs/text on this book's CD-ROM suggests a sample share, shown here:

```
[netlogon]
    path = /data/dos/netlogon
    writeable = no
    guest ok = no
```

These are the only requirements, although most Samba setups make use of the ability to include a logon script at this point that the user would run when logged in. The global parameter **logon script** identifies this script, which is placed within the netlogon share. The parameter can make use of macros so that a user or session variable identifies the script. An alternative is to use the macros within the parameter to pass the user or session variable to the logon script. In the DOMAIN.txt file, the suggestion for a script is

```
logon script = %U.bat
```

which would direct each user to a separate logon script for that user, with the **%U** being exchanged with the session username automatically. Any of the alternate % macros can also be used.

NOTE: *A list of alternate macros is included in Appendix A.*

The script can also be located in a subdirectory of the netlogon share and can be directed to by setting the parameter to that subdirectory by using the following value:

```
logon script = scripts\%U.bat
#or even a subdirectory per user as in
#logon script = %U\logon.bat
```

The script that is run on a Windows 9x PC should be ACSII and formatted to include the CRLF at the end of each line. If possible, it is better to create these on a Windows 9x PC using Notepad and to copy these onto the Samba server, preserving the line endings. A Unix editor, such as **vi** or **pico**, can also be used, but each line in the script should be appended with Ctrl+V and Ctrl+M to create the CRLF line ending. This ensures that the script will be understood when it is run on the Windows 9x client.

TIP: *It is advisable, although not essential at this point, to enable the Samba server as a WINS server if no other exists. You do this by setting the WINS support parameter to* ***wins support=yes****. Windows 9x clients can then make use of the WINS service.*

The sample smb.conf file to provide a simple Samba Windows 9x domain controller is shown in Listing 9.1.

Listing 9.1 A simple smb.conf file for a Windows 9x domain controller.

```
# Samba config file created using SWAT
   # from ntwdev02.domain (192.168.1.3)
   # Date: 1999/07/26 20:17:33
# Global parameters
   [global]
           workgroup = SAMBABOOK
           netbios name = LINUXSERVER
           encrypt passwords = Yes
           log file = /usr/local/samba/var/log.%m
           max log size = 50
           domain logons = yes
           logon script = confirm.bat
           os level = 32
           preferred master = Yes
           local master = yes
           domain master = Yes
           wins support = yes

   [homes]
           comment = Home Directories
           read only = No
           browseable = No

   [netlogon]
           comment = NetLogon Service
           path = /home/samba/netlogon
           guest account =
           browseable = No
```

```
locking = No
available = No
```

The Samba server should then be restarted to offer Windows 9x domain controller capability.

Setting Up A Samba Windows 9x Client

Configuring a Windows 9x client to use a Samba server acting as a domain controller is no different than setting up a Windows NT Server to perform the same task.

The essential configuration is that the Client for Microsoft Networks property for logon validation is enabled and the name of the domain entered. The domain name will be the same as that set in the **workgroup** parameter from the Samba server smb.conf file. If you take the suggested value from the smb.conf file used elsewhere as SAMBABOOK and enter this, the dialog box shown in Figure 9.1 should appear.

The system might prompt you for the Windows 9x installation CD-ROM and, once complete, will request a reboot. Following the restart, the Windows 9x client will attempt to log the user on to the SAMBABOOK domain using the new Samba Windows 9x domain controller.

Successfully Logging Into The Domain

If the logon script simply includes a command to echo a prompt to the screen, such as the command shown here

```
echo "Successfully logged into the SAMBABOOK domain ..."
```

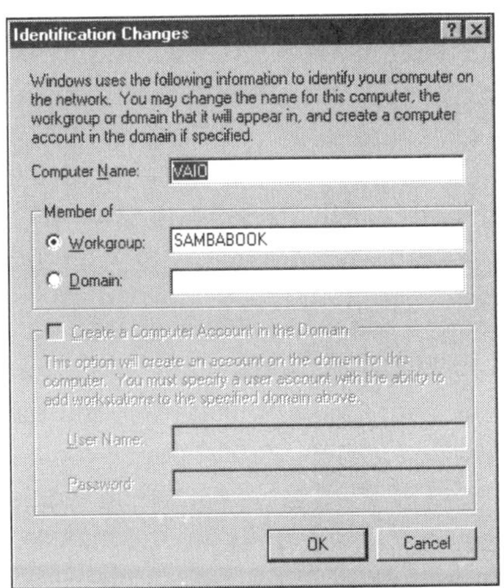

Figure 9.1 The Windows 9x SAMBABOOK domain configuration.

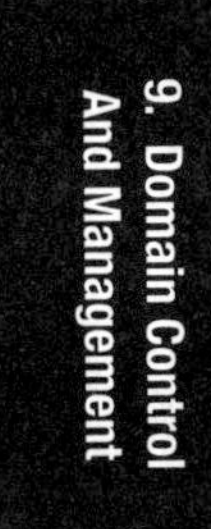

```
Successfully logged into the SAMBABOOK domain...
```

Figure 9.2 The DOS Command window with script prompt.

a successful logon to the SAMBABOOK domain controller will result in the DOS Command window appearing (see Figure 9.2).

If you receive any error messages at this point, follow the section on Windows 9x domain controller errors in Chapter 12 to solve the problem.

Explaining User Profiles

User profiles are a collection of setting and software details that a user has specified to customize the PC environment. These manifest for most users in the shortcuts, mapped drives, other system settings, application configuration details, and desktop settings.

For example, if you prefer a screen with a background image of Van Gogh's sunflowers, you can save this in your profile, and it will appear the next time you log in, assuming that the image to create the background is available. As another example, if you always want your email reader or some other application, say, a word processor, to start at login (or your system administrator would like it to start that way), you can add that to your Start menu.

Profiles work through the Windows Registry, which is rebuilt on system startup. The Registry contents are refreshed, with the contents coming from two data files: system.dat and user.dat. The Registry information, which includes essential system information for the hardware and software of the Windows system, is held within the system.dat file in the Windows home directory (normally c:\windows). The user profile information is held in the user.dat file for each user that uses the system. If more than one user make use of a PC running Windows 9x, these files are held in an individual users subdirectory within the \windows\profiles directory. This allows one system to hold different settings for a large number of users. The profile is highly configurable and can contain a large amount of information. In addition, it can include a considerable number of shortcuts and even data files. When a user first logs into Windows 9x, the user.dat file is created, as are the Start Menu, Desktop, Programs, and Nethood folders.

The standard practice is to allow users flexibility to configure their environment with different screen savers, backgrounds, and so on, but it is not uncommon for a mandatory profile to be used. The user.dat file is then named user.man, and in this case the system will always return to the same setting for each new login, and no user changes will be remembered. This is often used in large organizations—such as training companies, call bureaus, and some support organizations—where multiple workstations must always look and appear the same.

Explaining Roaming User Profiles

Roaming user profiles are an important part of Windows networking. The user profile detailed in the previous section can be transferred from one PC to another on a network as part of a logon process so that the settings for that user are also transferred from the server to the new system.

When a user logs in to a system, the system will check to see whether the remote profile contents are more up to date than the local contents. If they are, the contents will be merged with the local version stored in \windows\profiles\username. Immediately following a logout, the profile contents are written to the remote profile directory, which will be available for future sessions. This process repeats on all subsequent logins, with the system taking the most recent profile information each time.

TIP: *When establishing roaming profiles, it is essential to configure any Microsoft Office application to use an alternate location to the default if that location is included in the profile. In the case of Microsoft Word, the c:\My Documents directory is the default. However, for a user logged in with roaming profiles, the default user workspace is the personal folder and is located in the profiles directory. Not altering this can result in the contents being included in the roaming profile that is downloaded and can result in a considerable number of data files being transferred at each login. This sort of extra network traffic and the resulting delays at every login and logout can be frustrating in the long run and are better dealt with using a home directory.*

Setting Up Roaming User Profiles

To set up roaming user profiles in Samba, the **logon path** parameter from the [global] section of the smb.conf file should be set to the location of the profile download directory. The Samba distribution documentation suggests a possible value for this parameter, shown here:

```
logon path = \\profileserver\profileshare\profilepath\%U\moreprofilepath
```

This provides built-in flexibility so that a separate server can be used to store these user profiles to the logon server. When setting up Samba initially, the default value for this parameter is **\\%N\%U\profile**, which translates to \\sambaserver\userhomedirectory\profiledirectory. The root directory, **\\N%\%U**, is created automatically by the [homes] service when a user session is established with the Samba server.

It is important for Windows 9x clients to ensure that the profile share specified in the **logon path** parameter is also set with **browseable=yes**. Windows 9x clients need to confirm an ability to see the share and all subdirectories within that share specified by the **logon path** option before connection. Setting this share with **browseable=yes** will allow this access. The profile directory might not exist initially, and in operation the Samba server will attempt to create the components of the full path during connection. If the creation of any component fails or if it cannot see any component of the path, the profile creation/reading fails.

***WARNING!* Do not include the [homes] share within a profile path when using Windows clients. The Samba team determined that a problem exists regarding where Windows clients can maintain a connection to the [homes] share between logins. A better solution is to use a separate [profiles] share and to set logon path = \\%N\profiles\%U.**

Additional smb.conf parameters should be set to handle the case of file names and shortcuts and any profile folder names. Listing 9.2 provides suitable options.

Listing 9.2 Case preservation parameters in smb.conf.

```
In [global] section
preserve case = yes
short case preserve = yes
case sensitive = no
```

As previously stated, the user.dat file contains all the user's preferences, and this file is written to when the user logs out. If mandatory profiles are needed for a client, set up the settings for a user session as you require them, rename the user.dat file from the profile directory to user.MAN, and set the permissions to make this file read-only. This will be saved to the profile directory, and all future logins will make use of this file.

The Windows 95 system then needs to be configured to make use of roaming profiles. To configure the system, do the following:

1. In the Control Panel, double-click on Passwords, select the User Profiles tab, and set the level for roaming preferences. Figure 9.3 shows these settings.
2. Close the dialog box but do not allow the computer to reboot.
3. Now, in Control Panel, double-click on Network and select Client For Microsoft Networks|Preferences. Be sure that the Log On To NT Domain checkbox is selected, that the correct NT domain name is entered, and that the primary logon is Client For Microsoft Networks.
4. Click on OK and this time allow the computer to reboot.
5. On restart, the system will present a different login prompt, with the Microsoft Networks Login box requesting a username, password, and domain. At this point, enter the domain name, username, and user password for the Samba server.
6. Immediately following the successful authentication with the Samba server, the Windows 95 machine will prompt you with a notification that the user has not logged on before and asks you whether you want to save the user's preferences. To enable roaming profiles, click on Yes.

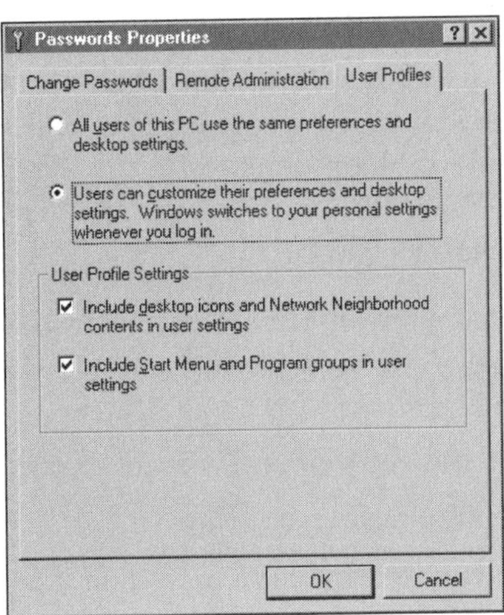

Figure 9.3 Setting roaming profiles in Windows 9x.

The Windows 95 client will function as before but now with roaming profiles enabled. The Samba server profile share specified in the logon path in the smb.conf file for that client will contain the necessary profile contents. When the client logs off, any changes are returned to the local profile directory on the client. When the user logs on again, the remote profile contents are compared with the local contents, and the most recent set is used. A copy is then cached to the Samba server.

If you receive any error messages at this point, follow the section on Windows 9x domain controller errors in Chapter 12 to solve the problem.

NOTE: *This behavior is the reverse of the Windows NT roaming profile, where the remote copy is downloaded from the logon server, the local copy is refreshed (unless it is more recent), the local copy is updated during use, and at logout the remote copy is replaced so that the most recent copy is maintained on the server and ready for the next logon.*

Understanding Policies

In addition to mandatory profiles, system administrators can restrict which applications a user has access to. The ability to map remote directories or printers other than those already in a mandatory profile might be denied. The concept of policies is one that needs an explanation beyond the contents of this chapter, and the appropriate references in Appendix B will provide a useful starting point to obtain this information.

In a Samba environment, policies can be used to disable password caching locally. Windows 9x has a Policy Editor (located on the Windows 95 installation

CD-ROM as \admin\apptools\poledit.exe) that allows you to disable the password caching capability. This is perhaps the most user-friendly method of doing this. A good alternative, especially if you have many systems to correct, is to delete all the *.pwl files on the workstations and to add an additional key to the Windows 9x Registry: HKEY_LOCAL_MACHINE\SOFTWARE\Microsoft\CurrentVersion\Policies\Network "DisablePwdCaching"=dword:00000001.

To replicate this change across other systems, there are two possible processes: make the change manually or export the key to a *.reg file and add it to other systems. To export a Registry key:

1. In the Registry Editor, regedit, highlight the key that you want to export.
2. Select the Registry|Export Registry menu option.
3. A dialog box will appear that will offer you the choice to export all Registry keys to a Registry file or just the highlighted key. Select the second option and save the *.reg file to an appropriate location.

TIP: *You have to use a Windows 98 Registry file on a Windows 98 system, a Windows NT file on an NT system, and so on.*

4. Either double-click the Registry *.reg file in Explorer, which will add it to the Registry, or use the Registry Editor to add the key by using the Import option under the Registry menu.

NOTE: *A copy of this Registry entry is on this book's CD-ROM as /registry/Win9xpwdcache.reg.*

If you receive any error messages at this point, follow the section on Windows 9x domain controller errors in Chapter 12 to solve the problem.

Using Windows NT Domain Control

Support for Windows NT domain control is still experimental and as such should be used with some caution. The Samba team will not officially state whether Samba 2 will support domain logons for Windows NT clients at this time. The use of Samba to act as a primary domain controller (PDC) for Windows NT domains providing all the required functionality is not complete. The Samba team and NTDOM email lists recommend using Samba 2.1 alpha (development code) for Samba NT domain control at this time. Considerable information is available on the use of Samba with NT on the Samba Web site at **www.samba.org**, and a mailing list is dedicated to NT domain support.

WARNING! The Samba 2.1 alpha code is considered experimental and under development.

The current state of the code means that much of the required NT domain control functionality indeed is available within the current 2.1 branch source code, which will eventually form the base for the next release. The supported functionality is as follows:

- Ability to act as a PDC for Windows NT 3.51 Service Pack 5 and Service Pack 4 clients (includes adding NT machines to the domain and authenticating users logging into the domain)
- Ability to act as a PDC for Samba clients (includes adding machines to the domain and authenticating users logging into the domain)
- Using User Manager for Domains to view domain accounts
- Using Server Manager for Domains from the NT client to view resources on the Samba PDC
- Using Windows 95 clients with user-level set (browsing of accounts is not supported)
- Updating machine account passwords
- Changing user passwords at an NT client
- Mapping username to RID (some tools work, whereas some, notably explorer.exe, do not)
- Mapping Windows NT groups and usernames
- Using an LDAP (Lightweight Directory Access Protocol) password database back end

In the current release, aspects of the program that are not functional include the following:

- Trust relationships
- PDC-to-BDC integration
- NT network printing
- Windows NT Access Control Lists (ACLs) (on the Samba shares)

Obtaining The Latest Samba NT Domain Controller Code

Although obtaining Samba source code was covered in Chapter 3, the version of the code that is being suggested here is not the stable release but the development code. The use of this code should not be undertaken on a production system, and you should always proceed with care in its use.

The section in Chapter 3 on obtaining Samba source code using CVS (Concurrent Versions System) should be reviewed along with the information on access at **http://cvs.samba.org/cvs.html**.

The steps to obtain the Samba source code with CVS installed are as follows:

1. Run the following command:

```
cvs -d :pserver:cvs@samba.org:/cvsroot login
```

   When you are prompted for a password, enter "cvs".

2. Run the following command:

```
cvs -d :pserver:cvs@samba.org:/cvsroot co samba
```

3. To update your source code, run the following command:

```
cvs update -d -P
```

   If you want to update the entire archive of the main branch code, make sure that you are located in the top directory of the Samba tree.

After you have the source code and before you continue, make a backup of the /usr/local/samba directory. Stop the Samba services. Starting from the location where you downloaded the CVS source, run the **./configure**, **make**, and **make install** sequence to create and install the latest version of the Samba executables. You will then need to start the services after having made any necessary alterations to the smb.conf and other files.

NOTE: *Be prepared for any part of the Samba server not to function at all; remember that at this point this is development code. In addition, a number of messages that are essentially debug in nature might appear as command line responses at the Samba server or fill the server logs. What this means is that the developers may have included some code that when actioned write a debug event—for example, writing a message that means "Did or could not do this..." into the logs as it is being tested for some new functionality. Defining a debug event usually involves these comments. Normally these additional debug event code sections would be commented out or removed when the code is stable, but sometimes they are left in. Overall these are intentional and might have no function other than to inform the developers as to what has happened. If you are serious about attempting to use the NT domain code, at the very least you should join and read the archives for the email lists listed at* ***http://samba.org/listproc****.*

Setting Up A Samba Server As The PDC For A Windows NT Domain

The following section assumes a Red Hat 5.2 installation of Linux or later with a kernel of 2.0.36 or later running. The original Samba version used in this book was 2.0.5a, and a CVS download taken at the end of August 1999 from the Samba CVS site was used for the NT domain controller section. A copy of the CVS code used in this section is included on this book's CD-ROM in /CVS/code.

Adding Clients To The Domain

To add any client to a Windows NT domain, follow these steps:

1. Using Server Manager, create the machine account in the NT domain.
2. Have the client machine log in to the NT domain.
3. Restart the client.

With a Samba-controlled NT domain, the steps are conceptually no different. Samba currently does not have a Server Manager GUI interface, so for now the addition of the machine account must be carried out manually. I am sure that a Samba-based GUI to reproduce Server Manager will appear at some time.

Creating Machine Trust Accounts

Currently, Samba has no Windows NT counterpart to the Server Manager utility, so the addition of other machines to a Samba-controlled domain cannot be automated with a GUI. There are two stages to manually adding machines. The first involves creating a standard user account. The only current method for doing this that is reliable across all circumstances is to add it manually by creating a line in the /etc/passwd file, similar to this:

```
machine$:*:9999:9900:WinNT trust account:/dev/null:/bin/false
```

The manual approach can create many machine trust accounts with identical settings; however, the user ID (UID) (first number) must be different in each case.

As you can see, the account has no ability to log in, as the password has been disabled and the home directory set to /dev/null; however, the UID of 9999 is the key, because this identifies the machine. Note that the machine trust account name is the NetBIOS name for the host with a "$" appended to it. In some Unix systems, usernames longer than eight characters are ignored or truncated to eight characters. (The Linux distribution Slackware also exhibits this behavior.) This means that you might need to manually add the line to /etc/passwd, as you cannot use the automated user creation facility in every circumstance because it will not allow user account creation with a username longer than eight characters. This occurs when using NetBIOS machine names to create machine trust accounts, because NetBIOS names can be as long as 15 characters.

Now that the simple machine account has been created, the second stage is for a client trust account to be created with the **smbpasswd** program using the options **-a** and **-m**. These indicate, respectively, that **smbpasswd** should first add an account and that it is a machine account.

Although it might seem odd to create a user account for a machine addition and then create the trust account, Samba currently treats new machines as user accounts for the purposes of authentication into an NT domain.

Joining The Domain (NT Clients)

An NT workstation or a standalone NT server that is to become a member of an NT domain that has the appropriate machine trust account on the Samba server can be added to the domain by editing the NT domain identification in the appropriate Network section in the Control Panel. Figure 9.4 shows the dialog box for an NT workstation, and Figure 9.5 shows the success dialog box that is returned upon a successful addition.

You should then reboot the NT client and be able to log in to the NT domain normally. If you receive any error messages at this point, follow the section on NT domain errors in Chapter 12 to solve the problem.

Understanding User Profiles In NT

User profiles in NT are similar to those in Windows 9x, but with additional NT security functionality available. If the administrator decides to remove a number

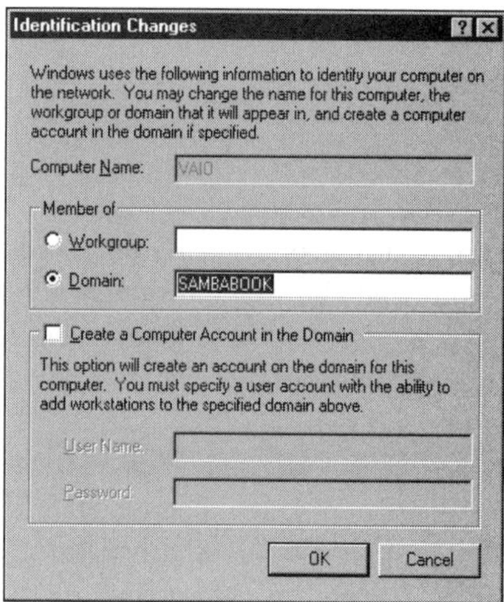

Figure 9.4 Joining a Windows NT domain.

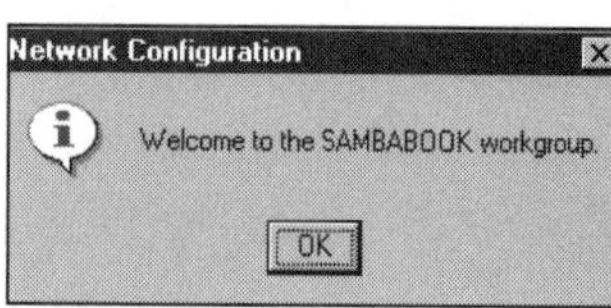

Figure 9.5 Success in joining the SAMBABOOK Windows NT domain.

of applications, such as games, from the Start menu under Windows 9x, the user might be able to re-add these to the Start menu through the Control Panel. Likewise, something more critical, such as the ability to reboot the system, can be added back in as well. Windows NT security enables the administrator to remove the programs and prohibits the user from adding them back once removed. It is even possible to remove the ability for the Windows NT user to reboot the machine.

The Registry is rebuilt on startup of a system and the Registry settings are refreshed from two data files: system.dat and ntuser.dat. The essential system information that refers to the hardware and required software of the Windows system is held within the system.dat file in the Windows NT System32 directory. The profile information for each user that uses the system locally is cached in the ntuser.dat file in the \\winnt\profiles\username directory.

The profile is highly configurable and can contain a large amount of information. As with Windows 9x clients, the default location for personal folders, used with word processors and so on, is included in the profile directory, which can contain a considerable number of data files. Once again, this is a good reason for considering using an alternate user home directory as the default location for these applications.

Setting Up Roaming User Profiles

Roaming user profiles for Windows NT Workstation clients are set up initially when a user first logs into an NT workstation. Windows NT Workstation contains a default user profile file called ntuser.dat, residing in the \winnt\profiles*DefaultUser* directory, that the system uses as a template to create the user's own ntuser.dat profile file. The system will have searched the logon path, but because the logon path and the local profile directory do not contain a profile for the user, the system will use the ntuser.dat file to create one. On logging out of the system, the profile information is copied to the logon server profile location for that user. It is also possible to place this default profile onto the logon server by creating a *Default User* directory in the profile share that contains the ntuser.dat file and the corresponding directory settings.

The second time the user logs on to the server, the ntuser.dat file from the logon server is compared with the local copy, assuming that it is the same workstation and that the more recent copy is used. If a different workstation is used, the remote user profile creates a local user profile and ntuser.dat file. At logout, the profile information is written back to the logon server, and the process repeats for next login.

You can create a mandatory profile in Windows NT just as you can in Windows 9x. Once again, the user profile file is renamed, but this time with a .man extension to become ntuser.man. This is set to read-only, and the user then is presented with the same profile on every logon.

The Samba logon server should have the smb.conf setting that is related to roaming profiles set to a share on the server. The Samba distribution documentation suggests the following value for this parameter:

```
logon path = \\profileserver\profileshare\profilepath\%U\moreprofilepath
```

This has built-in flexibility, in that a separate server can be used to store these user profiles to the logon server. When setting up Samba initially, the default value for this parameter is **\\%N\%U\profile**, which translates to \\sambaserver\userhomedirectory\profiledirectory. The user's root directory, **\\N%\%U**, is created automatically by the [homes] service when a user session is established with the Samba server.

The profile share specified in the logon path should be set to **browseable=yes**. Windows NT clients need to confirm an ability to see the share as well as all subdirectories within that share specified by the logon path option before connection. Setting this share to **browseable=yes** will allow this access. The profile directory might not exist initially, and the Samba server will attempt to create the components of the full path during connection. If the creation of any component fails or if no component of the path can be seen, the profile creation/reading fails.

***WARNING!* As with Windows 9x clients, do not include the [homes] share within a profile path when using Windows clients. The Samba team determined that a problem exists regarding where Windows clients can maintain a connection to the [homes] share in between logins. A better solution is to use a separate [profiles] share and to set logon path=\\%N\profiles\%U.**

Additional smb.conf parameters should be set to handle the case of file names and shortcuts and any profile folder names. Listing 9.3 provides suitable options.

Listing 9.3 Case preservation parameters in smb.conf.

```
In [global] section
preserve case = yes
short case preserve = yes
case sensitive = no
```

The extra parameters **logon drive** and **logon home** should also be used to set up users' home directories and to have these automatically mapped to a drive letter on successful login following authentication against the logon server. Suitable settings are shown here:

```
In [global] section
logon drive = H:  # H: meaning 'home'
logon home = //%N/%U # the user home directory
```

NOTE: *Any valid path can be specified for the location of users' profiles. The profiles can be located in another Samba server or any other SMB server as long as that SMB server supports encrypted passwords.*

Sharing Profiles Between Windows 9x And NT Clients

If you want to share the same Start menu/desktop between Windows 9x and Windows NT clients, specify "logon path=\\samba-server\username\profile" in the [global] section of the smb.conf file. Separate user.dat and ntuser.dat files will appear in the same profile directory. Note that any desktop shortcuts will need to include full paths and not a reference to the Windows directory, as some programs are not the same or are not available in both versions of Windows.

Using Access Control Lists

Setting up machine user accounts and profiles is not the whole picture for NT domain support within Samba. One area that has recently seen a number of improvements is that of ACLs. These include the permissions and security settings on the individual files and directories of an NTFS file system and the printers of an NT system. These permissions are similar to the Unix file and directory permissions and run along similar lines when the NT system makes use of the NTFS file system. They permit an administrator to assign user and group-level permissions for the files, directories, and printers of an NT system.

In an NT/Samba system, the username and group functionality of the NT User Manager for Domains can be replicated in the Samba server by making use of some Samba parameters, shown in Table 9.1.

Listing 9.4 domain group map and /etc/group.

```
#smb.conf entry
[global]
domain group map = /usr/local/samba/lib/domain-group.map
#contents of domain-group.map file
test = Test
admin = "Domain Admins"
#appropriate entries from /etc/group
users:*:500:test1, test2, test3, dbaines, bbaines
test:*:500:test1, test2, test3
admin:*:501:dbaines
```

Table 9.1 NT domain ACL parameters.

Parameter	Description
domain group map	This is the location of the file that contains the mapping between NT's global group names and those of the Samba PDC Unix group names. The groups listed will be global or domain groups and will be available domainwide. The file consists of plain text lines with the syntax *Unixgroupname=NTgroupname*. The *Unixgroupname* is the same as the entry in /etc/group on the Samba server. You might need to create a new group to create the ACLs you want. The *NTgroupname* is the same as would appear as the NT global group name. Group names that include spaces should be enclosed in quotes. Listing 9.4 provides an example of this file and the corresponding /etc/group file.
domain user map	This functions similarly to **domain group map** and contains the details of the file that contains the mapping for Unix usernames to Windows NT usernames. The file contains single-line entries with the syntax *Unixusername=NTusername*. In addition, it is possible to prefix the *NTusername* with an alternate NT domain name, and the entries will appear as *Unixusername=\\Domainname\\NTusername*. Listing 9.5 provides an example of this file and the corresponding /etc/smbpasswd file.
local group map	This is the location of the file that contains the mapping between NT's local group names and those of the Unix group names. The groups listed will be local to the Samba PDC server only. The file consists of plain text lines with the syntax *Unixgroupname=*[BUILTIN\]*NTgroupname*. The *Unixgroupname* is the same as the entry in /etc/group on the Samba PDC server. You might need to create a new group to create the ACLs you want. The *NTgroupname* is the same as would appear as the NT global group name. Note that the BUILTIN\ prefix should exist for all the normally available NT local groups. Listing 9.6 provides an example of this file.
logon home	When logged in, the NT user will use the share specified here as the login home directory. Figure 9.7 shows the User Environment Profile from Windows User Manager for Domains, where this value and the next two are usually applied.
logon drive	When logged in, the NT user will map this local drive to the logon home directory specified in **logon home**.
logon path	The NT user will attempt to download the roaming user profile from the path specified after a successful login.

Listing 9.5 domain user map and /etc/smbpasswd.

```
#smb.conf entry
[global]
domain user map = /usr/local/samba/lib/domain-user.map
#domain-user.map
root = administrator
```

```
#appropriate entries from /etc/smbpasswd
# Samba SMB password file
root:0:BC8AFF34937B5979F500944B53168930:FD0C144294BD58797C993A24AAD32AC8:
[U          ]:LCT-37A6F816:
```

Listing 9.6 local group map.

```
#smb.conf entry
[global]
local group map = /usr/local/samba/lib/local-group.map
#local-group.map
wheel = BUILTIN\Administrators
users = BUILTIN\Users
#appropriate entries from /etc/group
wheel:*:10:root
users:*:500:test1, test2, test3, dbaines, bbaines
```

User Manager for Domains is available from the Start|Administrative Tools menu, as shown in Figure 9.6.

The User Manager for Domains includes much functionality that has not yet been integrated with Samba. However, using these parameters allows the functionality of a PDC to be partly replicated with a Samba server.

The User Environment Profile in a Windows environment, which is shown in Figure 9.7, often makes use of the variable **%USERNAME%** when defining a pathname. In Samba, the replacement for this is **%U**, or the actual username may be used.

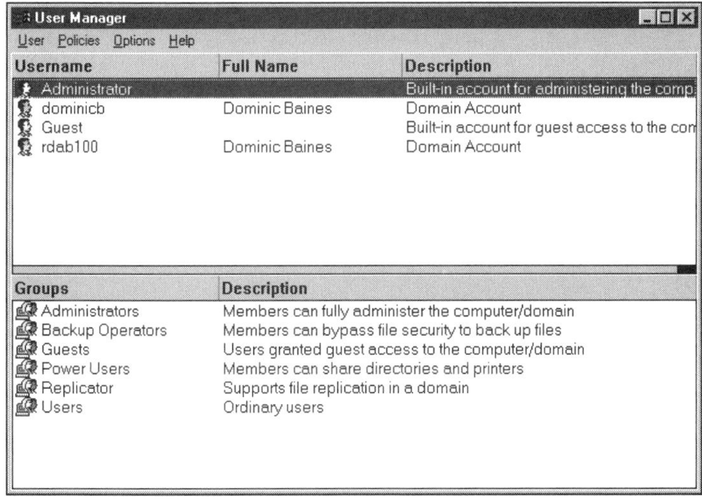

Figure 9.6 User Manager for Domains.

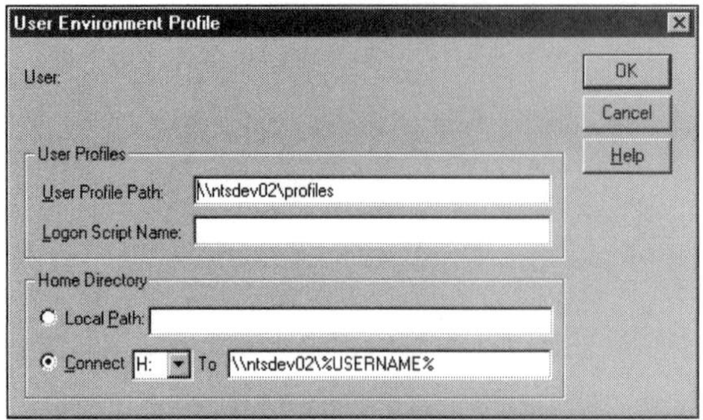

Figure 9.7 User Environment Profile.

Suitable values for **logon home** are of the form

```
logon home=\\servername\users\username
```

where *username* could be **%USERNAME%** when using User Manager for Domains on a Windows NT PDC, **%U** when using Samba, or the actual user home share name if this is not as specified in /etc/passwd, for the user home directory.

Suitable values for **logon path** are of the form

```
logon path=\\servername\profiles\username
```

where username could be **%USERNAME%** when using User Manager for Domains on a Windows NT PDC, **%U** when using Samba, or the actual share name for either a Windows NT server or Samba PDC as the location for the profile information. By default, the profile is stored in the user's home directory unless otherwise specified. This can cause problems, as shares remain open following a user logging out from a Windows session.

Replacing An NT Server PDC

Samba may not be ready yet to replace a functional PDC, but if you want to consider using Samba in this way, the following discussion provides details on how to proceed.

A caveat: Currently no way exists to successfully transfer the NT domain machine's database from an NT server PDC to a Samba PDC. This means that individual machine trust accounts for the NT domain must be set up on the Samba PDC first. Then the individual machines must, one by one, be added to the domain. See the "Adding Clients to the Domain" section earlier in this chapter for details of how to do this.

If you attempt to set up a Samba PDC to replace an existing NT PDC, you will need to follow a number of steps. For the purposes of this example, in addition to acting as the PDC, the server also has two shares—[work] and [research]—with different access requirements. The NT domain has two user groups: [test] and [research]. The NT domain users within those groups have separate home directories, and the users have roaming profiles. The PDC includes a central laser printer that is available to all users logged into the domain.

To perform this replacement, you first need to obtain information about the current setup, including the following:

- Domain name
- Group details
- User details
- Share names
- Printer names

If we assume that the domain name is SAMBABOOK, the group and user details are determined by knowing which users and groups exist on an NT system. The share names are [work] and [research], and the printer name is HP.

To determine the group and user details, use the **net** command, run from the Windows NT server PDC, which will return the information necessary to build a list of the groups and users included. Listing 9.7 contains the output following running **net group \SAMBABOOK** from the NT server PDC adminserver, which acts as the PDC for the NT domain SAMBABOOK. This lists the groups that exist on the server.

Listing 9.7 net group \SAMBABOOK output.

```
Group Accounts for \\ADMINSERVER
-----------------------------------------------------------------
*Domain Admins             *Domain Guests             *Domain Users
*research                  *test
The command completed successfully.
```

You will also need to know the user information from the NT server PDC, and the **net** command will return that information. Listing 9.8 contains the output following running **net user \SAMBABOOK** from the NT server PDC adminserver, which acts as the PDC for the NT domain SAMBABOOK that lists the users that exist on the server.

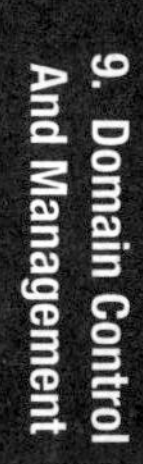

Listing 9.8 net user \SAMBABOOK output.

```
User accounts for \\ADMINSERVER
-------------------------------------------------------------------
Administrator            bbaines                  dbaines
Guest                    internet                 IUSR_ADMINSERVER
test1                    test2                    test3
test4
The command completed successfully.
```

It is necessary to capture and transfer this information into the appropriate location on the new Samba server PDC. To capture this information, send the output of the **net** command to a text file by using the command **net user*(or group)* \SAMBABOOK > filename.txt** and then extract the information of the users or groups. You could do this manually, but a member of the Samba team, Gerald Carter, has recently written some Perl-based scripts that make this transfer fairly painless. These are included on this book's CD-ROM under the directory \GeraldCarter. The readme.txt file included in the directory explains their use.

With the appropriate entries in the /etc/passwd and /etc/group files, and using whichever method you want, you now need to confirm the appropriate mapping for the groups and users and to create the files for them.

The domain-group.map, domain-user.map, and local-group.map files contain suitable entries for the group and user mappings. These files are shown in Listings 9.9 and 9.10 for the simple SAMBABOOK NT domain, which consists of a limited number of groups and users.

Listing 9.9 domain-group.map, domain-user.map, and local-group.map.

```
#contents of domain-group.map file
test = Test
admin = "Domain Admins"

#contents of domain-user.map file
root = administrator

#contents of local-group.map file
wheel = BUILTIN\Administrators
users = BUILTIN\Users
```

Listing 9.10 /etc/group, /etc/passwd, and /etc/smbpasswd.

```
#appropriate entries from /etc/group
users:*:500:test1, test2, test3, test4, dbaines, bbaines
test:*:500:test1, test2, test3
admin:*:501:dbaines
```

```
test1:x:503:
test2:x:504:
test3:x:505:
test4:x:506:
machines:x:1000:

#appropriate entries from /etc/passwd
dbaines:KUcgjh7c7mh9k:501:501::/home/dbaines:/bin/bash
bbaines:adf34fgnJHJk7:502:502::/home/bbaines:/bin/bash
test1:gto3cPyvDk9UA:503:503::/home/test1:/bin/bash
test2:ut8Q2L.ZGtR2Q:504:504::/home/test2:/bin/bash
test3:tc1CmZb10eWBw:505:505::/home/test2:/bin/bash
test4:fG1CmZbt8Qsdf:506:506::/home/test2:/bin/bash
testpc1$:*:9000:1000:WinNT trust account:/dev/null:/bin/false
testpc2$:*:9001:1000:WinNT trust account:/dev/null:/bin/false
testpc3$:*:9002:1000:WinNT trust account:/dev/null:/bin/false
testpc4$:*:9003:1000:WinNT trust account:/dev/null:/bin/false

#appropriate entries from /etc/smbpasswd
# Samba SMB password file - these entries are truncated

root:0:BC8AFF34937B5979F500944B53168930:FD0C144294BD58797C
rdab100:501:11FD0DFD5ECFE347C482C03F54CDB5D9:9F193D55A6C80
testpc1$:9000:396C951D07FD5154AAD3B435B51404EE:E6349B38689
testpc2$:9001:D5C65BBC2EA1A5DFAAD3B435B51404EE:09B325F1B76
testpc3$:9002:BF68BA831810B284AAD3B435B51404EE:40A12A08E55
testpc4$:9003:E4D9C024176098E5AAD3B435B51404EE:0F37A25D300
dbaines:506:11FD0DFD5ECFE347C482C03F54CDB5D9:9F193D55A6C80
bbaines:507:11FD0DFD5ECFE347C482C03F54CDB5D9:9F193D55A6C80
test1:502:AAD3B435B51404EEAAD3B435B51404EE:31D6CFE0D16AE93
test2:503:AAD3B435B51404EEAAD3B435B51404EE:31D6CFE0D16AE93
test3:504:AAD3B435B51404EEAAD3B435B51404EE:31D6CFE0D16AE93
test4:505:AAD3B435B51404EEAAD3B435B51404EE:31D6CFE0D16AE93
```

Users have their own home directories, so the new Samba PDC will need to include a [homes] section in the smb.conf file. A suitable version is shown here:

```
[homes]
comment = PDC users home directory
path = /%H
```

The two shares [work] and [research] must also be created in the smb.conf file, and the permissions associated with those shares will need to be applied to the underlying file system to allow the groups to read and write to the shares as appropriate. The [work] share is read-only by the "test" group and is read/writable by the "research" group. The [research] share is read/writable by the members of the "research" group. Listing 9.11 shows a suitable version of the smb.conf section for the two shares.

Listing 9.11 The [work] and [research] sections in smb.conf.

```
[work]
comment = department work directory for the testers
path = /export/work
create mode = 0660
directory mode = 0770
write list = @test @research
read list = @test @research
valid users = %S
[research]
comment = research group directory
path = /export/research
create mode = 0660
directory mode = 0770
write list = @research
read list =  @research
valid users = %S
```

The central printer, an HP LaserJet, has an appropriate entry in the /etc/printcap file, as shown here:

```
#
hp|hp laserjet:\
        :sd=/var/spool/lpd/lp:\
        :mx#0:\
        :sh:\
        :lp=/dev/lp1:\
        :if=/var/spool/lpd/lp/filter:
```

The Samba server will automatically read all the /etc/printcap entries at startup; however, we want to restrict printing to valid NT domain users only. Thus, appropriate entries are made to the smb.conf file, as shown in Listing 9.12.

Listing 9.12 [HP] printer smb.conf entries.

```
[HP]
print command = lpr -r -P%p %s
#the default
comment = HP laser printer
printable = yes
writable = no
public =no
```

The last line restricts access to only those users that have authenticated sessions with the server.

The Samba PDC will also have a section in the smb.conf file so that it can act as the PDC for the domain. Listing 9.13 shows the complete smb.conf file for the Samba PDC in this example.

Listing 9.13 Samba PDC smb.conf.

```
#Example Samba PDC smb.conf file
[global]
    netbios name = SambaPDC
    workgroup = SAMBABOOK
    security = user
    encrypt passwords = yes
    os level = 32
    domain master = yes
    local master = yes
    preferred master = yes
    domain logons = yes

    logon path = \\%N\profiles\%U
    logon home = \\%N\%U
    logon drive = H: #I've setup home directories to be drive H:
#The following files exist as above
    domain group map = /usr/local/samba/lib/domain-group.map
    domain user map = /usr/local/samba/lib/domain-user.map
    local group map = /usr/local/samba/lib/local-group.map
[homes]
    comment user home directories
    path = %H
    valid user = %S
    create mode = 0600
    directory mode = 0700
    locking = no
[netlogon]
    comment = NT Domain netlogon service share
    path = /export/smb/netlogon
    writeable = no
    guest ok = no
#     logon script = scripts\%U.bat
#Uncomment the above should you wish to use scripts
#don't forget to create it too !
[work]
    comment = department work directory for the testers
    path = /export/work
```

```
    create mode = 0660
    directory mode = 0770
    write list = @test @research
    read list = @test @research
    valid users = %S
[research]
    comment = research group directory
    path = /export/research
    create mode = 0660
    directory mode = 0770
    write list = @research
    read list =  @research
    valid users = %S
[HP]
    comment = HP laser printer
    print command = lpr -r -P%p %s
    printable = yes
    writable = no
    public =no
```

Logging A Windows NT Client Into A Samba-Controlled NT Domain

The current NT domain controller code is still under development, so this section is intended as a guide to logging into a Samba-controlled NT domain.

Follow the details in "Setting Up A Samba Server As The PDC For A Windows NT Domain" from earlier in the chapter, so that you have a functioning Samba PDC. The steps you need to confirm are as follows:

1. Ensure that the Samba server has **encrypted passwords=yes** in the smb.conf file.
2. Create the necessary machine trust account on the Samba PDC, first creating an account in /etc/passwd for the username *NTclient_workstation*$, where *NTclient_workstation* is the NetBIOS name for the NT workstation.

NOTE: *In the current NT domain controller code, the UID is all that is currently used to ensure that the Samba-generated machine RID (relative ID) for the NTclient_workstation account will be unique. The impact of this is that the UIDs in the /etc/passwd file should not be reused, even when machine accounts are removed. The machine user account is set up without normal login capabilities and no home directory, so the shell or home directory fields in /etc/passwd are used and should be set to /bin/False and /dev/null, respectively. The following shows sample /etc/passwd entries for two NT workstations:*

```
testnt1$:*:9008:1000:NT Workstation 1:/dev/null:/bin/false
testnt2$:*:9009:1000:NT Workstation 2:/dev/null:/bin/false
```

3. The Samba server now needs to create the **smbpasswd** for the machine accounts, so the **smbpasswd** command should be invoked with the **-a -m** options (**-a** creates the account, **-m** means that it is a machine account):

```
smbpasswd -a -m NTclient_workstation
```

The /usr/local/samba/private/smbpasswd file will have two machine account **smbpasswd** entries appended to it with the following syntax:

```
NTclient_workstation$:uid:LM_XXX:NT_XXX:[W        ]:LTC-XXXX:
```

The *LM_XXX* and *NT_XXX* fields are the ASCII representations of the 16-byte LanMan and NT MD4 hashes, respectively, of the password *NTclient_workstation* NetBIOS name.

NOTE: *When a client first joins an NT domain, it sends its password initially as the lowercase version of its NetBIOS name. After joining the domain successfully, the client will change its password to some random value using the old password as the encryption key. The impact is that if the client is removed from the domain for any reason and rejoins the domain, the machine trust account password must be reset on the server before proceeding. To do this, rerun the* ***smbpasswd -a -m*** *name command.*

If the client happens to be an NT server, you will need to set the capability to log in locally. This is available as an option within User Manager for Domains, Policies, and User Rights. Grant everyone (or authenticated users, assuming NT4 SP3 or later) the capability to log in locally. The NT user will then be able to log in locally. This process will need to be carried out if you are logging in to another NT PDC instead of a Samba PDC.

---

4. Confirm that the smb.conf parameters for the workgroup and domain logons are set correctly, as shown here (being corrected for your NT domain name):

```
workgroup = SAMBABOOK
domain logons = yes
```

If these are not already set, restarting **smbd** will create a file name /usr/local/samba/private/SAMBABOOK.SID with permissions rw-r--r--. The file contains the domain server ID (SID) for the Samba PDC.

The initial part of the file name will be taken from the value of the **workgroup** parameter. This file is the key identifier for the PDC and the domain, and the values are unique to the PDC and the domain for this creation. Importantly, if the file is damaged or altered, the machines in the domain will not be able to log on, and the machine trust accounts will need to be re-created.

5. Check that the Samba services are running (run a **ps x** and look for the **smbd** and **nmbd** services), as the NT client will now attempt to log into the domain controller. In the NT Network Settings dialog box, change the domain to SAMBABOOK. Figure 9.8 shows where to make this change.
6. After confirmation, the NT client should be welcomed to the NT domain, as shown in Figure 9.9.
7. Close the dialog box and allow the NT client to restart.

Obtaining User Manager For Domains, Server Manager, And Policy Editor

Versions of User Manager for Domains, Server Manager, and Policy Editor are available for Windows 95 and Windows NT 4 and can be obtained from Microsoft, from the Microsoft FTP site **ftp://ftp.microsoft.com/Softlib/MSLFILES**. The file to download for NT is called SVRTOOLS.EXE, and the Windows 95 version is called NEXUS.EXE.

It is important to use the correct version of the Policy Editor, because although the Windows 95 version will install on Windows NT, it is not capable of editing an NT policy file. The NT Server Policy Editor (poledit.exe) is included with the NT Server CD-ROM but, unfortunately, not with NT Workstation.

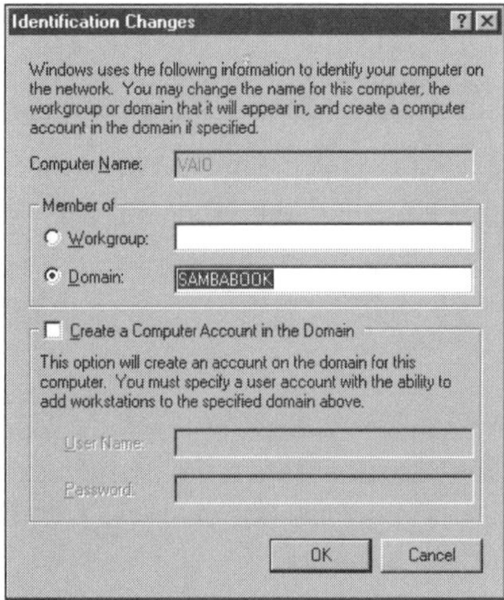

Figure 9.8 Changing the NT domain.

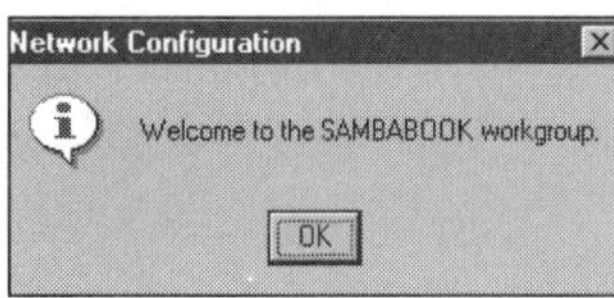

Figure 9.9 Welcome to the SAMBABOOK NT domain.

A copy of the Windows NT Policy Editor is included with Service Pack 3 and 4 for Windows NT 4. Copies of Service Pack 4 have been available on many *PC Magazine* CD-ROMs. The Policy Editor (poledt.exe) and the associated template files (*.adm) are available as well.

Office 97 also has policy template files that can be downloaded, including a copy of the Policy Editor.

Adding A Samba Host To An NT Domain

The previous sections have dealt with setting up an NT domain controlled by a Samba PDC. It is also sometimes necessary to add other Samba hosts to the NT domain (Samba controlled or not) just as you might need to add any Windows NT workstation clients.

The first task is to create a machine trust account on the PDC using the NetBIOS name of the Samba server. This can be created using either the Windows NT GUI Server Manager or the Samba PDC process described previously.

After the machine trust account has been created, all Samba services must be halted on the Samba client. The Samba **smbpasswd** program is used to add the machine to the NT domain. The **smbpasswd** option **-j** specifies that you want to join the given domain, having identified the domain PDC NetBIOS name, as shown here:

```
smbpasswd -j domainname -r domainPDC
```

The Samba host will join the NT domain, and a successful response should result.

In this example, if the NT domain name is SAMBABOOK and the PDC NetBIOS name is SambaPDC, the command and response shown here will be seen:

```
[root@sambaclient /root]# smbpasswd -j SAMBABOOK -r SambaPDC
smbpasswd: Joined domain SAMBABOOK.
[root@sambaclient /root]#
```

The Samba client then writes the new (random) machine account password into the file in the same directory in which the smbpasswd file will be stored. This is usually /usr/local/samba/private. The file name is a combination of the domain name and the client name and takes the form *NT DOMAIN NAME.Samba Server Name*.mac. The .mac suffix stands for "machine account password file." In this case, the file is called SAMBABOOK.SAMBACLIENT.mac. An example of the contents of this file is shown here:

```
AF133010172E406F7B3E1624087AAFE3:TLC-37A7316C
```

This is the trust account password for the Samba client. It is created and owned by root and is not readable by any other user, and it is the key to the domain-level security for your system. It is essential to maintain the permissions on this file and to ensure that it is backed up.

The Samba services on the client should now be restarted, but before you do so, you need to alter the smb.conf file to start to make use of the new domain security. The security parameter in the [global] section of the smb.conf file should be set to "domain," as shown here:

```
security = domain
```

If not already set, the **workgroup** parameter in the [global] section should now be set to the name of the NT domain that the Samba host has joined, as shown here:

```
workgroup = SAMBABOOK
```

For any NT PDC that is operating with a Service Pack later than 1, it is also necessary to set the parameter **encrypt passwords=yes** in order for your users to authenticate against the NT PDC.

Finally, the Samba client needs to be informed of the NetBIOS name for the NT domain authentication server. The **password server** parameter should be set to the PDC. If the PDC is a Samba server, that is all that can be entered; however, if this is an NT-controlled NT domain and a BDC is present, the **password server** parameter should list these in the order that they should be used. This can assist with spreading the load across several PDC/BDC servers in a busy network.

The following example shows the setting for the **password server** parameter:

```
password server = SAMBAPDC
#If this were an NT PDC and a number of BDC's (NTBDC1, NTBDC2 etc..) were
#present then this line should be written as
#password server = NTPDC NTBDC1 NTBDC2
```

The Samba client will attempt to contact these servers, in order, so you might want to rearrange this list to spread out the authentication load among domain controllers.

The current Samba development uses the model of needing to know the NetBIOS names of the PDC or BDC server. The standard NT client need not know this, and the PDC/BDC is determined by sending a broadcast to the local subnet to identify where the netlogon server is located. An alternative is that a WINS server, if the client is so configured, can be used to achieve the same goal.

The Samba client should then be able to begin using domain security to use resources on the NT domain.

Creating An Account To Act As A Domain Administrator

In a "normal" Windows NT domain, it is possible to use the Administrator account domainwide to perform administration tasks on any workstation. This functionality is also available in a Samba-controlled NT domain using three parameters:

- **domain group map**
- **domain user map**
- **local group map**

The syntax and function are described earlier in Table 9.1.

To create an administration account called "admin1" that exists in the Windows NT "Domain Admins" group, the process is as follows:

1. Identify a suitable Unix group. In this case, the administrator group is suitable.
2. Add the three parameters listed previously to the smb.conf file.
3. In the /usr/local/samba/lib directory, create three text files: domain-group.map, domain-user.grp, and local-group.map.
4. Direct the three parameters to these files, as shown here:

```
domain group map = /usr/local/samba/lib/domain-group.map
domain user map = /usr/local/samba/lib/domain-user.map
local group map = /usr/local/samba/lib/local-group.map
```

5. In the domain-group.map file, add the chosen administrator group from the Unix /etc/group file, as shown here:

```
adm="Domain Admins"
```

6. In /etc/group, add the Unix users to the adm group that are to be part of the Domain Admins group. Note that these users will be given Domain Admin rights on the workstations and are capable of altering the permissions on resources, including the creation and deletion of shares. A Domain Admin may remove the workstation from a domain, remove or edit profiles on the machine, create shares, delete shares, and so on, so this account should be created with care.

7. To create local administrators, choose a suitable Unix group, for example, “wheel,” and add the entry to the local-group.map file, as shown here:

```
wheel=BUILTIN\Administrators
```

8. In /etc/group, add the Unix users that you want to be local administrators in the group wheel.
9. The NT user accounts need to be mapped to the Unix accounts in the /usr/local/samba/lib/domain-user.map file, as shown in the following listing:

```
root=Administrator
username=Administrator
...(add for however many user accounts are involved)
```

username is the name of the Unix account that you have added to the domain or local group.

10. You need to create the appropriate **smbpasswd** entry, as shown here:

```
smbpasswd -a username
```

When prompted twice, enter the necessary smb password. The appropriate Domain Admin accounts will have been created.

Using rpcclient

Th **rpcclient** program does not appear to be used often in normal operation. It was designed to assist with development of Samba PDC functionality by being able to interrogate hosts with Windows NT networking for information during this development. The **rpcclient** utility does provide functionality to determine Windows NT client or server information quickly.

When run at the command line with no options, **rpcclient** returns a set of options, shown in Listing 9.14.

Listing 9.14 rpcclient options.

```
[root@linuxserver /root]# rpcclient
Usage: rpcclient service <password> [-d debuglevel] [-l log]
Version 2.0.4b
        -d debuglevel         set the debuglevel
        -l log basename.      Basename for log/debug files
```

```
        -n netbios name.      Use this name as my netbios name
        -N                    don't ask for a password
        -m max protocol       set the max protocol level
        -I dest IP            use this IP to connect to
        -E                    write messages to stderr instead of stdout
        -U username           set the network username
        -W workgroup          set the workgroup name
        -c command string     execute semicolon separated commands
        -t terminal code      terminal i/o code
                                {sjis|euc|jis7|jis8|junet|hex}
[root@linuxserver /root]#
```

The program functions similarly to the command line version of **smbclient** and is capable of communicating with Windows NT clients. Listing 9.15 shows a simple connection to a NTSDEV02 server by user rdab100. A list of internal commands can be returned with the **help** command once connected to a host.

Listing 9.15 Using rpcclient.

```
root@linuxserver /etc]# rpcclient -S ntsdev02 -U rdab100 W DOMAIN
Added interface ip=192.168.1.4 bcast=192.168.1.255 nmask=255.255.255.0
Enter Password:
smb: \> help
help

regenum          regdeletekey     regcreatekey     regquerykey      regdeleteval
regcreateval     reggetsec        regtestsec       ntlogin          wksinfo
srvinfo          srvsessions      srvshares        srvconnections srvfiles
lsaquery         lookupsids       enumusers        ntpass           samuser
samtest          enumaliases      samgroups        quit             q
exit             bye              help             ?                !
smb: \>
```

Some of the commands do not appear to produce much useful information, but the commands can provide information on the internal workings of the Windows NT machines and help with understanding the functionality of Windows NT networking. The command even provides the ability to interrogate the Registry settings of the remote Windows NT machine and to obtain user account information.

The **srvinfo** command will return information on the server, including details on whether it is a PDC and which version of NT is running. From Listing 9.16, it can be seen that the server is a PDC and is running NT 4.

Listing 9.16 srvinfo for NTSDEV02.

```
smb: \> srvinfo
srvinfo
```

```
Server Info Level 101:
        NTSDEV02        Wk Sv PDC PrQ NT BMB LMB PDC
        platform_id      : 500
        os version       : 4.0
smb: \>
```

It is possible to obtain the details for the SID by interrogating the server's Local Security Authority (LSA) database. Running the **lsaquery** command, the output, including the machine's SID, is shown in Listing 9.17.

Listing 9.17 LSA query for NTSDEV02.

```
smb: \> lsaquery
lsaquery

LSA Query Info Policy
Domain Member     - Domain: DOMAIN SID: S-1-5-21-312237597-911490962-
1558919984
Domain Controller - Domain: DOMAIN SID: S-1-5-21-312237597-911490962-
1558919984
smb: \>
```

The shares that are available, including the hidden shares, can be seen from the **srvshares** command. The output is shown in Listing 9.18.

Listing 9.18 srvshares for NTSDEV02.

```
smb: \> srvshares
srvshares
Share Info Level 1:
        NETLOGON        Disk        Logon server share
Share Info Level 1:
        c               Disk
Share Info Level 1:
        d               Disk
Share Info Level 1:
        e               Disk
Share Info Level 1:
        ADMIN$          ????        Remote Admin
Share Info Level 1:
        IPC$            ????        Remote IPC
Share Info Level 1:
        CDROM           Disk
Share Info Level 1:
        C$              ????        Default share
Share Info Level 1:
        D$              ????        Default share
```

```
Share Info Level 1:
       E$             ????      Default share
Share Info Level 1:
       print$         Disk      Printer Drivers
Share Info Level 1:
       CanonBJC       Printer   Canon BJC-4550
smb: \>
```

Chapter 10

Advanced Topics And Administration Issues

In Depth

Many organizations use a mixed Unix and Windows network environment. This should be a beneficial arrangement, and the advantages of both systems can be put to the best use. The problems are usually associated with sharing resources and files between the different types of clients.

Desktop applications, word processors, spreadsheets, and other integrated desktop and communications suites exist for these operating systems, and the ability to share data between them on a network can be very advantageous. When users are capable of roaming from one office to another or even moving from one operating system to another in this environment, the data files used by different users can be made available to them regardless of the operating system used on the desktop. Samba will allow these files and other resources to be shared within a mixed environment.

Samba also has the ability to aid the network administrator directly in addition to providing Windows Internet Name Service (WINS) and domain control support. Samba can successfully be used to back up the Windows clients and servers on a network to a Unix server and vice versa.

Using UNC Paths Inside Applications

You likely will find that almost all your usual desktop applications, be they Windows or Linux based, will use a Universal Naming Convention (UNC) path when specifying locations for files rather than a specific drive letter and directory location. Most single- and multiuser applications will benefit from a central template or configuration file location in addition to any location where work is saved. This is especially the case with the integrated desktop application suites, such as Microsoft Office and StarOffice, among others, that have a configuration option to specify file locations.

An ability to use UNC paths in applications exists not only for desktop applications but also for internal Web servers, such as Apache and Internet Information Server. This may occur within the content of the HTML pages where a suitable UNC path, such as *servername**sharename**filename*, will link to the file as appropriate. This functionality seems to be supported in Internet Explorer but not in Netscape when NetBIOS names are used. The configuration of the server can also use UNC paths for log files, directory aliases, and many other locations that would direct off the server. Email clients can also make use of this ability to retain the mail and news folders on SMB/CIFS servers.

Database servers, such as Oracle, running on NT systems can utilize the UNC path for the location of many database components. The archive log files, or copies thereof, from a running Oracle database are ideal candidates. The inclusion of a UNC path used in automated backup scripts for the database has proven successful. The creation of most output files from a Windows NT database can utilize UNC paths.

The limits of use are set only by the imagination of the network administrator, with some obvious application-imposed limitations. The use of UNC paths assumes that the application can support these paths.

Now that you can share resources between Unix and Windows machines across your network, it is important to take a look at some advanced topics that may affect the operation of the Samba server.

In addition, there is a section on performance tuning your Samba server. This section has been added so that you may fully take advantage of the capabilities of a Samba server in a production environment.

Immediate Solutions

Configuring Applications

Almost every desktop application today has the ability to use network resources directly without mapping a drive to the local system first. One of the more sophisticated uses of this is the ability to define a central template location for a particular application over a whole department.

A legal firm with which I consulted some time ago was having problems maintaining accurate, up-to-date copies of the case preparation notes needed by the partners when attending court. The court building happened to be around the corner from one of the offices. Much of the work carried out in other offices had to be rewritten in this office, and this entailed considerable administrative overhead. The problem was an inability to have the information made available to the legal secretaries in the other offices, where all of them were working off copies transferred between the offices on floppy drives by the network administrator using couriers and the postal system. Before I was called in, the firm had already started to consider setting up a small network between the offices to make their work easier, and this was an excellent opportunity to resolve the template issue as well. The firm relied on a group of legal secretaries in three offices spanning three counties in the United Kingdom using a word processor, Word 97, to write all case preparation notes.

The eventual network involved three subnets: 192.168.1.0, 192.168.2.0, and 192.168.3.0. A Linux/Samba primary domain controller (PDC) was set up, as were a WINS server and the logon server for the Windows 95 clients spread throughout the offices. A central file server, bigserver, also a Linux/Samba installation, existed in the offices close to the law courts. The three networks were connected using ISDN routers that connect the three networks on demand. The connection takes only a few seconds to complete.

The bigserver file server contains a [templates] share that holds the *.dot Word 97 templates for the firm's case preparation notes and other essential documents. The [templates] share was set read-only by all the legal secretaries and can be written to by any of the firm's partners. The users are in the appropriate groups, and the file permissions are set on the file system accordingly. The smb.conf share definition is shown in Listing 10.1.

Listing 10.1 The [templates] definition.

```
[templates]
        comment = Office 97 Templates
        path = /home/templates
        read list = @legal
        write list = @partners
        read only = No
```

In Word 97, the Tools|Options|File Locations menu item provides several choices for file locations, including the user templates and the default location for saving files. Figure 10.1 shows the settings used by one of the partners; the templates folder is clearly indicated, as is the default folder location to the partner's home directory.

Every member of the firm altered the location of the Word 97 user template to point to the central location, \\bigserver\templates, the *.dot files having been copied there previously. The impact is that whenever a new document is created, any of the members of the firm are always using the same template for the case preparation notes. One of the partners regularly ensures that the templates are up to date and, whenever one needs to be updated, creates a backup copy of the template (the [template] share has a backup directory) before altering it and saving it back over the original. Figure 10.2 shows the choice of document template, from the template folder, currently available when creating a new Word 97 document.

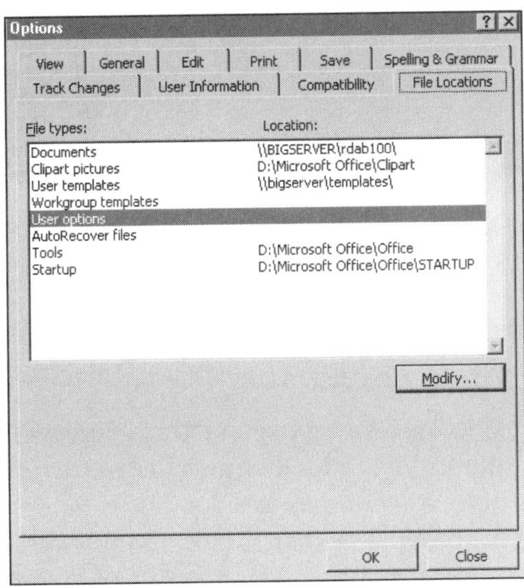

Figure 10.1 Word 97 file location options.

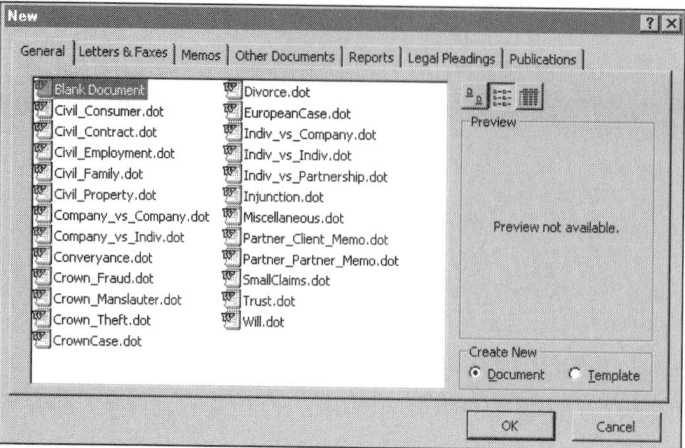

Figure 10.2 Word 97 document creation.

Fortunately for the network administrator, the users do not notice any difference between the templates being available on a local drive and being available over the network. In addition, because the templates are small, the maximum size is about 50K, and the bandwidth usage is not large. The partners soon were able to rapidly move the accounting packages and their expenses (calculated on Excel 97) to a similar system.

This sort of application of Samba or any SMB/CIFS server is readily reproducible and in this case led to considerable productivity increases, as the administrative overhead associated with multiple template copies on local machines was eliminated.

Coping With File Locking

File locking exists when two or more sessions attempt to open the same file. To prevent any secondary sessions from saving and editing a file that another process has already opened for editing, the system marks the file as already being open and so prevents the file from being saved. This is known as *file locking*.

Since version 1.9.18, Samba has included the SMB opportunistic locking mechanisms, also known as *oplocks*. The opportunistic locking mechanism is one in which the file is allowed to be opened by a secondary session but is marked as read-only and cannot be saved while the original version is open. Samba versions since 1.9.18 have included oplocks support by default. The function of oplocks is to stop two users from opening and editing the same file at the same time.

Note that oplocks will prevent multiple users from editing the same file only from another SMB session. The Samba server might have other connections that do not use SMB sessions, and so any oplocks will be ignored. This is shown in the following example, where both a Windows and a Unix system open and edit a file:

1. Create a document on a Unix box.
2. View the document on a PC via Samba.
3. Change the contents of the document on the Unix box.
4. Save it on the Unix box.
5. Look at the file again on the PC via Samba; the changes are not visible.

Currently, two solutions are available:

- Use a kernel-level interface that allows access from a Unix client via either Network File System (NFS) or a local process to notify Samba to "break" the oplock and thus force the correct data that has been added to Samba to be seen. This is currently supported only on SGI IRIX 6.5.3f and later. This interface might soon be included in some other Unix variants.
- Disable oplocks in smb.conf for those shares that will need to be accessed simultaneously from Unix and Windows clients. Set the parameter **oplocks=no** and veto **oplock files=no**. The impact of this might be to slow down file access, as the oplocks will now be checked more thoroughly.

No other option is available to allow access from both Windows and Unix at the same time.

It is also possible to alter the Windows Registry for Windows NT 4 so that oplocks on a Windows NT client are disabled. However, the Registry changes are not selective to the Samba server and will result in oplocks being turned off for all servers accessed from this client. Listing 10.2 contains the Registry keys that need to be altered. The Samba distribution includes a WinNT-locking.txt file that also lists these Registry changes.

Listing 10.2 Windows NT Registry changes to disable client oplocks.

```
[HKEY_LOCAL_MACHINE\SYSTEM\CurrentControlSet\Services\LanmanWorkstation\
 Parameters]
"BufFilesDenyWrite"=dword:00000000
"BufNamedPipes"=dword:00000000
"UseOpportunisticLocking"=dword:00000000
"DormantFileLimit"=dword:00000000

[HKEY_LOCAL_MACHINE\SYSTEM\CurrentControlSet\Services\LanmanWorkstation\
 Parameters\Linkage]
"UtilizeNtCaching"=dword:00000000
```

```
[HKEY_LOCAL_MACHINE\SYSTEM\CurrentControlSet\Control\Filesystem]
"Win95TruncateExtensions"=dword:00000000

[HKEY_LOCAL_MACHINE\SYSTEM\CurrentControlSet\Services\LanManServer\
 Parameters]
"EnableOpLockForceClose"=dword:00000001
"EnableOpLocks"=dword:00000000
```

The following Registry entry does the same under Windows 9x:

```
[HKEY_LOCAL_MACHINE\System\CurrentControlSet\Services\VxD\VREDIR]
"DiscardCacheOnOpen"=string:00000001
```

Managing Name Mangling

Name mangling of long file names can occur with DOS and Windows clients. Samba includes the name-mangling support that DOS and Windows clients use with files that do not conform to the 8.3 format. Samba can adjust the case of 8.3 format file names.

The parameters that control how name mangling operates are included in the smb.conf file. These parameters can exist at both the global and the service level and are shown in Table 10.1.

Table 10.1 Name-mangling parameters.

Parameter	Description
Mangled names	The default is **yes**. By default Samba will mangle file names into the 8.3 format so that DOS-based clients can read the files. If set to **no**, any files or directories with long names will not appear in listings for those clients.
Mangle case	The default is **no**. Samba will not mangle mixed-case file names if they are not in the default case, unless this parameter is set to **yes**.
Mangling char	The default character, "~", can be replaced by another character specified in this parameter.
Case sensitive	The default is **no**. By default, Samba will search directories and perform a case-insensitive file name match for all file names to check whether another file with the same name exists. If set to **yes**, Samba regards file names as case sensitive.
Default case	The default is to use lowercase. Options are **uppercase** and **lowercase**.
Preserve case	The default is to preserve case when files are created. Options are **yes** or **no**.
Short preserve case	The default is **yes**. The short (mangled) names are set to uppercase.

By default, Samba 2.0 has the same semantics as a Windows NT server; that is, it is case insensitive but case preserving.

To manage the Samba server, say, to use the default mangling options globally but for a [test] share to permit long file names, preserving their case while mangled or short names are lowered, the smb.conf file shown in Listing 10.3 could be used.

Listing 10.3 Name-mangling options in smb.conf.

```
[global]
#global section trimmed
Mangled names = yes
Mangle case = no
Mangling char = ~
Case sensitive = no
Default case = lower
Preserve case = yes
Short preserve case = yes

[test]
#share section trimmed
Short preserve case = no
```

Automating Samba

During the use of a Samba server, you might notice that—with no additional configuration—shares exist for users for whom shares have never been individually created or for printers that have never been shared. This was mentioned in Chapters 4 and 5. These are two indications that the Samba server might have some additional capabilities that will automatically create and manage resources for you. The automatic creation of user shares based on their home directories and the inclusion of printers from the /etc/printcap file are two examples. Samba also has a number of other capabilities, some of which are driven by parameters and some by the use of macros, both of which are configured in the smb.conf file.

The *exec Parameters

The parameters that can be used directly to automate tasks at the server are **preexec**, **postexec**, **root preexec**, and **root postexec**. These execute when any client either connects (pre) or disconnects (post) to any resource. These parameters are set at the resource level and do not apply at the global level.

The values for these parameters can include the details of a script or command that normally might be run only at the server. The use of these is limited only by the imagination of the administrator, but some tasks that have been created include removing the contents of the user's temporary directory following the closing of the home share, as shown here:

```
[homes]
postexec = /bin/rm -r /%H/tmp/*
```

You can also display a message of the day to a client on opening a share. The following message could be placed anywhere the user would have read access on the Samba server.

```
[sharename]
preexec = cat /user readable path/message | smbclient -M %m
```

Alternatively, a central message, perhaps informing users to make sure that they have cleared out folders at the end of a period (say, at the end of a term for students) could be invoked; the **root preexec** option would be used instead. If this is added to the [homes] section, the message will be guaranteed to get to the users on logon:

```
[homes]
root preexec = cat /secure path/message | smbclient -M %m
```

This can automatically create a backup copy of the user's home directory on closing the share, as shown here:

```
[homes]
root postexec = tar cf %H/* | gzip -9 > /%H/backup.tgz
```

When using a CD-ROM tower, wouldn't it be great to be able to automatically prompt a user to enter a CD-ROM to a share, mount the CD-ROM, and, when the share is closed again, to eject the CD-ROM after use? The **exec** and **preexec** messages are user driven and thus can be safely left as they are. The mount, unmount, and eject of the CD-ROMs in this case require root access, so the **root preexec** and **root postexec** parameters are used as well.

The cdrom*mount and cdrom*eject files in /messages are plain ASCII text and simply provide WinPopup a screen message that will be obvious to the user: "Place the CDROM in bay 1 in the tower," "Take the CDROM out of bay 1," and so on (see Listing 10.4).

Listing 10.4 Using a CD-ROM tower.

```
[cdshare0]
          path = /mnt/cdrom0
```

```
          comment = Bay 1 in CROM Tower
          exec = cat /messages/cdrom0mount | smbclient -M %m
          postexec = cat /messages/cdrom0eject | smbclient -M %m
          root preexec = mount /mnt/cdrom0
          root postexec = umount /mnt/cdrom0 | eject cdrom0

[cdshare1]
          path = /mnt/cdrom1
          comment = Bay 2 in CROM Tower
          exec = cat /messages/cdrom1mount | smbclient -M %m
          postexec = cat /messages/cdrom1eject | smbclient -M %m
          root preexec = mount /mnt/cdrom1
          root postexec = umount /mnt/cdrom1 | eject cdrom1
```

Adding a share access log entry to an administration file tracks who used the share, the user's name, where they logged in from, and when they logged in. The log.sharename administration file is located in the /usr/local/samba/lib/admin/ directory. The smb.conf entry is shown in Listing 10.5.

Listing 10.5 Auditing access to a share.

```
[sharename]
path = /somedirectory/sharename
comment = someshare
root preexec = echo "At %T, %U used %u, from %m on %M host, with %I" >>
/usr/local/samba/lib/admin/log.sharename
root postexec = echo "At %T, %U stopped using %u, from %m on %M host,
with %I" >> /usr/local/samba/lib/admin/log.sharename
```

The only difference between the root and nonroot version is that the later versions are run on the server as root and normally are required only when root privileges are necessary. The tasks that need to run as root usually involve file system changes (mounting or unmounting removable media, tape, CD-ROM, and so on), running backups, stopping processes, and the like.

Include

Samba is usually set up to include a complete smb.conf file on any server with all relevant parameters maintained in that file. An smb.conf **include** parameter will allow an external configuration file to be read in. The file name can include a number of macros that can be used to great effect, where different shares or resources can be defined from different users, group, or host operating types.

The **netbios alias** parameter in smb.conf can also be used to great effect, with the file name using the **%L** session variable or the NetBIOS name that the client is using. In operation, this means that the full smb.conf file for a specific user session from one type of client might be very different from that of another type of client.

The available macros are shown in Table 10.2.

Table 10.2 Macros.

Macro	Description
%S	Name of the current service, if any
%P	Root directory of the current service, if any
%u	Username of the current service, if any
%g	Primary group name of **%u**
%U	Session user name requested
%G	Primary group name of **%U**
%H	Home directory of the user given by **%u**
%v	Samba version
%h	Internet hostname that Samba is running on
%m	NetBIOS name of the client machine
%L	NetBIOS name of the server (if the **netbios alias** parameter has been set, this returns the alias name used when the connection was made)
%M	Internet hostname of the client machine
%N	Name of the NIS home directory server (this is obtained from your NIS auto.map entry. If you have not compiled Samba with the **--with-automount** option, this value will be the same as **%L**)
%p	Path of the service's home directory obtained from your NIS auto.map entry (the NIS auto.map entry is split up as **%N:%p**)
%R	Selected protocol level after protocol negotiation—either **CORE**, **COREPLUS**, **LANMAN1**, **LANMAN2**, or **NT1**
%d	Process ID of the current server process
%a	Architecture of the remote machine—Samba, Windows for Workgroups, Windows NT, and Windows 95 (anything else will be "UNKNOWN")
%I	IP address of the client machine

Using Samba For Backup And Recovery

The two main options are as follows:

- Copy the files off the remote host and create a tar file of them.
- Leave the files where they are and create a tar file of them.

Either option can use either the **smbtar** or the **smbclient** program, both of which, importantly, need not be run from a Samba server running **smbd** or **nmbd**. A suitable host would contain a standard Samba installation (with or without running **smbd** or **nmbd**), a suitable smb.conf file, and either extra hard drive capacity or a backup device where the backup tar files will reside.

The hosts that need to be backed up should have shares of the essential data created on them, and ideally these shares should have security applied to them so that only network administrators or a restricted backup group have access to them.

smbtar

The **smbtar** program syntax is shown here:

```
smbtar -s server [-p password] [-x service] [-X] [-d directory] [-u user]
[-t tape] [-b blocksize] [-N filename] [-i] [-r] [-l log level] [-v]
filenames
```

The **smbtar** program is a very small shell script on top of **smbclient** that dumps SMB shares directly to tape.

The following options may follow the command:

- **-s *server***—The SMB/CIFS server that the share resides on.
- **-p *password***—The password to use to access a share. The default is none.
- **-x *service***—The share name on the server to connect to. The default is **backup**.
- **-X**—Exclude mode. Excludes file names from tar create or restore.
- **-d *directory***—Changes to initial directory before restoring or backing up files.
- **-u *user***—The UID to connect as. The default is the Unix login name.
- **-t *tape***—A regular file or a tape device. The default is a tape environmental variable; if it is not set, tar creates a file called tar.out.
- **-b *blocksize***—A blocking factor. The default is 20. For a fuller explanation, see tar(1).

- **-N *filename***—Backs up only files that are newer than the file name. Could be used, for example, on a log file to implement incremental backups.
- **-i**—Incremental mode. Tar files are backed up only if they have the archive bit set. The archive bit is reset after each file is read.
- **-r**—Restore. Files are restored to the share from the tar file.
- **-l *log level***—The log (debug) level. It corresponds to the **-d** flag of **smbclient**(1).
- **-v**—Verbose mode.

smbclient

The **smbclient** program syntax is shown here:

```
ssmbclient servicename [password] [-s smb.conf] [-B IP addr]
[-O socket options][-R name resolve order] [-M NetBIOS name] [-i scope]
[-N] [-n NetBIOS name] [-d debuglevel] [-P] [-p port] [-l log basename]
[-h] [-I dest IP] [-E] [-U username] [-L NetBIOS name] [-t terminal code]
[-m max protocol] [-W workgroup] [-T<c|x>IXFqgbNan] [-D directory]
[-c command string]
```

The **smbclient** options are discussed in detail in other chapters; however, the **-T** options are of direct interest when discussing backup and Samba. **smbclient** can be used to create tar-compatible backups of the files on an SMB/CIFS share.

The secondary tar flags that can be given to the tar option are as follows:

- **-c**—Creates a tar file on Unix and must be followed by the name of a tar file, tape device, or "-" for standard output. If using standard output, you must turn the log level to its lowest value, **-d0**, to avoid corrupting your tar file. This flag is mutually exclusive with the **-x** flag.
- **-x**—Extracts (restores) a local tar file back to a share. Unless the **-D** option is given, the tar files will be restored from the top level of the share. This must be followed by the name of the tar file, device, or "-" for standard input. This flag is mutually exclusive with the **-c** flag. Restored files have their creation times (mtime) set to the date saved in the tar file. Directories currently do not get their creation dates restored properly.
- **-I**—Include files and directories. The default behavior when file names are those specified previously. It causes tar files to be included in an extract or create (and thus everything else to be excluded) File name globbing works in one of two ways (see **-r**).
- **-X**—Exclude files and directories. Causes tar files to be excluded from an extract or create. File name globbing works in one of two ways (see **-r**).

- **-b**—Block size. Must be followed by a valid (greater than zero) block size. It causes tar file to be written out in blocksize*TBLOCK (usually 512 byte) blocks.
- **-g**—Incremental. Backs up only files that have the archive bit set. Is useful only with the **-c** flag.
- **-q**—Quiet. Keeps tar from printing diagnostics as it works and is the same as tarmode quiet.
- **-r**—Regular expression include or exclude. Uses regular expression matching for excluding or excluding files if compiled with HAVE_REGEX_H. However, this mode can be very slow. If this is not compiled with HAVE_REGEX_H, it does a limited wildcard match on * and ?.
- **-N**—Newer than. Must be followed by the name of a file whose date is compared against files found on the share during a create. Only files newer than the file specified are backed up to the tar file. This is useful only with the **-c** flag.
- **-a**—Set archive bit. Causes the archive bit to be reset when a file is backed up. It is useful with the **-g** and **-c** flags.

Tar Long File Names

smbclient's tar option now supports long file names both on backup and on restore. However, the full pathname of the file must be less than 1,024 bytes. In addition, when a tar archive is created, **smbclient**'s tar option places all files in the archive with relative, not absolute, names.

Tar File Names

All file names can be given as DOS pathnames (with "\" as the component separator) or as Unix pathnames (with "/" as the component separator). The basic form for **smbclient** for use in tar mode is shown here:

```
smbclient //$client/backupshare -Tc
/backupdevice or location for the TAR file
```

Simple examples of backup and restore scripts appear in the following list:

- Restores from tar file backup.tar into someshare on testpc1 (no password on share):

  ```
  smbclient //testlpc/someshare "" -N -Tx backup.tar
  ```

- Restores everything except users/docs:

  ```
  smbclient // testlpc/someshare "" -N -TXx backup.tar users/docs
  ```

- Creates a tar file of the files beneath users/docs:

```
smbclient // testlpc/someshare "" -N -Tc backup.tar users/docs
```

- Creates the same tar file as in the previous entry, but now uses a DOS pathname:

```
smbclient // testlpc/someshare "" -N -tc backup.tar users\edocs
```

- Creates a tar file of all the files and directories in the share:

```
smbclient // testlpc/someshare "" -N -Tc backup.tar *
```

Using Samba To Back Up An Oracle Database

When running an Oracle database on an NT server with a Samba server available on a network, the Samba server can be used to assist in protecting the database. This process would also be possible for any database or software that could operate in a similar manner using extras or archives. Using a combination of **smbclient**, **smbtar**, and an NT server that would map a drive on the Samba host, allows the export and archive logs to be moved from the NT server to the Linux Samba server (which could be dedicated to the task). This might sound somewhat silly, but Unix has one great advantage over non-Unix systems: non-Unix systems cannot usually access a tape drive as a physical device. This means that the exports and logs could be written directly to the tape without using disk space. This can be useful for archive logs when databases are on systems running 24 hours a day, 365 days a year.

Using Samba As A Printer Server

The configuration of Samba as a printer server was covered in Chapter 5; however, some advanced topics were not included and so are discussed here.

Printer Drivers

Windows 95 and 98 have an ability to use printers without having a printer driver installed first. When such a printer is used, Windows automatically installs the required printer driver files.

A number of smb.conf parameters that affect printer operation are shown in Table 10.3.

Table 10.3 Printer-share-related smb.conf parameters.

Parameter	Description
load printers	If this is set to **yes** (the default), all the printers defined within the /etc/printcap file are loaded and made available for browsing. Set this parameter to **no** if you do not want the whole world to use your printers.
lppause command	This is one of the many parameters that you write into with the appropriate command line code to action something on the printer. It is used to stop the print job.
lpresume command	This parameter resumes the stopped print job using the **lppause** command.
lpq command	This parameter reads the printer queue status for clients. With BSD, the default is **lpq**.
lprm command	This parameter deletes the print job from the queue.
min print space	Specified in kilobytes, this parameter sets the minimum amount of space that must be available in the spool file location before a new print job can be accepted from a client. It is very useful when you have tree-size documents being produced on a busy printer. By default, this parameter is usually set to 0, meaning that all jobs are accepted.
postscript	Sometimes printers that are not PostScript seem to get confused because of the Ctrl+D characters appearing at the start of print jobs. The result is that the PostScript layout that is being printed is not PostScript. By default, this parameter is set to **no**, in which case it will add a **%!** to the beginning of each print job, forcing PostScript printing. It has been known to confuse real PostScript printers.
printing	This parameter sets the printer style to be used.
printer	If the /etc/printcap file does not have an entry for the printer share that you have defined, this parameter will tell Samba where to send the print job after spooling.
printable	This parameter defines what may or may not be a printer share and thus what may or may not be printed to. The default is **no**.
printcap name	Used in conjunction with the [printers] section, this parameter informs Samba of the printer definition file's location. This is an alternative to /etc/printcap.
printer	This parameter defines the printer name for the spool to be printed to.
printer driver	Windows clients need to know what the printer driver name is for the printer.
printer driver file	This parameter defines the location of the printer driver definition file.
printer driver location	This parameter defines the printer driver files.
queuepause command	This parameter defines the command used to pause a print queue.
queueresume command	This parameter defines the command to resume a print queue.

As in other sections, the printer parameters can make use of macros. Macros that can be used in printer shares are shown in Table 10.4.

The selection of the printer driver for Windows 9x clients requires some slight modifications to the smb.conf examples of printer shares provided in Chapter 5. To use the automatic printer driver installation, an additional share, [printer$], needs to be created. This share can be placed anywhere on the server and should be a directory where users have read access. The printer driver files will need to be copied to this directory. Listing 10.6 shows a sample [printer$] share.

Listing 10.6 A [printer$] share.

```
[printer$]
comment = printer drivers
path=/var/spool/lpd/printerdrivers
browseable = yes
public = yes
writable = no
```

The printer definition file in the **printer driver file** parameter needs to be created for the printer(s) on your system. The printer definition file is created from a copy of the original Windows-supported printer msprint.inf and msprint2.inf information files and any unsupported information files that might accompany the printer used. These files are ASCII and contain a list of the printer manufacturers, printers, and the details of the driver file names. The printer definition file is created using the make_printerdef script that is included with the Samba distribution; the appropriate information file (msprint.inf, msprint2.inf, or oem??.inf) and the printer driver name given in the smb.conf file are passed to the make_printerdef script, and the resultant printer.def file will contain the information needed by Samba to provide the files to the Windows 9x client. The format is:

```
make_printerdef msprint.inf "some printer name" >> printer.def
```

The printer.def file will contain all the entries that are passed to it using this process; thus, if five different printers are on your Samba server, this process will

Table 10.4 Printer share macros used in smb.conf files.

Macro	Description
%p	Replace with the printer name
%j	Replace with the job number
%s	Replace with the full pathname and file name of the spool file
%S	Replace with the file name of the spool file

occur five times, and five entries will be made in this file. The file should exist in the /lib subdirectory of the Samba home directory, usually /usr/local/samba/lib.

The full smb.conf file should then include the location of the printer definition file as a [global] parameter, and the **printer driver** and **printer driver location** parameters would be placed in the separate printer share section. Listing 10.7 shows the printer share [HP1] for an HP DeskJet.

Listing 10.7 The [HP1] printer share.

```
[HP1]
comment = old printer
path=/var/spool/lpd/hpl
printable = yes
printer driver = HP Deskjet
printer driver location = \\%h\printer$
```

The Samba server can now present Windows 9x clients with the correct printer drivers.

Printer Accounting

To enable printer accounting, first edit the /etc/printcap entries to provide for printer accounting. Listing 10.8 shows the /etc/printcap file for a Red Hat Linux system with an HP DeskJet printer on the LPT1 port.

Listing 10.8 The /etc/printcap file with accounting enabled.

```
##PRINTTOOL3## LOCAL djet500 300x300 a4 {} DeskJet500Mono 1 {}
hp|hp deskjet:\
        :sd=/var/spool/lpd/lp:\
        :mx#0:\
        :sh:\
        :lp=/dev/lp1:\
        :if=/var/spool/lpd/lp/filter:\
        :af=/var/spool/lpd/lp/accounting:\
```

To enable printer accounting for any printer, add an **:af** option and direct it to a file within the printer share /var/spool/lpd/lp/accounting. On use, the printer will automatically log its use. Running **pac-Php** will generate a list of users with the number and cost values for any jobs run.

Using Samba As A File Server

The configuration of Samba as a file server was covered in Chapter 4; however, some advanced topics were not included and so are discussed here.

Quotas

On systems where many users might use valuable resources, Linux offers the ability to impose quotas. Quotas limit the amount of hard drive space used in a number of ways. Quotas can be set by group, group ID (GID), or even individual users. If the system includes many critical systems, the use of quotas can be an invaluable aid when saving user files to the same location.

Quota administration and use is performed by the group of programs shown in Table 10.5.

Running **edquota -u *username*** will bring up the details of the file systems and the current quota levels for that username, as shown in Listing 10.9.

Listing 10.9 Editing user quotas for user testq.

```
#edquota -u testq
Quotas for user testq:
/dev/hda3: blocks in use: 0, limits (soft = 5000, hard = 10000)
        inodes in use: 1, limits (soft = 500, hard = 1000)
/dev/hdb1: blocks in use: 0, limits (soft = 5000, hard = 10000)
        inodes in use: 0, limits (soft = 500, hard = 1000)
```

The values for the soft and hard size and file number limits can then be edited directly. On saving the file, these are then activated. In this case, the user testq is

Table 10.5 Quota management commands.

Command	Description
quota	Returns quota information for the system. Options are: **quota [-guqvV]** **quota [-qv] -u *username*** **quota [-qv] -g *groupname***
quotaon	Enables quotas
quotaoff	Turns quotas off
repquot	Reports on quotas
edquota	Edits user quotas
quotacheck	Checks file system on quota usage

given soft limits of 500 files and 5MB and hard limits of 1,000 files and 10MB. The impact of this is that if the user creates files of a size or number greater than either number, the quota system is activated. Using **edquota -t *username***, as in Listing 10.10, sets the soft limits.

Listing 10.10 Setting quota grace periods.

```
#edquota -t testq

Time units may be: days, hours, minutes, or seconds
Grace period before enforcing soft limits for users:
/dev/hda3: block grace period: 0 days, file grace period: 0 days
/dev/hdb1: block grace period: 1 day, file grace period: 1 day
```

The user will be allowed to break the soft limit for the period of time given in the grace period for the file numbers or the size limit. If an operation occurs that breaks the hard limit, the system responds with a message similar to that shown in Listing 10.11.

Listing 10.11 Quota-exceeded message on a file copy.

```
Red Hat Linux release 5.2 (Apollo)
Kernel 2.0.36 on an i486
login: testq
Last login: Thu Aug  5 22:42:34 from ntwdev02
[testq@linuxserver testq]$ ls
[testq@linuxserver testq]$ cd ..
[testq@linuxserver /home]$ cp /tmp/files.tgz ~/
/home: warning, user disk quota exceeded
/home: write failed, user disk limit reached.
cp: /home/testq/files.tgz: Disc quota exceeded
[testq@linuxserver /home]$
```

When a Windows client connects to a Samba server with quotas enabled, the quotas set on the system will be active; if any operation is attempted that breaks the quota, an error message will occur, similar to that shown in Figure 10.3.

The system does not differentiate between the quota limits in the message.

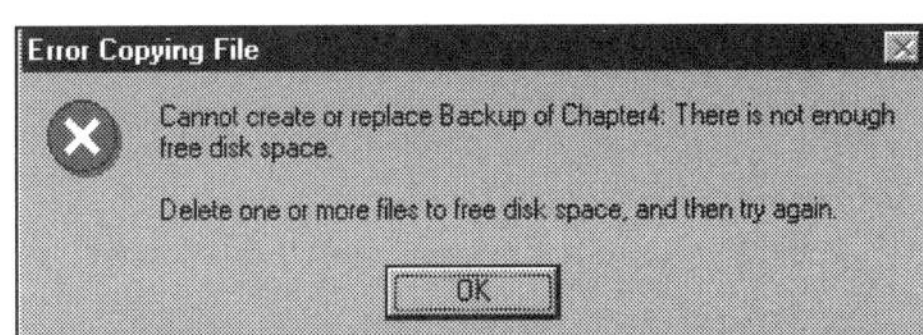

Figure 10.3 Windows message due to breaking a quota.

Using Samba As A Fax Server

Using Samba as a fax server for a network dominated by Windows is not difficult. A number of different fax software suites are available on the Linux distributions that can be used as a starting point. I will concentrate on the mgetty+sendfax package that is available from most Linux mirror sites. I assume that the Linux server already has a functional fax/modem. The important points are that it must be a fax/modem and should be capable of operating with Linux. There are several fax/modem devices available that rely on software drivers, usually Microsoft Windows only, for operation and these may not function with Linux.

In addition, it is necessary to obtain and install the following software for optimum results, as your goal is to configure the fax server as if it were a PostScript printer:

- The Ghostscript package
- A PostScript printer filter package
- The **pdm** image package

These are available as part of the standard Red Hat distribution.

Configuring mgetty+sendfax

The mgetty+sendfax distribution does not come as a binary to install, so you will need to compile mgetty+sendfax for the system. First, extract the distribution into /usr/src. Before continuing, you will need to determine the modem initialization string for your hardware, the telephone number from which the fax will operate, and the COM ports that the fax could use. After you have this information, edit the policy.h-dist file from the source directory from /usr/src/mgetty+sendfax, replacing the values present for the modem_init_string, fax_station_id, and fax_modem_ttys, and copy the contents to policy.h. Listing 10.12 indicates a sample set of values for a Motorola 33.6Kbps fax/modem, at 555-123-4567, using COM2 or COM3.

Listing 10.12 The mgetty+sendfax policy.h file.

```
#define MODEM_INIT_STRING "AT&F&C1&D2\\Q3S7=55\"

#define FAX_STATION_ID  "555-123 4567"

#define FAX_MODEM_TTYS  "ttyS1:ttyS2"
```

After the file is saved, compile and install the mgetty+sendfax distribution by using the standard Unix **make**, then **make install**. The mgetty+sendfax program will not start automatically, so you will need to configure the server startup routines. The program should be started with the fax/modem connected to one of the ports specified in the previous listing with a command similar to the following:

```
S3:45:respawn:/usr/local/sbin/mgetty ttyS1 vt100
```

Either the Samba server can be rebooted or issuing **kill -HUP 1** can restart the inetd daemon. The fax modem should then be installed and operational. At this point, the fax should be capable of receiving faxes and spooling them to an internal directory.

The default location for incoming faxes will be /var/spool/fax/incoming, and all faxes will be received into this location. The fax spool files are in PostScript format, so the final printer used should have a printer filter installed to be able to deal with PostScript input.

If you have a PostScript printer or a printer with a PostScript filter attached, you could pass one of the spool files to the appropriate printer definition from the /etc/printcap file, as shown here:

```
'spoolfile' | lpr -P printername
```

Creating The Fax Server

Obtain the mgetty+sendfax/frontends/winword/faxfilter file (this is in German on the distribution, but you will find an English version on this book's CD-ROM in /mgetty+sendfax) and place it in /usr/local/etc/mgetty+sendfax. The faxspool file should also be created, and a template for this is available in fax/faxspool.in. You will need to alter this file according to your system's requirements.

Every fax that is sent using mgetty+sendfax will need to create a header, and the **pbmtext** program (from the **pbm** package) is needed to create this. If you plan to install the complete **pbm** package, you need only **pbmtext** for generating the small line on top of each fax header page. Install this package before installing mgetty+sendfax.

Ensure that Ghostscript is functional and includes all the fonts. Prepare a fax header and place it in /usr/local/etc/mgetty+sendfax/faxheader. Edit the /etc/printcap file to account for the new printer, as shown in Listing 10.13.

Listing 10.13 The /etc/printcap file for the fax server entry.

```
# FAX
lp3|fax:\
        :lp=/dev/null:\
        :sd=/usr/spool/lp3:\
        :if=/usr/local/etc/mgetty+sendfax/faxfilter:sh:sf:mx#0:\
        :lf=/usr/spool/lp3/fax-log:
```

Edit the smb.conf file and make sure that an entry exists for the fax printer, as shown in Listing 10.14.

Listing 10.14 Suitable smb.conf entries for the fax server.

```
[global]
printcap name = /etc/printcap
print command = /usr/bin/lpr -r -P %p %s
lpq command = /usr/bin/lpq -P %p
lprm command = /usr/bin/lprm -P %p %j

[fax]
    comment = FAX Server (mgetty+sendfax)
    path = /faxserver
    printable = yes
    public = yes
    writable = no
    create mode = 0700
    browseable = yes
    guest ok = no
```

The fax server should now be ready for use by clients either through native Unix lpd printing (as it is a normal Unix printer) or as a Windows printer.

On any client workstation, install a PostScript printer and then map the fax server printer share. Using any Windows client software, you should now be able to send faxes to the fax server.

The mgetty+sendfax distribution is configured to expect every fax to contain a header page with at least the recipient's telephone number enclosed as a string in plain text of the following form: Fax-Nr: 123456789. It is important that this number be in plain text and that the format matches, or the fax filter will not be able to decode this information.

Print though the fax server as you would using another printer. All faxes will be queued for later transmission. The faxrunq manager will send the fax queue out.

Using Multiple Languages And Samba

The latest Microsoft operating systems come with the capability to choose and include different character sets. This might not appear to be an issue if you use only this one character set on the system. However, when Samba is used with other workstations and servers that might use alternate character sets, some complications can arise. In use, these differences manifest in the file names that are used on the client and server.

The parameters applicable to multiple language support in Samba include the following:

- **character set**
- **client code page**
- **codingsystem**
- **valid chars**

character set

The **character set** parameter provides **smbd** with a mapping for incoming file names from a DOS code page to a number of Unix character sets. Samba has a number of built-in code page translations:

- *ISO8859-1 Western European Unix character set*—If the **character set** parameter is set to ISO8859-1, the **client code page** parameter must be set to code page 850 in order for the conversion to the Unix character set to be done correctly.
- *ISO8859-2 Eastern European Unix character set*—If the **character set** parameter is set to ISO8859-2, the **client code page** parameter must be set to code page 852 in order for the conversion to the Unix character set to be done correctly.
- *ISO8859-5 Russian Cyrillic Unix character set*—If the **character set** parameter is set to ISO8859-5, the **client code page** parameter must be set to code page 866 in order for the conversion to the Unix character set to be done correctly.
- *KOI8-R Alternate mapping for Russian Cyrillic Unix character set*—If the **character set** parameter is set to KOI8-R, the **client code page** parameter must be set to code page 866 in order for the conversion to the Unix character set to be done correctly.

Normally, the **character set** parameter is not set, meaning that no file name translation is done. The default value is an empty string. If, say, the ISO8859-1 character set were required, the values would be set to **character set=ISO8859-1**.

client code page

The **client code page** parameter specifies which DOS code page the clients are using when accessing Samba. The value of the code page being used by a client can be determined by using the **chcp command** from within a DOS prompt. The output from **chcp** is the code page. This usually defaults to code page 437 in the USA for Microsoft operating systems and 850 for any Eastern European installations.

On startup of the **smbd** service, this value is used to instruct **smbd** as to which specific codepage.XXX file should be dynamically loaded. The codepage.XXX files inform **smbd** how to map lower- to uppercase characters to provide the case insensitivity of file names that Windows clients will expect.

The code page files included with Samba by default are the following:

- *Code Page 437*—MS-DOS Latin US
- *Code Page 737*—Windows 95 Greek
- *Code Page 850*—MS-DOS Latin 1
- *Code Page 852*—MS-DOS Latin 2
- *Code Page 861*—MS-DOS Icelandic
- *Code Page 866*—MS-DOS Cyrillic
- *Code Page 932*—MS-DOS Japanese SJIS
- *Code Page 936*—MS-DOS Simplified Chinese
- *Code Page 949*—MS-DOS Korean Hangul
- *Code Page 950*—MS-DOS Traditional Chinese

The parameter values would then be 437, 737, 850, 852, 861, 866, 932, 936, 949, or 950.

If an alternative code page is needed, it will need to be either created or obtained and included or created using the make_codepage script. The **client code page** parameter could be used in association with the **valid chars** parameter to specify which characters are valid in file names and how capitalization is performed. The **client code page** parameter must be set if the **valid chars** parameter is used, and importantly, the **client code page** parameter must be specified before the **valid chars** parameter in the smb.conf file. The default value for a Western European environment would be **client code page=850**. An example of an alternative would be **client code page=936**.

The text Samba code page definition file contains a description of how to map to characters, both upper- and lowercase, when the values are greater than ASCII 127 in the specified DOS code page. These mappings are not necessarily symmetrical, and some characters might map from lower- to uppercase consistently but not vice versa. The example given in the Samba documentation involves DOS code page 437, where lowercase acute “á” maps to a plain uppercase “A” when going from lower- to uppercase, but plain uppercase "A" maps to plain lowercase "a" when lowercasing a character.

The binary Samba code page definition file is a binary representation of the text code page information. The binary file will include a value that specifies which code page this file is describing.

Samba currently doesn't support Unicode Version 1 or Version 2. When working in an international environment, you must specify the client code page that your DOS and Windows clients are using to maintain the case insensitivity correctly for the particular language. The default code page that Samba uses is 850 (Western European) and the values this file contains are:

- **codepage_def.<*codepage*>**—The input (text) code page files provided in the Samba source/codepages directory. A text code page definition file consists of multiple lines containing four fields:
  - **lower**—The (hex) lowercase character mapped on this line.
  - **upper**—The (hex) uppercase character that the lowercase character will map to.
- **map upper to lower**—A Boolean value (either true or false) that tells Samba whether it is to map the given uppercase character to the given lowercase character when lowercasing a file name.
- **map lower to upper**—A Boolean value (either true or false) that tells Samba whether it is to map the given lowercase character to the given uppercase character when uppercasing a file name.
- **codepage.<*codepage*>**—The output (binary) code page files produced and placed in the Samba destination lib/codepage directory.

codingsystem

The **codingsystem** parameter is used to determine how incoming SJIS Japanese characters are mapped from the incoming client code page into file names in the Unix file system. This parameter is useful only if the client code page is set to 932 (Japanese SJIS).

The options are as follows:

- **SJIS (Shift-JIS)**—Does no conversion of the incoming file name
- **JIS8, J8BB, J8BH, J8@B, J8@J, J8@H**—Converts from incoming SJIS to 8-bit JIS code with different shift-in, shift-out codes
- **JIS7, J7BB, J7BH, J7@B, J7@J, J7@H**—Converts from incoming SJIS to 7-bit JIS code with different shift-in, shift-out codes

- **JUNET, JUBB, JUBH, JU@B, JU@J, JU@H**—Converts from incoming SJIS to JUNET code with different shift-in, shift-out codes
- **EUC**—Converts an incoming SJIS character to EUC code
- **HEX**—Converts an incoming SJIS character to a 3-byte hex representation, that is, :AB
- **CAP**—Converts an incoming SJIS character to the 3-byte hex representation used by the Columbia AppleTalk Program (CAP), that is, :AB (used for compatibility between Samba and CAP)

Creating Code Pages

Samba also has the ability to create code pages by using the make_smbcodepage script, which compiles or decompiles code page files for use with Samba in an international setting. The syntax for the command is:

```
make_smbcodepage [c|d] codepage inputfile outputfile
```

The **c** or **d** command line option instructs **make_smbcodepage** to either compile (**c**) or decompile (**d**) a text code page. The ***codepage*** is the numeric value for the code page being used.

inputfile is the input file being processed. When compiling, this will be a text code page definition file, such as the ones found in the Samba source/codepages directory. When decompiling, this will be the binary format code page definition file normally found in the lib/codepages directory in the Samba install directory path. outputfile is the output file that is to be produced.

valid chars

The **valid chars** parameter is an extra method of specifying other characters in the file names that should be considered valid by the server. The national character sets with accented or special characters, such as adding ü or å, would make use of this parameter. The values can be a list of characters in either integer or character form with spaces between them. Using a colon between values may pair upper- and lowercase characters.

The values may be represented in octal or be directly entered into the smb.conf file with an appropriate editor. Using SWAT might wipe out these values, so the **include** parameter to reference the share with the **valid chars** parameter might be an option.

The **valid chars** parameter must be set *after* any **client code page** parameter setting is used. Otherwise, the **valid chars** settings will be overwritten. The **valid chars** values in other languages, when using a Western European code page, are difficult to generate if the octal, hex, or decimal values are not known already. The Samba distribution contains the validchars package in the examples/validchars subdirectory of your Samba source code distribution. This package will automatically produce a complete **valid chars** line for a given client system.

Using SWAT

Although the use of a graphical user interface (GUI) was described briefly in previous chapters, it should be noted that several other GUI interfaces are now available for use with Samba. The Samba distribution includes one of these, known as SWAT, as part of the standard installation. Changes are automatically made to the etc/inetd.conf file on installation to allow for operation with the latest versions of Samba.

Only the SWAT interface configuration is discussed here. Appendix B, in the section for Chapter 10, contains details on where to find out about other alternatives. However, the SWAT interface does suffer from the requirement that the main system password be transmitted in plain text over any network. This can be a security risk, and currently no support is available for the SSL encryption of the SWAT authentication although that may change.

Swat does allow the configuration of the Samba server and corresponding smb.conf file in a manner that is much more user friendly. However, note that the SWAT tool will overwrite the current smb.conf file, having read its contents first, and this should maintain all current contents. However, any text or additional comment information will not be retained after SWAT updates the smb.conf file. If you have a situation in which any alterations must be documented, you should consider creating an additional backup copy of the smb.conf file before using the tool.

Note that SWAT does not perform any operation on the smb.conf file that could not be reproduced by editing it directly. Some advantages of using SWAT are the following:

- Uses separate configuration screens for global, file, and printer shares
- Includes basic and advanced configuration views
- Views the status of **smbd** and **nmbd** services remotely
- Stops, starts, and restarts the services remotely
- Manages users and passwords remotely
- Views the current smb.conf configuration file remotely

The installation of SWAT should be carried out at the same time as the normal installation, the details of which are given in Chapter 3. By default, SWAT is included in the build of the Samba executables when you compile your own. When you are using a package, such as a Red Hat RPM for Samba, it is included normally.

If you have created SWAT from source, you must remember to add the entries to the /etc/services and /etc/inetd.conf files to ensure that SWAT operates as expected. The entries are shown in Listing 10.15.

Listing 10.15 The /etc/services and /etc/inetd.conf entries.

```
/etc/services
swat        910/tcp

/etc/inetd.conf
swat   stream  tcp  nowait.400  root /usr/local/samba/bin/swat swat
```

You must now restart the inetd by entering a HUP command with the details of the process ID (PID) for the inetd process, as shown here:

```
kill -HUP <inetd PID>
```

With inetd restarted using a Web browser (I prefer Netscape, **www.netscape.com**, because it is also capable of running on Windows and Unix and because Netscape Corporation is a supporter of the Open Source Software community), enter the hostname or IP address of the Samba server, with the suffix :901. The :901 suffix makes the Web browser request a document from the service listening at port 901. This is the standard port that the SWAT process will listen for connections on. The SWAT process, a mini-Web server, listening at port 901, will then return the SWAT home page with a preceding authentication request. I have SWAT running on a server at 192.168.1.4, so I entered "http://192.168.1.4:901", and the result is the Authentication dialog box shown in Figure 10.4.

NOTE: *When you log in, the password is not shown at the browser but is replaced with "*" for each character. However, the username and password are sent in plain text over the network connection. If a sniffer were placed on the network between the Samba server and the client with the browser, this information would be captured.*

A successful login results in the main SWAT home page being displayed.

TIP: *If you have never used SWAT or read about it, the links to the HTML pages on this page should be viewed. Selecting any of them with Netscape will spawn another browser window displaying the contents. This can be very useful if you are following any of the links from the main pages. The main page will remain and the help text appear in the second window.*

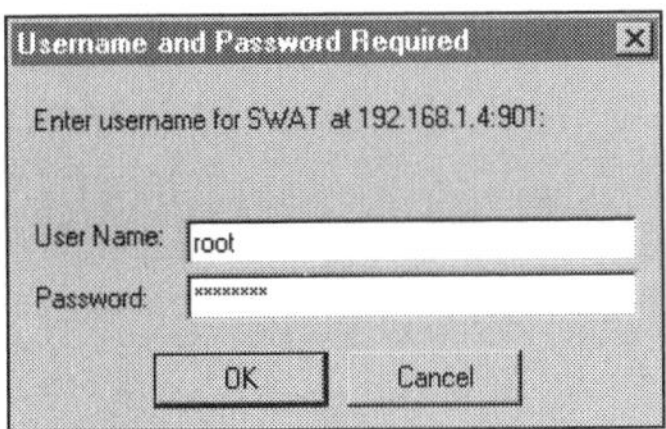

Figure 10.4 The Authentication dialog box.

Home

The main page has large buttons that link to the configuration and use pages and include the following:

- *Home*—The main SWAT server page.
- *Globals*—Configures the [global] section of the smb.conf file.
- *Shares*—Configures file shares.
- *Printers*—Configures printer shares.
- *Status*—A visual view of the **smbd** and **nmbd** services. Results are similar to running **smbstatus** on the server without the memory usage statistics being available. You can also start, stop, and restart the **smbd** and **nmbd** services from this page.
- *View*—Displays the current smb.conf. Full and normal (short) views are possible.
- *Password*—Configures passwords and users.

These appear at the top of every page and perform the navigation for SWAT configuration of the Samba server. Figure 10.5 shows the SWAT home page.

Global

The first page, Global, is shown in Figure 10.6.

Sufficient parameters are included in the basic view to configure the [global] section of a smb.conf file with many other [global] section parameters being available in the advanced view. As with all the other pages, the Help link to the left of each parameter will link to the smb.conf.html file or some other file and display the contents in a second browser window. The Reset Values button at the top will return any values to the original values from when the smb.conf file configuration was read. To change any values to the default, the Set Default button beside each parameter entry window will set this accordingly. After you are satisfied with your changes, click on the Commit Changes button, and the values will be written to the smb.conf file. The current functionality requires you to commit any

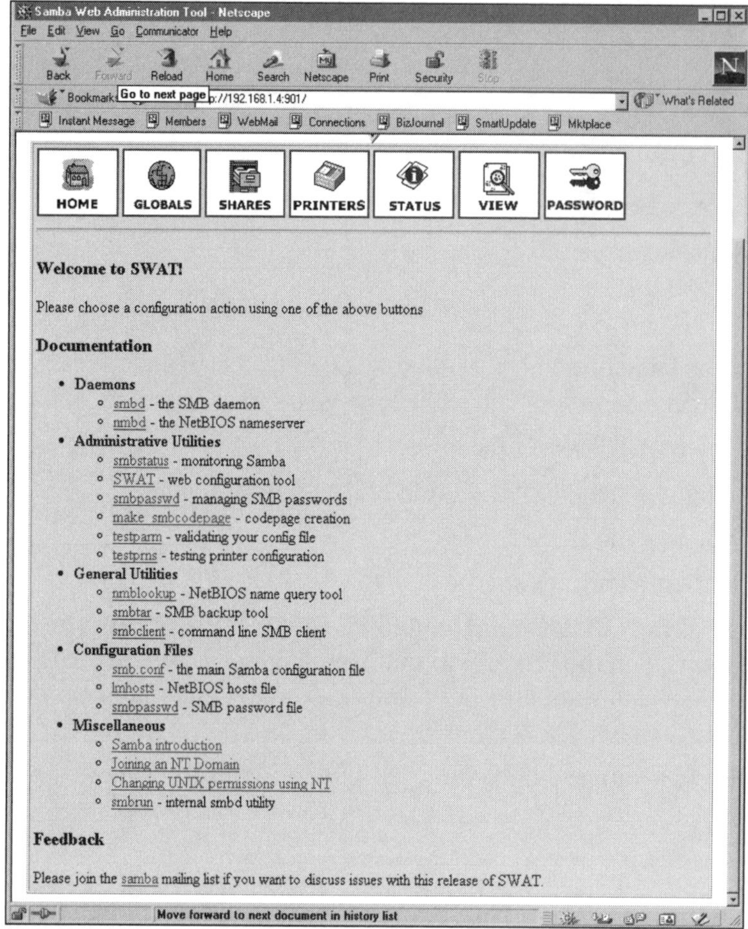

Figure 10.5 The SWAT home page.

changes before moving to the advanced view, as the changes are not retained but refreshed. The smb.conf file is also overwritten, and no backup of the previous configuration is kept.

The global parameters are gathered in SWAT under the advanced view. The parameters for base options are the following:

- **workgroup**
- **netbios name**
- **netbios aliases**
- **server string**
- **interfaces**
- **bind interfaces only**

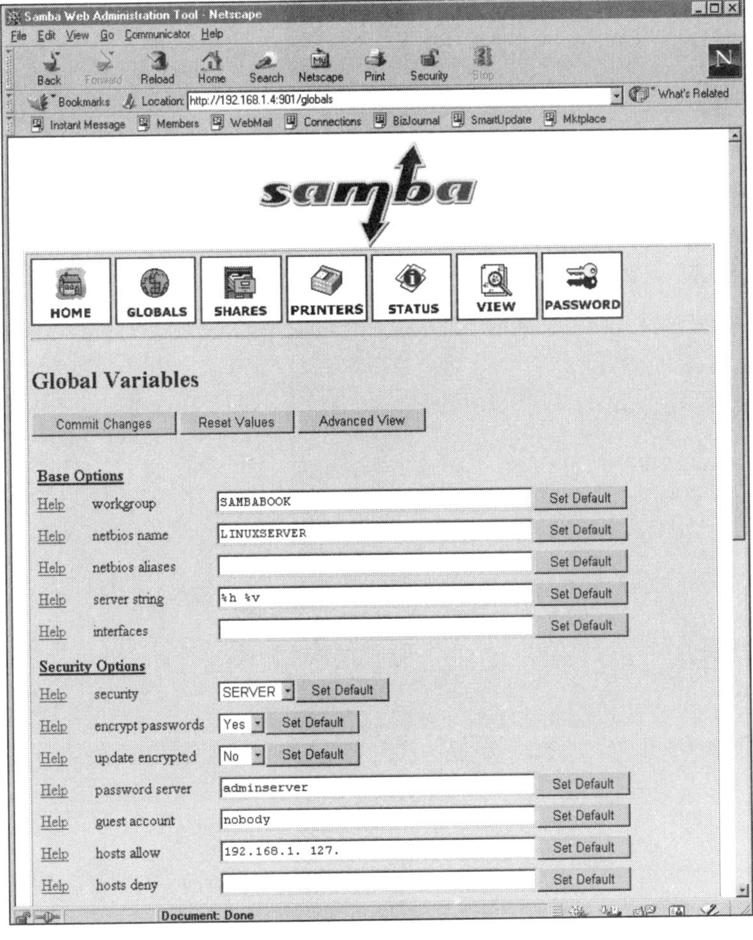

Figure 10.6 The Global page.

The parameters for security options are the following:

- **security**
- **encrypt passwords**
- **update encrypted**
- **allow trusted domains**
- **alternate permissions**
- **hosts equiv**
- **min passwd length**
- **map to guest**
- **null passwords**

- **password server**
- **smb passwd file**
- **root directory**
- **passwd program**
- **passwd chat**
- **passwd chat debug**
- **username map**
- **password level**
- **username level**
- **unix password sync**
- **restrict anonymous**
- **revalidate**
- **use rhosts**
- **username**
- **guest account**
- **invalid users**
- **valid users**
- **admin users**
- **read list**
- **write list**
- **create mask**
- **force create mode**
- **directory mask**
- **force directory mode**
- **hosts allow**
- **hosts deny**

The parameters for logging options are the following:

- **log level**
- **syslog**
- **syslog only**
- **log file**
- **max log size**

- **timestamp logs**
- **status**

The parameters for protocol options are the following:

- **protocol**
- **read bmpx**
- **read raw**
- **write raw**
- **nt smb support**
- **nt pipe support**
- **nt acl support**
- **announce version**
- **announce as**
- **max mux**
- **max xmit**
- **name resolve order**
- **max packet**
- **max ttl**
- **max wins ttl**
- **min wins ttl**
- **time server**

The parameters for tuning options are the following:

- **change notify timeout**
- **deadtime**
- **getwd cache**
- **keepalive**
- **lpq cache time**
- **max disk size**
- **max open files**
- **read prediction**
- **read size**
- **shared mem size**
- **socket options**
- **stat cache size**

The parameters for printing options are the following:

- **load printers**
- **printcap name**
- **printer driver file**
- **printing**
- **print command**
- **lpq command**
- **lprm command**
- **lppause command**
- **lpresume command**
- **queuepause command**
- **queueresume command**
- **printer driver location**

The parameters for file name handling options are the following:

- **strip dot**
- **character set**
- **mangled stack**
- **coding system**
- **client code page**
- **case sensitive**
- **preserve case**
- **short preserve case**
- **mangle case**
- **mangling char**
- **hide dot files**
- **delete veto files**
- **veto files**
- **hide files**
- **veto oplock files**
- **map system**
- **map hidden**
- **map archive**

- **mangled names**
- **mangled map**
- **stat cache**

The parameters for domain options are the following:

- **domain groups**
- **domain admin group**
- **domain guest group**
- **domain admin users**
- **domain guest users**
- **machine password timeout**

The parameters for logon options are the following:

- **add user script**
- **delete user script**
- **logon script**
- **logon path**
- **logon drive**
- **logon home**
- **domain logons**

The parameters for browse options are the following:

- **os level**
- **lm announce**
- **lm interval**
- **preferred master**
- **local master**
- **domain master**
- **browse list**

The parameters for WINS options are the following:

- **dns proxy**
- **wins proxy**
- **wins server**
- **wins support**

The parameters for locking options are the following:

- **blocking locks**
- **kernel oplocks**
- **locking**
- **mangle locks**
- **ole locking compatibility**
- **oplocks**
- **oplock break wait time**
- **oplock contention limit**
- **strict locking**
- **share modes**

The parameters for miscellaneous options are the following:

- **smbrun**
- **preload**
- **lock dir**
- **default service**
- **message command**
- **dfree command**
- **valid chars**
- **remote announce**
- **remote browse sync**
- **socket address**
- **homedir map**
- **time offset**
- **unix realname**
- **NIS homedir**
- **wide links**
- **follow symlinks**
- **delete readonly**
- **dos filetimes**
- **dos filetime resolution**
- **fake directory create times**
- **panic action**

Shares

The Shares page is shown in Figure 10.7. Current shares are available from a drop-down list.

Following the selection or creation of a new share, the share configuration page opens. Figure 10.8 shows the page for the [cdshare]. Note that the page provides the ability to create, delete, and modify the current shares on the Samba server.

An extra button, Delete Share, appears when a share has been selected. This provides the user with the ability to delete the current share. The share parameters are gathered in SWAT under the advanced view. The parameters for base options are the following:

- **comment**
- **path**

The parameters for security options are the following:

- **revalidate**
- **username**
- **guest account**
- **invalid users**
- **valid users**

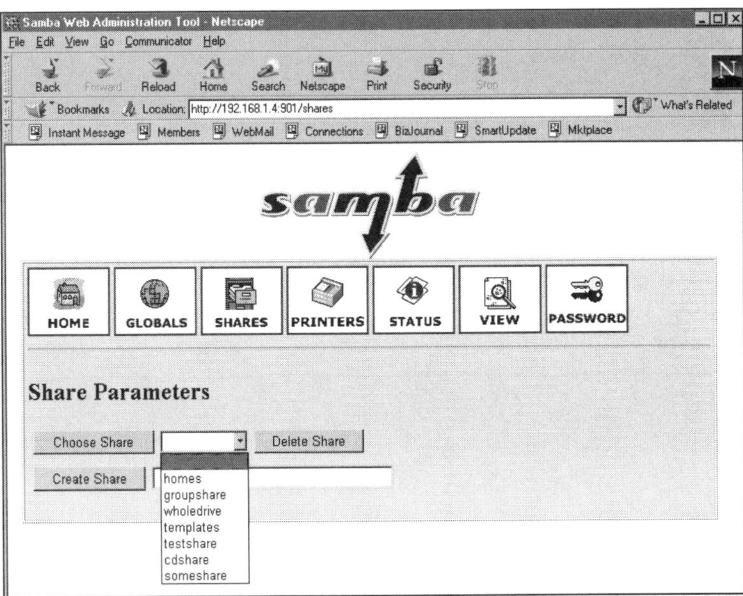

Figure 10.7 The Shares page.

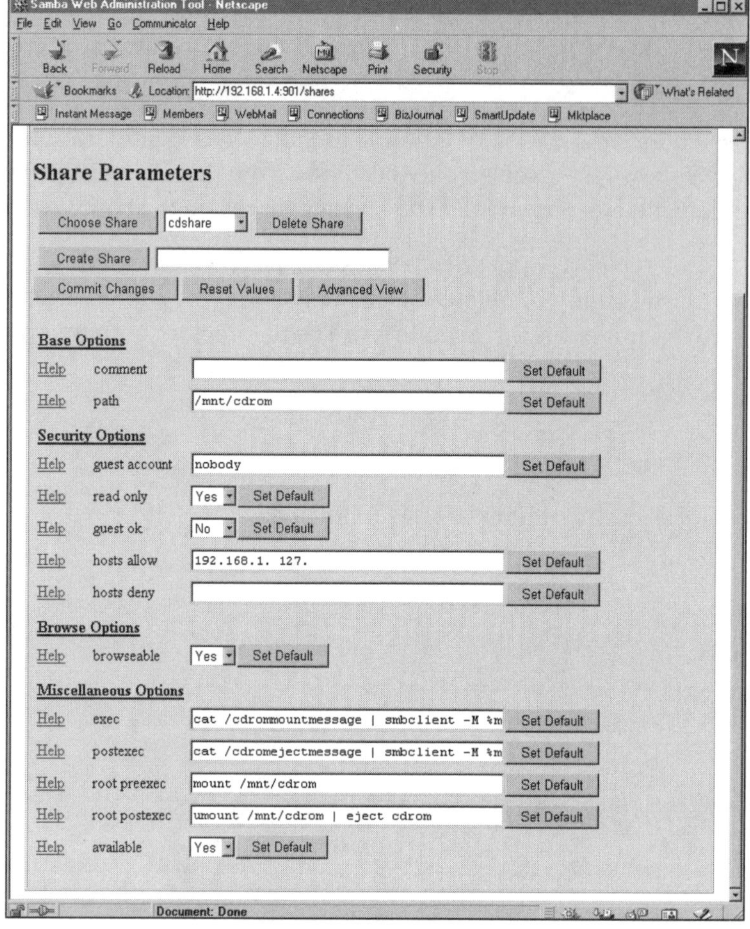

Figure 10.8 The [cdshare] share.

- **admin users**
- **read list**
- **write list**
- **force user**
- **force group**
- **read only**
- **create mask**
- **force create mode**
- **directory mask**

- **force directory mode**
- **guest only**
- **guest ok**
- **only user**
- **hosts allow**
- **hosts deny**

The parameter for logging options is the following:

- **status**

The parameters for tuning options are the following:

- **max connections**
- **strict sync**
- **sync always**

The parameters for file name handling options are the following:

- **default case**
- **case sensitive**
- **preserve case**
- **short preserve case**
- **mangle case**
- **mangling char**
- **hide dot files**
- **delete veto files**
- **veto files**
- **hide files**
- **veto oplock files**
- **map system**
- **map hidden**
- **map archive**
- **mangled names**
- **mangled map**

The parameter for browse options is the following:

- **browseable**

The parameters for locking options are the following:

- **blocking locks**
- **fake oplocks**
- **locking**
- **mangle locks**
- **oplocks**
- **oplock contention limit**
- **strict locking**
- **share modes**

The parameters for miscellaneous options are the following:

- **exec**
- **postexec**
- **root preexec**
- **root postexec**
- **available**
- **volume**
- **fstype**
- **set directory**
- **wide links**
- **follow symlinks**
- **dont descend**
- **magic script**
- **magic output**
- **delete readonly**
- **dos filetimes**
- **dos filetime resolution**
- **fake directory create times**

Printers

The Printers page is shown in Figure 10.9. The current printers are available in a drop-down list.

Following the selection or creation of a new printer share, the printer share configuration page opens. Figure 10.10 shows the page for [hp]. Note that the page

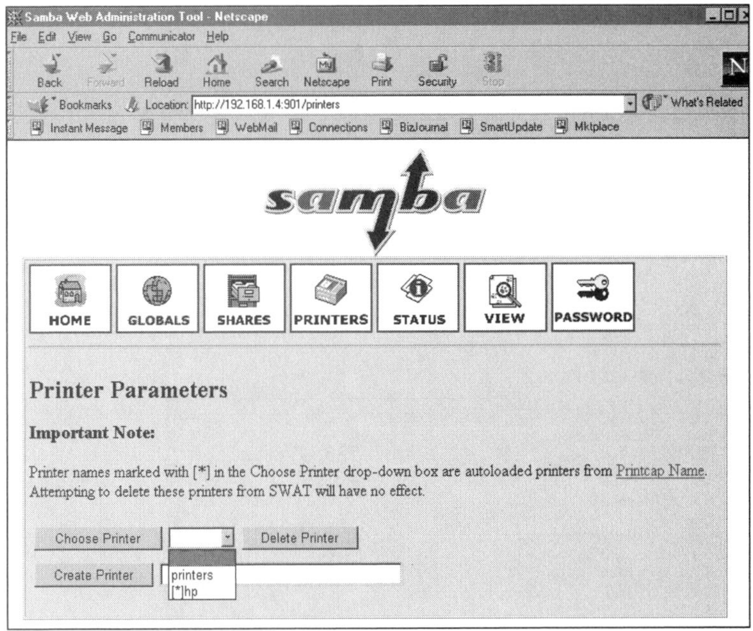

Figure 10.9 The Printers page.

provides the ability to create, delete, and modify the current printer on the Samba server.

This page provides the ability to create, delete, and configure, including modifying the current printers on the Samba server. An extra button, Delete Printer, appears when a printer has been selected. This provides the user with the ability to delete the current printer.

The printer parameters are gathered in SWAT in the following groups under the advanced view. The parameters for base options are the following:

- **comment**
- **path**

The parameters for security options are the following:

- **guest account**
- **guest ok**
- **hosts allow**
- **hosts deny**

The parameter for logging options is the following:

- **status**

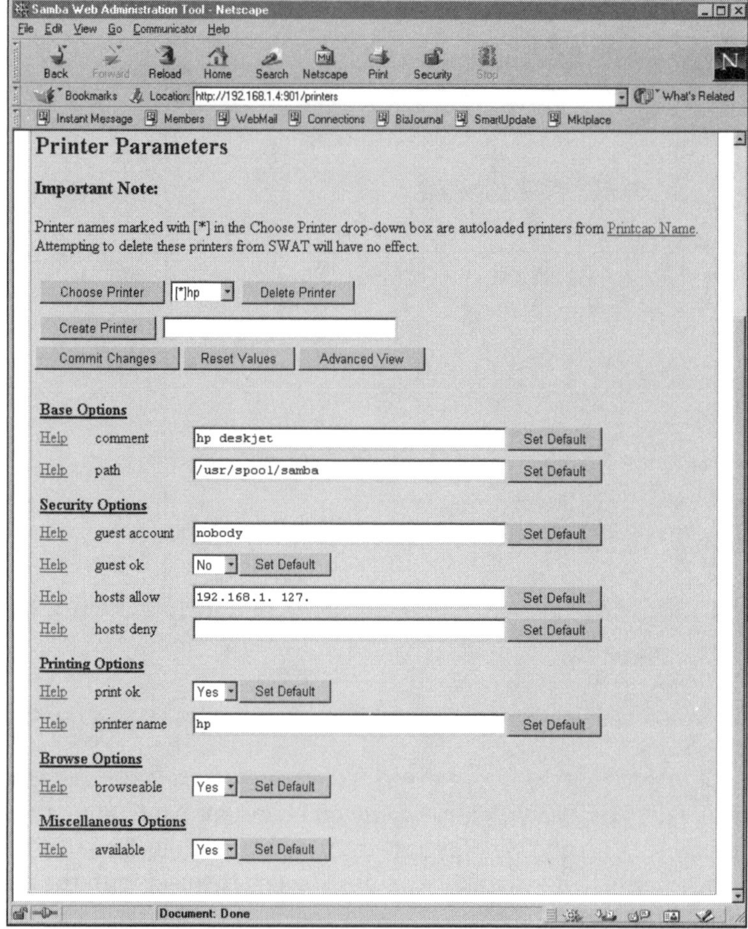

Figure 10.10 The [hp] printer page.

The parameter for tuning options is the following:

- **min print space**

The parameters for printing options are the following:

- **print ok**
- **postscript**
- **printing**
- **print command**
- **lpq command**
- **lprm command**

- **lppause command**
- **lpresume command**
- **queuepause command**
- **queueresume command**
- **printer name**
- **printer driver**
- **printer driver location**

The parameter for browse options is the following:

- **browseable**

The parameters for miscellaneous options are the following:

- **exec**
- **postexec**
- **root preexec**
- **root postexec**
- **available**

Using DNS, DHCP, And WINS

When using a Unix Samba server, it is possible to include all three of these capabilities at the same time. For the discussion in this section, assume that the Unix server is a Linux Red Hat server and that the distribution includes the DNS server software, a BIND distribution with the named daemon, and the DHCP server software. The essential steps to creating these services are outlined here.

Creating A DNS Server

To create a DNS server, you need to confirm that you can Telnet in and out of the server successfully. You should be able to do **telnet 127.0.0.1** and get your own machine. You also need the /etc/resolv.conf and /etc/hosts files. You will need to obtain and install **named** if you intend to run a DNS service.

Caching-Only DNS

To run a caching-only name server, create or obtain the files used with a Unix-named configuration:

- *named.boot*—This is the general parameters file; it indicates the source of the domain information for the DNS server.

- *named.ca*—This points to the root domain servers (you need to edit this file if you are not connected to the Internet).
- *named.local*—This resolves the loopback device address.
- *named.domainhosts*—This is the zone file that maps the hostnames for the domain to IP addresses.
- *named.reversedomain*—This is the zone file that maps the reverse domain IP addresses to hostnames.

A caching-only DNS server is a simple DNS configuration. A caching-only name server will find the answer to name queries and remember the answer the next time you need it. To start the process of installing a caching-only DNS server, the named.ca (Unix) file should be updated by downloading the domain/named.root file from **rs.internic.net** on a regular basis. The procedure is similar to the one shown in Listing 10.16, where the actual commands used in this example are highlighted.

Listing 10.16 Obtaining an update for the named.ca file.

```
C:\DNSSTUFF>ftp rs.internic.net
Connected to rs.internic.net
(a pile of messages)
user (rs.internic.net: (none)): anonymous
331 Guest login ok, send your complete e-mail address as password.
Password: dombaines@host.somewhere
230 Guest login ok, access restrictions apply.
ftp>BIN
200 Type set to I.
ftp> get domain/named.root
200 PORT command successful.
150 Opening data connection for domain/named.root (2769 bytes).
226 transfer complete
2769 bytes received in 1.3 secs (2 Kbytes/sec)
ftp>quit
221 Goodbye.
C:\DNSSTUFF>copy named.root named.ca
```

This code is in the correct format for immediate use. The code shown in Listing 10.17 shows a copy of the named.ca file for use with Unix DNS.

Listing 10.17 The named.ca file.

```
;       This file holds the information on root name servers needed to
;       initialize cache of Internet domain name servers
;       (e.g. reference this file in the "cache  .  <file>"
;       configuration file of BIND domain name servers).
;
```

```
;       This file is made available by InterNIC registration services
;       under anonymous FTP as
;           file                /domain/named.root
;           on server           FTP.RS.INTERNIC.NET
;       -OR- under Gopher at    RS.INTERNIC.NET
;           under menu          InterNIC Registration Services (NSI)
;              submenu          InterNIC Registration Archives
;           file                named.root
;
;       last update:    Aug 22, 1997
;       related version of root zone:   1997082200
;
;
; formerly NS.INTERNIC.NET
;
.                        3600000  IN  NS    A.ROOT-SERVERS.NET.
A.ROOT-SERVERS.NET.      3600000      A     198.41.0.4
;
; formerly NS1.ISI.EDU
;
.                        3600000      NS    B.ROOT-SERVERS.NET.
B.ROOT-SERVERS.NET.      3600000      A     128.9.0.107
;
; formerly C.PSI.NET
;
.                        3600000      NS    C.ROOT-SERVERS.NET.
C.ROOT-SERVERS.NET.      3600000      A     192.33.4.12
;
; formerly TERP.UMD.EDU
;
.                        3600000      NS    D.ROOT-SERVERS.NET.
D.ROOT-SERVERS.NET.      3600000      A     128.8.10.90
;
; formerly NS.NASA.GOV
;
.                        3600000      NS    E.ROOT-SERVERS.NET.
E.ROOT-SERVERS.NET.      3600000      A     192.203.230.10
;
; formerly NS.ISC.ORG
;
.                        3600000      NS    F.ROOT-SERVERS.NET.
F.ROOT-SERVERS.NET.      3600000      A     192.5.5.241
;
; formerly NS.NIC.DDN.MIL
;
```

```
.                           3600000      NS    G.ROOT-SERVERS.NET.
G.ROOT-SERVERS.NET.         3600000      A     192.112.36.4
;
; formerly AOS.ARL.ARMY.MIL
;
.                           3600000      NS    H.ROOT-SERVERS.NET.
H.ROOT-SERVERS.NET.         3600000      A     128.63.2.53
;
; formerly NIC.NORDU.NET
;
.                           3600000      NS    I.ROOT-SERVERS.NET.
I.ROOT-SERVERS.NET.         3600000      A     192.36.148.17
;
; temporarily housed at NSI (InterNIC)
;
.                           3600000      NS    J.ROOT-SERVERS.NET.
J.ROOT-SERVERS.NET.         3600000      A     198.41.0.10
;
; housed in LINX, operated by RIPE NCC
;
.                           3600000      NS    K.ROOT-SERVERS.NET.
K.ROOT-SERVERS.NET.         3600000      A     193.0.14.129
;
; temporarily housed at ISI (IANA)
;
.                           3600000      NS    L.ROOT-SERVERS.NET.
L.ROOT-SERVERS.NET.         3600000      A     198.32.64.12
;
; housed in Japan, operated by WIDE
;
.                           3600000      NS    M.ROOT-SERVERS.NET.
M.ROOT-SERVERS.NET.         3600000      A     202.12.27.33
; End of File
```

If your network is connected to the Internet, you could use this file as it is. If your network is not connected to the Internet, remove all the records and replace them with the NS and A records for the DNS server that is authoritative for the root domain at your site.

Create a named.local file, which is used to convert the address 127.0.0.1 into the name localhost. This is the zone file for the reverse domain 0.0.127.IN-ADDR.ARPA. Most if not all systems use a localhost 127.0.0.1 loopback address, so this file is similar on every server. A sample named.local file is shown in Listing 10.18.

Listing 10.18 The named.local file.

```
@    IN SOA    linuxdns1.domain.    root.linuxdns1.domain. (
             1           ;serial
             360000      ;refresh every 100 hours
             3600        ;retry after 1 hour
             3600000     ;expire after 1000 hours
             360000      ;default ttl is 100 hours
             )
     IN NS     linuxdns1.domain.
1    IN PTR    localhost.
```

This is the SOA and NS record for a system called linuxdns1.domain, with an IP address 192.168.1.1, and will vary from system to system. The root.linuxdns1.domain is the email address of the administrator of that system. The "@" that normally is included within an email address is not present; the "." is used instead.

The Unix DNS server is then created simply by using a named.boot file that contains the code shown in Listing 10.19.

Listing 10.19 The named.boot file.

```
; a caching-only DNS server
primary    0.0.127-IN-ADDR.ARPA    /etc/named.local
cache                              /etc/named.ca
```

That is all that is required to run the caching-only DNS server.

Primary DNS Server

For a Unix DNS server called linuxdns1.domain with an IP address of 192.168.1.1, the named.boot file would be altered to the code shown in Listing 10.20.

Listing 10.20 The named.boot file for a primary DNS.

```
; a primary DNS server
directory                                 /etc
primary       domain                      named.domainhosts
primary       1.168.192-IN-ADDR.ARPA      named.reversedomain
primary       0.0.127-IN-ADDR.ARPA        named.local
cache
                                          named.ca
```

The key line in this file is the first primary statement, which indicates that this is the primary server for the "domain" domain. The information for this domain is present in the named.domainhosts zone file. The line with named.reversedomain makes the local server the primary DNS server for the reverse domain 1.168.192-IN-ADDR.ARPA, and the resolution information for the domain is loaded from the named.reversedomain file.

The named.reversedomain file structure is almost identical to the named.local file. An example is shown in Listing 10.21.

Listing 10.21 A sample named.reversedomain file.

```
; IP address to hostname mappings
@     IN SOA   linuxdns1.domain.    root.linuxdns1.domain. (
                10000          ;serial
                36000          ;refresh every 10 hours
                3600           ;retry after 1 hour
                3600000        ;expire after 1000 hours
2592000) ; Minimum
      IN NS    linuxdns1.domain.
1    IN PTR    localhost.
```

The named.domainhosts file is the zone file that contains most of the domain information.

A sample named.domainhosts file for this system is shown in Listing 10.22.

Listing 10.22 A sample named.domainhosts file.

```
; IP addresses and other hostname information for the 'domain' zone
@            IN SOA   linuxdns1.domain.    root.linuxdns1.domain. (
                       10000          ;serial
                       36000          ;refresh every 10 hours
                       3600           ;retry after 1 hour
                       3600000        ;expire after 1000 hours
2592000) ; Minimum
; this zone has a couple of nameservers and a mail server
             IN NS    linuxdns1.domain.
             IN NS    linuxdns2.domain.
             IN MX    10   linuxmail1.domain.
             IN MX    20   linuxmail2.domain.
; it is necessary to define the localhost
localhost    IN       A     127.0.0.1
; list the hosts in this zone
linuxdns1    IN       A     192.168.1.1
linuxdns2    IN       A     192.168.1.2
linuxmail1   IN       A     192.168.1.3
             IN MX    5     linuxmail1.domain.
             IN CNAME       linuxmail1.domain.
linuxmail2   IN       A     192.168.1.4
             IN MX    5     linuxmail2.domain.
             IN CNAME       linuxmail2.domain.
linuxsmb1    IN       A     192.168.1.10
```

Secondary DNS Server

For a Unix DNS server called linuxdns2.domain with an IP address 192.168.1.2, the named.boot file would be altered to the code shown in Listing 10.23.

Listing 10.23 The named.boot file for a secondary DNS.

```
; a secondary DNS server
directory                                                /etc
secondary    domain                       192.168.1.1    named.domainhosts
secondary    1.168.192-IN-ADDR.ARPA       192.168.1.1    named.reversedomain
primary      0.0.127-IN-ADDR.ARPA                        named.local
cache                                                    named.ca
```

The key line in this file is the first secondary statement, which indicates that this is a secondary server for the "domain" domain. The information for this domain is present in the primary server at 192.168.1.1, and the information for this zone should be stored in the named.domainhosts file. Likewise, the reverse domain information should be stored in the named.reversedomain file obtained from the primary server at 192.168.1.1. In all cases, entering "named" at the command prompt or entering it as a command in a system startup starts the DNS service.

The hosts on your network then make use of the DNS service by referring to the DNS server, be it in the primary, secondary, or cache in the network configuration. The Windows 95/98 and NT versions are almost identical; under the DNS tab through the Network icon, the entries will read as shown in Figure 10.11.

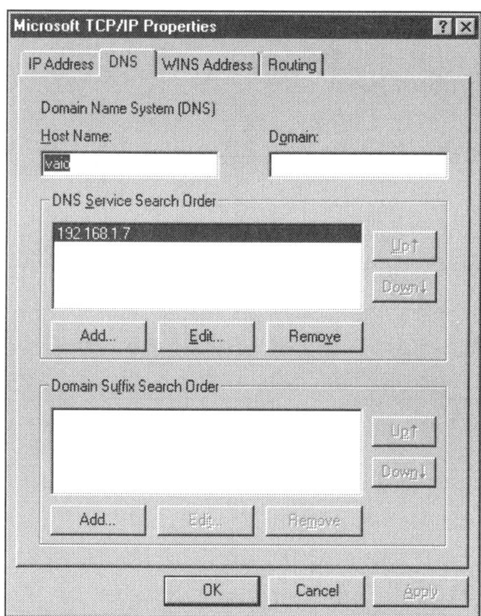

Figure 10.11 Windows client DNS entry.

In Unix systems, this is in the /etc/resolv.conf file. A suitable entry for the network is shown here:

```
# /etc/resolv.conf
domain   domain
nameserver   192.168.1.1
nameserver   192.168.1.2
```

Creating A DHCP Server

Obtain and install a **dhcpd** distribution. An ISC **dhcpd** distribution has been included on this book's CD-ROM from **www.isc.org**.

*Building The **dhcpd** Distribution*

To build the **dhcpd** distribution, unpack the compressed tar file using the tar utility and the **gzip** command and enter something like "tar zxvf dhcpd-2.0.tar.gz". Now, change (use **cd**) to the dhcp-2.0 subdirectory that you have just created and configure the source tree by entering "./configure". The configure utility should figure out what sort of system you are running on and will create a custom Makefile for that system; otherwise, it will complain. For more information, see the readme file that accompanies the distribution.

Following the successful creation of the Makefile, enter "make". The dhcp server will then be compiled. To install the **dhcpd** distribution, enter "make install".

Using The **dhcpd** Distribution

The **dhcpd** program is run from the command line. A number of options are available, and the syntax of the command is shown here:

```
dhcpd [ -p port ] [ -f ] [ -d ] [ -q ] [ -cf config-file ]
[ -lf lease-file ] [ if0 [ ...ifN ] ]
```

This DHCP server, **dhcpd**, implements the Dynamic Host Configuration Protocol (DHCP) and the Internet Bootstrap Protocol (BOOTP). As described in Chapter 2, DHCP allows hosts on a TCP/IP network to request and be assigned IP addresses and also to discover information about the network to which they are attached. BOOTP provides similar functionality, with certain restrictions.

The network administrator must allocate a pool of possible IP addresses in each subnet where the DHCP server is to run, and these values are set in the dhcpd.conf file. On startup, **dhcpd** reads the dhcpd.conf file and retains the list of available IP addresses on each subnet in memory. The **dhcpd** daemon will listen on port 67 of the primary Ethernet interface for UDP traffic. The **dhcpd** will transmit on port 68.

On startup a DHCP client, say, a Windows 9x workstation, requests an address using the DHCP protocol. The DHCP server (**dhcpd**) allocates an address for it. To make a limited number of IP addresses cover more hosts than might use the service in total over a period of time, each client is assigned a lease that expires after an amount of time chosen by the administrator; this defaults to one day. The clients to whom leases are assigned are expected to renew them in order to continue to use the addresses. Once a lease has expired, the client to which that lease was assigned is no longer permitted to use the leased IP address.

To keep track of leases across system reboots and server restarts, **dhcpd** keeps a list of leases that it has assigned in the dhcpd.leases file. Before **dhcpd** grants a lease to a host, it records the lease in this file and makes sure that the contents of the file are flushed to disk. This ensures that even in the event of a system crash, **dhcpd** will not forget about a lease that it has assigned. On startup, after reading the dhcpd.conf file, **dhcpd** reads the dhcpd.leases file to refresh its memory about what leases have been assigned.

New leases are appended to the end of the dhcpd.leases file. To prevent the file from becoming arbitrarily large, from time to time **dhcpd** creates a new dhcpd.leases file from its in-core lease database. After this file has been written to disk, the old file is renamed dhcpd.leases~, and the new file is renamed dhcpd.leases. If the system crashes in the middle of this process, whichever dhcpd.leases file remains will contain all the lease information, so a special crash recovery process is not needed.

TIP: *If the number of clients is more than the total number of IP addresses in the **dhcpd** address pool, errors will occur; thus, it is important not to set this to too small a range of addresses.*

Whenever changes are made to the dhcpd.conf file, **dhcpd** must be restarted. To restart **dhcpd**, send a SIGTERM (signal 15) to the PID contained in /var/run/dhcpd.pid and then reinvoke **dhcpd**. Note that **dhcpd** does not automatically restart itself when it sees a change to the dhcpd.conf file.

Configuration

The DHCP server (**dhcpd**) uses the dhcpd.conf configuration file.

Subnets

dhcpd needs to know the subnet numbers and netmasks of all subnets for which it will be providing service. To dynamically allocate addresses, it must be assigned one or more ranges of addresses on each subnet that it can, in turn, assign to client hosts as they boot. Thus, a very simple configuration providing DHCP support might look like this:

```
subnet 192.168.1.0 netmask 255.255.255.0 {
  range 192.168.1.120 192.168.1.170;
   }
```

Multiple address ranges may be specified as shown here:

```
subnet 192.168.1.0 netmask 255.255.255.0 {
  range 192.168.1.120 192.168.1.140;
  range 192.168.1.141 192.168.1.170;
}
```

Lease Lengths

DHCP leases can be assigned almost any length, from zero seconds to infinity. What lease length makes sense for any given subnet or for any given installation will vary, depending on the kinds of hosts being served.

In an office environment where systems are added and removed from time to time but move relatively infrequently, it might make sense to allow lease times of a month or more. In a final test environment on a manufacturing floor, it might make more sense to assign a maximum lease length of 30 minutes—enough time to go through a simple test procedure on a network appliance before packaging it up for delivery.

It is possible to specify two lease lengths: the default length that will be assigned if a client does not ask for any particular lease length and a maximum lease length. These are specified as clauses to the **subnet** command, as shown here:

```
subnet 192.168.1.0 netmask 255.255.255.0 {
range 192.168.1.120 192.168.1.170;
default-lease-time 600;
max-lease-time 7200;
```

This particular subnet declaration specifies a default lease time of 600 seconds (10 minutes) and a maximum lease time of 7,200 seconds (two hours). Other common values would be 86,400 (one day), 604,800 (one week), and 2,592,000 (30 days).

Each subnet need not have the same lease—in the case of an office environment and a manufacturing environment served by the same DHCP server, it might make sense to have widely disparate values for default and maximum lease times on each subnet.

Options

DHCP provides a mechanism whereby the server can provide the client with information about how to configure its network interface (such as a subnet mask) and how the client can access various network services (such as DNS, IP routers, and so on).

These options can be specified on a per-subnet basis. An initial DHCP server configuration might look something like the one shown in Listing 10.24.

Listing 10.24 Initial dhcpd.conf file.

```
subnet 192.168.1.0 netmask 255.255.255.0 {
  range 192.168.1.120 192.168.1.170;
  default-lease-time 600 max-lease-time 7200;
  option subnet-mask 255.255.255.0;
  option broadcast-address 192.168.1.255;
  option routers 192.168.1.254;
  option domain-name-servers 192.168.1.1, 192.168.1.2;
  option domain-name "sambabook";
}
```

The dhcpd.conf file is a free-form ASCII text file. The recursive-descent parser built into **dhcpd** parses it. The file may contain extra tabs and newlines for formatting purposes. Keywords in the file are case insensitive. Comments can be placed anywhere within the file (except within quotes) and begin with the "#" character and end at the end of the line.

The file essentially consists of a list of statements. Statements fall into two broad categories: parameters and declarations.

- *Parameter statements*—Indicate how to do something (for example, how long a lease to offer), whether to do something (for example, should **dhcpd** provide addresses to unknown clients), or what parameters to provide to the client (for example, use gateway 192.168.1.254).
- *Declarations*—These are used to describe the topology of the network, to describe clients on the network, to provide addresses that can be assigned to clients, or to apply a group of parameters to a group of declarations.

TIP: *In any group of parameters and declarations, all parameters must be specified before any declarations that depend on those parameters may be specified.*

Declarations about network topology include the shared-network and subnet declarations. If clients on a subnet are to be assigned addresses dynamically, a range declaration must appear within the subnet declaration. For clients with statically assigned addresses or for installations where only known clients will be served, each such client must have a host declaration. If parameters are to be applied to a group of declarations that are not related strictly on a per-subnet basis, the group declaration can be used.

For every subnet that will be served and for every subnet to which the DHCP server is connected, one subnet declaration must exist; this declaration tells **dhcpd** how to recognize that an address is on that subnet. A subnet declaration is required for each subnet even if no addresses will be dynamically allocated on that subnet.

Some installations have physical networks on which more than one IP subnet operates. For example, if there is a sitewide requirement that 8-bit subnet masks be used but a department with a single physical Ethernet network expands to the point where it has more than 254 nodes, it might be necessary to run two 8-bit subnets on the same Ethernet until such time as new physical network can be added. In this case, the subnet declarations for these two networks may be enclosed in a shared-network declaration.

Some sites might have departments that have clients on more than one subnet, but it might be desirable to offer those clients a uniform set of parameters that are different than what would be offered to clients from other departments on the same subnet. For clients that will be declared explicitly with host declarations, these declarations can be enclosed in a group declaration along with the parameters that are common to that department. For clients whose addresses will be dynamically assigned, there is currently no way to group parameter assignments other than by network topology.

When a client is started, its boot parameters are determined by consulting, in order, the following:

1. The client's host declaration
2. The group declaration
3. The subnet declaration for the subnet
4. The shared-network declaration
5. Any top-level parameters that can be specified outside of any declaration

When **dhcpd** tries to find a host declaration for a client, it first looks for a host declaration that has a fixed-address parameter that matches the subnet or shared network on which the client is booting. If it does not find any such entry, it tries to find an entry that has no fixed-address parameter. If no such entry is found, **dhcpd** acts as if no entry exists in the dhcpd.conf file for that client, even if an entry does exist for that client on a different subnet or shared network. To explain how these different settings may be employed for a DHCP server (**dhcpd**) in a network involving several subnets and DNS groups, an example dhcpd.conf file is shown in Listing 10.25.

Listing 10.25 A typical dhcpd.conf file involving different subnets and DNS groups.

```
global parameters...
shared-network SAMBABOOK-MAIN {
  shared-network-specific parameters...
  subnet 192.168.1.0 netmask 255.255.255.224 {
    subnet-specific parameters...
    range 192.168.1.10 192.168.1.30;
  }
  subnet 192.168.1.32 netmask 255.255.255.224 {
    subnet-specific parameters...
    range 192.168.1.42 192.168.1.62;
  }
}

subnet 192.168.1.64 netmask 255.255.255.224 {
  subnet-specific parameters...
  range 192.168.1.74 192.168.1.94;
}
group {
  group-specific parameters...
  host cornwall.sambabook {
    host-specific parameters...
  }
  host cambridge.sambabook {
    host-specific parameters...
  }
  host birmingham.sambabook {
    host-specific parameters...
  }
}
```

The dhcpd.leases file is the DHCP client lease database, and its default location is /var/state/dhcp. This database is an ASCII file containing a series of lease declarations. Every time a lease is acquired, renewed, or released, its new value is appended to the file. The last entry for a particular lease is the current version if more than one declaration appears for a given lease.

When **dhcpd** is first installed, no lease database exists. However, **dhcpd** requires that a lease database be present before it will start. To create an initial empty lease database, run the following command:

```
touch /var/state/dhcp/dhcpd.leases
```

This will create the file as required.

From time to time, the dhcpd.leases file is automatically resized by the **dhcpd** program and a dhcpd.leases~ file that contains older information is maintained.

The entries in the file for the lease descriptions are stored in the following format:

```
lease ip-address { statements... }
```

The statements define the duration of the lease and to whom it is assigned.

Start and end times of a lease are included with the prefix "starts" or "ends" within the statements as follows:

```
starts date;
ends date;
```

Dates follow this structure:

```
weekday year/month/day hour:minute:second
```

Typically, the MAC address of the network interface that was used to acquire the lease is recorded with the **hardware** statement as a series of hexadecimal octets, separated by colons:

```
hardware hardware-type mac-address;
```

If the client used a client identifier to acquire its address, the client identifier is recorded using the **uid** statement:

```
uid client-identifier;
```

The client identifier is recorded as a series of hexadecimal octets, regardless of whether the client specifies an ASCII string or uses the newer hardware type/ MAC address format.

If the client sends a hostname using the Client Hostname option, as specified in some versions of the DHCP-DNS Interaction draft, that hostname is recorded using the **client-hostname** statement:

```
client-hostname "hostname";
```

If the client sends its hostname using the Hostname option, as Windows 95 does, it is recorded using the **hostname** statement:

```
hostname "hostname";
```

If you are replacing an original installation, ensure that the current lease database is backed up before using the software.

Creating A WINS Server

The creation of a WINS server on a Samba server is as simple as adding **wins support=yes** to the smb.conf file. If you already have a Microsoft NT Server performing this duty on your network, do not add a Samba WINS server to your network, as a Windows NT Server would expect to adopt this function. In addition, the Microsoft WINS server is able to replicate its database with another NT WINS server, say, in a different building in a company. Samba does not support this ability and may be used only in a single configuration. The WINS database for a Samba server is contained in the WINS.DAT file, which is an ACSII text file in the <samba_home>/var/locks/ directory. An example of this file is shown in Listing 10.26.

Listing 10.26 Entries in the WINS.DAT file.

```
VERSION 1 170418
"SAMBABOOK#00" 930008238 255.255.255.255 c4R
"SAMBABOOK#1e" 930008238 255.255.255.255 c4R
"LINUXDNS1#00" 930008238 192.168.1.1 46R
"LINUXDNS1#03" 930008238 192.168.1.1 46R
"LINUXDNS1#20" 930008238 192.168.1.1 46R
```

In case of failure, say, for a WINS server that held the database for a couple of hundred hosts, it would make sense to be able to create a copy of this database for purposes of recovery. However, you cannot copy this file on a running Samba server. You need to shut down the **nmbd** service first. However, if the WINS server fails (either Samba or otherwise) and needs to be restarted, the NetBIOS hosts on the network will quickly reannounce themselves on the server starting up and the database will be quickly re-created. The browse service in Samba creates a database of machines that is held within the BROWSE.DAT file. An example of this file is shown in Listing 10.27.

Listing 10.27 Entries in the BROWSE.DAT file.

```
"SAMBABOOK"          c0001000 "LINUXDNS1"                      "SAMBABOOK"
"LINUXDNS1"          40019a03 "Linux DNS 1  Samba Server"   "SAMBABOOK"
"LINUXDNS2"          4006120b "Linux DNS 2  Samba Server"   "SAMBABOOK"
```

Discussions in the remainder of this book mention using a Unix/Samba server for file and printer sharing, domain control, and user authentication. However, it is also possible for the Unix/Samba server to form the backbone of the networking at an organization by offering DNS, DHCP, and WINS services.

NOTE: *Extensive details on the establishment of DNS and DHCP servers can be obtained from the references given in Appendix B.*

Obtaining Windows Network User And Group Account Information

You can obtain the information on the users and groups within a domain by using the **net** command. User information can be obtained using **net user** ***/domain:name***. This returns the list of user accounts in the domain as shown in Listing 10.28. The ***/domain:name*** is optional, as the current domain will be queried.

Listing 10.28 The net user command.

```
C:\>net user
User accounts for \\ADMINSERVER
-------------------------------------------
Administrator            bbaines                  dbaines
Guest                    internet                 IUSR_ADMINSERVER
IUSR_LAB1                rdab100                  test1
test2                    test3                    test4
The command completed successfully.
C:/>
```

Extensive information of an individual user can be obtained by sending the **net user** ***username /domain:name*** as shown in Listing 10.29.

Listing 10.29 A net user *username /domain:name* command.

```
C:\>net user dbaines
User name                  dbaines
Full Name
Comment
User's comment
Country code               000 (System Default)
Account active             Yes
Account expires            Never

Password last set          8/31/99 8:47 PM
Password expires           10/13/99 7:34 PM
Password changeable        8/31/99 8:47 PM
Password required          Yes
User may change password   Yes

Workstations allowed       All
Logon script
User profile
Home directory
Last logon                 Never
```

```
Logon hours allowed          All

Local Group Memberships      *Administrators
Global Group memberships     *Domain Users         *test
                             *research
The command completed successfully.
```

Group information can be obtained using **net group** * ***/domain:name***. This returns the list of groups in the domain. The ***/domain:name*** is optional, as the current domain will be queried as shown in Listing 10.30.

Listing 10.30 A net group * */domain:name* command.

```
C:\>net group *
Group Accounts for \\ADMINSERVER
-------------------------------------
*Domain Admins            *Domain Guests            *Domain Users
*research                 *test
The command completed successfully.
C:\>
```

A detailed list of the users within a group is returned using **net group *groupname*** as shown in Listing 10.31.

Listing 10.31 A net group *groupname* command.

```
C:\>net group "Domain Admins"
Group name     Domain Admins
Comment        Designated administrators of the domain
Members
-------------------------------------------------------------
Administrator
The command completed successfully.
C:\>
```

Creating User Accounts Automatically

In normal use, Samba requires that a Unix user account exists to enable any user to make use of the files on a server. Creating all the user accounts and maintaining the user database in sync with the Windows NT PDC can be a time-consuming task. When Samba is configured to make use of a Windows NT logon server with security being server based and a password server used to authenticate any connections, it is possible to have the Samba server automatically create the user account on the server. The **add user script** parameter specifies a script that creates this account. The value for the parameter will include the full pathname to a script that will be run as the root user by **smbd**. The security parameter in smb.conf has to be set to either **security=server** or **security=domain**, and **add user script** must include the full pathname for a script that will create a Unix user. The script must be capable of accepting one parameter, **%u**, which will become the Unix username created. This allows **smbd** to create a new Unix user account on demand when a previously unknown user accesses the Samba server.

When a user attempts to create a session using this configuration to the **smbd**, **smbd** will contact the password server and attempt to authenticate the given user with the given password. If the session authentication is successful, **smbd** will attempt to locate the user in the Unix account database and map the user to that account. If authentication is successful but no Unix account is located, the **add user** script will be triggered by **smbd**, and as root the script will be run using the **%u** session variable as a suggested username and create the Unix user account.

After an account is created, **smbd** will continue with the session request with the new Unix user account. New Unix user accounts are created dynamically on the Samba server with usernames that will match the Windows account database usernames.

By default, the value of this script is empty. A sample value is shown here:

```
add user script = /usr/local/samba/scripts/createuser %u
```

Creating Other Administrator Users For A Share

In almost all cases, the default administrative Samba user will be root. You might not want to use the root account to log in to perform administrative tasks on a share. This is largely due to the ability for the root user to do harm as well as good to the system if used unwisely. Samba includes the ability within the smb.conf file to set a share-level parameter that details other Unix users that may be set as administration users on that share. This parameter is **admin users**, which will include the user or list of users that would be capable of performing tasks on the share with the ability to run all operations as root.

The default value for this parameter has no entries. An example of this entry to provide administrative privileges to user dbaines is **admin users=dbaines**.

Performance Tuning Samba

Originally Samba was written to enable users to make use of the SMB services that a Samba server could provide. Gradually, as more and more users have started to use Samba to provide file and printer services (especially when used as a direct replacement for Windows NT Servers) the Samba software has been enhanced. With these enhancements and increased usage, demand has increased for better performance. This could mean allowing more users to connect to the server at once or allowing more data to be transferred between client and server in a shorter time. This is all still relatively new; however, the knowledge of how to tune or perform a sizing analysis of your Samba server to obtain maximum performance can be important.

Some of the time I work as a database architect and designer for very large databases (usually Oracle) and it is important to make sure with any database that you have the hardware and software configured to operate at the maximum efficiency for your users. An example of this would be, "The report that Jo in Accounts is trying to run is taking six hours when we need it to run in two hours." Sometimes it just is not possible to make the database produce this report as fast as the users need it with the current hardware—but this time can be reduced considerably by configuring the database correctly. To provide this improvement, and to know where to suggest further improvements, there are some procedures that when followed will allow this reduction in time to be obtained.

The first statement for this section is that there is no wrong or right way or complete answer to increasing the performance of a Samba server. Applying any of the suggested alterations to the current settings may provide some enhancements. When used individually the obtained improvements may be sufficient. There are considerable variations in the server hardware and set-ups where Samba is installed and the best thing to remember is that right out of the box Samba will allow you to use it with several users.

There are two important determinations that will need to be made when performance tuning your Samba server:

- Is the server hardware adequate or arranged appropriately?
- Is the Samba software configured correctly?

The answer to the first question may be that the server hardware needs to be enhanced or it could also be that if the disks were rearranged to be shared between the current controllers the necessary performance increase would occur. Sometimes this first task is referred to as *sizing*. It is important to note that sizing exercises do not always have to result in more hardware being purchased; often the reallocation of what is there already may be adequate.

The answers to the first question are often the easiest to obtain so we will start there.

Determining Your Current Hardware Performance Limits

The first task is to set out what you are trying to achieve, this usually takes the form of a simple statement like:

n users need to open and close (download and upload) x numbers of files of approximately y bytes each in s seconds.

Let's translate this into some real figures and give you an idea of what to expect. Table 10.6 contains the sizing data requirement for some of the situations that were mentioned at the end of Chapter 2.

Some of the users in these situations would have different user requirements, each involving different types of work these users were employed in. Some people in the administrative sections might require access to several small files, say Word 97 or Excel 97 documents. At the same time, the developers from the software companies may need access to as many as 100 files all at the same time, as well as large compile and test areas on the server. Some, especially the marketing or legal groups, may require access to large documents.

When you attempt to size server hardware, it is important to have some knowledge of the possible capabilities of the hardware. This will essentially fall into four main subject areas:

- CPU or Central Processing Unit
- Memory
- Disk I/O
- Network capacity

Table 10.6 Sizing requirements.

User Type	Users	Files	Average File Size (K)	Acceptable Time (seconds)	Bytes/Second Required
Admin	30	4	100	2	600K
Legal	30	2	500	2	1.5MB
Developer	30	100	150	4	112.5MB
Student	100	10	200	5	40MB
Research	100	100	500	5	1,000MB

CPU

The CPU value, in combination with the CPU memory cache size, will provide you with some idea of how much data can be handled by the server CPUs. The CPU details, in combination with the motherboard architecture, will provide a value for the number of operations that the server can handle every second. Combining this with the CPU cache size will provide you with a value for the maximum data throughput of the server. The larger the value the better. This is why the faster CPUs and motherboards generally cost more.

CPUs found in most PCs and smaller departmental servers can be expected to operate in the range of 1,000 to 3,000 I/O operations per second with a corresponding data throughput of 7,000 to 45,000Kbps. The larger and more powerful the processor and cache the larger this figure becomes. Multiple processor systems offer an increase in speed over that offered by a single CPU system as a reduced multiple of that possible from a single CPU system.

Memory

The Samba server, apart from any operating system requirements, will require memory to handle all the connections and the file transfers through the system. The **smbd** and **nmbd** services will also require memory. The allocations that have been reported are listing in Table 10.7.

This means that the memory capacity of the Samba server should be calculated with the number of user sessions expected and the corresponding memory demand included in any sizing.

Disk I/O

The type, speed, layout and disk controller type for disk drives on a server can have a huge impact on the performance of a server. Most disk drives available today operate at speeds of approximately 7,200 RPM in both EIDE or SCSI format. These disks should be capable of data throughput of approximately 500Kbps, with slower disks having a correspondingly slower throughput. There are 10,000 RPM SCSI devices available that would push this limit up to close to 700Kbps.

Table 10.7 Samba memory requirements.

Item	Memory Required
smbd	approximately 2.5MB
Each smbd client connection	approximately 700K
nmbd	approximately 2.6MB

The different hard drives have very different buffer sizes; most start at 128K. The larger the size the better, as this will allow disk write operations to be cached in the drive memory buffer.

In addition to the disk speed, the type of drive and the controller used are important. In most modern PCs, the standard disk controller is IDE and most motherboards contain two channels that can each handle two drives. The throughput would probably be limited by the drives but should be no more than 10Mbps. SCSI comes in many variants, and Ultra Wide Fast SCSI controllers can maintain data throughput at the 80Mbps level. In addition, SCSI has the ability to include multiple drives on a single controller, with some devices reporting up to 40 devices being possible.

The optimal setup would be to have the disk I/O balanced to provide maximum throughput for your server, based on the hardware available. You will see, though, that multiple Mbps throughput is going to be much easier with SCSI than IDE, and the better the hardware the better the throughput. Table 10.8 provides a comparison of the SCSI and IDE configurations.

RAID, short for Redundant Array of Inexpensive Disks, is an additional hard drive controller and comes with many different levels that reflect the different configurations involved. RAID is a hardware (and sometimes a software) method of automatically balancing the I/O on disks so that the maximum throughput is obtained. The fastest individual disk I/O would probably be in the region of 480Kbps, so the more disks in the RAID array the more throughput possible. The RAID configurations are the following:

- *RAID-0*—Arrays are groups of striped disk drives with no data redundancy and thus no fault tolerance. RAID-0 arrays can be configured with large stripes for I/O-intensive applications or small stripes for throughput-intensive applications. Because RAID-0 does not provide redundancy, a single drive failure will cause the array to crash. However, RAID-0 arrays deliver the best performance and data storage efficiency of any array type.

Table 10.8 Disk drive controller configurations.

Type	Description	Throughput
IDE	Standard PC hard drive controller, maximum of two disks per channel and two channels per PC	Maximum in the region of 10Mbps
SCSI	Higher spec hard drive controller, up to a maximum of 40 devices per channel with up to 3 channels on some controllers	Maximum in the region of 80Mbps

- *RAID-1*—Also known as disk mirroring, this consists of pairs of disk drives that store duplicate data, yet appear to the computer as a single drive. If one drive fails, the other drive of the pair is still available. A pair of mirrored drives has better read throughput than an individual drive because both drives of the pair can perform reads simultaneously. However, write throughput is the same as for a single drive, because every write must go to both drives of the pair. Striping is not used with a single pair of drives. However, multiple pairs may be striped together to appear as a single larger array. This configuration is sometimes referred to as RAID 0+1 or RAID-10. RAID-1 offers good performance and fault tolerance but has the least storage efficiency of any RAID level.
- *RAID-2*—Arrays are striped similar to RAID-0 except that disk fault tolerance is achieved by devoting some drives to storing ECC information. Since all disk drives today embed ECC information within each sector, RAID-2 is not used.
- *RAID-3*—Is similar to RAID-2 except that a single drive is devoted to storing parity information instead of one or more drives storing ECC information. If a drive fails, any missing stripe can be recovered by calculating the exclusive OR of similarly positioned stripes on the remaining drives. RAID-3 requires that records span across all drives in the array, so that pieces of each record are transferred in parallel, maximizing transfer rate. Therefore, the stripe size for RAID-3 must be small relative to the record size. As a result, RAID-3 can perform only one I/O at a time, limiting its use to single-user systems.
- *RAID-4*—Is identical to RAID-3 except that the stripes are larger than the typical record. As a result, records generally reside entirely on a single drive in the array. This allows multiple simultaneous read operations and, therefore, greater throughput in multitasking and multiuser systems. However, because all write operations must update the single parity drive, only one write can occur at a time. This architecture offers no significant advantages over RAID-5, and its write performance is slower.
- *RAID-5*—Avoids the write bottleneck caused by the single dedicated parity drive of RAID-4. RAID-5 uses *rotating parity*, evenly distributing parity information among all drives in the array. Multiple write operations can be processed simultaneously, resulting in improved throughput over RAID-4. Like RAID-3 and RAID-4, the equivalent of one drive's capacity is sacrificed for the array's parity data. RAID-5 arrays are versatile because they can be configured with small stripes to yield performance characteristics similar to RAID-3 or with large stripes for multitasking and multiuser environments. Multiple RAID-5 parity groups may be striped together to appear as a single larger array. This configuration is sometimes referred to as RAID 0+5 or RAID 50.

Network Capacity

The speed and configuration of the network hardware both on and off the server will also affect performance. The speed at which the network interface attached to the server will operate will be a pipe of a fixed capacity; likewise, the network that you connect the server to may have capacity issues associated with it.

The different type of network adapters start at the slower WAN type connections with RAS modem or ISDN dial-up usually limited to 128Kbps. The next step up would be token ring at 1,500Kbps and Ethernet at 1,113Kbps. The next step would be Fast Ethernet at 6,500Kbps, FDDI at 6,250Kbps, and Gigabit networking at throughput >10,000Kbps. There are additional levels within the higher range and it should be noted that as the speed goes up so does the price; conversely, the distances over which these speeds may operate, without considerable expense, also reduce.

The networking usually applies a bottleneck that is not restricted to the server alone, although upgrading a network adapter may be a wise first step in obtaining enhanced performance.

What does all this mean in relation to the examples given before? A server with a single CPU operating at say, 5,000Kbps will be capable of handling at least eight hard drives operating at 550Kbps. A network card at anything less than Fast Ethernet 6,500Kbps would be the bottleneck.

A server with a very large number of hard drives, say 40, would be capable of operating at some 20,000Kbps. The CPUs and the network would then become the determining factor to maximum throughput.

Identifying And Solving The Problem

With the necessary requirements identified, the task is then to determine where the problem exists. The best option would be first to perform the following operations on the server when it is not being used:

- Determine what file numbers and sizes are being used, when the problem appears to begin, and when it ends.
- Use a standard PC to look at the operations that are being performed on the Samba server from a user angle.
- Use a document or file that is 1MB in size or more, transferring this on and off the Samba server several times to ensure that the disk controller buffers are full.
- Use the Samba distribution client **smbclient** to capture and record the time taken to transfer the file to and from the server. Record the data throughput noted by **smbclient** during operation.

- Repeat the operation writing this to another part of the server, to determine any difference in hardware configurations.
- Repeat both when the server is quiet, or unused, and when it is in operation normally, and again during the problem periods, with care exercised not to stop others from working.
- Compare the times and see if there are any remarkable differences.
- Look at the server load statistics during these operations and determine what the CPU load was, how much free memory was available, what swap was being used.

The combination of all these values will help you to determine where a hardware bottleneck or sizing problem may exist.

Configuring Samba For Optimal Performance

The Samba software suite also has the ability to be tuned, and some of the parameters in the smb.conf file are important to review when looking at performance. The parameters most likely to affect performance and to be used in performance tuning are included in Table 10.9.

Table 10.9 The smb.conf parameters that can affect performance.

Parameter	Description
SO_SNDBUF	This is the TCP buffer limit that may be set, before Samba has to wait for an acknowledgement from the client. There can be visible improvements in increasing this above the operating system default. The value varies by OS, and this setting should be set after experimenting with your server. Setting this too high can cause a reduction in performance. It is not normal to increase this by more than a factor of two.
SO_RCVBUF	This value would mirror the behavior of the **SO_SNDBUF** value, and should be set as large as possible.
TCP_NODELAY	This is set by default from Samba 2.0.4 onwards. Its purpose is to instruct Samba to send as many packets as possible and not to delay between them.
ITOS_LOWDELAY	This TCP/IP setting is worth considering when routers are present on the network. This should be set at the same time as **TCP_NODELAY**.
SO_KEEPALIVE	The Samba client sessions that are dead or not responding are using up resources. When used in collaboration with the smb.conf parameters keepalive and deadtime, this will clean up these and return unused resources.
keepalive	The number of seconds between checks to see in a client session has crashed. This has a default value of 0.
dead time	Any inactive sessions will be terminated after the number of minutes provided by this value. This has a default value of 0.

(continued)

Table 10.9 The smb.conf parameters that can affect performance (continued).

Parameter	Description
log level	This may be obvious to some, but with larger log levels set, the Samba processes will write larger entries more regularly to the log files. If the log level is being set high to diagnose a problem with performance this is one time when it is counterproductive. Set log levels as low as possible.
read raw	Instructs Samba to use 64K buffers for faster reads. The values are either **YES** or **NO**; defaults to **YES**.
write raw	Instructs Samba to use 64K buffers for faster writes. The values are either **YES** or **NO**; defaults to **YES**.
max xmit	Sets the maximum packet size that Samba will attempt to use. This value can be useful when using older clients or when slow links are involved. Should not be set below 2,048 bytes.
lpq cache time	The time in seconds that the lpq print queue status cached. Default value is 0.
oplocks	This setting determines if Samba should support opportunistic locking of files on clients. A large (>25%) performance increase can result in this being set. The default is **YES**.
fake oplocks	Use this parameter *only when read only files are being used.* This instructs Samba to issue a false confirmation of a file lock on the server when requested to do so by a client. Defaults to **NO**.
veto oplock files	This parameter lists the files that should not receive oplocks (cached locally to clients). The files involved in database operations or those that require immediate visibility to other clients should be included in this list. There is no default value.
strict locking	This parameter if set can introduce a huge performance hit. The parameter instructs Samba to check the status of the locking on every session access to a file. Defaults to **NO**.
strict sync	This parameter will instruct Samba to write any data packet to disk that the client has set the sync bit for, and to wait for the write to complete before responding to the client again. If this is set the Samba server may appear dreadfully slow. The latest Windows 9x clients set this sync bit by default so if set the Samba server may appear slower than expected. Try turning it off to see if it improves performance. Default value is **NO**.
wide links	Samba will follow links that are not within the same share directory on the host file system if this is set to **YES** (the default). Turning this off will require Samba to check each file before sending to a client session. For performance it is best to leave this set to **YES**.
getwd cache	This parameter should be set when **wide links** is set to **NO**. A performance increase has been reported when a Samba server, operating primarily as a printer server, has the **wide links** parameter set to **NO** and this value set to **YES**. Defaults to **NO**.

These parameters could be used to enhance the performance of the Samba server and should be tried either singly or in the pairings suggested. At some point the performance improvements will be marginal and the server can be said to be tuned.

Other Considerations For Optimal Performance

The physical layout of the Samba server directories and resources is also important for optimal performance. An example that would highlight what is possible is for a Samba server that was in use at one of the above-mentioned companies. Sixty or so users were using this server and although not excessively stressed at the time, did appear to suffer from excessive delays. At time, delays on opening files were excessive. This appeared to occur at the same time as a number of database operations involving report production. The layout of the Linux operating system on the server was not optimal and although the server contained six separate drives, these were not being used with maximum efficiency. The disk layout details are given in Table 10.10 and again in Table 10.11 after some redesign of the server was completed.

It was identified that the clients and the database were all attempting to access work on the same drives, a number of database application and compile operations were also causing considerable disk I/O on the same drives. The server layout was reviewed and during a weekend the server hard drives and contents were rearranged with the structure shown in Table 10.11.

Table 10.10 Samba server disk layout before tuning.

Directory	Disk	Partition	Controller
SWAP	1	1	1
/	1	2	1
/usr	1	3	1
/home	1	4	1
/var	2	1	1
/data1	2	2	1
/data2	3	1	2
/data3	4	1	2
/tmp	5	1	2
/CDROM	-	-	2
TAPE	-	-	2

Table 10.11 Samba server disk layout after rearrangement.

Directory	Disk	Partition	Controller
SWAP	1	2	2
SWAP	1	1	1
/	1	2	1
/usr	1	3	1
/home	1	4	1
/var	2	1	1
/data1	2	2	1
/data2	3	1	2
/data3	4	1	2
/tmp	5	1	2
/CDROM	-	-	2
TAPE	-	-	2

The impact of these moves was to spread the disk I/O across the available drives and in doing so to maximize the possible throughput. The result meant that the noticed delays were removed and the users were no longer subject to strange work practices.

You want to think about splitting the system disk from the swap, moving the user areas to separate disks and even to separate controllers, likewise with any applications or database directories.

Chapter 11

Samba Security

If you need an immediate solution to:	*See page:*

In Depth

Every Samba server is vulnerable to attack from unauthorized users if not protected adequately. Some methods of protection involve the use of Samba smb.conf configuration parameters, whereas others involve external protection. This chapter investigates some of these options and will allow you to configure your Samba server for better protection.

Linux comes already configurable as a firewall. This chapter shows you one way to set up and configure a firewall for use with Samba.

Different Security Levels In Samba

Four security levels are currently available in Samba through the **security** parameter: share, user, server, and domain. All these parameters relate to how the server authenticates a session for a client connection request. The two main categories are share- and user-level permissions. In both cases, the authentication depends on user account details existing in the user account database.

Share permissions work on the premise that when a client connection request is made to use a share, the password associated with that share is sent during the connection request. Samba also requests the username and password for the session and then checks them against the username/password pairs held in the user account database until a valid match is obtained. If a match is obtained, the share is opened; if it is not, the connection is refused.

User permissions work on the premise that the username and password are sent during a client connection request. In any of the user-level modes, Samba takes the username/password pair and attempts to validate them against the user account database. The process is the same for any of the password encryption methods or alternate account databases used. There might be some translation of a username before authentication is possible, but the essential username/password pair authentication is common for all user-level security modes. Currently, these are user, server, and domain.

The essential details for the authentication of a client connection request when operating in each mode are the following:

- **security=share**—The client sends a tree connection request, including username and password. The Samba server validates that against the user account database and checks to see whether the user password exists. Samba will confirm that the user can access the share. If successful, the Samba server responds with a tree connection response. The session is successfully opened.

- **security=user**—The client sends a sessions setup request, including username and password. The Samba server validates that against the user account database and checks for a valid username and password match to see whether the user has access to the share. If successful, the Samba server responds with a valid session user ID (UID). The client then sends a tree connection request, including the valid UID. The session is successfully opened.
- **security=server**—The client sends a sessions setup request, including username and password. The Samba server sends a session request, including the username and password, to a password server that holds the user account database. The password server attempts to authenticate the user. If successful, the password server responds to the Samba server with a valid session UID. The Samba server sends the session UID to the client. The client then sends a tree connection request, including the session UID. The Samba server performs a Unix username lookup for the session UID on the password server to confirm that the client username contains a valid Unix UID and that the user has access permissions to perform the operation. If successful, the session is opened.
- **security=domain**—The client sends a sessions setup request, including username and password. The Samba server that is a member of a Windows NT domain sends a session request, including the username and password, to the Windows NT domain controller that holds the domain user account database. The domain controller attempts to authenticate the user. If successful, the domain controller responds to the Samba server with a valid session UID. The Samba server sends the session UID to the client. The client then sends a tree connection request, including the session UID. The Samba server performs a Unix username lookup for the session UID from the domain controller to confirm that the client username contains a valid Unix UID and that the user has access permissions to perform the operation. If successful, the session is opened.

Usernames

Samba has the ability to alter the usernames that are used when authenticating any session. The authentication parameters used with usernames are the following:

- **username level**—Samba defaults to checking any account database by using the default Unix practice of lowercase usernames. **username level** specifies the maximum number of uppercase letters that may exist in the username.

These do not have to be at the start of the username. Samba will attempt to authenticate with the username by altering the case of the username one character at a time, first with one uppercase letter, then two, with all possible permutations until the value of case substitutions specified has been attempted. After a valid combination validates the authentication, the process stops. If usernames were all lowercase, this parameter would not be required. Note that a larger value will include many more possible combinations and that because each is attempted, the authentication will take longer.

- **username map**—In Unix, the default superuser is known as root, Samba is usually installed by root, and the Windows NT superuser is Administrator. Windows NT will allow long usernames and spaces in usernames. Unix tends to be restricted to eight characters and the default practice is to use lowercase usernames.

With an attempt to use a central user account database to control operation, the username variations alone can provide a challenge to any network administrator. Samba permits the mapping of SMB/CIFS usernames received in session requests to Unix usernames by specifying these in a file. The **username map** parameter is a full pathname and file name value for the location of this file. The values in the file are single-line entries that list the mappings, as shown here:

```
Unix username = client username
```

Multiple client usernames may be specified for each Unix username.

In operation, a client user will need to provide the password for the Unix user account at the session request. This can also be used to map whole Unix user groups to single user accounts for SMB purposes with an @Unix User Group Name replacing the client username shown in the listing. Another option is to substitute the "*" character. This will attempt to map any users to that account, normally the Unix guest or nobody account.

The username map file is read completely during operation, meaning that a later mapping could overwrite a correct username mapping listed earlier. Prefixing the Unix username with "!" will instruct **smbd** to stop searching for a username map once a correct name is found.

Passwords

One of the most common questions that arises in many Samba discussion lists involves how to synchronize password across Samba- and Windows-based systems. This is a complex challenge, and some explanation is required.

The major issue with passwords in Samba and NT environments is that both operate different password account practices and NT keeps these passwords in a proprietary format and account database. Windows NT keeps all user authentication information in the SAM database, and Linux and Unix usually keep user account information in the /etc/passwd and /etc/shadow files. The passwords that are held in these systems are encrypted using different algorithms and formats.

Immediate Solutions

Changing Security Levels

To change between security modes, simply alter the **security** parameter value to either share, user, server, or domain.

Note that server or domain will require the presence of the appropriate password server or domain controller. In the case of domain security, the Samba server and client machines also need to be added to the domain. Chapter 9 contains the necessary details to implement domain security.

Managing Passwords With **smbpasswd**

The Samba suite includes programs and utilities to manage password encryption. The first of these is the **smbpasswd** program. A Samba server that is set up to use encrypted passwords will include the smbpasswd file.

The smbpasswd file is the Samba encrypted password file. This file contains, on a line-by-line basis, the username, the Unix UID, and the SMB-encrypted passwords of the user. The file also contains information on the account type, represented as an account flag, account information, and the time the password was last changed.

The current file format that includes this information is the latest of several different formats that were used by previous versions of Samba. The format used today resembles the Unix passwd file format. The file is currently ASCII, containing a single-line entry for each user. The lines contain several fields, each separated from the next by a colon. Commented-out lines are prefixed with the "#" character. The fields contained within this file are described in Table 11.1.

The format of the smbpasswd file is shown in Listing 11.1.

Listing 11.1 smbpasswd file format.

```
username:uid:XXXXXXXXXXXXXXXXXXXXXXXXXXXXXXXX:XXXXXXXXXXXXXXXXXXXXXXXXXXXXXX
XX:[Account type]:LCT-<last-change-time>:Long name
```

Table 11.1 The smbpasswd file fields.

Field Name	Description
Username	The username. This name must already exist in the standard Unix passwd file.
uid	The Unix UID for that user. This must exactly match the UID field for the same user entry in the standard Unix passwd file. Any other value will result in Samba being unable to recognize a valid entry in the smbpasswd file to the specific user.
Lanman Password Hash	This is the first of the encrypted passwords and is the LANMAN hash of the user password, encoded as 32 hex digits. DES encryption of a well-known string with the user password as the DES key is used to create this value. Windows 95/98 machines use this value directly. The password encryption used to produce the value is regarded as weak, as it is vulnerable to dictionary attacks, and if two users choose the same password, this entry will be identical. A Unix-encrypted password for two identical passwords will not appear identical because of the addition of a string to the password before encryption, ensuring that a difference will result. An entry for a null password would have the hex value for this field starting with the characters "NO PASSWORD". If the hex string is equal to 32 "X" characters, the user account is marked as disabled, and the user will not be able to log on to the Samba server.
NT Password Hash	The Windows NT hash of the user password, encoded as 32 hex digits. Encrypting a 16-bit little-endian UNICODE version of the user password with the MD4 (Internet RFC1321) hashing algorithm creates this value. The NT Password Hash is considered more secure than the Lanman Password Hash because the password's case is preserved, and a much higher-quality hashing algorithm is used. If identical passwords are used, the entries will appear the same.
Account Flags	Descriptions of the user's account. The Samba 2.0 release brackets this field with the "[" and "]" characters and is always 13 characters in length (including the "[" and "]" characters). The values are with U, N, D, or W: U indicates a user account. Only user and workstation trust accounts are currently supported in the smbpasswd file. N indicates a null password account. Any hash entries are ignored. This may be used if the smb.conf parameter null password is set to yes. D indicates a disabled account where no SMB/CIFS logins will be allowed for this user. W indicates a Workstation Trust account used when a Samba primary domain controller (PDC) is present and Windows NT workstations have joined a domain hosted by a Samba PDC. The rest of this field is padded out with spaces. The Samba team has indicated that further values will appear as necessary.
Last Change Time	Indicates the time of the last account modification. Prefixed with "LCT-" (last change time) followed by the number of seconds since 01-01-1970 00:00:00 (DD-MM-YYYY HH:MM:SS) that the last change was made. Currently, Samba ignores any additional fields.

The values and structure for the username, UID, XXXXXXXXXXXXXXXX XXXXXXXXXXXXXXXX, [Account type], and last-change-time sections are important, and these are used by Samba directly. The password hash following the UID is exactly 32 characters in length. If this file is damaged and this number is reduced, Samba will not be able to authenticate the users. The first 16 characters form the LanMan password hash, and the second 16 form the Windows NT version.

When new smbpasswd entries are created, the 32 characters exist as the "X" character. Following the successful change of the user's smbpasswd, the user may log into the system, and the 32 "X" characters will change to the hash values. If any user requires no password, an appropriate editor must edit the smbpasswd file and replace the first 11 "X" characters with the string "NO PASSWORD". A sample entry for a null password user is shown in Listing 11.2.

Listing 11.2 A null password user smbpasswd entry.

```
rdab100:100:NO PASSWORDXXXXXXXXXXXXXXXXXXXXX:
XXXXXXXXXXXXXXXXXXXXXXXXXXXXXXXX:[U          ]:
LCT-00000000:Dominic Baines:/home/rdab100:/bin/bash
```

A utility, mksmbpasswd.sh, is provided to generate an smbpasswd file for a Samba server from a Unix /etc/passwd file. The command to generate the smbpasswd file from the /etyc/passwd file is shown in Listing 11.3.

Listing 11.3 Generating an smbpasswd file from the /etc/passwd file.

```
cat /etc/passwd | mksmbpasswd.sh >/usr/local/samba/private/smbpasswd
#If you are running on a system that uses NIS, use
#ypcat passwd | mksmbpasswd.sh >/usr/local/samba/private/smbpasswd
```

This utility is included as part of the Samba distribution and can be found in the /source directory. The smbpasswd file is usually located in the /usr/local/samba/private directory.

The password hashes are known as plain text equivalent because of the nature of the password hashes involved when any SMB/CIFS client/server challenge-response occurs. The nature of the SMB/CIFS authentication protocol that is used allows anyone with knowledge of this password hash to impersonate the user on the network. Thus, the password hashes must not be made available to anyone but the root user. To protect the entries in this file, the owner of the /usr/local/samba/private directory should be set to root, and the permissions on it should be set to r-x------ or 500 using the command shown here:

```
chmod 500 /usr/local/samba/private
```

The smbpasswd file inside the private directory should also be owned by root, and the permissions on it should be set to rw------- or 600 using the command shown here:

```
chmod 600 smbpasswd
```


Using The **smbpasswd** Program

This program is responsible for setting and maintaining the smbpasswd file on the Samba server. The syntax for this command is shown here:

```
smbpasswd [-a] [-d] [-e] [-D debuglevel] [-n] [-r remote_machine]
[-R name resolve order] [-m] [-j DOMAIN] [-U username] [-h] [-s] username
```

As you can see, several different functions and operations are possible when using the program. Either a root or a normal user may also use it. When run as a normal user, it allows the user to change the password used for SMB sessions on any machines that store SMB passwords.

When run with no options at the command prompt, the program will attempt to change the currently logged-in user's SMB password on the local machine. The program will respond with a prompt to change the password, first requesting that the current password be entered. To change the password, **smbpasswd** will request that the new value be entered twice. If the entries match, the smbpasswd file will be changed. The **smbpasswd** program operates in a similar manner to the Unix **passwd** program. However, **smbpasswd** runs as a client application and expects to communicate with a locally running **smbd** daemon, whereas **passwd** runs **setuid**. The smbpasswd file contains the encrypted SMB passwords and usually resides in /usr/local/samba/lib. If you want to create a NULL password account by entering "no password" when prompted, the smbpasswd entry for that user will include the string "NO PASSWORD" in the smbpasswd file. Nonroot users may also use **smbpasswd** to change SMB passwords on other servers.

Finally, when run as root, the **smbpasswd** program will add, delete, or modify user entries to the smbpasswd file. In contrast to a normal user running **smbpasswd**, when the superuser (normally root) runs it, the **smbd** daemon need not be running, and changes can be made to the smbpasswd file directly.

Table 11.2 includes a description of the major **smbpasswd** options.

The **smbd** daemon must be running for a nonroot user to use the **smbpasswd** program. The **smbpasswd** command is useful only if Samba has been set up to use encrypted passwords.

Table 11.2 smbpasswd options.

Option	Description
-a	The username following this option will be added to the local smbpasswd file. The user is created, and the new password is prompted for. If this is a new user, the old password will be empty, so pressing Enter for the old password is sufficient. If the user already exists, this method can be used to change the password. When creating a user in smbpasswd, the user must already exist on the system. Note that this option is available only when running **smbpasswd** as root.
-d	The username following this option should be disabled in the local smbpasswd file. This involves writing a **D** flag into the account control space in the smbpasswd file. If this value exists, all attempts to authenticate via SMB using this username will fail. Note that this option is available only when running **smbpasswd** as root.
-e	The username following this option will have the entry in the smbpasswd file altered to reenable the username SMB authentication capabilities if the account has been disabled. If the account was not disabled, this option has no effect. After the account is enabled, the user will be able to authenticate via SMB once again. Note that this option is available only when running **smbpasswd** as root.
-D *debuglevel*	***debuglevel*** is an integer from 0 to 10; the higher this value, the more information concerning operation is written to the log files during **smbpasswd** operation. The default value is 0. Level 0 logs only critical errors and serious warnings. Levels greater than 1 generate a lot of information that might be useful only when diagnosing problems. Levels greater than 3 create data that is of value to developers.
-n	The password for the username should be set to null (blank) in the **smbpasswd** file. To permit users to log in with null passwords, the Samba server should have the **null passwords** parameter in the smb.conf configuration file set to yes or true. This option is available only when running **smbpasswd** as root.
-r *remote_machine*	The **-r** option is used when a user wants to change the smbpasswd on another machine whose name immediately follows the option. The smbpasswd will always default to local host unless this parameter is specified. The remote machine name is the NetBIOS name of the SMB/CIFS server. The remote server name is resolved to an IP address using the standard Samba mechanisms before the operation is attempted. The current Unix username from the session is the username whose password is changed. The **-U *username*** parameter can be specified to change the password of an alternate username. This option may be used to change the password of a

(continued)

Table 11.2 ***smbpasswd*** ***options*** **(continued).**

Option	Description
-r ***remote_machine***	user on an NT system; however, the remote machine must be the PDC for the domain. The account database on a backup domain controller (BDC) is read-only, and changes are not allowed. It is not possible to change pass words on remote Windows 9x machines, as these do not contain proper account databases.
-R ***name resolve order***	When the **-r** option is used, the **-R** option will specify which name resolution services to use and the order in which to use them when looking up the NetBIOS name of the host being connected to. The options are **lmhosts**, **hosts**, **wins**, and **bcast**. They cause names to be resolved as follows: **lmhosts**: Uses the lmhosts file to look up an IP address. **hosts**: Uses the system /etc/hosts file to perform a standard hostname-to-IP-address resolution or uses DNS. **wins**: Uses the WINS server specified to perform a name query. **bcast**: Performs a network broadcast on each of local subnets for the interfaces listed in the interfaces parameter in the smb.conf file. When used with smbpasswd, if this parameter is not defined, the name resolve order defined in the smb.conf file parameter ***name resolve order*** will be used. Without either entry, this defaults to **lmhosts**, **host**, **wins**, and **bcast**.
-m	This option specifies that a MACHINE account is involved and is used when the Samba server is acting as a PDC. This option is available only when running **smbpasswd** as root.
-j ***DOMAIN***	When this option is used, the Samba server is added to a Windows NT domain as a domain member. This Samba server will then be capable of authenticating user accounts to any domain controller in the domain in the same way as another Windows NT server. The Samba server must already have had a machine account created in the domain. This option is available only when running **smbpasswd** as root.
-U ***username***	When an alternate username on a remote server is required by the currently logged-on user, this option will allow the remote username account to be altered.
-h	As with many Unix programs, this option returns the help text from the **smbpasswd** program.
-s	This option allows **smbpasswd** to operate in silent mode without prompts appearing. It is usually used in scripts that include **smbpasswd** and do not require user intervention.

Using Older smbpasswd Files

Older version of Samba, prior to version 2.0.0, used a different smbpasswd file format that did not contain the Account Flags or Last Change Time fields. The current Samba 2.0 code is able to use the older smbpasswd file and may add new user entries, but might not be capable of modifying the older entries. Over time, the different username entries included new entries, and some did not. The older style of smbpasswd account may be converted to the newer version by running the script included in the /bin directory of the Samba distribution, convert_smbpasswd, on the older file. The syntax of the command is shown here:

```
cat old_smbpasswd_file | convert_smbpasswd > new_smbpasswd_file
#Note the syntax carefully as the convert_smbpasswd script reads from
#stdin and writes to stdout. Back up any smbpasswd file before use.
```

Following the running of the convert_smbpasswd script, the new smbpasswd file will contain the new entries. If the entries are intact, at this point the new_smbpasswd_file should be copied over the old file.

Encrypting Passwords

Password encryption for LanManager and Windows NT hosts is similar to Unix password encryption. In either case, the server uses a file containing a hashed value of a user's password. Performing an operation on the user's plain text password creates the hash values.

In the case of the LanManager hosts, this involves taking the user's plain text password, uppercasing it, and running an encryption on the value. The 16-byte encrypted value is known as the *hashed password*.

Windows NT encryption involves a higher-quality encryption that also produces a 16-byte encrypted value that is nonreversible.

In operation, for any client that wants to use a Samba server that is configured to use encrypted passwords and that attempts to mount a Samba drive (or to use a Samba resource), the first task is to request a connection and negotiate the protocol that the client and server will use. During the exchange between the server and the client, the Samba server generates and appends a random value to the reply to the client and then stores this value after the reply is sent. The value is known as a *challenge*. The value of the challenge is different for each separate client connection.

At the client, the challenge is encrypted using the hashed passwords from the smbpasswd file. The resulting value is known as a *response*.

On a client, during the SMB call to either SMBsessionsetupX (for user-level security) or SMBtconX (for share-level security), the client returns the response value to the Samba server. When Windows NT protocol levels are involved, the previously mentioned calculation is done on both hashes of the user password, and both responses are returned during the SMB call.

Following the receipt of the response, the Samba server reproduces the calculation for the challenge value, using its own stored value of the hashed password from the smbpasswd file. It then compares the challenge value that it kept from the negotiated protocol reply returned to it from the client. If the two values match, the client is permitted to access the resource. If they do not match, the client is denied access.

Setting Up Password Encryption Support

To configure Samba for password encryption, follow these steps:

1. Compile and install Samba as usual.
2. If your system cannot compile the getsmbpass.c module, remove the -DSMBGETPASS define from the Makefile.
3. Enable encrypted passwords in smb.conf by adding the line "encrypt passwords=yes" in the [global] section.
4. Create the initial smbpasswd password file in the place you specified in the Makefile by using the following command:

```
cat /etc/passwd | mksmbpasswd.sh > /usr/local/samba/private/smbpasswd
```

5. Change ownership of private and smbpasswd to root by using the following command:

```
chown -R root /usr/local/samba/private
```

6. Set the correct permissions on /usr/local/samba/private as shown here:

```
chmod 500 /usr/local/samba/private
```

7. Set the correct permissions on /usr/local/samba/private/smbpasswd as shown here:

```
chmod 600 /usr/local/samba/private/smbpasswd
```

8. Set the passwords for users using the **smbpasswd** command shown here:

```
smbpasswd username
```

The Samba server should now be configured to use encrypted passwords.

Controlling Access With smb.conf Security Options

Samba has the ability to control access to itself with a number of parameters that will screen the Samba server access to hosts with known IP addresses. It is able to do this using four parameters:

- **hosts allow**
- **hosts deny**
- **hosts equiv**
- **user rhosts**

The combination of these four parameters should allow a policy to be established that screens the Samba server to all but the allowed hosts with the correct IP address. The four parameters are discussed in more detail in the following sections.

hosts allow

This parameter is usually applied as a share-level parameter that may hold different values for each share. The parameter can also be applied in the [global] section of the smb.conf configuration file; if this parameter exists, the values will apply to all services regardless of whether the individual service has a different setting. The parameter is synonymous with the "allow hosts" file that exists in Unix systems.

The values that may be included with this parameter (separated by a comma, space, or tab) can identify single IP addresses, ranges of IP addresses, and even DNS hostnames. The local host address 127.0.0.1 will always be allowed access unless specifically denied by an entry in the **hosts deny** option. The hosts can also be specified by network/netmask pairs and by netgroup names if your system supports netgroups. The values can also include exclusions by use of the **EXCEPT** keyword, thus limiting a wildcard list. Examples of the use of **hosts allow** values include the following:

- Allow all IPs in 192.168.*.* except 192.168.1.250:

```
hosts allow = 192.168. EXCEPT 192.168.1.250
```

- Allow those hosts that match the given network/netmask:

```
hosts allow = 192.168.1.0/255.255.255.0
```

- Allow only a small number of hosts access:

```
hosts allow = testpc1, laptop
```

- Allow hosts from the NIS netgroup "sambabook" but deny access from the host router1:

```
hosts allow = @sambabook
hosts deny = router1
```

- Allow hosts from the sambabook.com domain

```
hosts allow = @sambabook.com
```

Note that the use of the **hosts allow** parameter does not preclude any other security settings and that the clients using these hosts will still require suitable user- or share-level access. This parameter has no default value, meaning that by default all hosts are allowed access.

TIP: *Be sure that in your configuration you do not leave unnecessary host values in the **hosts allow** parameter.*

hosts deny

This parameter is the counterpart to the **hosts allow** parameter and includes those hosts that are to be denied access to the server. The parameter can be set at the [global] or services level, with the [global] setting taking precedence. If the **hosts allow** and **hosts deny** values conflict, the **hosts allow** value should always win. This parameter has no default value, indicating that no hosts are denied access. The parameter values may exist in a similar form to the **hosts allow** values.

hosts equiv

This is a [global] parameter only, and it specifies the file name that contains those hosts that would be permitted access with no authentication requirement. The value often used is the /etc/hosts.equiv file. The Samba server will obtain the username from the session, and this will be used to define which services are offered. The use of this parameter has some serious security implications, as it could allow nonauthorized users to access the server in the instance of a host break-in. I do not recommend using this parameter if any sensitive information is contained on the Samba server. The parameter defaults to no value set.

use rhosts

The possible values for this parameter are **yes** or **no**. If set, it will indicate that Samba should use the entries in the ~/.rhosts file from the session user. The default is **no**.

In all four cases, the **testparm** program is designed to test the host access parameters, and the output values should correspond with your settings.

A number of other parameters may be set that Samba can use to add security to the server. These include the following:

- **create mask, create mode**
- **security mask**
- **directory mask, directory mode**
- **force directory mode**
- **force group**
- **force user**
- **map to guest**
- **root directory**

These are discussed in more detail in Table 11.3.

Table 11.3 Other security parameters.

Parameter	Description
create mask	This parameter sets the permissions on a file when it is created. This defaults to 0744, or rwx permissions for the owner and r-- for everyone else. The format set here will apply to all new files in the share, so the setting should be chosen with care.
security mask	This parameter indicates which Unix permission bits can be modified by a Windows NT client when using the native NT security dialog box. It is applied as a mask (logically AND'ed) to the changed permission bits, thus preventing any bits not in this mask from being modified. Essentially, zero bits in this mask may be treated as a set of bits that the user is not allowed to change. The parameter defaults to the same value as create mask if not set. To permit a user to modify all the user/group/world permissions on a file, this parameter should be set to 0777.
directory mask	This parameter sets the permissions on a directory when it's created. This defaults to 0755, or rwx permissions for the owner and r-x for everyone else. This parameter allows users other than the owner to change to the directory and list the contents. The format set here will apply to all new directories and new subdirectories created in the share, so the setting should be chosen with care.
force create mode	This parameter defaults to 0000, meaning that no additional parameters are set on new files created in the share. A setting of 0644 will overwrite the previous setting in create mask and set the permissions to rw-r--r--.
force directory mode	This parameter defaults to 0000, meaning that no additional parameters are set on new directories in the share. A setting of 0744 will overwrite the previous setting in create mask and set the permissions to rwxr--r--.

(continued)

Table 11.3 Other security parameters (continued).

Parameter	Description
force group	All Unix users will exist in a group. This parameter will force all new files in the share to be created, with the group owner set to the value provided. This defaults to no entry, meaning that normally any files created in the share are given the group of the parent directory.
force user	This parameter will force all new files in the share to be created, with the owner set to the value provided. This defaults to no entry, meaning that normally any files created in the share are given the owner of the user accessing the share.
map to guest	When a connection or user session fails because of a bad or an incorrect username, password, or combination thereof, it is possible to allow access to the guest-capable shares and services. This parameter defaults to never. The three settings are the following: **never**—User login requests with an invalid password are rejected. This is the default. **bad user**—User logins with an invalid password are rejected, unless the username does not exist, in which case it is treated as a guest login and mapped into the guest account. **bad password**—User logins with an invalid password are treated as a guest login and mapped into the guest account.
root directory	This parameter is a [global] setting and specifies which directory the server should change to as its root directory on startup. This is done by Samba chroot to the specified directory. The addition of a value for the root directory parameter, which defaults to "/," may provide additional security. This setting ensures that no files or shares that lie outside this directory tree are available during operation. However, this will also need to include all the system files, log files, printer spools, filters, and any other file or directory normally used. The use of this parameter might have serious implications for server administration, as all these files will need to be mirrored into this location.

Protecting A Samba Server

In the current world of networks, it is important for any network administrator to consider ways to protect the Samba server(s) on the network.

Using Antivirus Software

So far to date, no Unix virus has been detected that should cause a network administrator to worry unduly. This is perhaps due to the enhanced security and user and group permissions present in Unix environments. Unfortunately, however, this is not the case with Windows systems where viruses seem to proliferate. Opening up a Unix server to Windows users should not bring additional risks to the Samba server, but the files that are contained on the Samba server might not be cleared of trouble. The best way to protect any network is to stop all access to it from the outside, but this is not realistic in most cases, and so the only option is to use software that protects the systems from attack. The latest versions of antivirus software, such as Dr. Solomon's or McAfee's, are now sophisticated enough to detect and disinfect many different viruses, variants, and macros that exist within files. These protect the user's machine when opening any file for read, write, or delete individually and when used administratively to scan drives, network or otherwise, for the offending virus or macro.

The ideal configuration is to make a system independent from a network during any antivirus operation. The next best configuration is to have the file system automatically purged by an administrator.

To create an optimum installation, the antivirus software needs to be able to operate with sufficient file system privileges remotely to be able to delete, move, and rename files that might be infected. When operating on a local file system, administrator access is more typical.

One suggestion is to have a dedicated Windows NT workstation that contains a network edition of the antivirus software. The user that operates the software has the administrative privileges to map all the relevant file systems that are to be protected. The workstation contains a local share that also has a user-enabled version of the antivirus software installed. The installation, of the antivirus software, such as Dr. Solomon's Network Management Edition, adds a small component to all Windows, Novell, OS2, and other supported operating systems and clients on the network. This is configured to scan all removable devices, floppy disks, Zip disks, and CD-ROMs for any virus on opening a file. A Terminate Stay Resident (TSR) type of program is retained in memory on each of these workstations to protect against any macros or viruses not detected otherwise. The supported hosts can be configured to run regular file system checks.

Any Samba server share will need to be browseable by the NT workstation user with write privileges. If the Samba server were to have three main share trees—[homes], [profiles], and [work]—the smb.conf settings for these shares would also include the parameters **write list=@virusadmin** and **read list=@virusadmin** so that the software running from the NT workstation can access the shares.

An /etc/group entry that will allow this user to access these shares should also be present. An advisable option is to use an NT domain with the domain-group.map and domain-users.map parameters, which will allow domainwide authentication levels to be set for this user.

Adding The Secure Sockets Layer To A Samba Server

The standard way to transfer data between a client and a server in an SMB/CIFS environment involves sending the data unencrypted. The result is that a sniffer program running on a host on the network might be able to capture the contents of the files that are being shared by servers and read or written to by clients.

This sort of sniffing, if carried out in a secure network by a network administrator, should pose few problems. However, a major security risk can arise when such a transfer occurs and an unauthorized person using a host on a network carries out the capture. Suppose that the transfer involved a document that included personal or sensitive data.

Samba has been written to allow the use of the Secure Sockets Layer (SSL), more commonly seen with Web-based transactions. In simple terms, the SSL allows the client and server to pass any data between them encrypted with a 128-bit key. The major advantage of SSL is that it uses a well-established standard with public key cryptography and digital certificate authentication between client and server. The added ability to use symmetrical cryptographic encoding between the hosts with a random session key that exists for that session only also provides for a relatively secure mode of operation.

The version of SSL supported in Samba is known as SSLeay. This is a source library written by Eric Young. The FAQ for it can be obtained from **www.cryptosoft.com/ssleay**.The FAQ lists the master locations for SSLeay source and the SSLapps at the following:

- *SSLeay source*—**ftp://ftp.psy.uq.oz.au/pub/Crypto/SSL**
- *SSL applications*—**ftp://ftp.psy.uq.oz.au/pub/Crypto/SSLapps**
- *SSLeay Programmer Reference*—**http://www.psy.uq.oz.au/~ftp/Crypto/ssl.html**
- *Porting notes*—**ftp://ftp.psy.uq.oz.au/pub/Crypto/SSLapps/PORT4-5**

The site includes some additional FAQs and documentation that you should read. The current FAQ in particular raises some legal issues related to the use of some algorithms within SSLeay that you should read before using them. The inclusion of SSL support in Samba requires that you download this library and build your own Samba binaries. You will find details of how to build your own binaries in Chapter 3.

Steps to follow in addition to the standard build are the following:

1. Build Samba binaries with SSL support enabled. (You will need to obtain extra software to do this; see the following section "Compiling In SSL Support.")

2. Either obtain or create X.509 certificates that will enable you to use encryption on your Samba servers or clients as appropriate.
3. Configure Samba servers to make use of the X.509 certificates and private encryption keys.
4. Configure any clients that will access the SSL-secured servers.

Three groups of SSL-enabled client exist. Two of these involve using a third-party software add-on that copes with the encryption, and the third is the **smbclient** program with SSL support compiled in.

Windows NT, 9x, and 2000 hosts can make use of the sslproxy software that is available in much the same way as Linux and Samba under the GPL. When installed and configured, the software will allow these standard non-SSL-capable clients from operating with SSL servers and clients. If not using **smbclient** (with SSL), other Unix hosts can make use of the Sharity product.

Compiling In SSL Support

Obtain the SSLeay library source code from **www.cryptosoft.com/ssleay** and extract and build the enclosed software. This is done by using the **./configure**, **make**, and **make install** sequence.

The standard SSLeay distribution supports many different operating systems and uses the Perl programming language to create the Makefile. The standard expected Perl location is /usr/local/bin/perl, which might not be correct in some Linux distributions that install it in /bin/perl. Before running the **./configure** script, it is worth checking where Perl is installed with **which perl** and altering the first line accordingly. SSLeay will default install into /usr/local/ssl.

After SSLeay is installed, you can build the Samba binaries with SSL support. Support for SSL has been included since 2.0.3, so you should use only a distribution with a version later than that. To build Samba with SSL support, use the following commands:

```
./configure _with-ssl
make
make install
```

If SSL has been installed in an alternate location to /usr/local/ssl, the first line in the previous code should be written to reflect this alternate location, as shown here:

```
./configure _with-ssl -with-cclinc=<the directory where ssl is installed>
```

The Samba binaries will then be installed with SSL support enabled.

TIP: *If SSL is not present on your network, little can be gained by including SSL support. In fact, this can cause confusion if the smb.conf file is not configured correctly, even though SSL is not enabled by default.*

Using SSL

SSL operates by confirming the identity of the two hosts using the previously mentioned certificates when setting up the session and then encrypting all traffic that passes over the connection using a key that is part of the certificate. The following steps summarize the process:

1. The client connects to the Samba server. With SSL enabled and configured, the client/server exchange includes the information that the client is SSL-capable and which version of SSL is being used.
2. The Samba server responds to the client with a request for the client to confirm its identity. This includes a message from the server and a copy of this message that is encrypted and digitally signed by the server. The server also sends a copy of the certificate that it uses, including the public key to the encryption used for the message.
3. The client receives the message and deencrypts the encrypted message using the public key from the certificate. The client also takes the plain text message and encrypts it if the two results that match the client can be satisfied that the server really sent the message.
4. The client generates a random session key and, using the public key in the server certificate, encrypts it and sends this to the server.
5. The server is able to decrypt this random session key and to encrypt all transfers to the client for this session using this key.
6. The client and server are capable of sending any transfers over the network securely. The server may ask the client to authenticate itself in a similar manner, and this requires that the client also have a certificate.

Obtaining, Generating, And Using Certificates

Any host that intends to be set up using SSL needs to have a public and a private encryption key generated for it. If you have SSLeay installed, you will use this to generate the pair of keys needed.

The previously mentioned certificates provide a method of digital identification that includes a copy of the public encryption key that the host that owns the certificate will use. When created, the server takes certain identification information and uses the public key to encrypt it and send it to a Certificate Authority (CA). The CA digitally signs this information and sends it back to the server. This return forms the server certificate that confirms that the certificate belongs to the host, its DNS name, the email address of the certificate administrator, the host location, and additional information. The CA is used in this manner to confirm that the host is where it should be and that the public key that it uses is verified. If the server is present, say, on the Internet, the clients using it may trust the server certificate.

Obtaining A Certificate

You can obtain a certificate in a number of ways. If you need to have certificates residing on an external server, the commercial option is to use a CA such as VeriSign, but this can be expensive. However, this and other organizations that offer CA services are well trusted, and they sign many commercial certificates used on many different Web sites. However, as is probably the case here, if you are not running an external Samba server, you can set up your own CA, and SSLeay includes all the software required to do so.

To create a CA using SSLeay, follow these steps:

1. Add the location of the SSLeay binaries on your system to the **PATH** variable. On my system, this involved issuing the command **PATH=$PATH:/usr/local/ssl/bin**.
2. The SSLeay uses a random number generator that should be initialized. One method of doing this involves creating an ASCII text file that contains 10 lines or so of random keystrokes using both upper- and lowercase, and additional characters. (For the mathematicians out there, I know that this is not truly random, but for the purpose of the random number generator this should be adequate.) This file can be created using any text editor. The SSLeay documentation recommends using cat > /tmp/random.txt and Ctrl+D when complete. To initialize the random number generator, enter the following command:

```
ssleay genrsa -rand /tmp/random.txt
```

3. Delete the random.txt file from the computer, as it is no longer needed and could be used to "crack" any generated key.
4. Create a CA directory for the CA database. One suggestion, /usr/local/ssl/<*YOURCHOICE*>CA, uses the SSLeay-based directory if that is where it was installed. Set the directory mode to 700 to stop all but root access to the directory.
5. Edit the /usr/local/ssl/lib/ssleay.cnf file to reflect the directory entry to show the new location for the [CA_DEFAULT] entry. These will appear as shown here:

```
[CA_DEFAULT]
dir       = /usr/local/ssl/<YOURCHOICE>CA
```

6. Edit the /usr/local/ssl/bin/CA.sh script to reflect this database location as well:

```
CATTOP = /usr/local/ssl/<YOURCHOICE>CA
CATKEY = /usr/local/ssl/<YOURCHOICE>CA
CACERT = /usr/local/ssl/<YOURCHOICE>CA
```

7. Create the new CA by issuing the following command:

```
CA.sh -newca
```

8. The script will prompt for several entries, and these correspond to the following:
   a. Enter the password phrase for the CA's private key (NULLs not allowed)
   b. Reenter the password phrase for the CA's private key (NULLs not allowed)
   c. Enter the two-letter ISO code for your country (such as "US" for United States of America)
   d. Enter the region name (such as "Arizona")
   e. Enter the location (such as "Phoenix")
   f. Enter the name of the organization (such as "Coriolis")
   g. Enter the name of your department (such as "Editorial")
   h. Enter the fully qualified domain name of the server (such as "sambaserver.sambabook.com")
   i. Enter the email address of the administrator (such as "root@sambaserver.sambabook.com ")
9. The SSLeay program will create the CA database where you specified.

Creating A Key Pair

Creating a key pair can be done in two ways. You can use either **genrsa** for RSA keys or **gendsa** for DSA keys. To generate an RSA key with 1,024 bits written to the keypair.pem file, use the command shown here:

```
ssleay genrsa -des3 1024 > keypair.pem
```

The program will prompt you to enter a password phrase twice to protect the key pair. If no password phrase is required, remove the **-des3** parameter from the command.

The **genrsa** program defaults to a key size of 512 bits, although you might want to use an alternate length. The password phrase need not exist but should be used to maintain additional security. Do not forget to record this phrase elsewhere. To remove the password phrase for a key pair, use the following command:

```
ssleay rsa -in oldkeypair.pem -out newkeypair.pem
```

To replace the password phrase, use this command:

```
ssleay rsa -des3 -in oldkeypair.pem -out newkeypair.pem
```

Generating The Certificates For The Hosts

First generate the key pair for the required host, as was done previously, with the name identifying the host. Using the key pair, generate a Certificate Signing Request (CSR) by issuing the following command:

```
ssleay req -new - key hostkeypair.pem -out host-csr.pem
```

Here, **hostkeypair** and **host-csr** are named for the host as appropriate. This command will prompt you for all the information necessary to identify the host that requires a certificate. The fully qualified domain name or common name is the most important entry here.

Using The CA To Sign The Certificates

The CSR generated previously will need to be signed by your CA. To do this, issue the following command:

```
ssleay ca -policy <the policy you defined> -days <number of days>
 -infiles <host-csr.pem > host-cert.pem
```

The certificate for that host is now in the host-cert.pem file. The private key for that host is in the hostkeypair.pem file. These files need to be transferred to the host and will be installed into the /usr/local/ssl/certs file or whatever location has been specified for them. These files should be named to differentiate between the different hosts. The host applications that require a certificate to use the server should now be configured to use that certificate.

Configuring SSL For A Samba Host

To make use of SSL, you need to configure the server to use this added level of security. If you do not configure the server, Samba will operate as before without the added level of security. The smb.conf file has a number of extra parameters available that relate to SSL support. These are listed in Table 11.4.

Table 11.4 SSL parameters in the smb.conf file.

Parameter	Description
ssl	This variable enables or disables the entire SSL mode. When SSL is compiled into the Samba executables, this parameter defaults to no, which means that the SSL-enabled Samba behaves exactly like the non-SSL Samba. To enable SSL support, set this parameter to yes. The other parameters, **ssl hosts** and **ssl hosts resign**, will then determine whether an SSL connection is needed.
ssl CA certdir	The description reads almost directly from the parameter. This is the default directory for the CA certificates from all the sites that you want to trust. There is no default value. This parameter should not be set at the same time as **ssl CA certfile**.
ssl CA certfile	This parameter is set in the [global] section and specifies the file containing all the CA certificates. This file contains all the CA certificates concatenated into one file. This parameter should not be set at the same time as **ssl CA certdir**. The default is /usr/local/ssl/certs/trustedCAs.pem.
ssl client cert	When using **smbclient**, the certificate in this file is used, if it exists. It is needed if the server requires a client certificate. The default is /usr/local/ssl/certs/smbclient.pem.
ssl client key	When using **smbclient**, this is the location of the private key. This parameter should be set only if the client requires a certificate. The default is /usr/local/ssl/private/smbclient.pem.
ssl server cert	This parameter is set in the [global] section, and the value is the file that contains the server's certificate. To operate SSL, the server must have a valid CA certificate. The file may also contain the server's private key. This parameter defaults to an empty value.
ssl server key	This parameter is set in the [global] section, and the value is the file that contains the private key of the server. If this variable is not defined, the key is looked up in the certificate file specified under the ssl server cert parameter. To operate SSL, the server must have a private key, and the certificate must match this private key. This parameter defaults to an empty value.
ssl hosts	This parameter is set in the [global] section, and the value indicates the hosts (by IP address, IP address range, net group, or name) that will be forced into SSL mode. If no hosts are defined, Samba will allow only SSL connections, except to those hosts listed in the **ssl hosts resign** parameter. This parameter defaults to an empty string, requiring all hosts to use SSL mode.
ssl hosts resign	This parameter is set in the [global] section, and the value defines which hosts will not be forced into SSL mode. If no hosts are defined, Samba will allow only SSL connections. This parameter defaults to an empty string, removing no hosts from SSL mode.

(continued)

***Table 11.4 SSL parameters in the smb.conf file* (continued).**

Parameter	Description
ssl version	This parameter is set in the [global] section, and the value defines the versions of the SSL protocol that will be used. "ssl2or3" allows dynamic negotiation of SSL version 2 or 3, "ssl2" results in SSL version 2, and "ssl3" results in SSL version 3. A new development value of "tls1" results in TLS version 1. The Samba documentation with the distribution indicates that TLS (Transport Layer Security) is the new standard for SSL. This value defaults to **ssl2or3**.
ssl require server cert	This parameter is set in the [global] section and specifies whether **smbclient** requests a certificate from the server. The default is **no**. If a certificate is requested, the values for **ssl CA certdir** or **ssl CA certfile** on the client become relevant.
ssl require client cert	This parameter is set in the [global] section and specifies whether client hosts will be requested to present valid certificates. The default is **no** if the client hosts do not require a certificate. If a certificate is requested, the values for **ssl CA certdir** and **ssl CA certfile** on the server become relevant. Any connection that either does not or cannot present a valid client certificate on request is terminated.
ssl compatibility	This parameter is set in the [global] section and defines whether SSLeay should be configured for bug compatibility with other SSL implementations. Currently, no other clients with SSL implementations other than SSLeay exist. The default is **no**.

Using **sslproxy** With Non-SSL-Enabled Hosts

If you are unable to use **smbclient** or some other SSL-enabled client, **sslproxy** might enable a client to connect to an SSL-enabled server. The **sslproxy** operates by providing a connection to an SSL-enabled host for the non-SSL-enabled host. The use of **sslproxy** will allow operation with an SSL-enabled host, and the proxy may be installed on the client, the SSL-enabled host, or some third SSL-enabled host. The **sslproxy** is written by Christian Starkjohan and is available under the GPL license from **www.obdev.at/Products**. It is source code and can be installed under both Unix and NT.

Using External Protection (Firewall Operation)

Outside of the methods available to secure any Samba installation using software encryption or the smb.conf access configurations, one of the most secure and resilient methods makes use of a firewall. Many different kinds of firewalls are available, and Appendix B discusses some relevant texts and possible alternatives. One that might be worth considerable investigation involves TIS Firewall Toolkit. The **www.tis.com** Web site contains all necessary details on obtaining and using TIS Firewall Toolkit.

However, if you want to stick to a native Linux solution, without using software that's not available with a Linux distribution, two options are available. In both cases, these involve the filtering of all network traffic through the firewall on the basis of the IP addresses and the ports or services required. This approach is known as a *simple IP filtering firewall.* No user security is involved, and the firewall methodology assumes that the trusted hosts are running secure operating systems. This is by no means the most secure option, but I have found it acceptable in use in several circumstances.

Creating A Firewall For Use With Samba

The two options are basically the same, but they use slightly different syntax and programs. The programs are **ipfwadm** and **ipchains**, both of which forward IP (and in some cases IPX) traffic on the basis of rules that establish how the firewall operates. The method is fairly straightforward but does involve the compilation of the Linux kernel to act as a firewall with IP forwarding enabled.

The correct kernel options for IP firewalling using either **ipfwadm** or **ipchains** are listed in the Linux Firewalling-HOWTO, the IPCHAINS-HOWTO or the IPMASQUERADING-HOWTO. The options that are required might include the following:

- CONFIG_EXPERIMENTAL
- CONFIG_FIREWALL
- CONFIG_IP_FIREWALL
- CONFIG_IP_FIREWALL_CHAINS
- CONFIG_MODULES
- CONFIG_NET
- CONFIG_INET
- CONFIG_IP_FORWARD
- CONFIG_IP_MASQUERADE
- CONFIG_IP_MASQUERADE_IPAUTOFW
- CONFIG_IP_MASQUERADE_ICMP
- CONFIG_IP_ALWAYS_DEFRAG
- CONFIG_DUMMY

The Linux documentation for your kernel and **ipfwadm** or **ipchains** program will need to be consulted for the appropriate options to choose.

After the kernel has been configured and a new version compiled that includes the necessary support, the next stage is to establish the network connections to be used and then to set up the rules for the firewall operation.

Here, I provide an example of a firewall where a Linux host spans two networks, both involving "real" Internet IP addresses. This method is known as a *dual-homed host* and is just one possible configuration. Appendix B contains several references that show alternatives. Several hosts are external to the firewall and require access to one or more of the SMB/CIFS; other servers are inside the firewall. Likewise, several hosts are inside the firewall. These hosts require access to external hosts and services. Figure 11.1 shows the network configuration involved.

Packet Filtering Basics

All traffic through a network is sent in the form of packets. For example, downloading this package (say it's 50K long) might cause you to receive 36 or so packets of, say, 1,460 bytes each.

The start of each packet says where it's going, where it came from, the type of the packet, and other administrative details. This start of the packet is called the *header*. The rest of the packet, containing the actual data being transmitted, is usually called the *body*.

Some protocols, such as TCP/IP, which is used for Web traffic, mail, and remote logins, use the concept of a "connection." Before any packets with actual data are sent, various set-up packets (with special headers) are exchanged saying, "I want to connect," "OK," and "Thanks." Normal packets are then exchanged.

A packet filter is a piece of software that looks at the header of packets as they pass through and decides the fate of the entire packet on the basis of the information contained in the header. It might decide to deny the packet (discard the packet as if it had never received it), accept the packet (let the packet go through), or reject the packet (like denying it but telling the source of the packet that it has done so).

In Linux, packet filtering can be optionally built into the kernel. A few trickier things can be done with packets, but the general principle of looking at the headers and deciding the fate of the packet is still there.

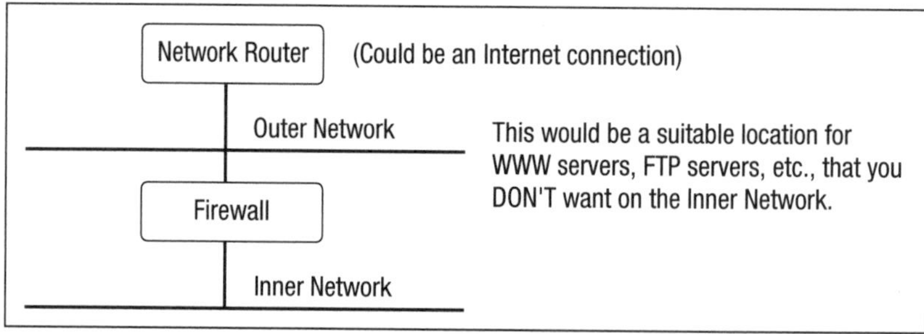

Figure 11.1 Firewall network configuration.

For the sample firewall shown in Figure 11.1, the kernel options were the following:

- CONFIG_EXPERIMENTAL
- CONFIG_MODULES
- CONFIG_NET
- CONFIG_FIREWALL
- CONFIG_INET
- CONFIG_IP_FORWARD
- CONFIG_IP_FIREWALL
- CONFIG_IP_ALWAYS_DEFRAG
- CONFIG_DUMMY

The firewall contained two Ethernet cards (NE2000 in this case), and these are enabled within the conf.modules file as shown here:

```
alias eth0 ne
alias eth1 ne
options ne io=0x300,0x220 irq=4,5
```

Running the script shown in Listing 11.4 as part of the startup process then configures the firewall. This script is a replacement for the standard **network** script in a Red Hat 5.2 installation.

Listing 11.4 The firewall configuration script.

```
#!/bin/sh -x
exec 1> /tmp/fw.out 2> /tmp/fw.err
# Activate the networking in a firewall configuration

[ -f /etc/sysconfig/network ] || exit 0
. /etc/sysconfig/network
[ ${NETWORKING} = "yes" ] || exit 0

[ -f /sbin/ifconfig ] || exit 0
IFCONFIG='/sbin/ifconfig'

[ -f /sbin/route ] || exit 0
ROUTE='/sbin/route'

[ -f /sbin/ipfwadm ] || exit 0
IPFWADM='/sbin/ipfwadm'
```

```
# Ethernet interfaces:
# eth0 faces outwards to the hostile exterior
# eth1 faces inwards to the protected interior
# ETH0 and ETH1 specify MAC addresses
# The lines will need to be changed if the ethernet cards are replaced
ETH0='00:xx:yy:aa:bb:cc'
ETH1='00:zz:ff:ee:bb:aa'

# Internet interfaces:
# Both interfaces will have the same IP address
# aaa.bbb.ccc.ddd replaces the real IP address in use
# substitute in your own
ADDR='aaa.bbb.ccc.ddd'
BCAST='aaa.bbb.ccc.255'
NMASK='255.255.255.0'
NWORK='aaa.bbb.ccc.0'
ROUTER='aaa.bbb.ccc.254'

# Load in the sets of trusted and untrusted systems
# from files in a directory.  Specify the filenames
# containing the information here:
FWDIR=/etc/fwconfig
[ -d ${FWDIR} ] || exit 0

case "$1" in
  start)

  # Interfaces
  ${IFCONFIG} lo inet 127.0.0.1 broadcast 127.255.255.255 netmask 255.0.0.0
  ${IFCONFIG} eth0 ${ADDR} netmask ${NMASK} broadcast ${BCAST}
  ${IFCONFIG} eth1 ${ADDR} netmask ${NMASK} broadcast ${BCAST}

  # Basic routing
  ${ROUTE} add -net ${NWORK} netmask ${NMASK} dev eth0
  ${ROUTE} add default gw ${ROUTER} dev eth0

  # Routing and proxyarping for systems within the firewall
  # The set of systems inside the firewall that are allowed out is
  # in the file internal_trusted_systems
  INSIDE='cat ${FWDIR}/internal_trusted_systems'
  for host in ${INSIDE}
  do
    # Access the system through eth1 (not the default interface)
    ${ROUTE} add -host ${host} dev eth1
    # Proxyarp on eth0
```

```
  arp -s -i eth0 ${host} ${ETH0} pub
done

# Routing and proxyarping for systems outside the firewall
# on the local subnet
# The set of all systems outside the firewall on the local subnet is
# stored in the file external_local_systems
OUTSIDE='cat ${FWDIR}/external_local_systems'
for host in ${OUTSIDE}
do
  # Systems are accessed by eth0 (the default interface) so no call to
  # route is needed.
  # Proxyarp on eth1
  arp -s -i eth1 ${host} ${ETH1} pub
done


# Now configure the firewall

# (1) Do not forward any packets unless overridden
#     but allow established TCP connections to survive.
ipfwadm -F -p deny
ipfwadm -F -a accept -P tcp -k

# (2) Systems in internal_trusted_systems are allowed to send out packets
for host in ${INSIDE}
do
  ipfwadm -F -a accept -S ${host}/32
done

# (3) Allow contact with the DNS ports of the external DNS servers
#     listed in external_dns_servers.
#     Port 53 is used for DNS (UDP and TCP)
DNSSVRS='cat ${FWDIR}/external_dns_servers'
for host in ${DNSSVRS}
do
  ipfwadm -F -P tcp -a accept -S ${host}/32 53
  ipfwadm -F -P tcp -a accept -D ${host}/32 53
  ipfwadm -F -P udp -a accept -S ${host}/32 53
  ipfwadm -F -P udp -a accept -D ${host}/32 53
done

# (4) Allow contact with the NTP ports of the external NTP servers
#     listed in external_ntp_servers.
#     Port 123 is used for NTP (UDP and TCP)
NTPSVRS='cat ${FWDIR}/external_ntp_servers'
```

11. Samba Security

```
for host in ${NTPSVRS}
do
  ipfwadm -F -P tcp -a accept -S ${host}/32 123
  ipfwadm -F -P tcp -a accept -D ${host}/32 123
  ipfwadm -F -P udp -a accept -S ${host}/32 123
  ipfwadm -F -P udp -a accept -D ${host}/32 123
done

# (5) Allow incoming telnet from the systems in external_telnet_systems
#     telnetd resides on TCP port 23
TELNET='cat ${FWDIR}/external_telnet_systems'
for host in ${TELNET}
do
  ipfwadm -F -a accept -P tcp -S ${host}/32 -D 0.0.0.0/0 23
  ipfwadm -F -a accept -P icmp -S ${host}/32 -D 0.0.0.0/0
done

# (6) Allow incoming SMB from systems in external_smb_systems
#     The complete netbios/smb protocol requires three ports
SMB='cat ${FWDIR}/external_smb_systems'
for host in ${SMB}
do
  ipfwadm -F -a accept -P tcp -S ${host}/32 -D 0.0.0.0/0 137
  ipfwadm -F -a accept -P udp -S ${host}/32 -D 0.0.0.0/0 137
  ipfwadm -F -a accept -P tcp -S ${host}/32 -D 0.0.0.0/0 138
  ipfwadm -F -a accept -P udp -S ${host}/32 -D 0.0.0.0/0 138
  ipfwadm -F -a accept -P tcp -S ${host}/32 -D 0.0.0.0/0 139
done

# (7) Allow incoming HTTP from systems in external_http_systems
#     http is on port 80.
HTTP='cat ${FWDIR}/external_http_systems'
for host in ${HTTP}
do
  ipfwadm -F -a accept -P tcp -S ${host}/32 -D 0.0.0.0/0 80
done

# (8) Allow SNMP management of systems in external_snmp_systems
#     from within the firewall
#     snmp is on port 161
#     NB This does not cover SNMP traps which are on 162
SNMP='cat ${FWDIR}/external_snmp_systems'
for host in ${SNMP}
do
  ipfwadm -F -a accept -P udp -S ${host}/32 -D 0.0.0.0/0 161
```

```
    ipfwadm -F -a accept -P udp -D ${host}/32 161 -S 0.0.0.0/0
  done

# (9) Allow Oracle connections from systems in external_oracle_systems
  #     Oracle is on TCP 1521 TCP 1525
  ORACLE='cat ${FWDIR}/external_oracle_systems'
  for host in ${ORACLE}
  do
    ipfwadm -F -a accept -P tcp -S ${host}/32 -D 0.0.0.0/0 1521
    ipfwadm -F -a accept -P tcp -S ${host}/32 -D 0.0.0.0/0 1526
  done


  # Register networking
  touch /var/lock/subsys/network
  ;;
  stop)
    # Turn off routing
    ${ROUTE} delete default gw ${ROUTER} eth0
    ${ROUTE} delete -net ${NWORK} netmask ${NMASK} eth0

    # Turn off the interfaces
    ${IFCONFIG} eth1 down
    ${IFCONFIG} eth0 down
    ${IFCONFIG} lo down

    # Deregister networking
    rm /var/lock/subsys/network
  ;;
esac
```

A cron job was established that reboots the server each night and thus kills any daemons that might be running. It also shuts down and starts up the networking at 1 A.M. and 7 A.M. every day. This is shown in the script in Listing 11.5.

Listing 11.5 The cron job script.

```
SHELL=/bin/bash
PATH=/sbin:/bin:/usr/sbin:/usr/bin
MAILTO=root

# Run any at jobs every minute
# * * * * * root [ -x /usr/sbin/atrun ] && /usr/sbin/atrun

# run-parts
01 * * * * root run-parts /etc/cron.hourly
```

```
02 1 * * * root run-parts /etc/cron.daily
02 2 * * 0 root run-parts /etc/cron.weekly
02 3 1 * * root run-parts /etc/cron.monthly

# Remove /tmp, /var/tmp files not accessed in 10 days (240 hours)
41 02 * * * root /usr/sbin/tmpwatch 240 /tmp /var/tmp

# Remove formatted man pages not accessed in 10 days
# To save space
39 02 * * * root /usr/sbin/tmpwatch 240 /var/catman/cat?

# Reboot every morning at 00:15
15 0 * * * root /sbin/reboot
#This enables the firewall IP files to be loaded daily

# Archives off all the directories to /misc (second HDD)
# every morning at 01:00
0 1 * * * root tar cvf - /lib/* | gzip -9 > /misc/lib.tgz
0 1 * * * root tar cvf - /etc/* | gzip -9 > /misc/etc.tgz
0 1 * * * root tar cvf - /bin/* | gzip -9 > /misc/bin.tgz
0 1 * * * root tar cvf - /home/* | gzip -9 > /misc/home.tgz
0 1 * * * root tar cvf - /usr/* | gzip -9 > /misc/usr.tgz
0 1 * * * root tar cvf - /var/* | gzip -9 > /misc/var.tgz
0 1 * * * root tar cvf - /root/* | gzip -9 > /misc/root.tgz
0 1 * * * root tar cvf - /sbin/* | gzip -9 > /misc/sbin.tgz

# Shutdown both ethernet cards at 1:00am
#0 1 * * * root /etc/rc.d/init.d/network stop

# Startup both ethernet cards and the firewall at 7:00am
#0 7 * * * root /etc/rc.d/init.d/network start
#at this point you could add a mail to root system to inform of the
#successful firewall startup or simply print the information to a log
```

This firewall configuration script makes use of several external files that list IP addresses of the trusted systems for that specific service. One of these files is external_smb_systems, which simply contains the IP addresses of the external hosts that require access to SMB/CIFS hosts inside the firewall. These IP addresses are read into the firewall script at the appropriate moment.

In the initial incarnation of this configuration, the IP files were maintained by a network administrator and FTP copied in ASCII to the firewall when any changes were required. The firewall automatically rebooted at 1 A.M. every day, thus automatically adding or removing new hosts as required. An alternative mode of operation might better suit your needs.

This type of firewall is only as secure as the host you are running. In this case, the Linux server has just about every possible service and package that is not required either removed or disabled in some form. On setup, the network script writes to two files that help in the diagnosis of the firewall. These are fw.out, which reads as the configuration output, and fw.err, which reports any errors. The cron jobs were added later and aided in both maintenance and security.

The latest Linux Red Hat version 6 also has an option to use **ipchains** instead of **ipfwadm**. The previous configuration will change when using **ipchains**, and a table for converting **ipchains** to **ipfwadm** is available in the IPCHAINS-HOWTO, a copy of which is reproduced here as Table 11.5.

Table 11.5 ipchains-to-ipfwadm conversion.

Ipfwadm Option	ipchains Option	Notes
-A *[both]*	-N *acct*	Creates an "acct" chain
& -I 1 input -j *acct*	Have output and input	
& -I 1 output -j *acct*	Packets traverse it	
& *acct*		
-A in	input	A rule with no target.
-A out	output	A rule with no target.
-F	forward	Use this as **[chain]**.
-I	input	Use this as **[chain]**.
-O	output	Use this as **[chain]**.
-M -l	-M -L	
-M -s	-M -S	
-a policy	-A [chain] -j POLICY	See **-r** and **-m**.
-d policy	-D [chain] -j POLICY	See **-r** and **-m**.
-i policy	-I 1 [chain] -j POLICY	See **-r** and **-m**.
-l	-L	
-z	-Z	
-f	-F	
-p	-P	
-c	-C	
-P	-p	
-S	-s	Takes only one port or range, not multiples.
-D	-d	Takes only one port or range, not multiples.

(continued)

Table 11.5 ipchains-to-ipfwadm conversion (continued).

Ipfwadm Option	ipchains Option	Notes
-V	**<none>**	Use **-i [name]**.
-W	**-i**	
-b	**-b**	Now actually makes two rules.
-e	**-v**	
-k	**! -y**	Works only if **-p tcp** is also specified.
-m	**-j MASQ**	
-n	**-n**	
-o	**-l**	
-r [redirpt]	**-j REDIRECT [redirpt]**	
-t	**-t**	
-v	**-v**	
-x	**-x**	
-y	**-y**	Works only if **-p tcp** is also specified.

Examples of translated **ipfwadm** commands are shown in Table 11.6.

In either case, the use of **ipfwadm** or **ipchains** requires a careful study and understanding of the options and syntax of both. The Linux HOWTOs for both are included on this book's CD-ROM under /docs with all the other Linux HOWTOs.

Sample copies of the scripts under either **ipfwadm** or **ipchains** can be found on this book's CD-ROM under /firewall/scripts.

An alternative type of Linux-based firewall that relies on free software can be found in the TIS Firewall Toolkit that can be found at **www.tis.com** or the SOCKS proxy. Details of both are available from the sources given in Appendix B.

Any serious inclusion of a firewall into a network requires much more information than is possible to include here, but I hope that this is sufficient to get you started.

Table 11.6 Old vs. new ipfwadm commands.

Old	New
ipfwadm -F -p deny	**ipchains -P forward DENY**
ipfwadm -F -a m -S 192.168.0.0/24 -D 0.0.0.0/0	**ipchains -A forward -j MASQ -s 192.168.0.0/24 -d 0.0.0.0/0**
ipfwadm -I -a accept -V 10.1.2.1 -S 10.0.0.0/8 -D 0.0.0.0/0	**ipchains -A input -j ACCEPT -i eth0 -s 10.0.0.0/8 -d 0.0.0.0/0**

Chapter 12

Troubleshooting Samba

In Depth

The Samba code is written by a diverse group of programmers and during its development is reviewed by many users and other programmers on a daily basis. Thus, in normal use you should not find any errors in the programs themselves. However, if you do find errors, several Samba-related newsgroups are available, and the samba-technical newsgroup is the place for reporting bugs. Appendix A includes details of these.

Configuring Samba, especially with the new Web-based interfaces (including SWAT, which comes with the distribution), is now extremely easy to do. The Samba distribution comes with a text on diagnosing problems, the details of which are summarized here. In addition, some of the more (and the less) common problems that I have experienced are listed along with their solutions.

This chapter will allow you to diagnose and solve most Samba-related issues; however, if all else fails, increase Samba's debug log levels to between 3 and 10 and/or run a packet trace program, such as **tcpdump** or **netmon**, and look for any error reports. Then, if you are still stuck, take a look at the news lists for similar problems and read all the Samba distribution documents again. If that still does not help, try posting a problem report to one of the technical Samba email lists.

The information that should be available before posting to the Samba lists should include the following:

- The version of the Samba software being used. If the Samba executable was compiled from a CVS source, you should include when you last checked out the main code via CVS.
- The operating system and version of the server on which you are running Samba.
- The sections of your smb.conf file that are involved with the error, at least the options in [global] and any service-level parameter sections.
- Partial log files written at a debug level of at least 20. Do not send the entire log, only enough to give the context of the error messages.
- If you have a complete netmon trace (from the opening of the pipe to the error), you can send the *.CAP file as well.
- Details of any error messages' output.
- A description of the error.

Immediate Solutions

Looking In The Samba Distribution Files

In the Samba distribution, the /docs directory contains a lot of information regarding the use and diagnosis of Samba, and considerable time and effort have gone into creating the contents. The bulk of documentation is available in text, in HTML format, and as Yodldocs. You will find more information on the readers of the various document formats in Appendix A.

The docs directory for the 2.0.4b distribution contents is shown in Listing 12.1.

Listing 12.1 The docs directory.

```
Volume in drive D has no label. Volume Serial Number is CC63-43E1
Directory of D:\Samba post SF\CDROM\distributions\samba-2.0.4b\DOCS
07/04/99  09:50a        <DIR>          .
07/04/99  09:50a        <DIR>          ..
11/23/98  10:11p                 5,917 THANKS
02/27/99  09:36p                 5,721 announce
07/04/99  09:50a        <DIR>          faq
10/29/98  01:00a                10,867 history
07/04/99  09:50a        <DIR>          htmldocs
07/04/99  09:50a        <DIR>          manpages
02/14/99  02:35a                   777 NT4-Locking.reg
08/21/97  11:51a                   303 NT4_PlainPassword.reg
11/23/98  10:11p                   986 samba.lsm
07/04/99  09:50a        <DIR>          textdocs
08/21/97  12:28p                   122 Win95_PlainPassword.reg
02/14/99  02:39a                   122 Win98_PlainPassword.reg
02/14/99  02:50a                   190 Win9X-CacheHandling.reg
07/04/99  09:50a        <DIR>          yodldocs
              16 File(s)         25,005 bytes
                             73,498,624 bytes free
```

The textdocs directory contents are shown in Listing 12.2.

Listing 12.2 The textdocs directory.

```
Volume in drive D has no label. Volume Serial Number is CC63-43E1

 Directory of D:\Samba post SF\CDROM\distributions\samba-
 2.0.4b\DOCS\TEXTDOCS
```

```
07/04/99  09:50a        <DIR>          .
07/04/99  09:50a        <DIR>          ..
11/23/98  10:11p                 3,154 PROJECTS
05/20/99  01:33a                 2,238 Application_Serving.txt
05/20/99  01:33a                10,092 BROWSING-Config.txt
05/20/99  01:33a                25,692 BROWSING.txt
05/20/99  01:33a                 5,643 BUGS.txt
05/20/99  01:33a                49,489 cifsntdomain.txt
05/20/99  01:33a                   831 CRLF-LF-Conversions.txt
05/20/99  01:33a                 3,935 CVS_ACCESS.txt
05/20/99  01:33a                 8,613 DHCP-Server-Configuration.txt
05/20/99  01:33a                12,389 DIAGNOSIS.txt
05/20/99  01:33a                 1,789 DNIX.txt
05/20/99  01:33a                17,916 DOMAIN.txt
05/20/99  01:33a                 6,001 DOMAIN_CONTROL.txt
05/20/99  01:33a                 6,010 DOMAIN_MEMBER.txt
05/20/99  01:33a                13,739 ENCRYPTION.txt
05/20/99  01:33a                 6,669 Faxing.txt
05/20/99  01:33a                 2,939 File-Cacheing.txt
05/20/99  01:33a                 2,918 GOTCHAS.txt
05/20/99  01:33a                 7,927 HINTS.txt
06/29/97  12:29a                   993 INSTALL.sambatar
05/20/99  01:33a                 1,148 Macintosh_Clients.txt
05/20/99  01:33a                   138 MIRRORS.txt
05/20/99  01:33a                 7,489 NetBIOS.txt
05/20/99  01:33a                 2,630 NTDOMAIN.txt
05/20/99  01:33a                11,005 NT_Security.txt
05/20/99  01:33a                 2,797 OS2-Client-HOWTO.txt
05/20/99  01:33a                 2,030 Passwords.txt
05/20/99  01:33a                 8,278 PRINTER_DRIVER.txt
05/20/99  01:33a                 5,915 Printing.txt
05/20/99  01:33a                16,071 PROFILES.txt
06/29/97  12:29a                 2,765 README.DCEDFS
08/13/96  09:40a                 8,616 README.jis
06/29/97  12:29a                 1,175 README.sambatar
04/09/99  02:29p                 2,453 README.smbmount
05/20/99  01:33a                12,158 Recent-FAQs.txt
05/20/99  01:33a                 2,569 RoutedNetworks.txt
05/20/99  01:33a                   830 SCO.txt
05/20/99  01:33a                 5,408 security_level.txt
06/29/97  12:29a                 1,777 SMBTAR.notes
05/20/99  01:33a                12,810 Speed.txt
05/20/99  01:33a                 2,418 Speed2.txt
05/20/99  01:33a                19,610 SSLeay.txt
05/20/99  01:33a                   222 Support.txt
```

```
05/20/99  01:33a              4,158 Tracing.txt
05/20/99  01:33a             10,858 UNIX-SMB.txt
05/20/99  01:33a             13,127 UNIX_INSTALL.txt
05/20/99  01:33a              2,039 UNIX_SECURITY.txt
05/20/99  01:33a              3,083 Win95.txt
05/20/99  01:33a              4,676 WinNT.txt
07/20/99  03:04p                  0 dir.txt
              52 File(s)        357,230 bytes
                            73,465,856 bytes free
```


The Samba diagnosis.txt distribution file contains troubleshooting information that can help diagnose and treat problems with the Samba server. This file consists of a series of tests that can be performed on the Samba server to validate the installation and operation of the software. The results from this series of tests also provide details of the most likely problems and the possible causes of those problems and, most important, how to correct them.

If your Samba server runs through all the tests successfully without failing, it is reasonable to assume that the software is installed and that the Samba server currently has a working configuration, although this might not be the configuration that you require.

The tests should be followed in order, as each subsequent test might depend on functionality in the Samba server that should be present and that should have been proven by passing the previous test. The versions of these tests make the following assumptions:

- Version 2.0.0 or later of the Samba Suite is installed on the Samba server.
- The Samba server is called BIGSERVER.
- A PC called ACLIENT is used.
- A suitable network connection is present between the client and the server, and the PC is running Windows 95 or Windows NT (Workstation or Server) or Linux.

NOTE: *The procedures are similar for other types of clients.*

The BIGSERVER server includes a share that is publicly available in the Samba distribution called *tmp*. The entry for the tmp share in the smb.conf file is shown here:

```
[tmp]
comment = temporary files
path = /tmp
read only = yes
```

Note all the messages that are returned so that you can confirm that the Samba server is configured as you expect it to be. It is especially important to record any error messages that are returned.

If any error messages appear that include a comment that the server is being unfriendly (what pleasing messages are used!), you should check your network configuration and determine whether IP name resolution is configured correctly and whether the /etc/resolv.conf entries are correct. You should also confirm that your server's hostname is registered in the DNS or that a hosts file entry for it exists on the client.

If the network does not contain any DNS server, an error will occur if the **DNS proxy** parameter is set to anything other than **no**.

Running The Samba Tests

The distribution suggests that several tests be conducted, as described in the following sections.

Test 1: Checking The smb.conf File

The first test uses the testparm application and involves running the **testparm** program. The **testparm** program is run from the directory that holds the smb.conf file, providing it with the name of the configuration file. Listing 12.3 shows the result of running this command.

Listing 12.3 testparm smb.conf run on LINUXSERVER.

```
[root@linuxserver /root]# testparm /etc/smb.conf
Processing section "[homes]"
Processing section "[printers]"
Processing section "[tmp]"
Loaded services file OK.
Press enter to see a dump of your service definitions

# Global parameters
[global]
   workgroup = SAMBABOOK
   netbios name = BIGSERVER
   netbios aliases = sambaserver
   server string = %h %v
   interfaces =
   bind interfaces only = No
   security = SERVER
```

```
   encrypt passwords = Yes
   update encrypted = No
   allow trusted domains = Yes
   hosts equiv =
   min passwd length = 5
   map to guest = Never
   null passwords = No
   password server = adminserver
   smb passwd file = /etc/smbpasswd
   root directory = /
   passwd program = /bin/passwd
passwd chat = *old*password* %o\n *new*password* %n\n *new*password* %n\n
*changed*
   passwd chat debug = No
   username map =
   password level = 0
   username level = 0
   unix password sync = No
   restrict anonymous = No
   use rhosts = No
   log level = 2
   syslog = 1
   syslog only = No
   log file = /usr/local/samba/var/log.%m
   max log size = 50
   timestamp logs = Yes
   protocol = NT1
   read bmpx = No
   read raw = Yes
   write raw = Yes
   nt smb support = Yes
   nt pipe support = Yes
   nt acl support = Yes
   announce version = 4.2
   announce as = NT
   max mux = 50
   max xmit = 65535
   name resolve order = lmhosts host wins bcast
   max packet = 65535
   max ttl = 259200
   max wins ttl = 518400
   min wins ttl = 21600
   time server = Yes
   change notify timeout = 60
   deadtime = 0
```

```
getwd cache = Yes
keepalive = 300
lpq cache time = 10
max disk size = 0
max open files = 10000
read prediction = No
read size = 16384
shared mem size = 1048576
socket options = TCP_NODELAY
stat cache size = 50
load printers = Yes
printcap name = /etc/printcap
printer driver file = /etc/printers.def
strip dot = No
character set =
mangled stack = 50
coding system =
client code page = 850
stat cache = Yes
domain groups =
domain admin group =
domain guest group =
domain admin users =
domain guest users =
machine password timeout = 604800
add user script =
delete user script =
logon script =
logon path = \\%N\%U\profile
logon drive =
logon home = \\%N\%U
domain logons = No
os level = 17
lm announce = Auto
lm interval = 60
preferred master = No
local master = No
domain master = No
browse list = Yes
dns proxy = No
wins proxy = No
wins server =
wins support = No
kernel oplocks = Yes
ole locking compatibility = Yes
```

```
oplock break wait time = 10
smbrun = /usr/bin/smbrun
config file =
preload =
lock dir = /var/lock/samba
default service =
message command =
dfree command =
valid chars =
remote announce = 192.168.1.255
remote browse sync = 192.168.1.255
socket address = 0.0.0.0
homedir map =
time offset = 0
unix realname = No
NIS homedir = No
panic action =
comment =
path =
alternate permissions = No
revalidate = No
username =
guest account = nobody
invalid users =
valid users =
admin users =
read list =
write list =
force user =
force group =
read only = Yes
create mask = 0744
force create mode = 00
directory mask = 0755
force directory mode = 00
guest only = No
guest ok = No
only user = No
hosts allow = 192.168.1. 127.
hosts deny =
status = Yes
max connections = 0
min print space = 0
strict sync = No
sync always = No
print ok = No
```

```
postscript = No
printing = bsd
print command = lpr -r -P%p %s
lpq command = lpq -P%p
lprm command = lprm -P%p %j
lppause command =
lpresume command =
queuepause command =
queueresume command =
printer name =
printer driver = NULL
printer driver location =
default case = lower
case sensitive = No
preserve case = Yes
short preserve case = Yes
mangle case = No
mangling char = ~
hide dot files = Yes
delete veto files = No
veto files =
hide files =
veto oplock files =
map system = No
map hidden = No
map archive = Yes
mangled names = Yes
mangled map =
browseable = Yes
blocking locks = Yes
fake oplocks = No
locking = Yes
mangle locks = Yes
oplocks = Yes
oplock contention limit = 2
strict locking = No
share modes = Yes
copy =
include =
exec =
postexec =
root preexec =
root postexec =
available = Yes
volume =
fstype = NTFS
```

```
   set directory = No
   wide links = Yes
   follow symlinks = Yes
   dont descend =
   magic script =
   magic output =
   delete readonly = No
   dos filetimes = No
   dos filetime resolution = No
   fake directory create times = No

[homes]
   comment = Home Directories
   read only = No
   browseable = No

[printers]
   comment = All Printers
   path = /usr/spool/samba
   print ok = Yes

[tmp]
   comment = test
   path = /tmp
   read only = yes
 [root@linuxserver /root]#
```

You should inspect the output from this command for any errors. If you find any errors, the smb.conf configuration file should be modified either directly with a text editor or by using **SWAT**.

The default location for smb.conf is /usr/local/samba/lib, although it might also exist in /etc.

Test 2: Checking The Network Connection

The second test confirms the networking connection from the client to the server, and this is accomplished by running a **ping *servername*** at the client command prompt. Following a successful ping, repeat the operation in reverse with the command **ping *clientname***. This will confirm that networking connectivity exists between the client and the server and that the IP name resolution from the client is functioning as expected. If any other message appears, this indicates an underlying network problem, related either to hardware or TCP/IP configuration. If either of these produces an error, you will need to consult your network administrator to correct the problem.

A Host Not Found or similar message might indicate a problem in resolving the IP address from the hostname. This would indicate a problem with either the DNS software or the /etc/hosts file setup. Although it is not necessary to use DNS for Samba operation, it is advisable to have the appropriate hosts file entries.

The network that you are using might use a router or firewall between the server and the client or have some additional network configuration that precludes normal operation. If this is the case, you will need to seek assistance from your network administrator.

Test 3: Confirming That **smbd** Is Running

The third test starts to use some of the Samba client software to confirm that the Samba server program **smbd** is running.

The command **smbclient -L BIGSERVER -N** is run on the Samba server. If successful, a list of available shares should be returned. Listing 12.4 shows this in operation.

Listing 12.4 smbclient -L BIGSERVER -N.

```
[root@linuxserver /root]# smbclient -L bigserver -N
Added interface ip=192.168.1.4 bcast=192.168.1.255 nmask=255.255.255.0
Got a positive name query response from 192.168.1.4 ( 192.168.1.4 )
Domain=[SAMBABOOK] OS=[Unix] Server=[Samba 2.0.4b]

   Sharename      Type      Comment
   ---------      ----      -------
   printers       Printer   All Printers
   tmp            Disk      tmp
   IPC$           IPC       IPC Service (linuxserver 2.0.4b)
   hp             Printer   hp deskjet

   Server              Comment
   ---------           -------
   BIGSERVER           linuxserver 2.0.4b
   LINUXSERVER         linuxserver 2.0.4b

   Workgroup           Master
   ---------           -------
   SAMBABOOK           NTSERVER
[root@linuxserver /root]#
```

If the connection is not successful or a Bad Password message appears, it is possible that the Samba server has smb.conf settings that deny this connection by the **hosts allow**, **hosts deny**, or **valid users** parameters. The **guest account** might also be invalid. The **testparm** program should output the details of which account is the **guest account** and should be enabled, and/or the settings for the **hosts allow**, **hosts deny**, **valid users**, or **invalid users** parameters might need to be altered, disabled, or removed.

A Connection Refused reply usually indicates that an **smbd** server might not be running. Using either an inetd.conf or an rc.local entry starts the program, and the syntax of either could be incorrect. The entry in the inetd.conf file especially causes problems if the full path is not correctly specified. If you use an rc.local entry, thus running the program as a daemon, you should check that the program is running and that the appropriate port maintains a LISTEN state. Listing 12.5 shows the result of the confirmation that the daemon is running.

Listing 12.5 smbd -D and netbios-ssn post LISTEN confirmation.

```
[root@linuxserver /root]# ps -aux | grep smbd
root       365  0.0  2.4  1896   764  ?  S   Aug 14   0:01 smbd -D
root       400  0.0  3.5  3140  1108  ?  S   Aug 14   0:00 smbd -D
root      1566  0.0  3.1  3116   956  ?  S    04:11   0:00 smbd -D
root      1567  0.0  3.1  3116   964  ?  S    04:12   0:00 smbd -D
root      1568  0.0  3.1  3116   964  ?  S    04:12   0:00 smbd -D
root      1569  0.0  3.1  3116   964  ?  S    04:12   0:00 smbd -D
root      1570  0.0  3.1  3116   964  ?  S    04:12   0:00 smbd -D
root      1574  0.0  1.1   836   348  p0 S    04:15   0:00 grep smbd
[root@linuxserver /root]# netstat -a

Active Internet connections (including servers)
Proto Recv-Q Send-Q Local Address          Foreign Address        State
tcp        0    132 linuxserver.doma:telnet ntwdev02.domain:1525
ESTABLISHED
tcp        0      0 linuxserver:netbios-ssn ntwdev02.domain:1029
ESTABLISHED
tcp        0      0 *:netbios-ssn           *:*                   LISTEN
tcp        0      0 *:swat                  *:*                   LISTEN
udp        0      0 linuxserver:netbios-dgm *:*
udp        0      0 linuxserver.:netbios-ns *:*
udp        0      0 *:netbios-dgm           *:*
udp        0      0 *:netbios-ns            *:*
[root@linuxserver /root]#
```

You might also see a Session Request Failed error message if the server refuses a connection. If the Your Server Software Is Being Unfriendly message appears, the startup of the **smbd** program might have a syntax error, the command line parameters might be invalid, or another fatal problem might exist. The **smbd** program also requires that, on startup, the lock and log files must exist and be in a location that can be accessed by the server. The quickest way to confirm the correct file locations is to note the locations returned from the **testparm /etc/smb.conf** run in Test 2. If the lock files or log files do not exist, you should create them in the correct locations using **touch *filename*** and then restart the server programs.

The other reasons for refusing a session's request might involve some smb.conf parameters, the prime culprits being **hosts deny**, **hosts allow**, and **bind interfaces** only.

The values in the following example would cause a problem because any session requests would automatically utilize the loopback adapter address 127.0.0.1:

```
hosts deny = ALL
hosts allow = xxx.xxx.xxx.xxx/yy
bind interfaces only = Yes
```

To solve this problem, change these lines to the following code

```
hosts deny = ALL
hosts allow = xxx.xxx.xxx.xxx/yy 127.
```

The **bind interfaces only** parameter should not be used when the local services are required for name resolution when using **smbclient** or when the Samba password change facility is used. This feature, whereby **bind interfaces only** stops only local attachment to the loopback interface, is a possible alteration in Samba that might be expected in the future.

If another service has already started that used port 139, the **smbd** service will not be able to bind to it. Check the inetd.conf entries to see whether another service is already present—Digital Pathworks is one possibility.

The last option when a failure to Test 3 occurs is to check the networking configuration closely between the client and the server. An incorrect value for the network IP address or subnet mask are common mistakes, as these would affect the parameters that use these values directly or when creating services. Samba will note the attempted values in the log.nmb file.

Test 4: Confirming That **nmbd** Is Running

The fourth test starts to use the Samba client software for name resolution and name services.

When you run the command **nmblookup -B BIGSERVER __SAMBA__**, you should get the IP address of your Samba server back. This would indicate both that **nmbd** is correctly installed and that the nmblookup client program is operating correctly.

Any other result being returned might indicate that **nmbd** is not installed correctly. The **nmbd** program is started either as a daemon process or from the inetd service. The inetd service is controlled from the /etc/services and the /etc/inetd.conf configuration files. To run **nmbd** as a service from inetd, the program should have an entry in the inetd.conf file that a UDP service is running and listening at port 137.

However, this is a simple process. From the Samba lists, many **nmbd** problems have been identified as being caused by a misconfiguration of the inetd.conf entry. Check both the spelling of the entry and the path being used. The default might not necessarily be correct for the **nmbd** location. An alternative problem will manifest in a similar error if the Unix variant does not allow inetd configuration to include the passing of parameters at the startup of the service. In these cases, the solution is to include all the command line options and parameters as an executable script that is subsequently called from the inetd service.

Test 5: Confirming That Network Broadcasts Are Running

The fifth test runs a simple **nmblookup** to confirm that network broadcasts are working and that the same local network and subnet mask for the client and the server are being used. The command **nmblookup -B *clientname* '*'** should respond with the correct IP address of the ***clientname*** host if the server is operating and configured correctly. The following shows the output for this command:

```
nmblookup -B laptop '*'
Sending queries to 192.168.1.88
192.168.1.88 *<00>
[root@linuxserver /root]#
```

If any other message is returned, you need to confirm that the client software is configured correctly, that the host is not started, and that no syntax error has occurred in the ***clienthost*** name.

Test 6: Confirming The Network Broadcasts From The Samba Host

The sixth test involves confirming that the network broadcasts from the Samba host are functioning correctly. The command **nmblookup -d 2 '*''** will send a broadcast to the local network, resulting in the hosts on the local network responding. Listing 12.6 shows the response.

Listing 12.6 nmblookup response.

```
nmblookup -d 2 '*''
Added interface ip=192.168.1.4 bcast=192.168.1.255 nmask=255.255.255.0
Sending queries to 192.168.1.255
Got a positive name query response from 192.168.1.180 ( 192.168.1.180 )
Got a positive name query response from 192.168.1.3 ( 192.168.1.3 )
```

```
Got a positive name query response from 192.168.1.7 ( 192.168.1.7 )
Got a positive name query response from 192.168.1.10 ( 192.168.1.10 )
Got a positive name query response from 192.168.1.200 ( 192.168.1.200 )
Got a positive name query response from 192.168.1.88 ( 192.168.1.88 )
Got a positive name query response from 192.168.1.169 ( 192.168.1.169 )
Got a positive name query response from 192.168.1.4 ( 192.168.1.4 )
192.168.1.180 *<00>
192.168.1.3 *<00>
192.168.1.7 *<00>
192.168.1.10 *<00>
192.168.1.200 *<00>
192.168.1.88 *<00>
192.168.1.169 *<00>
192.168.1.4 *<00>
[root@linuxserver /root]#
```


This test is very similar to the previous test, but this test confirms that the Samba host is sending a broadcast to the local network using the default broadcast address. If no NetBIOS and TCP/IP hosts are present on the network, the other hosts should respond to this request. The response that is displayed might not include all the hosts on the network, as the Samba host will listen for responses for only a short time. The fact that this list of hosts is not complete is normal and should not be a cause for concern. The important result is a list of hosts in which a Got A Positive Name Query Response message is included.

If this does not give a similar result to the previous test, **nmblookup** is not correctly getting your broadcast address through its automatic mechanism. In this case, you should experiment with using the "interfaces" option in smb.conf to manually configure your IP address, broadcast, and netmask.

If your PC and server are not on the same subnet, you will need to use the **-B** option to set the broadcast address to that of the PC's subnet.

This test will probably fail if the host subnet mask or broadcast address is not correct.

Test 7: Confirming That A Share Can Be Accessed Using smbclient

The seventh test starts to look at the connection to a share on an SMB host. The client command **smbclient '\\BIGSERVER\TMP'** instructs the client host to attempt to access and open the TMP share on the BIGSERVER server. The response might vary, but a common response is to prompt the client for a password to be entered. The correct password to be entered might vary, but it should be something like the password of the corresponding Unix user account that is being used at the client. This is normal Samba behavior in which the currently logged-in username is sent to the host when a connection request is made. It is also possible for other **smbclient** options to attempt to create the client connection with an alternate user account using the **-U *accountname*** option, the syntax of which is to append this option to the end of the command line (see Chapter 3), as shown here:

```
smbclient //bigserver/tmp -Usomeuseraccountname
#The smbclient program has many options and it would also be possible
 to connect to the server adding the required password in the command
 line with the % macro as in
 'smbclient //bigserver/tmp -Usomeuseraccountname%password'
```

On completion of a successful session, when the password has been accepted, the **smbclient** "smb>" prompt should appear.

At this stage, any error message that appears should indicate a problem, and the message should provide a clue to the problem. Table 12.1 provides some options.

A connection to a share can fail if the value for the path parameter for the share is either not present or incorrect. This includes a share path that does not exist on the server.

If the server or an authentication server does not have a valid user account for the current session username, the connection can also fail.

When connected, the **smbclient** session will allow a number of commands to be executed (these were described in Chapter 3). The simple **help** command will return a list of the possible options.

Table 12.1 smbclient errors.

Error	Cause And Cure
invalid network name	The share being accessed is probably configured incorrectly or is not present.
bad password	A shadow password or similar system is present. The smbd server should be compiled with support for the system being used. If the password is mixed case, the smb.conf parameter for "password level" might not be set at a high enough level. If passwords are encrypted, it is possible that this option was not set in the smb.conf file. If encrypted passwords are used, the SMB encrypted password file smbpasswd should exist. Simply create it.

Test 8: Confirming That Shares Can Be Accessed By DOS Clients

The eighth test involves using a DOS-based client session to view the shares on a server. This confirms that the Samba server can be browsed. The DOS **net** command includes many options, and in this test the objective is to view the shares on a Samba server, as shown here:

```
C:\net view \\BIGSERVER
Shared resources at BIGSERVER
Sharename      Type      Comment
----------------------------------
tmp            Disk      /tmp
user           Disk      Home Directory
```

The response should return a list of the available shares on the Samba server as shown. Any other response might indicate a problem.

A Network Name Not Found or similar message is probably due to NetBIOS name resolution not working correctly. A problem with the **nmbd** service is the most likely cause. These errors can be corrected in one of the following ways:

- Correct any error in an **nmbd** installation (inetd, paths, and so on).
- Add the BIGSERVER IP server address to the local WINS server that is being used by the client.
- Configure Windows name resolution to use DNS on the client.
- Add the IP address of the Samba server BIGSERVER to the lmhosts file on the client.

An Invalid Network Name or Bad Password Error message might indicate a similar problem as in the previous tests. The **hosts allow** and **hosts deny** parameters especially might be relevant if used.

As mentioned previously, the currently logged-in username is used when attempting to create the session. The username and password should match exactly, or else an error will occur.

Sometimes a message similar to Specified Computer Is Not Receiving Requests might be seen. This is most likely due to a TCP/IP network connection not being available between the host and the Samba server. The result could be due to a routing problem, a firewall, or sometimes a missing hosts.allow file entry for your client or subnet.

Test 9: Confirming That Remote Shares Can Be Mounted

The ninth test involves mounting a share on a remote server. For this test, you need to run the **net use x: \\BIGSERVER\TMP** command. This should be followed with a request for a password, and the successful entry of the password will be followed by a message that reports the successful mounting of the share: Command Completed Successfully. If this message does not appear, it could be due to either an incorrect software install of the client PC or an error in the smb.conf configuration. The most likely parameter that can cause a problem in the smb.conf, if incorrect, is the **hosts allow** parameter.

Another option might be that the server is unable to determine which username the session is attempting to use to connect to the share as. The **user** parameter can be added to the [tmp] share section, and the value should be set to the username being used by the PC. If this proves successful, the smb.conf parameters that involve username mapping should be employed.

Test 10: Confirming That The Samba Server Can Be Browsed

The final test recommended in the Samba distribution documentation is to use Windows File Manager or Network Neighborhood to attempt to browse the shares on the server. Before this is possible, the server must appear in the browse list for the PC and the local workgroup in the local subnet. This would require that the Samba server workgroup coincides with the PC being used. (In fact, the Samba server default workgroup, MYGROUP, should appear in the local subnet browse lists, but it is easier to run this test if both are in the same workgroup.) When the server name appears in the local Network Neighborhood, it should be selected and the server opened. The list of shares should then be visible.

The use of Network Neighborhood to browse a network and the servers in it depends on the NetBIOS networking (discussed in Chapter 8) being present and properly configured.

If an Invalid Password error message appears, check to see whether the PC is running Windows NT. This message might appear if the client is running Windows NT and no password encryption is enabled on the Samba server and if the Samba server is in user-level security mode.

If this is the correct configuration, the smb.conf file parameters for the **security** and **password server** should be amended and the **encrypted passwords** parameter set to true.

Using Samba's Own Test Programs

Two test programs are included with the Samba distribution:

- **testparm**
- **testprns**

testparm

The **testparm** program will check the smb.conf configuration file of a Samba server and report on the configuration currently employed. The program is called at the command line, and a number of options are appended to the program execution. The syntax for the program is:

```
testparm [-s] [configfilename] [hostname hostIP]
```

The options are to use an alternative smb.conf file or to run the **testparm** program against another system. The results from using **testparm** will not guarantee that all the services contained in an smb.conf file will be available, but the output from **testparm** will list the services contained within the smb.conf file.

When **testparm** is called using a script, the **testparm** program will return an exit code of 1 if an error is evident in the smb.conf file; otherwise, it will return an exit code of 0. This allows scripts to be used to run **testparm**.

The command line options are the following:

- **-s**—If **testparm** is run without this option, the program will immediately prompt for a carriage return after the service names have been returned. The service definitions are then listed.
- ***configfilename***—This option checks the specified configuration file or else checks the default smb.conf file.
- ***hostname***—If you run the program with the ***hostname*** option, the test program will run through the service entries in the smb.conf file and determine whether the host specified has access to the services. The **testparm** program will examine the **hosts allow** and **hosts deny** parameters in the smb.conf file to determine whether the hostname with this IP address is allowed access to the smbd server. If this parameter is supplied, the ***hostIP*** parameter must also be supplied.
- ***hostIP***—This value is the IP address of the host specified in the hostname parameter. The **testparm** program will demand that the IP address be included when specifying a hostname.

testprns

The program will check the printer entries in the /etc/printcap file that might be included as services in the smb.conf file. The syntax for the program is:

```
testprns printername [printcapname]
```

The **testprns** program is noted as being somewhat simple in the documentation that accompanies the Samba distribution, so you are advised to specify the full pathname and file name for the appropriate printcap file.

The program will respond with a Printer Name <printername> Is Valid message if the given printer name was found in the specified printcap file. Otherwise, the Printer Name <printername> Is Not Valid massage will appear.

The command line options are the following:

- ***printername***—Specifies the printer entry. This is the first field for each record in the printcap file, the individual printer names, and the aliases that are included in the printcap file, separated by vertical bars (|).
- ***printcapname***—The full pathname and file name for the printcap file that is being checked against smbd for a printer name.

If the **testprns** program is called with no value for the printcap file, the program will attempt to access the printcap file that is specified at the compile time of the program. By default, this is /etc/printcap.

Troubleshooting Problems

In any normal operation, you should not see any problems with your Samba server. However, some issues appear to be more common than others. The following section discusses one of these problems.

Browsing Nonnetworked Computers Over A RAS Connection

This problem is not specific to Samba and is common in Windows networking. You will likely see this problem the most when a remote user is trying to log in to the network when at home or "on the road" and you are unable to transfer the requested document or whatever was left on the office server. You will also notice this problem when a remote office dials into a central office; perhaps you want to send a message to the remote office printer, and you find that the remote office PC is unavailable to the central office for browsing. This can be frustrating, as it can stop work dead in its tracks.

A major problem is one in which browsing is automatically disabled on the client that is acting as the RAS client. This is the default in Windows NT and 9x if no network connection other than RAS is present. This behavior is based on the assumption that people will call only from a nonnetworked computer to a networked computer and will not allow or need any networked computer to browse the nonnetworked computer.

The solution to this problem is:

1. Ensure that the Entire Network option in the Windows Network Control Panel|Remote Access|Configure|Advanced dialog box is selected.
2. Ensure that the remote computer is a member of the domain or workgroup of the main office.
3. In the Network Control Panel, add an adapter, the Microsoft loopback driver on the remote computer, or a network card and driver. If this remote PC is already part of a network, you should not have to do this. The loopback driver will fake a network connection and will present all the normal network application options at the client, but none of these will be active unless a RAS session is active.

Troubleshooting Domain Controller Issues

When you arrange for a Samba server to operate as a Windows domain controller, either as a Windows 9x or a full Windows NT domain controller, some complex problems can arise.

Using Windows 9x Profiles

If you have made the folders/files read-only on the Samba server, you will get errors from the Windows 9x machine on logon and logout as it attempts to merge the local and the remote profile. If any errors are reported by the Windows 9x machine, check the Unix file permissions and ownership rights on the profile directory contents on the Samba server. You will likely find that the problem is permissions related.

If you have problems creating user profiles, you can reset the user's local desktop cache, as shown in the following list. When this user logs in again, they will be told that they are logging in for the first time:

1. Instead of logging in under the [user, password, domain] dialog box, press Esc.
2. Run the regedit.exe program and look in HKEY_LOCAL_MACHINE\Windows\CurrentVersion\ProfileList. You will find an entry called

ProfilePath for each user. Note the contents of this key (likely to be c:\windows\profiles\username) and then delete the key ProfilePath for the required user. Exit the Registry Editor.

***WARNING!** Before deleting the contents of the directory listed in the ProfilePath, ask the users whether they have any important files stored on their desktops or in their Start menus. When you delete the contents of the directory ProfilePath (making a backup if any of the files are needed), you will remove the local (read-only hidden system file) user.DAT in their profile directories as well as the local desktop, nethood, Start menu, and programs folders.*

3. Search for the user's .PWL password-caching file in the c:\windows directory and delete it.
4. Log off the Windows 95 client.
5. Check the contents of the profile path (see Step 2) and delete the user.DAT or user.MAN file for the user, making a backup if required.

If you have access to an NT server, first set up roaming profiles and/or netlogons on the NT server. Make a packet trace or examine the sample packet traces provided with NT Server and see what the differences are with the equivalent Samba trace.

No Domain Server Is Available To Validate Your Password

If the No Domain Server Is Available To Validate Your Password message appears, the problem is that the Windows 9x PC was not able to locate or resolve the domain master browser or the owner of the domain name <1b> NetBIOS name. This means that there was no netlogon service to connect to.

The Samba domain controller could be on a different subnet to the Windows 9x PC and the NetBIOS broadcasts are not being sent on the local subnet. In this case, the Windows 9x PC client should be configured to use the WINS server where the Samba 9x domain controller has been able to register its NetBIOS name.

The first possibility is that, although configured to be the domain master browser, the server was not able to register the domain name <1b> successfully. (Chapter 8 provided details of the setup of the different master browsers on a network.) The Samba domain controller needs to be the domain master browser for the domain; however, it is possible that another host registered the name and wins any NetBIOS election. Only one domain master browser should exist on a network. To determine which host is acting as the domain master browser, the **nmblookup** program from the Samba distribution can be used to identify the IP address of the host registered with the domain name <1b> NetBIOS name. Listings 12.7 and 12.8 show the response to **nmblookup** where a domain controller is present and not present, respectively. In this case, the host 192.168.1.88 has registered the name, and the configuration of the smb.conf file was incorrect.

Listing 12.7 Successful nmblookup for SAMBABOOK domain controller.

```
$nmblookup SAMBABOOK#1b
Sending queries to 192.168.1.255
192.168.1.88 SAMBABOOK<1b>
```

Listing 12.8 Unsuccessful nmblookup for SAMBABOOK domain controller.

```
[root@linuxserver /root]# nmblookup sambabook#1b
Sending queries to 192.168.1.255
name_query failed to find name sambabook
[root@linuxserver /root]#
```


Listing 12.8 could be the response when no host has yet been configured to be the domain master browser or is not in this subnet when no WINS server available.

On the host that is the intended domain master browser, a quick check of the nmbd log for the server is advisable. This file is located in /var/log/samba/log.nmb for a standard Red Hat install or /usr/local/samba/log/log.nmb otherwise. The file contents will appear as in Listing 12.9 for a successful <1b> name registration.

Listing 12.9 Successful <1b> NetBIOS name registration.

```
[1999/07/26 19:35:28, 1] nmbd/nmbd.c:main(677)
  Netbios nameserver version 2.0.4b started.
  Copyright Andrew Tridgell 1994-1998
[1999/07/26 19:35:28, 0]
  nmbd/nmbd_become_dmb.c:become_domain_master_browser_bcast(284)
  become_domain_master_browser_bcast:
  Attempting to become domain master browser on workgroup SAMBABOOK on
  subnet 192.168.1.4
[1999/07/26 19:35:28, 0]
  nmbd/nmbd_become_dmb.c:become_domain_master_browser_bcast(298)
  become_domain_master_browser_bcast: querying subnet 192.168.1.4 for
  domain master browser on workgroup SAMBABOOK
[1999/07/26 19:35:37, 0]
  nmbd/nmbd_become_dmb.c:become_domain_master_stage2(118)
  *****
  Samba server LINUXSERVER is now a domain master browser for workgroup
  SAMBABOOK on subnet 192.168.1.4
  *****
[1999/07/26 19:35:51, 0]
  nmbd/nmbd_become_lmb.c:become_local_master_stage2(406)
  *****
```

The Samba name server LINUXSERVER is the domain master browser and local master browser for workgroup SAMBABOOK. If the domain master browser and local master browser entry do not appear as in Listing 12.9, either the Samba server was not configured with the correct entries in the smb.conf file, as indicated in the following, or another server has registered the <1b> NetBIOS name:

```
[1999/07/06 21:04:11, 1] nmbd/nmbd.c:main(677)
 Netbios nameserver version 2.0.4b started.
 Copyright Andrew Tridgell 1994-1998
```

The final possibility is that the nmbd daemon was not started on the Samba server.

Incorrect Domain Password

The Domain Password You Supplied Was Incorrect message could mean three things:

- The password or username used was wrong. In this case, simply reenter it (check to see whether Caps Lock is on).
- The server is using plain text passwords when you are using a Windows 9x client that is encrypting them (or vice versa). In this case, either reduce the client to using plain text passwords with the Registry entry as appropriate or configure the Samba server to encrypt passwords using the smb.conf [global] parameter **encrypt passwords** as appropriate (**yes** or **no**).
- The server has been configured to deny access to the Windows 9x PC because either of the [global] smb.conf parameters, **hosts allow** or **hosts deny**, were incorrectly configured by including or excluding the IP address of the Windows 9x PC, respectively.

The Machine Account For The Computer Does Not Exist Or Is Not Accessible

The Machine Account For This Computer Either Does Not Exist Or Is Not Accessible message might require you to look at the entry for the machine account in the smbpasswd file on the Samba primary domain controller (PDC). If the entry was entered using the **smbpasswd** facility, it should be used with the **-m** option. If the machine account entry was added manually, the syntax of the entry should be checked. The account name that appears in the smbpasswd file needs to be the same as the machine NetBIOS name, with a "$" appended to it, such as hostname$. The password for this account is the machine name in lowercase letters. The account type should be Workstation or [W].

The Samba lists have reported that this problem has been defined as being due to subnet masks being different between client and server when a Samba server and Windows client are involved. When two hosts are meant to be part of the same network, it is essential that the subnet masks are identical.

Unable To Log In After Joining The Samba-Controlled Domain

When using a Windows NT client, the login process starts by pressing Ctrl+Alt+Delete. The NT login box should then prompt for three entries if the client is involved with a Windows NT domain (it should prompt for two entries, username and password, if the client is part of a workgroup only). A problem might be seen when the delay between the key sequence and the login prompt is excessively long. A period in excess of 20 seconds might indicate a problem. When this login request is sent, the workstation will issue a LSA_ENUMTRUSTEDDOMAIN request to the domain controller for the network.

The Domain drop-down combo box should have two entries: the hostname and the SAMBA domain. Any local accounts are under the hostname domain. Any domain accounts or global groups are defined using the domain group map parameter. Select the appropriate SAMBA domain and enter a valid username and password for a user account that exists in the Samba domain controller smbpasswd file.

If you follow this process by using NetMon or **tcpdump**, the login process will involve an LSA_REQ_CHAL, then an LSA_AUTH2, an LSA_NET_SRV_PWSET, and finally a SAM_LOGON. Of these components, the SAM logon will be the largest and could be more than 600 bytes, containing user session information. Additional traffic in the form of Net Server Get Info, Net Share Enum, and similar messages might also appear.

Once the SAM logon is successful, the Windows NT domain logon dialog box will disappear from the client, and the client will start to download the client profile information, stored in the location specified in the SAM user account database.

The first problem that might occur, other than getting a username or password incorrect, might be in either obtaining or creating a remote profile. If this occurs, the user session will probably terminate along with the login session (an LSA_SAM_LOGOFF would be seen in any trace).

This can be an annoying problem and is probably due to the user profile not existing on the Samba server in the location specified in the "logon path". The solution is to copy the contents of the user local profile directory (see /winnt/profiles directory) to the Samba server. Alternatively, you can use the Profiles application in the client Control Panel to make a copy of the local profile and place it onto the Samba server. The process is well documented in the Windows NT help files using "profiles" as the keyword.

Other problems might be due to either network or browse capabilities not being enabled or configured correctly. The use of a Samba server as a domain controller assumes that the server can be seen in the local network browse lists. You might have to log out following the failure and log in again, thus creating an LSA_SAM_LOGOFF. Copy the profile over as directed and try again.

You could also try to log in again, with the same username or with another. If a username mapping is required, check that the file exists, that the usernames exist in the databases, and that the username and password have the correct case and spelling. Also check that the **smbd** and **nmbd** services are running.

If nothing seems to work, contact the Samba NT Domain mailing list and send a bug report in. The Samba Web site states that such reports should be emailed, including "NTDOM:" at the start of the subject line, to **samba-bugs@samba.org**.

TIP: *Samba domain control is experimental, and you should join and/or read the archives from the Samba NT Domain mailing lists.*

Unable To Log In After Upgrading Samba

This can be extremely frustrating problem, especially after you have spent much time and effort creating a Samba-controlled NT domain where a number of Windows NT clients have been successfully added to the domain. You might have upgraded the Samba software and the NT domain no longer operates. Following the upgrade, error messages, such as The System Cannot Log You On (C000019B), Please Try Again Or Consult Your System Administrator, can occur when you attempt to log in with a Windows NT client.

During the upgrade process, you must be very careful which files are replaced. If you have a working Samba setup, it is essential that you back up the contents of the /lib, /private, and /var directories at least before the upgrade is applied. The /private and /lib directories contain the smb.conf file, the MACHINE.SID file that contains the server SID, the DOMAINNAME.SID file that contains the domain SID, and several other files essential for configuring Samba. If these are overwritten or replaced during the upgrade, you will find that the NT domain might not operate as expected.

If any of these files are replaced or damaged, replace them from a backup or reconfigure the Samba server. In the case of NT domain clients being unable to log in to the domain, correcting the problem requires the following steps:

1. Restore the original domain SID.
2. Remove the domain client from the domain (delete the smbpasswd machine trust account entry) and rejoin (replace the smbpasswd machine trust account entry).

Roaming Profiles That Do Not Seem To Be Updating On The Server

This problem can result from a number of things:

- The time on the PDC and client must be synchronized. The command **net time \\server /set /yes** might be replacing the server with the name of your SMB time server.
- Check that the logon path is writeable by the user and check that the connection to the logon path location is by the current user (use smbstatus). Windows clients sometimes maintain a connection to an SMB server even after logoff. A new user could be attempting to access the share with the incorrect authentication.
- The Samba lists have reported that the logon path had to be browseable from the network. It might be worth adding **browseable=yes** to the parameters for the logon path.
- The user might not be able to log in to the server if encrypted passwords are being used. If this is the case, the **security=user** and **encrypt passwords=yes** or the **security=server** and **password server=ip.address** parameters should be set. The client will then be able to access the Samba server using local area network (LAN) manager-encrypted passwords.

System Policies Do Not Seem To Work

To make use of system policies, you need to set several smb.conf parameters correctly. The first requirement is that a [netlogon] service entry exists and that the directory exists and the users have write access to that directory.

The service parameters should include the settings shown here:

```
[netlogon]
  #omitted entries for brevity
  locking = no
  public = no
  browseable = yes
```

The Windows NT policies are included in the ntconfig.pol file. The case used in this file can be important, and the Samba lists have indicated that entering the files as "NTconfig.pol", "NTconfig.POL", or "ntconfig.pol" have been successful. The smb.conf parameters that involve the case of file names are relevant. The following settings can be attempted:

```
case sensitive = no
case preserve = yes
default case = yes
```

Unable To Add An NT Client To A Samba-Controlled NT Domain

When the **smbpasswd** program is used with the **-m** option, which should add a client to a Samba NT domain controller, this problem might be caused by the Samba programs. The current advice is to increase the debug log levels of the Samba server programs and obtain a **tcpdump** (or preferably NetMon) trace of the session between the server and the client host. After both have been obtained, these can be carefully examined. The trace should show a NETLOGON and a SAMLOGON on UDP port 138. If not, it is possible that the parameter **domain logon** is not set. Confirm that this is set to **domain logon=yes**. An alternative might be that the NetBIOS name of the server is not being resolved properly.

Further analysis of the trace should reveal an LSA_OPEN_POLICY and two LSA_QUERY_INFO requests on port 139. The first should be for a domain SID of S-1-3... and another for S-1-5. The trace should then show an LSA_CLOSE or two. You might see a pipe connection to a wkssvc pipe, and you might also see a "Net Server Get Info" being issued on the srvsvc pipe.

Using A Command Line Tool That Fails

When using a Windows client at the command line to map to a Samba server share, with a domain user account the share mapping fails, and a message similar to No Mapping Between Usernames And IDs Was Done appears. The Samba code might still be highly developmental in this area. At the time of this writing, the Samba distribution notes referred to this problem as being due to a failure in the username <-> RID mapping, with some related remote procedure calls in the code being incomplete. At this time, the Samba team is requesting that this error be reported, with details on how to reproduce it, to the **samba-ntdom@samba.org** mailing list.

Using Tools

A number of tools and programs are available to investigate and diagnose Samba problems. Some are Samba tools, such as **nbtstat**, **netmon**, and **tcpdump**, and others are part of the Samba distribution.

Using **nbtstat** To Troubleshoot NetBIOS Name Resolution

NetBIOS over TCP/IP (NetBT) resolves NetBIOS names to IP addresses. TCP/IP provides many options for NetBIOS name resolution, including local cache lookup, WINS server query, broadcast, DNS server query, and LMHOSTS and HOSTS lookup.

Windows clients come with the **nbtstat** program, which is useful for troubleshooting NetBIOS name resolution problems. In addition, **nbtstat** can be used as a tool to remove or correct the preloaded entries in a client host browse list.

The **nbtstat** program runs at the command line with options, which are shown in Table 12.2.

The output from a Windows NT client, VAIO, is shown in Listing 12.10.

Listing 12.10 nbtstat -S output from NT client VAIO.

```
C:\>nbtstat -S
NetBIOS Connection Table
Local Name              State     In/Out  Remote Host            Input   Output
-------------------------------------------------------------------------------
VAIO           <00>   Connected     Out   192.168.1.7            543B     598B
VAIO           <00>   Connected     Out   192.168.1.3            614B     780B
VAIO           <00>   Connected     Out   192.168.1.169          432B     489B
VAIO           <03>   Listening
VAIO           <03>   Listening
C:\>
```

Using NetMon (Network Monitor)

Windows NT Server and Windows NT Workstation come with a network sniffer or monitor that is capable of operating on the local network adapters and will report on all traffic that has used those adapters. A version of NetMon is available in the SMS add-on for Windows NT Server that will permit you to capture network traffic. Another version uses the local network adapters and reports on wider network traffic issues.

NOTE: *A version of NetMon is also available for Windows 9x clients on the Windows 9x installation CD-ROM.*

Table 12.2 nbtstat options.

Options	Description
-n	Displays the names that were registered locally on the system by applications such as the server and redirector.
-c	Shows the NetBIOS name cache, which contains name-to-address mappings for other computers.
-R	Purges the name cache and reloads it from the LMHOSTS file.
-a *name*	Performs a NetBIOS adapter status command against the computer specified by ***name***. The adapter status command returns the local NetBIOS name table for that computer plus the MAC address of the adapter card.
-S	Lists the current NetBIOS sessions and their status, including statistics.

Installing Network Monitor On NT Workstation Or Windows 9x

To install NetMon on a Windows NT PC is not complicated and can be accomplished in a couple of steps.

The following instructions are for installing NetMon V4.00.349, which comes with Microsoft Windows NT Server 4 and Windows NT Workstation 4. The process should be similar for other versions of Windows NT/Netmon. You will need to do the following for an NT Server:

1. Install Network Monitor Tools And Agent on the NT Server from the Server CD-ROM.
2. Open the Network Control Panel. In Services, select Add and then select Network Monitor Tools And Agent from the list. Click on OK.
3. Close the Network Control Panel and insert the Windows NT Server 4 install CD-ROM when prompted. The necessary software will be added to the NT Server. The software should be added to the system in %SYSTEMROOT%\System32\netmon*.*. Two subdirectories exist as well: parsers\, which contain the necessary DLLs for parsing the netmon packet dump, and captures\.

To install the NetMon tools on an NT Workstation, do the following:

1. Install the Network Monitor Agent from the Workstation install CD-ROM.
2. Open the Network Control Panel. In Services, select Add and then select Network Monitor Agent from the list. Click on OK.
3. Close the Network Control Panel and insert the Windows NT Workstation 4 install CD-ROM when prompted. The necessary software will be added to the NT Workstation.
4. Copy the files from the NT Server in %SYSTEMROOT%\System32\netmon*.* to %SYSTEMROOT%\System32\netmon*.* on the Workstation and set permissions on these files as appropriate.

For either NT Server or NT Workstation, it is necessary to be logged in with an account that has administrative rights in order to run NetMon. The NetMon program is available from the Start menu under Administrative Tools.

To install NetMon on a Windows 9x box, do the following:

1. Install the network monitor agent from the Windows 9x CD-ROM (\admin\nettools\netmon). A readme file is available from the NetMon driver files on the CD-ROM if you need information on how to do this.
2. Copy the files from a working NetMon installation.
3. Run NetMon on Windows 9x.

Using Samba Software As A Tool

The Samba software executables have numerous logging and debug options available. Normally, these are set to record the minimum amount of information. The smbd and nmbd daemon processes can be started with a debug level up to 100 (1 is normal, and 20 should provide more information than is necessary), and the corresponding log files produced by these daemons will contain much information that can be used to diagnose any problem.

When writing Samba, the developers included the option of compiling the Samba executables with debug support included. To use this option, set the **-g** flag when compiling the executables.

WARNING!* *This option is best used by those that know what they are doing and who have experience with the gdb debugger.

Using **tcpdump**

This program puts the Ethernet card of the Unix host into promiscuous mode and allows it to capture all the network traffic. The standard version can be used, but the Samba team has produced a patch to **tcpdump** that captures the SMB messages as part of the capture. This program is capable of capturing the traffic between two separate clients and piping this to a text file for later analysis.

The **tcpdump** program is available with most Linux distributions, and the SMB-enabled version of **tcpdump** is available from the Samba FTP site or its mirrors: **ftp://samba.org/pub/samba/tcpdump-smb/**.

Using **capconvert**

capconvert is a small C program that will translate the output from a **tcpdump-smb** session to the CAP format that can be imported into a NetMon session. If you plan to use this program, the source is included with the Samba distribution. You will need to compile it yourself. In use, the **tcpdump** output must be saved in the raw output format if you intend converting to NetMon format.

Using **snoop2cap**

The Solaris **snoop** program output can also be converted to NetMon CAP format. The C source code for **snoop2cap** is available as part of the Samba distribution.

Miscellaneous Issues

There are some additional issues that are not really problems but often have troubleshooting associated with them. These are:

- Setting **shared mem size**
- Setting the **time offset**
- Creating a Time Server

Setting **shared mem size**

This parameter specifies the size of the shared memory (in bytes) to use between smbd processes. It defaults to 1MB of shared memory for use in the smbd process. If you know that many clients will be simultaneously accessing the Samba server, this value will need to be increased.

Problems with setting the parameter too low include the following:

- Users reporting strange problems trying to save files (locking errors).
- Error messages in the smbd log appear as "ERROR smb_shm_alloc : alloc of XX bytes failed."

Currently, no formula is available to define what this parameter should be set to. A suggested value is to increase it to the sum of the sizes of a sample series of files that is expected to be opened simultaneously. It is important to use real memory and not disk swap, so the exact value to which you set this parameter might depend on your circumstances.

If the value has been set too large for the operating system, the smbd process will not start. Set the value lower until the operating system allows the smbd process to request this memory area.

In installation, this value defaults to **shared mem size=1048576**, where the value is in bytes.

Setting The **time offset**

This is a global parameter, and the value specified is the number of minutes that needs to be added to the normal GMT to obtain the local time. The default value is for a setting of 0 minutes. You would use the **time offset** parameter in the [global] section of the smb.conf file.

Creating A Time Server

The Samba **nmbd** program might advertise itself as another time server for the local network by adding the parameter **time server=yes** to the smb.conf file. Windows clients would then be able to synchronize with this server using

```
net time \\sambaserver/set/yes
```

The default value for this parameter is **time server=no.**

Chapter 13

The Future

Samba development consists of a common set of outstanding tasks that are being addressed by a group known as The Samba Team. However, some ideas and patches often come from members outside this group. Some of the more recent visible additions have involved translations of Samba from the English-only version to other language versions.

Configuring Samba, especially with the new Web-based interfaces (including SWAT, which comes with the distribution) is now extremely easy to do. The Windows NT administrator might be put off by the lack of a suitable set of GUIs for user administration, profile or policy editing, and machine administration, but all these functions can be satisfactorily completed using non-GUI methods.

With every new Samba release, two documents should be read before proceeding with the installation of the new software. These are Whatsnew.txt and Roadmap, and you will find both in the root directory of the uncompressed Samba distribution. This book's CD-ROM contains the directories, /Samba-2.0.5a, and /Samba-2.0.6; these are copies of the current and other most recent distributions and they contain these files.

The Whatsnew.txt file will report what the current Samba release code is and what bug fixes, if any, have been incorporated. A synopsis of the Whatsnew.txt file is included here.

> The Samba Team is pleased to announce Samba 2.0.5a.
>
> This is the latest stable release of Samba. This is the version that all production Samba servers should be running for all current bug-fixes.
>
> Please read the "IMPORTANT NOTE" section of the release notes as this explains three security bug-fixes, which have been added in this release. It is vital that Samba administrators understand these issues.
>
> It may be fetched via ftp from:
>
> /samba/ftp/samba-2.0.5a.tar.gz

Binary packages will be available shortly for many popular platforms.

Please check the main Web site or email announcements for details.

If you think you have found a bug please email a report to:

samba-bugs@samba.org

The WHATSNEW.txt file follows.

As always, any bugs are our responsibility,

Regards,

The Samba Team.

WHAT'S NEW IN Samba 2.0.5a

========================

This is the latest stable release of Samba. This is the version that all production Samba servers should be running for all current bug-fixes.

IMPORTANT NOTE!

This version of Samba contains three security bug-fixes for problems in previous versions of Samba found by Olaf Kirch of Caldera Systems (www.caldera.com). The Samba Team would like to publicly thank Olaf for his help in doing a security review of our code and finding these bugs.

The three bugs are one potentially exploitable buffer overrun bug (although no current exploits are known) in smbd and two denial of service bugs in nmbd. By default the smbd bug was not exploitable as shipped (the problem parameter was disabled by default) but instructions on protecting any version of Samba prior to 2.0.5 are included below.

All these bugs have been fixed in Samba 2.0.5 and 2.0.5a.

If using any version of Samba prior to 2.0.5 the administrator *MUST NOT* enable the "message command" parameter in smb.conf, and *MUST* remove any "message command" that is listed in any existing smb.conf file. No known instances of this attack being exploited have been reported.

All Samba versions of nmbd prior to 2.0.5 are vulnerable to a denial of service attack causing nmbd to either crash or to go into an infinite loop. No known instances of this attack being exploited have been reported.

New/Changed parameters in 2.0.5 and 2.0.5a.

There are 5 new parameters in the smb.conf file.

security mask

force security mode

directory security mask

force directory mode

level2 oplocks

The first 4 parameters are used to control the UNIX permission bits that an NT client is allowed to modify. These parameters are now used instead of the older "create" parameters that were used in 2.0.4 to allow an administrator to separate the two functions.

Use of these new parameters is described in the smb.conf man page, and also in the documents:

docs/textdocs/NT_Security.txt

docs/htmldocs/NT_Security.html

The fifth new parameter is described in the following section.

Level II oplocks

Samba 2.0.5 now implements level2 oplocks. As this is new code this parameter is set to "off" by default. The benefit of level2 oplocks is to allow read-only file caching from multiple clients. This is of great speed benefit to shares that are serving application executable programs (.EXE's) that are usually not written to. To learn more about using level 2 oplocks read the parameter description in the smb.conf documentation or read the file:

docs/textdocs/Speed.txt.

Changes in 2.0.5a

----

1). Fix for smbd crash bug in string_sub(). smbd was miscalculating memmove lengths on multiple '%' substitutions.

2). Fix for wildcard matching bug for old DOS programs running on Win9x.

3). Fix for Windows NT client changing passwords against a Samba server, intermittently failing.

4). Fix for PPP link being detected as primary interface if using the same IP address as the primary.

5). Ensure smbmount is built with RPM build.

Changes in 2.0.5

----

1). smbmount for Linux systems has been re-written to use the libsmb code and clientutil.c is no longer used with it.

2). A bug preventing directory opens using the NT SMB calls has been fixed.

3). A related bug causing a file structure leak when directory opens were denied has been fixed.

4). Fix for glibc2.1 bug on 32-bit systems being reported as 64 bit.

5). Prevent timestamps of 0 or -1 corrupting file timestamps.

6). Fix for unusual delays when browsing shares using Windows 2000 - fix added by Matt.

7). Fix for smbpassword reading problems on Sparc Linux was fixed.

8). Fix for compiling with SSL library.

9). smbclient fix for crash when doing CR/LF conversion.

10). smbclient now reports short read errors.

11). smbclient now uses remote server workgroup to list servers by default.

12). smbclient now has -b option to change transmit/send buffer size.

13). smbclient fix for corrupting files when issuing multiple outstanding read requests.

14). Printing bug where Linux was using SYSV printing by default fixed. Linux now set to be BSD printing by default.

15). Change for Linux to use SYSV shared memory by default.

16). Fix for using IP_TOS options on some systems.

17). Fix for some systems that complained about static struct passwd buffers being modified.

18). Range checking applied to all string substitutions. Theoretically not a bug, but much more rebust now.

19). Level II oplocks implemented.

20). Fix for Win2K client printing added.

21). Always allow loopback (127.0.0.1) connects unless specifically denied.

22). Patch for FreeBSD interface detection code from Archie Cobbs (archie@whistle.com).

23). Return correct status from smbrun.

24). snprintf fixes for floating point numbers.

25). Force directories to always have zero size.

26). Fix for "force group" and "force user" options. "force user" now always uses primary group of user as well. Force group now enhanced with '+' semantics (see smb.conf man page for details).

27). Wildcard matching fix to get closer to WinNT semantics for Win9x clients.

28). Potential crash bug fixed in wildcard matching code. This bug could also cause smbd to sometimes not see exact file matches.

29). Read/write for sockets changed to use revc/send to allow optimisations later.

30). Oplocks added to client library.

31). Several purify fixes in IPC code.

32). nmbd crash bug in processing strange NetBIOS names fixed.

33). nmbd loop bug in processing strange NetBIOS names fixed.

34). Paranoia fixes to processing of incoming WinPopup messages in smbd.

35). Share mode code now auto initialised.

36). Detect dead processes in IPC lock code.

37). Explicit -V version switch added to command line processing.

38). WORKGROUP(1b) name processing with no WINS server fixed.

39). Win2k client detection code added by Matt.

40). Fix to allow really short changenotify times to be honoured.

41). Fix for NT delete finding the wrong file from Tine Smukavec (valentin.smukavec@hermes.si).

42). SWAT fix to prevent stderr messages from breaking the Web client.

43). testparm fixes to check more parameter conflicts.

44). Relative paths not fetched via SWAT in CGI scripts.

45). SWAT remote password change - remote host name not treated as a password field any more.

Changes in 2.0.4b

A bug with MS-Word 97 saving files with zero UNIX permissions was fixed. Even though a workaround is available (set force create mode = 644 on the share) Word is such an important application that a point fix was necessary.

Changes in 2.0.4a

The text and html versions of NT_Security were missing from the shipping tarball. Also a compile bug for platforms that don't have usleep was fixed.

Changes in 2.0.4

There are 5 new parameters and one modified parameter in the smb.conf file.

allow trusted domains

restrict anonymous

mangle locks

oplock break wait time

oplock contention limit

The modified parameter is:

nt acl support

Bugfixes added since 2.0.3

---

1). Fix for 8 character password problem when using HPUX and plaintext passwords.

2). --with-pam option added to ./configure.

3). Client fixes for memory leak and display of 64-bit values.

4). Fixes for -E and -s option with smbclient.

5). smbclient now allows -L //server or -L \\server.

6). smbtar fix for display of 64-bit values.

7). Endian independence added to DCE/RPC code.

8). DCE/RPC marshalling/unmarshalling code re-written to provide overflow reporting and sign and seal support.

9). Bind NAK reply packet added to DCE/RPC code, used to correctly refuse bind requests (prevents NT system event log messages).

10). Mapping of UNIX permissions into NT ACL's for get and set added.

11). DCE/RPC enumeration of numbers of shares made dynamic. Samba now has no limit on the number of exported shares seen.

12). Fix to speed up random number seed generation on /dev/urandom being unavailable.

13). Several memory fixes added by running Purify on the code.

14). Read from client error messages improved.

15). Fixed endianness used in UNICODE strings.

16). Cope with ERRORmoredata in an RPC pipe client call.

17). Check for malformed responses in nmbd register name.

18). NT Encrypted password changing from the NT password dialog box now fully implemented.

19). Mangle 64-bit lock ranges into 32-bits (NT bug!) on a 32-bit Samba platform.

20). Allow file to be pseudo-openend in order to read security only.

21). Improve filename mangling to reduce chance of collisions.

22). Added code to prevent granting of oplocks when a file is under contention.

23). Added tunable wait time before sending an oplock break request to a client if the client caused the break request. Helps with clients not responding to oplock breaks.

24). Always respond negatively to queued local oplock break messages before shutdown. This can prevent "freezes" on an oplock error.

25). Allow admin to restrict logons to correct domain when in domain level security.

26). Added "restrict anonymous" patch from Andy (thwartedefforts@wonky.org) to prevent parameter substitution problems with anonymous connections.

27). Fix SMBseek where seeking to a negative number sets the offset to zero.

28). Fixed problem with mode getting corrupted in trans2 request (setting to zero means please ignore it).

29). Correctly become the authenticated user on an authenticated DCE/RPC pipe request.

30). Correctly reset debug level in nmbd if someone set it on the command line.

31). Added more checking into testparm

32). NetBench simulator added to smbtorture by Andrew.

33). Fixed NIS+ option compile (was broken in 2.0.3).

34). Recursive smbclient directory listing fix. Patch from E. Jay Berkenbilt (ejb@ql.org).

Bug-fixes added since 2.0.2

---

1). --with-ssl configure now include ssl include directory. Fix from Richard Sharpe.

2). Patch for configure for glibc2.1 support (large files etc.).

3). Several bug-fixes for smbclient tar mode from Bob Boehmer (boehmer@worldnet.att.net) to fix smbclient aborting problems when restoring tar files.

4). Some automount fixes for smbmount.

5). Attempt to fix the AIX 4.1.x/3.x problems where smbd runs as root. As no one has given us root access to such a server this cannot be tested fully, but should work.

6). Crash bug fix in debug code where *real* uid rather than *effective* uid was being checked before attempting to rotate log files. This fix should help a *lot* of people who were reporting smbd aborting in the middle of a copy operation.

7). SIGALRM bugfix to ensure infinite file locks time out.

8). New code to implement NT ACL reporting for cacls.exe program.

9). UDP loopback socket rebind fix for Solaris.

10). Ensure all UNICODE strings are correctly in little-endian format.

11). smbpasswd file locking fix.

12). Fixes for strncpy problems with glibc2.1.

13). Ensure smbd correctly reports major and minor version number and server type when queried via NT rpc calls.

14). Bugfix for short mangled names not being pulled off the mangled stack correctly.

15). Fix for mapping of rwx bits being incorrectly overwritten when doing ATTRIB.EXE.

16). Fix for returning multiple PDU packets in NT rpc code. Should allow multiple shares to be returned correctly.

17). Improved mapping of NT open access requests into UNIX open modes.

18). Fix for copying files from an NTFS volume that contain multiple data forks. Added 'magic' error code NT needs.

19). Fixed crash bug when primary NT authentication server is down, rolls over to secondaries correctly now.

20). Fixed timeout processing to be timer based. Now will always occur even if smbd is under load.

21). Fixed signed/unsigned problem in quotas code.

22). Fixed bug where setting the password of a completely fresh user would end up setting the account disabled flag.

23). Improved user logon messages to help admins having trouble with user authentication.

Bug-fixes added since 2.0.1

Note that due to a critical signal handling bug in 2.0.1, this release has been removed and replaced immediately with 2.0.2. The Samba Team would like to apologize for any problem this may have caused.

1). Fixed smbd looping on SIGCLD problem. This was caused by a missing break statement in a critical piece of code.

Bug-fixes added since 2.0.0

---

1). Autoconf changes for gcc2.7.x and Solaris 2.5/2.6.

2). Autoconf changes to help HPUX configure correctly.

3). Autoconf changes to allow lock directory to be set.

4). Client fix to allow port to be set.

5). clitar fix to send debug messages to stderr.

6). smbmount race condition fix.

7). Fix for bug where trying to browse large numbers of shares generated an error from an NT client.

8). Wrapper for setgroups for SunOS 4.x

9). Fix for directory deleting failing from multiuser NT.

10). Fix for crash bug if bitmap was full.

11). Fix for Linux genrand where /dev/random could cause clients to timeout on connect if the entropy pool was empty.

12). The default PASSWD_CHAT may now be overridden in local.h

13). HPUX printing fixes for default programs.

14). Reverted (erroneous) code in MACHINE.SID generation that was setting the sid to 0x21 - should be *decimal* 21.

15). Fix for printing to remote machine under SVR4.

16). Fix for chgpasswd wait being interrupted with EINTR.

17). Fix for disk free routine. NT and Win98 now correctly show greater than 2GB disks.

18). Fix for crash bug in stat cache statistics printing.

19). Fix for file names ending in .~xx.

20). Fix for access check code wait being interrupted with EINTR.

21). Fix for password changes from "invalid password" to a valid one setting the account disabled bit.

22). Fix for smbd crash bug in SMBreadraw cache prime code.

23). Fix for overly zealous lock range overflow reporting.

24). Fix for large disk free reporting (NT SMB code).

25). Fix for NT failing to truncate files correctly.

26). Fix for smbd crash bug with SMBcancel calls.

27). Additional -T flag to nmblookup to do reverse DNS on addresses.

28). SWAT fix to start/stop smbd/nmbd correctly.

Major changes in Samba 2.0

This is a MAJOR new release of Samba, the UNIX based SMB/CIFS file and print server for Windows systems.

There have been many changes in Samba since the last major release, 1.9.18. These have mainly been in the areas of performance and SMB protocol correctness. In addition, a Web based GUI interface for configuring Samba has been added. In addition, Samba has been re-written to help portability to other POSIX-based systems, based on the GNU autoconf tool.

There are many major changes in Samba for version 2.0. Here are some of them:

1). Speed

Samba has been benchmarked on high-end UNIX hardware as out-performing all other SMB/CIFS servers using the Ziff-Davis NetBench benchmark.

Many changes to the code to optimise high-end performance have been made.

2). Correctness

Samba now supports the Windows NT specific SMB requests. This means that on platforms that are capable Samba now presents a 64-bit view of the file system to Windows NT clients and is capable of handling very large files.

3). Portability

Samba is now self-configuring using GNU autoconf, removing the need for people installing Samba to have to hand configure Makefiles, as was needed in previous versions.

You now configure Samba by running "./configure" then "make". See the CD-ROM /docs/textdocs/UNIX_INSTALL.txt for details.

4). Web-based GUI configuration

Samba now comes with SWAT, a Web-based GUI config system. See the swat man page for details on how to set it up.

5). Cross protocol data integrity

An open function interface has been defined to allow "opportunistic locks" (oplocks for short) granted by Samba to be seen by other UNIX processes. This allows complete cross protocol (NFS and SMB) data integrity using Samba with platforms that support this feature.

6). Domain client capability

Samba is now capable of using a Windows NT PDC for user authentication in exactly the same way that a Windows NT workstation does, i.e., it can be a member of a Domain. See docs/textdocs/DOMAIN_MEMBER.txt for details.

7). Documentation updates

All the reference parts of the Samba documentation (the manual pages) have been updated and converted to a document format that allows automatic generation of HTML, SGML, and text formats. These documents now ship as standard in HTML and manpage format.

NOTE - Some important option defaults changed

Several parameters have changed their default values. The most important of these is that the default security mode is now user level security rather than share level security.

This (incompatible) change was made to ease new Samba installs as user level security is easier to use for Windows 95/98 and Windows NT clients.

********IMPORTANT NOTE****************

If you have no "security=" line in the [global] section of your current smb.conf and you update to Samba 2.0 you will need to add the line :

security=share

to get exactly the same behaviour with Samba 2.0 as you did with previous versions of Samba.

> ********END IMPORTANT NOTE*************
>
> In addition, Samba now defaults to case sensitivity options that match a Windows NT server precisely, that is, case insensitive but case preserving.
>
> The default format of the smbpasswd file has also been changed for this release, although the new tools will read and write the old format, for backward compatibility.
>
> NOTE - Primary Domain Controller Functionality
>
> This version of Samba contains code that correctly implements the undocumented Primary Domain Controller authentication protocols. However, there is much more to being a Primary Domain Controller than serving Windows NT logon requests.
>
> A useful version of a Primary Domain Controller contains many remote procedure calls to do things like enumerate users, groups, and security information, only some of which Samba currently implements. In addition, there are outstanding (known) bugs with using Samba as a PDC in this release that the Samba Team are actively working on. For this reason we have chosen not to advertise and actively support Primary Domain Controller functionality with this release.
>
> This work is being done in the CVS (developer) versions of Samba, development of which continues at a fast pace. If you are interested in participating in or helping with this development please join the Samba-NTDOM mailing list. Details on joining are available at:
>
> http://samba.org/listproc/
>
> Details on obtaining CVS (developer) versions of Samba are available at:
>
> http://samba.org/cvs.html
>
> If you think you have found a bug please email a report to:
>
> samba-bugs@samba.org
>
> As always, all bugs are our responsibility.
>
> Regards,
>
> The Samba Team.

The Samba Team has created a set of goals for themselves, and in any distribution you will find a file named Roadmap. A synopsis of the contents of the file that accompanies the Samba 2.0.5a distribution is included here:

> The current Samba release 2.0.5a was the result of a series of enhancements and bug fixes to the Samba release 2.0.4 that The Samba Team referred to as the "NT Security Update". This version implements the Windows NT specific SMB calls, and will allow a Samba host to operate correctly as a client in a Windows NT Domain environment.

From Version 2.0.0 onwards the distributions have also included, SWAT, the first implementation of the Web-based GUI management tools. This was part of the ships with 2.0.0, thus fulfilling some of the commitments made in the 1.9.18 release Roadmap documents.

Some work has been done on ensuring compatibility with Windows NT 5.0 (now Windows 2000 :-) although this is a somewhat (slowly) moving target.

The following development objectives for future releases are in place:

2.0.x—"NT Security update"—Allowing Windows NT Clients to manipulate file security and ownership using native tools.

Note that the "NT Security update" part of the Roadmap has been achieved with the Samba 2.0.4 release.

2.0.xx—"Thin Server" mode—allowing a Samba server to be inserted into a network with no Unix setup required.

Some management capabilities for Samba using native NT tools.

Provision of command-line equivalents to native NT tools.

2.X—"Domain Controller"—able to serve as a Windows NT PDC.

X.XX—"Full Domain Integration"—allowing both PDC and BDC modes.

Note that it is a given that the Samba Team will continue to track Windows (NT/2000) update releases, ensuring that Samba will work well with whatever "Beta" releases Redmond throws our way :-).

You may also note that the release numbers get fuzzier the further into the future the objectives get. This is intentional as we cannot yet commit to exact timeframes.

Windows 2000 And Samba

The current beta release of Windows 2000 is beta 3, which can be installed and used with Samba. The release 2.0.5a at least is required. The Samba Team will not make many comments on the use of Windows 2000 or some of the latest functionality, especially as it is deemed to be software under development. The systems used to write this book will successfully run Windows 2000 and will connect to a 2.0.5a Samba server.

However, the password encryption used does seem to raise a few issues, and currently the only way to use the Windows 2000 client is with a plain text password Registry hack that is similar to the other Windows operating systems.

The Registry key involved is [HKEY_LOCAL_MACHINE\SYSTEM\CurrentControlSet\Services\LanmanWorkStation\Parameters]. The parameter

"EnablePlainTextPassword" set to dword:00000001. The latest Samba distributions also include this as a reg file. An alternative step that appears to function is to set the smb.conf parameter **nt pipe support** to **no**.

With a Samba-controlled NT domain, the steps are conceptually no different. Samba currently does not have a Server Manager GUI interface, so for now the addition of the machine account must be carried out manually. I am sure that a Samba-based GUI to reproduce Server Manager will eventually appear.

Windows NT Printer Support

Currently, Samba does not support Windows NT printing. Although a large amount of the development has been done, this is still very preliminary. Windows NT printer functionality will appear in the Samba distributions shortly.

Remote Procedure Calls Are Not Complete

If you use a share in Windows 9x, select Properties|Security in Explorer. The call will fail, because the remote procedure calls are not fully functional. This functionality should be complete within Samba shortly.

Other Samba Enhancements

Many other planned and "unplanned" enhancements are taking place all the time with Samba. The very nature of the Open Source concept allows a user to take the code, write some new functionality, and offer this functionality back to the wider community. Some additional functionality, some of which is available now and will have a large impact on the use of Samba, includes the following:

- NTFS and Access Control Lists
- Alternative user account databases
- WINS replication
- Distributed File System

NTFS And Access Control Lists

From the Samba 2.0.4 release onward, the ability to view and modify the Unix permissions on an underlying Unix file system by Windows NT clients using the security settings dialog box present in Explorer has been possible.

This works by modifying the file system and its Access Control Lists, which represents itself in Samba to a Windows user as an NTFS file system. An excellent document that describes these changes is included within the Samba distribution. Written by Jeremy Allison, it is present in several forms as NT_Security.

Alternative User Account Databases

Windows NT Domain control is rapidly followed in terms of Samba development with a requirement to look at alternative databases for user authentication. The current Unix user account databases are built around a number of ASCII text files and, although functional, are not very flexible. The most flexible and most talked-about alternative in the Samba technical lists is the LDAP (Lightweight Directory Access Protocol). This would make use of an API (Application Protocol Interface), which would query the user account database regardless of the operating system. A description of LDAP can be found at **www.whatis.com/ldap.htm** if you are curious about this.

WINS Replication

The functional ability for an NT Server, operating as a WINS (Windows Internet Name Service) server, to be able to replicate the database of NetBIOS names to IP addresses between servers is not currently available in Samba. At the moment, a Samba WINS server must operate in isolation and is not able to replicate its database with another WINS server, be it Samba or NT.

WINS replication is an important goal to achieve in terms of Samba's usability because of the requirement to load-balance NetBIOS name resolution across large and diverse networks and to provide an element of backup in case of the failure of a primary WINS server.

Samba, acting as an isolated WINS server, places much dependence on its continued operation in a network and introduces a single point of failure that could cause considerable disruption in a larger network.

Again, the Samba technical discussion lists contain threads on this subject if you are interested.

Distributed File System

The ability to offer a central server that can operate as a share manager, acting as a mount point for other shares, involves the Distributed File System (DFS). This is similar in many ways to the Network File System (NFS) in Unix and allows the distributed shares from many SMB/CIFS servers to be mounted and then shared from one central location. This topic occasionally appears in the Samba technical lists.

A healthy discussion on these and many other topics can be found in the Samba newsgroups and email lists, the details of which can be found in Appendix A.

Recent Default OS Level Changes

One recent change that MAY affect you is that in Samba version 2.0.5a, the default OS Level following a Samba installation was 0. Samba version 2.0.6 now defaults to 20. The thinking behind this change can be read in the Samba technical discussions groups; Andrew Trigdell suggested the change, and his comments are repeated here (the original can be found at **www.samba.org/listproc/samba-technical/4516.html**).

> ...
>
> I'm thinking of changing the Samba browse defaults as follows:
>
> preferred master = true
>
> os level = 20
>
> currently we have:
>
> preferred master = false
>
> os level = 0
>
> The idea is to put Samba ahead of any Win9X boxes on the net while still being behind NT. I've seen bug reports for cross-subnet browsing where Samba loses elections to Win9X boxes that don't know how to do browse sync operations across subnets. I think the above two changes make the defaults more reasonable. I want to make installing Samba with reasonable settings as simple as possible.
>
> ...

Appendix A

Samba Distribution

What Is On The Distribution?

The current Samba distribution is 2.0.5a, and it is possible to obtain this both as source and as precompiled binary for several systems.

The source distribution is available as a tar-gzipped archive from one of the mirror sites. This extracts to several directories, as shown in Listing A.1, as a directory list viewed in a browser.

Listing A.1 The samba-2.0.5a.tar.gz distribution.

```
COPYING                     17 Kb    Sat May 04 08:50:42 1996
Manifest                    3 Kb     Mon Nov 23 22:17:00 1998
README                      6 Kb     Wed Jul 21 02:23:32 1999
README-smbmount             2 Kb     Fri Feb 26 04:46:22 1999
Roadmap                     1 Kb     Sat May 15 03:03:14 1999
WHATSNEW.txt                19 Kb    Thu Jul 22 03:06:58 1999 Plain Text
docs/                                 Sun Sep 26 20:43:02 1999 Directory
examples/                             Sun Sep 26 20:43:04 1999 Directory
packaging/                            Sun Sep 26 20:43:04 1999 Directory
source/                               Sun Sep 26 20:43:06 1999 Directory
swat/                                 Sun Sep 26 20:43:16 1999 Directory
```

The source directory contains the Samba source code, and it is from this directory that any executables should be created. The current Makefile and Samba distribution supports the ./configure option to create a standard Makefile based on the system settings. This allows the Samba executables to be built by running the ./configure, make, make install series of commands. The source directory listing is shown in Listing A.2.

Listing A.2 The source directory from the samba-2.0.5a distribution.

```
Makefile.in             20 Kb     Wed Jul 21 02:24:32 1999
acconfig.h               2 Kb     Wed Jul 21 02:24:32 1999
aclocal.m4               2 Kb     Wed Nov 25 20:14:58 1998
```

```
architecture.doc        5 Kb     Mon May 03 18:32:18 1999 Winword File
change-log             79 Kb     Mon Nov 23 21:46:52 1998
client/                          Sun Sep 26 20:43:08 1999 Directory
codepages/                       Sun Sep 26 20:43:10 1999 Directory
config.guess           18 Kb     Tue Dec 22 23:38:22 1998
config.sub             23 Kb     Wed Jul 29 04:14:36 1998
configure             284 Kb     Wed Jul 21 02:24:52 1999
configure.developer   120 bytes Tue Oct 20 23:25:52 1998
configure.in           48 Kb     Wed Jul 21 02:24:54 1999
cvs.log              3347 Kb     Thu Jul 22 03:15:44 1999 Text Document
groupdb/                         Sun Sep 26 20:43:10 1999 Directory
include/                         Sun Sep 26 20:43:10 1999 Directory
install-sh              4 Kb     Wed Jul 29 04:06:48 1998
internals.doc           8 Kb     Tue Aug 13 09:57:46 1996 Winword File
lib/                             Sun Sep 26 20:43:10 1999 Directory
libsmb/                          Sun Sep 26 20:43:12 1999 Directory
locking/                         Sun Sep 26 20:43:12 1999 Directory
mem_man/                         Sun Sep 26 20:43:12 1999 Directory
nmbd/                            Sun Sep 26 20:43:12 1999 Directory
param/                           Sun Sep 26 20:43:12 1999 Directory
parsing.doc            12 Kb     Tue Oct 27 21:07:52 1998 Winword File
passdb/                          Sun Sep 26 20:43:12 1999 Directory
printing/                        Sun Sep 26 20:43:12 1999 Directory
rpc_client/                      Sun Sep 26 20:43:12 1999 Directory
rpc_parse/                       Sun Sep 26 20:43:14 1999 Directory
rpc_server/                      Sun Sep 26 20:43:14 1999 Directory
rpcclient/                       Sun Sep 26 20:43:12 1999 Directory
script/                          Sun Sep 26 20:43:14 1999 Directory
smbadduser              1 Kb     Mon Oct 13 13:13:12 1997
smbd/                            Sun Sep 26 20:43:14 1999 Directory
smbwrapper/                      Sun Sep 26 20:43:14 1999 Directory
tests/                           Sun Sep 26 20:43:14 1999 Directory
ubiqx/                           Sun Sep 26 20:43:14 1999 Directory
utils/                           Sun Sep 26 20:43:16 1999 Directory
web/                             Sun Sep 26 20:43:16 1999 Directory
```

The binary packages that are available from the mirror sites are shown in Listing A.3.

Listing A.3 Samba binaries.

```
AIX/                             Fri Jul 23 16:53:00 1999 Directory
BSDI/                            Sat Jul 17 10:29:00 1999 Directory
Bull/                            Sat Jul 17 10:30:00 1999 Directory
Caldera/                         Sat Jul 17 10:29:00 1999 Directory
Debian/                          Sat Jul 17 10:29:00 1999 Directory
```

```
DigitalUnix/          Sat Jul 17 10:29:00 1999 Directory
IRIX/                 Thu Jul 22 07:42:00 1999 Directory
OSF/                  Sat Jul 17 10:30:00 1999 Directory
SCO/                  Sat Jul 17 10:29:00 1999 Directory
Slackware/            Sat Jul 17 10:29:00 1999 Directory
SuSE/                 Thu Jul 22 07:40:00 1999 Directory
TurboLinux/           Sun Jun 06 06:40:00 1999 Directory
hp/                   Sat Jul 17 10:29:00 1999 Directory
mvs/                  Mon Feb 02 00:00:00 1998 Directory
novell/               Tue Aug 19 00:00:00 1997 Directory
redhat/               Mon Nov 16 00:00:00 1998 Directory
sinix/                Mon Jul 26 17:52:00 1999 Directory
solaris/              Fri Jul 23 16:53:00 1999 Directory
vms/                  Fri Oct 02 00:00:00 1998 Directory
```

Where To Get The Distribution

Start at **www.samba.org**, where you should immediately be provided with the option to visit a mirror site. Figure A.1 shows the current Web page.

The closest site to me is the Northern Europe Sunsite, which is shown in Figure A.2.

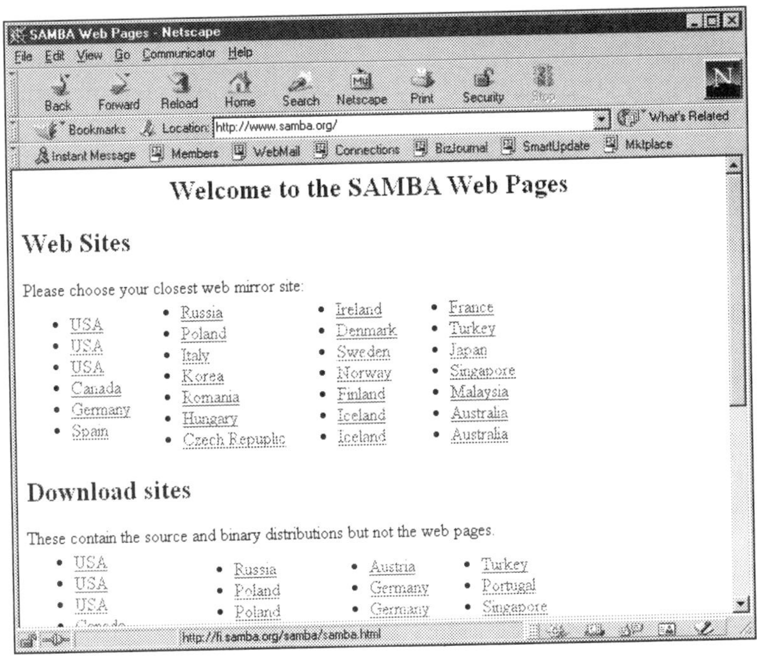

Figure A.1 The **www.samba.org** Web site.

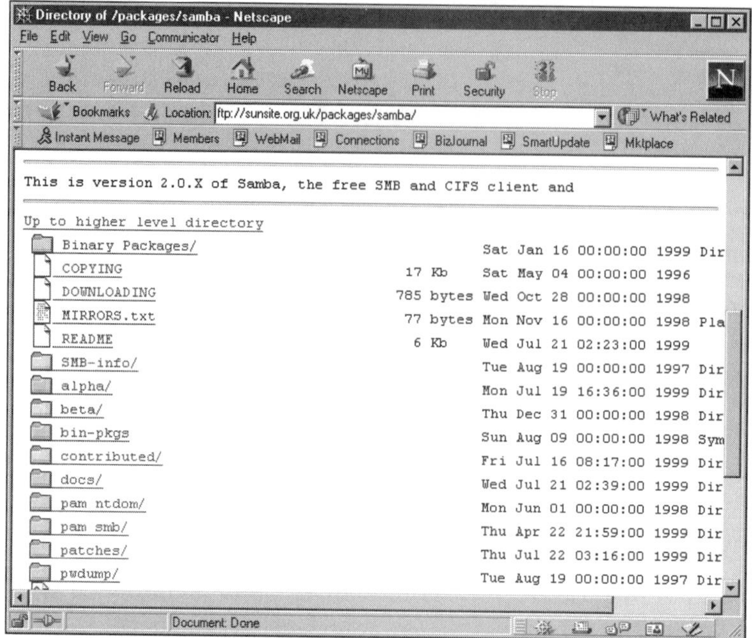

Figure A.2 The **ftp://sunsite.org.uk/packages/samba/** Web site.

You should download either the source or the binary that you need from the closest mirror site to you. The main Web site pages of each mirror site carry the brief announcement messages from the Samba development team concerning the latest releases and other Samba-related issues.

Samba Distribution Documentation

The Samba distribution comes with many documents. The latest source distributions are present in several different formats in the /docs directory. A copy of the samba-2.0.5a distribution is shown in Listing A.4.

Listing A.4 The Samba distribution documents.

```
Volume in drive D has no label.
 Volume Serial Number is 9803-15A7

 Directory of D:\samba-2.0.5a\docs

09/26/99  08:43p        <DIR>          .
09/26/99  08:43p        <DIR>          ..
02/27/99  09:36p                5,721 announce
10/29/98  01:00a               10,867 history
07/18/99  09:01p                1,079 NT4-Locking.txt
```

```
08/21/97  11:51a                 303 NT4_PlainPassword.reg
11/23/98  10:11p                 986 samba.lsm
11/23/98  10:11p               5,917 THANKS
07/16/99  05:36p                 303 Win2000_PlainPassword.reg
08/21/97  12:28p                 122 Win95_PlainPassword.reg
02/14/99  02:39a                 122 Win98_PlainPassword.reg
02/14/99  02:50a                 190 Win9X-CacheHandling.reg
09/26/99  08:43p        <DIR>          faq
09/26/99  08:43p        <DIR>          htmldocs
09/26/99  08:43p        <DIR>          manpages
09/26/99  08:43p        <DIR>          textdocs
09/26/99  08:43p        <DIR>          yodldocs
10/08/99  07:00p                   0 dir.txt
              18 File(s)        25,610 bytes
                           433,455,104 bytes free
```

The textdocs and htmldocs directories are especially worth browsing through, as both contain much information on the installation and configuration of any Samba installation.

The smb.conf.5.html file lists all the Samba smb.conf parameters and their descriptions, and this is currently more than 100 pages of paper, should you decide to print it all. This file will include the most current definitions of the smb.conf parameters for the Samba release that it accompanies.

The contents of the htmldocs directory are copied to the SWAT directories on installation and these become the online help pages for the Web-based interface.

The smb.conf File

The Samba software provides the possibility of operating in both server and client modes of operation. The central location for the configuration of Samba is the smb.conf file. The smb.conf file employs a specific format for its content that consists of sections that are grouped according to general and specific uses. Each of these sections starts with the section name in square brackets and all values and parameters that follow apply to that section until the next section starts. The sections include individual parameters and values that may be represented in the form:

```
name = value
```

The smb.conf file structure is such that each line that is included will be either a comment, a section name, or a parameter.

There is no ability to define multiple sections with different cases being employed and it should be noted that all of the section and parameter names used within the smb.conf file are not case sensitive.

The = that follows a parameter is significant; the value that immediately follows it will be the first value for the parameter to use. Further parameter values (usernames for example) may follow with a space separating the first and subsequent values. Should a space be a part of the value; then that value should be surrounded by single quotes. All other leading or trailing spaces are ignored.

Likewise any line within the smb.conf file that starts with either the semicolon (‘) or the hash (#) character is ignored, as are any blank lines or lines containing spaces.

To enable smb.conf files to include very long lines, the standard Unix continuation character (\) should be placed at the end of a line to indicate that this line should be followed or continued onto the next line as appropriate.

The values used with parameters, other than Boolean values, are treated as string literals; this means that the case used is preserved for any values entered. Any Boolean value may take any of the values **yes**, **true**, or **1** for a positive or **no**, **false**, or **0** for a negative value. The values used with create modes involved with Unix file systems are usually numeric.

The smb.conf file consists of a number of sections. These sections each describe and provide parameter values for the different resources, or shares, that the Samba server provides. The exception to this general rule is usually the first section that appears in the smb.conf file, the [global] section.

NOTE: *This section often is not explicitly referenced as [global] and any parameters placed at the beginning of the smb.conf file before any later section are assumed to be part of the [global] section.*

The section name placed in the [ ] brackets will be the name of the resource and the parameter values that follow will be the resource attributes. These resources are also referred to as shares, or shared resources.

In addition to the [global] section there are the [homes] and [printers] sections. The Samba documentation refers to these and the [global] section as “Special Sections” and there are a number of rules that apply to them.

[global]

All parameters in the [global] section will apply to the server as a whole, or will be accepted as the defaults for later sections that have not applied specific parameters.

[homes]

Samba servers commonly will be used to provide shared resources to other systems, for a number of users that exist on the Samba server as individual users. To aid in administration and ease of setup, the [homes] section may be employed to automatically, "on-the-fly", create shares for the home directories of the users that exist on the Samba server with no further configuration being necessary. The parameters listed in this section will, however, effect how these "home" directories may be used.

[printers]

The [printers] section operates in a similar manner to the [homes] section, but it is for printers. Should a [printers] section be included, then the printers specified in the server printcap file should be available to the clients.

[other user defined shares]

The user-defined shares will each be made up of a directory for which access permissions are specified. In addition to these basic parameters, the other parameters all relate to either format or conversion functions of one kind or another.

These sections can be for either filespace shares or printer shares.

The Parameters And Macros

The smb.conf parameters are listed elsewhere in this book according to function or appearance, as when using SWAT. Here they are arranged in Table A.1 and Table A.2 in alphabetical order including some of the more commonly used synonyms, or alias names. Table A.1 refers to parameters that are only available within the [global] section. Table A.2 refers to all other parameters. Any parameters that may accept a Boolean value (Yes or No) are marked (B).

Table A.1 Global section only parameters.

Parameter	Description
add user script	The value for this parameter is the full pathname to the script that will be run AS ROOT by **smbd** to create a Unix user account. The security parameter must be either **security=server** or **security=domain**. The script must be capable of creating a Unix user account with just one argument, **%u**, the current session username. There is no default for this parameter.
allow trusted domains	This parameter is effective when the **security=server** or **security=domain**. If the value is **No**, then a connection to the Samba server resource from a domain or workgroup other than the one in which **smbd** is running will fail, even if that domain is trusted by the remote server doing the authentication. This is an additional

(continued)

***Table A.1 Global section only parameters* (continued).**

Parameter	Description
allow trusted domains	security option where you want to restrict access to a Samba server to only those users within the domain of the Samba server, whilst permitting access to other domains. Should two domains exist, DOM1 and DOM2, DOM2 is trusted by DOM1, where the Samba server is a member. Normal Windows NT practice would then permit a user with an account in DOM2 to access the resources of either NT or Unix in DOM1 even if that user has no user account in DOM1. This definition of domain security can be a little open. This Samba parameter will allow the administrator to restrict access as necessary. The default value is **Yes**. (B)
announce as	The **nmbd** service will announce the server to a network browse list. This parameter allows the administrator to specify which type of server to announce, to a Network Neighborhood browse list. By default this is set to Windows NT. The valid options are: **NT**, which is a synonym for **NT Server**, **NT Server**, **NT Workstation**, **Win95** or **WfW** meaning Windows NT Server, Windows NT Workstation, Windows 95, and Windows for Workgroups respectively. Do not change this parameter unless you have a specific need to stop Samba appearing as an NT server as this may prevent Samba servers from participating as browser servers correctly. The default value is **announce NT Server**.
announce version	This parameter value provides the major and minor version numbers used by **nmbd** when announcing itself as a server. The default is **4.2**.
auto services	The list of shares that will always appear in any browse lists. The default setting is an empty string.
bind interfaces only	The Samba server may have more than one network interface. If some or all of these are listed in the **interfaces** parameter then this switches Samba to only provide shares and **nmbd** services on the interfaces listed. Note that 127.0.0.1 should appear in this list to allow password changes to be processed by **smbpasswd**. Default is **No**. (B)
browse list	Switch on or off the browse list from the Samba server. Default is **Yes**. (B)
case sensitive	Switch on the ability to change the case of a filename supplied by a client. Default is **No**. (B)
case sig names	A synonym for **case sensitive**. (B)

(continued)

Table A.1 Global section only parameters **(continued).**

Parameter	Description
change notify timeout	The number of seconds between checks for file name and directory changes. The default is **60**. A lower value may affect performance.
config file	The Unix pathname to an additional Samba configuration file. This may be used to redirect the Samba configuration or may be used with %-macros to define user or group configuration files. Default is empty string.
deadtime	Time in minutes between checks for sessions that are no longer active; Samba kills sessions that reach this limit. Default is **0**.
debug level	The value for the level of logging that Samba will run. Default is **0**. Log levels greater than 3 may affect performance; levels above 10 are used for development debugging.
debug timestamp	Every debug message can include date and timestamps. This switches timestamps on or off. Default is **Yes**. (B)
default	The name of the default service that a session should be connected to if requesting a connection that does not exist or that permissions to access are denied. Default is empty string.
default service	A synonym for **default**.
delete user script	The value for this parameter is the full pathname to the script that will be run AS ROOT by **smbd** to delete a Unix user account. The security parameter must be either **security=server** or **security=domain**. The script must be capable of deleting a Unix user account with just one argument, **%u**, the current session username. There is no default for this parameter.
dfree command	The system command required that returns the free disk space.
dns proxy	In collaboration with **wins server=Yes**, this parameter will switch on DNS name lookup for a host if not found in the WINS database. (B)
domain admin group	This parameter is part of the unfinished Samba NT Domain Controller Code.
domain admin users	This parameter is part of the unfinished Samba NT Domain Controller Code.
domain controller	This parameter is no longer used within the Samba source and should be removed from your smb.conf files. It remains in existence for compatibility reasons.
domain groups	This parameter is part of the unfinished Samba NT Domain Controller Code.

(continued)

***Table A.1 Global section only parameters* (continued).**

Parameter	Description
domain guest group	This parameter is part of the unfinished Samba NT Domain Controller Code.
domain guest users	This parameter is part of the unfinished Samba NT Domain Controller Code.
domain logons	Switch on or off Windows 9x- or NT-style domain logons.(B)
domain master	Set if the Samba server will act as the domain master browser. (B)
encrypt passwords	Set NT-style password encryption on or off. Requires an **smbpasswd** file to exist on the Samba server. (B)
getwd cache	Set the caching of current directory information on or off. Useful for performance if wide links is also switched on. (B)
homedir map	If the parameter **nis homedir = Yes**, and **logon server = Yes** then this parameter specifies the NIS (or YP) map location on the server for the user's home directory. The value takes the form: **username server:/some/file/system** and the program will extract the servername from before the first ':'. The default value is **auto.home**.
hosts equiv	If the value for this parameter is a non-null string, it contains the name of a file to read for the names of the hosts and users that may access the server without specifying a password. There are considerable security risks associated with setting this parameter, as you trust a foreign host and all logged in users from that host. The default value is an empty string.
include	This value specifies another config file to include within the current config file. The parameter may use any of the macro substitutions, except **%u**, **%P**, and **%S**, as none of these values will be set at the time the file is read.
interfaces	Samba may operate using several network interfaces; the values used will specify which network interfaces Samba should operate on. The values consist of a list of ip/netmask pairs. The netmask may either be a bitmask or a bitlength. By default, Samba will attempt to locate the primary network interface, usually eth0, and if no value is set will only configure for that interface. This can be useful if you have a multiple homed server operating on several subnets
keepalive	The value (an integer) indicates the number of seconds between checks to determine if any client has crashed. The **keepalive** parameter should not be set if the **socket options = SO_KEEPALIVE** is also set. The default value is **0**. A suggested setting, if needed, would be 4 hours or 3600.

(continued)

Table A.1 Global section only parameters **(continued).**

Parameter	Description
kernel oplocks	New to Samba 2.0, this breaks the oplocks on a file when a Unix client accesses a file that has been oplocked, preventing file corruption. Currently only SGI supports this; Linux and BSD should follow shortly. Once set, automatically at install, you should not have to alter this. (B)
ldap filter	This parameter is part of the unfinished Samba LDAP support and is currently a placeholder for information intended for use.
ldap port	This parameter is part of the unfinished Samba LDAP support and is currently a placeholder for information intended for use.
ldap root	This parameter is part of the unfinished Samba LDAP support and is currently a placeholder for information intended for use.
ldap root passwd	This parameter is part of the unfinished Samba LDAP support and is currently a placeholder for information intended for use.
ldap server	This parameter is part of the unfinished Samba LDAP support and is currently a placeholder for information intended for use.
ldap suffix	This parameter is part of the unfinished Samba LDAP support and is currently a placeholder for information intended for use.
lm announce	Switch on LAN Manager-style announcements for OS/2 SMB clients. There are three states: **Yes**, **No**, and **Auto**. **Auto** will wait for a client announcement to arrive first before responding. The default is **Auto**.
lm interval	The interval in seconds between LAN Manager broadcast announcements.
load printers	Switch on the load of printers present in the system. This defaults to **Yes**. (B)
local master	Switch on the **nmbd** as the local master browser in an election. The default is **Yes**. (B)
lock dir	Synonym for **lock directory**.
lock directory	The directory to keep lock file in. This must be writable by Samba and have world readable set. The default is **/usr/local/samba/var/locks**.
log file	The path and file name for the log file. All % macros are permitted.
log level	Synonym for **debug level**.
logon drive	Set the DOS drive name for the logon path for Windows NT. The default value is an empty string.

(continued)

Table A.1 Global section only parameters (continued).

Parameter	Description
logon home	Set the home directory of a Windows 9x or NT user. The default value is **\\%N\%U**.
logon path	Specify the path (Unix) to the Windows profile directory. This would contain the standard USER.DAT, USER.MAN and desktop, Start Menu, Network Neighborhood, and program folders used in Windows clients. The default value is **\\%N\%U\profile**.
logon script	Specify the pathname, relative to the [netlogon] share for a DOS script to be run on the client at logon time. This parameter allows all % macros. The default value is an empty string.
lpq cache time	In seconds specify the length to cache the print queue status. The default is **10**. Setting this to **0** disables lpq caching.
machine password timeout	The period in seconds between requesting a machine password change. Used in Windows NT domain control. The default is set to **604,800** seconds, or 1 week.
mangled stack	Specify the size of the cache of recently mangled filenames. The default is **50**.
map to guest	When using security modes other than **security=share**, i.e., user, server, and domain, the use of this parameter will inform **smbd** what to do with invalid login requests. The parameter has three possible values: **Never**—Reject user login requests with an invalid password. This is the default. **Bad User**—Reject user logins with an invalid password, unless the username does not exist, in which case it is treated as a guest login and mapped into the "guest account." **Bad Password**—All user logins with an invalid password are treated as a guest login and mapped into the "guest account."
max disk size	Specify the maximum number in megabytes (MB) to be returned to a client for the disk/free disk sizes. This defaults to **0**, which means no limit.
max log size	Specify the size in kilobytes (K) at which Samba will start to create a new log file. Meanwhile, the current log file will be renamed with the .old extension. The default is **5000**.
max mux	Specify the maximum number of simultaneous operations that the Samba server clients may make. The default is **50**.

(continued)

Table A.1 Global section only parameters **(continued).**

Parameter	Description
max open files	Specify the maximum number of files that a Samba process will attempt to keep open at the same time. The default is **10,000**.
max packet	Synonym for **packet size**. Now obsolete. Use the **max xmit** parameter instead.
max ttl	Time in seconds that NetBIOS names are held in **nmbd** cache before performing a lookup. The default is **14400** (4 hours).
max wins ttl	Specify the time limit in seconds that a NetBIOS name will remain in the nmbd WINS cache before performing a name lookup. The default is **259200** (3 days).
max xmit	Specifies the maximum packet size in bytes that Samba will negotiate. Default is **65535**; values below 2048 are not advised.
message command	Specify the command that must be run on the server when a client sends a WinPopUp message. The command MUST end with **&** to run the command immediately. The command may use the % macros, except **%u**, but including **%s** (file name), **%t** (destination), and **%f** (from).
min passwd length	Specifies the minimum length in characters of a plaintext password than **smbd** will accept when performing Unix password changing.
min wins ttl	Specify the minimum time limit in seconds that a NetBIOS name will remain in the **nmbd** WINS cache before performing a name lookup. The default is **21600** (6 hours).
name resolve order	Specify what naming services and in what order to resolve host names to IP addresses. The options are **lmhosts**, **wins**, **hosts**, and **bcast** with the default being the same options in that order.
netbios aliases	Specify the additional NetBIOS names that the Samba server will advertise itself as. The default is an empty string.
netbios name	Specify the NetBIOS name that the Samba server will advertise itself as.
nis homedir	Specify if the homedir map in NIS is switched on or off. The default is **No**. (B)
nt acl support	Specify if **smbd** will attempt to map Unix permissions into Windows NT access control lists. The default is **Yes**. (B)
nt pipe support	Switch on and off specific NT-pipe calls. This option is currently used in NT support development, including tuning, and may be removed in time. The default is **Yes**. (B)

(continued)

Table A.1 Global section only parameters (continued).

Parameter	Description
nt smb support	If **Yes** then allow NT-specific SMBs to be used. This option is currently used in NT support development, including tuning, and may be removed in time. The default is **Yes**. (B)
null passwords	Specify if the Samba server will allow client access to accounts with null passwords. The default is **No**. (B)
ole locking compatibility	Specify if Samba will allow an administrator to turn off the byte range lock manipulation, to provide compatibility for OLE applications. The byte lock range mapping above 32K stops some Unix locks crashing when opening locks above 32K. The default is **Yes**. (B)
oplock break wait time	Specifies the time (in milliseconds) that a Samba server will wait before sending an oplock break request to a client. The parameter is designed to stop Samba responding to an SMB that can cause an oplock break request. If it did, then the client redirector can fail and not respond to the break request. The default value is **10** milliseconds.
os level	Specifies the integer value for the level at which Samba advertises itself as for browse elections. This value will determine whether **nmbd** has a chance of becoming a local master browser for the WORKGROUP in the local broadcast area. The default is **zero**, which means **nmbd** will lose elections to Windows machines.
packet size	No longer used.
panic action	Specifies a system command to be called when either **smbd** or **nmbd** crashes. The default value is an empty string.
passwd chat	Specifies the "chat" conversation that takes places between **smbd** and the local password changing program to change the users password. The string may contain the % macros **%o** and **%n**, substituted for the old and new passwords respectively. Also the system macros **\n**, **\r**, **\t**, and **\s** to give line-feed, carriage-return, tab, and space. In addition a * character, which matches any sequence of characters, may be used. Strings containing white spaces should be contained within double quotes. If the **unix password sync = true**, then this sequence is called as root when the SMB password in the smbpasswd file is being changed, without access to the old password in cleartext. Then the old password in cleartext is set to an empty string. The default is ***old*password* %o\n *new*password* %n\n *new*password* %n\n *changed***.
passwd chat debug	Specifies if the **passwd chat** script parameter is run in debug mode. If in debug the strings passed through the passwd chat are listed to the smbd log with a debug level of 100.The default is **No**. (B)

(continued)

Table A.1 Global section only parameters (continued).

Parameter	Description
password level	Specifies the maximum number of characters that may be uppercase in passwords. The default is **0**.
passwd program	Specifies the program used to set Unix user passwords. The program or script should accept the %u macro replacing the value with the user name. Before executing, the existence of the username is checked. If **unix password sync = Yes** then this program is called as root before the SMB password in the smbpasswd file is changed. A change in SMB password will fail if the **unix pasword change** fails. The default is **/bin/passwd**.
password server	Specified NetBIOS name for the SMB server to which Samba passes all its username/password validation. The **security** parameter must be set to **server** or **domain** to apply. When using Windows NT Server, users should be able to log in from the Samba server. The default is an empty string.
preferred master	Specifies if Samba is preferred to become the master browser. The default is **No**. (B)
preload	Synonym for auto services
printcap name	Specifies the system printer configuration file that is loaded to form the [printers] section. The default is **/etc/printcap**; **/etc/lpstat** on System V.
printer driver file	Specifies the location of the msprint.def file used by Windows 9x clients. The default is **samba-lib/printers.def**.
protocol	Specify which SMB protocol version to use. The values available are **NT1**, **LANMAN1**, **LANMAN2**, **COREPLUS**, and **CORE**. The default value is **NT1**.
read bmpx	Obsolete, no longer used. The default value is **No**. (B)
read prediction	Obsolete, removed in Samba 2.0. For read-only files performs a read ahead.The default is **No**. (B)
read raw	Specifies if fast streaming reads are permitted over TCP using 64K buffers. The default is **Yes**. (B)
read size	Specifies the size of buffers to use on Samba servers where the disk and network throughputs are unbalanced. The size should not exceed 65,536 bytes, and the optimal value may require some experimentation. The default value is **2048**.
remote announce	Specifies the alternate workgroup list that a Samba server will announce itself. The values take the form of an IP address/ Workgroup name. The default is an empty string.

(continued)

Table A.1 Global section only parameters **(continued).**

Parameter	Description
remote browse sync	Specify the network broadcast addresses for those subnets where synchronization between Samba local master browsers is required. The default value is an empty string.
root	Synonym for **root directory**.
root dir	Synonym for **root directory**.
root directory	Specify the directory to chroot() to prior to the starting of any daemons. This may prevent access below that directory tree. The default is an empty string.
security	Specify the Samba server security policy. The allowable values are **share**, **user**, **server**, and **domain**.
server string	Specify the comment that will accompany the server NetBIOS name in browse lists. The default is **Samba %v in 2.0**.
shared mem size	Specify the shared memory size in bytes. The default is **102400**.
smb passwd file	Specifies the path and file name to the smbpasswd file to use instead of the compile time file location /usr/local/samba/private/smbpasswd, which is the assumed default.
smbrun	Specifies the path and file name to the **smbrun** progam, instead of the compile time location.
socket address	Specify which network interface, by IP address, to listen to for SMB connection requests. The default is to use all available network interfaces with this set to an empty string.
socket options	Specify the operating system socket options as a list. The list of possible values includes **TCP_NODELAY**, **IPTOS_LOWDELAY**, **SO_SNDBUF**, **SO_RCVBUF**, **SO_KEEPALIVE**, **SO_RCVLOWAT**, and **SO_SNDLOWAT**. The best option would be to run a **man setsocketopt** at a Unix prompt and determine which options your operating system supports.
status	Switches on the logging to a file or shared memory the connections to a server. The default is **Yes**. (B)
strip dot	Switches on the removal of trailing dots from file names. The default is **No**. (B)
syslog	Specify the level of Samba messages to send to syslog. The larger values contain more information. The syslog.conf must specify a suitable file and have logging enabled. The default is **1**.
syslog only	Switches Samba logging to the syslog only. The default is **No**. (B)

(continued)

Table A.1 Global section only parameters **(continued).**

Parameter	Description
time offset	Specify the number of minutes to add to any system time-zone calculation. The default is **0**.
time server	Switches on the Samba server **nmbd** to offer a time service to the network. The default is **No**. (B)
timestamp logs	Switches on the addition of timestamp to any log entry. The default is **Yes**. (B)
unix password sync	Enable the changing of the Unix password for a user that changes the SMB password. The default is **No**. (B)
unix realname	Switch on the sending to a client of the GCOS entry in the /etc/passwd file for the full username. The default is **No**. (B)
update encrypted	Switch on the update of the Microsoft-format password file when a connection from a user with unencrypted passwords occurs. The default is **No**. (B)
username level	Specifies the number of uppercase letter replacements to allow when attempting to match Unix usernames. The default is 0.
username map	Specifies the path and file name to a file that provides a list of Unix-to-Windows username mappings by listing the Unix and Windows usernames in pairs. The default is an empty string.
valid chars	Add a list of characters to a character set map. The default is an empty string.
wins proxy	Switch on **nmbd** name resolution requests to WINS servers for older clients that only use broadcasts. The default is **No**. (B)
wins server	Specify the DNS name or IP address of the WINS server. The default is an empty string.
wins support	Switch on **nmbd** as a WINS server. Must not be set when the **wins server** parameter has a value. The default is **No**. (B)
workgroup	Specify the workgroup or domain name that the server will belong to. The default value of **WORKGROUP** or **MYGROUP** should be changed.
write raw	This defines if the server will support raw writes SMBs when data is transferring from clients. The default value is **Yes**. It is not expected that this will have to be altered.

Table A.2 Service level parameters.

Parameter	Description
admin users	The list of users that will be granted root privileges on the share.
allow hosts	A list of hosts that may connect to the share. If **NULL** then any machine may access the server, except any listed in **deny hosts**.
alternate permissions	No longer used in Samba version 2. (B)
available	Sets a share access, defaults to **Yes**.(B)
blocking locks	New from Samba 2.0, sets if the server will honor byte range locks, with the request being queued for retries with time limits, until the time period expires. Default is **Yes** (B)
browseable	Can a share be seen in a browse list. Default is **Yes**.
browseable	A synonym for browsable for those that spell differently!
character set	Sets the character set for file name translations. The client code page value must be 850. The values are **ISO8859-1**, **ISO8859-2**, **ISO8859-5**, and **KOI8-R**. No default value.
client code page	Specify the DOS code page explicitly. The default is **437** (US MSDOS); **850** is Western European.
comment	A text string that accompanies the service in any browse list. The default is an empty string.
copy	Specify the previous section that should be copied into the current section. This is especially useful when used with the % macros to create custom smb.conf files. The default is an empty string.
create mask	Specify the Unix permissions for newly created files. This takes the form of the octal 0777 permissions. The default is **0744**.
create mode	Synonym for **create mask**.
default case	Specify which case is the default for the storage of new files. A little misleading as **LOWER** indicates mixed case is used, **UPPER** indicates uppercase only is used. The default is **LOWER**.
delete readonly	Switch on the removal of read-only files. The default is **No**. (B)
delete veto files	Switch on the deletion of directories containing files or directories that are invisible to the client through the **veto files** parameter. The default is **No**. (B)
deny hosts	List the machines that are to be refused connections or access to shares.
directory	Synonym for path.
directory mask	Specify the maximum allowable Unix permissions, in octal form, for newly created directories in a share. The default is **0755**.

(continued)

Appendix A
Samba Distribution

Table A.2 Service level parameters (continued).

Parameter	Description
directory mode	A synonym for **directory mask**.
dont descend	Specifies a list of paths that should not be changed to when browsing.
dos filetime resolution	Set the times on files created in Samba shares to use the DOS standards of rounding to the next even second. The default is **No**. (B)
dos filetimes	Switch on alteration of file times by non-owners if the non-owner has write access to a file. The default is **No**. (B)
exec	Synonym for **preexec**.
fake directory create times	Fix a bug in Microsoft **nmake** so that directory create times are faked so that users don't re-create file every time they run **nmake**.
fake oplocks	Specifies is a fake oplock created so that a client may request one and cache the file locally but the oplock is NOT enforced on the server. Should only be used for read-only file systems as Samba fully supports true oplocks. The default is **No**. (B)
follow symlinks	Allow the following of symlinks by a client when browsing shares. The default is **Yes**. (B)
force create mask	List the bits that will be ORed with the permissions of newly created files to maintain the necessary security settings on the server. The default is **0**.
force create mode	Synonym for **force create mask**.
force directory mask	List the bits that will be ORed with the permissions of newly created directories to maintain the necessary security settings on the server. The default is **0**.
force directory mode	Synonym for **force directory mask**.
force group	Specify the Unix group for all access to the share. The default is an empty string.
force user	Specify the Unix username for all access to a share. The default is an empty string.
fstype	Specify which file system the share reports to on the client. The values are **NTFS**, **FAT**, and **Samba**. The default is **NTFS**.
group	An alternate for **force group**; now obsolete.
guest account	Specify the Unix username to use for those tasks that require an unprivileged account, e.g., printing and access to shares with **guest ok = yes**. The default is an empty string.
guest ok	Switch on public, no passwords, required for this share. The default is **No**. (B)

(continued)

Table A.2 Service level parameters (continued).

Parameter	Description
guest only	Specifies that public or guest user only access to this share is permitted. The **guest ok** or **public** parameters must be set to **yes**. The default is **No**. (B)
hide dot files	Specify if the .* files in a directory should be hidden when browsing a share, in a similar manner to the Windows hidden property. The default is **Yes**. (B)
hide files	A more specific list of files and directories to hide in a share. The value may also include the ? or * wildcards and the value may also use the % macros.
hosts allow	Synonym for **allow hosts**.
hosts deny	A synonym for **deny hosts**.
include	Specify the pathname to an additional smb.conf file that should be included at the line where the **include** parameter is set. The % macros may be used, except **%u**, **%S**, and **%P**.
invalid users	A list of users that will be denied access to a share.
locking	Specify if file level locking is performed. Should this be set to **No**, then Samba will accept the lock request but will not perform the lock. Use with read-only file-systems. The default is **Yes**.
lppause command	The full Unix path and command that will pause a print job. The **%p** (printer name) and the **%j** (job number) macros are also supported.
lpq command	The full Unix path and command that would obtain the printer status. The **%p** (printer name) macro is supported.
lpresume command	The full Unix path and command to resume a paused print job. The **%p** (printer name) and **%j** (job number) macros are supported.
lprm command	The Unix path and command used to delete an entry from a printer job queue. The **%p** (printer name) and **%j** (job number) macros are supported.
magic output	Specify the output for the script specified in magic scripts. The default is **script.out**.
magic script	Specify the script path and name that will execute a shell script that is contained within this file whenever it is closed by a client. The default value is an empty string.
mangle case	Specify if a file name will be mangled if it is in mixed case. The default is **No**. (B)
mangled map	Specify a list of file name extensions to re-map as a list of from-to pairs. The default is an empty string. (B)

(continued)

***Table A.2 Service Level Parameters* (continued).**

Parameter	Description
mangled names	Specify if Samba will mangle long file names, or files that contain unsupported characters (e.g. white spaces in filenames) to an 8.3 format. The default is **Yes**. (B)
mangling char	Specify the character that will be unique in all mangled file names. The default is tilda, **~**.
map archive	Specify if the executable by user (0100) bit is set on Unix filenames if the DOS archive attribute property is set. The **create mask** parameter must contain the 0100 bit as part of its mask. The default is **Yes**. (B)
map hidden	Specify if the executable by world (0001) bit is set on Unix file names if the DOS hidden attribute property is set. The **create mask** parameter must contain the 0001 bit as part of its mask. The default is **No**. (B)
map system	Specify if the executable by group (0010) bit is set on Unix file names if the DOS system attribute property is set. The **create mask** parameter must contain the 0010 bit as part of its mask. The default is **No**. (B)
map groupname	Specify the path and file name for a file that does a mapping of Unix groups to NT groups. The default value is an empty string.
max connections	Specify the maximum number of client connections for a single client that are permitted to the share. The default value is **0**, which means unlimited connections.
min print space	Specify the minimum free disk space in K that must exist in the print spool before accepting a new print job. The default is **0**, which means no limit set.
only guest	Synonym for **guest only**.
oplocks	Switch on opportunistic locking of files on the server from client requests. The default is **Yes**. (B)
panic action	Specify the Unix command to run when an operation causes Samba to panic. The default is an empty string.
path	Specify the path for the directory that is to become the share. When the share section is [homes] this does not need to be set as this defaults to the users home directory or /tmp. The **%u** and **%m** macros are supported in **path**.
postexec	Specify the command to run after the resource has been closed by a client, running the command with that user privileges.

(continued)

Table A.2 Service level parameters (continued).

Parameter	Description
postscript	A parameter that will specify that a printer is capable of processing Postscript. This is accomplished by inserting a **%!** In the first line where a printer is so defined. The default is **No**. (B)
preexec	Specify the command to run before the resource has been opened by a client, running the command with that user privileges.
preserve case	Specify if the file names sent to the server by a client are to be forced to the case specified in the **default case** parameter. The default is **No**. (B)
print command	Specify the Unix print command to be used to send a spooled file to the printer. The printing parameter that specifies the default print style will automatically set this as appropriate. The macros **%p**, **%s**, and **%f** may also be used and it is possible to customize this command.
print ok	Synonym for **printable**. (B)
printable	Specify if a printer share will operate as a printer. The default is **No**. (B)
printer	Specify the name of the Unix printer. The default is **lp**.
printer driver	Specify the Windows printer driver name. This will inform Windows which printer driver to use. The default is an empty string.
printer driver location	Specify the location of the printer driver files. The default is a share **\\servername\PRINTER$**.
printer name	Synonym for **printer**.
printing	Specify the Unix printing style to use as default. The possible values are: **bsd**, **sysv**, **hpux**, **aix**, **qnx**, **plp**, and **lprng**.
public	Specify if a password is required for access to this share. The default is **No**. (B)
queuepause command	Specify the Unix command that is used to pause a print queue.
queueresume command	Specify the Unix command that is used to resume a paused print queue.
read list	Specify the list of users that will be permitted read-only access to the share.
read only	Specify that the share is to be read-only. The default is **No**. (B)
revalidate	Specify if the user is required to re-enter the password to access a share, even though a successful login to the server may already have occurred. The default is **No**. (B)
root postexec	Specify the command to run after the resource has been closed by a client, running the command with root privileges.

(continued)

Table A.2 Service level parameters (continued).

Parameter	Description
root preexec	Specify the command to run after the resource has been closed by a client, running the command with root privileges.
set directory	Permit a DEC Pathworks client to use the **set dir** command. The default is **No**. (B)
share modes	Specify if the server will apply Windows-style whole-file locks. The default is **Yes**. (B)
short preserve case	Specifies if the mangled 8.3 names sent to a server by a client should be left in the case that they are sent in or if they should be forced to the case specified in the **default case** parameter value.
strict locking	Specify if Samba operates by checking if locks are in place for every access, no just the initial opening or on demand. Setting this parameter to Yes may have severe performance implications. The deault is **No**. (B)
strict sync	Specifies if Samba should synchronize to disk when a client has the sync bit set on a packet. The default is **No**, which means that in normal operation Samba will only perform this operation once the buffers are full. The Samba team have reported that Windows 98 sets the sync bit incorrectly on all packets, which would make a Samba server appear slow on disk write access for these clients. (B)
sync always	Specifies if Samba should always flush the buffers and wait for every write to disk to complete before continuing. This may be useful when a server is unstable but will delay all write activity on the server. The default is **No**. (B)
user	Synonym for **username**.
username	Specifies a list of users to use when attempting to access a share when share-level security is being used.
valid users	Specify the list of users that are permitted to access a share.
veto files	Specify the list of files or file types (using ? or * wildcards) that a user should not be capable of viewing when browsing a share.
veto oplock files	Specify a list of files that should not have oplocks placed on them (so caching them to a client). The default is an empty string.
volume	Specify the volume label of a share.
wide links (B)	Specify if Samba will permit the following of symlinks outside of the current share directory structure. The default is **Yes**. (B)
writable	Specifies if a share may be written to. The default is **Yes**. (B)
write list	Specifies a list of users that are permitted write access to the share.
write ok	Synonym for **writable**.

The smb.conf macros and variables are listed elsewhere in this book and have also been listed in Table A.3.

Table A.3 Macros.

Macro	Description
%a	The architecture of the remote machine. Only some are recognized, and those may not be 100% reliable. It currently recognizes Samba, WfWg, WinNT and Win95. Anything else will be known as "UNKNOWN". If it gets it wrong then sending a level 3 log to **samba-bugs@samba.org** should allow it to be fixed.
%S	The name of the current service, if any.
%P	The root directory of the current service, if any.
%u	The user name of the current service, if any.
%g	Primary group name of **%u**.
%U	Session username (the username that the client wanted, not necessarily the same as the one they got).
%G	Primary group name of **%U**.
%H	The home directory of the user given by **%u**.
%v	The Samba version.
%h	The Internet hostname that Samba is running on.
%m	The NetBIOS name of the client machine (very useful).
%L	The NetBIOS name of the server. This allows you to change your config based on what the client calls you. Your server can have a "dual personality."
%M	The Internet name of the client machine.
%N	The name of your NIS home directory server. This is obtained from your NIS auto.map entry. If you have not compiled Samba with the **--with-automount** option then this value will be the same as **%L**.
%p	The path of the service's home directory, obtained from your NIS auto.map entry. The NIS auto.map entry is split up as "%N:%p".
%R	The selected protocol level after protocol negotiation. It can be one of **CORE**, **COREPLUS**, **LANMAN1**, **LANMAN2**, or **NT1**.
%d	The process ID of the current server process.
%I	The IP address of the client machine.
%T	The current date and time.

The use of macros, or variables as they are also referred to in the Samba Documentation, can provide for some complex and creative configuration options.

SSL

Should you have compiled-in SSL support into Samba, then the parameters listed in Table A.4 may also be used within the smb.conf file.

Table A.4 SSL parameters.

Parameter	Description
ssl	When Samba has been compiled with SSL support, this parameter switches on SSL support. When this value is **No**, Samba will continue to operate like the non-SSL Samba. When this value is **Yes**, the value for **ssl hosts** and **ssl hosts resign** will determine if an SSL connection is required. The default is **No**.
ssl CA certDir	Specifies the directory locations for the Certification Authorities. The location should contain one file for each CA that Samba will trust. This location is required if you intend to verify client certificates. The default value is **ssl CA certDir = /usr/local/ssl/certs**.
ssl CA certFile	Specifies the file that contains all the certificates of the trusted CAs. This file is required if you intend to verify client certificates. The default value is **ssl CA certFile = /usr/local/ssl/certs/ trustedCAs.pem**.
ssl ciphers	Specify the ciphers that should be offered during SSL negotiation.
ssl client cert	Specify the file that contains the certificate that will be used by **smbclient** on the Samba server. This value is required if the remote server requests a client certificate. The default value is **ssl client cert = /usr/local/ssl/certs/smbclient.pem**
ssl client key	Specify the location of the private key for **smbclient**. The value is only important if the client requires a certificate.The default value is **ssl client key = /usr/local/ssl/private/smbclient.pem**.
ssl compatibility	Specify if SSLeay is configured to include bug compatibility with alternate SSL implementations. This is of limited value, because currently no other SSL implementations exist. The default value is **No**. (B)
ssl hosts	List of hosts, by IP address, IP address range, net group, or name that will be forced into SSL mode. The default value is an empty string.
ssl hosts resign	Lists the hosts that will not be forced into SSL mode. The default value is an empty string.

(continued)

***Table A.4 SSL parameters* (continued).**

Parameter	Description
ssl require clientcert	Switch on the SSL check that clients must have a valid certificate. The contents of the directory or file specified in the **ssl CA certDir** or **ssl CA certFile** will be used to look up the CA that issued thecertificate to the client. Should a valid certificate not exist the connection will be refused. When set to **No**, the default, client certificates are not required. (B)
ssl require servercert	Specify that **smbclient** requests a certificate from the server. The default is **No**. (B)
ssl server cert	Specify the location of the file containing the server certificate. Note that in order for Samba to perform SSL operations the server Must have this certificate. The default is an empty string.
ssl server key	Specify the location of the private key of the server. If there is no value specified the key should exist in the certificate file. For SSL operation the server requires both a private key and the certificate must match this private key. The default value is an empty string.
ssl version	Specifies the version of the SSL protocol that will be used. The possible values are **ssl2**, **ssl3**, **ssl2or3**, and **tls1**. The default value is **ssl2or3**.

Appendix B

Further Reading

Chapter References

For the topics covered in some chapters, you might need additional background information. The following references are possible sources of that information.

Chapter 1

The main Web sites for Samba, Linux, and GNU are useful sources of information.

Chapter 2

The standard DNS book is *DNS and BIND*, by C. Liu and P. Albitz (O'Reilly & Associates; ISBN 0-937175-82-X).

A section on DNS can be found in *TCP/IP Network Administration*, by Craig Hunt (O'Reilly & Associates; ISBN 0-937175-82-X).

Online, the first source is **www.dns.net/dnsrd/** and **www.isc.org/bind.html**.

A FAQ, a reference manual (BOG, Bind Operations Guide), and papers and protocol definitions and DNS hacks (these and most of the RFCs mentioned here are contained in the bind distribution as well).

The newsgroup comp.protocols.tcp-ip.domains is about DNS.

A number of RFCs about DNS are available, the most important of which are the following:

- *RFC 2052*—A DNS RR for specifying the location of services (DNS SRV), October 1996
- *RFC 1918*—Address allocation for private Internets, February 29, 1996
- *RFC 1912*—Common DNS operational and configuration errors, February 28, 1996

- *RFC 1912 Errors*—Errors in RFC 1912; available at **www.cis.ohio-state.edu/~barr/rfc1912-errors.html**
- *RFC 1713*—Tools for DNS debugging, November 3, 1994
- *RFC 1712*—DNS encoding of geographic location, November 1, 1994
- *RFC 1183*—New DNS RR definitions, October 8, 1990
- *RFC 1035*—Domain names: implementation and specification, November 1, 1987
- *RFC 1034*—Domain names: concepts and facilities, November 1, 1987
- *RFC 1033*—Domain administrators operations guide, November 1, 1987
- *RFC 1032*—Domain administrators guide, November 1, 1987
- *RFC 974*—Mail routing and the domain system, January 1, 1986

These RFCs may be obtained from **www.cis.ohio-state.edu/hypertext/information/rfc.html**.

An online RFC search capability is available at **www.rfc-editor.org/rfcsearch.html**.

A copy of all the current RFCs has been obtained from **www.rfc-editor.org/tar/** and is on the CD-ROM in /doc/RFC as RFC-all.tar.gz

Chapter 3

The Samba documentation is relevant.

Chapter 4

The Samba documentation is relevant.

Chapter 5

The Samba documentation is relevant.

Chapter 6

The Microsoft operating system manuals and online help pages on the operation of the various operating systems prove useful.

Chapter 7

The Microsoft operating system manuals and online help pages on the operation of the various operating systems prove useful. The man pages for the Unix operating system are essential.

Chapter 8

For information on Remote Access Services (dial-in and dial-out), the Microsoft Windows NT Server Networking Guide in the Microsoft Windows NT Server Resource Kit (for Microsoft Windows NT Server 4.0) contains a wealth of valuable information that can be used when setting up an NT RAS server.

For information about installing TCP/IP protocol, see the Networking Supplement for Microsoft Windows NT Server 4.0.

For information about installing RAS, see the Microsoft Windows NT Server Resource Kit (for Microsoft Windows NT 4.0).

For information about NBFCP, see Request for Comments (RFC) 2097, The PPP NetBIOS Frames Control Protocol. IPCP is defined in RFC 1332, The PPP Internet Protocol Control Protocol (IPCP). IPXCP is defined in RFC 1552, The PPP Internetwork Packet Exchange Protocol (IPXCP).

For information on Linux PPP setup references, see pppd's manual pages, Robert Hart's PPP-HOWTO under the /usr/doc/HOWTO directory, Al Longyear's PPP-FAQ under the /usr/doc/FAQ directory, and relevant sections in the Linux Network Administrators Guide.

You can look at portions of your log to determine whether your modem or the ISP's modems are working. If you have problems connecting or setting up your scripts, take the time to read the chat and pppd manual pages along with the PPP-HOWTO and PPP-FAQ.

Chapter 9

Many sources of information on NT domain control are available in the form of mailing lists, RFCs, and documentation. The documents that come with the Samba distribution contain good explanations of general SMB topics, such as browsing. Several mailing lists might be of interest, including the following:

- **samba-ntdom@samba.org** is devoted to implementing support for NT domains for Unix. The list is archived at **www.samba.org/listproc/samba-ntdom**.
- **samba-technical@samba.org** is for normal Samba development. The list is archived.
- **www.samba.org/listproc/samba-technical** is the Samba Technical list in archive format.
- **samba@samba.org** is also for normal Samba deployment. This list is archived at **www.samba.org/listproc/samba**.

- **cifs@discuss.microsoft.com** includes a discussion of the CIFS (Common Internet File System) protocol; this list is archived at **www.discuss. microsoft.com/archives/cifs.html**.

Useful Web sites include the following:

- Samba home page: **www.samba.org**
- Miscellaneous links to CIFS information: **www.samba.org/cifs/**
- NT Domains for Unix: **www.mailhost.cb1.com/~lkcl/ntdom/**
- Microsoft's main CIFS page: **www.msdn.microsoft.com/workshop/networking/cifs/**
- FTP site for older SMB specs see the smb* files at: **ftp://ftp.microsoft.com/developr/drg/cifs/**

The following RFCs are of interest:

- RFC1001 (March 1987): Protocol standard for a NetBIOS service on a TCP/UDP transport: concepts and methods (from **www.ds.internic.net/rfc/rfc1001.txt**)
- RFC1002 (March 1987): Protocol standard for a NetBIOS service on a TCP/UDP transport: detailed specifications (from **www.ds.internic.net/rfc/rfc1002.txt**)

For CIFS Specifications, see the following:

- CIFS/E Browser Protocol: draft-leach-cifs-browser-spec-00.txt
- CIFS Remote Administration Protocol: draft-leach-cifs-rap-spec-00.txt
- CIFS Logon and Pass Through Authentication: draft-leach-cifs-logon-spec-00.txt
- Common Internet File System (CIFS/1.0) Protocol: draft-leach-cifs-v1-spec-01.txt
- CIFS Printing Specification: draft-leach-cifs-print-spec-00.txt

Chapter 10

For information on DHCP, see the following:

- RFC2131
- RFC2132
- RFC951

For information on Fax Server, see the following FTP sites:

- **ftp://Metalab.unc.edu/pub/Linux/system/serial/mgetty+sendfax***
- **ftp://ftp.leo.org/pub/comp/os/unix/networking/mgetty/mgetty+sendfax-1.0.0.tgz**

For information on pbm10dec91.tgz, see the following:

- **ftp.leo.org/pub/comp/networking/communication/modem/mgetty/pbm10dec91.tgz**
- **http://metalab.unc.edu/pub/Linux/aps/graphics/Converts/pbmplus-10dec91-bin.tar.gz**
- **ftp.gwdg.de/pub/linux/grafik/pbmplus.src.tar.Z** (this is 10dec91 source)

Chapter 11

The Linux HOWTOs for firewalling, IP masquerading, networking, Ipfwadm, and IP-Chains are all essential reading. The various Samba documents included with the distribution on security are also relevant.

Chapter 12

The main source is the diagnosis.txt file that comes with the Samba distribution in /docs/textdocs.

Chapter 13

Samba's home page **www.samba.org/** and the various email lists.

Other Samba Or Unix And Windows Integration Books

There are some recent texts on Samba and some more general ones on the integration of Unix and Windows:

Blair, John. *Samba Integrating Unix and Windows*, Specialized Systems Consultants, Inc., ISBN 1-57831-0067. The first text written on the subject.

Gunter, David, Steven Burett, and Lola Gunter, Osborne. *Windows NT And Unix Integration Guide*. ISBN 0078823951. Provides an alternative view of the subject.

Williams, G. Robert and Ellen Beck Gardner, *Windows NT &Unix*. Addison Wesley, ISBN 0-201-18536-9. A wider look at integration, covering wider issues.

Linux And Unix Books

There are many books available on Linux; my own library includes the following texts:

Gilly, Daniel. *Unix in a Nutshell*, O'Reilly & Associates. ISBN 1565920015. A useful reference that covers the essential commands used across the various Unixs.

Husain, Kamran and Tim Parker. *Red Hat Linux Unleashed*. Sams Publishing, ISBN 067231410X.

Johnson, Michael K. and Erik W. Troan. *Linux Application Development*. Addison Wesley, ISBN 0201308215. A useful text that will introduce development of applications to run on Linux for those who intend to look at a deeper integration between Unix and Windows.

Olaf Kirch. *Linux Network Administrator's Guide*. O'Reilly & Associates, ISBN 1565920872. The partner text to *Running Linux*.

Purcell, John. *Linux Man*. Red Hat, ISBN 188817272X. A useful hardcopy, if a little dated, of the man pages used with Linux.

Siegert, Andreas. *The AIX Survival Guide*. Addison Wesley, ISBN 0201593882. Useful for those with IBM systems running AIX.

Welsh, Matt and Lar Kaufmann, *Running Linux*. O'Reilly & Associates, ISBN 1565921003. One of the older and most read texts on the Linux operating system; later editions of this text now also exist.

Windows Books

Garms, Jason. *Windows NT 4 Server Unleashed*. Sams Publishing, ISBN 0672309335. A general NT book written by many authors.

Kaplan, Ari and Morten Strunge Nielsen. *NT5: The Next Revolution*. The Coriolis Group, 1-57610-288-2. A general look at NT5 as it was at the time of this writing.

Lambert, Nevin and Manish Patel. *PCWeek Microsoft Windows NT Security: System Administrator's Guide*. ZDPress, ISBN 1562764578. Covers most security subjects.

McMains, John and Bob Chronister. *Windows NT Backup & Recovery*. Osborne McGraw-Hill, ISBN 0078823633. A look at many disaster avoidance options.

Microsoft. *Microsoft Windows NT Server Resource Kit Version 4.0: Supplement Two*. Microsoft Press, ISBN 1572316268.

Meggitt, Ashley and Timothy D. Ritchey. *Windows NT User Administration.* O'Reilly & Associates, ISBN 1565923014. An aid to large scale user administration, excellently covered.

Microsoft. *Microsoft Windows NT Server Resource Kit Version 4.0: Supplement One.* Microsoft Press, ISBN 1572315598.

Microsoft. *Microsoft Windows NT Server Resource Kit: For Windows NT Server Version 4.0.* Microsoft Press, ISBN 1572313447. The Resource Kits that exist for the Windows NT Server and Workstations are valuable, if expensive references. The Server version is also known as Microsoft Windows NT Server—Technical References and Support Tools. The texts *Networking Guide* from the Resource Kit and *Concepts and Planning* from the NT Server Installation Documents both have many valuable sections.

Microsoft. *Microsoft Windows NT Workstation Resource Kit.* Microsoft Press, ISBN 1572313439.

Networking And Miscellaneous

These books contain sections or chapters on subjects that may prove useful reading:

Chapman, D. Brent and Elizabeth D. Zwicky. *Building Internet Firewalls.* O'Reilly & Associates, ISBN 1565921240. (You should definitely obtain the errata from O'Reilly & Associates Web site (**www.ora.com**) for this text.)

Hunt, Craig. *TCP/IP Network Administration.* O'Reilly & Associates, ISBN 1565923227.

Hunt, Craig and Robert Bruce Thompson. *Windows NT TCP/IP Network Administration.* O'Reilly & Associates, ISBN 1565923774

Minasi, Mark, Todd Lammle, and Monica Lammle. *Mastering TCP/IP for NT Server.* Sybex, ISBN 0782121233.

Parker, Timothy. *TCP/IP Unleashed.* Sams, ISBN 0672306034

Sun, Andrew. *Using and Managing PPP.* O'Reilly & Associates, ISBN 1565923219.

Appendix C

Linux Distribution

What Is Linux?

Linux is a free Unix-type operating system originally created by Linus Torvalds with the assistance of developers from around the world. Linux is an independent POSIX implementation and includes true multitasking, virtual memory, shared libraries, demand loading, proper memory management, TCP/IP networking, and other features consistent with Unix-type systems. Developed under the GNU General Public License, the source code for Linux is freely available to everyone.

What Do You Get With Linux?

Linux has many different distributions, some of which are highly marketed and packaged with manuals, bundled software, and support and others of which include little more than the source code or the compiled binaries that allow you to create a system.

Linux is capable of being installed on many platforms and with many different software packages and configurations. Most installations could include the following:

- X Windows
- Development tools, including compilers
- Desktop publishing and image and editing tools
- Databases
- Web server, FTP server, news server, email server

What Are The Different Linux Distributions?

The Linux home page **http://www.linux.org** provides a link to a page that briefly describes the different distributions. Figure C.1 shows the main page and the button link where the distribution page can be seen.

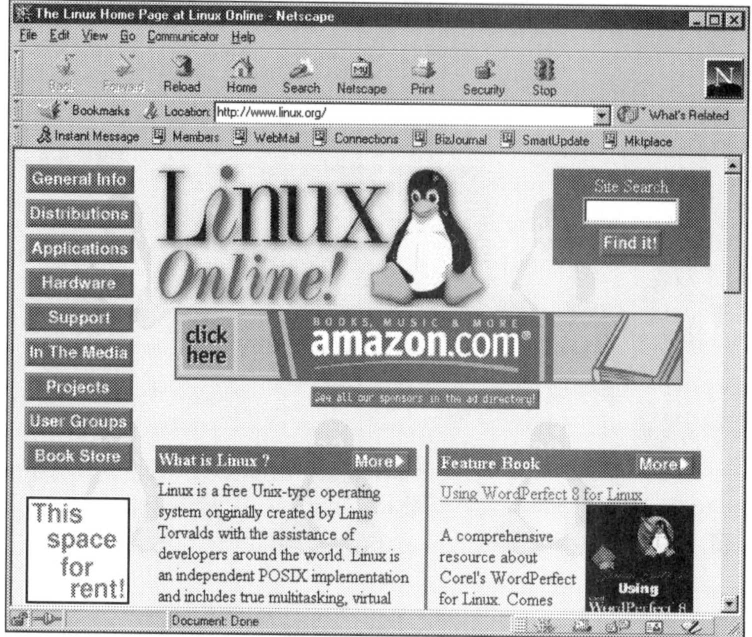

Figure C.1 www.linux.org.

The different Linux distributions can be seen on the page, currently **www.linux.org/dist/index.html**, as shown in Figure C.2.

The different distributions included on **www.linux.org/dist/index.html** are the following:

- Caldera OpenLinux
- Debian GNU/Linux
- Linux Mandrake
- LinuxPPC
- Linux Pro
- LinuxWare
- MkLinux
- Red Hat Linux
- Slackware Linux
- Stampede Linux
- S.u.S.E. Linux
- TurboLinux

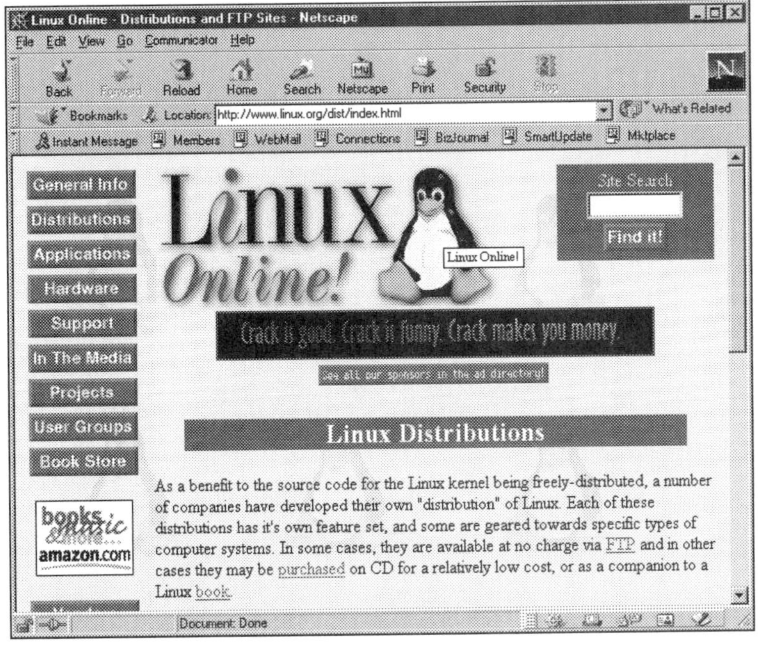

Figure C.2 **www.linux.org/dist/index.html.**

- Yggdrasil Linux
- DLX Linux
- DOS Linux
- hal91 Floppy Linux
- tomsrtbt

Where To Get Information On Linux

Start at **www.linux.org** and browse through the information on Linux; **www.linux-howto.com** or **www.metalab.unc.edu/linux/** are sites full of information on the different documentation that is available on Linux. *Linux Install and Configuration Little Black Book* (The Coriolis Group; ISBN 1-57610-489-3) is a good place to start learning about installing and setting up your Linux PC.

Which Linux Distribution To Choose

The Linux Documentation Project, written by Eric Raymond, includes a document called the Linux Distribution HOWTO, which contains a lot of useful advice on which Linux distribution to choose. A copy of this can be found on the CD-ROM in the /docs/LinuxHOWTO directory.

Index

E

F

G

H

I

J

K

L

M

N

O

P

Q

R

S

T

U

V

W

X

Z

What's On The CD-ROM

The *Samba Black Book's* companion CD-ROM contains elements specifically selected to enhance the usefulness of this book, including:

- Samba versions 2.0.5a and 2.0.6.
- A complete copy of the Samba FTP distribution site.
- Copies of all the configuration scripts mentioned in the text (including some brief firewall information).
- Request For Comments (RFCs)—An RFC is a formal Internet document or standard that is the result of committee drafting and subsequent review by interested parties.
- A variety of programs that are discussed in the book.

System Requirements

Software:

- Microsoft Windows (95, 98, or NT) on one computer.
- Another computer configured for Linux.

Hardware:

- At least two computers.
- An Intel (or equivalent) Pentium-class processor is the minimum platform required; an Intel (or equivalent) Pentium II 200MHz processor or better is recommended.
- 16MB of RAM is the minimum requirement (32MB is recommended).
- 500MB of hard drive space is the minimum for the Linux installation and Samba (1GB is recommended).
- A color monitor (256 colors) is recommended.
- A network connection between your computers (Chapter 1 should be enough to get you through networking).